Sub-Saharan Africa
From Crisis to Sustainable Growth

IBRD 21870

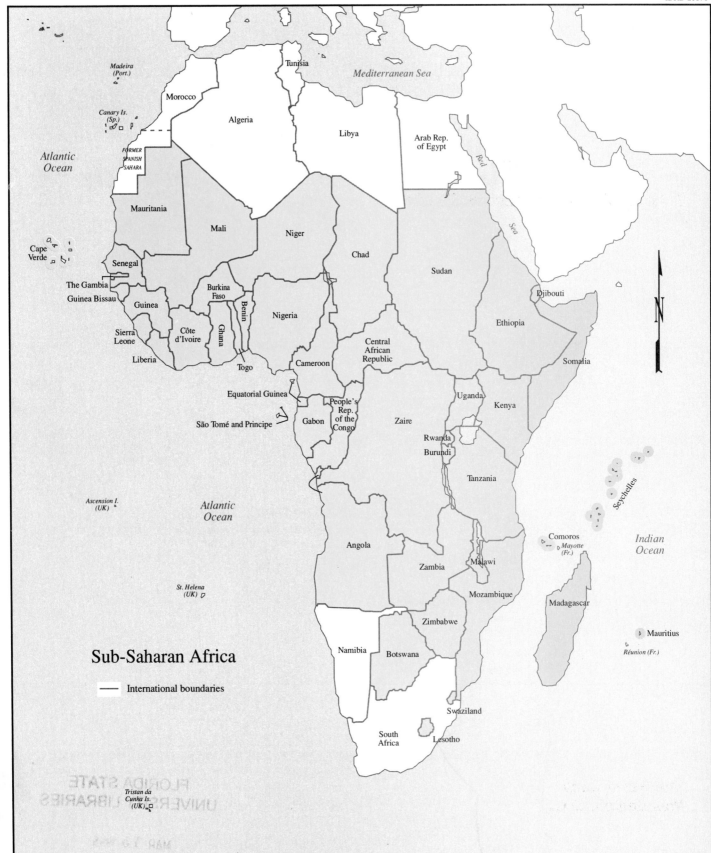

Madeira (Port.)

Tunisia

Mediterranean Sea

Morocco

Canary Is. (Sp.)

Algeria

Libya

Arab Rep. of Egypt

Atlantic Ocean

FORMER SPANISH SAHARA

Mauritania

Mali

Niger

Chad

Sudan

Red Sea

Cape Verde

Senegal

The Gambia

Guinea Bissau

Guinea

Burkina Faso

Benin

Nigeria

Djibouti

Sierra Leone

Côte d'Ivoire

Ghana

Central African Republic

Ethiopia

Liberia

Togo

Cameroon

Somalia

Equatorial Guinea

São Tomé and Principe

Gabon

People's Rep. of the Congo

Zaire

Uganda

Kenya

Rwanda

Burundi

N

Ascension I. (UK)

Atlantic Ocean

Tanzania

Seychelles

Comoros

Mayotte (Fr.)

Indian Ocean

Angola

Zambia

Malawi

St. Helena (UK)

Mozambique

Madagascar

Zimbabwe

Mauritius

Réunion (Fr.)

Namibia

Botswana

Sub-Saharan Africa

—— International boundaries

Swaziland

South Africa

Lesotho

Tristan da Cunha Is. (UK)

OCTOBER 1989

Sub-Saharan Africa

From Crisis to Sustainable Growth

A Long-Term Perspective Study

The World Bank
Washington, D.C.

The maps in this report are for the convenience of the reader. The denominations, the classifications, the boundaries, and the colors used in them do not imply on the part of the World Bank and its affiliates any judgment on the legal or other status of any territory, or any endorsement or acceptance of any boundary.

The material in this publication is copyrighted. Requests for permission to reproduce portions of it should be sent to the Office of the Publisher at the address shown in the copyright notice above. The World Bank encourages dissemination of its work and will normally give permission promptly and, when the reproduction is for noncommercial purposes, without a fee. Permission to photocopy portions for classroom use is granted through the Copyright Clearance Center, 27 Congress Street, Salem, Massachusetts 01970, U.S.A.

The complete backlist of publications from the World Bank is shown in the annual *Index of Publications*, which contains an alphabetical title list (with full ordering information) and indexes of subjects, authors, and countries and regions. The latest edition is available free of charge from the Distribution Unit, Office of the Publisher, Department F, The World Bank, 1818 H Street, N.W., Washington, D.C. 20433, U.S.A., or from Publications, The World Bank, 66, avenue d'Iéna, 75116 Paris, France.

Cover photograph credits (clockwise, from top right): (1) a chemist at a palm oil plant in Côte d'Ivoire (Ray Witlin), (2) a woman planting tree seedlings in Madagascar (Yosef Hadar), (3) a weaver in Mali (Yosef Hadar), (4) a self-employed father and son making charcoal burners in Zambia (Ed Huffman), (5) a boy drinking from a hamdpump in Lesotho (Curt Carnemark), (6) women voting in new officers for a village organization in Senegal (Nicla de Palma), and (7) a METEOSAT image supplied by the European Space Agency.

Library of Congress Cataloging-in-Publication Data

Sub-Saharan Africa : from crisis to sustainable growth.

  Includes bibliographical references.
  1. Africa, Sub-Saharan—Economic policy. 2. Africa, Sub-Saharan—Social policy. 3. Nutrition policy—Africa, Sub-Saharan. 4. Agriculture and state—Africa, Sub-Saharan. 5. Economic assistance—Africa, Sub-Saharan. 6. Technical assistance—Africa, Sub-Saharan. I. International Bank for Reconstruction and Development.

HC800.S825   1989   338.967   89-24925
ISBN 0-8213-1349-5

Contents

Figures

Tables

The co-authors of this report were Pierre Landell-Mills, Ramgopal Agarwala, and Stanley Please. Members of the core team included Osman Ahmed, Zafar Ahmed, Robert Barad, Kevin Cleaver, Jocelyn de Jong, Gladson Kayira, Barbara Pitkin, Raj Sharma, William Steel, Kalanidhi Subbarao, and Gertrud Windsperger. The team was assisted by Moussa Kourouma, Waheed Oshikoya, Sangeeta Parimoo, and Klaus Tilmes. The statistical appendix was prepared by Ramesh Chander and Sandra Gain, with the assistance of Smangele Mkhwanazi.

Many in and outside the Bank provided contributions, notably Claude Ake, Jacques Giri, Paul Harrison, Goran Hyden, Sanjaya Lall, Andrew Lemer, Janet MacGaffey, Jean Rabes, Pushpa Schwartz, Kifle Wodajo, and the members of the World Bank's Council of African Advisers. In addition a large number of African and non-African development professionals provided written inputs and contributed through about 20 workshops held in Africa and outside in the course of preparation of this report. Financial contributions for African inputs and workshops were made by the UNDP, the EEC, and the governments of Canada, Finland, France, The Netherlands, Norway, Sweden, and the United Kingdom.

The support staff was headed by Jean Ponchamni and included Barbara Dobrovodsky, Gloria Jackson, Patricia Moran, and Tatyana Ringland. Clive Crook was the principal editor.

Production for publication was directed by Virginia deHaven Hitchcock, with the assistance of Eileen Hanlon, Catherine Ann Kocak, Jeffrey N. Lecksell, Victoria Lee, Caroline McEuen, Jonathan Miller, Hugh Nees, Martin O'Hara, Jean Robinson, Michael W. Rollins, and Brian J. Svikhart. The French edition was translated under the direction of Jacqueline M. Gardes. The Portuguese edition was translated by Translex, Inc.

Foreword

Africa's continuing economic crisis presents an extraordinary challenge to the development community—to both intellectuals and policymakers. Responding to this challenge during the past decade, the Bank has issued a series of reports on Sub-Saharan Africa. These have increasingly concentrated on urgent measures needed to set Africa on the path to recovery, as have the efforts of the development community at large. Yet the crisis has continued to deepen. As we approach a new decade, the moment has come to step back from the immediate problems and take a longer view. How have the economies of Sub-Saharan Africa evolved during the first three decades of independence? What lessons have been learned? And what are the prospects for the next generation of Africans? This report attempts to provide such a long-term perspective.

The report is the product of a prolonged inquiry that has extensively involved African researchers, private businessmen, and public officials, as well as a broad spectrum of representatives of the donor community. In this sense the process has been as important as the product. The report builds on the many studies undertaken by the United Nations and African agencies, as well as by other scholars.

Clearly no single report can hope to do full justice to the diversity of African economies, the complexity of the problems they confront, and the differing views on how best to tackle them. We do not pretend to have complete answers; our goal has been to sift carefully through the evidence, to listen to the many viewpoints, and to set forth our best assessment of the policies and measures needed for Africa to achieve a sustained and sustainable improvement in welfare. The report is offered as a contribution to a continuing process of policy dialog and consensus building on programs to meet Africa's development needs. Our hope is that it will be seen by policymakers in Africa and in the development community at large as a resource on which to draw as they grapple with the task of formulating specific long-term country strategies.

Most African countries are now embarked on comprehensive programs of economic adjustment. The nature of these programs has evolved significantly as we have all learned from our experiences and mistakes. We have come to appreciate that fundamental structural change is needed to transform African economies and make them competitive in an increasingly competitive world. The adjustment efforts must be continued and the reforms broadened and deepened. The journey will be long and difficult, and special measures are needed to alleviate poverty and protect the vulnerable.

To achieve food security, provide jobs, and register a modest improvement in living standards, Sub-Saharan economies must grow by at least 4 to 5 percent annually. Compared with the region's past performance, even that target seems highly ambitious—but we believe it can be achieved. And for growth to be sustainable, major efforts must be made to protect, not destroy, the environment. During the next decade at least, agriculture will be seen as the main foundation for growth. Food production must expand twice as fast if Africa is to cope with the new mouths to be fed and slowly overcome malnutrition. The key to food security will be to develop and apply new technologies, as well as to slow population growth.

A central theme of the report is that although sound macroeconomic policies and an efficient infrastructure are essential to provide an *enabling environment* for the productive use of resources, they alone are not sufficient to transform the structure of African economies. At the same time major efforts are needed to *build African capacities*—to produce a better trained, more healthy population and to greatly strengthen the institutional framework within which development can take place. This is why the report strongly supports the call for a human-centered development strategy made by the ECA and UNICEF.

A root cause of weak economic performance in the past has been the failure of public institutions. Private sector initiative and market mechanisms are important, but they must go hand-in-hand with good governance—a public service that is efficient, a judicial system that is reliable, and an administration that is accountable to its public. And a better balance is needed between the government and the governed. Thus the report sets out a range of proposals aimed at empowering ordinary people, and especially women, to take greater responsibility for improving their lives—measures that foster grassroots organization, that nurture rather than obstruct informal sector enterprises, and that promote nongovernmental and intermediary organizations. The growing conviction is that development must be more bottom-up less top-down and that a learning approach to program design is to be preferred to the imposition of blueprints.

The difficulties facing Africa are formidable. The margin for maneuver is slim indeed. The risks of failure are devastating in human terms. So the need for concerted action among all the partners in development—African governments and mul-
tilateral institutions, the private sector and the donors, official and nongovernmental—has never been greater. We all share responsibility for the future, and the problems are big enough for all to have a role in their solution. By working together, African governments will hopefully achieve faster progress toward regional cooperation and integration, which was a central theme of the Lagos Plan of Action and has been once again stressed in the 1989 "African Development Report" issued by the African Development Bank.

Previous reports have all called for increased aid. This report is no exception, but clearly external finance must be matched by improved policies. In the long term, dependency on aid and technical assistance must be reduced. But in the immediate future the needs will continue to grow, and ways must be found to mobilize these resources, including measures to reduce Africa's debt burden.

A wide measure of consensus already exists on objectives and, with goodwill and open debate, the differences on policy can be progressively narrowed. So let us strive together to reach common ground—the high ground—that will permit concerted action on a strategic agenda for the 1990s and beyond—thereby ensuring Africa a more prosperous future.

This is a study by the staff of the World Bank, and the judgments in it do not necessarily reflect the views of the Board of Directors or the governments they represent.

Barber B. Conable
President
The World Bank

October 16, 1989

Definitions and data notes

Acronyms and initials

CEAO West African Economic Community (Communauté Economique de l'Afrique de l'Ouest)
CGIAR Consultative Group on International Agricultural Research
CPR Contraceptive prevalence rate
DAC Development Assistance Committee of the OECD
ECA UN Economic Commission for Africa
ECOWAS Economic Community of West African States
EEC European Economic Community
ESAMI Eastern and Southern African Management Institute
FAO UN Food and Agriculture Organization
GATT General Agreement on Tariffs and Trade
GDP Gross domestic product
GNP Gross national product
HIC Highly indebted country
IARC International agricultural research center
IBRD International Bank for Reconstruction and Development (World Bank)
ICIPE International Centre of Insect Physiology and Ecology
ICP International Comparison Project
IDA International Development Association
IEC Information, education, and communication
IITA International Institute of Tropical Agriculture
ILO International Labour Organisation
IMF International Monetary Fund

ISIC UN International Standard Industrial Classification of All Economic Activities
LSMS Living Standards Measurement Study
MUV Manufacturers' unit value
NGO Nongovernmental organization
NIC Newly industrializing country
NRR Net reproduction rate
OAU Organization of African Unity
ODA Official development assistance
OECD Organisation for Economic Co-operation and Development
OPEC Organization of Petroleum Exporting Countries
PTA Preferential Trade Area for Eastern and Southern African States
SADCC Southern Africa Development Coordinating Conference
SDA Social Dimensions of Adjustment Project
SDR Special drawing right
SFA Special Facility for Africa
SITC Standard International Trade Classification
SME Small- and medium-scale enterprise
SNA UN System of National Accounts
SPA Special Program of Assistance
SPAAR Special Program for African Agricultural Research
S&T Science and technology
TFR Total fertility rate
TNC Transnational corporation
T&V Training and visit system
UDEAC Central African Customs and Economic Union (Union Douanière et Economique de l'Afrique Centrale)

UMOA West African Monetary Union (Union Monetaire Ouest Africaine)

UN United Nations

UNCTAD United Nations Conference on Trade and Development

UNDP United Nations Development Programme

UNEP United Nations Environment Programme

Unesco United Nations Economic, Scientific, and Cultural Organization

UNFPA United Nations Fund for Population Activities

UNICEF United Nations International Children's Emergency Fund

UNIDO United Nations Industrial Development Organization

UNPAAERD United Nations Programme of Action for African Economic Recovery and Development

UNSO United Nations Statistical Office

UPE Universal primary education

USAID United States Agency for International Development

WHO World Health Organization

Data notes

- Billion is 1,000 million.
- Trillion is 1,000 billion.
- Dollars are current US dollars unless otherwise specified.
- Growth rates are based on constant price data and, unless otherwise noted, have been computed with the use of least-squares method. See the technical notes for the statistical appendix for details of this method.
- "World Bank data" refers to data obtained from various World Bank files, including the Bank Economic and Social Database (BESD), some of which are published from time to time (see the bibliographical note.) Historical data shown in this report may differ from those in previous publications because of continuous updating as better data become available and because of new group aggregation techniques that use broader country coverage than in previous publications.
- Country groups and economic and demographic terms are defined in statistical appendix.
- The symbol .. in tables means not available.
- The symbol - in tables means not applicable.
- The number 0 or 0.0 in tables means zero or less than half the unit shown and not known more precisely.

Introduction and overview

Africa[1] entered independence with high expectations. Most people believed that rapid progress would be made in raising incomes and improving welfare. And indeed in the early years many African countries successfully expanded their basic infrastructure and social services. Much effort was spent too on consolidating the fragile new nation states.

After an initial period of growth, however, most African economies faltered, then went into decline. There were some exceptions, but Sub-Saharan Africa as a whole has now witnessed almost a decade of falling per capita incomes, increasing hunger, and accelerating ecological degradation. The earlier progress made in social development is now being eroded. Overall Africans are almost as poor today as they were 30 years ago. This situation has spurred many governments to undertake far-reaching reforms. More than half have embarked on structural adjustment programs. The countries that have persisted with reforms since the mid-1980s are showing the first signs of improvement. These give grounds for believing that recovery has started.

The experience of the first generation of Africans after independence raises some searching questions. Does Africa face special structural problems that have not been properly under-

stood? Has the institutional dimension been neglected? Have the recent reform programs been too narrow or too shallow? Could the process of formulating and implementing reforms be improved? Has the effect of external factors been correctly assessed? Are external assistance and debt relief appropriate and adequate? More fundamentally, is there a long-term vision that is both credible and energizing?

These concerns—especially the last—lie behind this report. Drawing on past experience, it explores how programs and policies need to be changed to attain sustainable growth with equity in the next century. It is not sufficient for African governments merely to consolidate the progress made in their adjustment programs. They need to go beyond the issues of public finance, monetary policy, prices, and markets to address fundamental questions relating to human capacities, institutions, governance, the environment, population growth and distribution, and technology. Changes in perceptions and priorities, as well as in incentives, will be required to bring about improvements. Above all, to channel the energies of the population at large, ordinary people should participate more in designing and implementing development programs. Much of this will take time. But while the focus of the report is on the long term, the call is for action *now* to bring about long-run changes that will promote growth and reduce poverty.

This report emphasizes and embodies the process as well as the product. It is the result of an intensive collaboration with both Africans and donors and, as such, tries to reflect the evolution

---

1 Throughout this report, "Africa" when used is an abbreviation for Sub-Saharan Africa. The data given on Sub-Saharan Africa systematically excludes South Africa and Namibia.

1

in African views from the Lagos Plan of Action in 1980 to the program of action presented at the United Nations in 1986, the Abuja Declaration of 1987, the Khartoum Declaration of 1988, and the UN Economic Commission for Africa's (ECA's) 1989 report, *African Alternative Framework to Structural Adjustment Programmes*. The attention to human resources, technology, regional cooperation, self-reliance, and respect for African values that informs these African policy statements provides the main focus of the strategy proposed in the following chapters.

At various stages workshops were held in African countries as well as with donor agencies. Many eminent Africans contributed to the report's thrust and content. The report is intended to help in the design of a future development strategy for each African country. Policies and programs would then be formulated in detail on a country-by-country basis.

Some answers are readily suggested by past experience. But other issues, such as the apparent delay in the demographic transition in Africa or complex environmental questions, will require further research. Any report on Sub-Saharan Africa has to confront the continent's enormous diversity and the grave weaknesses of available statistics. We are all only too conscious of our inadequate understanding of many of the issues covered. But the report cannot be simply an agenda for research. It attempts to derive the elements of a future development strategy on the basis of present information, however incomplete. A long-term effort to improve African data is called for. Meanwhile the available figures, poor as they are, do provide enough evidence to establish the enormity of the problems, and they are used where possible to formulate policy recommendations.

Although much attention is inevitably given to Africa's failures, a lot can be learned from its successes. These show what can be done much more powerfully than any theories.

Responsibility for Africa's economic crisis is shared. Donor agencies and foreign advisers have been heavily involved in past development efforts along with the African governments themselves. Governments and donors alike must be prepared to change their thinking fundamentally in order to revive Africa's fortunes. However, Africa's future can only be decided by Africans. External agencies can play at most a supportive role.

What have we learned?

Overall economic growth in Sub-Saharan Africa has averaged 3.4 percent a year since 1961, only a fraction above population growth. By 1987 this region of 450 million people—more than double the number at independence—had a total gross domestic product (GDP) of around $135 billion, about the same as that of Belgium, which has only 10 million inhabitants. Growth was unevenly spread over time and across countries. There were three broadly distinct periods: 1961–72, when incomes per capita grew; 1973–80, a period of stagnation; and 1981–87, years of decline. For some countries (such as Liberia, Niger, and Nigeria) the decline in per capita incomes since 1980 has been calamitous—well over 25 percent. As always there were exceptions—notably Botswana, which has recorded an annual growth in per capita income of more than 8 percent a year for the past 26 years; Congo with 4 percent; and Lesotho, above 3 percent.

Africa's deepening crisis is characterized by weak agricultural growth, a decline in industrial output, poor export performance, climbing debt, and deteriorating social indicators, institutions, and environment. Agricultural output has grown annually by less than 1.5 percent on average since 1970, with food production rising more slowly than population. Although industry grew roughly three times as fast as agriculture in the first decade of independence, the past few years have seen an alarming reversal in many African countries where deindustrialization seems to have set in. With export volumes barely growing at all since 1970, Africa's share in world markets has fallen by almost half.

In the 1970s, to maintain income and investment, governments borrowed heavily from abroad. Africa's long-term debt has risen 19-fold since 1970 and is now equal to its gross national product (GNP), making the region the most heavily indebted of all (Latin America's debt amounts to only around 60 percent of GNP). Debt service obligations were 47 percent of export revenues in 1988, but only about half were actually paid. More than 100 debt reschedulings have been negotiated, and still arrears accumulate.

The crisis is taking a heavy toll in human terms. In several countries expenditure on social services is sharply down, school enrollments are falling, nutrition is worsening, and infant mortality continues to be high. Open unemployment in the towns, especially of educated youth, is also on the rise. And, threatening Africa's long-term productive capacity, population pressure on the land is accelerating desertification and deforestation; fuelwood is increasingly scarce, and soil fertility is being leached away, although none of these trends has been accurately measured. Last, institutional decay is symbolized by the poor conditions of once world-class universities, the disintegration of paved highways, and the collapse of the judicial and banking systems. Overstaffed and poorly managed public bureaucracies are deadweights on the productive sectors. Many governments are wracked by corruption and are increasingly unable to command the confidence of the population at large. In many places political instability, coup d'etats, and ethnic strife are exacting a terrible toll on helpless people. And the costs of destabilization in southern Africa have been enormous.

The factors behind Africa's economic decline are much debated. Some see mainly external causes, others internal. Changes in per capita income have three main sources: variations in the terms of trade, growth in population, and growth in production (GDP).

• For Africa as a whole the analysis in Chapter 1 shows that the income loss from changes in terms of trade since 1960 has been smaller than the gain. Other regions have suffered similar losses and performed better. Declining export volumes, more than declining export prices, account for Africa's poor export revenues. Low-income African countries have been the worst hit, with substantial income losses in the 1970s and 1980s.

• Population growth has steadily risen during the past three decades. Now well over 3 percent, it is outpacing GDP. In contrast, in most other developing countries population growth has declined.

• The region's disappointing GDP growth is partly a function of the level and efficiency of investment. Gross investment during the period first rose (from 15 to 20 percent in the 1970s), then fell back to 16 percent. The incremental output generated by this investment has dropped dramatically from 31 percent of investment in the 1960s to 2.5 percent in the 1980s.

Although many African countries have seen their development efforts disrupted by sharp falls in the world price of key commodities, viewed over the long term, falling per capita incomes for Africa as a whole since the late 1970s are explained largely by the declining level and efficiency of investment, compounded by accelerating population growth—and not primarily by external factors. Many countries, especially the poorer ones, did suffer severe external shocks. But the low return on investment is the main reason for Africa's recent decline. Africa's investment and operating costs are typically 50 to 100 percent above those in South Asia—the most comparable region. Weak public sector management has resulted in loss-making public enterprises, poor investment choices, costly and unreliable infrastructure, price distortions (especially overvalued exchange rates, administered prices, and subsidized credit), and hence inefficient resource allocation. Wage costs are high relative to productivity (particularly in the CFA franc zone), even though real wages have fallen by about a quarter on average across Africa since 1980. Intermediate technologies (such as pedal carts and animal draft power) are too little used. Even more fundamental in many countries is the deteriorating quality of government, epitomized by bureaucratic obstruction, pervasive rent seeking, weak judicial systems, and arbitrary decisionmaking. All of this adds heavily to the cost of doing business and discourages investors. For the most part Africa is simply not competitive in an increasingly competitive world.

The postindependence development efforts failed because the strategy was misconceived. Governments made a dash for "modernization," copying, but not adapting, Western models. The result was poorly designed public investments in industry; too little attention to peasant agriculture; too much intervention in areas in which the state lacked managerial, technical, and entrepreneurial skills; and too little effort to foster grassroots development. This top-down approach demotivated ordinary people, whose energies most needed to be mobilized in the development effort.

Outlook for the next generation

Certain fundamental forces will shape the context for Africa's development in the years ahead. The world is on the threshold of a new technological age—driven by rapid advances in information systems, in the biological sciences, and in materials research. High-speed, low-cost information processing and communications are transforming the way the world does business. Good market intelligence, flexible production structures, and a fast response to new opportunities will give firms and farms the competitive edge. Biotechnology and materials sciences will produce a dazzling array of new products that may quickly make conventional processes and products in Africa obsolete. Against this background, an improvement in raw materials prices is unlikely.

Genetic engineering, tissue cultures, and the like offer new opportunities as well as pose a significant threat. If Africa is not to be further marginalized, but rather benefit from these developments, two initiatives are crucial. Africa must:

• Improve its science and technology training and aim at the highest standards for at least a minimum core of specialists

• Forge new partnerships with qualified firms and research institutes in the developed countries.

Africa must grapple with two major trends: explosive population growth and accelerating environmental degradation. In 1983 the ECA sketched out a "nightmare scenario" that described the consequences of continuing high population growth and stagnant or declining incomes. On present trends the sheer growth in numbers is staggering: a continent that had fewer than 100 million inhabitants at the beginning of this century will have 1 billion by 2010. Without a decline in fertility the population will double in 21 years. This will place an unmanageable burden on social services and, in several parts of Africa (such as Burundi, Kenya, southern Malawi, Rwanda, and the Sahel), will put pressure on the land that can be relieved only by large-scale migration. This would cause mounting social and political tensions. It also implies continued rapid urbanization; by 2020 there will be some 30 cities with more than 1 million inhabitants. Depending on economic performance, these cities could be a force for growth and modernization or a wretched destabilizing element, with their inhabitants rebelling against squalid conditions in sprawling slums.

The degradation of Africa's environment has domestic and international dimensions. Unless halted, it threatens Africa's productive base. But deforestation in Africa is also of concern to the rest of the world because it threatens the loss of Africa's rich biological diversity—an irreplaceable gene bank of immense potential benefit. It also contributes to global warming.

The challenge now is for Africa to reverse its present decline. The potential is there—in its vast, poorly exploited resources of land, water, minerals, oil, and gas; in its underutilized people; in its traditions of solidarity and cooperation; and in the international support it can count on. The time has come to take up this challenge and to put in place a new development strategy for the next generation.

A strategy for sustainable and equitable growth

If Africa is to avert hunger and provide its growing population with productive jobs and rising incomes, its economies need to grow by at least 4 to 5 percent a year. This must be the minimum target. The primary source of this growth can only be agricultural production, which is itself targeted to expand annually by 4 percent. African countries could then not only meet their own food requirements, but also generate the foreign exchange needed for development. The target growth for industry—initially 5 percent rising to 7 or 8 percent a year—is higher than for agriculture, as is consistent with experience elsewhere. With all other sectors growing at around 4 to 5 percent, it should be possible to provide jobs for a labor force that will expand by about 380 million people between 1990 and 2020.

To meet these targets, Africa must not only dramatically raise the levels of domestic saving and investment, but also greatly improve productivity—by as much as 1 to 2 percent annually for labor and about 3 percent for land. This requires an *enabling environment* of infrastructure services and incentives to foster efficient production and private initiative. It also requires *enhanced capacities* of people and institutions alike, from the village to the upper echelons of government and industry. These themes recur throughout the following chapters.

For these targets to be achieved over the long term, the growth strategy must be both sustainable and equitable—sustainable because sound environmental policies can protect the productive capacity of Africa's natural resources and equitable because long-term political stability is impossible without this. Equitable means, in particular, that measures are taken to reduce poverty, especially by improving the access of the poor to productive assets.

The long-term strategy proposed here envisages a move away from earlier practices. It aims to release the energies of ordinary people by enabling them to take charge of their lives. Profits would be seen as the mark of an efficient business. Agricultural extension services would be seen as responding to farmers, not commanding them. Foreign investors would be welcomed as partners, not discouraged. The state would no longer be an entrepreneur, but a promoter of private producers. And the informal sector would be valued as a seedbed for entrepreneurs, not a hotbed of racketeers.

Enabling environment

Farmers and firms will be efficient only if the incentives they face encourage them to be. The enabling environment that promotes production and efficiency has two parts: incentives and the physical infrastructure. Both are crucial.

Experience worldwide convincingly demonstrates that the countries with the highest growth rates have kept their exchange rates competitive, avoided excessively protecting their manufacturing industry and underpricing their agricultural products, kept real interest rates positive and real wages in line with productivity, priced utilities to recover costs, and avoided high and accelerating inflation by following disciplined fiscal and monetary policies. Structural adjustment programs have reflected these themes, but as yet the policies have been only partially implemented. They are critical for Africa's recovery.

Exchange rate policy is perhaps the most controversial issue. Overvalued exchange rates encourage imports and discriminate against local producers. A competitive exchange rate is essential to boost domestic production and employment. The key is to keep farm prices remunerative and industrial wage costs internationally competitive. But for exchange rate adjustments to be successfully managed, there must be tight financial discipline and no artificially supported wage rates.

Neglected infrastructure—poorly maintained roads, inefficient ports, unreliable utilities, and the like—greatly increase the cost of doing business. Most African countries face this problem, but for some the situation is chronic. To tackle this issue, governments should give priority to rehabilitating infrastructure over investing in new facilities. Costs could be reduced by using small local contractors and revenues increased by raising charges, especially for utilities. Determined reforms in parastatal management could yield significant improvements quickly.

Tackling the backlog of deferred maintenance and rehabilitation will extend well into the next decade. This, together with the need for expansion and regular maintenance, will require an annual expenditure of 5 to 7 percent of GDP, accompanied by measures to increase user fees, foster the domestic construction industries, and reform public procurement, the administration of contracts, and transport planning. The consequences of poor planning and the cost of neglect, inefficiencies, and obsolescence are borne by a broad, but diffused, constituency. Systematic consultation with organized interest groups, such as chambers of commerce and industry, can strengthen accountability and responsiveness. There is ample evidence that businesses willingly pay the full cost of reliable services; without them, they fail.

Africa needs efficient cities to accommodate competitive businesses. Services can be largely self-financing. So can the upgrading of shelter, which at the same time would generate a great deal of employment. Pollution from waste disposal can be avoided by low-cost, on-site solutions.

Building capacity

Africa needs not just less government but better government—government that concentrates its efforts less on direct interventions and more on enabling others to be productive. Every level of government should take measures to improve the performance of public administrations and parastatal enterprises. Institution building is a long-term endeavor that requires a clear vision and a specific agenda. Several countries have already embarked on major reforms of central government, for example, Central African Republic, Ghana, and Guinea. They aim to create a leaner, better disciplined, better trained, and more motivated public service, with competitive salaries for highly qualified officials. Special attention needs to be given to strengthening the policy analysis and economic management capabilities of governments. Public enterprises need to be given clear mandates, managerial autonomy, and monitorable performance indicators. Local governments also could play a greater role if allowed more autonomy and regular, independent sources of revenue, especially in managing the expanding urban networks that link the towns to their hinterlands. In rural areas local services, such as water supply, could be better run at the communal level. This too requires genuine delegation of responsibilities.

Building private sector capacity should extend beyond helping community associations. Local nongovernmental associations can be drawn into the development effort as intermediaries to promote grassroots activities. Credit unions and informal savings and loan associations (such as *tontines*) could retail credit to farmers and microenterprises. Local consultants and professional associations could also be mobilized. All this requires a deliberate, carefully orchestrated effort by a country's leadership to build local capacities.

Ultimately, better governance requires political renewal. This means a concerted attack on corruption from the highest to the lowest levels. This can be done by setting a good example, by strengthening accountability, by encouraging public debate, and by nurturing a free press. It also means empowering women and the poor by fostering grassroots and nongovernmental organizations (NGOs), such as farmers' associations, cooperatives, and women's groups.

Investing in people

However well developed, institutions are only as effective as the people who work in them. Education and health were priorities in the strategies developed after independence and must remain so in the future. But better programs are essential. Previous attempts to achieve universal coverage in basic health, education, and food security failed, partly because the efforts were swamped by soaring population growth and partly because public expenditure was devoted to other priorities. But it is unthinkable that another generation should go by without a determined effort to attain this goal. By adjusting priorities and by cutting and recovering costs, it can be done. Moreover it can be done without setting aside the goal of better quality. Improved science and technology training is a high priority. Costs can also be reduced and efficiency increased by encouraging beneficiaries to participate in the design, delivery, and management of services.

SLOWING POPULATION GROWTH. Raising the GDP growth rate from the 2 percent of the recent past to 4 to 5 percent in the years to come would be a significant achievement. But incomes will improve little if population growth continues to soar. Increasingly, African governments are coming to accept that population policy should be an integral part of a sound strategy for human resource development.

Africa's situation is unique. Never in human history has population grown so fast. If current trends continue, Sub-Saharan Africa will have nearly 500 million inhabitants by 1990 and more than 1 billion by 2010. Africa will find it increasingly difficult to feed itself, educate its children, or find jobs for new entrants to its labor force. The absolute numbers are not so worrying in themselves—there are still vast underpopulated regions. But the high rate of growth means that Africa's economies and social services must sprint ahead for living standards even to stand still.

Family planning is the cornerstone for improved health care. Africa has some of the highest rates of maternal and infant mortality in the world. In the poorest countries—Burkina Faso, Ethiopia, and Mali—about one-quarter of all children die before the age of five. There is strong evidence from Botswana and Zimbabwe that, when family planning services are made widely available and especially when they are backed by mass media campaigns and community-based education programs, contraceptive use is high. The preference for large families has remained higher in Africa than elsewhere, even when mortality is falling. Families remain to be persuaded that better spacing and timing of births and fewer births can reduce infant, child, and maternal mortality and sickness. Most African governments now officially support family planning, but there is an urgent need to match expressions of commitment with adequate technical, financial, and managerial support. To reduce the population growth rate from the present high 3.3 percent a year to an average of 2.75 percent a year for 1990–2020, the total fertility rate will need to fall from 6.7 children per woman to 3.4 by 2020. An annual budgetary allocation for family planning programs of only 0.8 percent of GNP would establish effective family planning programs in most countries.

PRIMARY HEALTH CARE COMES FIRST. Major strides toward better health care are possible, even within the budgetary constraints facing African countries, if expenditures are redirected from high-cost curative medicine in modern hospitals to preventive and community-based systems. Mass immunization campaigns are cheap and effective against several major childhood killers. And even very poor people willingly pay for health care if they demonstrably get value for their money. This above all means ensuring a reliable supply of inexpensive drugs through better procurement procedures and regular delivery to clinics and health posts.

Two out of every three rural Africans are still without safe water. Universal access to clean water, which is a prerequisite for better health, should be an integral part of the long-term strategy. People themselves hold the key to achieving this target. Where communities are involved in designing, constructing, and installing water supplies and are made responsible for their maintenance, water projects tend to be more efficient, cost-effective, and hence sustainable. Once again much of the cost could be recovered through user charges.

ATTACKING HUNGER. More and more Africans are going hungry. Severe food shortages were exceptional in 1960; now they are widespread. It is estimated that about one-quarter of Sub-Saharan Africa's population—more than 100 million people—faces chronic food insecurity. In the first instance, this is a supply problem. Expanding food production is essential—the target is 4 percent growth a year—although that will be adequate only if food trade within Africa is also liberalized. This rate of growth would be enough to feed the growing population (2.75 percent a year), improve nutrition (1 percent a year), and progressively eliminate food imports (0.25 percent a year) between 1990 and 2020. An improved supply is not enough; the purchasing power of nonfarm families will also have to be sufficient. With the rising level of employment proposed in the target scenario, the number of low-income households unable to afford an adequate diet would gradually decrease. But recurrent droughts will continue to cause famine for a residual core of the poorest. For this vulnerable group, sharply targeted food subsidies or food-for-work programs will be needed, supplemented by direct feeding programs for malnourished women and children.

A BETTER EDUCATED POPULATION. School enrollments have been vastly expanded during the past three decades, but too often at the expense of quality. Improving quality is now the top priority. More must be spent on books and other materials. Raising annual expenditure on books at the primary level from $0.60 per pupil to about $5 would cost less than 5 percent of the amount donors spend each year in Sub-Saharan Africa on technical assistance. Countries also need the capacity to produce low-cost teaching materials adapted to local needs. The long-run goal remains to expand enrollments—especially of girls, because female education has a particularly strong effect on family welfare.

All this will require more money to be spent on basic education. The first step, however, is to use existing resources more efficiently. This could be done, for example, by moving to double shifts, increasing teaching loads, and strengthening management of the school system. There is scope to enlarge the education budget by charging fees, especially at the university level, and by redirecting some of the savings to basic education. Total expenditure on education can also be increased by encouraging private education and community contributions for school buildings, equipment, and housing for teachers.

Radical changes are called for in postsecondary education if Africa is to equip its labor force with the skills needed to survive in the new technological age. Resources should be shifted especially to science, engineering, accountancy, and other technical fields. Education subsidies should be reduced, and a better balance achieved between salary and nonsalary costs. Vocational training should be better attuned to employers' needs, employer participation in course design should be increased, and stronger links should be forged between the work place and training institutes.

BETTER MANAGED SOCIAL PROGRAMS. Placing management responsibility for basic social services in local hands makes the programs more responsive to users, who in turn become more willing to contribute to their cost. The watchwords for the future are delegation, community participation, and cost recovery. In this approach the central agency provides technical support through a training and visit system. NGOs can act as valuable and cost-effective intermediaries between the central agencies and community groups.

Women and women's groups can make a major contribution to improving delivery of social services. In Africa women are generally lead managers within the household; they are responsible for feeding the family; for providing water, education, and health; and for family planning. They are also active in production of food crops and in trade. Their role should be more explicitly recognized in design and implementation of human resource development programs.

SUSTAINABLE FINANCING. Even with the most strenuous efforts to put them to the best possible use, existing resources will not be enough. The proposed strategy calls for doubling public expenditure on human resource development—from around 4 to 5 percent of GDP to 8 to 10 percent—between now and 2000. This expansion can happen only if donors are willing to share the cost and, at the same time, if a greater effort is made to recover costs by charging fees, especially for postprimary education.

Raising agricultural production

In contrast to the past, the future strategy sees agriculture as the primary foundation for growth. This is where Africa has an immediate comparative advantage. Agriculture accounts for 33 percent of Africa's GDP, 66 percent of its labor force, and 40 percent of its exports. Moreover the links between agricultural and industrial growth are strong. Farmers need the urban market, and urban producers thrive in large part by selling to the rural population. Even taking full account of the environmental constraints, the scope for expanding agricultural production is great, although it varies from country to country. The target is to raise output growth from the 2 percent achieved since 1960 to 4 percent—the level that will be needed to achieve food security and to raise per capita incomes, initially by a modest 1 percent a year, and eventually by 2 percent. This in turn will require an annual increase in labor productivity of about 1.5 percent. Since the area under cultivation could not be expanded by more than 1 percent a year without adverse environmental consequences (the average rate of the past two decades was 0.7 percent a year), the productivity of cultivated land must rise by around 3 percent a year.

A 4 percent growth rate is ambitious, but not impossible. Cameroon, Côte d'Ivoire, Kenya, Malawi, and Rwanda have all achieved that or more for extended periods. Other countries have greater land potential, such as Ethiopia, Sudan, Zaire, and Zambia, to name the largest. At the same time a few—especially those in the Sahel—are unlikely ever to reach this target.

The overseas markets on which African agriculture depends will remain highly competitive. Long-term price trends cannot be expected to improve much. Only in rare cases—notably cocoa—will rising African production be likely to lower world prices significantly. Nevertheless African countries will need to diversify their production and seek out specialty markets—in off-season fruits, flowers, and vegetables, for instance. Greater regional integration would particularly help expand trade within Africa in agricultural products, especially food.

Despite the enormous range of ecological zones across the continent, there is surprising commonality in the kinds of policies needed to stimulate growth in Africa's agricultural sector. To achieve the growth target, all African countries will need to create an enabling environment, harness new technologies, build capacities, and safeguard natural resources.

• An enabling environment for agriculture means allowing prices to move flexibly in response to changing market conditions; turning over input supply, marketing, processing, and exporting largely to the private sector and reducing administrative controls; promoting credit at commercially attractive interest rates through private homegrown financial institutions such as cooperatives and credit unions (as already exist in Cameroon and Rwanda); gradually reforming systems of land tenure to enable titles to be registered (and in the interim codifying customary land rights), thereby increasing security and encouraging investment in land improvements; and upgrading rural roads using small local contractors and local community contributions.

• Harnessing technologies requires a new emphasis on agricultural research. This in turn calls for rehabilitating national research institutions, expanding the role for the international research centers, and establishing multicountry research networks to pool research efforts on specific topics. The core of the strategy must be a determination to improve research management and to link research to the farmer by putting in place better management systems for agricultural extension, which will be more responsive than in the past to farmers' needs and more efficient than the present situation in most African countries where donor-financed projects have created many extension services in the same country.

• Building capacities is a need that runs through all levels to produce better trained researchers, extension agents, and farmers and to strengthen rural institutions (such as farmers' associations, cooperatives, and women's groups) especially by training managers.

• Measures to protect the environment are needed to reduce soil erosion, deforestation, and desertification. Trees are being cut down 30 times as fast as they are being replaced. Possibly as many as 80 million Africans have difficulty finding fuelwood. In Ethiopia topsoil losses of 290 tons per hectare have been reported. Simple measures can have a large impact. In Burkina Faso lines of stones successfully reduce run-off and collect topsoil, communal tree planting in Ethiopia has slowed deforestation, and Kenyan farmers have terraced hundreds of thousands of smallholdings. These efforts need to be multiplied across the continent. The most pressing need is to plant more trees.

Although these ideas are not new, they are not yet widely applied. Controlled prices and restrictive marketing, disorganized research, and weak extension services, poor rural roads and few effective farmers' associations, insecure land tenure and poor environmental practices are still the rule rather than the exception. Only by concerted action will it be possible to achieve and sustain the agricultural growth targets on which Africa's future development hinges.

A new start to industrialization

Since independence Africa's labor force has acquired technical skills and industrial experience—as workers, managers, and entrepreneurs. Indigenous businesses range from self-employed metalworkers making cookstoves from scrap metal in Kenya to a firm making paper from sugarcane waste in Ghana. African countries today export not only processed raw materials but also manufactures, such as garments from Madagascar, electronics from Mauritius, and car radiators from Tanzania. The challenge is to build on this base and achieve the industrial transformation envisioned by African leaders in the 1980 Lagos Plan of Action.

Preparation for a Second Industrial Development Decade for Africa, first formulated by the ECA and the UN Industrial Development Organization (UNIDO) in 1981, has stimulated systematic reevaluation of industrial policies and strategies. While deteriorating economic conditions impeded implementation of ambitious industrial investment proposals, it has become increasingly evident that the earlier industrialization efforts focused on state-led creation of capacity without adequate regard to cost or markets. The result was highly inefficient industrialization, heavily subsidized by consumers and taxpayers. In recent years the emphasis has been on restructuring that capacity (including divestiture of large, unviable public enterprises) and on substituting market prices for direct controls. Success so far has been limited. Indeed output has continued to decline. This is partly a necessary adjustment—a weeding out of misconceived production operations that have no chance of becoming viable. But for industrial production to respond positively to the reforms, there must again be an enabling environment, together with measures to generate market demand and build industrial capabilities.

AN ENABLING INDUSTRIAL ENVIRONMENT. Because of their high operating costs, African countries will have to be all the more determined in using exchange rate policy, undertaking infrastructural investments, forging international partnerships, and providing incentives to raise productivity if they wish to be competitive. Besides lowering the direct costs of business by investing in infrastructure, governments need to lower the administrative costs and financial risks of private investment. This means moving from a controlling approach to a facilitating one, from protecting existing business to promoting competition. The aim must be to reward efficiency and innovation. Regulations and controls should be removed unless there are compelling reasons to retain them.

Although the public enterprise sector has expanded industrial capacity in many countries, it is hobbled by poor management, political interference, and weak financing. The private sector holds the key to future industrial growth, but private entrepreneurs have often found more enticing opportunities outside industry (especially in taking advantage of the scarcity rents created by controls). To attract investors, a stable economic and political environment is essential. Governments need to support private investors both in words and in deeds—and in particular by establishing a well-functioning judicial system that can be relied on to protect property and to enforce contracts.

EXPANDING MARKETS. Industry should be developed in response to market opportunities. Thus sustained industrial growth will depend in part on a broadly based expansion of domestic demand for local manufactures. The key will be to take advantage of demand and supply linkages between agriculture and industry and to aim for complementary growth in both. Higher agricultural incomes raise the demand for consumer goods and farm inputs in the rural areas and generate increased surpluses for processing, while the availability of appropriate, low-cost manufactures stimulates farmers to invest in order to raise income and also provides them with the means to raise productivity.

The small market in most African countries has two strategic implications. Small-scale producers can play a special role in meeting localized demand and providing competition; but rapid industrial growth will depend on penetrating external markets. African leaders have correctly placed priority on enlarging markets through regional integration. In practice, however, progress has been far too slow. Greater access to neighboring markets would be a stepping stone to markets beyond Africa. Competition in regional markets would stimulate efficiency and help prepare African producers to compete globally.

BUILDING INDUSTRIAL CAPABILITIES. Industrialization in Africa has so far engendered too little indigenous technological development to be self-starting and too few labor and management skills to generate steadily rising productivity. The core of a future strategy to transform African industry from infancy to maturity is a deliberate plan to acquire the necessary entrepreneurial, managerial, and technical skills. Incentives should focus on in-firm training and adapting technology to local conditions. Industry associations should be encouraged to set up advanced training courses. Postprimary education should aim to furnish the work force with technical and commercial skills.

The business of manufacturing is learned mostly on the job. In Africa's case this should mean in partnership with foreign investors, who have the skills as well as the capital. The transfer of capabilities, however, is not automatic. It can be helped along by building links between industries—through subcontracting, for example—and by promoting local consultants.

Fostering African entrepreneurship

In the coming decades Africa's entrepreneurs face a monumental challenge—to find productive employment for a labor force that will surpass 600 million workers by 2020—about three times the present number. These jobs are more likely to be created in a myriad of small and microenterprises than in a few large firms. Fortunately there is no shortage of entrepreneurship in Africa. During the recent years of economic crisis, small firms in the informal sector have provided a growing

share of jobs and output. Estimates indicate that these enterprises currently provide more than half of Africa's urban employment and as much as one-fifth of GDP in many countries.

Unregulated and unrecorded, the informal sector is home to small firms in agriculture, industry, trade, transport, finance, and social services. It is not static and not necessarily traditional in its techniques, but it undertakes innovations and adaptations indicated by market forces. In the informal sector enterprises find a business environment that is competitive, free from unjustified regulatory constraints, and well-adapted to local resource endowments and demand. These enterprises are also supported by a system of grassroots institutions: on-the-job apprenticeships that provide training and small associations that can represent group interests and improve access to credit and other resources.

But the capacity of Africa's small and microenterprises as a seedbed for entrepreneurship and jobs remains limited by restrictive business environments and inadequate links with formal markets. Governments can help these enterprises to grow in several ways.

• Improving the business environment. Regular consultations with private sector associations can increase confidence in the stability of reforms. Specific actions include regularizing the legal status of enterprises in the informal sector, eliminating unnecessary taxes that stifle initiative, removing excessive regulatory constraints, protecting property and contract rights, and ensuring fair settlement of disputes.

• Expanding access to credit. Banks should be allowed to charge market-based interest rates that reflect the costs of small-scale lending. For the smallest enterprises, informal groups can provide mutual guarantees that mobilize resources and use social pressures to ensure repayment.

• Encouraging self-sustaining services. Trade and professional associations, NGOs, and grassroots organizations are often better at delivering extension services and technical assistance than government agencies. Policies that support subcontracting links between firms and encourage local consulting firms can improve access to technology and inputs.

• Stimulating local markets. Government purchase of goods and public services, such as refuse collection, transport, vehicle repair, and road maintenance, can all be contracted out to small firms. Improved infrastructure linkages and targeted assistance programs can also help accelerate entrepreneurial responses to market incentives.

Unlocking Africa's mineral wealth

Africa is well endowed with minerals (including oil), and so far only a fraction of this wealth has been extracted. But these riches are a mixed blessing. Large revenues received by governments in the past have too often disrupted rather than promoted real development. The income has been spent unwisely, compounded by heavy borrowing secured on future revenues, which led to an excessive debt burden. Massive distortions have entered the pricing system and have obstructed agricultural and industrial growth. The development of mines and oil wells will make its proper contribution to Africa's long-term growth only if governments exercise tight financial discipline, rigorously appraise new investment, and prevent exchange rates from becoming overvalued.

Very little mineral exploration has been undertaken in Africa in recent years because transnational mining companies (the most important potential source of investment in mining development) have found Sub-Saharan Africa the least attractive place to operate. Unfortunately, for their part the foreign companies that do invest have often contributed to the malaise by withholding information and by failing to train local staff or to build links with the local economy. Managing this relation successfully—to the benefit of both parties—is another challenge for the future.

During the past two decades, African production of 10 major minerals has declined by an average of 2 percent annually, whereas that in Latin America and Asia has grown. But with more favorable policies this trend could easily be reversed. A feasible target would be to expand output by 5 percent a year over the long term, although it will take time to build up to that level. It will require an annual investment (largely private) of around $1 billion in exploration and development, about five times present spending. As before this will be possible only within an enabling environment of competitive exchange rates; guaranteed repatriation of profits; stable, transparent, and equitable fiscal management; and an attractive mining code that clarifies reciprocal obligations. In short governments need to build a new, more balanced partnership with foreign investors. The alternative approach—state mining companies using hired expertise, with the country itself bearing all the risk—has performed poorly in the past and is better avoided in the future. All this applies equally well to oil and gas production.

Energy for growth

The demand for energy grows roughly in step with GDP—possibly a little faster in the lower-income countries. Without assured energy supplies, African economies will not grow. To achieve the needed 5 percent expansion in energy production, Africa will have to invest some $28 billion during the next 10 years, equivalent to about 2 percent of GDP annually.

Africa has abundant energy resources, although these are unevenly distributed. Proven oil reserves alone are equivalent to 120 years of current consumption. Less than 4 percent of Africa's hydroenergy potential has been developed. Known reserves of gas are equivalent to 20 times current installed hydropower capacity; exploitable coal reserves amount to 135 billion tons.

To meet Africa's energy needs, formidable technical, financial, and environmental problems must be overcome. Careful planning will be needed to establish the least-cost mix of energy sources. Opportunities exist to reduce overall costs through intercountry cooperation, using Africa's oil reserves to earn more foreign exchange and making full use of natural gas, which causes less pollution and is difficult to transport to overseas markets. Large savings are possible simply from better management of power utilities and more efficient energy use.

Household energy poses a special problem. Four-fifths of Africans depend on woodfuels—but well over 50 million people face acute shortages, and the number is growing rapidly. Measures to promote tree planting and to encourage the use of more efficient stoves or alternatives, such as bottled gas and kerosene, are urgently needed. Charging fees for fuelwood and charcoal would help, but means would have to be found to assist the poorest families. Measures to overcome the household energy crisis should be an integral part of each country's environmental action plan.

Closer ties among African states

African leaders have long recognized the need for closer regional ties. Most African economies are too small to achieve economies of scale or specialization without trade, and their firms too new and inexperienced to compete with established overseas exporters without some protection. But progress toward economic integration has been disappointing. Official intraregional trade has hardly grown in 20 years. Nonetheless the case for larger integrated markets is confirmed by thriving unofficial trade.

Only one trade group—the francophone West African Economic Community (CEAO)—has scored some success. Thanks to lower nontariff barriers, a common convertible currency, a satisfactory compensation mechanism, and labor mobility, trade among the members has grown to around 10 percent of their total trade. That contrasts strikingly with the 3 percent for the larger Economic Community of West African States (ECOWAS).

If the goal of greater regional integration is to be realized, bolder efforts will be needed to create an enabling environment. First, there must be much greater harmonization of macroeconomic policies, particularly exchange rate policy, which can be part of a phased program of trade liberalization favoring African products over those from abroad. A top-down dirigiste approach—governments deciding which enterprises will go where—will work at the regional level no better than at the national level. Rather, integration must follow market signals. Second, experience suggests that the approach most likely to succeed will be pragmatic and incremental, allowing two or more countries to move forward wherever opportunities arise. For instance two countries with nonconvertible currencies could agree to allow market clearing of their payments imbalances through the open market operations of commercial financial institutions. This would be consistent with the Lagos Plan concept of phased integration. Third, needless obstacles to movements of capital, labor, and goods should be removed. Simpler administrative procedures, uniform national standards, and better communications would make a big difference. (At present up to 70 separate steps may be necessary to take goods across a border legally.) Infrastructure investments should still be made only in response to established demand. Fourth, through chambers of commerce the private sector can do more to disseminate market information.

The proliferation of regional institutions, created ad hoc over the years, has made coordination and financing difficult. Rationalizing these institutions should be high on the agenda. This would promote not only economic integration, but also greater regional cooperation across a broad range of issues, such as education, research, and watershed management. Consistent with the priority proposed for capacity building and technology training, particular attention should be given to creating regional centers of excellence.

Sustainable funding for development

REORIENTING DEVELOPING EXPENDITURE. For output to grow at the target of 5 percent a year, Sub-Saharan Africa will need to raise investment from the present 15 percent of GDP to 25 percent. Total expenditure on human resource development should be steadily expanded until it reaches 8 to 10 percent of GDP annually, about double present spending (with donors meeting about half the total). Infrastructure spending should rise to around 6 percent of GDP. This would cover capital and recurrent expenditure and ensure adequate resources for maintenance and running costs. In contrast to the past, the bulk of investment in the productive sectors (estimated at 4 percent of GDP for agriculture and 3 percent for industry) would come from private investors. Rigorous appraisal of all public investment is essential to raise the efficiency of investment.

HIGHER PUBLIC SAVINGS. A significant effort is needed to generate public savings by both raising revenues and controlling expenditures and to do so in a way that is consistent with the priorities of the future development strategy. Thus, progressively and as far as feasible, taxes on trade—that is, on producers (and especially exporters)—should be replaced by taxes on consumers. For example, higher tariffs could be charged for utility services and fees collected for certain social services. Revenue measures should be matched by much stricter financial discipline to limit waste, to ensure that spending reflects development priorities, and to achieve a better balance between expenditure on wages and materials. The goal would be to lower the public wage bill, which currently absorbs as much as 60 percent of revenues in some countries, and to raise expenditures on materials needed for the staff to work efficiently and for maintenance. Savings could also come from lower subsidies to the parastatals and from reduced military expenditures.

MOBILIZING PRIVATE SAVINGS. Africa's traditions of sharing and community-based development provide an avenue for mobilizing private savings. Contributions might be in cash or labor and be applied to a wide range of local community projects, such as primary schools, health clinics, and the supply of drinking water. Strongly supported by government, these grassroots initiatives could make an important contribution.

There is also considerable potential for mobilizing additional household savings through the formal and informal financial systems. In many African countries the formal financial system has deteriorated in recent years. Reforms are urgently needed. These should aim to bring about market-determined interest rates and credit allocation, stronger bank supervision, and adequate prudential ratios and debt collection. The broad objective is to deepen and diversify financial intermediation. There is further scope, too, for encouraging informal savings and credit institutions, which can extend financial services to farmers and to informal sector enterprises, especially in remote areas. More attractive investment opportunities for the informal sector will, by themselves, promote savings by those seeking to expand their household enterprises—for example, by buying plows, oxen, or fishing nets.

THE EXTERNAL RESOURCE BALANCE. If Africa's economies are to grow, they must earn foreign exchange to pay for essential imports. Thus it is vital that they increase their share of world markets. The prospects for significant increases in world prices for most primary commodities are poor, so higher export earnings must come from increased output, diversification into new commodities, and an aggressive export drive into the rapidly growing Asian markets. In the proposed growth scenario the ratio of exports to GDP is targeted to rise from 19 percent in 1986--87, to about 24 percent by 2000, and to 28 percent by 2020. To make up for the compression that has occurred during the past decade, imports in the early 1990s would need to grow significantly faster than overall GDP—to about 33 percent of GDP in 2000—and thereafter they would grow in step with GDP.

Several assumptions underlie the overall resource balance: an initial target GDP growth of 4 percent a year, rising later to 5 percent; total investment of 25 percent of GDP throughout the period; and domestic savings of 18 percent of GDP by 2000, increasing to 22 percent by 2020. The net transfers (including all forms of financing) required to close the gap are estimated to be 9 percent of GDP by 2000. Thereafter the need for

foreign savings would decline, and drop to 5 percent of GDP by 2020.

While average per capita income will grow by less than 1 percent during the 1990s and overall per capita consumption will stagnate, the impact across income groups will vary. The top 5 percent of income earners, who belong to the modern sector, will contribute most to increased public savings, and consequently their consumption will be compressed, while the rest of the population— those working in the rural areas and in small and microenterprises— will enjoy a rising level of consumption of about 2 percent a year.

The proposed scenario for sustained growth is fragile. It is built on the assumption that targets for the key parameters (levels of investment, savings, incremental capital-output ratios, and the like) will be achieved. These targets are all ambitious. Some countries will not meet them. Some should do better. To the extent they fail, the outlook will be that much bleaker.

Development assistance in the 1990s

The momentum of the growth of aid during the past few years will have to be maintained during the 1990s if the reforming African countries are to persist with their difficult adjustment programs and if the countries that have not yet embarked on reform are ever to do so. Adding to the demands, there may be some new entrants (currently classified as middle-income) to the list of IDA-eligible countries. Moreover special efforts will be needed in the 1990s to reverse Africa's backsliding in areas such as food security, human resource development, and infrastructure and to fund new initiatives in family planning and environmental protection.

The external resource requirements of Sub-Saharan Africa could be met if the donor community:

• Increased gross official development assistance (ODA) during the 1990s at about 4 percent a year in real terms (which is below the rate achieved during the 1980s)

• Put in place concessional debt relief mechanisms (preferably debt reduction) so that debt service payments are at most no greater than in recent years (that is, no more than $9 billion for all Sub-Saharan Africa). To this end, the middle-income countries should be considered eligible for concessional debt relief measures.

The above assumptions lead to a gross ODA requirement of $22 billion a year (at 1990 prices) by 2000. These estimates imply that if the critical minimum needs for reversing Africa's decline are to be met, ODA needs to grow at 4 percent a year in real terms. The combination of low *and* declining per capita incomes create special difficulties for Africa that require special assistance efforts. Furthermore, during this period there may be special new ODA needs if more African countries are added to the list of IDA-eligible countries. If these efforts are not forthcoming, Africa's decline is likely to continue in the 1990s. If, however, the special programs of assistance started in the 1980s can be continued for another decade, Africa should be able to reverse its decline and level off, and eventually reduce, aid.

AID COMPOSITION. In line with the strategy proposed in this report, ODA should be increasingly focused on four priorities:

• Supporting public expenditures on physical infrastructure and human resource development. As far as possible external financing should fund "time slices" of sector and subsector expenditure programs, including recurrent outlays for operation and maintenance.

• Using structural adjustment financing more selectively, although it will remain an important component of aid in the 1990s and beyond. Policy lending should be given increasingly in support of measures already adopted, rather than with conditionality based on promises of future action.

• Assisting private sector initiative at all levels and using NGOs to channel more ODA, particularly for grassroots development.

• Fostering regional integration by supporting the rationalization of regional institutions and helping to cover the transitional costs of trade liberalization within Africa.

With these priorities, the suggested composition of ODA would be 25 percent each for social and physical infrastructure and 50 percent for the productive sectors, technical assistance, and program assistance.

MAKING AID EFFECTIVE. The financing gap is large and growing. The aid required can be justified only if it is used effectively and only if it is clear that the need for aid will eventually decline. Neither donors nor recipients can accept a strategy that envisages permanent dependency. There must be a credible commitment to ensure that aid funds do not go, even indirectly, to finance military spending, luxury consumption, or capital flight.

If a new and more equal partnership is to make aid more effective, then the design and monitoring of macropolicy and the related aid program should be placed on parallel tracks. The dialogue would be as intense and disciplined as under structural adjustment lending. But it should be clear that the reform program is the government's—expressed in its own policy papers and internalized through local seminars and workshops. Then donor support linked to specific programs or project expenditures would reflect overall performance. Assistance should become far more selective among countries and be biased strongly in favor of sound and sustained reform programs.

Reflecting the priority accorded to capacity building, technical assistance will remain a crucial component of donor support. But with about $7 per capita being spent annually, donors and recipients are clearly not getting value for their money. Most technical assistance is uncoordinated, improvised, poorly managed, and rarely fitted into a comprehensive strategy for capacity building or institutional development. A radical reappraisal must be undertaken on a country-by-country basis. Greater use should be made of consultants from Africa and other developing countries and much more attention given to transferring skills. The long-term target must be to reduce technical assistance sharply. The first step is to replace long-term experts with short-term consultants.

A strategic agenda for the 1990s

This report sketches a menu of options and ideas to guide the formulation of long-term development strategies. Its conclusions are inevitably couched in general terms; they do no more than indicate the directions forward. Each country must develop the approach that suits its particular circumstances. Debate, even over these general propositions, will continue among Africans and between African countries and their external partners. But the aim must be to seek the highest common ground for joint action.

Already a consensus seems to be emerging on some important points. As a result, a strategic agenda for the 1990s can be suggested.

• Adjustment programs should continue to evolve. Programs must take fuller account of the social impact of reforms (and increase budget expenditures on human resource development), and investment needs to accelerate growth and measures that are required to assure sustainability.

The goal is not simply to achieve macroeconomic balance but over time to fundamentally transform Africa's production structures.

• The strategy should be people-centered. Human resource development and meeting basic needs are top priorities.

• Capacity building needs to be deliberately pursued through institutional reforms at every level of government and by measures to foster private sector and nongovernmental organizations and to enable women to play their full role in economic and social development.

• An enabling policy environment that fosters private investment should be put in place. Greater efforts to provide efficient infrastructure services are crucial, as is support to the informal sector for generating income and employment.

• To overcome the nexus of weak agricultural production, rapid population growth, and environmental degradation, agricultural research and extension services would have to be strengthened, family planning services expanded, and environmental action plans adopted.

• Regional integration and coordination should be pursued through a series of pragmatic, incremental steps to facilitate trade across borders, labor mobility, education, research, and natural resource management. A first step would be to rationalize regional institutions.

• Special programs of assistance to Africa should be continued throughout the decade.

None of these measures will go far, nor will much external aid be forthcoming, unless governance in Africa improves. Leaders must become more accountable to their peoples. Transactions must become more transparent, and funds must be seen to be properly administered, with audit reports made public and procurement procedures overhauled.

The challenge facing Africa is exceptional. The cost of failure would be appalling. Much depends on the relation between African governments and their foreign partners. New and closer forms of collaboration should be devised to ensure that policy is continuously reviewed. To facilitate this dialogue, a global coalition for Africa should be created. This would provide a forum in which African leaders in the public sector, private business, the professions, and the universities and their key partners could agree on general strategies that would provide broad guidance for the design of individual country programs and on specific action programs for greater African cooperation.

The coalition could give particular attention to reaching the high ground of agreement on actions to tackle the priorities identified in the following chapters: environmental protection, capacity building, population policy, food security, and regional integration and cooperation. And it could provide impetus for channeling aid to these priority programs. Such a coalition would be a concrete demonstration of a shared new resolve to work together pragmatically to build a better future for Africa.

1

A thirty-year perspective: Past and future

Past patterns and trends

At independence Africans had high hopes of rapid development. New energies were released by the ending of colonialism, and African leaders were determined that their countries should catch up with the developed world. "We must run while they walk" well summarizes the spirit in those early days. No time was to be lost in overcoming "ignorance, poverty, and disease." Africans were encouraged to be bold by the many who argued that Africa could find shortcuts to development. The donor community shared this optimism and contributed substantial resources.

The first generation of African leaders adopted economic strategies that echoed the ideas of prominent economists of the day. Industrialization was believed to be the engine of economic growth and the key to transforming traditional economies—partly because the prospects for commodity exports were thought to be poor and partly because of a strong desire to reduce dependence on manufactured imports. Agriculture was relegated to a secondary role of supplying raw materials and providing tax revenues to finance other development. To implement these strategies, African leaders believed that government had to play the dominant role. That view reflected their mistrust of foreign business, the perceived shortages of domestic private capital and entrepreneurship, and an underlying distrust of market mechanisms. As a result, and generally with full donor support, governments drew up comprehensive five-year plans; invested in large, state-run core industries; and enacted pervasive regulations to control prices, restrict trade, and allocate credit and foreign exchange.

Much was achieved. Starting from a low base, African countries have significantly raised life expectancy and expanded literacy and health care. There has been enormous growth in the number of trained people, and major investments have been made in Africa's infrastructure: roads, ports, telecommunications, and power. The region has seen important successes, as well as failures, and has accumulated valuable experience in managing development. Countries born with arbitrary colonial borders have struggled to establish nation states and to put new governmental structures in place. In some—notably Angola, Mozambique, Somalia, and Sudan—the struggle continues and takes precedence over economic and social development. South Africa has been a further source of conflict and destabilization throughout southern Africa.

Overall economic growth in Sub-Saharan Africa has averaged 3.4 percent a year since 1961, a fraction faster than the increase in population. By 1987 this region of some 450 million people—more than double the number at independence—had a total gross domestic product (GDP) (at market prices) of nearly $135 billion, about that of Belgium, which has only 10 million inhabitants.

Economic growth initially was moderate—although slower than the average for other developing countries. The pace quickened after 1967. Record commodity prices and high investments financed from export earnings, commercial borrowing, and aid helped raise the growth rate. But then, as the 1970s advanced, countries began to

Figure 1.1 Gross national income per capita in Sub-Saharan Africa and other developing countries, 1967-87

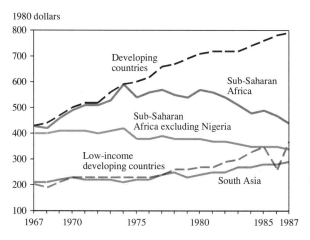

1980 dollars

Source: World Bank data.

stumble. By the middle of the decade Africa's performance had fallen below that of other developing countries. By the 1980s output was actually declining (see Figure 1.1).

Throughout Africa much of the modern sector has been in malaise for nearly a decade. In contrast, the nonformal sector (broadly defined to include indigenous, mainly unregistered, enterprises in both urban and rural areas as well as local intermediary, nongovernmental, and grassroots organizations) has shown remarkable dynamism. This applies to a broad range of activities in agriculture, industry, trade, transportation, finance, social services, and even regional trade and integration.

Behind the broad trends experience has varied greatly from country to country (see Figure 1.2). Average annual GDP growth during 1961–87 ranged from 8.3 percent (Botswana) to minus 2.2 percent (Uganda). Oil accounts for much of the variation, with oil exporters doing well or badly according to fluctuations in the oil price. Excluding the oil economies, aggregate annual growth initially rose but generally declined in the late 1970s and 1980s.

These variations in country experience reflect the rich diversity in Sub-Saharan Africa. Even within countries there are often large differences. The region contains a multiplicity of ethnic groups, languages, and religions. Almost no country is culturally or socially homogeneous. Governments vary from working democracies that encourage debate and dialogue to authoritarian regimes that trample dissent. Some economies are

tightly controlled, while others operate largely on market principles. The climatic zones span the whole spectrum from temperate, well-watered highlands to arid deserts and from dry savannah to tropical rainforests. Countries vary from tiny to vast. Five alone account for more than half the inhabitants of the region. The population of Nigeria is more than 100 million, while nine countries have less than 1 million. Population densities are very uneven, with more than 246 persons per square kilometer around Lake Victoria to less than 1 in Mauritania. Fifteen countries are landlocked, and six are islands. Incomes per capita vary by a factor of 20. Some countries have considerable mineral or oil wealth, while others have almost none.

Despite this diversity there are surprising commonalities in the problems facing Sub-Saharan countries: high rates of population growth, low levels of investment and saving (except in a few of the mineral-rich economies), inefficient resource use, weak institutional capacity and human resources, and a general decline in income and living standards. It is therefore possible to draw out common themes that provide a framework for discussing the problems of Sub-Saharan Africa as a whole—themes that will then merit further exploration country by country to take account of specific country circumstances, a task that can be effectively tackled only by country specialists.

The deepening crisis

Sub-Saharan Africa has now witnessed almost a decade of falling per capita incomes and accelerating ecological degradation. Per capita food production first fell, then rose, but remains lower than in 1980. Africa has lost a substantial part of its share in the world market for its exports. Some African countries have surrendered some of the gains they made earlier in human resource development—notably in school enrollments. Open urban unemployment is a growing problem in many countries.

In the past decade six countries—Equatorial Guinea, Ghana, Liberia, Nigeria, São Tomé and Principe, and Zambia—have slipped from the middle-income to the low-income group (as classified in the *World Development Report*). If overvalued exchange rates were taken into account, more would have slipped. In the early 1960s Sub-Saharan African countries had per capita incomes similar to those in other developing countries. But African incomes began to fall behind in the 1970s,

Figure 1.2 Diversity of economic performance in Sub-Saharan Africa

Per capita GDP growth rate, 1961-87

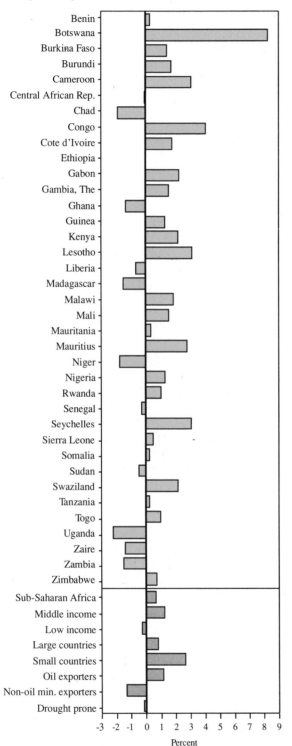

and, if present trends continue, they will be on a par with those of the poorest countries of Asia by the turn of the century (see Figure 1.1 above). Thirteen African countries—accounting for a third of the region's population—are actually poorer in per capita terms today than they were at independence.

Several countries stand out in contrast against this picture of general decline. Botswana, Cameroon, Congo, Lesotho, Mauritius, Seychelles, and, to a lesser extent, Gabon and Kenya achieved significant per capita income growth between 1961 and 1987. But in recent years the oil producers experienced dramatic declines when oil prices collapsed.

Africa's generally poor performance during the past 10 years has been reflected in weak growth in the productive sectors, poor export performance, mounting debt, deteriorating social conditions, environmental degradation, and the increasing decay of institutional capacity. Each of these trends, and the reasons for them, is discussed below.

Weak growth in the productive sectors

During the past two decades the contribution of agriculture to production has declined to less than one-third of GDP; industry (including mining and oil production) grew much faster, at 6 percent a year, and rose to 28 percent of GDP (see Figure 1.3). But these broad trends do not reflect any fundamental transformation in Africa's productive structure, diversification of exports, or change in trade patterns. For the region as a whole, new oil extraction simply made up for lagging agricultural production. Manufacturing remained at about 10 percent of GDP and contributed less than one-tenth to exports.

During the 1960s agricultural production grew at 2.7 percent a year, about the same as population. Thereafter agricultural growth slowed considerably, averaging only 1.4 percent from 1970 to 1985—half the rate of population growth. This decline was due to many factors, including severe

Note: Large countries are Ethiopia, Kenya, Nigeria, Sudan, Tanzania, and Uganda. Small countries are Gabon, The Gambia, Mauritius, Seychelles, and Swaziland. Non-oil mineral exporters are Liberia, Mauritania, Togo, Zaire, Zambia, and Zimbabwe. Drought-prone countries are Burkina Faso, Chad, Ethiopia, Mali, Mauritania, Niger, Senegal, Somalia, and Sudan.
Source: World Bank data.

Figure 1.3 Structure of GDP in Sub-Saharan Africa

(percentage of GDP)

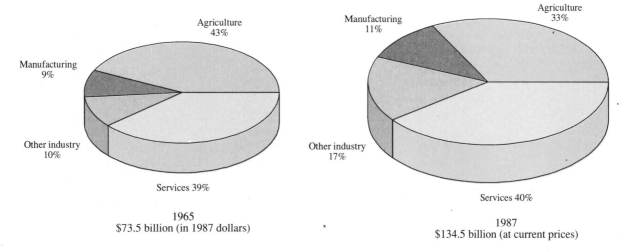

Note: Other industry includes mining and petroleum.
Source: World Bank data.

droughts in 1972–73 and 1983–84. But it also reflects the low priority accorded to farming by Africa's postindependence development strategies. Policies kept farm prices low; encouraged labor and capital to flow into cities; promoted cheap imports of foods such as wheat and rice, which are preferred by urban consumers; and neglected agricultural research.

With population growing faster than food production, higher commercial food imports and food aid have been necessary, although not sufficient. But lack of purchasing power and other distributional factors have meant that hunger has nonetheless become more widespread (see Chapter 3).

Some of the other productive sectors did better, but not by much. Although in the 1960s manufacturing grew by more than 8 percent a year, this initial spurt did not last; the average growth rate for 1965–87 was about the same as total GDP. The volume of mineral production, as measured by exports, grew only 1.7 percent a year, no faster than agricultural output, because of inadequate exploration and excessive taxation, which prevented maintenance and modernization. Only petroleum output expanded substantially during the period, although output (again measured by exports) has fallen by more than a third since its peak around 1980. Rising petroleum production accounts for the 5 percent annual growth of industrial GDP during 1965–87.

Poor export performance

During the 1960s the volume of exports from African countries grew on average by 6 percent a year. Almost all countries shared in this growth. Since 1973, however, export volumes have remained stagnant or declined significantly in most of the countries. For Sub-Saharan Africa as a whole, including oil exporters, the total volume of exports has declined, on average, by about 0.7 percent a year (see Figure 1.4).

During the 1960s agricultural exports (which now account for one-fifth of agricultural production) grew at nearly 2 percent a year. But since then they have declined sharply—by more than 3 percent a year (see Figure 1.5). As a result Africa's share of world exports for most of its major crop exports fell during the 1970s and early 1980s. For example, between 1970 and 1984 Africa's world market share for three main agricultural exports—coffee, cocoa, and cotton—shrank by 13, 33, and 29 percent, respectively. Of the six major agricultural exports, market share rose only for tea.

The share of African exports in all world trade fell from 2.4 percent in 1970 to 1.7 percent in 1985 (see Figure 1.6). Its share of non-oil primary commodities declined even more dramatically, from 7 percent to well below 4 percent. The implications are substantial: if Sub-Saharan countries had maintained their 1970 market share of non-oil primary exports from developing countries and prices had remained the same, their export earnings would have been $9 billion to $10 billion a year higher in 1986–87. The difference is approximately equal to the region's total debt service payments in this period. In practice part of this gain might have been lost because of lower prices resulting from increased supplies; however, Africa's competitors might not have expanded their exports so much had African countries been stronger exporters (see Chapter 8).

The structure of Sub-Saharan exports has remained largely unchanged since the early 1960s. The heavy reliance on primary commodities (including oil) persists; they accounted for 93 percent

most have been written by a lawyer!

Figure 1.4 Merchandise exports from Sub-Saharan Africa, 1965-87

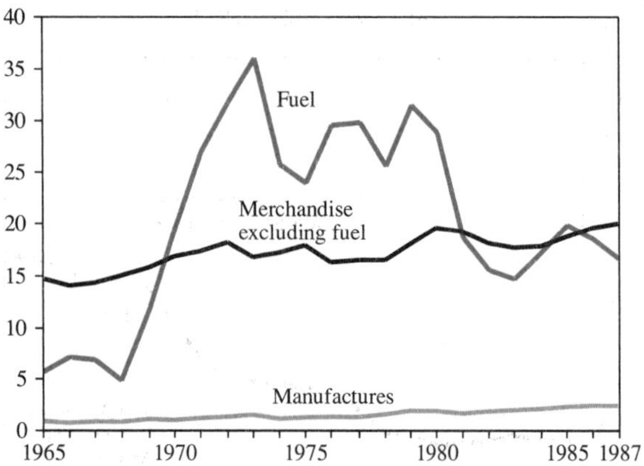

Billions of 1980 dollars

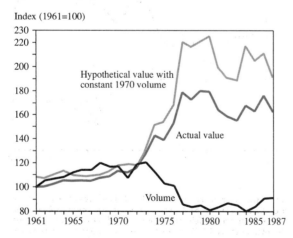

Source: World Bank data.

Figure 1.5 Volume and value of Sub-Saharan Africa's agricultural exports, 1961-87

Index (1961=100)

Note: The dashed line shows that export value would have been higher if export volume had kept up to its 1970 level.
Source: FAO data.

Figure 1.6 Sub-Saharan Africa's share in the value of exports, 1960-85

Percent

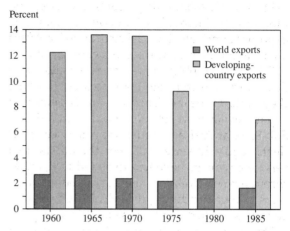

Source: UNCTAD data.

of total export earnings in 1970, declining to 88 percent by the mid-1980s. A few countries, such as Kenya and Mauritius, have partly diversified out of primary products, but they remain the exceptions. The markets for Sub-Saharan African exports have also changed little. Roughly half the region's exports still go to the European Community. African exporters have yet to take advantage of the booming markets of Asia.

Mounting debt

In the face of declining commodity prices, many African countries resorted to heavy external borrowing to sustain levels of expenditures made possible by earlier booms. Sub-Saharan Africa's total debt increased from about $6 billion in 1970 to $134 billion in 1988. By the end of that period the region's debt was about equal to its gross national product (GNP) and three-and-a-half times its export earnings. Roughly 70 percent of total debt, including short-term commercial trade credits and drawings from the International Monetary Fund (IMF), is at market rates.

Sub-Saharan Africa's debt has grown faster than that of other developing regions, especially since 1980. Long-term debt has increased 19-fold since 1970 and is now the heaviest of all; Latin American debt, for example, is only about 59 percent of GNP. But Sub-Saharan Africa owes less to private creditors (39 percent compared with 73 percent), and about a third of their private debt is guaranteed by creditor governments. Sub-Saharan Africa's difficulties in servicing its commercial debt have received relatively little attention because its share in total developing-country debt is small (about 10 percent) and poses no threat to the international banking system. The exposure of private financial institutions in Africa is concentrated in a few middle-income countries.

Debt service obligations, the real measure of debt burden, rose in the 1980s to a point where they could not be met. They stood at 47 percent of export revenues in 1988. No more than a dozen Sub-Saharan African countries have serviced their debts regularly since 1980. For the others debt service payments have had to be reduced, either through rescheduling or the accumulation of arrears. Altogether during 1980–88, 25 Sub-Saharan countries rescheduled their debts 105 times.

Debt service actually paid averaged 27 percent of Sub-Saharan Africa's exports in 1985–88 (see Figure 1.7). This represented only about three-fifths of the region's obligations. Low-income countries had an even higher debt service ratio—30 percent, a crippling burden for countries where poverty remains so widespread.

The debt crisis in Sub-Saharan Africa is not uniform in its origins or its effects. By virtually every measure the low-income countries face the harshest difficulties. Their debt ratios are nearly double those in the highly indebted middle-income countries and more than triple those of low-income Asian countries. Because much of this debt is concessional (almost half of total debt in low-income Africa compared with 5 percent in the highly indebted countries (HICs)), the usual debt ratios may overstate the real debt burden borne by low-income Africa. The estimated grant equivalent in low-income Africa's existing debt is about $17 billion. But even adjusting for this greater concessionality, the bite that debt service payments take out of countries' capacity to import each year is clearly unsustainable in an environment of low investment and stagnant GDP.

The debt burden of the middle-income countries in Sub-Saharan Africa is also more severe than that of other HICs. Although their ratio of debt to exports is only slightly lower, these economies have a lower capacity to adjust to their debt overhang. Their per capita GNP is only about a third that of the other HICs. Their economies are, on average, smaller. Their export structures are generally more rigid, with a higher share concentrated in a few primary commodities; export growth has been erratic and lower on average. Their economic performance has in general been much more negative than that of the other HICs,

with stagnating GDP growth and drastically declining per capita consumption. Their imports have been compressed even more than those of the countries eligible for the Special Program of Assistance (SPA), which have benefited, at least recently, from rising official development assistance (ODA) disbursements. Projected debt service ratios are considerably higher than those of the HICs. A higher share of their debt is owed to official creditors, while their commercial debt is generally worth less on secondary markets.

Figure 1.7 External debt of Sub-Saharan Africa and highly indebted countries, 1970-87

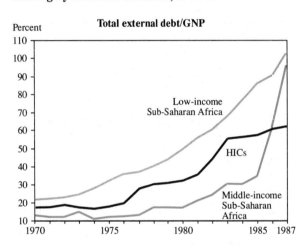

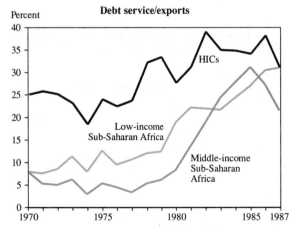

Note: HICs refers to the group of 17 highly indebted developing countries, listed in World Bank 1988h, of which two are in Sub-Saharan Africa. Total external debt is outstanding and disbursed long-term debt, short-term debt (1977–87), and IMF credit. Debt service is interest and amortization for long-term debt. Exports are goods and services. Percentages are based on debt in current dollars.
Source: World Bank data.

Deteriorating social conditions

There is growing evidence of deterioration in the social sectors. Primary school enrollment rates have declined since 1980, and life expectancy is lagging well below South Asia's. The problem of food insecurity is becoming ever more daunting; in the 1970s the proportion of Africans with deficient diets increased slightly (while the population increased substantially). The adverse economic environment of the 1980s has accelerated the deterioration. In the 1980s barely a quarter of Sub-Saharan Africans lived in countries in which food consumption per capita was increasing; in the 1970s the corresponding proportion had been about two-thirds.

Despite slowing economic growth, government spending per person in the social sectors continued to rise in real terms until the early 1980s. After 1981–83, however, these expenditures began to fall, reflecting the acute financial difficulties faced by an increasing number of governments. The cuts tended to fall mainly on nonwage recurrent costs. Spending here was already too low—in 1983 a mere $0.60 on each primary school pupil annually.

Growing open unemployment is becoming a significant concern in virtually every African country. This is partly a consequence of urbanization, which transforms rural underemployment into urban open unemployment. A particularly worrisome aspect is the mounting number of educated unemployed, in part a result of an educational system that is insufficiently responsive to local needs.

Environmental degradation

Within Sub-Saharan Africa's 21 million square kilometers natural water and land resources hold vast potential for growth. But the ecology of Africa is fragile, and there are clear signs of ecological degradation. The pressure of population is causing desertification to accelerate, because it forces people and their livestock farther onto marginal grassland. The productive capacity of land is falling because of shorter rotations, soil erosion, and overgrazing. Growing population also raises the demand for fuelwood and cropland, and the resulting deforestation increases runoff and erosion, lowers groundwater levels, and may further reduce rainfall in arid areas. Pollution is a growing problem, especially in poorly serviced urban areas. And, to compound these problems, some

industrial countries are trying to dump their toxic waste in Africa.

Against this background of growing, continent-wide damage to the environment, certain ecological zones have special problems. The Sahel and areas bordering the Kalahari face encroaching deserts and soil degradation accelerated by drought. Countries with tropical rainforests have to contend with accelerated deforestation. Soil erosion is particularly acute in areas of dense settlement and cultivation—for example, in parts of Burundi, Ethiopia, Kenya, and Uganda.

Institutional decay and political instability

In many African countries the administrations, judiciaries, and educational institutions are now mere shadows of their former selves. This widespread institutional decay is symbolized by the poor physical condition of once world-class institutions such as the University of Legon in Ghana and Makerere University in Uganda, by the breakdown of judicial systems in a number of countries, by the poor state of once high-quality roads, and by the dilapidation of once well-functioning railways.

Equally worrying is the widespread impression of political decline. Corruption, oppression, and nepotism are increasingly evident. These are hardly unique to Africa, but they may have been exacerbated by development strategies that concentrated power and resources in government bureaucracies, without countervailing measures to ensure public accountability or political consensus. On the one hand, in several countries the neglect of due process has robbed institutions of their legitimacy and credibility. On the other hand, the proliferation of administrative regulations such as licensing, controls, and quotas has encouraged corruption and set the individual against the system.

Sometimes the military have deposed unpopular regimes. But often this has led to more, not less, state violence and lawlessness. Occasionally it has led even to civil war. These disruptions have driven many to become refugees, both directly by threatening lives and indirectly by making drought and other natural calamities harder to cope with. Sub-Saharan Africa, with one-tenth of the world's population, now accounts for about a third (or almost 4 million) of the world's officially recognized refugees. In addition the region has another 12 million or so displaced persons. In southern Africa destabilizing policies have dis-

The human and economic costs of conflict and destabilization in southern Africa have been staggering. Studies undertaken by SADCC, the ECA, and UNICEF point to quantifiable costs approaching 25 to 40 percent of GDP annually and even greater in Mozambique and Angola, the most devastated nations.

The costs cut across all sectors of the economy. Military spending has diverted enormous resources from southern Africa's development, and has consumed nearly 50 percent of government expenditures in the countries experiencing the worst destabilization. Exports have suffered throughout the region, and import costs have risen as transport routes have been disrupted, forcing landlocked countries to use circuitous routes through South Africa. This has resulted in lost revenues and higher costs for these countries (as much as 40 percent higher for Malawi). In addition there has been the heavy burden of emergency assistance to the 5 million to 7 million displaced persons who have been forced to flee their land and homes; in financial terms alone this has exceeded 1 billion dollars during the 1980s, over and above the contributions of international relief efforts. Again, Mozambique and Angola have had to bear the bulk of these costs, but the capacity of neighboring countries has also been strained. Malawi, already one of the most densely populated countries in Africa, is host to some 600,000 to 700,000 refugees.

The lost resources, destroyed assets, and foregone income as a consequence of destabilization have further handicapped these economies. In Mozambique the capacity of the economy to respond to the far-reaching set of economic reforms has been severely constrained.

Angola's incipient reforms have been hampered by continuing instability. The interruption of transport routes in Malawi, necessitating further costly measures, set back the good progress made in structural adjustment in the early 1980s. The costs of adjustment have been significantly increased, especially in Zimbabwe and Zambia. While reform measures combined with international support and improved regional security should help growth rates to recover, the accumulated losses of the past decade will depress aggregate income levels for years to come.

The loss of lives and human potential defies quantification. Apart from the human suffering and misery, the death of hundreds of thousands of people, the rise in infant and child mortality, the stunted potential from famine and malnutrition, and the lack of progress in, and in some cases the virtual disintegration of, education and health service delivery systems have immeasurably set back the development in southern Africa. Building national capacities for economic and social administration and creating an environment conducive to entrepreneurial activity have been largely precluded because scarce managerial talent has been siphoned off into military and relief operations.

The prospects for establishing political stability have gradually improved, however; recent developments are especially encouraging. The economies have begun to recover, reflecting a growing momentum of policy reform and enhanced donor assistance. Nevertheless they remain highly vulnerable to destabilization. Further progress toward peace is essential to translate the recovery of recent years into sustained growth.

rupted the development of South Africa's neighbors (see Box 1.1).

Crisis of confidence

Many people in and out of Sub-Saharan Africa feel a growing sense of hopelessness. This crisis of confidence has been reinforced by the adverse external image of Africa in the global media, which focuses mainly on Africa's economic, social, and political woes—famines, desertification, refugees, human rights violations, coup d'etats, internecine violence, and health problems. Sometimes this image is projected from within Africa itself, in an effort to call forth additional exceptional external support. Yet many in and out of Africa feel that Africa may become too dependent on external financial assistance and on foreign advice and expatriate personnel. The danger is that pessimism can become self-fulfilling: weak performance breeds disappointment, responsibility is shifted to others, inaction undermines self-

confidence, and performance sinks even further. The process undermines the very basis on which to build growth and to develop African responsibility for Africa's destiny.

Factors behind the decline

Some lay the blame for the region's economic decline on factors beyond Africa's control—bad weather, weak world commodity prices, fluctuating international interest rates, and too little aid. Others blame policies, especially poor management of public resources and inappropriate incentives. Most recognize the importance of structural factors, especially high population growth.

Changes in per capita income have three main components: domestic economic growth, population growth, and changes in the terms of trade. Because Africa's problems are so frequently attributed to adverse external factors, the impact of changes in terms of trade is discussed before the internal causes.

Figure 1.8 Terms of trade and income effect in Sub-Saharan Africa, 1961-87

All Sub-Saharan Africa

Index (1961=100)

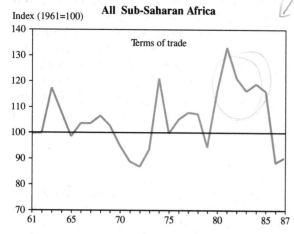

Income effect/GDP (percent)

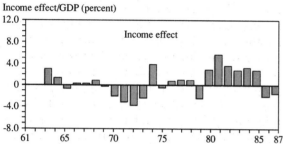

Low-income countries

Index (1961=100)

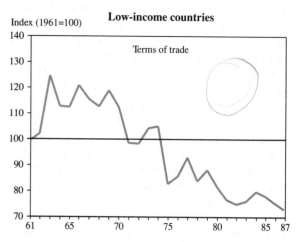

Income effect/GDP (percent)

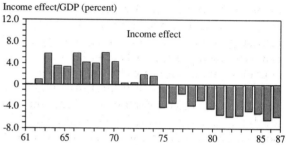

Note: Estimating terms of trade is complex, and alternate methods may be applied. Here it is defined as the ratio of export and import unit values derived from series in current and 1980 dollars for goods and nonfactor services. The "income effect" of changes in the terms of trade in a given year is calculated by multiplying the value of exports of goods and nonfactor services in 1980 dollars for that year by the percentage change in the terms of trade index. The result is shown as a percentage of GDP in 1980 dollars for that year.
Source: World Bank data.

Middle-income oil importers

Index (1961=100)

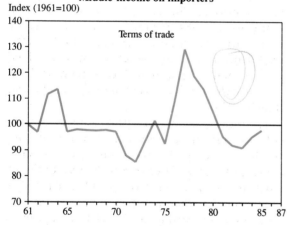

Income effect/GDP (percent)

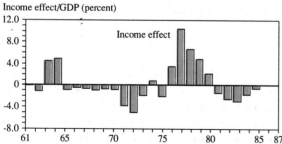

Terms of trade

The evolution of the barter terms of trade varies for different groups of countries and has changed significantly over the longer term. For the region as a whole terms of trade fell sharply in the 1980s, although the decline was from the historically high level attained in 1981. Despite the fall the terms of trade were still higher during the first half of the 1980s than in the 1960s—although by 1986–87 they were lower. The loss in income caused by deteriorating terms of trade since 1985 is far less than the earlier gains. Although declining terms of trade result in depressed levels of income, the region has gained more income (at constant prices) since 1961 from terms of trade changes than it has lost (see Figure 1.8). Except in 1986–87 the effect on per capita income growth has been small—less than one-tenth of a percentage point a year, on average, during the entire period, 1961–87. However, unstable prices have made economic management far more difficult.

Several African countries have been hard hit by persistently declining commodity prices; many had little scope to shift resources to more promising exports. The low-income countries suffered sharply declining terms of trade in the 1970s—partly because of rising oil prices. The 1980s brought them greater stability, but their terms of trade remain lower than in the past. The steady increase in aid has only partially offset this. The pattern for the middle-income oil importers is more complex, with terms of trade rising rapidly in the late 1970s followed by a general decline into the early 1980s. This decline was at first cushioned by rising commercial borrowing, but these inflows declined precipitously after 1983.

Even so, many countries in other regions have suffered similar terms of trade losses and have coped better. Africa's declining income must be attributed in large part to a combination of high population growth and low GDP growth. It is instructive to compare African per capita GDP growth since 1961 with that of South Asia, the only comparable large group of low-income countries (see Figure 1.9). Until the first oil shock, per capita GDP grew almost twice as fast in Sub-Saharan Africa. Since then, despite the fact that more than half of the region's GDP comes from oil-exporting countries that benefited from the oil shock, per capita GDP growth has been negative, and increasingly so. During this time, however, it has been increasingly positive in South Asia. On average since 1973 annual per capita GDP growth has been four percentage points lower in Africa than in South Asia.

Population growth

Sub-Saharan Africa now has twice the population it had in 1965 and more than five times the population it had at the beginning of the century. The upward trend in population growth has greatly handicapped Africa's efforts to raise per capita incomes. Had the region's population growth followed South Asia's or Latin America's declining trend since the early 1970s, per capita incomes might now have been as much as 10 percent higher than they actually are, assuming the same growth in GDP. Instead Africa has witnessed an increasing dependency ratio and, more

recently, a fall in the proportion of its people who are literate, numerate, adequately fed, and healthy, and this has had an obvious negative effect on long-term productivity. While high population growth contributes to the decline in per capita income, it is not a sufficient explanation. A crucial factor is also the low GDP growth rate, which, in turn, is a consequence of declining investment rates and the low efficiency of investment.

Declining investment

Average investment rates were roughly the same in both South Asia and Sub-Saharan Africa until 1980—roughly 16 percent of GDP in the 1960s, rising to 20 percent in the 1970s—although in real terms Africa's investment rate was less because of higher costs. Since then investment rates have declined by a quarter in Africa, while continuing to rise in South Asia. Moreover the growth of investment in Africa stopped just after the mid-1970s and has since generally declined, reflecting the drop in both the domestic and foreign savings rates. The domestic savings rate fell as declining terms of trade and production reduced real incomes and as large public sector deficits emerged. The foreign savings rate fell because nonconcessional capital flows declined dramatically in 1984–85 and because worsening domestic economic performance reduced Africa's creditworthiness. But foreign savings remained positive and, even at their lowest point in 1985, real net capital inflows were only 8 percent lower than in 1975–77.

The recent low investment rates point to difficulties in restoring growth in the future (see Chapter 8). Because its investment rates were comparable with those of South Asia until the 1980s, however, it is hard to conclude that too little investment has caused Africa's poorer economic performance since the mid-1970s. Low returns to investment are what made the difference.

Low returns to investment

Measured simply as the ratio of the growth of output to the rate of investment in a given year, Africa's returns on investment have fallen steadily. By the 1980s they were only about one-tenth of the levels in South Asia; they had been more than one-third higher in the 1960s and early 1970s. If the returns were calculated by setting investment in the late 1970s against growth in the 1980s

Figure 1.9 Sub-Saharan Africa and South Asia: Components of per capita income growth

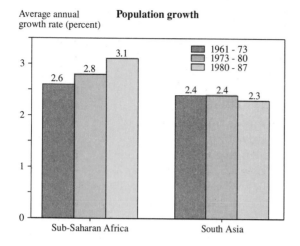

Average annual growth rate (percent)

Population growth

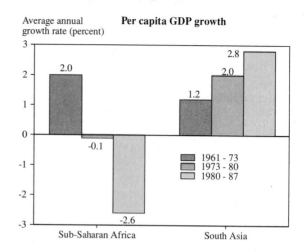

Average annual growth rate (percent)

Per capita GDP growth

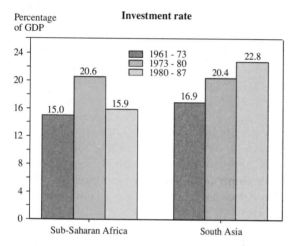

Percentage of GDP

Investment rate

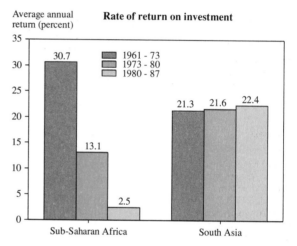

Average annual return (percent)

Rate of return on investment

Note: Ideally this measure (as well as the more conventional incremental capital-output ratio) should use *net*, rather than gross, investment. Use of gross investment means that the returns thus calculated can go down when the gross investment rate goes down, even though net returns have not. In practice the depreciation figures necessary to calculate net investment are seldom available. Assuming a depreciation rate of 10 percent of GDP (which is on the high side), the calculated net returns on investment are as follows:

This modification changes the levels of the rates of return, but the basic conclusion regarding a sharp decline in returns on investment in Africa remains unchanged. In this calculation, however, these returns are also declining in South Asia, although not as rapidly as in Africa.
Source: World Bank data.

Net rate of return
(percent)

Region	1961–73	1973–80	1980–87
Sub-Saharan Africa	83.8	23.5	6.2
South Asia	47.8	38.5	36.5

(allowing for some lag in the supply response), the decline would look even larger.

What caused the returns on investment to decline? Drought is not the answer; its effects on production in the 1980s were hardly any worse than in the early 1970s. Falling world demand is

not the reason; African exports have actually lost market share. The greatest fall in the region's terms of trade happened after 1985, and by then the stagnation and decline in GDP growth were already well established. Everything points to declining productivity. Africa's crop yields are

Table 1.1 Typical costs in Sub-Saharan Africa and Asia

	Sub-Saharan Africa	Low-income Asia	Africa relative to low-income Asia
Investments and construction			
Irrigation (in thousands of 1984 dollars per hectare)	6.0–10.0	2.5–6.0	1.4–2.4
Urban water supply (1985 dollars per unit)	55–106	35–60	1.8
Vocational school boarding (thousands of dollars per place)	5.0	3.0	1.7
Roads (thousands of dollars per kilometer)	250	190	1.3
Recurrent costs			
Primary education (1980 dollars per pupil)	92	17	5.4
Transportation			
Road maintenance (thousands of dollars per kilometer)	4.8	2.2	2.2
Rolling stock cost (dollars per ton/per kilometer)	0.09	0.04	2.3
Wages			
Central government (multiple of per capita income, median annual, 1977–82)	5.5	2.0	2.8
Unskilled construction (median, dollars per day, 1989)	1.91	1.35	1.4

Note: Country coverage varies by indicator, depending on available data.
Source: World Bank project files and various reports. For details see the background paper by Singh. Data on central government wages are from Heller and Tait 1984.

smaller, its cropping cycles on irrigated land are fewer, its transport costs are higher, and its utilization rates for factory capacity are lower.

Higher investment costs have contributed to lower productivity. Investment costs are usually more than 50 percent higher in Africa than in South Asia (see Table 1.1). Part of this difference may reflect overvalued currencies in Africa, although the effect of exchange rates is reduced to the extent that investments are more import-intensive. These costs have risen in the 1970s and 1980s as infrastructure and institutional constraints have become more binding. Costs of operating and maintaining investments are higher, too, in Africa—often more than double South Asia's.

Costs are high partly because of Africa's particular circumstances. Difficult topography makes road construction and irrigation expensive. Low population densities and widely dispersed settlements (20 persons per square kilometer in Sub-Saharan Africa compared with 146 in low-income Asia) also increase costs. Landlocked countries face even greater difficulties. Undiversified economies short of skilled local labor depend on expensive imports of skills and goods. But a large part of the explanation for Africa's present economic crisis also lies in poor public resource management and bad policies. Together these have undermined the efficiency of the private sector and have added greatly to the high cost of doing business in Africa.

POOR PUBLIC SECTOR MANAGEMENT. Because the state is dominant—public expenditures in 1986 were more than 27 percent of GNP (compared with only 19 percent in low-income countries outside Africa)—its interventions strongly affect the overall efficiency of resource use. There are countless examples of badly chosen and poorly designed public investments, including some in which the World Bank has participated. A 1987 evaluation revealed that half of the completed rural development projects financed by the World Bank in Africa had failed. A cement plant serving Côte d'Ivoire, Ghana, and Togo was closed in 1984 after only four years in operation. A state-run shoe factory in Tanzania has been operating at no more than 25 percent capacity and has remained open only thanks to a large government subsidy.

African governments and foreign financiers (commercial banks and export credit agencies as well as donor agencies) must share responsibility. Foreign financiers and suppliers promoted capital exports with attractive credits, and poor coordination among donors caused duplication and waste. Governments also agreed to—and often pressed for—grandiose or inappropriate investments. Moreover the rapid increase in foreign exchange resources—about fivefold in nominal terms between 1970 and 1982—tended to relax investment criteria and undermine financial discipline. The region's public enterprises expanded tremendously during this period. Governments (and donors) have preferred to invest in new buildings and equipment rather than maintain their existing facilities and to hire new staff instead of giving their existing staff the resources they need to work effectively. As a result the capital stock has deteriorated, and many investments yield little or nothing. Poorly maintained and managed infrastructure has added enormously to the cost of doing business (see Box 1.2).

PRICE DISTORTIONS. Large state monopolies, controlled prices, and centrally allocated credit and foreign exchange have been common. The departure from market prices and the resulting inefficiency in resource allocation have grown worse as governments have tried to use administrative measures to cope with tightening foreign exchange and shortfalls in public revenue. The failure to adjust policies promptly to the decline in primary export prices following the boom years of the mid-1970s, to the shrinking nonconcessional flows in the early 1980s, and to the rising debt service payments on earlier borrowing deepened the crisis.

Widening budget deficits prompted more borrowing and higher taxes in the first instance, not less public spending. The deficits fueled inflation despite price controls. Because parities were not adjusted, real effective exchange rates appreciated steadily after the first oil shock, and parallel exchange rates increasingly diverged from nominal

rates (see Figure 1.10). The inability to meet debt service obligations in the 1980s disrupted international financial relations. Increasingly stringent price controls and the growing currency overvaluation affected traded goods most. Real agricultural prices declined during the second half of the 1970s as real effective exchange rates rose. Public enterprises began to run bigger operating deficits, and before long the banks that were called on to finance them were showing losses.

These events hit producers hard. Overvalued exchange rates, together with export taxes, undermined export performance from the early 1970s. The region's market share in the major non-oil commodities declined sharply.

These price distortions caused longer-run damage, too. Farmers chose not to invest in soil fertility, mining companies undertook little exploration and depleted their reserves, and manufacturers underutilized their capital assets. At the same time governments let the physical infrastructure deteriorate. Because countries lacked flexible, diversified, and dynamic economic structures, their budget and balance of payments gaps became unmanageable. Governments, forced to

Box 1.2 The cost of infrastructure deficiencies: The Nigerian experience

Recent research in Nigeria has demonstrated that poor infrastructure services have imposed heavy costs on manufacturing enterprises. To overcome these deficiencies, firms have had to incur considerable expenses. Although all 179 of the firms studied were connected to the power grid, all those with more than 50 employees had their own standby generators and had invested, on average, $130,000 (at an exchange rate of 7.5 naira per dollar) in their own power facilities. Of firms with fewer than 20 employees, only one-third generated their own power.

Water supply is a similar case. While none of the small enterprises was able to install its own supply to overcome poor public water services, 14 percent of firms with between 20 and 50 employees did. More than two-thirds of larger enterprises (those with more than 100 employees) had invested in private boreholes.

Poor public telephone and postal services are yet another constraint on business. Firms have tried to overcome the difficulties by using messenger motorcycles or radio transmitters. As the size of firms increased, so did their reliance on their own supply of such services. The importance attached to communications services was as great as for water supply. Of larger firms, 70 to 90 percent had their own radio transmitters.

The study showed that although the capital value of private facilities was about 10 percent of the total value of machinery and equipment for large firms, it was on average 25 percent for small firms. This share varied widely

across states, by firm size, and by type of service. Expenditure was highest on electricity generation—almost four times that for boreholes and treatment facilities.

Box figure 1.2 Nigerian enterprises with their own infrastructure

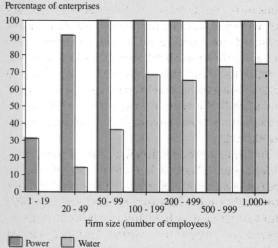

Source: Lee and Anas 1989.

Figure 1.10 Real effective exchange rate index, 1970-87

Index (1980=100)

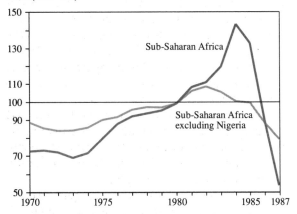

Note: Group averages weighted by 1985 GDP in dollars. Sub-Saharan Africa here includes only 30 countries.
Source: IMF data.

retrench, often cut back first on social expenditures, thereby further eroding the human resource base.

HIGH WAGE COSTS. Because the direct and indirect labor content in final production can exceed 50 percent, Africa's high cost of labor relative to its productivity matters all the more. High salaries are a legacy of colonialism. Real wages in the first half of this century reflected abundant natural resources, plentiful private venture capital, easy access to protected markets, trained and experienced expatriate managers, and stable colonial administrations. Expatriates, employed to compensate for the shortage of skilled African personnel, were paid above European scales. As Africans acquired comparable skills, their salaries were linked to (but remained lower than) those of the expatriates. After independence the pay of skilled nationals was brought closer to that of expatriates, and unskilled wages, at least in the formal sector, were increased through minimum wage legislation.

But what seemed justifiable and sustainable at independence became less justifiable with the increased availability of educated Africans and less sustainable with less experienced management and less efficient infrastructure services in an increasingly competitive world. In most African countries at the beginning of the 1980s public sector wages, measured as a multiple of per capita income, were several times those in Asia. For instance official Tanzanian wages, which were relatively low for Africa, were more than double those in Sri Lanka.

Adjustment is well under way. The International Labour Organisation (ILO) reports that real wage rates in Sub-Saharan Africa have fallen by a quarter since 1980. This is a brutal but necessary adjustment to reflect labor underemployment caused by a growing labor force that has outstripped job creation and by the need to become internationally competitive. Devaluation has helped to bring the dollar cost of African wages close to its competitors'—in Ghana, Guinea, and Tanzania, for example—although official wage rates in the CFA franc zone remain high.

Market forces have kept real wages in the informal sector more closely linked to productivity. Until recently, these forces did not touch governments, where much of the educated labor was employed, nor the parapublic and large-scale private sectors, where rents created by trade protection and subsidies helped to finance wages that were higher than labor productivity would otherwise justify. Now in several countries public sector wages are barely enough for subsistence, and the wage structure has become highly compressed. In those cases the correction has gone too far, and productivity has plummeted as a result.

THE MISSING MIDDLE. A unique feature of African economies is the dualistic character of consumption and production. Intermediate technologies are scarce. Transportation is mostly by motor vehicle or on foot (see Box 4.5). In some countries there are surprisingly few bicycles, mopeds, carts, and the like. (Burkina Faso, where the moped is ubiquitous, is an exception.) Africa has nearly 7 cars for every thousand inhabitants (Zimbabwe has 30, Côte d'Ivoire 17, and Senegal 13); the Republic of Korea has only 6, India 2, and Bangladesh 0.3. When farmers modernize, they switch from the hoe to a tractor; few use oxen, even where the tsetse fly is absent. On the production side there are countless microenterprises and a few medium to large modern firms, but not much in between. Almost everywhere one looks there seems to be a "missing middle." Investments and operating costs are higher than they would be if appropriate technologies were used more. Consumers with little alternative tend to spend heavily on imports. All this adds to the high cost structure of African economies.

DETERIORATING GOVERNANCE. At independence Africa inherited simple but functioning administrations. They were managed largely by expatriates and were not geared to the development role assigned to them by African leaders. The responsibilities of the state were enormously expanded. But at the same time the rapid promotion of inexperienced staff and the gradual politicization of the whole administrative apparatus led to declining efficiency. A combination of administrative bottlenecks, unauthorized "fees" and "commissions," and inefficient services imposed costs on businesses that have progressively undermined their international competitiveness. The gradual breakdown of the judicial systems in many countries left foreign investors doubtful that contracts could be enforced. The ones that did invest insisted on large profit margins to compensate for the perceived high risks. Authoritarian governments hostile to grassroots and nongovernmental organizations have alienated much of the public. As a result economic activity has shifted increasingly to the informal sector. Too frequently ordinary people see government as the source of, not the solution to, their problems.

The outlook for the next generation

What kind of environment will Africa face during the next 30 years? The future is likely to bring accelerating technological change; new patterns of industrial organization, competitiveness, and trade; mounting pressures on the world's ecological resources; and a demographic outlook that threatens to blight the region's prospects for a better future. Their impact cannot be ignored. Most important, Africa should not turn in on itself and risk being completely peripheral to the global economy.

The technological revolution

The world is on the threshold of a new technological age, driven by advances in information technology, microelectronics, biotechnology, and materials sciences. This will have implications for virtually all sectors, not just those considered to be high tech.

Fast and cheap communication and information processing will transform business and administration. Global information networks will integrate markets and facilitate the global management of dispersed industries. Access to ideas will be the key to competitiveness. Technological breakthroughs have already created new opportunities to trade long-distance services, such as accounting, tourism, or education. The ability to transfer funds instantly anywhere in the world has already led to a 24-hour-a-day global financial market. Industrial applications of information technology are starting to change the face of manufacturing and the division of labor within the global economy.

Certain labor-intensive service industries could thrive in developing countries with flexible links to knowledge-based markets abroad. But a continent with a weak telecommunication system and tightly regulated service industries will be isolated from the mainstream of progress. Africa's prospects for competing effectively will depend on greater efforts to create an efficient basic telecommunication structure and to obtain access to global information networks by building links with international partners.

Advances in biotechnology also hold enormous potential for Africa and could raise its agricultural production and protect its population, crops, and livestock from disease (see Box 1.3). In contrast to the Green Revolution, which required irrigation and focused on just a few crops, the biorevolution can reach the entire rural population. At the same time tropical countries, which control around 70 percent of the earth's biogenetic resources, may seek to barter the increasing value of their biogenetic pool for economic development. Partnerships with private companies in the United States, Japan, and Europe that attempt to forge globe-spanning alliances uniting capital, research capacities, marketing channels, and access to biological resources suggest new patterns of technology transfer. However, the commercialization of biotechnology also poses risks. Laboratory production and product substitution can threaten the markets for Africa's traditional export crops. The extent to which companies can claim property rights to biotechnology applications will influence the spread of new crop varieties in Africa.

Advances in materials sciences will be no less far-reaching. Optical fibers made from silicon have virtually replaced copper in telephone cables. Current research promises fuel-saving engines based on high-temperature ceramics. The accelerating substitution of advanced materials—superconducting substances, optical transmission fibers, advanced plastics, metal alloys, and so on—for traditional raw materials will put pressure on minerals producers. The implications for Africa will vary according to the ability of its

Box 1.3 The promise of biotechnologies for Africa

The direct use of biotechnology for plant propagation and breeding could dramatically raise crop productivity and overall food production in developing countries. Tissue culture techniques are creating more drought- and disease-resistant varieties of cassava, oil palms, and groundnuts. Plant genetic engineering may also result in coffee beans with less caffeine, in response to new consumer preferences, or faster-growing tree species, which make reforestation easier. Better fermentation techniques in solid media, such as protein-enriched cassava flour, improve the nutritional value of crops. Embryo transfer may raise the reproductive capacity of livestock. Genetically engineered vaccines may overcome trypanosomiasis, thus opening up tsetse-infested grazing areas. Medical research on monoclonal antibodies, presently the fastest growing branch of biotechnology, is expected to result in more accurate medical tests and diagnostics. New vaccines against killer diseases are being developed. And integrated bioenergy systems may simultaneously generate food, animal feed, and fuel through microbial conversion of biomass.

The commercial use of new bioindustrial products may result in dramatically different patterns of agricultural production and trade. This may pose a threat to Africa's export crops. Laboratory-produced vanilla may soon put the livelihood of 70,000 vanilla bean farmers in Madagascar in doubt. And it is not unthinkable that consumers will soon have a choice between Kenya AA and biocoffee beans made in the United States. Another concern involves the privatization of research results. The current practice of patenting first-generation biotechnology products to cover any further use of bioengineered material will severely limit future competition. For developing countries this may also entail high licensing fees for seeds, which will make it harder to disseminate new crop varieties to smallholders. The widespread distribution of new bioengineered plant material may decrease the genetic diversity and may make crops increasingly vulnerable to new diseases.

A flexible African response to these competitive dynamics must be based on a close monitoring of biotechnological trends, more joint research and development partnerships with Western companies, and the development of substitute products. At the same time Africa will need dramatic improvements in its science education and agricultural training.

exporters to adjust to shifts in world demand. Policies that favor efficient production methods, the development of new raw materials, and increased exports of food and manufactures will help to reduce the region's dependence on primary products in declining demand.

Changing industrial organization and managerial practices

A new perception of technological progress as a function of organizational flexibility and access to information is emerging and is forcing a reassessment of organizational structures. New business methods, derived partly from Japan's experience, may be more relevant to Africa than developments in high-technology machinery. These innovations include "best-practice" production methods, such as flexible specialization, total quality control, and "just-in-time" inventory management. Collectively, they improve a firm's ability to respond to shifts in consumer preferences, often at lower cost and with higher quality. They may also transform relations between firms by extending longer contracts to fewer, more reliable suppliers or by promoting cooperation between potentially competing suppliers. Overall

these management practices contrast sharply with previous industrial country concepts that focused on mass production and economies of scale and considered labor as a cost factor rather than as a resource.

Africa can draw important lessons from these new perspectives on technological progress and competitive advantage. The introduction of "best-practice" production systems may offer the most cost-effective and rapid way for Africa to improve its competitiveness quickly. With a critical minimum of complementary technical and managerial skills, the pursuit of better product quality and the new forms of industrial organization may be particularly well-suited to a variety of labor-intensive sectors such as textiles, clothing, and light assembly. The transfer costs are low, consisting mainly of improving the skills of the labor force. Moreover the benefits of longer-term technological innovation may not materialize unless flexible production management methods have been introduced in the meantime. Africa will have to overcome enormous hurdles to exploit this potential, including making up the skill deficits in the work force, providing appropriate incentives for organizational change, and raising awareness of the links between information, technology, and

Figure 1.11 Export prices for five major Sub-Saharan African export commodities, 1961-87

Index (1961=100)

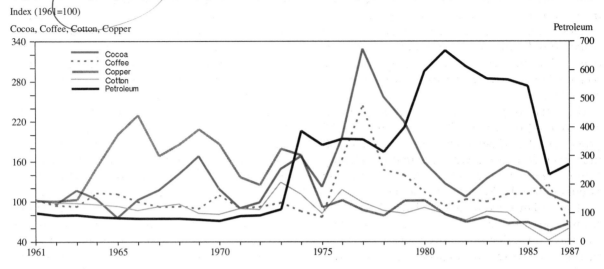

Note: Prices deflated by the manufacturers unit value (MUV) index.
Source: World Bank data.

competitive structures. Much will depend on the region's ability to make partnerships with firms and institutions in the more advanced countries.

Evolving patterns of production, trade, and finance

Far-reaching changes are also occurring in the global pattern of trade and production. The Pacific Basin is emerging as the fastest growing area for world trade and capital flows. By 2020 it will probably have become the center of economic power. Sub-Saharan Africa, historically focused on the North and the West, will need to also look to the East from now on.

Africa will be affected more than any other region by the likely slow growth in demand for primary commodities. Any hope of a revival of economic growth predicated on the recovery of primary commodity prices would seem to be misplaced. The price forecasts for Africa's five major primary commodity exports up to 2000 do not show any significant increases. Except for oil, prices are currently close to their long-term trend, and, while sharp fluctuations are to be expected, it is most unlikely that there will be significant or lasting gains from the terms of trade (see Figure 1.11). However, Africa can and must seek to expand its market share wherever it has a comparative advantage.

Commercial capital flows are unlikely to be much help either. Many African governments enjoyed a favorable credit rating in the past and

attracted credit from commercial sources quite easily. However, the debt crisis and Africa's poor economic performance have frightened most lenders away. This situation is not expected to change in the near or medium term. Fundamental changes must occur, including the establishment of political confidence, before these channels open up again. Equally, capital flight will be reversed only when confidence has been restored. Africa's best option for obtaining nonofficial finance is to create conditions that are attractive for direct private investment, since by definition such finance would be linked to expanding production. Steps must also be taken to reduce Africa's debt (see Chapter 8).

African megatrends

The UN Economic Commission for Africa (ECA) was among the first to dramatize the long-term consequences of recent trends. In 1983 it presented a "nightmare scenario," which underlined the urgent need for fundamental reform. Since then the outlook has deteriorated further.

DEMOGRAPHIC TRENDS. The two key assumptions underlying the ECA's scenario were population growth and GDP growth. The alarming vision portrayed by the "nightmare scenario" comes from the extremely rapid and immense increase in the number of people who will populate the continent if current rates continue. Africa's population would double every 20 years, reaching 1 billion in 2010. Even if fertility follows the declining pattern in South Asia, Africa's population will reach 1.7 billion by 2050. A turnaround in fertility behavior will not occur easily and certainly not over a short period. This makes the "nightmare scenario" more than a bad dream—it is a very real possibility.

The consequences of the soaring populations are striking (see Figure 1.12). During the next 30 years the rates of entry into the labor force will more than double and will exacerbate an already acute employment problem. Rapidly growing populations will also soon lead to a switch from land abundance to increasing land shortage in several countries. Land-to-people ratios, already a constraint on agricultural development in several places, will worsen. Ecological degradation will accelerate.

This exceptional demographic surge will be accompanied by massive pressures for migration—both national and regional—creating social and political tension. Most of the migrants will settle in the expanding urban centers, creating megacities. By 2020 there are likely to be about 30 cities with more than 1 million inhabitants. Several can be expected to exceed 10 million.

THE GLOBAL VILLAGE. Desertification and deforestation in Africa are increasingly of worldwide concern, just as the heavy pollution coming from industrial countries is of concern to Africa. International attention is especially focused on the effect these processes are having both on the rate of habitat loss and species extinction and on changes in the global climate. The global impact of environmental trends in Sub-Saharan Africa can be expected to command increasing attention in the future, as environmental issues become increasingly prominent in world affairs.

Sub-Saharan Africa is endowed with an abundance of wild plants and animals. It is home to an estimated 300,000 species out of a global total of 5 million. The Tai Forest of Côte d'Ivoire, the Montane forests of East Africa, and a small slice of Madagascar are among the most biologically diverse areas of the world. Many plant and animal species in Sub-Saharan Africa are unique to restricted locales. For example, more than 6,000 flowering plants, 106 different birds, and half the world's chameleon species are found only on the island of Madagascar.

The disappearance of Africa's plants and animals has implications beyond the extinction of species. It means the loss of genetic material for the future development of crops, medicines, and industrial products. The reduction of Africa's forests and other vegetation cover can also contribute to large global climate change. The widespread burning of forests and scrub to clear land adds large amounts of carbon dioxide to the atmosphere, thus contributing to global warming. If deforestation were slowed, these emissions would be reduced. If reforestation efforts were accelerated, the role of these forests as a vast carbon sink, which removes large amounts of carbon dioxide from the atmosphere through photosynthesis, would be enhanced.

Even though Africa's contribution to global pollution is minor compared with that of the industrial countries, the twin threats of loss of biological diversity and global climate change are of increasing international concern. They present an opportunity to mobilize international resources to reduce the poverty that drives deforestation.

The challenge

Africa's crisis is deep seated. But while great problems lie ahead, Africa also has important assets on which to draw. First, despite the population pressure in certain areas, its land and water resources are vast. Agricultural production, with the right technology, could be greatly expanded. The considerable mineral potential has yet to be tapped. Africa has massive energy resources in

Figure 1.12 Population and urbanization in Sub-Saharan Africa, 1960-2020

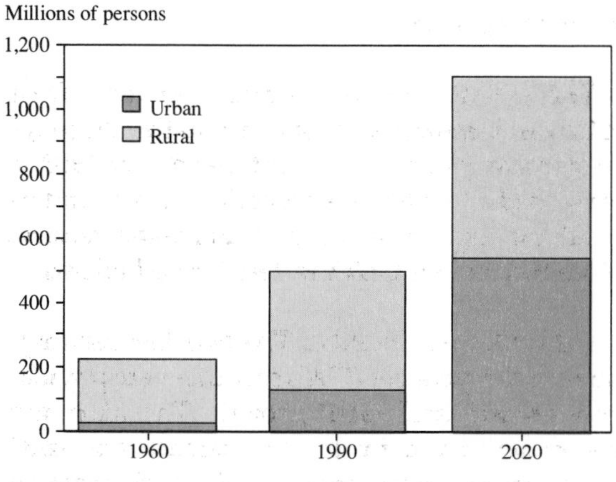

Millions of persons

Note: Figures for 1990 and 2020 are projections based on declining fertility rate.
Source: World Bank data.

gas reserves and hydropower potential. These resources are unevenly distributed across Africa; for the most part they are not where the population is. That is the region's first challenge: to realize the vision of pan-African cooperation by allowing freer movement of supplies and people.

Second, women in Africa, although more fully involved in production activities than in many other developing countries, face innumerable obstacles to the true fulfillment of their potential. Given the right opportunities, they can have much greater impact on the development of the continent than in the past.

Third, the informal sector has great vitality. African traditions of solidarity can be of tremendous value in mobilizing populations at the community level. The widespread practice of sharing among people can be used to mobilize private savings for local social investments. Informal enterprises have demonstrated remarkable dynamism and can be counted on to continue to be a significant source of income and employment. In country after country the informal sector has exhibited a resiliency and a responsiveness to changing conditions and opportunities that goes beyond an existence predicated simply on policy distortions and the general poor performance of the largely statist, formal, modern sector.

This locally based dynamism has channeled the continent's traditions of community welfare into self-help—as in Kenya's *harambee*. These movements, often supported by foreign nongovernmental organizations, are now active in many fields: education and training, health care and family planning, village water supply, agricultural production, storage, marketing, agroforestry, housing, slum improvement, and small enterprise development (see Box 2.9). They have been effective intermediaries between grassroots organizations and those providing public, commercial, and private forms of support.

Fourth, Sub-Saharan Africa's vast endowments of diverse flora and fauna and its spectacular scenery and fine beaches make tourism a very promising sector, as a few countries such as Kenya have already shown. Africa's biological diversity is of enormous international interest. Considerable resources can be attracted to ensure its protection

---

Box 1.4 Mauritius: From Malthusian gloom to sustained development

The socioeconomic structure of Mauritius in the early 1960s had the same ingredients for poor prospects as many other countries in Africa have today. Population was growing at almost 2.5 percent a year, and per capita income was barely rising. In 1965 the crude birth rate was 36, the total fertility rate was 4.8, and the infant mortality rate was 64. A population explosion of that magnitude would have large-scale economic and social repercussions. For example, the working-age population (aged 15 years and over) was projected to increase by some 50 percent during 1957–72. This, combined with low savings and investment rates (below 12 and 15 percent, respectively) and exports exclusively based on sugar, made the prospects for growing out of the vicious circle of poverty quite poor.

The sustained pursuit of sound macroeconomic and population policies, among others, has completely transformed the outlook. The import replacement strategy followed in the 1960s was not a viable long-term option, although it did enable industrialists to acquire experience and allowed a new industrial culture to take root. To build on this experience, incentives have been provided to overseas manufacturing firms to locate labor-intensive activities in Mauritius and to convert imported raw materials into finished goods for export. The structure of the economy has, as a result, also been transformed. The country has taken advantage of opportunities in world markets and has exploited its resource endowments—an adequate infrastructure and a literate and adaptable labor force paid competitive wage rates. Exports represent 63 percent of GDP, but the economy has moved away from its earlier dependence on sugar. Manufactures—notably textiles—now account for 39 percent of exports. Spurred by continuing growth in per capita income (3 percent a year on average between 1965 and 1986), investment and domestic savings have been growing and are now above 20 percent of GDP. Domestic policies have also promoted equitable development—spatially, by diminishing the rate of urban population growth; sectorally, through favorable agricultural pricing policy; and intergenerationally, through conservative debt and borrowing policies.

Undiminished emphasis on programs for human resource development, including perhaps the most successful population program in the region, has placed Mauritius among the top performers in Sub-Saharan Africa. Its population growth rate (1 percent a year during 1980–86) is the lowest in the region, with life expectancy at 68 years (1987). Other health and fertility indicators also show significant improvement: a crude birth rate of 19 (1987), a total fertility rate of 2.2 (1986), an infant mortality rate of 24 (1987), and a child death rate of 1 (1984, down from 9 in 1965). Enrollment ratios of 100 percent for primary schools and above 50 percent for secondary education are high for a developing country with Mauritius's level of per capita income. Mauritius has shown that the right policies can overcome poor initial conditions and work an economic transformation.

and more generally to protect the environment (see Box 2.1).

The history of economic development has witnessed some remarkable transformations. Countries once considered economically weak have later prospered. Within Africa several countries have done consistently well since independence (see Box 1.4). There is no insurmountable reason why the others cannot succeed as well.

Since the mid-1980s Africa has seen important changes in policies and in economic performance. Although per capita incomes declined more steeply in the two years 1986–87 than in 1980–85, this must be put in the context of other important signs of improvements since the mid-1980s. The large fall in regional per capita incomes in 1986–88 was caused by a combination of especially sharp deteriorating terms of trade and continued high population growth. These negative factors swamped the growth in domestic output. Comparing the past four years to the early 1980s for Africa as a whole, however, there is some indication of better performance. The region's aggregate GDP grew at 2.1 percent a year on average during 1985–88, reversing the 1.2 percent annual decline of the previous four years. For 17 countries, accounting for a third of the region's population, output grew faster than population during this period. For some the annual rates of growth were impressive: 9.1 percent in Mauritius, for example, and around 5 percent in Ghana and Kenya. Terms of trade declined largely because of falling oil prices, which have since stabilized. Preliminary data for 1988 show that the terms of trade improved for the non-oil-exporting countries.

On average, agricultural production and exports have grown faster since 1984 than during the previous two decades. Even when the recovery from drought in 1985 is excluded, recent annual growth rates appear well above the longer-term average of the 1970s and early 1980s, thus reflecting a positive response to incentives, although good weather also helped. Africa's most recent export performance is encouraging, with non-oil export volumes rising in aggregate by almost 10 percent during 1985–87, in sharp contrast to the declining trend of the past 15 years. Moreover, Africa's declining share of world markets for non-oil exports began to reverse in 1984 (see Figure 1.13).

The improvements are often small and could be reversed. Africa's undiversified economies remain especially vulnerable to external shocks. Past low investment rates have weakened the eco-

Figure 1.13 Recent economic trends in Sub-Saharan Africa, 1980-88

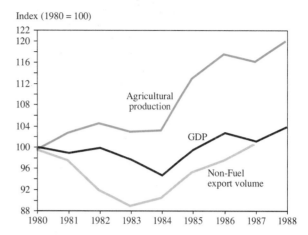

Index (1980 = 100)

Source: FAO and World Bank data.

nomic basis for renewed growth. Nonetheless stronger efforts to improve domestic economic management may help to sustain these recent improvements.

About half the countries in Africa have adopted major policy reform programs during the 1980s. Initially these programs mainly addressed the short- to medium-term macroeconomic imbalances. Over time they have evolved significantly, with measures being introduced to tackle the underlying structural constraints. Exchange rate adjustment has been crucial to this objective. In response, their real effective exchange rates began to decline in the early 1980s, following a decade of growing divergence from those of other developing regions. A combination of nominal devaluations and market liberalization led to rising real agricultural prices in many countries, especially for export commodities. The immediate response to these price increases has been dramatic in some cases, as for cocoa in Ghana, for instance. In other cases the response to reforms has been slow. Many countries have also seen a realignment of real factor costs; real interest rates are becoming less negative, and real wages for both skilled and unskilled labor are continuing to decline. In some countries, such as Tanzania, real wages are now less than half of their 1980 levels, although in others, particularly in the CFA franc zone, adjustment is still delayed.

Economic performance has also been spurred by large increases in aid. In 1987 net international capital flows were 10 percent above the 1975–79 average in real terms, and estimates for 1988 point to continued increases.

The social impact of these improvements is difficult to assess. Up-to-date data are patchy. Better delivery of public services will in any case improve conditions only after a lag. Nonetheless, the evidence from several African countries suggests that real per capita spending on public health and education services is no longer falling. In countries in which adjustment programs were adopted early with strong donor support, per capita expenditures may now be rising.

Africa's economic problems cannot be solved quickly or through a single focus on capital accumulation or economic adjustment. Africa's production structures need to be transformed; in many countries policies need to be reoriented radically. Each country is unique, and there are no magic answers. Many factors—the pace of technological advance, the weakening market for primary products, and the changing structure of world production—are beyond the control of African policymakers. A long-term perspective is essential. The necessary decisions are hard—for donors as well as Africa's governments—because big changes will be needed in the way aid is dispensed. Above all each country will need to establish a development strategy appropriate to its own particular circumstances.

2

Sustainable growth with equity

A strategy for the next generation

Governments have been struggling to reverse the relentless decline in African living standards. They can succeed. Indeed, if Africa is to avoid a major human catastrophe, they must. In their declarations at the UN Special Session on Africa in 1986, the region's leaders clearly recognized the need for radical reform. This chapter draws on the debate taking place within Africa and on the experience of the past three decades. Building on measures already initiated, it describes the main elements of a long-term strategy to set Africa on the path to recovery and growth.

The need for new measures

The nightmare scenario projected in Chapter 1 is not far-fetched. Indeed, without resolute new measures, it will almost certainly come to pass. Yet Africa has unexploited land and minerals and a population that can be mobilized to develop them. During the past five years broad-ranging reforms have been widely initiated, but these are no more than a beginning. The reforms, although courageous, are incomplete because they fail to address fully the long-term constraints. The challenge for African governments is to forge comprehensive and coherent programs of action that will attract broadly based support.

To be credible, any new long-term strategy should be based on a hardheaded examination of the lessons of the past. The first generation after independence assumed that development meant achieving Northern standards of living. To that end countries concentrated on import-substituting manufactures, and industrial investment was largely state-led. The strategy failed in part because it was based on poorly adapted foreign models. The vision was couched in the idiom of modernization—meaning the transfer of Northern values, institutions, and technology to the South. In recent years, however, many elements of this vision have been challenged. Alternative paths have been proposed. They give primacy to agricultural development and emphasize not only prices, markets, and private sector activities, but also capacity building, grassroots participation, decentralization, and sound environmental practices. So far such ideas have been accepted and tried only halfheartedly, if at all. The time has come to put them fully into practice.

Both in the broad conception and detailed elaboration of the development strategies adopted after independence, non-Africans played an overly dominant role. There are now a significant number of experienced African policymakers who will decide future strategy. Nonetheless an important supportive role will remain for Africa's external partners. Self-reliance and the assertion of African leadership should not mean cutting links with the global economy and turning away outside assistance. Yet, partly as a consequence of its policies, Africa is in danger of being increasingly marginalized in its participation in both the world economy—Africa's share in world trade has fallen from 3 percent to less than 1.5 percent since 1960—and in global strategic decisionmaking as superpower competition in Africa ebbs. For Africa to become isolated from the mainstream of global development would be disastrous. The rapid development of the world economy, the huge expansion of population, and the dangerous pressures on the global environment are leading irresistibly to growing global interdependence. Africa and its external partners have a compelling mutual interest in building a stronger and more equal basis for collaboration.

Key features of a future strategy

To ensure Africa's future welfare, the next generation must first build solid foundations for sustainable and equitable growth: *sustainable*, because care must be taken to protect the productive capacity of the environment, and *equitable*, because this is a precondition both for political stability and ultimately for sustained growth. The focus here is on access to assets and poverty alleviation, not on the distribution of wealth. Creating wealth, in contrast to rent seeking, is seen as essential for growth. By giving the poor access to assets and promoting their productivity, a higher level of growth can be ensured. These aims will take time to achieve. Institutions will need to be strengthened and capabilities enhanced. The task will require sustained effort and far-sighted political leadership.

To prosper in an increasingly competitive world, Africa must radically improve the productivity of its labor, capital, and natural resources. This requires two things:

• An enabling environment of sound policies and efficient infrastructure and services to foster productive activities and private initiative.

• A much enhanced capacity, from the village to the highest echelons of government, to cope with change.

Weak capacity in both the public and private sectors is at the very core of Africa's development crisis. In the most fundamental sense development depends on the capacity to initiate, sustain, and accommodate change. Africa's governments were grafted onto traditional societies and were often alien to the indigenous cultures. Its economies were dualistic, with modern sectors that remained highly fragile. Many governments proved unable to cope with the political stresses of rapid modernization and the unstable external environment of the 1970s and 1980s.

The structural adjustment programs of the early 1980s aimed to improve resource allocation primarily by correcting distortions in prices and markets. But these programs only set the stage for increasing production. It was soon appreciated that, to bring about real and enduring development, a transformation of the production structures was required and, furthermore, that the capacity of people and institutions to deal with change must be enhanced. This means strengthening institutions and investing in people. A start has been made, but much more remains to be done. Development in this widest sense is the theme of this report. It is consistent with the human-centered strategy recently recommended by the ECA. Both reports see people as both the ends and the means of development.

Building capacity is also a prerequisite for greater self-reliance, the dominant objective of the Lagos Plan of Action. Self-reliance, so essential for Africa's long-term development, has an evident regional dimension. In the past the rhetoric in favor of greater regional cooperation and integration has been insistent, but the actions disappointing. The time has come for determined and pragmatic action; Chapter 7 sets out specific proposals to this end.

Growth that is sustainable and equitable

Even at current levels of per capita income there are many opportunities to meet basic needs more effectively. Over the longer term, however, welfare cannot be steadily improved unless economic growth significantly exceeds population growth. This is the clear lesson from countries such as Ethiopia, Ghana, and Tanzania. What are to be the sources of economic growth? To what extent will Africa's soaring population and accelerating environmental degradation compromise its development? And how can growth be made equitable?

Sources of growth

There is a growing consensus that postindependence strategies pinned too much hope on rapid state-led industrialization. Domestic markets were too small for the capacity created, while the state proved to be an uninspired entrepreneur and a bad manager. In contrast almost everywhere the informal sector has been a thriving success—in part because it escapes government regulation. This is a measure of the vitality and potential of the neglected African entrepreneur. The earlier strategy also neglected agriculture, a sector in which Africa has a clear comparative advantage. Exploiting Africa's land resources offers the best immediate opportunity for raising incomes. Over the longer term and with policies that foster private investment and entrepreneurship, the industrial sector could undoubtedly contribute increasingly to Africa's economic growth. But it is to agriculture that Africa should look for the primary foundation for growth during the coming years.

Agriculture currently provides 33 percent of Africa's GDP and 40 percent of its exports. Yields are far below potential. Even when full account is taken of the environmental limits to land exploitation, the scope for expanding production is great. Of course this potential varies among countries. Over the long term it must be assumed that people will migrate away from the arid lands and that the resulting inflow of labor will spur growth in the better-endowed areas, as it has in Côte d'Ivoire during the past 30 years.

Chapter 4 argues that agricultural growth can be doubled to 4 percent a year—as it must be if African living standards are to improve. This target is ambitious. Industrial growth, starting from a much smaller base, could be significantly higher. But neither sector will prosper unless the linkages between the two are strengthened. In most African countries these linkages are weak because of poor infrastructure and the failure to gear production to rural needs and to overcome the fragmentation of rural and urban markets.

Savings in the agricultural sector provide the basis for capital formation in the cities, and surplus earnings in the urban sector are in part channeled back to rural areas. In Kenya, for example, urban workers remit an average 21 percent of their earnings. Migration from the countryside provides labor for urban industries, while some workers in industry and in the nonfarm sector return to work in agriculture, thus bringing a new dynamism to farming. Agricultural growth stimulates the demand for consumer goods and for agricultural inputs produced by industry, and in turn industrial growth stimulates the demand for food and for inputs into agroprocessing industries.

This stress on agriculture does not imply a minor role for industry. African industry has performed disappointingly during the past 25 years; growth in output has slowed particularly in recent years. But with sound policies there is no good reason why the rate of growth of industry should not recover in the 1990s and rise gradually toward 8 percent a year during the next two decades. In individual countries, of course, higher rates of growth are possible. For these to be achieved, industrial policies will need to be overhauled in the early 1990s. The key is the transfer to Africans of industrial skills: management, marketing, technology, and finance. This can occur most easily through a collaborative partnership with local investors who have the necessary expertise and access to markets. This in turn implies a radical reappraisal of the current industrial strategies. The precedents in Asia and elsewhere are well established, and there are already good examples in Africa of what can be done.

African entrepreneurs able to participate in such partnerships are emerging in increasing numbers from the indigenous informal sector. The explosive growth of the informal sector has gone largely unrecorded in the national accounts data. For example, Zaire's value added in the manufacturing sector is estimated to be possibly 25 times the official figure. Policy has often discriminated against the informal sector, yet it has been the most dynamic part of most African economies and is by far the largest source of new employment.

Although agriculture and industry constitute the first and second sources of growth, other sectors could also make vital contributions. Africa will need to exploit every opportunity. Mining, oil production, and tourism all have good potential. Mining in the 1980s contributed 13 percent to Sub-Saharan Africa's GDP and earned some $8 billion in foreign exchange in 1988. But growth has been limping along at no more than 0.2 percent annually in the 1980s, a tenth of the world average. Here, as in manufacturing, attracting private investors will be a decisive factor. Despite known reserves richer than those elsewhere, the major mining companies have preferred to invest outside Africa, where they found conditions more attractive. There has been comparatively little serious exploration in Africa during the past decade. The same is true of oil. Chapter 5 suggests policy reforms that could help the sector eventually to achieve growth of 3 to 5 percent. Equally, however, the exploitation of mineral and oil resources should not be viewed as an easy option. It is no substitute for fiscal discipline and sound policies. As Nigeria and Zambia have shown, poor management of oil or mining revenues can easily undermine the foundations of long-term development.

Despite huge worldwide expansion tourism has made very slow headway in Africa. Global spending on tourism is about $160 billion and growing at 15 percent a year. Africa's share is just 2 percent, and falling. Nonetheless a few African countries have booming tourist sectors. For example, Kenya's gross foreign exchange receipts from tourism are more than from any single commodity export. Tourism is also an important revenue earner in The Gambia, Mauritius, Senegal, and the Seychelles. Africa's tourist assets are remarkable—and, in countries such as Ethiopia, Madagascar, and Tanzania, largely unexploited. Europe's resorts are rapidly reaching saturation, and the market can be expected to continue expanding vigorously. Europeans are increasingly looking for recreation farther afield. Unless Africa becomes more welcoming, tourists will travel instead to Asia and Latin America.

As in tourism, so in industry and agriculture: the challenge is the same. Markets exist, but the competition to satisfy them is fierce. In the years to come this competition will get even tougher. The pattern of demand is changing as is the technology to supply it. Only those flexible enough to adapt will succeed. Comparative advantage is swinging in favor of those with good market intelligence, a grasp of the relevant technologies, and a capacity for rapid response. Abundant labor is no longer enough.

Taking all this into account, the recent decline in per capita incomes can be arrested in the 1990s and the foundations laid for modest growth thereafter. It will require fundamental reforms and a new vision of the contribution to be made by the rural sector, of the route to industrialization, and of the strategy for human resource development. But it will also require measures to slow the rise in the region's population.

Slowing population growth

Raising Africa's overall GDP growth from the 2 percent a year achieved during the past decade to 4 to 5 percent in the years to come—the target proposed in this report—would be a major achievement. But if most of that is eaten away by surging population growth, per capita incomes will hardly rise. Significant improvement in living standards cannot be achieved over the long term unless population growth is slowed. On current trends Africa will increasingly be unable to feed its children or find jobs for its school leavers. The burden of dependents on active workers is overwhelming if half the population is under 18. Traditionally children contributed significantly to farm work; if children are to attend school, as they should if they are to become more productive adults, that can no longer be true. In any event

increasing numbers live in urban areas where there is much less demand for child labor. With development, intergenerational income flows from children to parents are gradually reversed.

For a major region Africa's situation is unique. Its population growth rate is the highest seen anywhere, at any time, in human history. Whereas in Asia and Latin America better health care and extension of education have been accompanied by falling population growth, in Africa the reverse has been true. In 1960 African and South Asian population growth rates were around 2.5 percent a year; Latin America's was reaching 2.9 percent. Today, South Asia's and Latin America's have fallen to 2.1 and 2.5 percent, respectively—but Africa's has risen to 3.2 percent. Even if fertility fell tomorrow to two children for each African family, the continent's population would continue to expand for the next 60 to 70 years. On current trends it will double in 22 years. No region of the world has ever managed to develop with so high a rate of population growth.

Each year Africa's school-age population increases by 4 million (3.22 percent). There is a corresponding increase in the number of mouths to be fed, bodies to be clothed, health services to be provided—all just to maintain the existing level of health, education, and nutrition. The public and the private purse are thus depleted. Too little is saved or invested to improve living standards.

For Africa as a whole land is still abundant, but in some countries the transition from abundance to scarcity is already affecting agriculture and the environment. This transition took centuries in Europe and Asia. It is taking place over decades in Sub-Saharan Africa. The image of Africa as a continent of vast empty spaces is less and less true. In some places the pressure of population on arable agricultural land and other natural resources is already intense (for example, in much of the Sahel, Burundi, western Cameroon, Kenya, eastern Nigeria, and Rwanda). It is true that many areas are substantially underpopulated. Some could easily support much larger numbers, but here too very high population growth makes it difficult for people to escape grinding poverty. The urgency of curbing Africa's population explosion is not due to the present size of the population, but rather to the unmanageable rate of increase.

The link between accelerating population growth and environmental degradation is especially worrying. In several countries overpopulation is putting unsustainable pressure on agricultural land. In many places traditional farming land is already overcultivated, and more fragile land is being exploited to meet the needs of the growing population. Without agricultural modernization the result is rapid desertification, deforestation, and loss of vegetation cover. With sound practices and technological innovations Africa might eventually accommodate several times its present population. But this will take time, and, meanwhile, high population growth spells disaster.

Few Africans are yet persuaded of the advantages of smaller families; they see land as abundant and labor as scarce. But these conditions are changing. Family size is a highly personal and sensitive subject. In most cases it will be necessary to bring down infant mortality rates if parents are to be persuaded to accept a smaller family size. Each country must, of course, attune its policies to its own culture and economic circumstances. Often donors approach the issue in inappropriate or ineffective ways. But the demographic realities facing Sub-Saharan Africa remain: exceptionally high population growth is compromising economic growth and family welfare, adding to environmental degradation, and thus seriously jeopardizing Africa's long-term development.

This nexus of rapid population growth, the slow modernization of agriculture, and consequential environmental damage is a stark reality that must be faced boldly and urgently. It implies a change in fundamental societal values as profound as has already occurred on other continents. The future strategy would be gravely deficient were it not to include measures to slow population growth (see Chapter 3). A reasonable target would be for Africa to follow the rate of fertility decline already achieved by other developing countries. This would result in an average population growth of 2.75 percent a year for 1990–2020.

Employment and wages

Rapid population growth is causing an acute employment problem. The creation of jobs for the rapidly expanding labor force must be a central objective. Nearly half those who will enter the labor force in the next three decades are already born. Therefore, even if the population growth rate during 1990–2020 slows down to 2.75 percent, the labor force will continue to grow more than 3 percent a year. If the unemployment rate by 2020 is to be no more than 10 percent, employment will have to grow around 3.4 percent a year. In other words about 380 million new jobs (more than twice the current level of employment) must be created by 2020 (see Table 2.1).

Agriculture occupies about two-thirds of the labor force in Africa, and it will continue to be an important source of new employment during the next generation. For instance horticulture, dairying, and forestry could expand rapidly, and all these activities are labor intensive. However, there are limits to agriculture's capacity for labor absorption. To achieve food security throughout the continent, average per capita food consumption has to increase by about 1 percent a year during 1990–2020 (see Chapter 3). For this to occur, and to provide for the needed growth in agricultural exports, value added per worker in agriculture has to grow by about 1.5 percent a year. Thus an agricultural growth of 4 percent would imply employment growth of no more than 2.5 percent a year in agriculture; this would enable the sector to provide jobs for almost half the increase in the labor force.

Only a fraction of the new workers who come on the job market each year will be able to find employment in the modern sector, even under the most optimistic of scenarios. The public sector is

Table 2.1 Indicative projections of employment in Sub-Saharan Africa, 1985–2020
(millions of persons unless otherwise specified)

	1985	1990	2000	2020	Annual growth rate, 1990–2020 (percent)
Population	423	497	677	1,107	2.8
Labor force	198	230	318	610	3.3
Employment	168	199	279	549	3.4
(employment rate, percent)	(85)	(87)	(88)	(90)	–
Agricultural sector	131	148	190	311	2.5
Modern wage sector	10	12	17	32	3.4
Small and microenterprise	27	39	73	206	6.0

Sources: ILO 1988, World Bank 1989b, and World Bank data.

chronically overstaffed and needs to be trimmed back rather than expanded. In some countries budget constraints are already forcing cuts in public employment. Large-scale modern industries will be important sources of employment only in a few countries. However, much simple manufacturing—for example, furniture, clothing, and household goods—can be undertaken by small- and medium-scale firms. Employment in these firms and in construction could be important. In the longer term it is to these expanding modern enterprises and their supporting services that countries must look for new jobs. But in most countries they will fail to absorb more than a fraction of the new workers who come onto the job market each year. At best, wage employment in the modern sector as a whole can be expected to grow at around 3 to 4 percent annually.

This leaves small and microenterprises, now mainly in the informal sector, to absorb about half the new entrants to the labor force. Construction to meet the fast-expanding demand for housing is likely to be an important source of jobs, especially through owner-managed businesses that employ just a few laborers. The same is true of much construction of infrastructure, such as school buildings and clinics, as well as small sewerage, rural road, and other rural and secondary-city infrastructure. A myriad of other activities and services can be imagined.

Overall, employment in small and microenterprises will need to grow on average by 6 percent a year. It would be reasonable to assume that value added per worker in these areas will grow at least as fast as in agriculture (1.5 percent a year) and that the small and microenterprise sector would grow by 7.5 percent annually, thus contributing about 1.5 percent to overall GDP growth—about the same as each of the other sectors (see Table 2.2). Such growth will also be nec-

essary to create effective demand for agricultural products.

Wage legislation has a direct effect on job creation in the modern sector. Governments have typically attempted to set minimum wages higher than market-determined wages. Such regulations are widely ignored in the informal sector, but, where wage legislation has been effectively enforced, it has led to higher costs and lower competitiveness. Experience shows that this legislation reduces overall employment.

The impact of wage controls is well illustrated by the experience of Kenya, where real wages quadrupled between 1949 and 1968 (to several multiples of average rural farm incomes) as a result of wage fixing. Later the government ceased administratively raising private sector wage rates and allowed the labor markets to function. Within a decade the wage rate for unskilled labor was little higher than the mean income of farmers, which broadly eliminated the urban income bias. The effect on employment was striking. In the decade before 1968 urban formal employment expanded at a sluggish 1.6 percent a year; in the decade after 1968 it grew at more than 6 percent a year, only part of which can be explained by greater public sector employment. In the 1980s government policy has been to allow official wage contracts to rise by no more than 75 percent of inflation. As a consequence real wage rates in the private sector have continued to fall.

The policy conclusions are clear. Experience suggests that, except on grounds of health and worker safety, governments should resist interfering in labor markets. If left alone, they work well. The political imperative is to interfere, but the economic logic is not to. Minimum wage legislation, regulations restricting the ability of employers to hire and fire, and related interventions tend to raise costs, reduce competitiveness, and con-

Table 2.2 Contributions to the growth of GDP in Sub-Saharan Africa, 1990–2020
(percent)

| | Sector | | | |
	Agriculture	Modern wage	Small and microenterprise	Total
GDP distribution (1987)	33	47	20	100
Growth of employment	2.5	3.4	6.0	3.4
Growth of value added per worker	1.5	0.2	1.5	–
Sectoral growth rate	4.0	3.6	7.5	–
Contribution to GDP growth	1.3	1.7	1.5	4.5

Source: World Bank data.

strain the growth of employment. Equally, for countries in which public sector salaries act as pacesetters—which is common—wage rates fixed at higher than the market rate will tend to raise wage costs in the economy as a whole. This is no longer true in countries such as Ghana, Liberia, Sudan, and Uganda, where real wages have collapsed, but it still applies in other countries, especially those in the CFA franc zone. During the next generation the rapidly expanding labor force will tend to drive wages down. In these cases any attempt to obstruct this process administratively will fail in the long run, at the cost of lower growth in production and employment in the short run.

If farmers and firms are to raise their production and employment as intended, they will have to be competitive both at home and abroad. This means letting wages and salaries reflect labor productivity in agriculture and industry. Thus, as part of the future development strategy, pay should largely be determined by the market.

Urbanization and migration

The corollary of rapid population growth is rapid urbanization. This, of itself, is not alarming, since urbanization and economic development are mutually reinforcing. People migrate in response to economic opportunity and should not be discouraged from doing so. As cities grow, they generate economies of scale and, through complementarities, achieve a higher level of productivity than the rural areas. Cities foster modernization and change and consequently are the nerve centers of the development process. Nonetheless they must be in economic balance with their rural hinterland.

Agricultural growth creates a demand for transport, processing, and various other support services. Through increased cash incomes it also creates a demand for urban goods and services. The associated multiplier effects are typically very strong as further increases in income and employment are generated in the towns. This leads in turn not only to increased demand for agricultural products but also to greater efficiency in the production of agricultural inputs. Improvements in transporting, storing, and marketing agricultural products allow farmgate prices to rise while consumer prices fall.

Comparisons during the past 30 years suggest that countries that have pursued policies leading to sustainable development and diversification of

their agriculture have also had the best relative success in equipping their cities and developing their urban networks. Conversely, the countries that have stifled or neglected their agriculture also have the most dilapidated urban infrastructure even when they have benefited from large surpluses from extractive industries. Agriculture and urban development go hand-in-hand.

Yet many African governments have pursued macroeconomic policies with a distinct urban bias. Their past trade and credit policies have encouraged the establishment of large-scale, capital-intensive industries that locate in large cities, while agricultural procurement, food subsidy, and exchange rate policies have tended to keep food prices low for urban consumers at the expense of the farmers. Partly as a response to this urban bias, Africa's urban growth has been markedly faster than average for developing countries. Efficiency and equity call for a neutral policy framework. Indeed adjustment processes presently under way in much of Africa are dramatically reducing urban policy biases, with a marked impact on urban incomes. In Tanzania farm incomes rose by 5 percent in real terms between 1980 and 1984, while urban wage earners faced a decline of 50 percent; in Ghana, during the same period, farm incomes stagnated while urban incomes fell by 40 percent; in Côte d'Ivoire the ratio of urban to rural incomes fell from 3.5 in 1980 to about 2 in 1985. In Nigeria higher farm incomes have caused workers to return, at least temporarily, to farming.

Whereas in the past urban dwellers in many African countries have benefited from subsidized investments in infrastructure, urban enterprises—and especially the small- and medium-scale ones that provide the bulk of new employment—are nonetheless suffering from inadequate and unreliable infrastructure services. To ensure the efficient functioning of Africa's cities—and thus future economic growth—the key urban services need to be made self-financing, and local governments have to be allowed to mobilize more of their own resources, rather than relying on transfers from the central government. Past investments in certain primary cities—Brazzaville and Lusaka to name but two—also seem disproportionate when compared with the poor infrastructure in secondary and minor towns. The benefits of urbanization depend partly on the efficiency of the overall urban network linking farmers to the domestic and international markets. Thus it is imperative that the infrastructure needs of the secondary towns are given due weight in public investments, as has been done in Kenya.

Since population will more than double between 1990 and 2020, certain areas will be subject to intense population pressure. To accommodate this growth, migration between countries must occur. Based on past trends and differences in resource endowment, rates of such migration may range up to 1 percent a year.

This would be nothing new. Africa's populations have always been highly mobile. Even with the imposition of colonial boundaries, considerable migration occurred between territories and over long distances. Since independence Côte d'Ivoire has accommodated more than 2 million people from the Sahel. The willingness to accept migrant workers has been of great economic benefit both to Côte d'Ivoire and to the countries of origin (see Box 7.7). Migration gives low-wage farm labor to the former and substantial remittances to the latter. On present demographic trends it is vital for countries to facilitate rather than frustrate migration.

Sustainability

Sustainable growth calls for a development strategy that does not compromise the welfare of future generations. Until recently, public policy and donor programs have largely neglected the issue of sustainability. Instead spurts of growth have been based on external borrowing, inflationary financing, rapid depletion of natural resources, and the degradation of ecological systems. Such growth cannot last.

When growth depletes capital, it must eventually slow down. Capital, in this context, includes not only plant, machinery, and infrastructure, but also natural resources such as land, water, and minerals and human capital in the form of knowledge, health, and social organizations. Thus, to ensure sustainable growth, the future strategy will need to emphasize both sound environmental management and human resource development. Unlike physical capital, human capital grows through use. Moreover the health and education of parents improves the health and education of their children.

Properly managed, renewable natural resources can last forever. However, there is a pervasive tendency to consume or destroy them through overuse. Throughout Sub-Saharan Africa forests are being cut down, crop lands turned into

deserts, species of flora and fauna lost, and water and air polluted. These are losses not just to the present generation, but to all future generations. Environmental sustainability is a critical issue that cuts across all sectors.

Environmental management and economic development are intimately connected. The environment consists of intricate ecological systems. Trees and grass, for example, not only provide fuel and fodder, but also build soil fertility, prevent erosion, provide water catchment, ameliorate climate changes, and provide wildlife habitats. These systems are the underpinnings for human welfare and survival.

Sub-Saharan Africa's environment is easily damaged. Eighty percent of the soils are fragile, 47 percent of the land is too dry to support rainfed agriculture, and average rainfall varies from year to year by an enormous 30 to 40 percent. In many areas population pressure is pushing farmers onto marginal lands and causing deforestation, severe soil erosion, and declining productivity. Poor families cut whatever wood they can for essential fuel. The result is ever-widening circles of bare and infertile soil around settlements, ever more time and effort required simply to obtain fuel and raise enough crops to survive, and less time and energy to improve welfare. Where environmental abuse leads to loss of arable land, wildlife, and water supplies and even to local climate change, the effects are felt in declining incomes and a diminishing quality of life. Inevitably the poor suffer most.

After a while environmental damage may reach a critical point. In the Sahel expanding populations and accelerated deforestation have triggered a cascading decline in biological and economic productivity and have created what is now the world's largest area threatened by desertification. Hardship is widespread as people seek refuge in the cities. The Sahel's urban populations have quadrupled in the past 20 years. Air and water pollution in these areas and their growing demand for raw materials (such as fuelwood) in turn accelerate deforestation and environmental degradation.

This downward cycle can be reversed through sound environmental management. Strategic tree planting, for example, can significantly reduce pressures on the land. In Rwanda communal forests, village nurseries, tree planting, and agroforestry have helped to provide fuelwood, fodder, and erosion control for the rural population. Throughout Africa the rural populations should be mobilized to plant trees around their homes.

For some countries the costs of environmental degradation could be clear and immediate; in Kenya, for example, one-quarter of the nation's total foreign exchange earnings come from tourists mainly attracted by its wildlife. In other cases the impact of natural resource depletion and pollution on economic growth is less clear. Many costs take years or decades to appear. Traditional measures of economic well-being, such as per capita GNP, fail to capture them. At the same time spending on pollution abatement, for example, is counted as consumption rather than investment.

Rapid population growth and a declining resource base lead inevitably to conflicts over resource management. Environmental issues involve externalities. Powerful groups will try to impose environmental costs on weaker ones. Developed countries may try to transfer the costs of their environmental problems to developing countries. The export of toxic wastes, for example, must be vigorously discouraged.

Earlier approaches to environmental management were based on environmental impact assessments of individual projects and on investment in programs such as pollution abatement, afforestation, or water management. These are useful, but inadequate. The project-by-project approach tends to address the symptoms, rather than the root causes, of environmental problems. Future strategies should look beyond projects to the broader issues and explicitly recognize intersectoral links and intergenerational concerns. To this end a few African countries are preparing national environmental action plans, which describe how population growth, land tenure, livestock management, and other agricultural methods need to change to attain sustainable growth. A wide range of people and organizations have been involved in these discussions. This should help to secure a consensus on the actions that are needed and broad support for their implementation (see Box 2.1).

Government's awareness of environmental factors and the willingness to take politically difficult measures will largely determine whether the degradation of natural resources will continue to threaten economic growth in Africa. Integrating natural resource management into country economic planning will require political courage. To overcome the financial and institutional constraints, substantial concessional assistance from abroad will be needed. Since there are global benefits in resource conservation, this seems amply justified. A compact might be envisaged in which donor assistance would be provided if credible programs of environmental protection are implemented. Without such programs assistance cannot in any case expect to achieve lasting benefits.

Equity and poverty reduction

Growth does not necessarily reduce poverty or provide food security. Thus the future development strategies of African countries need specifically to address poverty alleviation and better income distribution as issues in their own right. These strategies need to address two critical needs: first, how to make the poor more productive and, second, how to provide productive assets to the poor. Earlier policies tended to favor the urban elite at the expense of the rural poor and men at the expense of women. Establishing a neutral structure of incentives is an important first step toward a fairer society. In addition ensuring better access to food, clean water, health and nutrition, education, and sanitation for everyone is a central objective. Improving human capital is an effective way to promote social mobility and more equal economic opportunities.

In the 1970s increasing attention was paid to the importance of meeting basic needs, not just for welfare reasons but because a work force that was deprived would not be able to generate growth. The economic crisis of the early 1980s diverted attention from basic needs programs. This was a mistake; every effort should be made to protect basic needs expenditures in times of recession. The challenge now is to make up for lost time. Also important to long-term equity are measures to improve the access of the poor to assets, especially for women. Throughout Africa land reform and credit for microenterprises are good examples of this.

Structural adjustment programs already incorporate components intended to assist the poor (see Box 9.2). For example, higher agricultural prices benefit the rural areas in which most of the poor live. Several countries are planning to help redundant workers through food-for-work programs. But more needs to be done. Above all it is essential for governments to maintain, and as soon as possible expand, expenditures on basic health and education.

The issues of growth and equity underlie the dualism that is found in most African countries. Public sector employment has expanded enor-

Box 2.1 Madagascar's environmental action plan

The Malagasy government has initiated decisive action to forestall the serious environmental degradation that now threatens the country's long-term development. With donor assistance it has prepared an environmental action plan with five key sets of measures aimed at:
- Limiting deforestation and soil erosion
- Protecting Madagascar's unique biological patrimony
- Monitoring environmental trends
- Educating the population on environmental issues
- Controlling urban pollution.

Madagascar was initially endowed with about 80 percent of forested land and an exceptionally diverse flora and fauna. Now only 16 percent of forest land is left. If current trends are not reversed, Madagascar's natural forests will disappear altogether within about 30 years. This would cause calamitous soil erosion and an irreversible decline in its exceptional biological diversity, which would represent a permanent loss to future generations. As a consequence of deforestation, land fertility is steadily decreasing, while investment and maintenance costs for major irrigation schemes and dams have increased dramatically. The annual cost of environmental damage is estimated to be between 5 and 15 percent of GNP.

The environmental action plan has been conceived as an on-going process with three features.
- Strong political commitment. Initiated by the prime minister, the plan has effective political support and is considered an integral part of Madagascar's development program. A National Charter for Environment is being prepared for approval by the National Assembly. Although donors have strongly supported the government's initiative, they have been no more than catalysts for a truly national process.
- Intense participation and communication. To prepare the plan, about 150 local specialists have been mobilized in a range of disciplines from a great variety of public, semipublic, and private organizations. Furthermore a vast multimedia campaign has been launched to increase awareness of the environment at all levels of Malagasy society. Environmental issues are being progressively introduced into primary, secondary, and university education.
- Quick progression from studies to action. Studies have already led to actions in the field, pilot operations, the preparation of a major investment program, and proposals for policy and institutional reforms.

The planned investment program includes watershed management projects to protect large irrigation schemes, hydropower dams, and reservoirs; the development of environmental information systems (mapping, remote sensing, and cadastral records) to improve resource management; and education programs. Among the legal and policy changes being elaborated are land legislation and taxation to increase land security and thus to provide incentives for reforestation and conservation practices, procedures for systematically screening large investments, and the monitoring of endangered species.

Madagascar's drive to protect its unique biological diversity is of long-term global concern and has stimulated strong donor support. It will also bring economic benefits in the form of ecological tourism. A large tourism project, which would open parks under strict control, has been initiated with private funding. Tourism will create much-needed employment opportunities in addition to generating revenues from taxation and fees.

So far Ghana, Lesotho, Mauritius, and Rwanda have also begun to develop environmental action plans, and other countries have expressed their interest in doing so. They will benefit from Madagascar's pioneering efforts.

---

mously since independence. Educated Africans have assumed that they would be found jobs in the civil service, in the military, or in parastatals—jobs that paid better than others elsewhere in the economy. Public sector pay often set the standard for firms in the formal private sector. Public spending would be better devoted to meeting basic needs than to creating unproductive jobs and providing social welfare to a privileged minority.

Allied to these concerns is a growing recognition that many officials with power over scarce inputs (such as import licenses or foreign exchange) have prospered unfairly in recent years. They have sold these inputs at parallel market prices, sometimes in collusion with firms from developed countries. "Rent-seeking" and the capital flight that goes with it have undermined development and corroded the fabric of society.

Corruption is not, of course, unique to Africa. But perhaps Africa can least afford it.

The rapid growth of population during the 1990s implies that even the ambitious targets proposed for agricultural and industrial growth would leave room for only limited improvements in per capita incomes. Moreover the increased level of domestic savings required would mean that per capita consumption would remain stagnant. However, the strategy would still imply a significant increase in income and consumption of the vast majority of the population working in agriculture and in the informal sector providing goods and services. The squeeze would come mainly on the consumption of the top 5 percent belonging to the formal modern sector and to the recipients of "rents." Beyond the 1990s even this top 5 percent of income earners can expect rising levels of consumption, although it is important that these increases are related to real increases in productivity.

Strengthening the enabling environment

The first element of the proposed two-part strategy is to strengthen the enabling environment. Chapter 1 makes clear that low productivity lies at the heart of Africa's economic problem. A fundamental reorientation of the pattern of incentives seems essential. On the one hand, consumers need to be more attracted to domestically produced goods; on the other, new entrants to the labor market should no longer aspire to employment in the public sector and nowhere else, but instead seek to use their skills in industry or agriculture. Policies on pricing, the exchange rate, and taxation can be attuned to this goal.

Reoriented incentives

Economic distortions in African economies have had a pervasive and damaging effect on patterns of household consumption, income distribution, and growth. The countries with relatively high growth rates have avoided the worst of these pitfalls. Specifically, they have kept their exchange rates competitive, avoided strong or discriminatory protection of their manufacturing industry, avoided underpricing their agricultural products, kept real interest rates positive, kept real wages at levels justified by productivity, applied cost recovery in pricing infrastructure services, and avoided high and accelerating inflation by following disciplined fiscal and monetary policies.

Structural adjustment programs are helping to reduce distortions in many countries, but much more remains to be done (see Box 2.2). Chapters 4 and 5 return to the question of incentives in agriculture and industry. Exchange rate policy is so central, however, that it merits further examination here.

EXCHANGE RATE POLICY. Discussions of exchange rate policy usually focus on the short-run macroequilibrium. Devaluation has therefore come to be associated with austerity. This ignores its structural implications. Import-intensive patterns of consumption are largely attributable to exchange rates that discourage domestic producers. By influencing a country's internal terms of trade—that is, by raising the return to domestic producers and the prices consumers pay for imports—exchange rate policy can tackle some of Africa's major barriers to growth.

An active exchange rate policy ought to be part of any long-term program to boost production and employment. For farm and factory employment to increase rapidly, external and internal demand for local products must rise. A devaluation raises the price of imports, which switches demand from imports to local goods. Exchange rate adjustments are a simpler and more effective way to promote domestic production than tariffs or other trade restrictions.

After independence most African countries adopted levels and patterns of personal consumption in the modern sector that could not be sustained at prevailing levels of productivity; this was especially true of public employees. Tanzania was a notable exception in holding public sector pay in check. In some countries, such as Ghana and Uganda, general economic collapse has forced a brutal fall in consumption. A better way to bring consumption into line with productive capacity is an across-the-board "tax" on all forms of consumption that, directly or indirectly, require foreign exchange. This, in effect, is what an active exchange rate policy implies. The most obvious result would be a greater demand by the prosperous for domestic goods and services—household workers, drivers, and other personal services—and a corresponding drop in their demand for imported clothes, electronic appliances, and the like. Such a switch would be wholly beneficial since it would generate employment and save foreign exchange. Admittedly consumption habits are difficult to change in the short run. Imported products easily come to be regarded as conventional necessities, and the vested interests of suppliers and consumers accumulate around them. In the longer run, however, consumption is flexible.

Exchange rate policy can also stimulate regional economic integration in Africa—an important political objective and a necessary condition for sustained growth. Greater trade among African countries will not happen as long as foreign goods are made cheap by an overvalued exchange rate. In theory fiscal measures such as tariffs and export subsidies could substitute for devaluation. But their administrative and economic shortcomings are evident. The extensive and porous borders of African countries offer many opportunities for smuggling. The best way to make imports from

Box 2.2 Nigeria's lessons of adjustment

Nigeria's economy illustrates the distortions caused by a commodity boom, the positive impact of decisive government action to reorient incentives, and the need to moderate the adverse social impact of adjustment measures. Sharply rising oil prices boosted exports from $4 billion in 1975 to $26 billion in 1980, while GNP per capita rose from $360 to more than $1,000. Rising public expenditures fueled by oil revenues shifted production from agriculture to services. When the price of oil collapsed, so did Nigeria's export receipts. By 1986 they were down to $6 billion, while external debt rose form $5 billion in 1980 to $25 billion in 1986. Real imports contracted at an average annual rate of 20 percent. Growth rates turned sharply negative, and GNP per capita fell to $370.

After intensive public debate the government adopted a program to liberalize the economy and move to market prices by

• Introducing a market-determined exchange rate system
• Eliminating import licensing and liberating export regulations
• Removing price controls and abolishing agricultural marketing boards
• Adopting supporting monetary and fiscal policy.

The program, initiated in 1986, has transformed the incentive structure of the economy. A fourfold depreciation of the currency sharply increased the relative prices of internationally traded goods. This has revitalized the tree crop sector. But, as farmers shifted production toward exports and substituted for imports, food prices rose, which made food production more profitable. These improved incentives for agriculture have reversed the strong urban bias that had developed during the oil boom.

Exchange rate adjustment and trade reforms have redirected foreign exchange to where it is more productive. Manufacturing firms have switched from assembly operations and other import-dependent lines of production to activities based on local materials. After five years of contraction at an average rate of 4 percent a year, manufacturing output began growing again in 1987. The new exchange rate and price regime have improved resource use in the economy and encouraged exports. Although investment and import levels have continued to decline since the program was adopted, output has started to recover. In the five years from 1982 to 1986, real non-oil output, excluding agriculture, dropped 15 percent. More than half of this loss was recouped in 1987 and 1988, despite a 30 percent decline in the real value of imports.

Non-oil exports, particularly cocoa and other agricultural products, have risen sharply—by 40 percent a year in 1987 and 1988.

In contrast to the program's effectiveness in improving efficiency, it has not yet led to a recovery of private investment—the key to future growth. To revive private investment, the authorities have recently liberalized the regulatory environment for private investment (including relaxing restrictions on direct foreign investment) and have begun to commercialize major public enterprises and privatize minor ones.

Partly because of the sluggishness of private investment, GDP growth has barely kept up with population growth, and per capita incomes have stagnated. Unemployment remains high, because the labor force is growing faster than employment, although the situation has been partially alleviated by a strong migration back to the land to take advantage of the increased economic opportunities in the rural sector. Real wages, which fell by more than 50 percent in 1982–86, declined by an additional 10 percent in 1987, and a poor harvest in 1987 ratcheted up prices. Relaxed financial policies in early 1988 exacerbated these price pressures. Although civil service wages were increased in early 1988, sharply rising food prices more than eroded that gain. In mid-1988 fiscal stabilization and a good harvest slowed the increase in food prices until the first part of 1989. But prices then began to rise quickly, in part reflecting exchange rate depreciation and reduced government funding of the foreign exchange market. The social impact of these trends has been harsh.

Several lessons emerge from Nigeria's experience. Most prominent is the need for prudence in spending the proceeds of a commodity boom. Cutting public spending when a boom ends is difficult, as is adapting the structure of an economy to lower spending levels. These difficulties delayed Nigeria's response to the collapse of oil revenues and led to a buildup of foreign debt that it could not service. The second lesson is that devaluation can successfully promote agricultural production and enhance the efficiency of resource use. Third, enough time must be allowed for macroeconomic measures to have an effect. Stop-go policies undermine investor confidence and deprive the economy of investments essential for its recovery. Finally, adjustment must be viewed as an ongoing process, and, unless fiscal discipline is maintained, inflation can easily undermine the reforms and cause undue social distress.

outside Africa less attractive than those from within Africa is to keep exchange rates competitive.

For all the above reasons active management of the exchange rate is central to achieving sustained growth and greater regional integration. The precise form of exchange rate policy can vary. Operating a free market in foreign exchange, possibly using an auction system, has been useful in coun-

tries such as Guinea—especially for breaking away from highly overvalued currencies. Other countries, such as Botswana and Malawi, have successfully adopted more managed systems.

A managed system is particularly relevant where a country has abundant inflows of foreign exchange from oil or mineral sales or from a windfall caused by a temporary peak in the price of some other export commodity, or even from a high level of capital inflows (see Box 8.1). In these situations a free market in foreign exchange will result in a currency that is overvalued, as judged by the need for long-term incentives in favor of domestic production. The aim should be to make farm prices remunerative and industrial wages internationally competitive.

Effectiveness of exchange rate adjustments will be thwarted if the patterns of consumption and production are not flexible enough to redirect expenditures from imports to domestic sources. The problem of the "missing middle" in the consumption and production systems in Africa thus contributes to the slow response to exchange rate adjustments. Government action to promote "intermediate technology" would be an important element in the overall strategy for structural adjustment.

Financial discipline is essential if nominal devaluations are to result in real devaluations—that is, if they are not merely to cause higher inflation, as happened in some African countries. Timing is vital. Governments should, for instance, take advantage of improvements in their terms of trade or of bumper harvests. This implies the opposite of the conventional (and politically convenient) view. It requires governments to recognize the central importance of exchange rate policy for long-term development and to see a short-run balance of payments improvement as an opportunity to devalue rather than an excuse to do nothing—or, even worse, to revalue. Indonesia skillfully followed such a strategy in 1978.

For exchange rate policy, as for the management of other key prices, the objective should be to avoid major distortions, even when fully market-determined prices are not feasible for economic, social, and political reasons. Experience also suggests that when the country starts from a situation of high distortions, the process of adjustment has to be managed carefully with regard to timing, pace, and scope to avoid disruption. The benefits of liberalization operate primarily through changes in relative prices, with resultant changes in the flows of new investment, and they are easier to bring about in an environment of economic growth. Thus, adjustments and growth have to go hand in hand.

Improved infrastructure

A key component of the enabling environment is good infrastructure. Despite the heavy investment in the past, services remain extraordinarily poor. In many countries much of the population lives more than a day's travel from an all-weather road. Average road densities are one-half to one-third of those in other developing regions. Fewer than 20 percent of attempted telephone calls are actually completed; in many countries the figure for international calls is less than 10 percent. Shortages of drinking water and problems in waste disposal are all too common. In Zaire, for example, urban infrastructure services reach less than half the urban dwellers. Further, lack of maintenance is eroding the infrastructure base. Urban buses are out of service as much as 90 percent of the time. Private motor vehicles are reported to last only three years on Zairian roads. Road maintenance equipment in West Africa typically operates at between only 30 and 60 percent of capacity. Government-owned civil aviation services are fragmented and suffer from lack of coordination. The examples are endless. All this greatly raises the cost of doing business in Africa.

There are many reasons for the poor state of Africa's infrastructure. First, except for railways, independent Africa inherited a very meager base. Second, public infrastructure agencies have performed badly and have generally failed to develop a professional cadre of managers and technicians. Third, policies have failed to emphasize financial viability and service quality; underpricing has led to decay and scarcity. Prices for petroleum products, kept low by administrative controls, for example, have resulted in waste and shortages, especially in the rural areas.

Sound infrastructure is particularly important for cities and towns to develop and function efficiently. In Africa, as in other parts of the developing world, rapidly expanding urban centers are crucibles of acculturation to modernity and to the market economy. The earlier development strategy gave prominence to the primary urban centers. In many instances it adopted distorted pricing and investment policies, which stifled the links between urban centers and their hinterland. As a result the urban networks that are vital for the development of domestic markets were not established. Postindependence strategies have also done little to develop the institutions that are necessary to manage urban growth, particularly local government. Given projected population pressures, the long-term trend toward rapid urbanization will not abate despite the drive to modernize agriculture. And since efficient urban networks foster both urban and rural development, provision has to be made for a faster expansion of infrastructure. In this, policy should recognize the role of secondary towns in supporting agriculture.

In the coming information age rapid access to data and new ideas worldwide will be the key to national success. This is as true for Africa as anywhere else. Improving and expanding the telephone service is therefore an essential component of the new development strategy. Recent studies on the relationship between the supply of telecommunications services and economic development have shown benefit-cost ratios of five to one and in some sectors even higher. In Africa less than one person in 300 has access to a telephone. This coverage is half that of Asia and one-sixteenth that of Latin America. The figures understate the difficulty because the service is generally poor. At any time between 20 and 40 percent of the connected lines are out of service for lack of maintenance, and the service is unevenly distributed, with remote areas often lacking any service at all. So large is the unmet demand that a well-managed telecommunications sector could easily pay for itself and generate substantial surplus revenue for other uses (see Box 2.3).

Neglect of road maintenance multiplies the eventual cost of repair by 200 to 300 percent and increases costs to vehicle owners and shippers by up to 50 percent for paved roads and much more for gravel and earth roads. It is estimated that $5 billion is required to clear Africa's maintenance and rehabilitation backlog and that a further $700 million is needed each year to avoid further deterioration. This will require big changes in spend-

ing. During the past 15 years donors and governments have begun to address the problem of road maintenance, but lasting results have been achieved in only a handful of countries. Some have developed innovative labor-intensive methods for road maintenance in rural areas (see Box 2.4).

Faced with tight budgets, the huge backlog of maintenance needs, and rapid urban growth, how can governments hope to provide essential infrastructure services? Several broad recommendations merit consideration:

• Give priority to rehabilitation instead of investment in new facilities
• Make greater use of the private sector
• Improve cost recovery from public services
• Ensure consistent long-term financial support.

RESPONDING TO DEMAND. Political and commercial interests both in Africa and in the donor countries find it advantageous to expand facilities and especially to undertake the large projects that were typical of past infrastructure programs. But too often overly optimistic forecasts of demand and revenue have been used to justify investments that later proved unviable. Pressure to construct new roads that will benefit only a limited constituency should be resisted while portions of the existing network are deteriorating. Responding to proven demand itself poses problems of phasing and sequencing. Infrastructure improvements with high rates of return deserve priority. These include telecommunications and rural roads serv-

---

Box 2.3 Telecommunication in the information age

In an increasingly information-driven world, Africa's competitiveness will depend on its ability to access and exchange information globally. Informatics are dramatically improving decisionmaking processes, raising productivities, and transforming the map of comparative advantage. New technologies—from personal computers and telefacsimiles to digital networks—are revolutionizing the way the world does business. None of this equipment can be used if the basic telecommunication network is not in place. At present Africa's unmet demand for lines is estimated at more than 60 percent of current installed capacity.

Experience elsewhere suggests that with a GDP growth rate of 4 percent, the number of telephone lines should expand by 10 percent. In recent years the expansion rate has been 7 percent annually. To make up the backlog, a 12 percent annual growth rate in the number of lines would

be a reasonable target for Sub-Saharan Africa and would require an investment of around $800 million each year, or about 0.5 percent of GDP. This target is modest compared with the headlong expansion taking place in the developed countries. Europe currently allocates 0.7 percent of GDP, while Africa's figure is only 0.3 percent.

To meet this challenge, the traditional approach to telecommunications in Africa will need to be rethought. Existing public monopolies are already overwhelmed and lack the managerial, technical, and financial resources to cope. The commercialization, and in some aspects the privatization, of telecommunications services would be a more effective way to mobilize the resources and skills that are needed. The benefit-cost ratios of good communication are so high, and the economic losses caused by the current poor services so great, that a ready interest on the part of the private sector is assured.

Box 2.4 Labor-intensive road maintenance

Road rehabilitation and maintenance, whether of trunk or feeder roads, generally relies heavily on costly equipment. With the acute lack of foreign exchange facing many countries, such equipment has been scarce. In its place labor-based techniques can save foreign exchange and generate jobs.

In The Gambia a pilot project on labor-based maintenance has shown that employing small-scale, village-based contractors (both men and women) is feasible and economic. The small contractors quickly learned the necessary skills and effectively organized workers for the jobs. This was possible because simplified procedures for the awarding, control, and payment of contracts and for monitoring performance and productivity were developed.

Other examples of successful labor-intensive rural road rehabilitation programs exist in Ghana, Kenya, and Malawi. Labor-based techniques were successfully used in the Kenya Rural Access Roads Project and the Minor Roads Project. Malawi has also demonstrated the viability and effectiveness of labor-intensive techniques for road

rehabilitation in their District Roads Improvement Program.

Ghana has decided to use labor-based methods for about 25 percent of its annual feeder road rehabilitation and maintenance. Feeder roads could be rehabilitated 15 percent more cheaply than those done by conventional methods, with up to a 40 percent savings in foreign exchange. Small contractors, after four months of practical training followed by two months of trial contracts, can now each produce on average two kilometers of high-quality gravel road a month. They employ about 200 persons (about 30 to 40 percent women) a day compared with about 50 persons under the capital-intensive method. Wages contribute to cash earnings, which stimulate the rural economy. Nineteen such firms have been trained in the World Bank/UNDP-financed project executed by the ILO. Spending on equipment was limited to tractors, trailers, and manual compaction equipment costing about $100,000 per contractor, compared with the $1.0 million to $2.0 million needed by each contractor under the capital-intensive method.

---

ing areas with good agricultural potential or towns with strong economic links to the agricultural hinterland.

USING THE PRIVATE SECTOR. Infrastructure is long-lived and, as a rule, inherently monopolistic. Governments must therefore take overall responsibility for it. But an important distinction can be made between the *facilities* and the *services* they provide. The private sector can play a useful role in managing the services, even when government builds and controls the facilities. Box 2.5 describes cases of private sector participation in water supply, solid waste disposal, and public transport. In Nigeria a privately owned power company serving the Jos Plateau sells electricity to the National Power Authority. However, subcontracting to private firms is a viable option only if the government respects its contracts and pays its bills.

While recognizing that local governments are the appropriate managers for infrastructure services (see "Strengthening local government," below), most countries would also benefit from greater reliance on the private sector. Nowhere is this more evident than in transport. In Khartoum the informal *bakassi* continue to operate profitably while the public bus fleet accumulates deficits. So it is in many cities. Wherever private operators have been permitted to enter the market—and where monopolies and restrictive practices were held in check—transport services have generally improved. In many countries the failure of public

services has forced individuals and companies to invest in electric generators, boreholes, radio-equipped couriers, and the like. This demonstrates both the scope for private services and the willingness of users to pay for them (see Box 3.2). Programs for the sector should consider ways to promote such interaction.

Many governments are already relying more on the private sector. Their policies range from outright privatization to divestiture of ancillary activities (for example, stevedoring and freight forwarding) and management contracts. In some cases public agencies have narrowed their role to intermediation and planning—as in Malawi, where the housing project agency is being recast as a lender rather than a developer. Contractors are now used for road maintenance in several countries, such as Ghana, Madagascar, and Senegal.

REDUCING COSTS. Although experience varies from country to country, the unit costs of infrastructure investments in Africa are as much as twice that in Asia and even higher for maintenance services. This is partly because domestic markets are small and fragmented. But it is also because of poor methods of public procurement and contract administration, low labor productivity, and the dearth of indigenous machine shops and other support. Some African economies are too small to support a construction sector that can undertake major rehabilitation and development, so it makes sense to foster the emergence of firms that will serve subregional markets. Measures to do this would include harmonizing the regulations that apply to public procurement.

Reducing the cost of infrastructure is vital if African producers are to compete successfully internationally. Most infrastructure agencies have opportunities to cut costs without affecting the quality or the volume of their services. Cost reduction programs require careful monitoring and, above all, strong commitment from senior managers. Sector agencies under financial pressures have seen that such programs are needed; for instance, the managers of Africa's railways are struggling to rehabilitate their bankrupt systems (see Box 2.6). Greater use of infrastructure is possible with better management and modest investment. This applies to the turnaround time for wagons, to the berthing time for ships, and to the use of urban streets. In Abidjan, for example, new parking restrictions recently increased rush hour capacity in the central downtown area by about 30 percent.

Africa has so far failed to take full advantage of the available small-scale, labor-intensive procedures for developing, maintaining, and supplying infrastructure services. Attempts to use appropriate technologies have been too quickly abandoned. The comprehensive programs launched under the UN Water Decade to develop handpumps for rural use and to design low-cost sanitation have shown that the keys to success in this area are extensive field testing and a multidisciplinary scientific approach. Regulatory obstacles and institutional weakness often frustrate the use of new technologies; this is true of containers used for transport, for example.

Box 2.5 Private participation in infrastructure

Private enterprise can provide infrastructure services efficiently, as the following cases demonstrate.

Private water supply. Successful private provision of infrastructure is demonstrated in Côte d'Ivoire, where drinking water is supplied by the Société de Distribution d'Eau de la Côte d'Ivoire (SODECI) to 130 cities and towns—from Abidjan's extensive piped network to well-based systems in smaller towns. SODECI is jointly owned by private Ivorian interests, the government, and a French firm. SODECI has operated under a system based on the French *affermage* model, in which the public authority handles the construction of the system but contracts out its operation, maintenance, and collection of charges to a private operator, the *fermier*. This arrangement has recently been extended to a concession contract that also makes SODECI responsible for investment in expanding the water system. Investment plans need to be approved by the government.

SODECI's revenues derive from a fee that is about one-third of the water tariff. Although the tariff structure provides for a lower tariff for small consumers, which helps the poor to afford water, overall it is set to reflect total costs, financing of debt service, and cash generation for future investments. The water tariff and the fee are related to the volume of water sold, so consumers rather than taxpayers pay for the service received, and, since consumption is metered, water losses are low. SODECI has consistently shown a profit and has expanded rapidly, because it supplies water at standards among the highest in West Africa.

Refuse collection. Another example is the collection of municipal waste by a private company in Togo. The private Togolese Refuse Collection Company (SOTEMA) was formed as a Togolese private corporation with French technical participation and financial support and began collecting and disposing Lomé's municipal solid waste in 1974. An annual tax, specifically designated for waste collection and applied to the properties served, is the principal source of government revenue to pay the company, and the municipality's excellent performance in revenue collection is one of the reasons for the success of the operation.

SOTEMA started with a one-year renewable contract to collect, transport, and dispose of the full range of wastes and by now collects annually an average of 284,000 tons of waste. The company has maintained responsible disposal standards and has established a good record of environmental improvement. Management practices have been sound, and the company has grown steadily and profitably. Substantial savings were achieved by manufacturing collection equipment locally under license. Now, after nearly 15 years of successful operation, SOTEMA has obtained financial support from local banking institutions and is studying proposals to expand operations to other cities in Togo and abroad.

Public passenger transport. Private bus operators are making a breakthrough in Accra, Ghana, in providing much-needed public transport. A small private firm, started by a mechanic in 1985, purchased some old buses that were auctioned off by a state-owned bus company. The buses were rehabilitated in the informal sector and put into service. Now the firm has about 40 buses that provide regular passenger services on many routes in Accra. The firm has a staff-to-bus ratio of five—about one-fourth of the staff-to-bus ratio of state-owned bus companies. The success of this private firm in providing efficient services at a profit within government tariff levels is a good example to policymakers trying to reorganize state-owned bus companies more efficiently.

RECOVERING COSTS. Except perhaps where facilities are underused, there are no good reasons for charging the users of infrastructure less than it costs to provide the service. In fact these services may sometimes be priced above long-run costs to recover some of the consumer surplus; most of these services are consumed by the higher-income groups, so this approach would also be equitable.

Often cost-based pricing alone can increase revenues by 20 to 30 percent. Adjusting the charges for water, electricity, roads, and telecommunications so that they better reflect marginal costs can increase public revenues by between 5 and 10 percent. For water supplies special arrangements may be justified to protect the very poor.

Setting prices properly is only part of the answer: fees and charges also have to be collected. Revenue-gathering in Sub-Saharan Africa has been notoriously poor. Frequently this is because people cannot see what they are getting for their money or because they subvert the cost-recovery process for personal gain. In Tanzania, where the roads have deteriorated because of poor mainte-

nance, only 60 percent of the tolls are collected, according to recent estimates. Such figures are common. By contrast, recent rural water-supply projects—which users themselves have helped to operate and maintain—have collected charges successfully.

Operational discipline is also needed to minimize capacity losses and service leakages. Accurately metering water and electric power, enforcing motor vehicle regulations, and monitoring shipping and air traffic may be particularly cost-effective. These measures can add the equivalent of 40 to 50 percent to the capacity of many systems at relatively little cost.

MAINTAINING THE CRITICAL FINANCIAL COMMITMENT. Financial uncertainty has added to the problems of planning and maintaining infrastructure. World Bank studies find that erratic payments by governments to contractors are one of the main risks facing indigenous construction companies. In several African countries utility companies have trouble collecting fees from ministries and parastatals, and contractors are not paid on time for road maintenance. In some cases cash shortages are to blame since they lead finance officials to divert funds to seemingly more pressing areas. This is a costly mistake. It increases future demands on government funds and slows economic growth. Timely and reliable funding is essential. Earmarking revenues—although undesirable in principle—may in practice be needed to protect infrastructure assets and to build fiscal discipline.

The gulf between current spending for infrastructure in Africa and the amount needed to develop and maintain a system to support economic growth is huge. Africa cannot achieve sustainable development unless this gulf is bridged through a long-term commitment of public funds. Annual infrastructure investment equivalent to at least 4 to 6 percent of GDP on average is warranted in most countries, and $10 per capita annually (1980 dollars) may be a suitable absolute minimum target in all but the poorest nations. Spending for normal maintenance must keep pace with new investment. An additional 1 percent of GDP is needed annually over 10 years to catch up on the substantial backlog of deferred maintenance.

Building capacity

An enabling environment creates the conditions for higher productivity, but growth rates will be raised and sustained only if African capacities are much enhanced. Capacity-building has three distinct elements:
- Human development, especially the provision of basic health, education, nutrition, and technical skills
- The restructuring of many public and private institutions to create a context in which skilled workers can function effectively
- Political leadership that understands that institutions are fragile entities, painstakingly built up, easily destroyed, and therefore requiring sustained nurturing.

Often African countries have been lacking in all three elements. Too frequently national institutions have become politicized and hence used for narrow, sectional ends rather than to achieve national objectives.

Human development and labor productivity

In the first 15 years after independence Africa made impressive gains in literacy, public health,

and life expectancy. Since then, however, it has seen reverses in these as in other areas. Vocational training is poor, and labor productivity remains very low. A high priority for the new development strategy must therefore be to restore momentum in human development. In particular the *quality* of African education and public health must be improved. Where access to education, training, and health services has been widened, it has generally been at the expense of quality.

Education must be relevant to the real needs of African economies. The allocation of spending among primary, secondary, and tertiary education, between academic and vocational training, and among the different disciplines must likewise be related to development needs. Above all, education should aim to engender an analytical frame of mind and receptivity toward technology.

Another aspect of capacity-building is training for excellence. To make progress every country needs a technocratic elite of entrepreneurs, civil servants, administrators, academics, and other professionals. Although few in number, they will be important catalysts for development. With technology advancing rapidly, Africa will need scientists and technicians if it is not to be left behind. This question is addressed in Chapter 3.

Public versus private institutions

The postindependence development strategy accorded the state a lead role in producing many goods and services. This approach foundered on the weak capacity of public institutions. At the same time, far from promoting the private sector, the state often actively curbed private initiative, including cooperatives and grassroots organizations. These policies have been partly reversed, but where to draw the boundary between the private and the public sectors remains controversial and must be settled on a country-by-country basis.

The debate is not simply about the division of responsibilities between the state and the private sector, but also about the division among the central authorities, local government, and local communities. The goal is to reduce the number of tasks performed by central government and to decentralize the provision of public services. Many basic services, including water supply, health care, and primary education, are best managed at the local level—even at the village level—with the central agencies providing only technical advice and specialized inputs. The aims should be to empower ordinary people to take charge of their lives, to make communities more responsible for their development, and to make governments listen to their people. Fostering a more pluralistic institutional structure—including nongovernmental organizations and stronger local government—is a means to these ends.

The state has an indispensable role in creating a favorable economic environment. This should, in fact, be its primary concern. It is of the utmost importance for the state to establish a predictable and honest administration of the regulatory framework, to assure law and order, and to foster a stable, objective, and transparent judicial system. In addition it should provide reliable and efficient infrastructure and social and information services—all preconditions for the efficiency of productive enterprises, whether private or state-owned.

The division of responsibilities between the state and the private sector should be a matter of pragmatism—not dogma. Often public services can be provided by private contractors at very competitive rates—road maintenance, transport, water supplies, refuse collection, and public vehicle repair to name but a few. At the same time consumers have sometimes been exploited by private business monopolies. What matters is reliability and cost-effectiveness. There need be no preconceptions about the "right" type of organization; appropriate incentives count for much more.

Most state enterprises have a poor performance record, although there are some notable exceptions (see Box 7.3). Managers have suffered from political interference. But it has also proved difficult to devise incentive systems to motivate employees and managers when entrepreneurship, commercial judgement, and risk-taking are needed. Increasing recognition of these problems has spurred a worldwide trend toward privatization. If Africa wishes to remain competitive, it should not resist this trend. State-owned enterprises will still be appropriate in many cases, especially in providing utilities and some public goods. In some cases the private sector lacks the capacity to take over, but in time and with imagination privatization can work.

Much can be done to strengthen the performance of those state enterprises that are retained. Efficiency has less to do with ownership than with the conditions under which enterprises operate. Experience shows that state enterprises are more likely to succeed when they are given clear and attainable objectives, day-to-day managerial autonomy, and unambiguous performance indicators, which permit the supervisory body to monitor progress without undue interference. So far in Africa this has rarely been the case.

Development takes place through institutions, including markets, whether private or public. Institution-building in the widest sense is essential and must for the most part be nurtured by governments. But few African governments have paid much attention to the task. Agencies are created or disbanded without much attention to the interrelationships and respective roles of the different institutions involved. Once created, they are often allowed to decay as their initiators move on. The turnover of senior staff is frequently kaleidoscopic; yet prolonged inaction in the face of urgent problems is also common—and equally damaging. Thus, to overcome these weaknesses during the next generation, governments need an explicit strategy for institution-building for both the public and private sectors.

Better government

In the words of President Abdou Diouf of Senegal, Africa requires not just less government but better government. Despite reforms in the 1980s Africa's public administrations remain woefully weak. The principal causes are:
- The uncontrolled expansion of staff in the civil services and public enterprises, which have often functioned as welfare agencies for unemployed school leavers
- The rapid promotion and turnover of poorly qualified staff who have little in-depth understanding of either the institutions they manage or of the broader context in which they are expected to function
- Difficulties faced by managers in motivating and disciplining their staff owing to the social and political context in which they operate
- Insufficient appreciation in government that public agencies work best if staffed and run by professionals according to objective rules and criteria
- In an increasing number of countries the compression of civil service pay scales at the expense of higher level staff.

Recognizing the urgency of this problem several governments—notably Central African Republic, The Gambia, Ghana, Guinea, Mauritania, and Senegal—have launched, although not yet completed, comprehensive programs of administrative reform. The key measures include:

• New and clearer mandates for the agencies, with staff planning based strictly on need

• Staff testing to help select the best qualified candidates and the release of redundant staff with compensation and assistance to enter the private sector

• Better personnel management, with competitive entrance examinations, regular staff appraisals as the basis for promotion based on merit (rather than patronage and longevity), and accurate personnel records that correspond exactly to the payroll

• Selective improvements in the pay structure to attract and retain highly qualified staff.

Public employment accounts for more than 50 percent of nonagricultural registered employment in Africa, compared with 36 percent in Asia and only 27 percent in Latin America. Chronic overstaffing has damaged performance severely, partly because staff are badly deployed and denied adequate material support and partly because idle staff undermine the morale of those who want to work. Many ministries in Africa would probably function better with a fraction of their present staff. Often the application of existing regulations—dismissing persistent absentees, requiring retirement at the mandatory age, laying off temporary staff when they have completed the task for which they were hired—would reduce staff substantially. Pressure on the wage bill can be eased by eliminating ghost workers, double payments, and automatic promotion. Merit-based pay systems, which relate bonus payments to performance and not status and which pay a greater part of salary in that form, help to motivate staff.

In many African countries compensation for civil servants has been severely eroded during the past decade, if only by inflation. This erosion has often affected positions requiring higher skill levels disproportionately, precisely those where the greatest shortages exist and migration occurs. By many measures of internal and international comparisons, compensation levels were too high at independence, and in a few cases they may have to fall further. In a growing number of countries, however, compensation has fallen below levels necessary for the government to compete for indispensable skills and for government workers to support their families on their official income alone. The adverse effects—low morale, moonlighting, and petty corruption—have been unmistakable. Despite the many competing claims on the public purse, in countries in which civil service wages have collapsed, systematic progress must be made over time to reduce the numbers of public employees and to reallocate the savings to improve wage scales if performance incentives are to be restored.

Staffing is but one aspect of the problem, albeit a crucial one. Complicated staff and financial regulations that are barely known and erratically applied contribute to a gross lack of accountability. Overspending and misappropriation of funds occur routinely and pass unnoticed because of poor accounting and the lack of audits. Even when audits are conducted, they are rarely acted on. Such laxity can and must be stopped. Administrative reform takes time and persistence, but it can be done. Guinea's administration, which was enormously weakened during the 1970s, has successfully instituted far-reaching reforms and has laid off 16,000 civil servants in the past two years. The Gambia's government has gone even further and has still maintained its political support; despite heavy redundancies, it was returned to office in a free and open election held soon after the reforms (see Box 2.7).

Despite overstaffing and growing numbers of educated unemployed, there is a great shortage of competent officials, especially at the higher technical levels. This is partly because of poor training and partly because many well-trained nationals join private firms or emigrate. For example, 10,000 highly trained Nigerians are reported to be working in the United States. With the right incentives it should be possible to persuade many to return home. So producing skilled people is only half the battle; the other half is to recruit and retain them, not so much by high pay (which can be ill-afforded) but by ensuring that they have productive jobs, satisfying work, and secure conditions.

Effective economic management

African governments have depended heavily on external agencies and foreign consultants for the analytical work on which key policy decisions have been based. If governments are to become more self-reliant, their capacity to undertake this work for themselves must be improved. In the 1980s governments had to design adjustment programs to attract external support—notably from the IMF and the World Bank. This stimulated a demand for policy analysis, but progress was slow. Governments should plan ways to build up

Box 2.7 Reforming the civil service

Civil service reform is high on the agenda for many African governments, such as the Central African Republic, The Gambia, Ghana, and Guinea. In these four countries civil services have expanded very fast and have served in part as welfare programs in a period of economic decline. Consequently the salary bill absorbed a very large part of government revenues. By 1986 Guinea's 75,000 civil servants' wages accounted for 50 percent of current expenditures. In The Gambia the civil service doubled between 1974 and 1984. In Ghana the civil service increased at a rate five times the growth of the labor market—14 percent each year between 1975 and 1982. In the Central African Republic civil service salaries absorbed 63 percent of current revenues. Recent hiring freezes have helped to contain the wage bills, but they remain unsustainable. The capping of wages and promotions have demotivated staff whose morale was already very poor. Generally, productivity was extremely low, discipline was largely lacking, and overall there was little accountability.

To tackle this situation, the first step has been to conduct a staff census to eliminate from the payroll departed staff (ghosts), overage employees, and unwarranted promotions and allowances and to determine precisely the numbers and deployment of civil servants. In The Gambia more than 20 percent of the civil service was identified as superfluous following such a census and was subsequently retrenched. The Central African Republic terminated automatic recruitment of graduates and introduced competitive entrance exams; a census allowed savings of 7 to 8 percent of the wage bill.

As a second step staff audits have been undertaken to match staff requirement to actual staffing, thereby establishing appropriate staffing structures and identifying surplus staff. To ensure that the most competent staff were retained, Guinea required all civil servants to be tested. As a result 14,000 staff have been placed on administrative leave pending retrenchment, and 9,000 have opted for early retirement. Ghana carried out a systematic job inspection program that involved up to 60 job inspectors and removed some 24,000 civil servants from the payroll over two years.

To avoid costly repeats of census and competency tests, the third step has been to develop and maintain an effective personnel information system to provide up-to-date data on staff numbers and their distribution among administrative units by occupational category. Foolproof procedures needed to be put in place to ensure that each

personnel action (such as hiring, promotion, transfer, or retirement) is promptly recorded in the personnel information system and the payroll simultaneously adjusted. By creating a personnel data system linked to the payroll, governments have been able to prevent salary payments to nonexistent or unauthorized personnel. Moreover computerization permits regular updating and quick verification. In The Gambia the staff audit was followed by the rigorous monitoring of salary payments and control of new hiring, and similar measures are being instituted in Ghana and Guinea.

Fourth, basic and in-service training is being designed in the context of a comprehensive civil service human resource plan and clearly linked to planned career development. More specifically, to overcome weakness in personnel management, specialized in-service training is being provided to personnel staff. In The Gambia and Ghana the staff audits were undertaken by selected officials, who were first given intensive training in staff inspection and job analysis techniques.

Fifth, the rehabilitation of a civil service also required the reform of the statutory and legal framework. The objective is to revise and simplify the civil service code, personnel statutes, and employment conditions to reflect the need for a streamlined, motivated, and cost-conscious civil service. Linked to this in The Gambia was a revision of the civil service pay and benefit structure and related reward systems (special bonuses and allowances) aimed at harmonizing special arrangements and linking salary premiums to individual performance. In Ghana, based on comparator surveys, pay was improved in two ways for higher-skill levels to reverse a severe brain drain out of government and to fill critical long-standing vacancies.

In all four cases reform involved laying-off staff. The success of the reform hinged on the political skill with which this task was approached. In The Gambia a staff resettlement scheme to assist redundant employees was put in place and in Ghana a redeployment committee was established to help former civil servants find gainful private sector employment. In Guinea the government has introduced a redeployment program assisted by a credit scheme administered by local banks.

The implementation of civil service reforms is a long and politically difficult process. Securing acceptance of the reforms by ensuring transparency and fairness is important for their success; so too is assisting retrenched staff to find productive work in the private sector.

---

local capacities to meet this need. External advisers can continue to help as both analysts and trainers during the transition. But in the longer run both the demand for, and the supply of, policymakers should come from within. A starting point would be for government leaders to make fuller use of the trained nationals who are already available. The present failure to do so increases Africa's already excessive dependence on foreign advisers.

Developing an internal capacity for policy analysis takes a long time. This capacity is like a pyramid. Typically, its apex is a small team of advisers concerned primarily with economic strategy and other major issues. This group has to be ideologically close to the government and must enjoy the confidence of the political leadership. Below the apex are the analysts who work on particular aspects of policy, such as agriculture, conservation, pricing, budget, and balance of payments.

Box 2.8 Capacity building for economic policy analysis in Tanzania

The University of Dar es Salaam (UDSM) is one of the few examples in Africa in which faculty and research economists are contributing significantly to national economic policy analysis. Its Economic Research Bureau, started in 1965 with Rockefeller Foundation support, was staffed initially by expatriates while Tanzanians were sent abroad for postgraduate training.

This effort to create a center of excellence was set back by the phasing out of Foundation support in 1971. Core staff were attached to jobs in the public service, and expatriates left. This decline was reversed in 1979 when Sweden agreed to sponsor technical support and training for the bureau and for the economics faculty at the University of Lund.

The current program also provides for short-term study visits, sabbatical leave for senior staff, assignments by visiting professors, and equipment. As a result the UDSM now provides more than a dozen Tanzanian professional economists with strong capabilities in independent research and policy analysis.

These UDSM economists have been increasingly drawn into policy work by the government in recent years. They were seconded to government and parastatals, where they participated in working parties and advised on the formation of the Economic Recovery Programme and external negotiations. Donors funded policy and project studies (on inflation, tariff reforms, and crop marketing as well as the collection and analysis of data on parastatal performance and government recurrent costs). UDSM economists have also promoted informal discussion of policy options by organizing workshops with senior government officials; in 1988 they launched a quarterly publication reviewing economic trends and contemporary policy issues.

All this proved possible for three reasons. First, the strong foundations laid 20 years ago with external assistance sustained the faculty through the 1970s and helped produce a large enough second generation of well-trained economists to provide a critical minimum mass. Second, the authorities sought an open debate on difficult policy issues and were willing to draw on nationals outside government to reinforce policymaking capacity. Third, there was increasing awareness by donors that local experts are a knowledgeable and cost-effective resource for their own program work.

These technocrats provide the continuity when governments change. To improve the quality of the work and to ensure that the structure will survive periods of neglect, the pyramid must extend beyond government. This can be done by developing analytical capacity in universities and other independent research institutions, as well as in economic consulting firms. The donor community has made a useful contribution to institutional development by building up this nongovernmental component—mainly through private foundations for research into long-term development. Several countries have institutes of this kind, which are scarcely used by governments. Tanzania is an exception; its university economists played a valuable role in preparing its economic reform program (see Box 2.8).

The aim must be professional excellence, and one way to promote this is by building professional links between economists within Africa. The creation of a professional network of economists in East Africa is an important step in that direction, which could well be replicated elsewhere and in other disciplines (see Box 7.5).

Policy analysis is very difficult in the absence of reliable and timely data. Africa's statistical services are woefully inadequate. Most need comprehensive upgrading and increased funding as a matter of urgency. Their data collection activities should be redirected to give priority to the needs of decisionmakers. This issue is discussed more fully in the Statistical appendix to this report.

Strengthening local government

In most countries urban growth has far outstripped planning and administrative capacity at both the central and local levels. The task of meeting mounting infrastructure needs has increasingly fallen on local governments. This is as it should be. Alhough weak and underfunded, local governments are best suited to meet the needs of local communities. This is as true for the rural areas as it is for the towns. The initiative shown by Rwanda's communes in mobilizing citizens for road improvements, tree planting, and soil conservation illustrate the potential. Developing competent and responsive local governments is central to capacity-building. It implies stronger powers to raise revenue locally and a clearer delegation of authority and responsibility. Many of the problems of the towns and rural communities can only be solved locally; solutions imposed by central authorities are likely to fail. The objective should be to capitalize on the energies and resources of the local people.

Decentralization in Africa has so far mainly concentrated on strengthening the field agencies of central government. This has been justified by the fear of corruption and inefficiency in poorly supervised local governments. But a change of heart is now apparent. Francophone West African states have embarked on fresh efforts at decentralization; Nigeria is reappraising its local government systems; and Tanzania is in the midst of reviving local government. These are all moves in the right direction. They need to be extended and reinforced.

Fostering private sector capacities

Recognizing the drawbacks of relying too heavily on public bureaucracies, future development strategy could make greater use of the private sector. Often, despite considerable hostility from central government, local entrepreneurs have shown remarkable vitality (see Chapter 6). In Guinea, for example, private traders continued to supply the population with essential goods even when severely harassed by officials under the pre-vious regime. The new approach should try to reconcile efficient government with the common desire of individual Africans to be independent economic operators and of social, religious, and community groups to play their part (see Box 2.9). This latent local capacity can readily be tapped by removing administrative restrictions and providing positive support.

The objective should be to release private energies and encourage initiative at every level. At the grassroots level this means village and ward associations; at the intermediate level, various local nongovernmental and cooperative unions and other organizations; and at the national level, chambers of commerce and industry, trade associations, umbrella NGO organizations (such as CONGAD in Senegal and VADA in Kenya), and professional associations of bankers, doctors, lawyers, accountants, and the like. Such groups and communal actions can build on the African tradition of self-help (see Box 8.3).

Box 2.9 Self-help community participation

Undugu, which means brotherhood in Swahili, is the name of a private society that is helping poor urban youth in Kenya to find gainful employment through training and communities to alleviate poverty and provide low-cost housing. Started by a Catholic action group, it began its work in 1972 by offering shelter and food to young "parking boys" who lived off tips on the streets of Nairobi. To provide vocational training for the boys, it developed a "village polytechnic" system, which later evolved into a very successful apprenticeship program. Under this program Undugu pays roughly half of the boys' wages to the tradesmen willing to train them and has developed simple business training specifically for these trainers. Apprentices are required to attend classes to acquire a minimum of theoretical knowledge, and at the end of the apprenticeship period they take trade tests given by the government. They generally pass these tests after nine months instead of the two years that is normal for those who attend the government's "village polytechnics."

Related to training is Undugu's objective to create gainful employment for the youths; to find sources of income, it created its own training and production units in carpentry, metalworking, motor mechanics, and tailoring. A vehicle maintenance contract from the Norwegian aid agency (NORAD) was so successful that an independent maintenance facility was established in 1986.

Undugu's involvement in housing projects started in 1983, following a large fire in one of Nairobi's "slum villages." With community participation in planning and self-help contributions for construction work, about 500 one-room, mud-and-wattle houses; a second community hall; and a nursery school were built. The next project was the rebuilding of 250 houses destroyed by a heavy flood, augmented by the provision of pit latrines, footpaths, and a road. A third project provided housing for about 6,400 squatter residents. Some 1,070 houses were built at an average cost of less than $300 per house, including self-help labor—far less expensive than the government-assisted, low-cost, sites-and-services housing. Although somewhat lower in standard, they are much better than the flimsy cardboard and paper dwellings that they replaced.

The range of Undugu activities grew. Trying to get at the roots of poverty, it became involved in primary school education, adult literacy classes for women, and the provision of basic health services. Income-generating activities for women and youths included the formation of a cooperative to sell items salvaged from Nairobi's main dump. By early 1986 Undugu participated in more than 20 programs and needed to rethink its role and the focus of its future work. It decided to concentrate on employment generation, through continuation of training and small-enterprise development; low-cost housing; and community development through the formation of interest groups.

Today the Undugu Society has a salaried staff of more than 100 Kenyans and two or three volunteers. Its 1987 budget was more than $1 million, almost half of which is derived from its income-producing activities, among them a craft shop in one of Nairobi's well-to-do areas and a growing number of consultancies to outside groups who draw on Undugu's experience and know-how.

The political and cultural dimensions

History suggests that political legitimacy and consensus are a precondition for sustainable development. A sound strategy for development must take into account Africa's historical traditions and current realities. This implies above all a highly participatory approach—less top-down, more bottom-up than in the past—which effectively involves ordinary people, especially at the village level, in the decisions that directly affect their lives.

Modernization

African intellectuals have emphasized in their writings the widespread failure of the postindependence development strategies to build on the strengths of traditional societies. Modernization theories in the early years of independence tended to make rigid distinctions between modern—that is, "Western"—societies and premodern or traditional societies. Modern society represented "progress." The approach led to many mistakes, especially in land reform, livestock projects, consolidation of rural populations, and integrated rural development.

Future development strategies need to recognize that, far from impeding development, many indigenous African values and institutions can support it. For instance the persistence of primary group loyalties, although often deplored by outsiders, has been a significant force for development. Communal culture, the participation of women in the economy, respect for nature—all these can be used in constructive ways. The informal credit systems successfully draw on customary values and patterns of social organization (see Boxes 4.2 and 6.3). Many indigenous cultivation practices, such as mixed cropping, were once much criticized but are now seen to have technical merit. More generally, while the modern sector has been in malaise, the informal sector, strongly rooted in the community, has been vibrant. In particular it has shown a capacity to respond flexibly to changing circumstances.

This is not to lessen the importance of the modern sector. Certainly if agricultural growth is to be raised, higher productivity through the adoption of modern agronomic packages, tools, and machinery is essential. Other sectors need modernization too. But increasingly it should be a modern sector that *supports* the traditional sector, rather than one that aims to *replace* it. Nonetheless, the traditional sector, despite its strengths, should not be romanticized. On the contrary, the aim must indeed be change, but change that is securely rooted in a country's social context.

Customary institutions are not stagnant, but rather constantly evolving in response to the changing environment. To be successful, development programs need to take fuller account of a country's social context and cultural dynamics. Each country has to devise institutions that are consonant with its social values without losing sight of the basic objectives. In some spheres, however, there can be little compromise. The family and ethnic ties that strengthen communal action have no place in central government agencies, where staff must be selected on merit and where public and private monies must not be confused.

Empowerment of women

That women play a central role in development is becoming increasingly recognized. They are the principal producers of food, the managers of household resources, and the custodians of family welfare (see Chapter 3). This is a case in which tradition and development really do seem to clash. African women face a variety of legal, economic, and social constraints. Indeed some laws still treat them as minors. In Zaire, for instance, a woman must have her husband's consent to open a bank account; the new civil code presumes that a wife's property will be managed by her husband unless he is proved incompetent, and, although she may manage goods acquired in the pursuit of her profession, her husband is allowed to usurp them if he deems it in the interest of the household. Such legal constraints have confined many women, in their role as economic agents, to the informal sector.

Future development strategies should favor women. Government and donors should help women's groups to contribute more fully to economic and social development through training and access to credit and by giving them equal status in their dealings with formal institutions.

Governance for development

Underlying the litany of Africa's development problems is a crisis of governance. By governance is meant the exercise of political power to manage a nation's affairs. Because countervailing power has been lacking, state officials in many countries have served their own interests without fear of being called to account. In self-defense individuals have built up personal networks of influence rather than hold the all-powerful state accountable for its systemic failures. In this way politics becomes personalized, and patronage becomes essential to maintain power. The leadership assumes broad discretionary authority and loses its legitimacy. Information is controlled, and voluntary associations are co-opted or disbanded. This environment cannot readily support a dynamic economy. At worst the state becomes coercive and arbitrary. These trends, however, can be resisted. As Botswana has shown, dedicated leadership can produce a quite different outcome. It requires a systematic effort to build a pluralistic institutional structure, a determination to respect the rule of law, and vigorous protection of the freedom of the press and human rights.

Intermediaries have an important role to play; they can create links both upward and downward in society and voice local concerns more effectively than grassroots institutions. In doing this, they can bring a broader spectrum of ideas and values to bear on policymaking. They can also exert pressure on public officials for better performance and greater accountability. The National Christian Council of Kenya has played this role for some time. Others are now emerging in several countries. The intermediary's role can be politically controversial, yet it is essential for greater citizen involvement. In relating to the local organizations, it is the intermediary that must exercise restraint. A common mistake is to ignore local leadership, often on the grounds that it is exploitative, but there is little empirical evidence to support that view. On the contrary, studies show that working with existing leaders produces more effective development programs. Better information is crucial for generating greater public awareness. Too often political consciousness and participation are stymied—sometimes deliberately so—by lack of information about government policy.

Curbing corruption

The extent of corruption is largely determined by the example set by a country's leadership. And once bad habits have become entrenched, they are hard to undo. Unfortunately foreign aid has greatly expanded the opportunities for malfeasance exacerbated by the venality of many foreign contractors and suppliers. Hundreds of millions of dollars have been siphoned off to private bank accounts outside Africa. The cost is not just the waste of funds, but also more seriously the profound demoralization of society at large.

Corruption can be countered in several ways. The elimination of unnecessary controls greatly reduces the scope for "rent seeking." Transparent procurement procedures, scrupulous and prompt accounting, the publication of audits, and the vigorous prosecution of those misusing public funds all contribute to financial propriety. External agencies providing aid have a right to insist on such measures. Donor governments also have a responsibility to prosecute their own firms when they pay bribes to obtain business; regrettably so far the United States is the only developed country that has outlawed such practices. A free and vigilant press—all too rare in Africa—is as important for good governance in Africa as elsewhere. The two countries with the best economic performance in Africa—Botswana and Mauritius—both have effective parliamentary democracies and a vigorous free press.

International dimensions

If Africa's efforts are to succeed, the international environment must be supportive. Four aspects are particularly important:

• A renewed effort to promote regional integration and cooperation
• A growth-oriented, liberal trade environment
• Sustained and assured long-term financial assistance
• Reduced donor dirigism.

Africans have long seen greater regional integration and cooperation as prerequisites for sustained development—and rightly so. But real progress will be made only if there are new initiatives (see Chapter 7). This report does not address the issue of South Africa. Nonetheless it is reasonable to assume that solutions will be found to the problems that have divided the peoples of that region and that South African economic cooperation will eventually transform the prospects for the whole of southern Africa.

Growing international trade is essential for Africa to expand and diversify its exports. Africa is a beneficiary of the generalized system of preferences under the General Agreement on Tariffs and Trade (GATT), while the Lomé Convention grants African countries virtually free access to the European Community market. Thus market access for manufacturers is not a problem. However, African countries do frequently encounter obstacles to trade in the very agricultural commodities in which they could be competitive, such as beef. The dumping of dairy products in Kenya severely damaged its dairy export prospects; US restrictions on cut flowers did the same. Protectionism that keeps out African products serves the interests of neither the importing nor the exporting countries and should be vigorously opposed. Equally, the newly industrializing countries should be encouraged to open their markets to African produce.

To reduce and eventually eliminate Africa's dependency on foreign resources must be the goal. Aid has negative, as well as positive, effects, not the least of which is enabling hard decisions to be postponed. The development community must be vigilant that the negative effects do not become predominant. In the medium term Africa's minimum requirement of foreign assistance will remain high (see Chapter 8). It is important for donors to ensure the continuity and growth of their support for countries willing to undertake sustained reforms. Prompt and far-reaching measures to reduce Africa's debt, as outlined in Chapter 8, are also essential.

In assisting Africans to develop their own capabilities, donors should be willing to be flexible. It is increasingly clear that the approaches applied in the North are inadequate even for tackling northern problems: the war on poverty has not been significantly more successful in some northern countries than in the South. Development practitioners from the North have often prepared programs for the South without the participation of local officials—or still less, that of the general public. These programs often inspire little commitment from the countries involved and as a result have often been ineffective. New and more effective aid modalities are discussed in Chapter 8.

In conclusion

The central objective of the future country development strategies is to transform production structures, to reverse the decline in institutions, and to build the foundations for sustainable and equitable growth. The recent structural adjustment programs are important first steps in the right direction—but much more is needed, and greater care should be taken to mitigate their adverse social impact. The fundamental weakness in these programs is the lack of local capacity, both private and public, in their design and execution. Too often conceived by outsiders, the reforms are not adequately internalized and do not inspire commitment. A deep political malaise stymies action in most countries, and the citizenry sees the elite as self-serving. Governments have failed to rally the people for development.

Africa has abundant resources. It could achieve an economic growth rate of 4 to 5 percent a year—the target proposed—if bold actions were taken. Future country strategies should:

• Continue to pursue adjustment programs, which should evolve to take fuller account of the social impact of the reforms, of investment needs to accelerate growth, and of measures to ensure sustainability

• Stress capacity-building through a new drive for human resource development, especially a radical reorientation of education and training to improve quality, relevance, and cost-effectiveness and through the adoption of a systematic approach to strengthening institutions, both public and private, by paring down overblown public agencies, directing their activities from controlling to promoting development, and fostering nongovernmental intermediate and grassroots organizations

• Foster an enabling environment for productive activities by removing unnecessary regulations that add to the costs borne by enterprises, keeping exchange rates competitive, and strengthening infrastructure services

• Overcome the nexus of weak agricultural production, rapid population growth, and environmental degradation through enhancing agricultural research and extension services, promoting family planning, and elaborating and implementing country environmental action plans

• Pursue regional integration and cooperation to overcome the fragmentation of African economies

• Forge a genuine partnership between governments and donors that builds on all these elements.

The following five chapters address in greater detail the main issues that will arise in putting this strategy into effect. The report then discusses financing needs, the role of the donors, and the steps that are needed to build a global coalition in support of a jointly agreed future development strategy for Africa.

3

Investing in people

Toward human-centered development

People are both the ends and the means of development. Although improved health, nutrition, and education are ends in themselves, healthy and educated human beings are also the principal means for achieving development.

Measuring development in terms of access to basic health services, education, and food is more satisfactory than using most other yardsticks. Social indicators, such as life expectancy, reflect more accurately the condition of most of the population than per capita incomes because of their much broader distribution across households. Kenya, for example, with a GNP of only $330 per capita, has lower infant mortality and higher primary school enrollment rates than, say, Côte d'Ivoire, with a GNP of $740 per capita.

Narrowing the gap in access to basic services between Africa and the more developed countries is a more feasible goal than narrowing the gap in income. The gaps in access to basic needs have considerably narrowed during the past 30 years and can be narrowed even faster in the next 30. Countries such as China and Thailand made much progress toward meeting their social goals by devoting about 5 percent of GDP to health and education when their per capita incomes were no higher than those of present-day Sub-Saharan Africa.

Africa has made impressive progress in human development since independence, but there has been a disquieting setback due mainly to fiscal difficulties and expanding populations. If the current trends persist, the basis for long-term development will be undermined.

The future development strategy calls for a new commitment to developing Africa's human resources. There are two immediate priorities: to improve the quality and relevance of education at every level and to redirect public resources toward basic education and health care, including family planning. For the longer term, and by 2020 at the latest, African countries could realistically aim for universal food security, primary education, and primary health care.

Synergism in human resource development programs

The components of human resource development programs are linked in a mutually reinforcing way. Family planning, for example, is more accepted when overall mortality is relatively low and levels of education relatively high. Family planning improves maternal and child health by allowing the spacing of births. Similarly, clean water and sanitation produce more benefits when provided along with health education, which improves hygiene, and nutrition education, which promotes better dietary habits. Providing clean water reduces infection in children and boosts nutritional status.

Healthier children are more likely to attend school and to learn than the sick or malnourished. Education, in turn, enables people to understand health problems and to act in their prevention and cure. In general the incidence of mortality is found to be lower among children of educated mothers.

A mother's knowledge, in particular, about inexpensive health and nutrition measures such as immunization, oral rehydration, breastfeeding, and hygiene can have a significant effect on a child's survival. Educated and healthy parents are the most likely to have educated and healthy children. Similarly, raising educational levels enhances agricultural productivity and contributes to the effectiveness of agricultural extension and, therefore, to food security. A healthier population can produce more food and generate higher incomes, which can lead to further improvements in nutrition, health, and education. Improved access to health and education are thus crucial for Sub-Saharan Africa's long-term development.

Poor quality of, and declining access to, social services

The quality of social services varies throughout Sub-Saharan Africa, but it is generally poor and has declined in the 1980s. Urgent corrective measures are required. Improvement in the quality and content of education is especially important to support sustainable growth.

In most African countries human resource programs have been geared to meet the needs of the elite. Health, education, water supply, sanitation, and other services for most of the poor are either nonexistent or represent the efforts of local communities and NGOs, poorly supported financially and technically by the state. Few government efforts have been made to elicit community participation—and this in societies that have a long history of group decisionmaking. Africa's social indicators will improve only if public policy and money are focussed more on delivery systems that respond to the basic needs of a wide spectrum of beneficiaries, especially the poor.

With the recent decline in public resources caused by Africa's poor economic performance, social services in many countries have deteriorated as budgets have been cut (see Figure 3.1). There is evidence also of stagnating or falling primary school enrollment rates; infant mortality rates in some poor countries continue to be very high. Where there are serious inequalities in access to public health and education, even a small reduction in aggregate social expenditures may have a disproportionate effect on the health of poorer households. Therefore it is important during fiscal crises to protect public expenditures on basic social services.

Figure 3.1 Central government expenditures on health and education, 1975-87

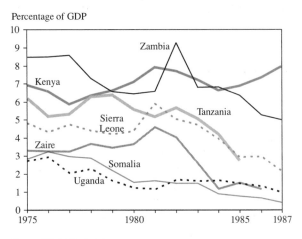

Source: World Bank data.

How can universal food security, primary education, and primary health care be accomplished by 2020 in Sub-Saharan Africa? First, it will be imperative to reverse the decline in per capita incomes and to achieve a modest but sustained improvement in living standards. The targeted 4 percent a year GDP growth rate would generate comparable increases in public revenues for investment in human resource development—itself essential to sustain the projected growth. Second, fertility rates must be lowered, without which improved access to, and the quality of, education, health, and other services necessary to accumulate human capital and social development will be constrained. Third, although all levels of education and health care require more resources, relatively more public resources need to be allocated to primary education and primary health care services. With a targeted GDP growth of 4 percent a year, additional public financial resources will continue to be available for hospitals, curative medicine, and higher education, but their relative share in total public budgetary resources should decline. Moreover, given the prevailing overall budget constraints in many countries, there is an urgent need to tap additional private sources of funding for higher education and curative health care. Parallel measures need to be taken to reorient higher education toward effective and relevant skills training. Fourth, serious efforts have to be made to reduce costs, promote cost sharing, encourage people's participation in service management, expand outreach, and raise the efficiency of social services. Fifth, mainstream programs must be designed to reach both genders effectively. Finally, additional resources should be committed to the social sectors.

Providing universal primary health care and reducing the population growth rate

Critical health threats

In 12 out of 29 countries for which data are available, the maternal mortality rate is higher than 500 for every 100,000 live births, compared with 44 in China and 90 in Sri Lanka. Each year about 150,000 mothers in Africa die and roughly the same number suffer permanent disabilities because of complications from pregnancy and childbirth. The infant mortality rate for most of Sub-Saharan Africa ranges between 100 and 170 for every 1,000 live births, compared with 33 and 32 in Sri Lanka and China, respectively. In many countries deaths of children under five represent close to half of total deaths. In the poorest countries, such as Burkina Faso, Ethiopia, Mali, and Niger, only 70 to 77 percent of children live to the age of five. In most countries progress toward improving child survival is slow. The progress achieved in seven countries is shown in Figure 3.2.

Africa also faces some of the gravest—and most intractable—general health problems, especially tropical endemic diseases. The environment favors the survival of vectors (such as airborne in-

sects) that transmit diseases. Only large-scale—and expensive—efforts can control diseases such as river blindness and schistosomiasis. Campaigns have reduced their prevalence, but many of the control efforts have lapsed since 1970. Besides reinstating disease control efforts, programs are also needed to efficiently administer the drugs that have recently become available to reduce the intensity of infection and to control morbidity.

The declining availability of food has worsened malnutrition. Moreover high fertility leads to low birth-weight babies, who have the poorest chance of withstanding malnutrition and infection. For those who survive childhood disease, morbidity remains high; an estimated 200 million Africans have chronic malaria and live disabled lives. Between 1979 and 1983 life expectancy declined in nine Sub-Saharan African countries.

On top of all this has come the AIDS epidemic, which is likely to strain the capacity of already weak health sectors in the countries to which it spreads during the next decades (see Box 3.1). The potential cost of caring for AIDS patients is high, in addition to the indirect cost to society of the loss of labor and family caretakers. It is also likely to divert resources from the treatment and control of other diseases.

Improved health care

The economic crisis facing many African countries has not only depressed already low incomes and poor living conditions, but has also dealt a blow to the ability of the health care sector to cope by constraining public expenditures on drugs and medical supplies. Safeguarding budget allocations for health care, especially for the provision of primary health care, is essential if health services are to achieve their potential contributions to improved health, productivity, and development. These might be best accomplished in many African countries, if people—individuals, families, and communities—take responsibility for their own health care. Government, NGOs, and the private sector need to provide support for these efforts. Communities must be consulted and encouraged to participate in setting their own priorities and in the design and delivery of health care programs.

In many cases the new investment in health care has not been distributed equitably nationwide. Poor communication and transportation keep meager services outside the reach of most of the population. Clearly, priorities must be reassessed

Figure 3.2 Mortality rates of children under five in selected Sub-Saharan African countries

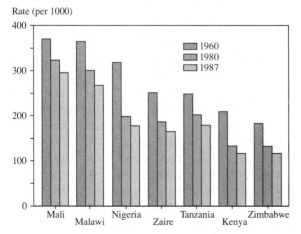

Rate (per 1000)

1960
1980
1987

Mali Malawi Nigeria Zaire Tanzania Kenya Zimbabwe

Note: The mortality rate is the number of deaths of children under age five per 1,000 live births.
Source: UNICEF data.

Box 3.1 AIDS: The demographic and economic consequences

The World Health Organization (WHO) estimates that more than a million people in Africa are infected by the HIV virus and that 30 percent of these will evolve into AIDS cases in a few years. The countries most affected, in the central belt of Africa, are Burundi, Kenya, Rwanda, Tanzania, Uganda, and Zaire. Surveys in these countries show seropositive prevalence rates from 5 to 20 percent among urban adults and higher rates among high-risk groups.

AIDS can spread quickly in Africa. The prevalence of sexually transmitted diseases (STDs) reflects widespread high-risk sexual behavior, which also facilitates the transmission of the HIV virus. In Bangui, Central African Republic, seroprevalence among adults rose from 2.1 percent in 1985 to 7.8 percent in 1987. Among prostitutes in Kenya it rose from 4 to 59 percent in five years.

The mortality rate from malaria is higher than that related to AIDS, but the death rate, and infant mortality in particular, could rise during the next decades as a result of the AIDS pandemic. Different models show the crude death rate rising from 20 to 100 percent over what it would otherwise be in only two or three decades. Infant mortality rates could rise 50 percent or more.

The treatment of AIDS patients will increase demand on weak health care systems in the countries to which it spreads. In a cost analysis in Zaire the costs of treating AIDS ranged from a low of $132 for each patient (in Public Health Center facilities) to a high of $1,585 (for private treatment). A weighted average (70 percent of patients attend public facilities, 25 percent are insured, and 5 percent use private facilities) yields an average cost of $229 for each AIDS patient. Multiplying the number of people likely to seek AIDS treatment by this average cost gives an estimate of total direct annual cost of $49 million by 2010. To finance this, the national health budget would have to increase by 58 percent in 1993 and up to 244 percent in 2010. Cost sharing may relieve some of the burden, but it will be too great after 2000 to be borne without subsidies. Thus AIDS has budgetary implications, apart from the physical strain on the health care delivery system.

To combat AIDS, resources are likely to be diverted from the treatment and control of other important diseases. At the Mama-Yemo hospital in Zaire, which has 2,000 beds, 50 percent of the medical or surgical patients test positive, and 25 percent of deaths are AIDS-related. AIDS treatment also will increase demand for foreign exchange for pharmaceuticals. The WHO Essential Drugs Program risks facing even more acute shortages, as increasing numbers of AIDS patients seek treatment for recurrent infections, which are more resistant to treatment and require higher levels of drug use.

There are other costs. AIDS predominantly affects young and middle-aged people in their prime productive years. Among African adults the highest proportions of infected people are between 16 and 29 years old. A cost study prepared for Zaire estimates the number of healthy years saved for each case of HIV prevented as 6.2 on average. The value of these healthy years would be $5,512 in urban areas and $893 in rural areas. Weighting costs by the percentage of population in rural or urban areas gives an average indirect cost of $4,600, or 20 times the direct cost of each AIDS case.

The impact of AIDS cannot be projected with precision, but the urgent need for AIDS control is clear. Strategies to combat AIDS depend on the specific epidemiology of AIDS within the country concerned. The following are necessary components:

- Programs integrated with existing primary health care, family planning programs, maternal and child health services, and STD control programs
- Effective and continued counseling of people who test positive for the AIDS virus, to reinforce behavioral patterns that could reduce the spread of infection
- Quick diagnosis and effective treatment of STD victims, who are especially vulnerable to HIV (Targeted condom distribution has been effective in Kenya, and free condoms to prostitutes have meant lower infection rates.)
- Information and education campaigns targeted to school-age populations, sexually active people, and prostitutes.

---

and the coverage of services broadened. Besides, consideration should be given to increased private and NGO involvement in nonprimary levels of care, especially curative care. The large amounts (relative to income) being spent by people on private health services, often of dubious quality, make cost sharing seem feasible for public and NGO health care systems too.

Rationalizing drug procurement and dispensing could reduce costs. Improved procurement methods can save 40 to 60 percent on budgets. A study in Mali showed that 15 to 20 percent of the drug budget could be saved if the procurement strategy for one widely used antibacterial drug—injectable ampicillin—were improved. Tanzania provides a good example of an effective low-cost

drug procurement and distribution program; its Essential Drug Program ensures a regular supply of essential drugs for most of its rural population of 20 million for about $0.30 per person a year. Better storage and security would also reduce costs. A study in Cameroon found that 35 percent of medicines were lost from central medical stores because of bad storage and expiration due to poor inventory management and control. Big savings can be achieved too by better prescription practices and by improved compliance with directions for drug use. In each area the most effective roles for the public and private sectors and the NGOs should be considered.

Rationalizing the use of labor in the health sector could raise efficiency. Delegating simpler procedures to less-trained staff, particularly in hospitals, would allow doctors and nurses to devote more time to complex and unusual problems. In rural Africa community health workers are the front line of the health care system; their often weak performance could be improved if links to higher levels of the health sector were strengthened to provide efficient training and supervision. Also many superfluous unskilled workers (such as groundkeepers and janitors) could be reduced without affecting the quality of health care.

Primary health care services can expand more rapidly with cost-effective delivery. For example, preventative activities can have large-scale results at low cost. Many maternal deaths can be averted by community-based family planning, prenatal care, and delivery of infants. Traditional birth attendants can be trained to identify high-risk mothers and refer them to adequately staffed and equipped health facilities, which could reduce birth-related injuries or illnesses and improve these mothers' chances of survival. By encouraging birth spacing, breastfeeding (which provides passive immunity to the newborn, as well as nutritional benefits), and appropriate weaning and feeding practices, infant deaths can be reduced.

With a small cost (and supervision) immunization is effective against the main childhood killers. For example, one measles shot costing $0.06 is 95 percent effective in preventing the disease. The total cost of immunizing one child against the six target diseases—measles, polio, whooping cough, diphtheria, tetanus, and tuberculosis—is estimated to be $5.00. Rapid strides have been made through the Expanded Programme on Immunization campaign in developing countries, yet only about one-third of children in Africa are immunized against these diseases. There are variations among countries; Botswana, The Gambia, and Tanzania have almost reached their target of 80 percent coverage, while Kenya may reach it in 1991. In many countries, however, serious efforts are required to speed up the coverage, and significant management reforms are necessary to make these programs sustainable.

Most countries in Sub-Saharan Africa endorsed the Alma-Ata declaration on Primary Health Care, supporting the goal of "health for all." Yet the influence of urban and upper-income elites on public policy and the lack of health policies to redress distribution problems have skewed the distribution of resources away from the rural poor and more preventative services. For example, in Senegal, the Dakar-Cap Vert region—where less

than 30 percent of the population lives—took almost 60 percent of the annual drug budget in 1979–80, 70 percent of the Senegalese physicians, 60 percent of the midwives, and more than 40 percent of the nurses. Donors contribute to this curative bias in health care by supporting capital-intensive large hospitals in urban areas. Yet the irony is that the urban poor may have no better access to effective health care than the rural population.

Expenditure on hospital services has been disproportionate to that on primary health care, and the consequent burden of large hospitals on recurrent budgets is often overwhelming. For example, the cost of operating the main hospital in Brazzaville equals the total Congolese expenditure on primary health care. There are exceptions to this, however. For example, since 1972 Tanzania has limited hospital construction in order to channel resources to basic rural and community health services. As a general rule for future development strategy, investment in new hospitals or in expanding existing hospitals for curative services should be made only if it can be demonstrated that public health would not be better served by increased expenditures on primary health care, including the facilities necessary for their support. Much-needed improvements in hospitals (and elsewhere in the health care system) will require improved management and training. Basic health centers are needed to encourage people to seek care at an early stage of sickness, which would thereby reduce the crisis morbidity situation that prevails in most hospitals.

Pressures on women's time have an adverse effect on the efficacy of health care. Women are limited in their ability to travel to service points (for immunizations, for example); thus outreach clinics may be more cost-effective than they appear to be when the cost of women's time is taken into account. Apparently low-cost health interventions, such as oral rehydration therapy, may have hidden costs in that they divert women's time from productive activities. Therefore policies that free women's time will have to go hand-in-hand with community-based health care interventions.

Improvement in health care delivery in Sub-Saharan African countries is contingent on safeguarding and improving budgetary allocations to the sector and increasing the efficient use of these resources. In health care a little money can go a long way. According to the World Health Organization (WHO), depending on the level of infra-

Box 3.2 Willingness to pay for improved water supply

In urban areas, middle- and upper-income households typically receive subsidized piped water. Households without municipal water service, particularly the poor, often purchase water from private sellers at high prices—thus incurring an expenditure amounting to sometimes more than 5 percent of income. Private water vending is inefficient and expensive. In Onitsha, Nigeria, an important market town in West Africa with a population of about 700,000, only 8,000 households (or about 50,000 people) had functioning connections to the public water supply in 1987. Most of the population obtained water from an elaborate and well-organized private sector system. Approximately 275 tanker trucks purchase water from about 20 private boreholes and sell it to households and businesses equipped with water storage facilities, many of which then resell the water by the bucket to individuals.

This provides a reliable, relatively high-quality water supply, but the price is high. Transporting water by tanker truck and on foot is inefficient, and tanker owners have been able to control prices. Households were paying on average 120,000 naira a day ($28,000 in 1987), about 24 times more than the revenue of the water utility, which supplied only 1.5 million gallons a day—half of the amount supplied by the vending system. Even during the rainy season households were paying about 51,000 naira a day ($12,000) to the vending system, which is more than 10 times the revenue of the water utility. In total, households in Onitsha were paying water vendors about twice the annual operation and maintenance costs of a new piped distribution system and 70 percent of the total annual costs of a new system serving the city of Onitsha.

Poor households pay more for water than the middle- and upper-income groups. In Onitsha low-income households (less than 100 naira, or $23 per capita per month) pay as much as 18 percent of income during the dry season versus 2 to 3 percent for the upper-income households. In Addis Ababa the urban poor spend a high proportion of their income on water.

What people are *actually* paying is not the same as the amount they are *willing* to pay. In a study of households' willingness to pay in the Newala district of southern Tanzania, it was estimated that most were willing to pay more than 8 percent of their income for water from public taps in their village.

Many factors besides income determine how much a household is willing to pay for improved water supply. An important determinant is the time spent collecting water from existing sources. On average women in the Newala district were willing to pay 20 percent more than men for improved water service. Women frequently walk eight hours a day to collect water from traditional sources, and a bucket of water from vendors often costs 50 to 100 percent of a day's wages in agriculture. Considering the opportunity cost of labor spent in collecting water, it is not surprising that poor people are willing to pay a substantial portion of their income for water despite limited cash resources.

Willingness to pay also depends on the perception about entitlement to free water from government. Those who no longer believed that it is the state's responsibility to provide water were willing to pay 14 percent more than those who still felt it was the government's responsibility. There is thus a need for governments not only to institute sound cost sharing practices, but also to make a special effort to change people's perception that free water is a basic right.

---

structure development, it should be possible to provide essential primary health care with a recurring cost of $10 per capita per year. For even the poorest countries with GNP per capita of around $200, the public expenditure for gradually achieving universal primary health care would be no more than 2 percent of GNP, increasing to 3 percent by 2000, provided measures for improving efficiency are adopted.

Water for better health

Access to safe water, accompanied by improvements in sanitation and personal hygiene, contributes to better health. Not only the quality, but also the quantity of water can affect health. In many parts of Africa families devote inordinate amounts of time to collecting water. In the Lesotho lowlands, 30 percent of families spend more than two-and-a-half hours a day collecting water. In eastern Nigeria it can take up to five hours a day.

This puts great physical strain on the water carriers—women and children—who tend to be the most nutritionally vulnerable. It also means time lost that could be spent on childcare, crop cultivation, food preparation, education, or other activities that could improve health. Unlike the health benefits, the economic benefits arising from time savings that improved water supplies contribute are measurable; recent research has established that these benefits can be substantial.

Although coverage has increased in the 1980s, an estimated two-thirds of rural Africans are without access to improved water supplies. Until recently, the high per capita cost of water supply systems has been a primary obstacle to increasing Africa's water supply coverage. Improved technologies have reduced the per capita cost of safe water; the capital cost of handpumps and simple gravity-fed systems is estimated to be about $5 a person, although there are regional variations. Low cost does not necessarily ensure success. People hold the key to success. Women, in particular, have the incentive to make water programs work since they are generally the most affected by poor access to water. Wherever communities are involved in the design, construction, installation, and maintenance of water supplies, water projects are more efficient, cost-effective, and hence sustainable. In Malawi nearly 1 million people have access to clean water through systems that are owned, built, and largely maintained by the communities they serve. And consumers seem willing to pay for safe water (see Box 3.2). With community participation and cost sharing, an expenditure of about 0.5 percent of GNP (net of cost sharing) would ensure widespread access to safe water.

Health and fertility

Better spacing and timing of births as well as fewer births can reduce infant, child, and maternal mortality and sickness. A baby born within two years of its mother's previous delivery has a 90 percent greater chance of dying during its first year of life than one born two years or more later. As child survival rates increase, fertility rates decline; parents no longer have too many children to insure against future deaths. Declining fertility through family planning leads to healthier families.

Unregulated population growth strains the capacity of social services throughout Sub-Saharan Africa. It imposes a burden that takes its toll on individual, household, and state savings; weak-

ens national efforts to improve the quality of life and productivity of the population; and exacerbates the problem of declining per capita health care expenditures. Policies to improve health care have to go hand-in-hand with those to reduce fertility levels and vice versa.

Reducing population growth

The total fertility rate (TFR)—the number of children born to a woman during her childbearing years—in all African countries (except Mauritius) is significantly higher than in developing countries with comparable levels of per capita income, life expectancy, female education, and contraceptive prevalence rate (CPR) (see Table 3.1). This reflects not only the high economic value of children in rural Africa, but also the many sociocultural factors that determine the fertility aspirations of households. Knowledge of the latter is scanty. The high economic value of rural children in the African context, however, is understandable. Rural Africans spend long hours farming and performing other household activities. Children contribute labor in cropping, livestock herding, fetching water and fuelwood, and child rearing. As the frontier for fuelwood recedes and water and soil resources are depleted, the need for children to share the increased work burden intensifies. The problem is further aggravated by the prevailing high levels of infant mortality. The nexus of population, poverty, mortality, and the environment is complex; hence population control policies must be integrated with policies that

Table 3.1 Fertility rates in Sub-Saharan Africa and South Asia

(percent unless otherwise specified)

Region and country	Total fertility rate 1987	Per capita income (dollars) 1987	Life expectancy (years) 1987	Infant mortality rate (per 1,000 live births) 1987	Female education (enrollment rates) Primary 1986	Secondary 1986	Contraceptive prevalence rate (most recent estimate)
Sub-Saharan Africa							
Botswana	5.0	1,050	59	67	109	33	29
Kenya	7.7	330	58	72	91	15	17
Mauritius	2.1	1,490	67	23	106	49	78
Nigeria	6.5	370	51	105	..	..	5
Zimbabwe	5.9	580	58	72	126	37	40
South Asia							
Bangladesh	5.5	160	51	119	50	11	25
India	4.3	300	58	99	76	24	35
Nepal	5.9	160	51	128	47	11	15
Sri Lanka	2.7	400	70	33	102	70	62

Source: World Bank data.

Box 3.3 Family planning: Zimbabwe and Botswana

Zimbabwe and Botswana are the leaders in family planning in Sub-Saharan Africa. Their programs are available to most citizens. Knowledge of modern contraception is widespread, and levels of modern contraceptive use—in 1988, 36 percent in Zimbabwe and 32 percent in Botswana—are the best in Africa. Both seem now to be achieving a significant decline in fertility levels.

Yet the two countries have followed different approaches, illustrating that there is no blueprint for success in this field and that all strategies must start from the unique situation of each country. Both countries, however, share a favorable mix of background factors, including good-to-excellent economic growth and per capita incomes, excellent infrastructure and administrative systems, high levels of education and modernization among their populations, the lowest levels of mortality in Sub-Saharan Africa, and strong government commitment to family planning (although officially only as a health intervention).

Zimbabwe has an impressive family planning program. Because of the successful history of a nongovernmental family planning association, the newly independent government elected to work with this association, now a parastatal body called the Zimbabwe National Family Planning Council (ZNFPC) and to give it much of the responsibility for delivering and promoting family planning services. The government now funds about 70 percent of ZNFPC's budget, although there has been significant donor support—mainly from the US Agency for International Development and, to a lesser extent, the UN Population Fund.

The ZNFPC runs a network of family planning clinics, but more important, a community-based distribution outreach program, which employs about 600 community-related educators and distributors and accounts for about half of family planning services. Program workers concentrate solely on family planning and are well paid (more than $100 a month). The ZNFPC has also been responsible for an impressive IEC (information, education, and communication) strategy and a monitoring, evaluation, and research unit.

Recently, the government, with help from the World Bank-assisted health project, decided to offer family planning services through its network of health facilities, which are expected to become the main providers. Coordination and cooperation between ZNFPC and health personnel are good. Nevertheless, the outreach system has remained the backbone of the Zimbabwe family planning program in rural areas.

Botswana's low-key program differs in almost every respect. It has never had an independent family planning association, and the government was, and is, virtually the sole provider of family planning services and accounted for about 95 percent of contraceptive use in 1988. Family planning services are based in clinics and delivered entirely through an integrated Maternal and Child Health (MCH)–Family Planning program, which operates in every health facility. Clinic nurses do the bulk of family planning work. There is also a rudimentary outreach network of the community-selected workers—family welfare educators—who are supposed to carry out preventive health activities in their villages and do some family planning promotion, referral, and supplying. In practice most work mainly in MCH clinics as assistants to nurses.

Botswana's health service network is so good and widespread—80 percent of the population live within 15 kilometers of a health facility—that access to family planning services is not a constraint for most people. A more serious one is the inadequate coverage and quality of IEC activities for both health and family planning, coupled with the lack of services geared to men and to teenagers, neither of which normally use MCH services. Nevertheless the program has achieved widespread knowledge and acceptance of the benefits of family planning.

---

help to reduce women's work burden, protect the environment, and control infant mortality.

Required efforts

The Bank's standard projections assume that the TFR will fall in Sub-Saharan Africa by 50 percent within the next generation, from 6.7 in 1990 to 3.4 by 2020. This implies annual population growth rates for the next three decades of 3.0, 2.6, and 2.1 percent, respectively. Even so, Africa's population will exceed 1 billion by 2020.

During the past two decades many non-African countries have reduced their TFR from around 6 to 3. Zimbabwe and Botswana seem determined to do the same (see Box 3.3). All African countries should strive to obtain similar results. Considering the inadequacy of family planning programs throughout most of Sub-Saharan Africa, however, it is unlikely that the fertility reduction assumed in standard projections will occur. To achieve World Bank projections, CPRs would need to rise from the current 0 to 10 percent to 50 to 60 percent by 2020. In the few African countries where this represents no more than a doubling or a trebling, it should not be an insuperable problem if strong governmental commitment is forthcoming. In others that have weak family planning programs, it represents up to a tenfold increase in the CPR during the next three decades. In all cases far more strenuous efforts in female education and community-based family planning are needed.

More than three-quarters of African governments have expressed their commitment to family planning, but few countries have matched these expressions with adequate technical, financial,

70

and managerial support to promote and deliver family planning services. At the 1974 World Population Conference in Bucharest all Sub-Saharan African countries (except Botswana, Ghana, and Kenya) were satisfied with their fertility and population growth rates and thought that population growth did not contribute to their economic development problems. Most found family planning acceptable as a way of improving maternal and child health. By 1986 only Chad, Côte d'Ivoire, Gabon, Guinea-Bissau, and Mauritania were pronatalist or gave little support to family planning; seven countries had explicit population policies by 1989, and five (Ghana, Mauritius, Nigeria, Uganda, and Zambia) had declared specific targets for fertility reduction. Even so, support needs to move from expressing concern in policy documents to acting and committing public resources.

Besides Mauritius, Botswana and Zimbabwe are the only African countries to achieve a sizable decline in fertility—from high rates of 8 and 6.9, respectively, in 1965 to 5.7 and 5.0, respectively, in 1988. They have the highest rates of modern contraceptive use in Sub-Saharan Africa among married women of childbearing age—36 and 32 percent, respectively. Government policies have played a key role through education and ensuring that family planning services are widely available. Experience has shown that official endorsements of family planning have to be buttressed with clear fertility reduction goals and followed by specific operational strategies to ensure success.

Demand for family planning

Only 3 to 4 percent of couples in Africa use contraception. Pockets of demand for family planning are emerging, however. Field investigations suggest that roughly a third of all African women desire child spacing; younger, more-educated women want fewer children. In Ghana, for example, women aged 40 to 44 want seven children, but those aged 15 to 19 want only five. On average African women with at least 10 years of education want three fewer children than women with no education. Finally, 25 to 50 percent of maternity-related deaths are associated with abortion, which suggests an unmet need for family planning services.

There is increasing evidence that where family planning services are available, contraceptive use is high. In Chogoria, Kenya, a rural area of 200,000 persons, a pilot program provides accessible health and family planning services and follow-up. In 1985 about 35 percent of couples in Chogoria used modern contraception, compared with 8 percent nationally. In a rural project in Zaire the rate is roughly 25 percent compared with a national average of 3 percent. In Zimbabwe the rate increased from 14 percent in 1980 to 36 percent in 1988 with an intensified national program. There are, however, cases in which demand could not be created (such as Ghana), even when women had the required knowledge about the supplies of contraceptives. In such cases more needs to be learned to achieve better results.

Even with present levels of demand for family planning, the CPR in Africa could be increased to 25 percent compared with present rates of 0 to 10 percent in most countries. To do so will require a significant expansion of family planning services, helped by the private and commercial sectors, which can also provide information and training.

Among urban and educated groups the main objective should be to publicize where to obtain services and to raise awareness of the benefits and risks of different methods. Among rural, uneducated, and more traditional groups the aim should be to prepare for the arrival and acceptance of modern family planning services. Family planning programs can be extended by mobilizing community and women's groups. The key, as Kenya shows, is to get both *education* and *community-based* family planning to women.

The scope for stimulating demand through information, education, and communication (IEC), so successful in other regions, remains virtually unexploited. IEC activities include mass media campaigns, talks by health workers, campaigns in schools and workplaces, promotion by outreach workers, and seminars and study trips for high-level officials and religious leaders. The private sector can also play a part. In Kenya, as in India, it offers effective and innovative family planning programs for company employees, as well as for the community. Over the long run it would also be necessary to address the major research needs, especially how to create demand and to make services more efficient in small, scattered communities and among people with little education.

Supply of family planning services

Studies have shown that increasing the availability of services raises the level of use; in Taiwan in the mid-1960s, for example, each 1 percent increase in the number of family planning fieldworkers produced a 1 to 2 percent decline in fertility. According to the Contraceptive Prevalence Surveys and Demographic and Health Surveys carried out in Africa during the 1980s, 30 to 40 percent of women not using modern family planning cited lack of access (such as ignorance of methods or of where to get contraceptives or the high costs) as their reason for not practicing contraception.

In many African countries information and services do not exist outside the big towns. In a few countries, notably Botswana and Zimbabwe (see Box 3.3 above), most urban and rural communities have easy access to family planning services. Others, including Burkina Faso, Kenya, Mali, Mozambique, and Tanzania, are gradually introducing such services nationally, but progress is slow.

In Africa most family planning services are delivered through, or integrated with, the public health care system, usually as part of maternal and child health care. IEC is handled in parallel by the health and educational systems. This can be successful where public health and education networks are strong and widespread, as in Botswana and Zimbabwe. In many countries, including most of the poorest and neediest, the public health care system (like other social services) is so weak and limited in coverage that it cannot deliver widespread and effective family planning services.

Thus the rapid expansion of access to family planning in most parts of Africa will require strengthening and expanding public health care systems as well as developing alternative and supplementary channels to deliver family planning services and IEC. These include private family planning organizations; nongovernmental health care networks (such as missions, employers' schemes, and private practitioners); other nongovernmental groups working in development (such as women's groups and community-based associations); non-health-based government outreach networks (such as agricultural extension workers and community development workers); and the commercial sector (such as pharmacies, rural general stores, and market traders). At the same time efforts must be made to relieve both the environmental degradation (for example, loss of soil fertility, deforestation, and depleted water resources) and the overall work burden on women, which can fuel the demand for additional family labor.

In some African countries women prefer to have fewer children but are discouraged from adopting family planning because of many socio-cultural factors, including their husband's wishes. This suggests the importance of reaching men, either at the workplace or through other means, such as the agricultural extension system. It also suggests that women's groups would be a good channel for delivering family planning services because they foster solidarity among women and may help them make fertility decisions on their own.

Costs

What would a large-scale family planning program cost? Based on recent experience, Zimbabwe, spending 0.6 to 0.8 percent of GNP annually, could reduce fertility by 50 percent from a rate of roughly 6 in 1985 to about 3 in 2010. Botswana could halve its total fertility rate of 6.5 by 2010 by spending annually an average of 0.8 percent of its 1986 GNP. Annual costs of 0.6 to 0.8 percent of GNP are not only modest, but are also more than offset by the savings in education and health budgets and in food imports that lower fertility would produce.

Food security and nutrition

Chronic hunger saps people's productivity and increases vulnerability to disease. Food security has deteriorated since independence in Sub-Saharan Africa, and severe food shortages, exceptional in 1960, are now widespread. Food security at the household level is directly influenced by agricultural performance. In many countries malnutrition is seasonal and increases before the harvest, when food supplies have dwindled. The gap in food intake widens further in years of drought. Recurrent famines in the 1980s have graphically illustrated the high degree of food insecurity in the region.

In terms of energy value food consumption in Sub-Saharan Africa between 1965 and 1986 averaged 2,100 calories per person per day, or about 85 percent of recommended requirements. It is estimated that about one-quarter of Sub-Saharan Africa's population—more than 100 million people—obtain, on average over good and bad crop years, less than 80 percent of the daily calorie supply recommended by FAO and WHO. In drought and other bad years the numbers would be even larger.

The Sahelian countries and the southern central region (Botswana and surrounding areas), where rainfall is meager and unreliable, form a core area years, less than 80 percent of the daily calorie supply recommended by FAO and WHO. In drought and other bad years the numbers would be even larger.

The Sahelian countries and the southern central region (Botswana and surrounding areas), where rainfall is meager and unreliable, form a core area of food insecurity, but all subregions have countries with the same problem, albeit with varying intensities. Apart from those vulnerable to periodic droughts, such as Ethiopia, there are countries in which income distribution is particularly skewed and a part of the population is very poor, even though the agricultural base and national income levels are strong (such as Kenya). Food insecurity is also common in countries with civil wars (Angola, Ethiopia, and Mozambique); countries with poor infrastructure (Uganda and Zaire); those with large poor urban populations (such as Zambia and perhaps Sudan); and others in which economic management has either stunted growth or not supported equitable distribution of its benefits.

Any public program addressing minimum food intake must distinguish between chronic food shortages (that is, trend-level shortfalls) and transitory food crises caused by crop failures, economic crises, and civil disturbances. Further, within poor households, women and children are more susceptible to malnutrition, which suggests that interventions should be designed to reach specific vulnerable groups.

To provide universal food security by 2020, action is needed on both the demand and supply sides. Improving agricultural production is imperative, because widespread access to food is ensured by agricultural growth. Public action on the demand side is also necessary, however, especially for households with low or fluctuating incomes or purchasing power.

Projected food needs

Assessing the food needs of African countries for the next 30 years is difficult because any such projections have to be based on assumptions about the prevailing levels of calorie consumption, future population growth rates, and future production performance. It is, however, necessary to estimate requirements in order to project future needs for imports and food aid. The methodology used is outlined below.

The *average* daily calorie consumption in Sub-Saharan African countries in 1986 was about 85 percent of the nutritional requirement. Although in eight countries in 1986 the average calorie intake was 80 percent or less of the recommended intake, for the purpose of projection it is assumed that no country had an average calorie intake less than 80 percent of the required minimum in 1988.

Table 3.2 Population and food security in Sub-Saharan Africa, 1990–2020

	1990	*2000*	*2010*	*2020*
Case I				
1. Population (millions of persons) (with constant fertility)	500	700	1,010	1,500
2. Food production (mtme) (at current trend growth rate of 2 percent a year)	90	110	135	165
3. Food requirement (mtme for universal food security by 2020)	100	160	250	410
4. Food gap (mtme)	10	50	115	245
Case II				
1. Population (as in Case I)	500	700	1,010	1,500
2. Food production (at 4 percent annual growth)	90	135	200	300
3. Food requirement (as in Case I)	100	160	250	410
4. Food gap (mtme)	10	25	50	110
Case III				
1. Population (millions of persons) (with total fertility rate declining by 50 percent to 3.3 by 2020)	500	680	890	1,110
2. Food production (mtme at 4 percent annual growth)	90	135	200	300
3. Food requirement (mtme)	100	150	220	305
4. Food gap (mtme)	10	15	20	5

Note: mtme = millions of tons of maize equivalent.
Source: World Bank data.

tween requirements and regional-level food supply is derived under three alternative sets of assumptions:

• Production grows at 4 percent a year, and population growth gradually declines to 2.75 percent during 1990–2020.

• Domestic production grows at 4 percent a year and population at 3.3 percent.

• Domestic food production and population grow at 2 and 3.3 percent, respectively.

These alternatives are shown in Table 3.2. The *sharp* widening of food imbalance in the latter two cases (see Figure 3.3) shows how crucial it is to maintain a production growth of 4 percent a year and to reduce population growth in order to ensure long-run food security throughout the region.

A growth rate of 4 percent a year in food production allows for an average population growth of 2.75 percent during 1990–2020, a 1 percent annual growth in per capita food availability, and a 0.25 percent growth to reduce dependence on food imports. Even if domestic food production grew 4 percent a year, food imports would double from about 10 million tons to 20 million tons by 2010, but then would decline to 5 million tons by 2020. Food import needs would have to be met through a combination of commercial imports and food aid and in ways that will not discourage domestic food production.

Supply side

To meet the growing food needs from traditional crops, complementary improvements are needed in the technology for processing and storing local foods. Rising demand for foreign grains in Sub-Saharan Africa is due, in part, to their faster preparation time; this characteristic will become increasingly valued as urbanization proceeds and as women face more demands on their time. Varieties of grain amenable to central processing and easier transportation need to be developed. Improved storage means a regular supply of foods to local markets.

A large part of the food insecure population in Africa consists of small farmers—often women— in isolated parts of the country with high transport costs and little or no access to markets. In most of these cases increased production of food and greater stability in availability are likely to be the only ways to provide assured food security. Food security considerations on the supply side indicate the need to redress the biases against women

Figure 3.3 Projected food gap: Alternative scenarios for Sub-Saharan Africa, 1990-2020

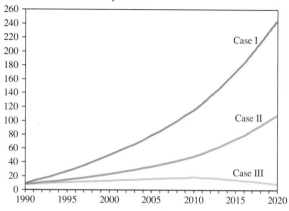

Millions of tons of maize equivalent

Note: Case 1: a 2 percent annual growth rate in agricultural production and a constant fertility rate. Case 2: a 4 percent annual growth rate in agricultural production and a constant fertility rate. Case 3: a 4 percent growth rate in agricultural production and a declining fertility rate.
Source: World Bank data.

farmers in access to credit, extension, and research and development. Reform of financial institutions through liberalization of lending criteria and repayment procedures would also increase the productivity of women in agriculture and their income from trade.

Chapter 4 examines the critical issues of agricultural policy, including the technological and institutional needs that must be addressed if domestic food production is to grow at a high rate. This chapter emphasizes that the pervasive discrimination against agriculture in general, both for food and export, has to be reversed. Although aggregate growth in production may ensure long-run food security for the region as a whole, it may not be achieved for every country; food trade within Africa is therefore essential (see Chapter 7).

The demand side

Even if food supply improves, the distribution of income and wealth and regional concentration of production may leave large segments of society without the purchasing power to buy enough staple foods. The long-run solution is to improve income and employment.

In the short to medium term, interventions such as food subsidies or programs to support employment and income may be needed during crop failures, in addition to direct nutrition support programs to overcome chronic maternal and child malnutrition. Women constitute a large portion of the vulnerable population, and they should be helped to participate in employment and feeding programs. In many countries subsidies have been misdirected, often for political reasons, toward urban residents who are not poor. Food subsidies must be sharply targeted to vulnerable groups. Given weak institutional and administrative structures, it seems imperative to introduce self-targeting into programs by using economically (but not nutritionally) "inferior goods," such as coarse grains. Following the Indian model, "area targeting," which restricts programs to regions in which a large percentage of the population has a history of food insecurity and malnutrition, can be tried. Food subsidies managed by government are inconsistent with the objective of removing the state from food marketing. Therefore, unless food aid is made available directly to vulnerable groups, such as those hit by famine, the link must be broken between the provision of subsidized food and food aid. New initiatives are necessary. For example, the counterpart proceeds from the sale of food aid (through commercial channels and auction) could be used for food subsidies and income supplements for vulnerable groups. If effectively targeted to the food insecure, the expenditure on food subsidies could be modest.

Income support schemes for low-income groups can provide cash or food in return for work or as a transfer. There is no single prescription. Income generation through public works, which add to infrastructure, is particularly relevant in Africa. Payment for labor should not be above the basic market wage if public works are to meet targeting criteria. The cost to government of such schemes is variable, ranging from $0.50 to $5 or $10 to increase income by $1, depending on the wage offered and the costs to participants of traveling to the site.

The absence of discrimination in wage payments can attract women to public works schemes, as happened in the Maharashtra region of India. Such productive employment of women helps improve nutritional status, especially of children. Public works have the potential to help women whose livelihoods in traditional activities are being increasingly threatened, although only Botswana and Mauritania have implemented such schemes.

Nutrition programs

Suboptimal feeding practices, household constraints from pressures on women's time, lack of essential micronutrients, and poor sanitation and water supplies all affect nutrition. So do specific behaviors, such as how mothers feed children and treat diarrhea, how household income is controlled and spent, and how food is selected and prepared. These behaviors appear to be independent of income levels attained by most in Sub-Saharan Africa and are compounded by poor health. This explains the persistence of malnutrition despite rising incomes, as in The Gambia, Kenya, and Rwanda. Until progress is made in lowering birthrates and increasing food availability, hope for nutritional improvements must rest primarily on family-centered interventions to modify feeding practices.

Nutritional risk begins before birth. Millions of African women are malnourished and suffer from chronic iron deficiency anemia, which, along with malaria and intestinal diseases, weakens their ability to cope with the physical demands of pregnancy, childbirth, and breastfeeding. Undernourished pregnant women are more likely to have low birth-weight babies, who, in turn, are susceptible to infection, disease, and early death. If the infant dies, the mother stops nursing, and ovulation resumes prematurely, which enables the mother to get pregnant sooner than if the infant had lived. The next baby will be weaker, and so the vicious circle continues—maternal malnutrition, infant death, and high fertility.

Children who survive the neonatal period enjoy a few months of adequate nutrition during breastfeeding (which is nearly universal in Africa, although declining in urban areas). Between 6 and 18 months is the most critical period for child survival, partly because 0–3 years is the time when the highest percentage of energy intake (approximately 27 percent) is needed for growth. Solid food is often introduced too late, too few calories are offered, or feeding is infrequent. The resulting inadequate food intake, combined with diseases (often due to unhygienic feeding), constitutes the classic interaction between infection and malnutrition that explains much of the high child mortality in Africa.

Nutrition strategies should be directed toward overcoming poor dietary habits and specific deficiencies. Nutritional status can be improved at any level of food availability. Women are obviously the main (although not the exclusive) audience for nutrition education programs, especially those on the value of breastfeeding and young children's needs at weaning and beyond. Growth monitoring serves both as a screening device and as an excellent way to impart nutritional information. At weighing sessions mothers (and fathers) can be shown how to identify and treat the causes of inadequate growth. Beyond better information, other supports will be needed, such as energy-dense foods for children to make extra meals unnecessary and time-saving devices for women.

Direct feeding programs are also necessary for malnourished children. A project in Zaire exemplifies a low-cost approach to nutrition interventions (see Box 3.4). Such programs should be established with primary health care provision; growth monitoring should identify children in need of extra food as well as disqualify those who no longer need it.

Direct feeding programs need not be expensive, if effectively targeted to those children most at risk nutritionally. India has developed such a system in Tamil Nadu State (see Box 3.5). Notwithstanding the differences between Africa and Asia, the management systems developed in the Tamil Nadu project could be replicated in combating malnutrition in Sub-Saharan Africa. The Iringa project in Tanzania has achieved similar results in nutrition improvement through social mobilization and community involvement, such as making effective use of local media, although more could be done by integrating complementary services. Given the prevalence of serious (second-and-third degree) malnutrition among 20 to 30 percent of the child population (age 1 to 5) in Africa, the cost of nutritional programs comparable with that in Tamil Nadu would be about $200 million annually, or roughly 0.1 percent of the GDP of Sub-Saharan Africa.

Box 3.4 Cost-effective nutrition interventions: producing a low-cost weaning food in Zaire

The US Agency for International Development (AID) in Zaire used donated food to help Victoria Assorted Products (VAP), a private company, reduce the cost of manufacturing CEREVAP, a nutritious food mixture designed for weaning children and women at risk of malnutrition.

AID assisted VAP in purchasing an extruder which was subsequently used to make weaning food from locally-produced foods. In exchange for this equipment, VAP agreed to sell its weaning food at a reduced price both to the public and for NGO feeding programs. In the public MCH clinics, a similar corn-soy weaning food (based on food aid corn and local soya) was mixed and sold at a price that varied with household income. CEREVAP was the only manufactured weaning food able to maintain a low price during the foreign exchange crisis because it was made entirely from local commodities. The commercial sales of CEREVAP expanded, thanks in part to the market development effect of the government distributions. By reducing the risks to private investors in nutrition programs, this coordination among a local business, a government program, and international food aid has given Zaire a low-cost, nutritious weaning food that helps poor urban mothers meet family nutritional needs easily and inexpensively.

Box 3.5 Integrating health and nutrition services for children under three

India's Tamil Nadu project, initiated in 1980, was targeted to children 6 to 36 months old, and expectant and nursing women. Key aspects of the project were a growth monitoring system to enable mothers and health workers to identify children who were nutritionally at risk, short-term supplementary feeding to help seriously malnourished children reach an acceptable pattern of weight gain, food supplements to mothers at risk (mothers with a malnourished child or who had lost a child), and a comprehensive communications program that included both face-to-face instruction and mass media.

Nine thousand community nutrition centers were established in four years, each staffed by a locally recruited community nutrition worker who had completed the eighth grade and was considered a model mother. The workers were reinforced by health outreach and referral services from the health department. The centers weighed children monthly and provided food for 90 days for children who were not growing properly.

Preliminary findings indicate that after seven years the program had reduced malnutrition in Tamil Nadu by approximately 50 percent, at an annual cost of $8.10 per beneficiary—achieved, incidentally, in a period of economic decline. The program's success is attributable to the "training and visit" nutrition delivery system, with thorough training and close supervision of the nutrition workers. Growth monitoring proved to be an accurate screening device for spotting children at greatest risk and an effective vehicle for educating mothers to maintain their children's nutrition through permanent behavior changes. Finally, once at-risk children were identified, the program could immediately provide supplementary food "as a prescription for malnutrition."

The project was so cost-effective because it closely targeted beneficiaries; minimized the need for food supplements by detecting problems early; limited supplementary feeding to a short-term, therapeutic remedy until the mother could take over on her own; and was operated with significant community involvement.

Micronutrient deficiencies are a serious nutritional problem in Sub-Saharan Africa. Three conditions are widespread. Blindness (xerophthalmia) is caused by vitamin A deficiency, which is also linked with pneumonia, measles, and diarrhea in children. Iron deficiency, the most common cause of widespread anemia, undermines work and health and may also affect psychological functioning and cognitive development. At least half of all women of reproductive age, more than 60 percent of pregnant women, and about half of all children under 12 years suffer from anemia. Iodine deficiency, also widespread, is the cause of goiter among 30 million Africans and of cretinism among half a million more.

These disabling conditions can be overcome at only modest cost, and African governments could plausibly aim to eradicate them before 2020 (see Box 3.6). The iodizing of common salt costs $0.04 a person a year and the addition of iron another $0.05 to $0.09. Since centrally processed grain, which could be fortified with vitamins and minerals at low cost, is little consumed outside urban areas, micronutrient supplements could be provided in rural areas alongside health services, such as immunizations. This is a cost-effective approach, since young children, who are immunized, and the reproductive-age women, who accompany them, are the primary targets.

Thus a comprehensive approach to food security would involve not only the critically important programs to augment domestic food production, but several other programs targeted toward vulnerable groups. The cost of a comprehensive food security and nutrition program may thus range between 1 and 2 percent of GDP for different countries. Such an approach is administratively feasible, as Botswana's experience shows (see Box 3.7).

Primary education: revitalization and universalization

Increased investment in education can accelerate growth in several ways. For example, educated farmers have been found to achieve higher productivity levels than those who have not gone to school. Research has also established that a mother's education enhances the probability of child survival. Cost-benefit studies during the past decade in 16 African countries suggest that the social rates of return to investment in education are 26 percent for primary, 17 percent for secondary, and 13 percent for higher education. Education is intrinsic to development in the widest sense; empowering people, especially the poor, with basic cognitive skills is the surest way to render them self-reliant citizens.

The goal of universal primary education, however, has often been interpreted as simply expansion of enrollment. This will not serve any purpose if quality is not ensured. In Africa not only are enrollments stagnating, but the quality of primary education is low and declining. Tests on reading comprehension, general science, and mathematics suggest that many African students are learning very little. Ensuring quality is, therefore, an important prerequisite to expanding enrollment.

One reason for the low quality of primary education is the low expenditure on educational materials per student—$0.60 per student a year in Africa, or 1.1 percent of recurrent primary education expenditures. This situation has been aggra-

Box 3.7 Botswana's food security program

Botswana has less malnutrition than any other drought prone country in Southern Africa, thanks to its comprehensive food security program. Since its inception in the early 1980s, the program has eliminated severe malnutrition among children under five and has reduced moderate undernutrition substantially, despite a series of drought years and drastic falls in local grain production.

The principle underlying the design, organization, and management of the program was to expand the capacity and flexibility of institutions concerned with different aspects of food security. The program comprises:
• Direct feeding through primary schools and health centers
• Additional water supply
• Emergency public works schemes to provide short-term supplementary income
• Farm support and rehabilitation programs to expedite recovery from drought.

The program involves several ministries. The Ministry of Local Government and Lands handles food aid imports, local purchases, and distribution to schools and health facilities. The Ministry of Health monitors the nutrition situation and organizes on-site feeding in clinics, and the Ministry of Education oversees the feeding of primary school children. When there is no drought, a limited feeding program reaches young school-age children, pre-school children, and pregnant and lactating women. During a drought the program is stepped up to feeding all children up to 10 years and vulnerable groups on a daily basis. Its food supplies come mostly from food aid, but when supplies cannot be secured quickly enough, the government purchases foodgrains on the international market out of its cash reserves; these are reimbursed later by donor agencies. The Ministry of Mineral Resources and Water Affairs handles domestic water supply in consultation with local government, and extra domestic water is supplied as necessary through temporary drilling or other means. The whole country is covered, so that no community is without reasonable access to water.

To provide short-term supplementary income, labor-intensive projects are available in all rural settlements. Each year 60,000 to 90,000 people earn cash wages from building local infrastructure or from other activities sug-

gested by village committees. The Ministry of Agriculture administers the farm relief and recovery program through the extension and veterinary services. A basic seed package is given to all farmers, and low-cost draft power is provided to those who have few or no animals. To protect farmers' and pastoralists' productive capacity, older cattle are purchased at a floor price to reduce grazing pressures and to provide household income. These measures help minimize the need for emergency camps and resettlement, although in some years the incentives to reduce grazing pressures were not sufficient.

Program components are coordinated by an Inter-Ministerial Drought Committee, serviced by staff of the Ministry of Finance and Development Planning. This committee also has an important role in monitoring moisture and cropping conditions and in providing early warning information to the concerned ministries. The involvement of many ministries has enabled Botswana to handle droughts regardless of the level of foreign assistance. Although the staffing involves some costs, the gains in flexibility of response are more valuable.

The budgetary cost of these interventions has varied with the severity of the drought. In 1982–83 total cost, excluding food aid, amounted to 3.4 percent of all development expenditure, and in 1985–86 it was 18 percent. The donor-funded share dropped from 33 percent in 1982–83 to 9 percent in 1984–85. The value of food aid, which was efficiently coordinated by donors, was about 20 percent of total cereal consumption, or almost 39 kilograms for each person in 1984, higher than the average for all Sub-Saharan Africa and even for many other (much poorer) drought prone countries.

Botswana is to some extent a special case. Most of the population is concentrated in the country's eastern region. The regularity of drought predisposes the government to take stabilization measures. The country's relatively high national income, good foreign exchange position, and reserves from mineral revenues provide a helpful financial base for the program, in particular for flexibility in importing food. Nonetheless Botswana's case demonstrates that institutionalized support systems can be developed to provide food security.

---

vated in recent years as salaries have been protected relative to other parts of the budget. It is estimated that the minimum requirements of books and materials cost $5 per pupil a year. But the problem goes beyond money. It is also due to the limited national capacity of most African countries to develop low-cost teaching materials that are pedagogically sound and relevant to the national curriculum. Depending on individual circumstances, countries will need to develop national skills at least in the areas of adapting and editing materials and, in some countries, in writing, publishing, and printing their own materials.

Enhancing the quality of education will also require raising the professional competence of teachers while keeping the costs of teacher training down. This can be done. Some countries have shortened the duration of preservice training (as in Burkina Faso), while others have incorporated distance-teaching techniques in preservice training (as in Nigeria, Tanzania, and Zimbabwe) and innovative in-service training (as in Ethiopia) (see Box 3.8).

Improved testing can help monitor the quality of schools and ensure that students are developing cognitive skills and not merely engaging in rote recall. Quality can also be improved by ensuring that curriculums and teaching materials meet the needs of the African environment. Finally, using the local language in the first years of primary school may also contribute to quality.

Although improving quality is paramount and the immediate priority, the long-run goal is also to expand enrollment, especially of girls. There is wide variation in gross enrollment ratios—from Niger and Somalia with ratios of 29 and 20, respectively, to Kenya, Madagascar, Togo, and Zambia with ratios of around 100 in 1986. Female enrollment ratios are generally lower than those of males even in countries with high total gross enrollment ratios; see, for example, the situation in six countries shown in Figure 3.4.

Figure 3.4 Primary school enrollment ratios by gender in six Sub-Saharan African countries, 1986

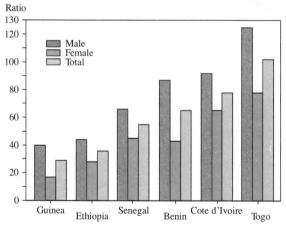

Note: The primary school enrollment ratio is the number of children enrolled in primary school as a percentage of the primary school age population.
Source: World Bank data.

In 1983 girls in Sub-Saharan African countries accounted for only 44 percent of the students in primary school, 34 percent of the enrollment in secondary school, and 21 percent of those enrolled in higher education. Female students are more likely to drop out than male students, in part because of the demand for female labor within the household. Illiteracy is much higher among females.

The gender gap in education comes at a high cost. Evidence shows that the mother's education is perhaps the single most important determinant of a family's health and nutrition and that education enhances agricultural productivity. Thus, since most agricultural subsistence producers are women, basic education can be expected to improve their incomes, opportunities, and decisionmaking power within the household. Further, even a few years of learning at the primary level has been shown to lower women's fertility either directly, by increasing awareness of contraception, or indirectly, either by reducing the demand for children because women perceive enhanced earnings opportunities or by raising the age of marriage and thereby reducing the number of childbearing years.

For many countries improved quality and expanded enrollments in primary education imply an increase in total expenditure on the education sector as a percentage of GNP, as well as a gradual increase in the relative share of primary education in total education budgets. There are, however, significant differences among countries. Some countries may reach universal primary education (UPE) well before 2020; others may not. Figure 3.5 illustrates the recurrent budget implications of achieving UPE *with an improvement in educational quality* for five low-income countries with low

Figure 3.5 Universal primary education: Cost scenarios for countries with low enrollments

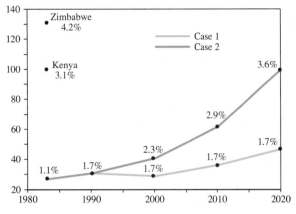

Gross enrollment ratio

Note: Figures on the graph are actual (1983) and projected (1990–2020) expenditures on primary education as a percentage of GNP. For comparison, actual (1983) expenditures are given for Kenya and Zimbabwe, which have already achieved gross enrollment ratios greater than 100. Case 1: expenditure on primary education as a percentage of GNP remains constant at estimated 1990 levels. Case 2: expenditure on primary education as a percentage of GNP increases to accomodate a gradual increase in gross enrollment so as to achieve UPE by 2020; this case includes a provision for quality. The low-enrollment countries are Burkina Faso, Ethiopia, Mali, Niger, and Somalia, whose per capita incomes range between $130 and $290. Per capita incomes for Kenya and Zimbabwe are $330 and $580, respectively.
Source: World Bank data.

enrollments. These projections are based on four assumptions.

• A systemic provision of $5 for teaching materials is added to the public recurrent expenditures for each primary pupil (observed in 1983) to enhance quality

• The revised country-specific expenditures on each pupil remain constant in real terms

• School-age populations grow in line with the standard fertility reduction, and GNP grows at 4 percent a year

• Substantial community contributions are available to build schools

Given these assumptions, it is projected that these countries would have to gradually increase recurrent expenditures on primary education from 1 to 2 percent of GNP to 3 to 4 percent of GNP to achieve UPE by 2020. Case 1 shows that if the present level of expenditures continues, these countries will fall short of the goal even by 2020. These projections do not represent a uniform policy recommendation for all countries. Some countries that have nearly achieved UPE are already spending 3 to 4 percent of GNP on primary education (such as Kenya). In these countries the goal

can be reached well before 2020 with only modest additional expenditure.

Although a reduction in cost for each pupil in primary education appears unlikely in most African countries, there is some scope for using resources more efficiently. In certain circumstances double shifts can be introduced, teaching loads increased, and distance-teaching techniques implemented, although care must be taken to ensure that quality is not jeopardized. Planners in Senegal, for example, expect to raise by 6 percent the number of students enrolled by 2000 through a double-shift system in 20 percent of the overcrowded classrooms. In Burundi double shifts have helped lower unit costs to $35 (compared with the African average of $52), without any noticeable adverse effects on quality. Increasing class size is another way to reduce costs, especially in the rural areas. Finally, as Kenya's experience shows, interactive radio can be used to improve the quality of teaching and to enrich the classroom environment.

For every 1,000 children who enter primary school in Africa, only about 600 enter the final year. Dropouts and repeaters increase the cost for each completer of primary education by an average of 150 percent; in many low-income countries the cost is more than doubled. Students repeat years in the highest levels of primary school to better their chances of getting qualifying marks on primary completion examinations to enter secondary schools. The change to a separate test for entering secondary school has been shown to reduce the number of repeaters. In some cases dropping out and repetition may be due to impaired mental abilities resulting from poor nutrition and micronutrient deficiencies. In such cases appropriate interventions, such as targeted school-feeding programs, complemented by supplements of micronutrients, could improve learning abilities and reduce dropout rates.

Most African countries face a growing demand for the limited number of secondary school places. Here too expansion should not take precedence over improving quality. The key lies in reducing costs, especially through measures directed at teacher training and utilization. In many countries capital and teachers are seriously underutilized at the secondary level; the student-teacher ratio is 23 to 1 at the secondary level compared with about 30 to 1 in South Asia. Making use of distance teaching in secondary education is another way to reduce costs, as Malawi has shown. Finally, increased cost sharing is imperative, provided bursaries are offered to those from the lowest income groups, based on merit. Given the paucity of public resources, private resources should be mobilized for investment in secondary education, as is being done in Kenya. Although the scope for rationalization, cost reduction, and cost sharing is considerable in secondary education, it is even greater in higher education.

Higher education, skill formation, and training

To survive and compete in a competitive world in the 21st century, Africa will require not only literate and numerate citizens, but also highly qualified and trained people to perform top-quality research, formulate policies, and implement programs essential to economic growth and development. Institutions of higher learning must be able to produce, at an affordable and sustainable cost, well-trained people in academic and professional disciplines applicable to diverse African work environments.

Higher education

A new spectrum of scientific and technological knowledge is unfolding outside the continent. Universities in Africa will have to develop a few world-class postgraduate programs in sciences and engineering if these countries are to have access to the new frontiers of science and technology. Unfortunately, given the present state of higher education in Africa, the continent is unable to prepare itself to take advantage of the expanding frontiers of knowledge. At present higher education in Africa is confronted by an inappropriate mix of outputs, overproduction of poor-quality graduates, and high costs.

Since independence, special emphasis has been given to higher education. African governments, acutely aware of their dependence on expatriate skills, have spent lavishly on universities and training centers. Enrollments for higher education have increased from a few thousand in 1960 to half a million today. The aspirations of people for higher education are high, and governments have responded to this demand. Public subsidization has been so high that the direct private cost of higher education has been kept close to zero, which has further fueled demand. In the past the private rate of return to higher education has been about 30 percent (higher than anywhere else in the world), but the social rate of return has been only 13 percent. With the growing unemployment of graduates, however, the rate of return may have fallen recently.

Notwithstanding the growing number of graduates and the rising rate of unemployment among them, there is a scarcity of skilled workers in fields such as science, engineering, auditing, and higher-level accounting and management. Despite the large share of government budgets going to higher education, the number of expatriate teachers as well as technical experts in science, mathematics, and other professional fields remains high; there is apparently an excess of graduates in some disciplines and too few in others.

One explanation for the shortages in high-level skills is the brain drain. The United States alone had more than 34,000 African students in 1985, many of whom are unlikely to return to Africa; there are reported to be more than 70,000 trained Africans who have opted to remain in Europe. Underlying this migration was (among other things) a fall in real incomes of 16 percent between 1980 and 1985, which increased the attractiveness of overseas salaries. Other factors include unfavorable working conditions and political instability. On the positive side, migration of skilled workers within Africa also has been significant, especially into Côte d'Ivoire, Gabon, Kenya, Nigeria, and Zimbabwe, which indicates a growing market for skills within the region.

The quality of higher education is low and possibly declining. One reason is the low and declining quality of primary and secondary education. Another reason is the shrinking of resources for nonsalary inputs (such as physical plant and equipment) on which only 2 percent of total recurrent expenditure on tertiary education is being spent. The immediate consequence is that academic standards of many graduates are unacceptably low. As a result Africa is falling further behind in its stock of high-level skills and in its ability to manage its economy. And yet the dilemma is that by the beginning of the next century, the quality of African higher education must be much better than it is today if African development is to become self-sustaining.

For Sub-Saharan Africa as a whole the cost for each student-year of public higher education was $3,655 in 1979–80 and ranged from $895 in Somalia to $11,081 in Zimbabwe. As a percentage of GDP per capita these costs are six to seven times higher than in some Asian countries and nine times higher than in some Latin American countries. Wastage, proliferation of small institutions, excessively large staffs (especially nonteaching staff), and the nearly universal policy of charging no fees all contribute to higher costs. In Nigeria, for example, only 10 to 20 percent of the actual costs are recovered from tertiary education, whereas 30 to 40 percent are recovered from primary and secondary education. The subsidized allowances for housing, food, transportation, and health care for each student of higher education, as a percentage of the average public sector salary, amounted to 62 to 63 percent in Benin and Burkina Faso, 43 percent in Cameroon and Niger, and 24 percent in Côte d'Ivoire and Kenya. A similar situation prevails in most other countries. Not only does charging no fees lead to an increase in publicly borne costs, but it also contributes indirectly to high costs, since beneficiaries have no incentive to contain nonessential expenditures.

To meet the crisis in university education, radical measures are needed to improve quality, reduce costs for each student and graduate, constrain output in fields that do not support economic development, and relieve the burden on public sources of financing by increasing the participation of beneficiaries and their families. If the principal objective of improving quality is to be achieved, additional resources will be required. Given the current budgetary constraints, these resources will need to be found mainly through the reform of the higher education system itself. Only by implementing policies to decrease unit costs, constrain output, and expand cost sharing by beneficiaries will it be possible to free the necessary resources to restore quality.

In the longer term, improvements in quality can be realized and sustained by establishing programs or centers of excellence for postgraduate education and research. These could concentrate staff and resources to achieve a critical mass in priority areas. By establishing such specialized high-quality programs and institutions, African governments would provide able students with an attractive alternative to foreign study, create incentives for university researchers to pursue their work on the continent, and thereby also address the serious problem of "brain drain." To economize and to ensure high quality, these centers of excellence should be developed on a regional basis (see Chapter 7).

Vocational training

In response to the pressing need to provide the work force with skills for specific occupations, many countries have invested in skills-training institutions. Few have, however, a coherent policy and institutional framework for effective, relevant vocational education and training.

The efficiency and quality of vocational training are improved by training oriented toward meeting employment demand, increasing employer participation, and strengthening the transition from training to work. Apprenticeship complemented by theoretical training off-the-job has been successful in many countries. Experience shows that this can be effective for both larger firms in the modern sector and the smaller enterprises, in which the bulk of new jobs will be created (see Box 3.9).

Response to employment demand is central to vocational training, including apprenticeship, and to improving the quality of training. A first step is to create a national training agency to finance and administer training in collaboration with industry. It could focus on a range of nonformal training activities and be located in the ministry of labor to facilitate flexibility in staffing and responsiveness to employers' needs. Existing vocational schools and training centers should be consolidated and reformed to conserve scarce resources and enhance quality, and only those responsive to labor market demands should be maintained. Curriculums should be broadened to include such areas as management training so as to be of assistance to enterprises. Some countries with strong modern sectors will be able to recover part of the costs from employers or individuals, but in most countries costs will be met from public revenues.

The training scheme now being devised in Mauritius reflects many of these elements. The objective is to respond to short-term labor market signals through rapid adjustments in the size and content of training. Short-term, nonformal training will be administered through an autonomous Industrial and Vocational Training Board, governed by an Industrial and Vocational Training Council composed of representatives from both government and industry. The scheme will be financed by a 1 percent payroll tax levy that will be matched by government budgetary allocations.

Where civil services are chronically overstaffed, governments need to reassess their approach to training. The intake of the training institutes needs to be curtailed and training reoriented to upgrade the skills of incumbent civil servants. Public service training should also be linked to opportuni-

Box 3.9 Training for employment

Formal education and vocational schools in most of Sub-Saharan Africa are oriented toward the modern sector. They are expensive and hence inaccessible to many people and are a considerable budgetary strain on the government. The training offered is inadequate to prepare school leavers for the work place. As such, promotion of training systems that combine on-the-job experience with theoretical training have considerable potential to provide the crucial "missing middle" in Sub-Saharan Africa. This is especially so, given the unrelenting demographic pressures, which are bound to continue, widening the gap between those with jobs and the jobless. Deteriorating economic conditions and low labor productivity and skill levels, combined with declining public sector employment, further aggravate the problem of labor absorption. Innovative methods are needed to train people cost-effectively in a wide spectrum of skills, improve the quality of training, and offer incentives for self-employment after training.

A change from the present preservice, formal training system toward on-the-job and in-service training in the work place, complemented by theoretical training, would require private sector involvement and local efforts (such as craft and worker organizations) while retaining overall public management of training. Once such apprenticeship supplemented by theoretical training is established, it would:

• Transmit a broad range of skills in production and service sectors, technical and administrative fields, and traditional and modern occupations to all levels of school leavers
• Establish norms to introduce comparability of skills attained into the system; this also could adjust to changing patterns of skills demanded
• Reduce unit costs of training, which are borne partially by those who benefit.

An example of a training system that combines traditional on-the-job apprenticeship training with formal, theoretical training is the National Open Apprenticeship

Scheme in Nigeria. Launched by Nigeria's Directorate of Employment, the scheme, in its first year of operation (1987–88), successfully persuaded public and parastatal enterprises and private sector employers, including informal sector workshops, to take on apprentices. The directorate provides financial and logistic support at 50 naira a month for each trainee and 150 naira a year to the trainer for each trainee. Details of training received and the resulting performance are logged and checked by monitors at least once every two weeks, thus ensuring quality.

The Nigerian example demonstrates the potential for cost sharing in demand-oriented training schemes—the employer provides training and the trainee works for lower wages. Better use of formal training institutions could further lower unit costs, thus allowing more apprentices to supplement practical training, and ameliorate the present scarcity of qualified trainers. Training institutions and trainers benefit from the contact with, and feedback from, enterprises.

There are other similar initiatives. Togo has established regional vocational training centers to boost apprenticeship by providing complementary theoretical training and by supplying teaching materials for enterprises and an advisory apprenticeship inspectorate. New forms of training are also tested in programs sponsored by German technical assistance. In Sudan and Botswana, three-year apprenticeships are split between practical on-the-job training and theoretical courses in vocational schools. In Zimbabwe students receive one-and-a-half years of pre-occupational training followed by another one-and-a-half years of practical training on the job. A training system has been developed in Malawi that combines institution-based training with apprenticeships of two to three years, which lead to competency-based certification as skilled craftsmen or technicians. Part of the training is financed by a head tax on enterprises. Such flexible approaches can strengthen training systems and improve the transition to work for school leavers.

ties for career development. The experience of Malaysia, which has a strong public sector training system, has shown that close contact between trainers and managers is vital to this process. To upgrade skills systematically, governments need to establish detailed long-term public sector training programs, which is rarely done.

In much of Africa the small number of skilled personnel required for each country and the high costs of providing good quality training (including curriculum design, staff development, and materials and equipment) can render the unit cost of training prohibitive. For this reason it is important for governments to support cooperative training efforts at a regional level (see Chapter 7).

Science and technology

In the 1960s and 1970s national and regional research institutes were established in many countries. World-class research is carried out at some centers, such as the International Centre of Insect Physiology and Ecology (ICIPE) in Kenya (see Box 7.4) and international agricultural institutes under the Consultative Group on International Agricultural Research (CGIAR) system, such as the International Livestock Center for Africa in Ethiopia. In general, however, national research systems have not been successful. In some cases they have created an isolated layer of modern research that is neither supported by a broad base of technically trained personnel nor by an informed public able to use the research products. Moreover, despite its training effort, Africa lacks the middle-level technicians essential to underpin science and technology work.

Scientific work is seldom subjected to peer review. With shortages in research budgets, there are often drastic cuts in funding for equipment, fieldwork, periodicals, or much else beyond salaries. Too often government research depends on donor support and collapses when it is phased out. In this light a systemic provision for research and development expenditures of about 1 percent of GDP is essential over the long term.

Improvements in the quality of research depend on greater interaction between the users and producers of technology and on a greater commitment to science and technology (S&T) at the top levels of government. The entrepreneurial class is constrained by the business environment in their efforts to demand and produce adaptive technology (see Chapter 6). Elsewhere this group produces low-cost, intermediate, and energy-saving equipment geared to the local market and acquires a set of technical skills to identify indigenous needs and search for their solutions. Creating an enabling environment and fostering entrepreneurial development should help. To this end research institutes should involve the private sector in their management. Research quality also can be improved by networking with other institutes. This can be promoted by conferences, workshops, and joint publications by African institutes with their counterparts in other developing countries. Witness those organized by the African Academy of Sciences in Nairobi.

The long-run effectiveness of an S&T infrastructure in Africa will depend on the commitment of both the public and the government to provide sustained support for national and regional S&T institutions in which excellence and relevance are fostered. Excellence must be built upward by improving the quality and relevance of educational systems and by recognizing the role of universities in producing scholars to fill teaching, research, and leadership roles within the universities. Research must be an intrinsic and fundamental part of this process if the universities are to attract and retain high-caliber staff, who should not be relegated solely to teaching, as is done in many countries.

There are no shortcuts to an environment conducive to research and innovation. Both donor and government support must be sustained. Sharp fluctuations in support and unpredictable changes of direction are damaging to the development of a technological infrastructure in any society.

Donor support should thus be devoted to building excellence and relevance in African S&T and helping to link institutions to others outside Africa. This will mean redefining the mission of African universities and research establishments to achieve excellence and relevance, pursue and support first-class talent, and, particularly, promote the infusion of young scientists into S&T institutions. Creating networks of institutions and scientists in Africa with counterparts elsewhere will be an integral part; linking with the international S&T community will help overcome the isolation of African researchers and help enhance quality.

Three levels of technology—high technology, middle-enterprise applications, and village-level requirements—need to be considered in the new strategy. To mesh S&T with economic and social development, effective tripartite arrangements will need to be developed among teaching, research, and delivery of services. Acquisition of less costly, intermediate technology is important for tackling the problems of the "missing middle" (see Chapter 1). It would be desirable to explore more thoroughly opportunities for obtaining products and services from other developing countries.

The design and efficient management of human resource programs

In most of Africa the planning and management of human resource development activities need to be considerably strengthened. There is widespread inefficiency in the operation of health, education, family planning, nutrition, and water supply services. Schools are operating without books and clinics without medicines, and neither schools nor clinics are properly repaired and maintained. Likewise, water supply facilities are widely unusable because of inadequate maintenance. Experience suggests that the management of primary services could be placed with decentralized agencies—local government, local communities, or NGOs. Services such as primary schools, clinics, and water pumps are best managed by users or by agencies working close to them. When services deteriorate or break down,

Box 3.10 Malawi: successful community participation in water supply

The Malawi Rural Piped Water Program is widely regarded as one of the most successful and sustainable water programs in Africa, with implications for other Sub-Saharan African countries. The program
• Is based on strong community involvement with limited, but defined, responsibilities of government
• Started small, with technology that could be easily understood and maintained by local residents
• Was expanded gradually, once experience was acquired and lessons learned concerning program design and the appropriate technologies.

Beginning in one community of 2,000 people in 1968, the Department of Community Development used a pilot project to gain experience in mobilizing community involvement, and to optimize construction and operational techniques. The project was confined initially to areas where gravity-fed piped water could be used, and the technology could be easily maintained. It has now been extended to different conditions, where groundwater is available.

The program has defined the responsibilities of community and government well. The communities, which organize and manage the water facilities, are responsible for identifying sites, electing water committees, organiz-ing digging, electing repair teams, raising funds for replacement parts, and enforcing community water use rules. The government commits funds for the initial capital investment, sets standards, and adopts technical responsibilities, such as hydrological surveys, engineering design, provision of materials, and monitoring system performance. The government also trains community members, which avoids involving a large number of government extension workers and engineers, but at the same time ensures good maintenance.

One drawback is that the role of women in the provision of water is not adequately taken into account. Women provide over half of the self-help labor for the program, and over two-thirds of the committee members responsible for tap maintenance are women. Yet only 10 percent of planning committees—which make decisions on responsibilities and design—and of repair teams are women.

The government has helped communities to provide nearly 1 million people with reliable and accessible water supplies. The success of the program has encouraged public health workers to begin complementary health programs, which ensure that the health effects of the improved water supply are realized.

users can determine the cause and the responsibility for action. If money is required to maintain or repair the facility or to provide books or medicines, there is no need to wait for the central government to appropriate money. Users are more willing to contribute to the cost if they are directly involved in the management.

Encouraging decentralized participatory management does not imply an idealized view of local communities. Elites and powerful vested interests can subvert the wider interest. But in an imperfect world user-oriented management is more likely to be responsive to the needs and demands of the intended beneficiaries. This is particularly important in Africa, where the availability of experienced managers for highly centralized agencies is limited and where group effort and community action are entrenched.

Centrally managed agencies have an important role to play in supporting local groups with technical services. This is well illustrated by the cases of Kenya, Malawi (see Box 3.10), and Zimbabwe, which have well-run water supply programs. In these cases centralized engineering services provide technical guidance, support, and supplies to locally managed user groups. In primary schools and in family planning, health, and nutrition services, local staff need to be kept abreast of techni-cal developments in their field. The interface of the centrally provided technical services and the local staff and management is best developed through programs based on regular visits and interaction between central agencies, trained local people, and beneficiaries. This training and visiting (T&V) method is used in agricultural extension and conveys information on production techniques to a wide group of people. The T&V approach, suitably adapted for human resource development, could help to reach those with least access to social services in a cost-effective manner.

The T&V system is particularly amenable to health delivery because there is already a range of low-cost technical innovations that can be effective against the main causes of mortality and morbidity among infants and children. One such innovation is oral rehydration therapy to counter diarrhea. T&V workers working one-on-one with community members can teach women about the nutritional needs of their children and family planning. By using local people as community health workers, who are trained at regular intervals and work under close supervision, the messages of the T&V system are more likely to be accepted. A cost-effective T&V system was implemented successfully in the Tamil Nadu nutrition project in India, in which a small number of low-paid workers was locally recruited and trained.

Implementing reforms and quality improvement programs requires a well-functioning administrative system that can provide schools with teaching materials and health centers with medical supplies, as well as supervision and support. In many African countries health, education, and food security are handled by various parallel administrative structures that have little functional integration among them. These administrative structures limit the coordination of activities and programs. Horizontal integration is needed, especially at the village and community levels, to maximize the synergistic relationships among these sectors.

User charges

Encouraged by donors, many governments insist on providing water free. But because there are no funds to install or maintain pumps or taps, there is no water. Consumers must either pay a high price to private water vendors or walk long distances to find water (see Box 3.2, above). This is an all too familiar story also in education and health services. Whatever the merits of free social services, the reality in Africa is that it means inadequate provision or no provision at all to many people and particularly to the poorest and most vulnerable. If universal primary education, primary health care, and water supply are to be achieved by 2020, then each country must reexamine its policy toward user charges.

In UNICEF's 1987 report, "Adjustment with a Human Face," the need for a case-by-case approach is emphasized. There is scope for partial cost recovery, especially for such services as water supply and sanitation. Full economic cost recovery from beneficiaries for nonbasic services—such as university education and nonessential health services—deserves to be encouraged. Selective charging can be practiced for such services as secondary education, curative health services, and residential piped water. In all cost-sharing schemes, however, exceptions have to be made for cases of extreme economic hardship or outstanding merit. Cost sharing is a means not only of contributing modestly to the cost of social services—perhaps 10 to 20 percent of total costs can be met in this way—but also of empowering the beneficiaries to demand improved services and of fostering a sense of individual and community responsibility for their delivery.

Women as lead managers

African women are the lead managers within the household for providing food, nutrition, water, health, education, and family planning to an extent greater than elsewhere in the developing world. They have always been active in agriculture, trade, and other economic pursuits. Women are guardians of their children's welfare and have explicit responsibility to provide for them materially.

But women's economic capabilities, and in particular their ability to manage family welfare, are being threatened. "Modernization" has shifted the balance of advantage against women. The legal framework and the modern social sector and producer services developed by the independent African nations (and also most externally sponsored development projects) have not served women well. Legal systems have discriminated in land titling, by putting newly registered land in men's names (in their purported role as head of household), often overriding women's traditional rights to land use; similarly, payments for family labor under contract growing schemes are typically made to the male. It is often more difficult for women to gain access to information and technology, resources, and credit. Agricultural extension and formal financial institutions are biased toward a male clientele, despite women's importance as producers. Women have to pay higher prices for finance and for material inputs such as fertilizer (or have to do without them altogether). Female education affects family health and nutrition, agricultural productivity, and fertility, yet there is a wide gender gap in education. Lack of resources and pressures on time and energies put enormous constraints on the ability of women to maintain their own health and nutrition as well as that of their children.

As a result, women are less well equipped than men to take advantage of the better income-earning opportunities that have emerged in Africa. Despite the facts that food and nutrition are women's prime concern in Sub-Saharan Africa and that they are the principal participants in agriculture, women's independent farming has been relatively neglected. By contrast, women's family labor contribution has increased, but goes unpaid; in industry and trade women have been confined to small-scale operations in the informal sector; however vibrant these operations are and despite the trading empires built up by the most successful female entrepreneurs, women's aver-

Table 3.3 Financial requirements for broad-based human resource development for Sub-Saharan Africa
(percentage of GNP)

Component of human resource development	1985 actual	Immediate required expenditure	Required by 2000
Food security interventions	..	0.5	0.5
Nutrition	..	0.2	0.2
Universal primary education and quality improvement	1.3	1.5	2.2
Family planning	..	0.8	0.8
Water and sanitation	..	0.5	0.5
Primary health care	1.35[a]	2.0	2.5
Subtotal		5.5	6.7
Other related investments			
Science and technology	..	0.5	0.8
Secondary and higher education	1.7	2.5	2.5
Total	4–5	8.5	10.0

.. = Negligible.
a. Total health care, including primary and nonprimary.

age incomes are relatively low. Women are also handicapped in access to formal sector jobs by their lower educational attainments, and those who succeed are placed in lower-grade, lower-paid jobs. Lower income prejudices their ability to provide for their children's welfare.

Alongside these disadvantages in the "public" (income-generating) realm, women are facing increasing pressures domestically. The natural fuels and domestic water supply necessary for health care and food preparation are becoming increasingly scarce, expensive, and time consuming to obtain. Women are obliged either to devote more time to stretching available resources, or to draw more on the labor of children, or to cut down the level of feeding and nurturing. Time-saving devices, such as light grinding machines, efficient cookstoves, reforestation schemes, and, probably most important, more abundant water supplies can be a highly cost-effective way of relaxing some of the constraints on women in their household nurturing capacity. By taking account of the difficult circumstances in which women have to manage household resources, it may be possible to increase the efficiency and cost-effectiveness of human resource development interventions.

Sustained financial support for human resource development

Even if all the necessary steps are taken to improve the efficiency and effectiveness of service delivery, to reduce unit costs, and to improve user charges, a doubling of annual investment in people from about 4 to 5 percent of GNP to about 8 to 10 percent of GNP is called for in the future development strategy to 2000 and beyond (see Table 3.3). This is higher than in countries such as China, Republic of Korea, Mauritius, and Sri Lanka, which managed to ensure broad access to human resources by spending about 5 percent of GNP. But in Sub-Saharan Africa populations are widely dispersed, and infrastructure is generally poor. Significant variations in resource needs among countries have to be expected, given the variation in the levels of human resource development already reached in different countries.

In conclusion, the recommendation to increase domestic and donor expenditures on human resource development programs must be seen as part of a broad strategy in which programs to develop an enabling environment to stimulate growth in the productive sectors of agriculture and industry are to be formulated and implemented. In summary, the strategic agenda for the 1990s should aim to:

• Double total spending from 4 to 5 percent to 8 to 10 percent of GNP from now to 2000 and beyond to achieve universal primary education, health and family planning, food security, and nutrition—a substantial part of these funds may be expected to be contributed by donors

• Improve the quality of all services, especially education and health care

• Improve the effectiveness of expenditures by appropriately reallocating resources within each sector, by targeting resources toward the less advantaged, and by sharing costs

• In implementing programs, increase the use of community-based NGOs and women as lead managers in all areas of human resource development.

4

Agriculture: The primary source of growth and food security

The task facing African agriculture in the 1990s and beyond is formidable indeed. It must cope with the needs of a rapidly growing population. It must achieve sufficient growth in foodcrops not merely to maintain output per person, but also to reduce food calorie deficits and to lower food imports. In the process it must be a major employer of Africa's growing labor force and compete on world markets to earn the foreign exchange that Africa needs to fuel its economic growth. And it must do all that while reversing the degradation of natural resources that threatens long-term production. This challenge requires a transformation of agriculture.

The challenge of transforming agriculture

Transforming agriculture and expanding its productive capacity is the prerequisite for improving living standards in Sub-Saharan Africa. To achieve food security, as set out in Chapter 3, food production will have to grow at about 4 percent a year. Beyond that, to raise incomes and meet Africa's import needs, the production of export crops must grow by no less than 4 percent a year (see Chapter 8). Thus Africa must set its target for long-term agricultural growth no lower than 4 percent a year.

This will be no easy task. During the past 30 years, agricultural production in Sub-Saharan Africa has risen by only 2 percent a year. Agricultural exports have declined, and food imports are increasing at about 7 percent a year. Despite the rapid growth in food imports, an average of about 100 million people in the early 1980s were undernourished—many more in years of poor harvests. Severe food shortages are now widespread; drought and famine have been common in the 1980s. Such transitory shortfalls are even more damaging against a background of chronic food insecurity.

The agricultural potential of African countries varies widely. Central Africa, humid west Africa, and southern Africa have large cultivable areas and low population density. In contrast, most of the Sahel, parts of mountainous east Africa, and the dry belt stretching from the coast of Angola through Botswana, Lesotho, and southern Mozambique all support unsustainably large populations, and hence need food imports. To cope with these difficulties, the productivity of cultivable land must be raised. Where land is still abundant and labor scarce, increased labor productivity is required. Land scarcity is more common—and is becoming more so as the population expands. Many African countries or regions have large surface areas but considerably less cultivable land. A recent FAO study showed that only 30 percent of Africa's land area is capable of sustained production of rainfed crops. About one-quarter of this is used. However, much of the rest is under primary forest that ought to be conserved for environmental reasons.

The FAO reports that acreage expanded by only 0.7 percent annually during the past 20 years. Assuming that the rate of expansion cannot be any higher in the future, productivity must rise by more than 3 percent a year—three times faster than in the past. The necessary productivity gains can come only from technological change. This will involve a more intensive use of chemical and organic inputs; the integration of livestock into farming systems to use animal power and manure; the introduction of new higher-value crops; better irrigation methods, hand tools, and crop storage techniques; and improved animal and crop husbandry. The policy environment will need to make these changes profitable to farmers. Better rural infrastructure, particularly roads, would make it easier for farmers to obtain inputs and market crops; it would also give rural families better access to consumer goods. Greater security of land tenure would encourage investment and land conservation. Improved financial services would help farmers to save, or borrow, for investment. Better educated and healthier farmers are more likely to aim for higher productivity and to conserve resources. More thorough investment appraisal would help governments to avoid environmentally damaging schemes, such as large irrigation and settlement projects involving deforestation. A combination of incentives and sanctions is needed to deter businessmen from supplying environmentally damaging chemicals, from logging destructively, and from dumping pollutants into rivers and groundwater.

Migration from areas of high to low population density should be encouraged, although this alone will not solve the problems of the highly populated countries. The less populated areas—for example, the rain forests of central Africa and the arid and semiarid areas of the Sahel and much of southern Africa—are unsuited to supporting significantly more people. That is why improving the productivity of land is so critical for Africa.

What, then, is the long-term vision? In the years ahead African agriculture can be transformed. Africa's plentiful labor, proximity to Europe, and seasonal patterns give parts of the region a comparative advantage in the production of several crops. By 2020 better educated farmers could be using land, labor, and capital much more efficiently. A vigorous private sector could process and market agricultural produce efficiently, and rising investment could combine with new agricultural technology to steadily raise yields. Additional domestic and foreign markets for new as well as traditional products could be opened, which would permit, in particular, trade in food

within Africa. All this would require a better quality of produce, more aggressive marketing, and less government interference. Farmers would play a bigger role in shaping agricultural policy and rural development. Increased income, improved social services, and food security would make rural areas more attractive and would encourage further development of dynamic farming communities.

Despite the enormous variety of ecological zones, microclimates, and soil conditions—each requiring its own specialized crops, seeds, and farming techniques—throughout Africa there is a remarkable commonality in the principal policy measures required to spur agricultural development. Specifically those measures aim:

• To increase the role of the private sector in pricing and marketing agricultural products and farm inputs and in improving financial intermediation services for farmers
• To identify and disseminate new technologies to increase productivity
• To improve the security of land tenure and enhance environmental protection
• To develop rural infrastructure in order to strengthen rural-urban economic links and improve marketing
• To encourage rural peoples and associations, including women, to play a greater role in decisionmaking
• To promote regional cooperation, especially in food trade and joint research.

The first two priorities—involving the private sector and harnessing technology—are the most important. But too few African governments or donors are addressing them. The unsuccessful agricultural policies of the 1960s and 1970s are still common today. They include:

• Administering prices, input subsidies, markets, and input supplies through the government
• Financing farmers through parastatal agricultural credit banks
• Financing rural development through government-managed regional development projects
• Marketing export crops through parastatal enterprises, usually dealing with a single commodity
• Providing irrigation through medium- and large-scale government-managed schemes.

These policies have depended excessively on public administrations unequal to the task. Issues relating to land tenure, the environment, the role of women, and the need for capacity building have been neglected. Governments have relied heavily on technical assistance. And the farmers have been left out of decisionmaking. Progress is more likely to be made if farmers are put in control—and allowed to market freely; to invest freely; to establish their own cooperative credit, input supply, and marketing enterprises; to manage their own irrigation facilities; to own the land they work; and to take responsibility for protecting the environment. Africa's future is at stake. The best minds must be put to work, the best policies and practices must be sought, and a new sense of urgency must drive efforts on every level to accomplish the task.

Mobilizing the private sector

In agriculture, as elsewhere, many African governments have put little trust in the market. They believed that markets would fail because they would be controlled by rapacious traders—often foreigners or people from ethnic minorities. And they thought that profit margins would be excessive. Most governments, therefore, imposed controls on the marketing of key crops (cereals in much of East Africa and export crops in West Africa). Private trade was often banned outright. Government participation in, and even monopolization of, agricultural marketing and processing was widespread. The state-owned enterprises concerned were frequently costly and inefficient. Where the private sector was left to operate largely unhindered, as for tree crops in Kenya, food crops (other than rice and wheat) in West Africa, and livestock in many countries, marketing remained relatively efficient. By suppressing private marketing and processing, governments have blocked the potential for African entrepreneurship. For their part, public sector agricultural agencies have failed to seek out new export markets, new crops, and new product lines and technologies.

Most African governments have long regarded volatile prices as a deterrent to investment in agriculture. In addition volatile producer prices for food are seen to lead to volatile consumer prices, which may harm poor consumers. In response many governments have tried to stabilize producer prices. In due course the aim became not merely to stabilize prices for farmers but to keep consumer food prices low. But prices were often set so low that farmers had little incentive to supply the official marketing channels. Parallel markets, where prices were uncontrolled, expanded as a result. This reduced the negative impact of poor policy on farmers, but it did not eliminate it. Price stabilization funds established to even out prices have rarely succeeded. When the funds are in surplus, they tend to be diverted to other purposes, so that when deficits occur, there are no funds to cover them. One way forward is to put the stabilization funds under the control of management boards representing producers and consumers so that governments cannot have access to the funds. This approach is being tried in the Central African Republic.

Often governments have kept farm prices (in real terms) artificially low by allowing their exchange rates to become overvalued. Alongside price subsidies for imported wheat and rice, this distortion accelerated the substitution of imports for domestic produce. The markets for locally produced traditional foods (such as sorghum, millet, roots, and tubers) have consequently been compressed. These policies have also reduced the incentive to process traditional foods into forms more acceptable to urban and high-income households. An overvalued exchange rate has the same effect on export crops as it does on import substitutes—reducing their local currency value and discouraging production.

Flexible prices, reflecting demand and supply in local and world markets, are the best way to signal to farmers what, how much, and when to produce. Local prices would then be free to rise when supply is short—helping to stabilize both farmer income and supply itself. A market-oriented approach can also insulate governments from the political pressures to keep consumer (and hence producer) prices low. As for export crops, if farmgate prices reflect world market conditions when the world price of an export crop is low, farmers will have an incentive to switch their efforts to other crops with relatively higher value. Domestic prices of export crops fixed by governments prevent farmers from making an economically rational response to changing world market conditions.

Flexible prices call for a marketing system in which private traders are allowed to compete. When trade is monopolized, governments may feel compelled to set minimum prices to protect farmers from price fixing by the monopoly. A better solution is to encourage broader participation in trade. In contrast, African countries that have allowed free domestic trade and export and have left agricultural prices relatively uncontrolled have had higher agricultural growth than those that have not—witness Kenya (for coffee, food crops other than maize, wheat, and fruits and vegetables, as described in Box 4.1); west and central Africa (for food crops other than rice and wheat); and Ghana, Guinea, and Nigeria, following the recent liberalization of price controls and marketing restrictions (for all crops). Where exchange rates are overvalued and where monopoly food buyers persist, however, protecting farmers through setting minimum purchase prices may be justified as a "second-best" solution. Apart from these cases, the clear lesson is that, except for food security reasons in certain extreme circumstances (discussed in Chapter 3), price intervention is best avoided. Governments do of course have an important role in pricing and marketing beyond that defined in food security strategies: for example, providing market and price information, promoting private and cooperative marketing activity, building market infrastructure, ensuring the proper use of weights and measures and the qual-

ity control for export products, and establishing a legal framework that permits the development of competitive marketing activities.

A controversy continues over whether incentives should promote self-sufficiency in food by favoring food crops over export crops. The argument is misplaced. The distortion that needs correction is the one that favors food over export crops or vice versa. Once the bias against agriculture is corrected, the remaining incentives should be neutral between food and export crops, and farmers will be guided by their comparative advantage. Countries with a comparative advantage in export crop production should exploit it and import food if necessary. This will promote not only growth and higher incomes, but food security as well. In practice the policies advocated in this report would significantly increase the production of food in most African countries and substantially reduce the food gap by 2020 (see Table 3.2). This conclusion is justified by the improving comparative advantage of many African countries in food production that results from

Box 4.1 Kenya succeeds in horticulture

Productive land in Kenya has become scarce relative to the growing supply of labor. In this situation horticultural cultivation, by making intensive use of both land and labor, is highly appropriate. It employs about 20 percent of the labor force (1.8 million people) during the harvest season, and it provides small-scale landholders with an additional source of income and improved food security. International and domestic demand for horticultural products is high; the growing domestic market alone absorbs 90 percent of the fruits and vegetables produced, thus replacing imported apples, bananas, and grapes.

Kenya's favorable climate makes it possible to produce tropical, semitropical, and temperate fruits and vegetables. The range of products has increased steadily. More than 50 varieties of flowers are being grown. Kenya, which had almost no flower exports 15 years ago, is now the world's fourth largest exporter of flowers; roses, orchids, and carnations are the most popular.

Production of fresh horticultural exports increased dramatically from about 1,500 tons (worth $434,000 equivalent) in 1968 to 36,500 tons (worth $54.7 million) in 1987. They are the third largest source of foreign exchange among agricultural exports. Horticultural products go to some 30 countries, the largest single market being the United Kingdom, with a share of more than 40 percent. Middle Eastern countries are also becoming an increasingly important market.

Horticulture was able to expand because local entrepreneurs, foreign investors, and the government collaborated, facilitated by the Horticultural Crops Development

Authority (HCDA), set up in 1967. The HCDA is a parastatal institution that markets some of the produce from smallholders. It developed a market information system with the International Trade Centre, licensed horticultural exporters, established packing stations, participated in allocating air cargo space, and worked to standardize containers. The Ministry of Agriculture, helped by the HCDA, provides extension and marketing advice. The ministry also controls the quality of produce to maintain international standards. The Kenya Agriculture Research Institute, under the Ministry of Science, Research, and Technology, carries out new crop trials and supervises the sale of planting material. The private sector and the HCDA compete freely in harvesting, transportation, marketing, and pricing.

The private sector has been the main source of finance. Marketing costs have been modest because of the close links many exporters, especially foreign companies, have with external markets. Bilateral assistance and private foreign investment from several countries financed horticultural research and production, agricultural training, crop research, water development, and technical assistance.

The success of Kenya's horticultural production holds important lessons for other countries in Africa. The government, through the HCDA, acted as a facilitator and coordinator but did not create a large bureaucracy. It did not interfere with the market mechanism, but relied on private incentives.

these policies, the added focus on food security, and the relative stagnation in the real prices of some commodity exports.

Trade within Africa in agricultural products, especially food, should grow as domestic distortions in exchange rates, agricultural prices, and marketing systems are eliminated. Reducing the barriers to regional trade will open up opportunities for specialization, depending on the comparative advantage of each country, and will expand markets.

It is sometimes argued that because world prices for most African agricultural products have fallen, government intervention is needed to protect export producers. Agricultural prices have indeed declined. Sluggish growth in developed countries reduced demand in the late 1970s and early 1980s. At the same time the supply of some export crops increased, especially from Asia and Latin America (notably coffee, palm oil, and cocoa). New substitutes for some tropical products (synthetic rubber and sugar made from corn syrup and sugar beets) appeared. Because of Africa's low market share, except for cocoa, world prices are not significantly affected by the level of production in Africa.

Lower prices, however, do not explain why Africa has seen its share of the world markets in cocoa, coffee, palm oil, rubber, copra, tea, and cotton shrink in the past 20 years. Asian countries—with more liberal trade regimes, stronger private investment, and growing productivity—have taken up the slack. Africa's experience has shown that governments cannot afford to protect farmers from sustained declines in world prices for their export crops. Instead, farmers should be allowed to adapt and respond through free and open price and marketing regimes. Africa's best hope for the future is to become increasingly competitive. Government's role is to help farmers to improve their productivity. Encouraging cost cutting and maintaining a policy environment that permits diversification in response to market signals is the best way to beat depressed world market prices.

Wide short-term fluctuations in world agricultural prices are disruptive. Efforts have been made to mitigate such fluctuations through international commodity agreements, as has been attempted, for example, by the international coffee and cocoa agreements. In practice, international price stabilization schemes have proven to be extremely difficult to manage effectively; however,

ways to improve their operations are under study. Given the sophistication and complexity of world commodity markets for agricultural products and the conflicting interests among producer and consuming countries, this will be no easy task. Schemes that resist long-term price trends created by changes in world supply and demand are almost inevitably doomed to failure, possibly at considerable cost. Compensatory finance, such as the EEC's STABEX scheme or that provided by the IMF to countries demonstrating a need based on significant short-term shifts in terms of trade, makes more sense. They provide relief without intervening in markets that are increasingly difficult to manipulate.

Subsidies in North America and Western Europe have created abundant supplies and have lowered prices of cereals and livestock products that are imported by African countries in competition with local production. In this situation tariff protection from subsidized and dumped exports is justified; recent examples include dairy products, cereals, and edible oils from Europe and North America. For these commodities, production costs are lower in many African countries than in exporting countries. If these subsidies were to disappear, Africa would have much to gain. Tariff protection will permit production capacity and enterprises that market domestic produce to develop.

A role for medium- and large-scale farmers

Better incentives should benefit not only smallholder agriculture, but also medium- and large-scale private farming. Enterprises that can integrate agricultural production, marketing, and processing are more likely to develop new products and markets. They will often sign production contracts with smallholders, who will thereby receive the benefits of modern technologies, quality control, marketing, and other services. Côte d'Ivoire, Kenya, and Malawi have attracted private money to plantations producing export crops—bananas, pineapples, fruits, and rubber in Côte d'Ivoire; coffee, tea, fruits, and vegetables in Kenya (see Box 4.1, above); and tobacco in Malawi. A more open policy for such investment attracts domestic and foreign capital, as well as technical and marketing expertise. Educated Africans who might spurn peasant agriculture could be attracted to work in such modern agricultural enterprises.

Fostering rural savings and credit

To provide funds for farm investment and to improve farmers' cash flow, efficient financial intermediaries are needed to serve rural areas. Many parastatal credit institutions established to serve the agricultural sector have been unsuccessful, mostly owing to poor management. Politically motivated loans have been common and their default rates high. Governments have also tended to maintain below-market interest rates. Consequently, the demand for credit invariably exceeded the supply. Credit was rationed and distributed according to criteria that often failed to take account of the quality of the investments proposed. It is hardly surprising that these institutions have suffered big losses.

A better approach would be to let interest rates balance supply and demand. Funds could then be allocated by the market. Higher interest rates would also make the banks less dependent on government for funds and would increase the incentives for savings. The banks would gain the resources needed to strengthen the management of their rural operations. Commercial banks might also be attracted into agricultural lending or encouraged to lend to farmers through intermediaries (such as traders who sell farm inputs and equipment on credit or who market crops). This has begun to happen in Kenya, for example. However, significant agricultural lending by private commercial banks will develop only in the long run. Even then there will be little progress unless the banks are allowed to enforce the default clauses in their loan agreements.

For smaller farmers the most promising way to provide credit is to encourage the development of informal sector financial institutions (see Chapter 6). These combine savings by members with lending to groups that assume collective liability for the debt. Peer pressure increases the likelihood of repayment, since nonpayment by one results in

Box 4.2 Savings and credit cooperatives in Cameroon

Cameroon's credit unions (CU) are an impressive example of efficient rural financial institutions. They have been built on informal savings and lending associations (*tontines* or *njangis*), which have a long history dating to premonetized times in many areas of Cameroon. These associations foster savings through regular contributions and oblige members to make regular debt repayments. CUs formalized their short-term temporary arrangements into permanent institutions. The first CUs were formed in 1963 in the northwest, an area in which tontines were prevalent. From this start CUs spread progressively to neighboring areas, and nationwide expansion is planned.

CUs meet the needs particularly of the low-income urban and rural population. Rural families need a safe place to deposit their savings. CUs offer at least the same degree of safety as tontines, a far greater variety of savings instruments, and a higher degree of accessibility to deposits in case of a need to withdraw. Although the formal banking sector in Cameroon is undergoing a very difficult period, the CU movement is thriving; savings growth rates averaged some 25 percent for 1982–87, and, by the end of 1987, 231 CUs with some 68,000 members had savings deposits and loans of $33 million and $24 million equivalent, respectively.

Although many members use CUs exclusively to accumulate savings, CUs illustrate the importance of savings for credit operations. The repayment capacity of a member is easier to assess when the lending institution knows the potential borrower's saving habits. CUs, which mobilize funds for onlending exclusively from member savings, tend to behave more prudently than institutions that finance lending operations from resources provided by external sources.

The CU movement has a long-term vision to develop solid institutions. To promote institutional standards, the Cameroon Cooperative Credit Union League (CAMCCUL) was established in 1968 as an apex organization to provide support services (bookkeeping and management assistance, a central finance unit, training, and audit and insurance services) to its members. Before registration a new CU operates provisionally as a precooperative savings club. Existing CUs that fail to meet established professional standards are downgraded to precooperative status and are subject to the sanction of eventual closure.

The CUs and CAMCCUL are genuine cooperatives, established and controlled by members and their representatives. Although CUs are state-registered formal cooperative organizations, the government has not intervened in their operations.

Instead the affiliated CUs control and supervise CAMCCUL operations and finances through their board of directors and supervisory committee, which are elected by, and responsible to, the members. Depending on their size, CUs are managed by voluntary or paid managers. Paid managers and the senior staff of CAMCCUL are banking and cooperative professionals, and considerable resources go to staff training.

The CUs' success can be attributed to the adaptation of an indigenous institution to modern business concepts. They are accountable to their members and serve their members' needs. Through the years the CU movement has maintained its autonomy, and its unique private nature is attractive to its many shareholders.

the loss of credit to the group. Defaults are few. Savings and loan organizations operate successfully, for example, in Benin, Burundi, Cameroon, Côte d'Ivoire, Rwanda, and Togo (see Boxes 4.2 and 8.4).

Harnessing technology

African soils need skilled management to ensure sustainable production. Dry areas are dominated by sandy porous soils lacking nutrients. Much of the humid lowlands have acid soils, where aluminum toxicity can damage plants. The continent's most fertile soils are in the east African highlands, where slopes increase risk of erosion or where dark clay and alluvial soils are prone to waterlogging. Most African soils are easily degraded when vegetation is weakened or removed. All but the most humid zones have unpredictable rainfall. Much of the continent (by some estimates two-thirds) has a significant chance of drought each year. Even in years of adequate overall rainfall, rains can start late or finish early, and dry spells can arrive at crucial times in the growing season. Potential for irrigation is much smaller than in Asia, where it has been the major source of agricultural growth. Moreover the continent's diverse patterns of rainfall, soil, and slopes combine to produce a bewildering diversity of micro-environments.

Nevertheless, over centuries, Africans have developed ways of coping with these difficulties. Nomadic livestock raising was perhaps the only practical system for the arid areas of Africa, in which sparse and erratic rainfall necessitated the movement of livestock in search of good pasture and water. Slash and burn agriculture was appropriate in forest and savanna areas with abundant land and low population density, because it allowed long fallow periods for the land to regenerate.

The problem is that, with rapid population growth, the land and resource base has not been adequate in most of Africa to maintain these traditional extensive farming and livestock systems. Pressure on the land is resulting in declines in crop yields and in overgrazing. Vegetative cover is weakening, erosion accelerating. Hence more productive technologies must be rapidly developed and adapted to respond to the special needs of African farmers and to the needs of their environment.

Attempts to introduce technology into Africa in the past 30 years have been disappointing. Wit-

ness the 1960s and 1970s, when "modern" technologies were planned for cereals, tree crops, oil seeds, cotton, and other crops based on higher-yielding varieties, fertilizer, chemical pest and disease control—and in some cases mechanization. This "off the shelf" technology was frequently a failure. Often farmers lacked the labor, capital, or land necessary to use the technology properly. Mechanization, fertilizers, chemical pest and weed control, and high-yielding seeds all cost money—hard to acquire for African farmers operating at or near subsistence levels. Farmers adapted slowly to using modern inputs and equipment. Chemicals for plant protection were not widely understood. High-yielding seed performed no better than traditional seed if not fertilized and correctly grown. Moreover government price and marketing policies often made it impossible to use the technologies profitably. Fertilizer arrived only when governments had both the necessary foreign exchange and the inclination to spend it accordingly. Finally, "modern" technologies were sometimes disseminated without adaptation to local conditions. In these circumstances farmers were understandably reluctant to switch from traditional practices. A new effort to harness agricultural technology to the needs of African farmers is now required.

The search for higher-yielding varieties

The success of new varieties of crops introduced into Africa in the past 30 years has been limited. High-yielding maize, grown by many smallholders in Zimbabwe and Kenya, is spreading in western Africa. Improved varieties of lowland rice and wheat can also be used in some areas of Sub-Saharan Africa. The International Institute of Tropical Agriculture (IITA) is developing disease-resistant cassava varieties, which offer modest yield increases over existing varieties. Many other new varieties of crops did well on research stations, where soil, management, and water availability were good, but did not thrive under farm conditions. New crop varieties must be widely tested on-farm to make sure they perform at least as well as local varieties.

Expanding fertilizer use

Africa's average use of chemical fertilizer is less than 10 kilograms per hectare, compared with about 90 kilograms per hectare in China and India. Demand is low because traditionally farmers have used only limited amounts of organic nutrients, such as decayed vegetation, ash from burning, and manure, and because traditional crops often show little response. At the same time fertilizer has been in short supply because of ineffective government agencies, poor transport systems, limited foreign exchange, and restrictions on private sector fertilizer marketing.

Chemical fertilizers will be in demand as farming systems change and new agricultural technologies and crop varieties are introduced. However, there is generally no justification for subsidizing fertilizer use; that only encourages waste. The key is to ensure that reliable supplies are readily available at full cost. In many African countries shortages prevent existing demand from being met. Public enterprises typically manage fertilizer distribution inefficiently. To reduce supply bottlenecks, private traders and enterprises should be

allowed to import, produce, and distribute it themselves. Controls on fertilizer prices and marketing margins merely discourage private enterprise. Finally, foreign exchange should be available to pay for fertilizer imports as demanded (preferably through the exchange rate management reforms outlined in Chapter 2), and fertilizer distribution should be considered in planning transport networks.

Organic fertilizers will always be needed because they increase the soil's ability to hold water and nutrients and to resist erosion. They also reduce the amount of chemical fertilizer needed. This is desirable both for cost and environmental reasons. Agroindustrial wastes, such as coffee pulp and husks, rice husks, spent tea leaves, molasses, and distillery waste from sugar refineries, should be used as organic fertilizer, in addition to the more common animal dung and crop residues.

Box 4.3 Fighting insects with insects

Cassava is the staple crop for more than 200 million people in more than 35 African countries and is particularly important during partial or complete crop failure. A few years ago it was reported that "a small bug is eating the heart out of Africa"—the cassava mealy bug first identified in Zaire in 1973. Together with the cassava green spider mite (first reported in Uganda in 1971), the mealy bug has spread rapidly in a wide belt from Mozambique through Zaire and the Central African Republic, across coastal west Africa to Senegal and Guinea Bissau. Severe attacks of either pest can reduce yields by up to 80 percent. Economic losses are estimated at almost $2 billion a year; some farmers have abandoned the crop.

Now, however, thanks to the International Institute of Tropical Agriculture (IITA) in Ibadan, Nigeria, a successful biological control program has begun to reverse the tide. The story of the Africa-wide biological control program for the mealy bug is one of remarkable persistence, regional and international cooperation, and technical and economic success. The program's benefit to cost ratio is conservatively estimated at 150:1.

The program merits special attention because it:
• Uses nonchemical pest control, which is environmentally sound and does not drain foreign exchange resources
• Offers a permanent and self-sustaining solution to a major agricultural problem
• Benefits mostly subsistence farmers
• Is a national program with inputs of technical assistance and training from outside the region
• Is also a good example of the benefits derived from regional cooperation (for example, the Organization for African Unity (OAU) helped to facilitate cross-border flights, regional workshops, and information exchange).

The program grew out of an international workshop

cosponsored by the IITA and the government of Zaire in June 1977. Because cassava is a low-value crop grown primarily by widely scattered, poor farmers and because the mealy bugs are hard to control with chemical pesticides, a dual strategy was recommended: breeding cassava varieties resistant to the pests and implementing a biological control program.

The IITA located nearly 30 species of predators and parasites, the most promising being a tiny parasitic wasp (*Epidinocarsis lopezi*). It has become the star of the world's largest and most successful biological control program. Under a variety of ecological conditions, it rapidly multiplies and disperses. By 1985, after four years of releases, the parasite's presence was confirmed in 11 countries. Indications are that it can establish itself throughout the cassava belt. However, the situation is too urgent for this passive approach.

There is large and growing demand from more countries for training inputs and technical assistance to set up national programs. Because of skilled labor and production shortages at the control program headquarters at the IITA, not all of this demand can be met, although new facilities have been constructed in Cotonou, Benin. The greatest needs are for skilled technicians to run the parasite breeding operations and to direct and implement the national programs.

Many donors have supported the core program, but there is still a chronic shortage of funds due in part, ironically, to its success, which gives the mistaken impression that the cassava pest problem in Africa has been solved. In fact more work is needed to distribute the parasites in the affected region and to support a parallel program that is searching for biological control of the cassava green spider mite.

Controlling pests and diseases

Pests and diseases such as rice blast, cassava bacterial blight, and green spider mite cause heavy preharvest losses in Africa—ranging from 10 percent up to 80 percent. There will be increasing demand for chemical pest and disease control material, much of which has undesirable environmental effects. Planned programs of disease and pest control will be necessary, using limited quantities of pesticides and fungicides, but increasingly relying on cultural and biological controls (see Box 4.3). Pest- and disease-resistant crops will have to be developed. Improved cropping and cultivation methods are needed that reduce the spread of pests and diseases.

Irrigation and water availability and control

In Sub-Saharan Africa 5 million hectares are irrigated—just over half by modern means, the rest by small-scale traditional methods. Some 70 percent is in three countries: Madagascar, Nigeria, and Sudan. The area potentially suitable for irrigation is estimated at nearly 20 million hectares. Further irrigation could contribute significantly to expanding agricultural production in Chad, Ethiopia, Malawi, Mali, Mauritania, Senegal, and Uganda, in addition to the three countries cited above. These countries have dry areas that are cultivable with water, which could be obtained from rivers or from groundwater resources. The most promising possibilities are schemes costing $1,500 a hectare or less, which could be built and maintained by farmers with some government assistance. These include surface irrigation from wells, controlled flooding, and development of inland valleys and basins, swamps, and flood plains. Such developments have often spread spontaneously. Private small-scale schemes by Mauritanian farmers in the Senegal valley are one example. In addition expenditure on the proper operation and maintenance of existing schemes and on rehabilitation will be money well spent in many countries.

Water management and conservation for rainfed crops is important. In semiarid areas and where dry spells are a danger, it is essential to maximize the proportion of rainfall that filters into the soil for crops to use rather than washing off uselessly or destructively. This can be helped by waterspreading (diverting it from gullies onto cultivated fields) and water harvesting (directing runoff from a broad area by earth or stone bunds and canals onto smaller areas growing crops or trees) (see Box 4.4).

Agricultural equipment

In many parts of Africa it will be necessary to raise the productivity of labor by using improved agricultural equipment. Past experience has shown that full-scale mechanization is not the answer for the short or medium term. Tractor plowing and bulldozer land clearance have accelerated soil degradation in many areas. Maintenance of machinery has been poor, partly because of lack of foreign exchange for spare parts. Animal power is often a more profitable alternative. In addition many small "appropriate technology" projects run by private voluntary agencies have introduced simple mechanical devices that require little maintenance and are cheap and easy to use. The jab planter is an example of a hand tool that can halve the time needed to sow a hectare by hand. Animal-drawn equipment, such as plows and seeders, has an enormous potential. So too do improvements in on-farm storage facilities and machines for dehusking and the initial conditioning and processing of crops.

Livestock

Livestock offers good opportunities for rural income growth in Africa. Small stock (sheep and goats) and poultry have a large potential, which has not been exploited in much of the region. Cattle production is currently the most important and provides a large proportion of agricultural value added—more than half in some countries. Africa's 160 million head of cattle are distributed unequally across the continent. Mountainous east Africa, relatively free of the tsetse fly, has one-fifth of all livestock on only 11 percent of Sub-Saharan Africa's land. The Sudano-Sahelian zone, with another third of the total, is crowded with cattle, while humid central Africa, where the tsetse is endemic, has only 3 percent of the stock on 18 percent of Sub-Saharan Africa's area.

Livestock can also be part of an integrated farming system by providing both manure and draft power. However, livestock also contributes to the progressive removal of Africa's vegetative cover. The task is to increase underused livestock for production and draft power, while reducing the pressure on the environment.

Solutions will vary. In the mountainous areas integration of livestock in farming systems is al-

Box 4.4 Soil conservation and water harvesting in Burkina Faso

An agricultural research and extension project, Projet Agro-Forestier (PAF), in the Yatenga region of Burkina Faso, launched in 1979, aimed at reducing soil erosion and water runoff. It used simple, inexpensive, labor-intensive earthen basins to catch rainwater for trees. Rock bunds, built to slow the runoff of rainfall from terraces, have proved effective in reducing erosion and retaining moisture in the soil.

The Yatenga region is located in the Sahelian area that borders the southern edge of the Sahara desert. It is dry, with annual rainfall of 350 to 650 millimeters and is prone to drought. Traditional agricultural techniques cause considerable soil erosion and depend on long fallow times to restore the soil's productivity. Yet strong population pressure forced farmers to shorten and eventually eliminate the fallow periods, and the traditional methods of stemming soil erosion proved insufficient. Past efforts by government and international organizations to improve the situation had largely failed.

To halt further environmental degradation, the PAF, funded and managed by Oxfam, persuaded eight village cooperatives to volunteer land for the experiment. Skeptical at first, the participants became more interested when large amounts of water built up in the microcatchments. Several decided to plant upland rice in the basins, and sorghum was introduced. These crops did well, and soon farmers shifted their attention from the group plots to their own land.

When PAF staff found that the farmers were more interested in planting crops than trees, they shifted their focus. The PAF also accommodated farmers' preference for less labor-intensive construction of the rectangular microcatchments and began to use a method similar to a traditional technique that had been abandoned. For more effective water collection, the PAF developed an inexpensive and rather ingenious device: the water-tube level, which accurately identified the contour lines on the gentle slopes common to the Yatenga. The technique is now used by thousands of farmers.

The PAF found that they could train villages in two or three days. Despite a field staff of fewer than six persons, the PAF's training record is impressive. Today, soil conservation measures cover more than 60,000 hectares and extend to the northern region.

Crop yields have improved because the bunds hold rainwater on the fields, which increases the absorption of water into the land and thus by the crops. Fertilizer (usually manure and organic material) applied to the fields is less likely to be washed away, which makes the soil directly behind the bunds more fertile. As much as 200 millimeters of soil had accumulated behind some of the barriers after their first year of use. First-year yield increases can be a dramatic 15 to 30 percent, but the system needs to be managed well, with restitution of organic matter and fertilization, for yields to be sustained. The project is successful because:

- The technology is simple. Yatenga farmers were familiar with the general principles of soil and water conservation, so they could understand the technology and do the basic work and maintenance themselves.
- The extension program is simple. A few extension workers can help many farmers so that an elaborate network is not needed.
- The benefits are obvious and the costs minimal. Farmers are not required to move, to grow crops they are unfamiliar with, to borrow money to purchase a new technology, or to do anything very different from what they have been doing. For a small investment of time and effort, they can increase output and reduce risk.

The PAF can be copied cheaply. The techniques identified and developed are now widely disseminated by other NGOs and by the national extension services. This gives hope that a much larger area will be reclaimed or protected during the next 10 years.

---

ready under way. In humid and subhumid zones tsetse can be controlled, but not eliminated, through low-cost traps and spraying. So a priority should be the spread of dwarf cattle tolerant to trypanosomiasis (the disease carried by tsetse), along with the development of lightweight transport and draft equipment that such cattle can power. In drier cultivated zones there will be increasingly intense grazing pressure from farmers' expanding herds, compounded by those of pastoralists, who graze their animals on crop stubble and bushy fallows in the dry season. Greater control of grazing is desirable, but no effective means of achieving this has been found. The drier pastoral areas have different problems. Although pastoralists efficiently exploit the meager and shifting resources of the rangelands, the potential for increasing their output and productivity is low.

Overgrazing is acute around public waterholes and urban centers and is a major cause of environmental degradation. New water points should be widely dispersed in pastoral areas and allocated to user associations to help avoid the excessive concentration of livestock.

Veterinary services are essential for livestock development in all areas, and they can be provided mainly by the private sector. National animal health services should concentrate on regulating private veterinarians, organizing and subsidizing mass vaccinations, and undertaking other emergency measures that veterinarians in commercial practice are unlikely to undertake, except under contract with the government. Since few private veterinarians will choose to practice in the more remote pastoral areas, improved livestock care will also depend on "para-vets" paid from drug sales. In all areas extension workers should teach improved animal husbandry and forage production to livestock owners.

Measures to promote fisheries

The potential of African fisheries, both marine and continental, is large, with a maximum sustainable yield estimated at 8 million tons a year. However, the catch is declining (it fell from 7.5 million tons in 1977 to 5.9 million tons in 1985) because of overfishing, climatic factors, and reductions in river flows and lake levels. The value of African fish exports is about $650 million a year. African fleets account for about 30 percent of the total, foreign fleets 45 percent, inland fisheries 24 percent, and aquaculture 1 percent.

Many African countries need fisheries resource management plans that identify fishing potential and the opportunities for exploiting this potential in a manner consistent with long-term conservation and with environmental considerations. The plans must also provide for the necessary policies and institutional development.

Systems to monitor and control foreign fleets are needed in many coastal countries. Such systems will increase the amount of taxes taken from foreign fishing, which is necessary since foreign fleets are usually self-contained and provide little benefit other than taxes and royalties to the countries whose waters are fished. Licensing agreements with foreign fleets generally need to be improved. Increasingly, coastal states should develop their own fisheries capabilities through policies and financing that encourage private sector involvement.

Development of aquaculture can be greatly encouraged through both adaptive research and extension of aquaculture techniques to farmers and other interested individuals. Integrated agriculture and aquaculture farming packages have considerable interest. The artificial stocking of natural and man-made bodies of water has some potential. Finally, artisanal ("canoe") fisheries can be assisted through support to organizations of fishermen; this support should also be given to women, who have an important role in small-scale fisheries and in fish marketing.

Better agricultural research

Better technology will be essential to achieve the targeted growth in output of 4 percent a year over the medium and long run. The slow development of new agricultural technology in the past two decades reflects the decline in the quality of agricultural research in Africa. Often rudimentary and carried out by just a few scientists, agricultural research nonetheless contributed greatly to African farming in the first 60 years of the 20th century. It enabled cocoa, rubber, mangoes, tea, citrus, maize, and later hybrid maize to be introduced to African farmers—as were fertilizer and new agricultural implements and equipment. Weak government commitment and poor management, rather than a lack of money, have caused the current failure. In many African countries more researchers than before are spending more money, with little to show for it. Donor-financed projects have not helped. More has been spent on agricultural research in Sub-Saharan Africa per farmer than elsewhere in the developing world—about $360 million in 1980, the most recent year for which data are available, compared with roughly $190 million in South Asia, which has many more farmers. It is an urgent priority for Africa to rehabilitate its agricultural research institutes, and tough action on the part of result-oriented managers is required so that they can once again perform their critical role of creating, adapting, and disseminating improved agricultural technology, including new products.

Most African countries are too small to afford the agricultural research they need. Basic research (as well as much applied research) will need to be done at the international agricultural research centers (IARCs) and at universities and research centers in the industrial countries. The international agricultural research effort devoted to Africa, particularly in technology improvement, must be strengthened. Promising research on biotechnology in agriculture, which will have a profound effect on the world's agriculture by 2000, will be done initially in industrial country research centers and the IARCs because it requires high expenditure and high technical competence. These institutions must play an increased role in the transferring and adapting of new technology to Africa (see Box 7.4).

International research will have an impact in Africa only if it can be adapted to local circumstances, so it is crucial to rehabilitate national agricultural research systems. The first step is to draw up national action plans in which priorities are identified and provision is made for monitoring and evaluating results and for translating those results into recommendations for farmers. Faculties of agriculture should be drawn in. Donor efforts need to be firmly coordinated; the recently created Special Program for African Agricultural Research (SPAAR) is an important step in this direction. The IARCs must also be drawn closer into technical support for national systems. Greater sharing of results among researchers in various countries would be one way to achieve this. Regional networks would allow smaller African countries to participate in specialized research.

Improving agricultural extension and the supply of inputs

Extension services, which transfer the results of research to the field, have a further important role in transmitting information about farmers' needs to researchers. Farmers experiment to adapt research results to their own circumstances; extension services could do more to tap this source of information. However, few African countries have effective nationwide services. Most are fragmented, with separate systems for different crops or with special systems contained in various area development projects. Multiple donor-financed extension services in the same country have often caused confusion and have made the development of efficient national extension programs more difficult. Management and supervision are typically lax, links with research are weak, training of extension agents is poor, and feedback from farmers is almost nonexistent. A nationwide public extension system for every African country, to which the donors could contribute collectively, would be more cost-effective. One extension worker would ideally be provided for about 200 to 1,000 farmers, depending on the population density. These workers would deal with all farming activities. Techniques that have been proven in similar environments could be suggested, with a preference for low-cost, low-risk techniques. Extension workers should offer farmers, through options rather than a single "package", the best techniques to suit their circumstances. This would not preclude private companies or cooperatives from offering extension services for crops that they market (as for tobacco in many countries). Also, where a single crop extension service is operating successfully (such as in certain cotton programs), its activity could be expanded to cover other crops in collaboration with the national extension service.

Programs based on the T&V system of extension, developed successfully in Asia, are being tried in Africa. Supervisors check that fieldworkers are visiting farmers as they should, while regular training sessions and links with research allow extension workers to be continually upgraded and to feed results and farmers' questions back to researchers. T&V is a good example of capacity building. It focuses on improving African skills, on management, on building African institutions, and on channeling information from farmers to government institutions. By consolidating various public agricultural extension services into a single system, costs can be kept down. In Kenya some farmers have increased maize yields up to 50 percent as a result of a national extension system run along these lines. The T&V system has also been widely and successfully introduced in Burkina Faso, Côte d'Ivoire, Nigeria, Senegal, and Togo, and is being started in other African countries.

Efficient mechanisms for supplying farm inputs, equipment, and livestock are crucial, but they have largely been lacking. As a rule these are best handled by the private sector. The role of government should be to provide adequate foreign exchange, to undertake research, and to pass the results on to farmers. Government research and extension services, along with private voluntary organizations, should be developing inputs and investment goods (such as new hand tools, animal-drawn equipment, crossbred cows, grain storage facilities, and energy-efficient stoves) that can then be produced and distributed by the private sector.

Reorienting agricultural education

In most African countries agricultural institutions presently provide inadequate training to students. After graduation students usually prefer to join the public service rather than become farmers. Jobs in the private agricultural sector are scarce. The costs of training are high. Better training should be focused on three distinct groups: on agricultural technicians, who will serve as staff or owners of private agricultural and agroindustrial enterprises; on the staff of the research, veterinary, and extension services; and on high-level agricultural researchers and policymakers. This is an area where donors can greatly help.

Protecting the rural environment

Reliable data on the state of environmental degradation do not exist for most of Africa. However, deforestation is clearly a problem that calls for urgent attention. The most recent survey (in 1980) showed that Africa's 703 million hectares of forests were being cleared at the rate of 3.7 million hectares (or 0.6 percent) a year. Deforestation outstripped the rate of new tree planting by 29 to 1. At the same time 55 million Africans faced acute scarcity of fuelwood. Deforestation is causing the destruction not only of much of Africa's unique animal and plant life, but also of its preagricultural cultures, such as the pygmies.

What little evidence is available indicates that 80 to 90 percent of Africa's rangelands and 80 percent of cropped land in the dryland areas may be affected by soil degradation. Soil erosion, widespread in all areas of Sub-Saharan Africa, is perhaps most serious in Ethiopia, where topsoil losses of up to 290 metric tons a hectare have been reported for steep slopes. In west Africa, losses of 10 to 20 metric tons of soil per hectare have been reported even for very gentle slopes. Wind erosion is significant in drier areas. There are numerous reports of a decline in the fertility of cultivated land in many parts of the region.

A common feature of degradation is the removal or weakening of vegetative cover by overgrazing, overcultivation, or deforestation, which exposes the soil to rain and wind. With several notable exceptions government efforts to combat soil degradation have failed because soil conservation usually requires the farmer to provide extra labor—labor that is often unavailable. Moreover low prices for produce coupled with uncertain land tenure make conservation financially unattractive. It is cheaper to move on to a less-degraded patch than to rescue a degraded one. A more prosperous rural environment—resulting from the removal of price, exchange rate, and fiscal and other distortions together with greater security of tenure and improvements in productivity—is necessary for farmers, forest dwellers, and pastoralists to have an interest in conservation. Conservation will fail unless it appeals to the farmer's self-interest.

Successful conservation efforts show what can be achieved. Kenya's national soil conservation program, launched with Swedish funding in 1974 and continuing through Kenya's national extension project, has terraced hundreds of thousands of smallholdings, with farmers doing most of the work without pay. Other successful techniques include the use of surface mulches, the development of crop varieties that emerge early and protect the soil against early rains, and intercropping,

which provides denser soil cover, increases output, and provides more stable yields. Minimum tillage (planting crops through a sod of dead weeds or stubble) can reduce erosion and increase yields. A technique suitable for hilly areas is the planting of infiltration bands of fodder grass, such as vetiver, along the contours. Vetiver, which produces a dense hedge and is a complete filter, is cheap and self-sustaining. Simply farming along the contours in hilly areas will be beneficial. In Burkina Faso farmers are placing lines of stones across the contours of land prone to soil erosion. The lines slow down runoff, increase water infiltration, and collect topsoil. They can restore desertified land (see Box 4.4, above). To stand any hope of adoption, the soil conservation must increase crop yields, cost little or nothing in cash, and involve no expensive machinery. If tree planting is involved, it must produce timber and fuelwood or fodder and not conflict with the labor needs of crop production.

In Africa's often fragile soils trees protect the soil against wind and rain, provide organic matter to improve soil structure, and draw on deep groundwater and nutrients that the roots of annual crops cannot reach. In many areas fallow periods have been cut too short for naturally regenerating trees to reach maturity and fulfill these functions. Expanding herds of livestock exert a heavy grazing pressure, reducing the ability of forests to regenerate naturally. The tree cover of Africa is declining rapidly, and clearance for farming will continue. If trees are to play an increased role in soil conservation and agricultural production, it must be in the farmed areas, through agroforestry. This takes many forms, such as planting shade trees around living areas or planting trees and shrubs in tight lines along the contour of fields to prevent soil erosion. Crops such as cocoa, coffee, and tea have value as trees in agroforestry systems. More species that produce fruit, nuts, or fodder should be added to diversify food production. For semiarid areas windbreaks of mixed heights and species seem promising. For humid areas multilevel farming, which involves intercropping trees, shrubs, and crops of various heights for total ground cover, may be desirable. Pruning provides fuelwood, stakes, and fodder or nitrogen-rich mulch for fertilizer.

The fuelwood crisis in many parts of Africa can be only partially alleviated by communal woodlots and plantations of fuelwood species. In addition measures are needed to ensure the systematic management of forest cover. The lack of financial and other resources places this task beyond the capacity of the forestry services in the Sub-Saharan countries. If it is to occur, responsibility will have to be transferred to local communities. The goal is to limit forest exploitation to what is necessary to meet rural energy needs and part of the urban energy needs without causing environmental damage. This will require a capacity to decide where fuelwood should be harvested, to provide for regenerating stocks (calling in some cases for a change in traditional land rights), and to ensure that costs are recovered. Trees for fuelwood will be planted on a significant scale (there is some subsistence planting) only when wood becomes a marketed commodity and prices are attractive to growers. This is already happening in much of east Africa. There are also efforts to slow down the rise in fuelwood consumption by introducing more fuel-efficient wood and charcoal stoves (see Box 5.7).

Changing agricultural practices to conserve soil and water and to reduce the destruction of forests will not be enough, however. Tropical forest action plans recently completed by the FAO, the UNDP, the World Bank, and the World Resources Institute for a number of African countries call for a range of additional measures (see also Box 2.1). These include strengthening forestry and park services, which protect existing forests and wildlife and replant where forests have been destroyed; changing agreements with logging companies to induce them to become partners in forest protection and replanting; and changing fiscal policy applied to logging companies so that they pay the real economic and social cost of the trees they sell.

Africa's lakes, swamps, rivers, and coastal waters are important resources to protect. They provide a habitat for fish and wildlife and perform other significant ecological functions. Claims on Africa's surface waters come from irrigation, hydropower, navigation, water supply, and fisheries. These water resources may be seriously affected by other economic activities. For example, agricultural or industrial chemicals may pollute drinking water. Soil erosion adds to the sedimentation of reservoirs and irrigation systems. Dumping urban wastes in rivers and coastal lagoons reduces fishery production, which provides food as well as income and employment. Yet few countries have effective policies or institutions for managing water and fishery resources.

Africa's unique wildlife is threatened in many countries by uncontrolled harvesting, poaching, and loss of habitat in both forest and rangeland areas. Large and diverse populations of wildlife are commonly found in marginal land areas, which offer relatively low returns to other forms of land use. Wild plants and animals provide subsistence resources. Their preservation is an important factor in food security and quality of life for rural communities. Some African countries can use commercially managed wildlife to generate significant economic returns (often in foreign exchange) from meat and processed animal products as well as from tourism. Involving local

Box 4.5 Bicycle transport: The "missing middle"

Transport services for hire are scarce in the rural areas of Africa, and long-range motor transport services on roads often operate only when the nearest market is open—once a week in some locations. This results in the paradox that in villages just outside cities locally grown produce is sold at low prices and still finds few buyers, while less than 10 miles away in an urban center fresh produce is expensive and hard to find. But few rural people can afford any form of transport, so almost all trips are made on foot, with rural women bearing the brunt of the transport burden. For the many who live away from available motor transport, a trip on a bus or a bush taxi still entails a long walk from the village.

Because of this lack of transport, a high percentage of commodities is back- or head-loaded. Consequently, transport consumes inordinate amounts of household time and energy. For example, a recent survey found that the average time spent by village households on transport ranged between 417 hours per person a year in Tanzania and 522 hours in Ghana. Women accounted for more than 70 percent of goods carried in Tanzania.

Intermediate forms of transport can greatly reduce the amount of time and human energy spent on carrying by back or head load, if both speed and payload are taken into account. Studies in northern Ghana demonstrated that a bicycle trailer could increase each person's capacity at least five times by enabling the rider to carry up to 440 pounds. A specially designed small handcart carries as much as 330 pounds, six times the maximum head load, and considerably reduces the potential for neck or spinal injuries. Ghana's Technology Consultancy Center is now promoting the production and use of such bicycle trailers and handcarts. Both vehicle designs have been adapted to local conditions. The project includes plans for credit lines and technical assistance for local firms to start manufacturing, assembling, and maintaining the vehicles.

communities in managing wildlife can help to reverse present destructive trends and yield both economic and ecological benefits.

Providing rural infrastructure

For the most part rural infrastructure is highly deficient. Improving rural infrastructure is an essential requirement for the modernization and growth of agriculture. Better market incentives to farmers will be blunted if the physical barriers and economic costs of transporting goods to and from local markets are too high (see Box 4.5). The development of roads in rural areas is crucial.

The construction and maintenance of rural roads should not depend on central road organizations alone. These are already overburdened by their responsibilities for main roads and are often far removed from the areas served by rural roads. Distinct institutional and funding arrangements for rural roads will be required. These should include the decentralization of some existing institutions, with the appropriate involvement of local communities, and the use of local contractors and technicians. Labor-intensive techniques can be used to keep costs down and to provide local employment (see Box 2.4).

Although rural infrastructure is an important requirement, agricultural development also needs the support of market towns. Most of the nonfarm activities could be carried out efficiently by the private sector, such as transport, trade, repair services, and the provision of consumer goods. The necessary infrastructure will have to be provided in local market towns. Health facilities and schools will also be needed (see Chapter 3). In setting priorities for infrastructure investment, the usual bias against rural and secondary town development must be corrected.

Developing farmers' associations and recognizing the role of women

The political and economic elite are more likely to take note of farmers' needs if farmers have their own organizations. These, if genuinely representative, constitute a step toward empowering local people. Group action is deeply rooted in African societies. Many groups already exist—for land management, for cooperative marketing and input supply, for savings and credit, and so on. Cooperatives in Africa have worked best when organized to market and process cash crops such as coffee and milk—crops for which a simple tech-

nology can provide substantial value added to distribute to members. Savings and credit cooperatives also work well. Cooperatives are generally unsuccessful when organized by government or if based on high-bulk, low-value commodities that are easily sold through private traders. To succeed, cooperation has to be voluntary and managed from below. Grassroots management is one way to ensure this. Alternatively, cooperatives can be based on customary social structures and groups, as they often are. Governments can, however, provide technical assistance, such as advice on accounting, legal rights, and technology. Laws that make it easier to set up or dissolve a cooperative are also helpful.

Women are perhaps the most important, and the most neglected, rural people. They are responsible for an estimated 70 percent of staple food production. In most African cultures women's rights and duties are complex. Women may be allocated fields (usually from their father's or husband's land), be responsible for specific crops and operations, and enjoy independent income from certain crops or, as in West Africa, from marketing. Often benefits of initiatives such as promoting cash crops, mechanization, extension, and resettlement flow to men, who manage these activities. Finally, as farms shrink through inheritance and population pressure and men turn to outside work and become part-time farmers, women increasingly manage the family farm. In many areas half of all farms are managed by women; in some, such as Congo, 70 percent. Women's agricultural workload grows while their traditional work burden in childcare, wood gathering, water fetching, and staple food pounding remains the same—or grows too. The burden on women means that land preparation, planting, and weeding are often delayed, which depresses yields.

African land rights that give women the use of land owned by a close male relative are being eroded as population pressure makes land more valuable. Land registration and land settlement schemes have usually resulted in husbands registering as sole owners. Without land titles or security of tenure, women's access to credit has been limited, thus making it harder for them to buy inputs.

There are several ways to help African women in agriculture. Where land is being registered, women's rights to their share of land during their husband's life and after his death should be acknowledged and protected. Even where communal tenure still prevails, women's rights should be formalized. The labor burden falling on women could be reduced—for example, by providing sources of water and wood closer to home. Fuel-efficient stoves can decrease time spent collecting fuelwood. Agricultural research and extension systems also need to be responsive to women's needs. Women farmers should be involved in on-farm research to make sure that the new varieties and technologies recommended largely correspond to their needs and constraints. Women's representation in agricultural training, currently only about 20 percent in Africa, should be brought closer to Asia's 50 percent. Male extension workers should be trained to be aware of women's roles, needs, and problems, and women should be selected as contact farmers in proportion to their numbers as farm managers. In many parts of Kenya women already make up one-half of all contacts of extension workers, many of whom say they find women more interested and committed than men. Women's groups need to be fostered. They could then be used, for instance, not only as contacts for extension services but also for channeling credit for the purchase of inputs. Finally, female education needs to be expanded, since farmers with higher levels of education have been shown to achieve higher increases in output from new technology.

Redefining land rights

The rights of African farmers over land vary between the extremes of communal and individual ownership. A commonly perceived paradigm of the situation runs as follows. Initially, when there was surplus land, rights were defined for groups rather than individuals. Within the groups, individual or family rights rest on elaborate traditions and customs, which serve to enforce group control over the use and disposition of land. To minimize social friction and to ensure the group's survival, the entitlement of individuals to specific tracts of land is transitory. As population increases and land becomes scarce, long fallow periods can no longer be relied on to maintain land fertility, and the transitory nature of land use rights fails to provide incentives for individuals to improve their land. Technologies to restore fertility require the investment of capital and effort, but must be adopted. Accordingly, farmers must be given incentives to change their ways. One important incentive is the right to permanently cultivate land and to bequeath or sell it.

Secure land rights also help rural credit markets to develop, because land is good collateral.

Since many countries (and regions) are at different stages of this transition, Africa has diverse and changing land rights. Agricultural modernization combined with population pressure will make land titling necessary. Traditional tenure systems need to be codified. Titles could also be provided to groups for collective ownership. The transition to full land titling will take time to achieve in most African countries and should be attempted only in response to demand by rural people. Nationally legislated land rights are likely to conflict with prevailing customary rights. Judicial mechanisms for dealing with disputes between owners claiming traditional versus modern land rights are urgently required. As with other actions needed for agricultural growth, the critical element in any new land policy will be the administrative capability to manage it.

Can the challenge be met?

The importance of an improvement in agricultural growth for Africa's development objectives, especially to achieve greater food security, cannot be overemphasized. Yet enormous internal and external difficulties must be surmounted. One constraint is Africa's lack of competitiveness. International markets for Africa's output exist. The challenge for Africa is to recapture them by becoming more competitive. For that African governments will need to undertake the whole range of policies described above, but especially those concerned with exchange rates, marketing, and technology. The target growth of 4 percent a year requires an increase in labor productivity of only 1 to 2 percent a year, because the labor force is itself growing. Land productivity must grow by at least 3 percent a year. Many other countries have achieved that sort of productivity growth in agriculture and thus have become competitive on world markets.

The domestic market for food already exists but is being partially met from imports. This market will expand with population growth, industrialization, urbanization, and improved food security programs. With appropriate policies domestic and export markets will be found to absorb a 4 percent increase in agricultural output. Africa cannot afford to stand still but must actively seek market outlets worldwide. Eliminating regional barriers in food trade would be an important step in this direction.

Africa's institutional weaknesses and its fragile and deteriorating physical environment are difficult problems. But if they can be remedied, then most countries in Sub-Saharan Africa could meet the 4 percent target for agricultural growth. Several countries did so for extended periods between 1965 and 1987—Botswana, Cameroon, Côte d'Ivoire, Kenya, Malawi, Mauritius, and Rwanda (see Box 4.6). Except for Côte d'Ivoire and Cameroon, these are countries in which the natural conditions were not particularly favorable. Indeed, at independence, countries such as Botswana, Malawi, and Rwanda were regarded as having little potential. Equally few people would have expected Ghana, Sudan, Uganda, Zaire, and Zambia to become agricultural failures. In the four largest countries (Ethiopia, Nigeria, Sudan, and Zaire), which accounted for 47 percent of Sub-Saharan Africa's population in 1986, agricultural production increased by 1.5 percent a year during the past two decades; this implies a decline in per capita production. Yet these countries (except per-

---

Box 4.6 Rwanda: A case of successful adaptation

Rwanda stands out among the handful of countries that have increased agricultural production faster than population. It has done so without the inequities that have sometimes accompanied development elsewhere or the land abundance of Côte d'Ivoire and, so far, largely without chemical inputs or improved varieties.

Food production in Rwanda grew at 4.7 percent a year between 1966 and 1982, while population grew at 3.4 percent. Rwanda avoided the urban bias so common in Africa. Government remained attentive to the farming majority in determining pricing policy, exchange rate policy, fiscal priorities, and effective rural institutions.

Market forces fixed the level of food prices, which rose by 10 to 17 percent a year during the 1970s; indicative prices set by government at a relatively high level were not enforced, but served as guidelines. A realistic exchange rate, coupled with an absence of excessive taxation, ensured that producers of the main export crop, coffee, received a high share of the border price. A parastatal company was in charge of grading and processing coffee, but purchasing was left to private merchants.

Within this enabling environment output grew largely because of spontaneous changes undertaken by farmers. The major source of production increase was an expansion in area, averaging 3.7 percent a year from 1966 to 1983. Part of this was into Rwanda's drier savannah regions, which had lower potential than its volcanic highlands. Much came from draining fertile marsh and valley bottoms. Many parts of the highlands now grow three crops a year, one in each of the two main rainy seasons, a third in the dry season.

There also have been shifts in production patterns. Bananas, grown mainly for fermentation into beer, declined from 62 percent of production by volume in 1966 to 48 percent in 1984. The share of cereals and legumes declined from 16 to 13 percent, whereas root crops, with their higher yield of calories per hectare, grew from 22 to 39 percent of production. As farm size grew smaller and fallows and fodder dwindled, there was a shift from cattle to smaller livestock; cattle numbers declined by 19 percent between 1970 and 1981; small livestock grew by more than 80 percent.

Rwanda is facing increasing constraints to expanding production. Virtually all cultivable land is already in use, except for the valleys of two large rivers, which could be opened up by expensive drainage schemes. Population is now growing at 3.7 percent a year. Fertility and birth rates are the highest in Africa, and the use of modern contraceptives in 1983 was less than 1 percent.

The average farm size in 1984 was only 1.2 hectares, and, as land is subdivided among male heirs, the size is dwindling with each generation. Already in 1984 more than a quarter of all farms occupied less than half a hectare. The practice of fallowing has virtually disappeared. Rwandan farmers have a long tradition of using organic fertilizers and mulches, but manure is in increasingly short supply as farms grow too small to provide fodder for cattle or sufficient mulching material. As a result the yields of some major upland crops—bananas, beans, coffee—have been declining.

Solutions that have worked in the past cannot be the solutions for the next generation. The population growth must be curbed. Agricultural strategy must focus now on intensification and on sustainable growth in yields, not on extension of the area or continued shifts into low-protein root crops.

The change has begun. Rwanda's program of soil and forest conservation has become one of the most effective in Africa. Thanks to a nationwide community tree-planting program, Rwanda now has more trees than it had at independence and has attained self-sufficiency in fuelwood. Soil conservation was first introduced by the Belgian colonial authorities. By 1960 more than 750,000 hectares were covered by antierosion ditches, but in the next decade most of the conservation works were abandoned or destroyed. Since 1973 priority has again been given to conserving resources, but efforts became intense only after 1980. At that time only 15 percent of farms were protected by terraces, infiltration ditches, or bands of deep-rooted fodder grasses along the contour. By 1985 coverage had reached 63 percent; the target is 100 percent by the end of 1989. New varieties (of potato, for instance) and the use of chemicals are beginning to spread. New maize and bean varieties have been identified. Fertilizer trials have given mixed results, but chemical fertilization is economically attractive for potatoes, sweet potatoes, and rice. But to spread new varieties and techniques, Rwanda needs to create an effective, responsive extension network.

Box 4.7 The growth of smallholder maize production in Zimbabwe

Zimbabwe's recent cereal production contrasts sharply with African trends. Per capita cereal production increased 80 percent and maize production doubled between 1979 and 1985.

Smallholders contributed most of Zimbabwe's post-1979 maize production gains. During the 1970s productivity was low, yields averaged one-seventh of those obtained by the commercial farming sector, and maize sales accounted for less than 5 percent of total deliveries to national markets. The war, lack of inputs (particularly seeds and fertilizer), and low prices hampered production. After 1979, however, maize production by smallholders tripled. Areas under cultivation increased more than 90 percent, yields doubled, and by 1985 smallholders produced more than half of the country's maize supply. Sixty percent of the production gains were marketable surpluses, and smallholder maize accounted for one third of total maize deliveries to the Grain Marketing Board.

This increase in production between 1979 and 1985 was facilitated by the rapid expansion of input and product marketing infrastructure, by an increase in the availability of credit, and by a rise in producer prices. Between 1979 and 1981 the government increased the real producer price by 80 percent and allowed the ratio of the producer price of maize to the price of fertilizer to rise by 50 percent. Although the real producer price of maize declined after 1981, the price ratio of maize to fertilizer did not fall as much. The government's Agriculture Finance Corpora-

tion also improved smallholders' access to credit, with about 10 percent of them receiving loans by 1985.

Improved technologies became available and were rapidly absorbed. Hybrids were developed for both high- and low-potential zones, and between 1979 and 1985 hybrid seed supplies to the smallholder sector increased fivefold. Fertilizer trials provided recommendations suitable to the agroecological conditions of the small farm sector; by 1986 fertilizer purchases by smallholders had increased by 400 percent.

Distribution of inputs improved as shopkeepers began to stock fertilizers, seeds, insecticides, and farm equipment. Fertilizer and agrochemical companies began to promote agricultural inputs with village-based sales and demonstration trials. Access to markets widened when the Grain Marketing Board expanded the number of collection points. Meanwhile private sector investors established buyer facilities authorized by the board and farm-to-market transport operations.

The Zimbabwean experience shows that if technologies are perceived as profitable and supportive agricultural services are available, smallholders will respond with increased production. Maize production grew because available technologies increased the profitability of maize above most competing crops. Production for the market expanded when producer prices increased and when market access improved. The market structure allowed private sector investments that complemented those of the government.

---

haps Ethiopia) have an agronomic potential that exceeds that of the successful countries.

If Botswana, Malawi, and Rwanda could achieve a 4 percent growth rate over an extended period, then it is only the shortcomings of policies and programs in other countries that prevent them from doing the same. A comparison of the more successful performers with the less successful shows that in almost every case the former pursued policies to promote the private sector, technology improvement, rural infrastructure, agricultural education, and in some cases land reform. These are the policies proposed in this chapter. Recent agricultural policy in Ghana, Guinea, and Zimbabwe has moved in the same direction, and agriculture has responded favorably (see Box 4.7).

Success will not be universal. In the countries with low agricultural potential—for instance in the Sahelian belt—higher incomes will come mainly from temporary, seasonal, or more permanent employment in agriculture and industry in neighboring countries. Such migration could be mutually beneficial (as discussed in Chapter 7).

Furthermore some countries will fail to adopt the needed reforms. Projections of agricultural growth in Sub-Saharan Africa made by various organizations are lower than 4 percent. The FAO, for example, predicts about 3.5 percent. A 3 percent growth rate would just keep pace with population growth. The 100 million people who are inadequately fed would grow in numbers, rather than diminish, unless food aid were greatly increased. No economic surplus would be available from agriculture to contribute to the development of industry and the social sectors.

In summary, the principal elements of an action plan to raise agricultural growth are as follows.

• The private sector, including cooperative and grassroots organizations, should be given a bigger role. Agricultural products should be freely marketed. Prices should reflect supply and demand to stimulate and regulate production. Private investment in production, agricultural processing, and farm input supply should be promoted, not constrained by excessive regulations and administrative controls or legislation. Rural financial intermediation by commercial and cooperative banks and credit unions should be encouraged, rather than hampered by government regulations.

• Intensive new efforts are required to strengthen the management of agricultural research at the national level, linked to streamlined national extension services. The international research centers and multicountry research networks need to focus a more intensive research effort on Africa. But the quality of agricultural training must improve for this to occur.

• The development and maintenance of rural infrastructure needs to be given greater attention, and beneficiaries should be involved in maintenance and operation.

• Environmental protection action plans for each country are needed to address issues of soil erosion, deforestation, and watershed management.

• Programs to assist women as farmers and traders require government assistance and encouragement. Women's groups should be fostered; they are good channels for providing extension and credit services in rural areas.

• Governments should assist the evolution of land tenure systems by providing legal and administrative mechanisms to ensure greater security of tenure.

This strategy differs significantly from present practice in most countries. Governments still manage agricultural prices, markets, and the supply of farm inputs; use parastatal rather than private credit and crop development agencies; emphasize large-scale rather than small-scale irrigation; and provide agricultural research, extension, and animal health services through separate donor-financed area or crop development projects rather than through coherent national programs. With some notable exceptions little attention is being given to the environment, to land tenure, or to enabling men and women in the rural areas to take full charge of their lives. Agriculture can become the engine of growth only if all this changes. More public investment in agriculture is not the critical factor. The key to success is to make the farm sector more productive through better policies and stronger institutions and, most of all, by developing people.

5

Industry, mining, and energy

Industry: Responding to markets

In Africa industrial growth will depend heavily on the success of raising agricultural output and incomes. Rising agricultural incomes would mean a growing demand for manufactures, and the availability of affordable consumer goods would give farmers an incentive to expand production. Industry can process surplus agricultural output and provide farmers with the inputs and equipment required to raise productivity. Savings generated by agriculture can be used to finance industry, and the labor released by rising agricultural productivity can be used to staff it. Agricultural exports will still be needed to pay for industry's growing import requirements while industry itself gradually generates more foreign exchange.

The challenge of industrialization

Since African nations gained independence, their labor forces have acquired technical skills and industrial experience—as workers, managers, and entrepreneurs. Indigenous businesses range from self-employed metalworkers making cookstoves from scrap metal in Kenya to a firm making paper from sugarcane waste in Ghana. African countries today export not only processed raw materials but also manufactures, such as garments from Madagascar and car radiators from Tanzania. The challenge is to build on this base to achieve the dynamic transformation of industrial structures envisioned by African leaders in the Lagos Plan of Action and the Industrial Development Decade for Africa.

For all the encouraging achievements, there have been setbacks. In the 1980s industry declined in many countries, partly as a result of poor agricultural performance, excessive dependence on imported inputs, and a growing crisis in foreign exchange earnings and debts. Too few businesses made appropriate use of local resources or built up industrial skills.

To stimulate an innovative and competitive spirit, three issues need to be addressed:

• *Expanding markets* by increasing agricultural incomes (and thus demand) and opening up interregional and overseas export markets

• *Creating an enabling environment* for industrial investment by providing reliable physical infrastructure and business services; improving financial intermediation; encouraging self-employment and small-scale businesses, as well as bigger firms; and facilitating competition by cutting red tape and rationalizing protection (among as well as within countries)

• *Building capabilities* by strengthening education, training, on-the-job learning, research, technology transfer, foreign partnerships, subcontracting, information, and business associations.

A future strategy

Africa's postindependence industrialization concentrated on creating physical capacity. Consistent with development theory at the time, it assumed that lack of capital constrained growth. Import substitution policies attracted foreign investment through protected markets. Agricultural taxation and foreign borrowing helped to finance public investment in heavy industry, which served a narrow market at high cost. The capacity created was not well adapted to local demand and supply conditions, and much of it cannot be sustained.

Modern manufacturing remains mostly small, stagnating at around 10 percent of GDP and 9 percent of employment between 1965 and 1987. Most industries remain isolated from world markets and new technology, with high costs relative to best-practice operations elsewhere. Protectionism has stimulated investment but not innovation to raise productivity or export growth to finance rising import requirements. The future lies in shifting industrial structure toward high-growth, competitive enterprises that are linked to the domestic economy. Reviving investment for this purpose will require restructuring or removing loss-making firms and substantial efforts to mobilize domestic and foreign investible resources.

At a meeting held in May 1989, African ministers of industry committed themselves to working with UNIDO and the ECA to prepare a new industrial strategy for the Second United Nations Industrial Development Decade for Africa. A consensus has emerged that this strategy must address functional issues, such as the underlying human, technological, and institutional capabilities, and not concentrate simply on creating or rehabilitating industrial capacity. A focus on building flexibility into the process by which industrial transformation occurs is less risky than promoting specific products; witness the various high-cost, underutilized steel, fertilizer, and automobile assembly plants across Africa.

The most successful newly industrializing countries (NICs), while protecting local markets, have gradually opened them to competition, provided export incentives, and identified the educational and technical skills that build a flexible labor force. In Africa this implies a shift from central planning to a market-oriented approach, from regulation to competition, and from failed attempts to transplant technology to systematic building up of capabilities.

The core of this strategy is the step-by-step acquisition of skills necessary to operate and adapt

new techniques. Industrial strategy in Africa has tended to overstress hardware (plant and machinery) and neglect training labor and management to master new technologies. Good working relations with international investors and marketers can help close the technology gap; this will require stable economic and political conditions to build confidence over time.

Each portion of the size continuum of African industry should be allowed to develop its strengths. Despite official neglect, the informal sector has played a dynamic role in providing income-earning opportunities and serving the demand of the low-income population for inexpensive manufactures. Small- and medium-scale enterprises (SMEs), however, tend to be under represented (the "missing middle," discussed further in Chapters 1 and 6). SMEs can adapt techniques to local resources and products to changing niche markets at home and abroad. They also build the technical, managerial, and entrepreneurial experience necessary to expand the large-scale sector efficiently. Regulatory reform and institutional support would help informal and SME firms as well as large-scale industries, to grow.

As the experience of the NICs has shown, growth can be accelerated by penetrating export markets. It helps industry to transform by infusing new technology and competition and by enabling some industries to expand beyond the domestic market. In contrast, overvalued currencies and import substitution policies have discouraged investment for export in Africa. Subregional markets can provide an important stepping-stone to international competitiveness, as well as build regional self-reliance. With more favorable policies and agricultural growth around 4 percent a year, it should be possible to raise industrial growth gradually to an average of 7 percent a year for Africa, with some countries doing better.

Each country must combine these strategic elements according to its particular circumstances. Low-income, agrarian, landlocked countries such as Burkina Faso, Burundi, Chad, Malawi, Mali, Rwanda, and Uganda are likely to emphasize the links between industry and agriculture. Countries in the earliest stages of industrialization will be looking to build a foundation of education, skills, and infrastructure to support future industry. Nontraditional export markets could be exploited by the more industrially advanced nations, such as Côte d'Ivoire, Ghana, Kenya, Nigeria, Senegal, Zaire, Zambia, and Zimbabwe.

The current state of industrial development

During the colonial period manufacturing was mainly in export processing (for example, in Cameroon, Côte d'Ivoire, Ghana, Nigeria, and Senegal); bulk low-value consumer goods (particularly in settler colonies, such as Kenya and Zimbabwe, but also in Ghana, Mauritius, Nigeria, Senegal, and Zaire); and light engineering linked to mining (in Zaire, Zambia, and Zimbabwe). In the 1960s, when independence and protective policies prompted international trading houses to produce consumer goods locally, expansion took off. During the 1970s direct state investment in heavy industries dominated capacity creation (for example, in Côte d'Ivoire, Ghana, Nigeria, Tanzania, and Zambia).

The initial results were promising. In Sub-Saharan Africa during the 1960s manufacturing value added grew at more than 8 percent a year— nearly double the rate of GDP growth. By 1965 manufacturing exceeded 15 percent of GDP in 12 countries (Botswana, Cameroon, Chad, Côte d'Ivoire, Ghana, Kenya, Madagascar, Mauritius, Senegal, Togo, Zaire, and Zimbabwe) and by 1973 in 6 more (Burkina Faso, Ethiopia, Mozambique, Rwanda, Swaziland, and Tanzania). Production became more diversified in the number of products, although consumer goods remained dominant. The share of intermediate goods industries rose in the 1970s from about 30 percent to around 40 percent, mainly through investment in oil refining in a few countries.

Stagnation, not transformation

The 1970s, however, showed that simply substituting local for imported consumer products brought neither economic independence nor technical efficiency. The import substitution industries depended heavily on imports for inputs, spare parts, and equipment and were vulnerable to shortages of foreign exchange as export commodity prices fell and oil prices rose. The growth of manufacturing value added in the low-income African countries fell to 2 percent a year in the first half of the 1970s and was negative in the second half. In the middle-income oil importers it fell from 8 to 4 percent a year between the two halves.

Only oil exporters were able to sustain the growth of manufacturing during the 1970s—at 9 percent a year. Although manufacturing grew at 11 percent a year from 1980 to 1986 in China and India and 5 percent in other low-income economies, it was virtually stagnant in Sub-Saharan Africa, and its 10 percent share of GDP was barely higher than in 1965.

"De-industrialization"—a decline in manufacturing output—occurred in 10 countries during the 1970s and in another 11 in the early 1980s. Among the most seriously affected were Benin, Ghana, Liberia, Madagascar, Mozambique, Tanzania, Togo, and Zaire. Some reported capacity utilization rates below 30 percent. Installed industrial capacity was susceptible to underutilization because of:

- Constricted demand from falling real incomes and stabilization measures
- Unsuitable scale, design, or cost, particularly in some public investments
- Shortages of foreign exchange to support import-dependent industries
- Poor maintenance and lack of spare parts, resulting in the total deterioration of some capacity.

Policies such as heavy protection, extensive regulation, and directed investment contributed to these problems and to more fundamental ones, such as weak links to the domestic economy, high costs of production, and lack of incentives to raise productivity. Attempts to promote particular industries have foundered because success depends on much more than product category. Whereas passenger car assembly plants have consistently proven uneconomic, for decades lorry bodies constructed on imported chassis have provided without official support efficient vehicles for transporting passengers and goods.

The public sector's ability to operate efficiently those investments that it retains clearly will influence overall industrial performance for some time. Governments are likely to remain involved in decisions on major new industrial investments, whether or not as a direct investor. But many governments are downplaying their proprietary role to avoid several tendencies of a centrally directed approach that have run counter to the long-run objectives of industrialization:

- Political rather than economic criteria guiding investment choice, location, and management
- Regulation and wage controls that raised unit costs and undermined competitiveness

- High costs passed on to downstream users of the output of heavily protected and inefficient basic industries

- Expatriate entrepreneurs and managers removed before qualified nationals were available to take their place

- Private investment crowded out where the state controlled profitable monopolies.

An import substitution strategy can be combined with competitive pressures to ensure efficient production, as in the NICs. Few African industries have so far been able to raise productivity enough to graduate from infancy to become international competitors. There are several differences between African countries and the NICs.

- The domestic market size is relatively small, which makes it difficult to foster competition and efficient size for that market alone.

- The construction of capacity was not accompanied by the development and application of knowledge and skills, whereas most NICs systematically infused literacy, numeracy, sciences, and engineering through their education systems.

- Domestic competition was forestalled by regulating new investment, whereas the NICs used domestic competition and export incentives to make firms reduce costs if they wanted to survive and grow.

- Imports were reproduced using transplanted techniques and equipment, without sufficiently adapting the technology and product design to local conditions and materials. The NICs often produced a simpler version for the domestic market before upgrading it for export markets.

World trends in technology and information

Technological innovation and competition in world industry has accelerated in the past decade, thanks partly to the use of computers. Production processes need to be flexible to respond to high-profit opportunities. Access to market information and global marketing networks is needed for an industry to grow rapidly. Cheap labor and economies of scale are less important than prompt information—and response.

To take advantage of this global market, African industry will need links with foreign partners and stronger incentives to export. In Mauritius the buildup of industrial skills, good external con-

---

Box 5.1 Mauritius' success in export-led industrialization

Manufacturing played a small part in Mauritius' sugar-based economy before independence in 1968. Low income and small size offered little opportunity for efficient import substitution.

After independence, export-oriented manufacturing and tourism were identified as potential sources of growth, along the lines of small Asian economies such as Hong Kong, Singapore, and Taiwan. The Export Processing Zone Act of 1970 aimed to attract domestic and foreign investors in export processing. Its incentives included tax holidays on retained earnings and dividends, duty-free imported inputs, free repatriation of capital and dividends, flexible employment, and land and factory space. Exchange rate and wage policies also were designed to ensure the profitability of export-oriented production.

The results in the 1970s were impressive. Industrial investment quadrupled in a few years and was financed largely through profits from the buoyant sugar industry. Real GDP grew at an average annual rate of around 10 percent during the first half of the 1970s.

Manufacturing growth halted in 1979–82, however, as the decline of sugar prices, the second oil price shock, and worldwide recession generated serious financial and economic imbalances. The government responded rapidly with short-term stabilization measures, exchange rate adjustment, trade policy reform, and an effective incomes policy to hold down labor costs. Other measures to revive industrial exports included bilateral agreements to avoid

double taxation of dividends, an export credit guarantee scheme to protect commercial banks against default, duty drawbacks for new exports from firms oriented toward the domestic market, and export promotion abroad.

These adjustments coincided with the emergence of capital from Hong Kong searching for investments abroad, pushed by political uncertainties in the colony, and seeking alternatives to countries in which the growth of textile exports was constrained by quotas. Industrial investment surged in 1983--84, with the number of export-processing industries increasing from 195 in 1984, to 408 in 1986, and to 586 in 1988. Led by woven and knitted garments, manufactured exports grew at 30 percent a year and overtook sugar as Mauritius' main export (see Box table 5.1).

Box table 5.1 Composition of Mauritius' exports, 1970–88
(percentage)

	1970–71	*1980–81*	*1987–88*
Sugar	93.5	60.0	33.9
Export processing zone	..	32.6	61.2
Other	6.5	7.4	4.9
Total	100.0	100.0	100.0

Source: World Bank data.

tacts, and supportive fiscal policies and infrastructure allowed garment exports to expand phenomenally in the mid-1980s (see Box 5.1). On a smaller scale Botswana, Madagascar, Malawi, and Mozambique are following this strategy.

Vertical integration into domestic basic industries is less important for successful industrialization today. Reduced bulk transport costs have fostered integration across national boundaries. Products ranging from sweaters to computers involve processing and component assembly in different countries.

Unless Africa can take advantage of these global trends, technology and information gaps could widen. As world producers raise productivity, the costs to African consumers of protecting industries with outmoded technologies will increase. For example, blast-furnace steel technology requires large-scale production and incurs high costs; some countries have achieved high efficiency in steel "minimills." Key elements of an effective strategy for technology acquisition for Africa include obtaining good technical advice on suitability, adaptability (especially using intermediate technology), and design; providing effective management of the technology transfer process; and training workers to apply it.

Positive developments on which to build

Experience demonstrates that African industry can compete on world markets. In Tanzania an automobile radiator producer uses Indian technology and trainers to develop small-scale but efficient production; more than 10 percent of output is exported to neighboring countries, India, the Middle East, and the United Kingdom. A Botswana garment manufacturer sells its fashion designs in London and New York. Côte d'Ivoire exports cocoa products and chocolate from unexportable beans. A state-owned engineering firm in Zambia has rectified bus design flaws with minimal assistance from the foreign supplier. Nigeria exports cloth, Senegal plastics, and Kenya jewelry and basketry.

African industry has often taken advantage of market opportunities and adapted to locally available materials. Small enterprises in Nairobi turn waste-packing materials into low-cost housing. Firms in Côte d'Ivoire and Ghana can specialty foods for Africans overseas. A firm in Zimbabwe exports custom-made parts for old automobiles to Europe. When imports were unavailable in Ghana, local distillers used molasses instead of sugar, and mechanics learned to make automobile spare parts and water pumps.

Some countries have started to improve the policy environment for sustained, efficient industrialization and for private entrepreneurs to play a bigger role. Removal of price controls and more flexible exchange rates have reduced the risk that profits will be squeezed by arbitrary decisions. Import liberalization in, for example, Ghana, Kenya, Madagascar, and Nigeria has reduced scarcity rents, increased access to needed inputs, and forced monopolistic firms to cut costs to compete. Improved agricultural prices have raised both rural demand and the supply of raw materials in countries ranging from Guinea to Zimbabwe. Government withdrawal from industrial ownership in countries such as Côte d'Ivoire, Guinea, and Togo has opened opportunities for private investors and created the potential for greater efficiency through increased competition.

These measures, however, often involve politically painful choices and do not guarantee an adequate supply response. The future strategy should attempt to create the complementary market and supply conditions needed to transform industrial structures successfully.

Opening up market opportunities

To revitalize industry and to sustain manufacturing growth at 7 percent a year in Africa requires building, seeking, and responding to domestic, regional, and overseas demand. Policy changes are needed to link industrial production closely to domestic product and input markets and to orient firms toward exports. Backward linkages will then stimulate the expansion of competitive, domestic intermediate and capital goods industries and supporting services.

Domestic demand

One objective for the Second United Nations Industrial Development Decade for Africa in the 1990s will be to reorient manufacturing industries toward serving the needs of the three-quarters of Africa's population found in agriculture. Even in the mining economies of Botswana, Zambia, and Zimbabwe agriculture (which provides only 3 to 12 percent of GDP) accounts for more than half the labor force. The potential demand represents a powerful engine of growth, if it can be met at affordable prices.

Past industrialization based on import substitution has fostered large firms catering to urban demand, with little regard for cost. The rural population has a relatively high propensity to spend increased income on simple, inexpensive products of local, small enterprises. Besides clothing and furniture they need inputs and equipment to increase productivity. Women need tools, food-processing equipment or services (such as corn milling), and devices to lighten household work, which would release more time for agricultural production and other income-earning activities.

Small enterprises are meeting these needs. Since Africa's agricultural population is spread widely and transportation is poor, small-scale producers using local materials often have advantages over centralized mass production. Low incomes make low cost and serviceability more important than standardization, and payment terms can be negotiated between buyer and seller. Stimulating the growth of rural income and recognizing the complementary role small manufacturers can play in an economic development strategy centered on agriculture would help start the engine. Removing barriers to growth and competition by these firms will also encourage large firms to raise productivity. Additional measures are needed to facilitate subcontracting and other relations between larger and smaller firms; such links have helped improve SME technical capabilities in Asian countries.

Rising agricultural incomes will also generate demand for mass production goods. In the towns rapid migration ensures continued growth in demand for such products; but firms serving this market have grown inefficient behind excessive protection. They will find it hard to adjust as protection is lowered unless they can reduce costs by, for example, exporting to neighboring countries to raise capacity utilization.

Although informal enterprises producing for low-income earners do not provide a major share of GDP, they make a significant contribution to the long-term growth of output by building up the seedbed of experienced entrepreneurs from which the "missing middle" can emerge, grow, and generate the successful investors and managers of larger enterprises in the future. Less restrictive regulations would facilitate the dynamic process of informal firms becoming SMEs.

The exchange rate is a key tool for linking industrial growth more effectively to domestic supply. Incentives to use local suppliers are few when currencies are overvalued and duties on imported inputs are low. Until Ghana liberalized foreign exchange markets, the large soap factory imported vegetable oil because it had access to import licenses at the official exchange rate, whereas small soap producers used local palm oil because it was cheaper than the parallel market rate for imports. Devaluation favors substitution of local labor and inputs in which the country has a comparative advantage; it also favors the growth of activities that use local resources intensively, including agriculture.

Regional markets

Regional integration in Africa (discussed in more detail in Chapter 7) is important for the efficient development of many intermediate and capital goods industries, because few countries have a big enough internal market to achieve adequate scale and competition. Investment for a multinational market requires both competitive costs and stable trade policy regimes.

Neighboring countries can provide an outlet for excess capacity and experience for tackling larger overseas markets. A Zambian garment firm survived the collapse of its domestic market by exporting uniforms to Tanzania and the Federal Republic of Germany, by drawing on the experience and contacts of its German partner (see Box 5.2). Kenya's breweries have moved from neighboring to overseas markets. The role of African entrepreneurs in developing regional export markets can be expected to increase the more easily they can travel and transfer their foreign exchange earnings.

Liberalizing trade barriers against African manufacturers can help underutilized and overprotected firms to adjust by increasing markets and competition, without exposing them too quickly to international competition. Some firms might be unable to compete with those in neighboring countries. Others would—and consumers would benefit from lower prices. At present some manufacturers export informally through traders rather than through official channels, where costs often exceed any benefits. Although difficult to achieve, an across-the-board approach to trade liberalization is more likely to be effective than product-by-product negotiations in creating new trade and

Box 5.2 A Zambian-German joint venture

After a promising start in Zambia's domestic garment market, Serioes Ltd., a Zambian-German joint venture company founded in 1973, was hit by shrinking domestic demand and restrictions on imported inputs in the late 1970s. To overcome this, Serioes searched for markets abroad. It emerged as a strong exporter by exploring a niche in the international market—military and airline uniforms. The company was successful because of its entrepreneurial ability to find a market niche, its managerial skills to achieve competitive costs and quality, and technology transfer through training.

The firm produced men's wear, sports clothing, uniforms, and ladies' wear. Its output soon reached all of Zambia and adjoining countries, and the company expanded into retail clothing.

The company's manager, a Sri Lankan, was flexible in adjusting to African conditions. Together with the high-quality equipment came training on the factory floor by experienced German technicians. This training ensured technology transfer rather than technology acquisition, and it enabled local staff to replace expatriates at the middle and higher levels of management.

Contraction in the domestic market and lack of foreign exchange for imported inputs led Serioes to lay off 50 percent of its workers in 1983. The founder's accumulated experience in production and exporting led him to seek a specialized niche to survive. Building on an initial sale of military uniforms to Tanzania, the company marketed uniforms in other African countries and recently broke into the German market. Another niche was found by supplying airline uniforms.

Serioes' success shows how a foreign partner can be a key catalyst, bringing together the experience, vision, technical skills, managerial competence, and creative marketing necessary for an African company to find a niche in a highly competitive international market.

---

developing compensatory mechanisms to deal with the possible adverse effects on some firms.

Overseas markets.

The rate of industrial growth that rising agricultural productivity and increasing urbanization can sustain within national and even regional markets is limited. Although penetrating new markets overseas is a difficult and lengthy process, it offers a critical means to accelerate industrial output growth and foreign exchange earnings, especially in

* Processing exportable raw materials, which has suffered from a policy bias against exports
* Handicrafts, although this market suffers from the vagaries of fashion
* Other niche markets that offer high returns from meeting specialized demand (such as wooden toys and tropical fruit juices)
* Standardized products, in cases in which local labor and costs meet the requirements of international producers or buyers (such as knocked-down furniture from Ghana).

Successful, diversified export development requires a realistic exchange rate policy, a supportive and stable policy environment, and time for investors to respond. Liberalizing foreign exchange markets can have some immediate effects, as in the recovery of Ghana's timber and pineapple exports, but the case of Mauritius shows the importance of policy flexibility over time (see Box 5.1, above). Positive policies include promotional measures such as export financing schemes and processing zones. Meanwhile increased manufactured exports for many countries will come mainly from first-stage processing of exportable raw materials. Although such processing can increase value added, countries must be careful to avoid the danger of turning high-quality raw materials into medium-quality processed products. Converting nonexportable-grade raw materials into exportable semiprocessed products is a promising innovation (for example, chocolate from Côte d'Ivoire).

Countries looking for rapid growth of standardized or niche market products should expect foreign entrepreneurs to play a significant role, as in the case of the Zambian-German uniform exporter (see Box 5.2, above). Taiwan's success derived partly from direct investments and subcontracting by American and Japanese firms. Bangladesh expanded garment exports rapidly after workers learned skills and technology from a Korean firm and went into business for themselves. Côte d'Ivoire's success with chocolate exports was achieved through the technical and marketing expertise of the French partner. More developed countries can encourage such developments by lowering their tariff and nontariff barriers.

To reduce Africa's dependence on foreigners, partnership agreements should be designed to ensure training and technology transfer (as discussed below). African entrepreneurs should be encouraged also through a less restrictive and more supportive policy environment. A Malagasy woman's success in exporting children's clothes to Europe was achieved through improved incentives and without outside support (see Box 5.3).

Creating an enabling environment

To sustain relatively rapid industrial growth, African entrepreneurs must respond to improved domestic demand and export incentives. In the past domestic competition has been constrained by restrictive licensing, direct allocation of credit and foreign exchange, price controls, selective investment incentives, and complex administrative requirements. In some cases public policy has even been hostile to private investment. Governments can help by

• Deregulating to encourage competitiveness
• Rationalizing distortions in the structure of protection
• Investing in infrastructure (and taking other measures) to reduce the high costs of doing business
• Improving access to credit.

Mozambique has shown that major changes in the policy environment can be achieved quickly. In two years the government has switched from a centrally planned, price-controlled economy to one in which even state-owned enterprises operate on a commercial basis in a liberalized market environment with a competitively valued currency. This policy and the reduced labor cost in

dollar terms have induced a Hong Kong firm to establish an export joint venture with a state-owned garment maker.

Competition policies

Future industrial policy must go beyond market incentives. Governments need to back them up with drastic changes in regulations and their implementation. Measures to make the business environment more positive and competitive (discussed further in Chapter 6) include:

• Eliminating restrictive licensing of capacity for most industries and facilitating legal status for smaller firms
• Automatic investment incentives based on eligibility criteria and consistent with employment and efficiency objectives
• A well-administered legal framework that enforces contracts, facilitates asset transfers through bankruptcy, and establishes property rights
• Labor laws and policies that protect workers' rights without hamstringing firms.

Rationalizing protection

Protection has been a source of industrial profits and incentives to invest but has also fostered uncompetitive behavior. In many countries past policies have permanently shielded industries both

---

Box 5.3 Madagascar exports high-quality children's clothing to Europe

Madagascar's traditional skills in embroidery and the competitive edge provided by devaluation have enabled a Malagasy woman to penetrate the European market for high-quality children's clothing. Two years after moving from interior decorating into embroidered tablecloths, she was exporting more than $1 million of children's clothing and tablecloths to Europe.

Embroidery is a well-known art in Madagascar. To provide high-quality embroidered tablecloths to her clients, the young interior decorator hired women to work in her backyard in 1986. She also had dresses made for her daughter, and they attracted favorable attention during a visit to Europe. In 1987 she presented a line of high-quality embroidered children's clothes at a salon in Paris. She chose classic designs that change little over time and emphasized the perfect finishing to cater to the highest end of the market. By choosing this niche, she could minimize her dependence on fashion trends.

Her ability to compete in international markets, especially against Philippine exporters, was enhanced by

Madagascar's major devaluation in 1987. Her business mushroomed on export orders, and within two years she was employing 300 women. Faster growth might have been possible had bank financing been available, although the owner is reluctant to overextend her operations.

Virtually all the primary inputs are produced locally, including cloth manufactured from domestic cotton. In the absence of adequate cardboard packing, she adapted traditional baskets woven from natural fibers to protect the clothes in shipment. After becoming president of the garment exporters association, she negotiated with Air Madagascar to reduce air freight rates to Europe, which had been much higher than those from Europe to Madagascar.

The government helped by making exports more profitable and by simplifying procedures. The local entrepreneur responded by adapting available skills and materials to a specialized international market. In this case the capabilities existed and lacked only a favorable environment and marketing acumen to add considerable value.

from import competition, through tariffs, quantitative restrictions, and foreign exchange rationing, and from domestic competition, through restrictions on new entry. Import restrictions generate scarcity rents that enable firms to survive despite low capacity utilization and negligible foreign exchange savings, such as automobile assembly plants in Kenya, Nigeria, and Zambia. A patchwork of quantitative restrictions, high tariffs on some items, and exemptions on others for selected firms and government agencies has created a distorted pattern of protection.

The challenge is to balance protection, which nurtures domestic industries, with competition, which forces firms to innovate, raise productivity, and reduce costs. Although industrialization normally involves business failures as markets and productivities change, much African industry has been insulated, at a heavy cost in lost efficiency and high prices to consumers. The costs of dislocation in terms of lost output and employment when firms are suddenly exposed to competition also can be high. The gains from lower costs and new growth may come only slowly and only to firms that can survive and adapt to greater competition.

Quantitative restrictions make protection excessively high, variable, and hard to calculate. When imports are restricted (or tariffs high), the price consumers pay for the scarce goods rises to the point at which people risk smuggling. Substituting exchange rate adjustment and moderate tariffs for quantitative restrictions and very high tariffs reduces smuggling, increases revenues, and makes the level of protection transparent. Ghana shifted imports to legal channels and raised revenues by liberally issuing licenses for prepaid imports and imposing on them a 20 percent up-front tax. Exchange rate adjustment also helped increase official imports by reducing the gap between official and parallel exchange rates.

Tariff collections, lower than high nominal rates would suggest, have averaged about 13 percent of the value of imports during the 1980s for 35 countries. Only Madagascar and Sudan averaged more than 20 percent for 1984–86 (compared with 14 countries in the 1970s). Chad, Guinea, Guinea-Bissau, Mali, Tanzania, Uganda, Zaire, and Zambia had average collections of less than 10 percent in 1986. These rates are lower than the average of all nominal rates because:

• Official imports tend to be concentrated in low-duty capital and intermediate goods

• Government agencies and many firms are exempt from duties on inputs

• Restricted and highly taxed imports enter clandestinely or under the guise of lower-duty items.

When duties are high on consumer products and low on inputs, firms can profit from the difference by importing the inputs and incorporating them into a protected product. There the protection on the value added (which is the "effective rate of protection") can be very high, and sometimes the real costs can exceed the benefits. Many countries have assembly industries in this category. When tariffs and import content vary widely, so do the rates of effective protection. A Zambian study, for example, showed that in 1975, 24 percent of its consumer goods had effective protection rates above 500 percent, while 17 percent were penalized by negative effective protection; for intermediate goods, only 5 percent had rates above 500 percent, and 30 percent had negative effective protection. The resulting distortion of investment incentives toward the most highly protected products (often consumer durables and luxuries with high duties for revenue purposes) helps explain the bias of industrial structure toward the upper-income urban market. The very high rates of protection explain why many firms could survive despite severe inefficiency and even foreign exchange losses.

A more uniform tariff structure would reduce interindustry distortions in incentives by eliminating differences between inputs and outputs. Guinea shifted from a complex system of multiple duties to a dual rate, with a standard 30 percent and a lower rate for basic necessities such as pharmaceuticals; luxuries are now subjected to an additional excise tax on both imports and local production, which is a desirable shift toward consumption taxes for raising revenue.

Tariffs on inputs generally ought not to be raised, however, to avoid penalizing export industries by making them pay more than the world price for inputs. Although drawback or rebate schemes theoretically can compensate for taxes paid, up-front temporary waivers or tax credits to exporters work better.

The key issues are how to reduce excessive protection and give firms sufficient time to adjust and how long to carry firms that fail to reduce excessive costs. High protection should be lowered gradually enough for firms to adapt through rehabilitation investment, changes in product line, and cost-cutting measures. Governments can assist by ensuring that finance and technical assistance are available. Exchange rate adjustment can help replace reduced protection, although it will increase the financial requirements of firms that depend on imported inputs. Devaluation of the naira enabled a Nigerian tire producer to offset increased competition in the domestic market by exporting to neighboring countries.

¸Once they have established a reasonable schedule for lowering high tariffs and eliminating exemptions and quantitative restrictions, governments should avoid selective protection, so resources can be released to growth industries. Adjustment policies stimulate industrial growth when supported by liberalized access to imports (see Box 5.4).

Overcoming the high costs of production

African firms often invest in transport for materials, goods, and workers. Poor road systems raise the cost of maintenance. Small firms without vehicles have difficulty reaching beyond their local

---

Box 5.4 How adjustment programs have affected the industrial sector

Adjustment programs initially have both positive and negative effects on industry, and the net effect varies widely by product and firm. Devaluation raises the profitability of import substitutes, as well as exports, and higher agricultural prices raise rural demand for basic consumer goods and farm inputs. But stabilization measures dampen overall demand. Lending in support of adjustment relieves the foreign exchange constraint and improves the access of firms to needed inputs, but liberalizing imports increases competitive pressures on inefficient firms.

Industries that faced imported input constraints or that could export have responded positively to adjustment measures. Industries that were highly protected and depended on imported inputs were most likely to suffer. The overall effect has been positive, according to evidence from countries in which industrial output switched from decline to growth, so long as the adjustment efforts have been maintained (which was not the case in Côte d'Ivoire or Zambia) (see Box table 5.4).

Manufactured exports responded strongly to improved incentives, and overall output grew in all cases, albeit from a small base. Devaluation in several countries led to increased utilization of local inputs, and export-processing industries, such as timber and cocoa, have revived. Much of the increase represents the recovery of export markets and the expansion of existing operations, for example, in textiles from Ghana and Nigeria to neighboring countries and in cocoa products from Côte d'Ivoire and Nigeria to Europe. More firms are seeking export opportunities, including new export products such as garments from Madagascar and glycerol from Ghana.

Capacity utilization rates improved significantly and rapidly, partly because lending in support of adjustment eased the constraint on imported inputs. The average utilization rate in Nigerian industry increased by about a third to 40 percent, mainly in consumer goods industries. The intermediate and capital goods industries, however, were adversely affected by the reduced protection, and firms with 66 percent import content have utilization rates below 50 percent. Adjustment policies appear to bring the strongest competitive pressures on large, highly protected, often public enterprises in basic industries. For instance in five of Zambia's less-efficient parastatals capacity utilization fell from 56 to 25 percent.

In some countries labor costs have become more internationally competitive as a result of devaluation. Hourly compensation in dollar terms fell in Madagascar to $0.29 in 1987, as against $0.40 in India and $1.89 in Hong Kong, which induced some Hong Kong firms with garment operations in Mauritius to invest in Madagascar. Some large-scale firms have responded to increased competition and relaxation of labor regulations by reducing employment to cut labor costs. Expatriate labor was cut back sharply as devaluation made foreign labor more expensive. However, Nigeria's experience suggests that employment may rise in smaller firms that previously were less affected by restrictions on excess labor.

Structural shifts within industry are being induced by adjustment policies as highly protected, import-dependent firms contract and exports and the processing of domestic inputs increase. Industrial output as a whole—exports in particular—improved in the short term in adjusting countries, but domestic demand must be revived to sustain the recovery and ensure long-term growth.

Box table 5.4 Growth in manufacturing output, exports, and capacity utilization before and during the reform period in Sub-Saharan Africa
(percent a year)

Country	Output		Exports		Capacity utilization	
	Before	During	Before	During	Before	During
Côte d'Ivoire	−1.8 (81–83)	5.8 (84–86)	− 6.9	12.3	..	..
Ghana	−17.1 (80–83)	15.0 (84–87)	−10.4	51.0	19	32
Nigeria	−7.8 (82–85)	0.2 (86–87)	− 15.4	18.1	30	40
Zambia	−3.1 (82–84)	4.0 (84–86)	5.4	7.2	38	54

Source: World Bank 1989g.

market. In Nigeria an unreliable electricity supply has led virtually all larger firms to invest in backup generators to avoid temporary shutdowns. Extractive industries and others outside large towns have to build housing for their workers. A comprehensive approach to industrialization should include public infrastructural investment (see Chapter 2) and other measures to lower some of these costs.

Some infrastructural investment by firms justifies compensatory assistance, such as subsidies or tax credits. Extractive and processing industries, such as mining, timber, and vegetable oils, help to open up rural areas. Many cases also exist in which high costs have been imposed by political decisions. Many of Nigeria's steel mills are far from both their ore supplies and their market. Ghana's attempt to develop an integrated shoe industry foundered partly because the shoe factory was located far away from the tannery and the main urban markets.

Without local suppliers of spare parts and repair services, maintenance of equipment is costly. Firms either must carry an excessive stock of spares or risk curtailing production while awaiting air shipment of parts. Development of the parts industry has generally been discouraged by cheap imports and the concentration of protection on consumer goods and basic industries (raising the cost of materials to intermediate industries). Devaluation in Nigeria has already led firms to switch to maintenance instead of replacement.

The ideal is domestic production of equipment that suits local conditions and can readily be repaired. An Indian entrepreneur has designed simple, durable grinding equipment for cassava and maize in Ghana. Zimbabwean agricultural equipment is exported to neighboring countries with similar soil characteristics. When imported equipment is purchased, the ability of local technicians to service it and produce spare parts should be considered.

Equipment leasing companies could help solve technical and financial problems of SMEs. They could achieve the economies of scale needed to develop technical and repair facilities that would be beyond the ability of individual firms. By leasing equipment, firms could overcome the difficulty of obtaining credit to purchase machinery and could ensure that foreign suppliers pay attention to the suitability and servicing of their equipment. Cameroon, Côte d'Ivoire, Gambia, Kenya, Malawi, and Tanzania have extended the hire-purchase system to investment goods and have

encouraged leasing companies. To follow suit, other countries may have to modify their legal and tax frameworks.

Financial intermediation

The financial system in Africa, like the size distribution of firms, suffers from a "missing middle." The commercial and development banking system serves large, well-established customers, often at subsidized rates of interest. Microenterprises can usually be established from family savings and can get credit if needed through informal mechanisms, although at very high rates. But new investors in SMEs have little access to the investment capital required, and small enterprises languish for lack of working capital at reasonable rates.

Financial systems have worsened with economic decline and often with adjustment policies that suddenly increase the funds firms need to repay foreign loans or import inputs. When Ghana raised the official cost of foreign exchange by a factor of 10 in one year, the banking system was not prepared to handle the increase in credit needed for firms to utilize increased foreign exchange for imported inputs. Now Ghana has begun to restructure its financial sector. So too have Cameroon, Guinea, and Madagascar (see Chapter 8).

Efforts are also needed to link formal financial institutions with informal credit mechanisms. Even poor, self-employed persons can meet much of their modest investment needs through savings. Credit unions, *tontines*, and *susu* groups could form a basis for credit from formal financial institutions or provide business capital, perhaps through nascent capital markets (see Boxes 4.2 and 6.3).

Building industrial capabilities

Acceleration of industrial capacity growth will be wasted unless the capability to design, manage, and use it is also improved. Both the failures and the successes of industrialization are often traceable to a flaw or flair in entrepreneurship, management, or technology.

The lack of domestic industrial entrepreneurs and private capital led most African governments to approach industrialization by courting foreign investors and by investing in state-owned industries. Domestic entrepreneurial energies followed more profitable opportunities in informal activities and other sectors. Even so, the pool of entrepreneurial talent and experience has greatly expanded. Releasing this talent is critical to industrialization (see Chapter 6).

Improving technical and managerial capability is important to raise productivity and move from small- to medium- and large-scale modern enterprises. Although many countries have a surplus of well-educated labor, they do not always have the middle-level technical and supervisory skills needed. "Africanization" programs by foreign firms tend not to give local managers sufficient responsibility for decisions. Nevertheless some countries, such as Ethiopia, have succeeded in building competent management. Good production engineers in Kenya and Zimbabwe enable textile industries to operate closer to international best practice than those in Somalia and Tanzania. Better education and on-the-job training efforts are needed to raise the supply of good African professional managers and engineers.

Both public and private investors need technical advice on project feasibility, design, alternative technologies, sources of equipment, specification, and technology transfer. Examples in which inappropriate technology resulted in unsustainably high operational costs include a fertilizer plant in Benin, a denim factory in Côte d'Ivoire, a steel mill in Nigeria, and a shoe factory in Tanzania. Adapting product design, equipment, and production processes to local needs and resources requires skilled technicians and management, as in the case of a firm producing automobile radiators profitably in Tanzania.

Development of technical capabilities in these areas varies with the complexity of the technology, market opportunities, and labor participants. The key to building these capabilities is to identify functional skills that can be adapted to different applications.

Education and training

The approach to education and training in Africa, with foreign assistance, has emphasized bricks and mortar rather than the "software" of teaching methods, programs, equipment, and practical experience. This is particularly true of formal education. Expanding general education can enhance the productivity even of informal entrepreneurs, many of whom have little or no education. At the lowest level, literacy and numeracy would help. Inclusion of elementary bookkeeping skills in the curriculum would assist graduates who end up in business for themselves. In middle and secondary schools, basic technical, bookkeeping, and managerial skills, including hands-on experience, would help prepare the majority who will not enter professional occupations.

Some advanced professional skills, such as accounting and engineering, may justify higher education programs. Some that are industry specific (for example, textile design and electronics) should be supported by the industry by, say, endowing a professorship. Industry associations also can set up training institutes, with manufacturers providing tutors, as the Sri Lanka textile industry has done to improve its export potential.

The possibilities for formal education, however, depend on scarce budgetary resources. A large share of technical training is provided informally through the apprenticeship system, especially in tailoring, carpentry, metalworking, and vehicle repair, although governments hitherto have had little to do with this system. On-the-job training, one of the weakest areas in African industry, is the means by which workers assimilate technology (See Box 3.9). Overseas training in firms for managers and technicians exposes them to the best practices in organizing production, quality control, marketing, and distribution. Expatriate technicians working alongside the trainees can be effective if training is practical and responsibilities shared. The government can assist by easing regulatory constraints on expatriates and by providing fiscal incentives for training programs. Nigeria and Zaire offer rebates (funded by a small payroll tax) to firms that institute in-house training.

Science and technology

Countries that have universities and research centers can adapt them to serve industry better. Laboratories should seek contract work for manufacturing enterprises. Adapting products and technologies to the local environment should be a priority. For example, the Technology Consultancy Center of the University of Science and Technology in Ghana has worked extensively on using local materials in construction.

National standards bureaus should not only regulate, but should help firms improve standards and quality control. Côte d'Ivoire provides a testing service for agricultural machinery. Korea's experience suggests that industry may benefit from establishing its own quality control centers, especially to break into export markets.

Governments can support technological research and development in firms. State agencies may be able to assist trade associations by providing information and contacts with counterparts and suppliers overseas. Fiscal incentives are needed for firms to set up their own research and quality control units, paid for by tax credits or industry taxes. Firms should also develop salary and incentive structures that encourage innovations to enhance productivity and the promotion of the technically astute.

Transferring technology from industrial countries to Africa has not been very successful. Effective technology transfer requires technicians who can teach what they have learned from experience and local technicians to absorb and apply it. The NICs can offer fruitful partnerships, since they have recently gone through a process of learning and adapting technology. Mauritius' export success has been catalyzed by entrepreneurs from Hong Kong. Technical assistance from Taiwanese equipment suppliers enabled a Ghanaian entrepreneur to overcome foreign exchange scarcity by making toilet paper from bagasse (waste sugar cane from local distillers).

Linkages

Efforts should be made to promote linkages among industries to enhance the spread effects of industrial growth and to facilitate the transfer of technology and skills. A firm in Zimbabwe has designed agricultural equipment that is suited to local conditions and can be manufactured from domestically produced steel. In Côte d'Ivoire a large shoe manufacturer shifted to marketing shoes made on contract in small, more cost-effective firms set up by former employees. With subcontracting, larger firms train their suppliers in technical skills, procurement, and quality control. Industry associations can help by finding local suppliers and putting them in touch with buyers. An exchange rate and tariff environment that favors local sources is a necessary precondition. Direct assistance can be provided to subcontractors on both legal and technical aspects.

Consultancies are important for technology transfer. Governments should foster the growth of consulting agencies, especially in the private sector by, for example, using domestic consultants as much as possible and by encouraging foreign technical assistance agencies to work with local counterparts.

Developing industrial capabilities is self-reinforcing, with different elements interacting to support each other; the rate and continuity of economic growth affects the speed of development. Sustained rapid growth permits basic education and training to expand and allows new technologies to be deployed faster. It also permits firms to take the long-term risks involved in research, development, and training. Basic research in scientific institutes and applications in industry are needed to adapt technologies and processes to local conditions (see Box 5.5).

Meeting the challenge

The role of government implied by the strategy outlined above differs significantly from that followed since independence. Instead of directing industrial development, governments would be facilitators. Regulatory actions would be confined to only a few overall concerns, such as protecting health, the environment, and the banking system. Government efforts would concentrate on building the institutional and human resources that enable entrepreneurs to respond to market opportunities. They would provide adequate infrastructure and basic education, maintain supportive technical and training institutions, assist industry associations, and ensure that the legal and financial systems function smoothly.

In time the increasing vigor of the private sector and the constrained budgets of the public sector will greatly reduce the latter's share of industry in most countries. But public sector restructuring is a difficult and lengthy process in countries that have decided they can no longer subsidize loss-making state enterprises. The first step is to divide public firms into those that are viable; those that can survive only on a short-run, sunk-cost basis and that the government wishes to divest; and those that need to be closed.

Closing down firms is a difficult political hurdle. But the middle group poses more complex issues. Some expenditure may be needed before buyers can be attracted. As in Guinea, private sector buyers may demand special concessions that are anticompetitive. Nigeria is trying to offer shares in state enterprises to the public, but this approach is less feasible in smaller countries. Meanwhile the public sector can try to improve efficiency by setting policies, guidelines, and performance criteria and leaving managers free to

Box 5.5 Ghana's Suame Magazine: Building indigenous engineering capabilities

Small-scale industries in Ghana have shown resilience and growth since the early 1970s. The informal sector proved particularly resourceful in surviving the economic crisis of the late 1970s and early 1980s. Under the economic recovery program initiated in 1983, the informal industrial and service sector has been a springboard for import-substituting, labor-intensive technological innovation. Efforts are under way to improve institutional and financial conditions so that entrepreneurship and industrial technology can develop.

An example of ingenuity and entrepreneurship is "Suame Magazine" in Kumasi—about 5,000 craftsmen working in makeshift sheds. The mechanics in these small garages and workshops repair and rehabilitate old vehicles and machinery and transform scrap materials using relatively primitive tools. As much as 80 percent of Ghana's aging vehicle fleet is serviced and rebuilt through these informal garage complexes, in which specialists perform the mechanical, body, electrical, and other work.

These mechanics learned to make vehicle and machinery spare parts that were unavailable during the economic crisis. They have flourished under the economic recovery program because the 100-fold increase in the official price of foreign exchange since 1983 has made imported spares relatively expensive and because liberalization of imports has increased the availability of inputs and tools.

The government has supported these indigenous engineers through technology services, training, and credit. The Technology Consultancy Centre of the University of

Science and Technology has operated in Suame Magazine for more than a decade through its Intermediate Technology Training Unit. The Centre now operates with little government funding. The government has extended the training unit concept nationwide through an innovative organization, Ghana Regional Appropriate Technology Industrial Services, which provides on-site training in product development. This organization and the Centre research and develop appropriate technology and the use of local materials in important areas such as agricultural implements, intermediate transport, and building materials. They also provide advice to entrepreneurs in developing new products.

Training through institutions such as the Kumasi Technical Institute is popular and effective. Through its IDA-supported Transport Rehabilitation Project, the government is providing training to upgrade the skills of mechanics in informal workshops and to teach them basic accounting and management methods.

The government has also helped to establish a pilot program to provide credit to small operators in complexes like Suame Magazine. Recipients include a mechanics' cooperative established to purchase and share equipment, such as lathes and crank-shaft grinders. The National Garage Owners Association guarantees the loans, which are provided through the Social Security Bank on commercial terms. Averaging about $3,000, the money has already helped small mechanics make significant gains in quality and competence.

---

manage. Operating by competitive rules is more important than outright ownership.

Privatization offers a unique opportunity to build up industrial capabilities by bringing in outside technical assistance to advise on and assist in rehabilitating potentially profitable enterprises. But privatization is not the only way forward. Partnerships and management contracts with foreign firms are alternatives; they should be designed in a way that maximizes the transfer of technical skills and know-how. In Senegal, Belgian investors who took over a defunct state agricultural machinery plant were able to diversify the product line into metal components for construction and to export half the production to neighboring countries. Likewise in Togo an American investor rehabilitated a former state steel rolling mill, changed product lines, and now exports within the region.

Government attitudes toward regulation must change in many countries for a competition-driven strategy to work. They can encourage private investors to take up the slack left by failed public industries by making entry and exit easy

and free from political risk. But private industry will be inefficient unless there is constant pressure from domestic competitors and imports to stimulate cost-cutting innovations.

Strategic choices, policy instruments, and industrialization paths will vary by country. Mining and petroleum will stimulate associated industries and influence trade policies in countries such as Angola, Cameroon, Congo, Gabon, Nigeria, and Zambia. In low-income agricultural countries initial growth is likely to occur mainly in industries based on growing rural demand and agricultural inputs, including textiles, basic furniture, and hand tools. In time these will be able to diversify into a wider range of industries.

Some countries, for example, Ghana, Madagascar, Senegal, Zaire, and Zambia, face difficult transitional problems in industries that were established under heavy protection. Like Côte d'Ivoire, Kenya, Mauritius, and Zimbabwe, these countries have the experience and skills to expand nontraditional exports to neighbors and overseas, if export policies are favorable and regional markets are more integrated. Nigeria has the size to develop industries with significant economies of scale but has to ensure that technologies and location permit efficient production.

The strategic elements suggested here are only inputs into decisions that each country must make according to its circumstances. Four important themes stand out for each country's strategy:

• Industrial structure must transform in response to market opportunities, both domestic and foreign; it cannot be determined by supply-side decisions.

• To avoid a widening gap with the rest of the world, industry must become competitive. For this countries need to acquire from foreign partners technical know-how and market intelligence.

• A positive environment for private entrepreneurship, which involves minimal control through regulation and investment in complementary services, is essential to permit a competitive, innovative response to opportunities, especially in smaller firms.

• The key to an efficient, well-adapted industrial structure is the gradual, time-consuming process of building entrepreneurial, managerial, and technical capabilities through education, research, and, above all, on-the-job training and experience.

Mining prospects

Minerals: A mixed blessing

Africa is well-endowed with minerals (including oil). The potential of this resource, however, has only begun to be realized in most of Sub-Saharan Africa. For many countries relative mineral abundance has been a mixed blessing. Often the increased revenues generated have been dissipated and high debts incurred, leveraged on the mineral wealth. Massive distortions in incentives made possible by mineral revenues have hindered the development of agriculture and industry. The result is that some countries with developed mineral sectors have grown no faster than those without. Liberia and Niger, for example, each have substantial mineral sectors but have experienced negative annual growth rates in GDP in the 1980s.

World mineral markets are inherently volatile. Recurring periods of boom and slump have had a severely disruptive effect on economies dependent on minerals. Only Botswana has established effective mechanisms for building savings during mineral boom periods to help offset the economic shocks that arise during lean periods (see Box 8.1).

Africa presently needs the risk capital and technical expertise of the transnational mining companies to help unlock its mineral wealth. In the past, relations with foreign companies have often not been well managed. At the same time foreign companies have not always dealt fairly with their host countries in sharing the revenues of profitable mines. Moreover foreign companies have frequently withheld information and paid too little attention to training nationals for senior positions and building links between the mines and the local economy.

Mineral production could (and should) become an important source of growth in many African countries. But this potential will not be fully realized unless a mutually beneficial partnership is established between government and investors. Such a partnership should incorporate management and technical training. A policy framework must also be put in place that ensures that mining revenues are used to promote sound long-term development and that systematic steps are taken to build African capacity to develop the mineral industry.

Potential and importance

Geologically, Africa's mineral potential is equal to, if not greater than, that of other continents. West Africa, for example, is geologically similar to Brazil, where there has been a mineral boom—especially in gold, tin, and iron ore—during the past 20 years. The southern African countries have much in common geologically with South Africa, where mineral production increased strongly in the 1970s and 1980s. Evidence suggests that Sub-Saharan Africa has potential for high-value minerals—gold, diamonds, and other gemstones; industrial minerals; and rare earths. These can be developed over relatively short periods, without the massive investments for infrastructural support required for bulk minerals.

Botswana's diamond deposits are among the richest in the world. Guinea has some of the world's highest-quality bauxite reserves, and its iron ore deposit at Mifergui Nimba is exceptionally high grade. Ghana has considerable potential in gold, as do other countries (such as Burkina Faso, Mali, and Sudan) in the precious metals. Another major gold belt has recently been found in southern Ethiopia, while western and northern Ethiopia contain promising mineral belts that

Figure 5.1 Value of mineral exports in Sub-Saharan Africa

(1987 dollars)

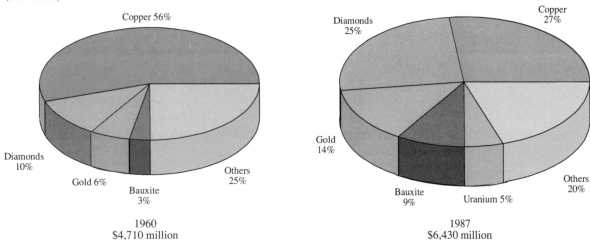

Note: Prices deflated by manufacturers unit value (MUV) index. Bauxite includes alumina and aluminum.
Source: World Bank data.

have been barely explored. Zimbabwe has platinum potential. The copper ore in Zaire and Zambia is generally three to four times higher grade than that in North America and is frequently rich in cobalt. Zaire not only has copper reserves sufficient for 40 years, but has the world's richest undeveloped copper deposits at Tenke and Fungerume.

Despite limited progress in exploiting this potential, mining already plays a significant role in Sub-Saharan economies. Excluding South Africa, they produce about 5 percent of the world's mineral resources, the major ones being copper, diamonds, gold, uranium, and bauxite (see Figure 5.1). Zaire and Zambia together produce 74 percent of the world's cobalt and 15 percent of its copper. Nine other Sub-Saharan countries account for more than 40 percent of world diamond production. Guinea is the world's second-largest bauxite producer, Sierra Leone the second-largest rutile producer. Zimbabwe is the third-largest producer of asbestos and Gabon the third-largest manganese producer. Africa also mines significant quantities of uranium, chromite, iron ore, nickel, lead, zinc, phosphate, and cadmium. African mineral output is important to the world's nuclear, aerospace, steel (titanium), oil (platinum and alloys), precious metals, and abrasives industries.

Mining contributes to foreign exchange earnings and fiscal revenues. Exports (excluding oil and coal) averaged roughly $5 billion a year from

Table 5.1 Contribution of mining to selected Sub-Saharan countries in 1987

Country	Mining exports (dollar million)	Mining exports as percent total exports	Mining value added as percent GDP	Mining taxes as percent total taxes
Botswana	1,420	90	44	55
Zaire	1,266	73	24	37
Zambia	836	93	15	7
Zimbabwe	609	43	8	..
Guinea	584	92	21	82
Niger	290	80	8	13
Liberia	217	58	14	..
Ghana[a]	159	19	2	..
Gabon	120	9	3	..
Mauritania	127	31	12	2
Sierra Leone	113	74	13	67
Togo	87	29	7	11
Senegal	65	9	2	2
Burkina Faso	50	20	3	..
Total	5,943	55	12	20

Note: Mining includes smelting and refining.
a. Excludes aluminium.
Source: World Bank data.

1980 to 1987—representing about 30 percent of non-oil exports (and around 14 percent of total exports) for the region. With improved prices for minerals in 1988, mining exports exceeded $8 billion. Mining makes a noteworthy contribution to 14 economies in Sub-Saharan Africa by contributing 55 percent of exports, 12 percent of GDP, and some 20 percent of fiscal receipts (see Table 5.1).

Figure 5.2 Mineral production in Sub-Saharan Africa, Asia and Latin America and the Caribbean

Billions of 1980 dollars

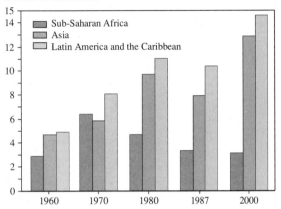

Note: The data are actual and projected gross values for aluminum, copper, iron ore, zinc, nickel, lead, tin, bauxite, alumina and gold.
Source: World Bank data.

Past experience

The late 1950s to early 1970s was a period of growth and diversification for African mining. Big new mines were developed, including bauxite in Guinea, manganese in Gabon, iron ore in Liberia and Mauritania, copper and nickel in Botswana, asbestos and nickel in Zimbabwe, uranium in Niger, and phosphate rock in Senegal and Togo. Copper and cobalt production was expanded in Zaire and Zambia, and diamond production in Zaire. Many of these new mines were joint ventures between government and private sector operators and owners.

In contrast, during the past 15 years new investment has been modest, save in Botswana. As a result Africa has lost its market share in many metals and minerals, including copper, tin, chromite, and diamonds. Foreign investors have shown little interest in new investments in Africa, and state mines have generally been limited at best to sustaining investments to replace depleted reserves. The low level of private investment has slowed diversification away from these traditional minerals into more profitable precious metals and industrial minerals. As a result, since 1970 the value of African production of 10 major minerals has declined by 2 percent annually in real terms, whereas that in Asia and Latin America has grown. Based on presently known investment plans, the divergence between Africa and the other two continents will increase in the 1990s unless new initiatives are taken (see Figure 5.2).

Mining investment has been held back by restrictions on ownership, cumbersome regulatory procedures, unattractive taxation arrangements, and unstable macroeconomic performance. Witness Zambia and Zaire, which previously dominated Africa's mining exports. Zambian mining has declined since it was nationalized in 1969; in Zaire state mining has been adversely affected by government intervention. Zambia and Zaire both have large copper ore reserves, but their share of world mine production has declined from 24 percent in 1960 to 15 percent in 1987.

In the past two or three decades there have been few significant mineral discoveries in Africa. In contrast, large deposits have been discovered and developed elsewhere—copper in Chile, base metals and tin in Brazil, bauxite in Venezuela, gold in Papua New Guinea, and industrial minerals, gold, and diamonds in Australia. The lack of new discoveries in Africa is not because mineral prospects are poor, but because insufficient exploration has taken place.

During the past decade half of the world's expenditures for mining exploration and development has been for gold. The bulk has been in Australia, Canada, and the United States—which provide a combination of good resource potential, strong local investors, and attractive investment incentives for both local and foreign investors (especially in Australia and Canada). Developing countries that have good gold potential and provide attractive incentives to private investors—such as Brazil, Chile, Indonesia, Papua New Guinea, and the Philippines—have also shared in this boom. Except for Botswana, Sub-Saharan African countries have missed out. Even where there has been gold or diamond development—in Burkina Faso, Ghana, Guinea, and Zimbabwe—the projects have been generally small and the investments modest.

Higher investment in prospecting

Mining depends on high-risk investment in exploration. Companies mining base metal ores typically spend 1 to 5 percent of annual sales on exploration, some even more. For precious metals and other minerals with faster market growth, exploration expenditures are usually much higher. For example, in 1987 Australia produced $2.1 billion of gold and spent $280 million—or approximately 13 percent of sales—on exploration. Canadian mineral production in that year was roughly $15 billion and exploration expenditure around $900 million. With an estimated annual production of $5 billion in Sub-Saharan Africa, an annual expenditure of at least $250 million on exploration would seem to be justified; in fact, it is running at only about $100 million. Considering the long lead time between discovery and production (typically 5 to 15 years), this shortfall threatens to condemn Africa's industry to little better than stagnation.

The reason for the low level of investment in exploration can be traced to the early 1970s. As state control of the big mining operations increased, many international mining companies retreated from Africa because they preferred to do business in countries such as Australia and Canada or in other developing countries—such as Brazil, Indonesia, and Papua New Guinea—in which the investment climate was more conducive to high-risk capital.

State mines have generally failed to mobilize the investment funds necessary to maintain a steady growth of production. Constant political intervention in mine operation and management has jeopardized efficiency. Given the heavy indebtedness of many mining-dominated economies and their overdependence on mineral exports, state mining production has become insensitive to mineral market conditions; high-cost mines have failed to improve efficiency and have continued in production even when making losses. Profitable mines have been strapped for exploration and development funds because revenues have been channeled elsewhere, with little provision for reinvestment. Most African states have been unwilling (or unable) to establish joint ventures with international mining companies, and few have had a private sector strong enough to take up the slack.

The stagnation in Africa's mining is due not only to low investment, but also to management deficiencies, shortages of technical skills, an unsupportive policy environment, and political interference. Sub-Saharan countries, however rich in resources they may be, are free market competitors; if the investment climate does not attract the financial resources and technical expertise of the big mining houses—either directly or in joint ventures—African mines will continue to stagnate. Guinea's strong bauxite mining sector (from which it derives more than 90 percent of its export earnings and more than 80 percent of its public revenues) is due to effective collaboration with its foreign partners when the rest of its economy was in disarray.

Past experience indicates that, as a general rule, expenditure of about $100 million annually on exploration leads to the discovery of two small- to medium-size economic deposits. On average a new mine for such a deposit will require an investment of around $60 million and can be expected to result in an annual value of output equal to the cost of developing the mine. Although it will take time to reestablish investor confidence, it should be possible to double Africa's present level of exploration investment within the short to medium term and to raise it to between $400 million and $500 million during the next 10 years. This should enable mining sector output to grow progressively and to reach a growth rate of 5 percent a year by the late 1990s.

An enabling environment for mining

Unlike Australia or Canada, mining companies in Africa face difficult infrastructural problems and high exploration costs owing to the need for technical expatriate staff, imported equipment, lack of local contractual services, and the absence of support facilities. However, there are better chances of discovery in Africa. Most of the easy-to-find deposits elsewhere are already being mined.

Setting in place the conditions for the long-term recovery of the sector will require a partnership between private mining companies, which can provide the capital, management, and technology needed to revitalize the mining sector in Africa, and host governments, which can create a conducive investment environment that also protects the interests of the country. Successful cooperation depends on recognizing reciprocal obligations and the equitable sharing of benefits. Taking a minority interest in new ventures is sufficient for governments to keep abreast of mine developments and protect the national interest. All this will require African governments to rethink their roles and their policies for the mining sector. The main elements of an enabling environment relate to the foreign exchange regime, taxation, repatriation of profits, and the regulatory and institutional framework. By financing specialized advisory services, the donor community could help African governments to negotiate technically sound and fair mining agreements.

Exchange regime

Since most mineral production is for export, mining profitability is sensitive to exchange rate policy. It can be quickly eroded by currency overvaluation—as happened to gold mining in Ghana in the early 1980s. Overvaluation provides a powerful incentive for gold and gemstones to be smuggled through neighboring countries, as were Zaire's diamonds in the early 1980s. Furthermore mine performance can be hamstrung by inadequate access to foreign exchange. Mines require imports of spare parts and materials and of capital goods to replace or expand capacity. Shortages of foreign exchange contributed to the difficulties of the Zambian state mining company in the 1980s, and restricted access to foreign exchange in Zimbabwe has held back mining investment in recent years.

Fiscal regime

Equitable and stable tax arrangements are crucial to a durable partnership between private investors and the state. Investors require a return that justifies their capital investment; governments expect a share of the profits to compensate for the use of national assets and to ensure that mining will contribute to economic development. Tax formulas can be negotiated case-by-case to take account of the special circumstances of individual projects. What is vital in building long-term investor confidence is scrupulous respect for agreements reached.

Repatriation of profits

Foreign investors will be unwilling to risk money—hundreds of millions of dollars for large projects—unless there are ironclad assurances that they can repatriate earnings. This may involve not only legal agreements between investors and government, but also the use of offshore trusts to service foreign loans, pay suppliers, and provide for dividends and capital recovery to the foreign investor. Given the high risks and large investments involved, such exceptional arrangements are justified.

Regulatory and institutional framework

The importance of stability and transparency extends to the rules governing access to land, the granting of exploration licenses and mining rights, mine development agreements, and management, marketing, and export arrangements, which are normally regulated in a mining code, as are mine safety and environmental standards. Investors need to be sure of their legal title to mining properties and will look for simple and objectively applied labor regulations. In short, private investors look for explicit, well-specified, nondiscretionary regulations that are broadly in line with industry standards worldwide. It is not a question of removing necessary controls, but rather of reassuring investors that the controls will not be implemented arbitrarily.

Even with a sound regulatory framework investors may still hold back if the mining sector institutions are too weak to ensure the sector's orderly administration or to assist prospecting through the systematic acquisition of basic geological and mineral exploration data. In most countries the government's mining and geological survey departments need to be strengthened. Improving technical and managerial training is critical to strengthening the role of Africans in developing the sector. Mining, like all industries, also needs good transport infrastructure and efficient utilities and other support services. Too often these are lacking, which adds considerably to the costs of mine operations.

Future prospects

Recent weakening demand for traditional minerals (iron, lead, and copper) is balanced by a new trend toward high-technology products (lightweight alloys, ceramics, and rare earths). For the next decade or so demand for traditional metals is expected to grow at 1.5 to 2.5 percent a year. For some chemical industry metals and other industrial minerals the rates could be much higher. The mining industry will continue to face a volatile world market. The African mining industry will have to be ready to adapt to new opportunities with the production flexibility to take advantage of booms and the technical efficiency and financial strength to endure slumps.

A resurgence in Sub-Saharan mining will depend on governments putting in place the necessary enabling environment and attracting international mining companies who will need to see Africa as a place in which the political risks are not prohibitive. For example, exploration by private companies has picked up in Ghana following a more promotional mining and investment code introduced in the mid-1980s (see Box 5.6), and

Box 5.6 A revival of gold mining in Ghana

At independence Ghana was the leading gold producer in West Africa, with an output close to 1 million ounces a year. Production dropped steadily for two decades and hit a low of 277,000 ounces in 1983 owing to currency overvaluation, numerous barriers to private investment, and a lack of funds for public investment in the sector. Ghana's gold mining industry has the mineral potential to recover to, and even exceed, the past peak level of production. The government has made increasing gold production a key objective of its economic recovery program.

The government's strategy has been to encourage investment in the mining sector by reforming the policy environment. In 1986 the government introduced a new, coherent mining code; taxation rules; and a regulatory framework to attract private investors. A Minerals Commission now negotiates foreign exchange access and fiscal arrangements according to well-defined procedures, uniformly applied, and issues leases and exploration permits.

These measures reinforce macroeconomic reforms—most notably a significant exchange rate adjustment—by attracting foreign capital and, at the same time, badly needed managerial and technical expertise. In this way improvements in mining and recovery technology, such as heap leaching, already widely utilized elsewhere, have been introduced to Ghana.

The government's new approach is already paying off. Gold production is expected to reach about 400,000 ounces in 1989—about 50 percent above the 1983 low point. In mid-1988 Southern Cross Mining, owned 70 percent by private investors and 30 percent by the State Gold Mining Company, opened the first new gold mine in Ghana in more than 40 years, and production is currently running at about 36,000 ounces a year and is likely to expand. Three other mines—Canadian Bogosu Resources, Ghanaian Australian Goldfields, and Teberebie Goldfields—each owned 90 percent by the private sector and 10 percent by the government, are expected to begin operation in the next two years. Other new gold mines are in various stages of exploration and planning. Finally, Ashanti Goldfields, another private sector-government joint venture and the largest and most profitable gold mining company in Ghana, has almost completed a major expansion to increase its mostly underground production from 280,000 ounces in 1987 to 400,000 ounces a year by 1991. It is also about to start a second expansion project to produce an additional 100,000 ounces a year from surface deposits by 1993. By that time Ghana's gold production could exceed 1,000,000 ounces a year and will continue to grow into the next decade.

foreign mining companies have recently negotiated exploration licenses or mine development agreements in Botswana, Guinea, Madagascar, Mali, and Zimbabwe. They are also in various stages of negotiation in Burkina Faso, Liberia, and Tanzania. The success of these early initiatives may prove critical to the resurgence of mining in Africa, since other companies, less willing to venture into new territory and less familiar with Africa, will look for successful examples before taking the plunge themselves. The alternative approach—state mining companies using hired expertise, with the country itself bearing all the risk—has performed poorly in the past and is best avoided.

During the past three decades investments in existing mines in Africa have declined. This trend should be reversed. Most large mining projects are generally designed with a life of 20 to 25 years. As the mine ages, investment is needed to prove new reserves, replace aging plant and equipment, and open up new mining areas. Long-term sales contracts may also need renewal. Many of the larger mines developed in the mid-1960s and early 1970s are now entering this phase. If the work is not done, there may be unnecessary mine closures. The decline of copper production in Zambia, for example, is partly due to lack of funds for adequate reinvestment, and the future of bauxite mining in Guinea will depend partly on investments in the early 1990s.

The value of world mining production is expected to increase from about $140 billion in 1987 to about $200 billion by 2010 (in 1987 prices). Provided an enabling environment is established, a production growth rate rising to 5 percent a year in real terms in Africa should be possible between 1995 and 2010. Sub-Saharan Africa might then increase its share of world production from about 5 percent now to around 8 percent by 2010—or $16 billion in exports (in 1987 prices). This growth rate would require annual capital expenditures of $1 billion a year from 1995 to 2005—on top of spending necessary to maintain present levels of production, which would largely have to come from private companies. This would be a substantial increase above present investment levels but is by no means impossible if the right policies are now put in place.

African countries should be able to attract high-risk capital for exploration and development from foreign mining companies. The improving macroeconomic environment in many countries and the willingness of some governments to promote and encourage new foreign investment have helped to stimulate renewed interest in African mining.

Mining investors generally take a 10- to 20-year view of a prospective investment and look not only at the ore body, location, market prospects, technical risks, and cost competitiveness in relation to other projects, but also at the investment environment of the host country—political stability, macroeconomic prospects, exchange rate risk, access to foreign exchange, ability to repatriate profits and dividends, and taxation arrangements.

In this situation multilateral and bilateral agencies may have a valuable catalytic role to play. Even marginal participation can help to guarantee fair conditions; provide governments with an independent, expert assessment of investment proposals; and assure mining companies of an atmosphere in which sound concession agreements can be negotiated.

Energy for growth

Inadequate and unreliable energy supplies have contributed to Africa's slow growth during the past three decades, and the increasing demand for household woodfuels is leading to chronic deforestation. Ways must be found to overcome these problems if Africa's economies are to grow.

During the past 25 years consumption of commercial energy in developing countries has risen in step with GDP growth. Assuming the same is true for Africa, commercial energy production will need to expand by about 5 percent a year if Africa's economies are to achieve the targeted annual growth rates of 4 to 5 percent (see Table 5.2). This implies that commercial energy supplies would increase sixfold between 1986 and 2020, with a total investment rising from around $2 billion in 1990 to $4.7 billion in 2000 (at 1989 prices)—equivalent to 2 percent of GDP. By subsector, electric power generation should expand sevenfold, natural gas tenfold, and solid fuels (coal and lignite) about threefold. The balance of commercial energy needs would be met by petroleum products.

Natural energy resources are abundant in Sub-Saharan Africa; an energy growth rate of 5 percent would consume only a fraction of the known oil, gas, coal, hydro, and geothermal resources. Known petroleum reserves are, for example, equivalent to 120 years of supplies in the region at the current rate of consumption, and it is believed further exploration will reveal many more reserves. Africa's vast hydro resources have an estimated gross potential of about 300 gigawatts, less than 4 percent of which has been developed. Known reserves of natural gas are equivalent to 250 gigawatts of electricity—20 times current installed hydropower capacity and 5 times the hydropower that could be tapped economically during the next 30 years. However, unequal distribution of resource endowments, large transmission distances, and the size of markets impose limits on the supply development that is feasible. Africa faces formidable obstacles to realizing its potential and to securing the economic energy supplies needed to sustain growth.

The environmental costs need to be carefully considered in formulating energy strategies. Dam construction for hydropower floods forests and agricultural land. The production, refining, and transport of petroleum can pollute air and water. Hydrocarbon combustion releases carbon dioxide into the atmosphere—contributing to the "greenhouse effect" now threatening the earth's climate.

Environmental regulations for the energy sector need to be established, their implementing institutions strengthened, and appropriate pollution control technologies adopted. Gas releases only about half as much carbon dioxide as coal per unit of energy and contains fewer pollutants, so its exploration and development should be increased wherever possible.

Greater energy efficiency in industry, households, commercial buildings, transportation, and

Table 5.2 Total primary energy supply projections in Sub-Saharan Africa
(mtoe)

Energy source	Actual		Projected 2020
	1960	1986	
Commercial			
Petroleum	5.6	24.0	140
Natural gas	0.0	3.0	30
Power[a]	0.5	3.0	20
Coal	3.5	4.0	10
Subtotal	9.6	34.0	200
Woodfuels	..	66.0	200
Total	..	100.0	400

mtoe = million tons of energy equivalent; percentages are of total primary energy supplies.
a. Hydro and geothermal.
Source: UNSO, *Energy Statistics Yearbook.*

the power sector both save money and, by reducing the growth in energy consumption, slow the growth in the emission of "greenhouse" gases. Several countries (such as Senegal) have mounted successful programs to assist high-energy-using enterprises to adopt more energy efficient technologies. Policies must be designed to accelerate the rate at which energy efficient technologies are adopted.

The cornerstone of any energy efficiency program is a pricing system that reflects the economic cost of providing power. Underpricing electricity not only encourages higher consumption, but also critically impairs the operating revenues of utilities. Marginal cost pricing of electricity could help ensure the long-term financial equilibrium of utilities and provide the resources for expansion to meet demand (see Chapter 8).

Long-term strategies for sustainable growth in energy supply should include research and development of renewable resources such as solar, wind, biomass, and small-scale hydro. Small-scale, decentralized energy generation from these resources might be particularly useful in the rural areas, where electrification can have an impact on agriculture and rural industry, as well as living conditions. Alternative fuels, such as those derived from biomass, can be utilized in small-scale industry and transportation.

A 30-year perspective

The energy sector covers noncommercial primary energy sources (mainly woodfuels) and commercial energy (petroleum, natural gas, hydroelectricity, coal, and some geothermal). Renewables (such as solar) could become important, especially in remote inland areas.

Woodfuel: A growing crisis

Four-fifths of the population of Sub-Saharan Africa relies for energy wholly or partly on woodfuels (fuelwood, charcoal, and agricultural residues), which account for two-thirds of energy consumption. Already more than 50 million Africans face acute scarcity. Based on present trends, the demand for woodfuels would at least triple by 2020. Demand is growing among the urban population, which is expected to double in 12 to 15 years. If urban households continue to consume woodfuels at the present rate, urban demand will represent between 50 and 75 percent of total woodfuel use in most Sub-Saharan countries by

2000. The rate of consumption of fuelwood greatly exceeds the rate of natural growth in many areas. Even if tree planting is accelerated (see Chapter 4), chronic shortages are almost inevitable. The main reasons for the uncontrolled exploitation of the forest cover, apart from land clearing, are that in most countries there are neither incentives for its sound management nor for optimization of its yields. Restoring a balance between supply and demand involves:

• Improving the management of forest cover by transferring control over exploitation to local communities; local people need to have secure rights to an adequate return from the resources that they manage and questions of land tenure, usufruct, and revenues will therefore have to be resolved in a manner satisfactory to the rural populations involved.

• Pricing woodfuels economically (as is being attempted in Malawi and Niger) to encourage conservation and interfuel substitution, as well as fostering exports of efficiently produced charcoal from surplus areas, such as Congo and Zaire.

• Encouraging the use of more energy efficient charcoal and wood stoves, including stoves and ovens used by rural industries (see Box 5.7), as well as encouraging the adoption of more efficient carbonization techniques through a better incentive system.

• Developing reliable, economically accessible, and appropriately priced alternative energy supplies, such as kerosene and liquified petroleum gas, and assisting low-income urban families with appropriate credit or subsidy schemes for purchasing stoves and appliances that use these fuels.

• Upgrading institutional development through planning, management, and training to enable the public sector to formulate, monitor, evaluate, and adjust effective fuelwood strategies.

Commercial primary energy

Sub-Saharan Africa produces about 1.8 percent of the world's commercial primary energy (before conversion to other energy forms) and consumes 0.5 percent of it. The main sources are petroleum (70 percent of consumption in 1988), natural gas (9 percent), hydroelectricity (9 percent), and coal (12 percent). Per capita consumption is the lowest in the world and has been increasing by only 0.9 percent a year in the 1980s. By comparison, per capita commercial energy consumption in India is now double Africa's, having risen at 4.9 percent a

Box 5.7 Energy efficient stoves in Niger

As in most Sub-Saharan African countries, wood is the main source of energy in Niger and accounts for four-fifths of the country's gross energy supply. About 98 percent of the households in the urban areas use it for food preparation. The increasing consumption of fuelwood and the inefficient way it is harvested and consumed have had a deleterious impact on the country's environment and on its economy. To address these issues, the government mounted a program to improve the efficiency of fuel consumption by urban households.

The objectives were to replace the inefficient traditional woodstove with a new improved portable metal stove and to establish an unsubsidized, autonomous, and self-sustaining production and marketing network using existing commercial networks. Several activities were carried out simultaneously. A more efficient stove (known as the Mai Sauki) was designed, artisans were trained to produce it, the marketing network was improved, and the new Mai Sauki was advertised. During the two-year implementation of the project nearly 40,000 stoves were produced and sold, 200 percent more than originally planned.

The Mai Sauki was successful because it met the needs of both consumers and producers. It was easy to use and suited local cooking habits. Household expenditure on fuelwood fell by 30 percent, sufficient savings to cover the cost of the stove in only two months. The 116 independent metalsmiths, who were trained by the project and now sell the Mai Sauki, have virtually doubled their profits.

The project was successful because it was open to suggestions and flexible in incorporating activities already involved in stove promotion. Many Nigeriens, ranging from the district chiefs to the Women's Organization and the Youth's Organization of Niger participated in the project, and technicians and engineers of the National Solar Research Laboratory collaborated in designing and testing the stoves. The project also worked with NGOs, grassroots associations, and volunteers such as Church World Service, Association Bois de Feu, the Peace Corps, and the European Volunteers for Development. In working closely with the different national and foreign organizations, the project was able to benefit from their experience and, in turn, to assist them in their activities by channeling their efforts within the project framework.

---

year from 1970 to 1986. Assuming a 5 to 6 percent growth in energy supplies during the next 30 years, the share of petroleum in the commercial primary energy mix is projected to hold at 70 percent, natural gas to rise to 15 percent and hydroelectric power to 10 percent, and coal to fall to 5 percent.

Oil and gas rich . . . and poor

Proven reserves of petroleum in Sub-Saharan Africa at the beginning of 1989 were estimated at 20.5 billion barrels (2.3 percent of the world total), most of which is located in the Gulf of Guinea. Angola and Nigeria together account for 80 percent of the region's annual production of 2.2 million barrels a day, of which 84 percent is exported. The other African countries spend a crippling 20 to 40 percent of their annual export earnings on oil imports. However, it is widely believed in the industry that important oil deposits remain to be discovered in some of the relatively unexplored areas outside the Gulf of Guinea.

Although Sub-Saharan Africa has 3.5 percent of the world's known natural gas reserves (four-fifths in Nigeria), consumption is limited. Most gas is produced in association with oil and is flared. Considerable proven but undeveloped reserves of non-oil-associated gas exist offshore of Nigeria and, to a lesser extent, in such countries as Cameroon, Côte d'Ivoire, Sudan, and Tanzania.

PROMOTING EXPLORATION AND DEVELOPMENT. Oil and gas exploration have lagged. In 1987, 2,303 wells were drilled in Latin America, while in Sub-Saharan Africa only 237 were drilled—and they were concentrated in three countries. The success rate has been good; in the Gulf of Guinea there has been one discovery for every 2.5 exploratory wells, compared with a world average of one for every 5.6. Further, production costs are competitive with areas such as Indonesia, the North Sea, and Alaska, where there has been intensive exploration and development despite difficult physical conditions.

Countries with potential for exploration and development fall into three groups:

• Existing oil producers (such as Angola, Cameroon, Congo, Côte d'Ivoire, Gabon, and Nigeria), in which most of the proven reserves lie. Development costs and risks are relatively low, and exploration will probably focus on known offshore fields, such as in the Gulf of Guinea.

• Countries in which exploration is likely to result in discoveries of gas fields (such as Mozambique, Tanzania, and offshore Sudan). The main obstacles are uncertain prospects for foreign exchange earnings from the export of liquid hydrocarbons, small local markets for natural gas, long gestation periods for investments, and the high cost of infrastructure. The Pandi field in Mozambique and the Songo Songo field in Tanzania remain undeveloped for these reasons.

- Interior countries (such as Central African Republic, Chad, Niger, and south Sudan), in which limited local markets for petroleum and gas, the cost of infrastructure, and transport difficulties across frontiers to local markets or to coasts for exporting have discouraged exploration. Intercountry cooperation and a favorable environment for investors would facilitate their exploitation.

Exploration and development of Africa's oil and gas resources presently depend on a partnership with multinational oil companies that can provide investment and expertise. To attract the large oil companies, countries must put in place favorable enabling environments for exploration and development. In Kenya, for example, oil companies were willing to enter into exploration agreements once legislation, taxation, and royalties policy were revised. Many potential oil basins extend over several countries. Cooperation among countries—such as the preparation of reliable multicountry technical data bases, consistent legislation across neighboring countries, arrangements for regional transport corridors, and defined national boundaries to prevent disputes—would facilitate exploration in these areas. A good example is the Rift Valley, a particularly promising area, where exploration has been modest so far.

RATIONALIZATION OF REFINERIES. Africa has 23 refineries with a capacity of about 44 million tons a year—almost double the region's demand. High costs and poor cooperation among neighboring countries make exporting unviable. Capacity utilization averaged about 60 percent in 1986; 13 refineries have a capacity of only 30,000 barrels a day or less, low for an industry where economies of scale are significant. Except for Côte d'Ivoire and Nigeria, old technology limits the proportion of higher-value products to low-cost heavy fuel, maintenance is poor, and domestic markets are small. Average refinery operating costs in Africa are $2 a barrel, against $0.75 elsewhere. State refineries suffer many of the problems that afflict parastatals in Africa (see Chapter 2).

African countries continue to operate uneconomic refineries for several reasons: some because the price-setting mechanisms for petroleum products produced in the refinery generate rents that subsidize costly parastatals (such as Cameroon and Congo); others to maintain access to credit made available by suppliers of crude oil in government-to-government contracts; yet others for reasons of status or as a training ground for engineers (such as Côte d'Ivoire and Nigeria). Most of these refineries are poorly adapted to local markets and produce a surplus of fuel oil, which must then be exported to Europe or North America at considerable loss. More than half of total production at the SONARA refinery in Cameroon, for example, is surplus and must be exported.

Some countries have also invested heavily in surplus storage facilities that greatly add to cost. Côte d'Ivoire, for example, possesses unutilized publicly financed storage facilities that can hold the equivalent of four months of domestic demand; meanwhile private sector storage is adequate to meet requirements. The cost of financing the capital immobilized in strategic stocks of petroleum products is another burden on public finances. In some cases these stocks could be reduced without jeopardizing national security.

Rationalizing refineries on a regional or subregional basis could raise capacity utilization, improve efficiency, and save more than $300 million annually. Doing so will require improving the efficiency of modern plants (such as those in Côte d'Ivoire and Nigeria) and pooling the product requirements of small markets on a regional basis around them as well as closing uneconomic refineries.

LOWERING THE COST OF OIL SUPPLY AND DISTRIBUTION. The supply of petroleum in Sub-Saharan Africa is the most costly in the world, only in part because of the inefficient refineries. Shortages of foreign exchange lead countries to buy oil in small batches, which allows little flexibility to take advantage of market conditions. A poor infrastructure makes supplies unreliable.

These problems can be overcome. The Tanzanian government, for example, has enlisted the help of the private sector and international lenders to rehabilitate its old system. Chronic fuel shortages in the interior have cost some $100 million annually in avoidable losses. In other cases intercountry cooperation could improve the supply and distribution of petroleum products. A particularly interesting example is found in Togo, where the local uneconomic refinery has been closed and certain of its facilities converted into a transit depot for reexport to other countries in the region, both inland (Burkina Faso and Mali) and coastal (Guinea and Liberia). The Lomé storage depot now generates profits, whereas the refinery previously incurred losses.

Coal prospects

More than 90 percent of Africa's coal deposits, estimated at 135 billion tons, are in three land-locked countries—Botswana, Swaziland, and Zimbabwe. Lack of capital, trained labor, demand, and infrastructure, as well as high transport costs, will continue to restrain development unless the price of petroleum increases dramatically. Nonetheless there is scope to make greater use of coal to meet Africa's long-term energy needs. Any large-scale future development should be accompanied by measures to protect the environment.

Cheaper and more reliable electric power

Installed capacity for electric power in Africa in 1986 was 19 gigawatts, of which two-thirds came from hydro and the rest from thermal plants, mostly oil-fired. Consumption of electricity, less than 200 kilowatt-hours per capita, is low even by developing-country standards (in India it is 435 kilowatt-hours per capita). Consumers are mainly households and the public sector since industrial and commercial use is limited. In 1986, 86 percent of electricity came from public utilities and 14 percent from commercial plants for their own use or for sale. Because of limited cooperation among countries only 8 percent or so of the electricity was traded. The share of self-producers could grow considerably if regulations would permit.

Power utilities are mostly small and rarely can afford the economies of scale needed to justify large hydroelectric schemes or the costly infrastructure needed to use gas. Installed capacity exceeds 1 gigawatt in only seven countries, the largest being Nigeria. Electricity losses are high—30 percent or more in some countries, of which a portion is attributable to pilfering. Supplies are unreliable, and much demand unmet (see Box 1.2).

Poor energy planning has led to costly investments in excess generation capacity and too little expenditure on distribution facilities and maintenance. In Zaire, for example, because of inefficient load distribution between hydroelectric plants, capacity utilization is no more than 25 percent. Although utilization of existing plant may be only 50 percent or less, poor maintenance—resulting in breakdowns and lengthy unit outages—tends to force investment in new plant. Nigeria, for example, has approximately 5 gigawatts of installed capacity to serve a power market that is today

slightly less than 2 gigawatts. In many cases the capital stock has deteriorated seriously. Investment in maintenance could be a cost-effective way to expand the energy supply.

Several severe problems face Africa's public utilities—overstaffing (averaging around 30 percent) and tariffs too low to generate adequate revenue for basic operations, let alone maintenance and investment. Moreover arrears range from six months to one year; collection rates rarely exceed 80 percent of the power sold. On top of that debt is debilitatingly high, reflecting overinvestment and poor cost control.

Africa's untapped hydro power potential is enormous and its abundant natural gas reserves largely unused (many gas wells are plugged or, where gas is produced in association with oil, it is flared). Priority should be given to using these indigenous nonexportable energy resources by developing larger markets on a multicountry basis to allow the economies of scale required for the massive capital investment involved; by economic pricing and improved collections, which are vital to assuring financial viability and raising capital for new investments; and by attracting foreign capital for investments without government guarantees or through privatization. Innovative financing is needed; for example, an operator builds a facility, runs it until the investment is recouped, and then transfers it to the government.

There is much scope for rationalizing power generation during the next 30 years, especially through connections between national grids that have been operating successfully, for example, between Benin, Côte d'Ivoire, Ghana, and Togo in West Africa and between Kenya and Uganda and between Zambia and Zimbabwe in East Africa. Ultimately all of West Africa could be interconnected. A similar scheme may become feasible in East Africa, but it is not likely within the next two decades. Increased integration of power systems and improved capacity utilization could make 60 gigawatts of additional hydroelectricity economically viable. This could lead to the projected sevenfold increase in hydro generation of primary energy by 2020, when hydroelectricity would meet 10 percent of commercial primary energy demand.

Africa has 107 trillion cubic feet of natural gas, yet gas production accounts today for only 3 percent of Africa's energy consumption. In comparison Argentina's 25 trillion cubic feet of reserves (one-quarter that of Africa) supply more than one-third of its energy needs, which are 50 percent greater than those of all Sub-Saharan Africa. Assuming a tenfold increase in gas consumption during the next 30 years, current reserves would last more than a century. Moreover the investment cost of gas-fired power plants is below that for hydroelectricity. The projected investment of $10 billion by 2020 for natural gas infrastructure would yield savings, at 1989 oil prices, of $3 billion to $4 billion a year.

A good example of the potential to optimize the use of indigenous primary energy resources through cooperation is the interconnected grid of Benin, Côte d'Ivoire, Ghana, and Togo. In times of drought the region is prone to power outages. Coordinated operation of the interconnections would optimize the use of hydro energy stored in Côte d'Ivoire and Ghana and also ensure benefits from the existing thermal capacity in the four countries during dry periods. Substantial additional advantages would be derived from coordinating expansion programs, which would enable some countries to defer major investments for two or three years to take advantage of a temporary surplus elsewhere, and vice versa. In the longer run, regional cooperation would be further enhanced by extending the interconnection to Nigeria, thus permitting the import of the low-cost energy produced by gas-fired thermal plants and the export of surplus hydro energy in wet years. Similar opportunities exist in east Africa among countries with large hydroelectric or gas potential (Ethiopia, Mozambique, Rwanda, Tanzania, Uganda, and Zambia) and energy-poor countries (Kenya, Sudan, and Zimbabwe), but they are unlikely to be viable within the next two decades.

Solar energy

Electricity from solar energy remains a high-cost source of power and is as yet economically feasible mainly in remote areas where the cost of other energy sources is prohibitive. Simple thermal solar technologies can be used for such purposes as crop drying and heating water and would ease demand for woodfuels. Photovoltaic energy can be used, for example, to provide refrigeration for vaccines in rural health clinics.

The main drawback with solar energy is that it is available only during the day, but in Sub-Saharan Africa the main power demand is for lighting. Large-scale application of solar energy technology would thus become practical in Africa only when ways are found to store power more cheaply. Africa's Solar Energy Research Center should help to identify long-term economic technologies for solar-based energy applications in the region (See Chapter 7).

A future energy strategy

To realize a sustainable expansion in energy supplies to underpin economic growth, Africa needs to:

• Develop long-term national strategies for the energy sector based on implementing the least-cost mix of domestic, imported, and inter-country energy resources. Key elements of such strategies are the ranking of investments, with a better balance between expenditure on maintenance and rehabilitation and investment in new capacity; efficient use of local resources and facilities; conservation of costly sources of energy, including petroleum and woodfuels; sound pricing policies; strengthening of energy institutions; and maintenance of existing installed capacity.

• Promote strong intercountry cooperation for optimum exploitation and delivery of energy to create larger markets that permit economic investments and optimum utilization of hydroelectric, gas, and other primary energy resources; to reduce administrative barriers to joint procurement, processing, and distribution of petroleum products by the private sector and to eliminate barriers to intercountry trade; and to jointly promote the exploration and development of geological basins underlying several countries by establishing favorable investment conditions.

• Create an enabling environment that will attract high levels of investment, chiefly for oil and gas. The key elements are similar to those for mining discussed earlier and involve creating a contractual framework that creates a conducive investment environment while protecting the interests of the country.

• Encourage improved end-use efficiency and accelerated research and development of energy efficient technologies, promote marginal cost pricing of electricity and improve the efficiency of price-setting mechanisms for petroleum products, and pursue research and development of renewable energy resources.

• Introduce concerted measures to tackle the woodfuel crisis.

Efforts to develop the energy sector at present are haphazard and poorly coordinated. A rigorous and systematic approach—which takes into account environmental considerations—is essential at the national, subregional, and regional levels. Multilateral and bilateral aid agencies have a large role to play in promoting and supporting these national and regional efforts.

6

Fostering African entrepreneurship

The entrepreneurial catalyst

Africa needs its entrepreneurs. Achieving sustainable growth will depend on the capacity of people from all levels of African society to respond flexibly as new market and technical opportunities emerge. During the next three decades the population of Sub-Saharan Africa is expected to grow by at least 600 million persons—more than doubling the size of the labor force. Africa's entrepreneurs must create these jobs. Only their initiative can ensure that the long-term demand for low-cost products and services will be met.

Entrepreneurs are people who perceive profitable opportunities, are willing to take risks in pursuing them, and have the ability to organize a business. In every country the number of people who are inherently entrepreneurial is limited. Market incentives, not innate instincts, are the primary motivation for most entrepreneurs. They are attracted to any activity that generates profit: restrictive business environments generally channel entrepreneurial energies into rent-seeking activities. Potential profits to be gained by taking on additional employees and new machines to pursue productive business opportunities will be judged against these "softer" options. For entrepreneurs to sustain productive activities over the long term, they must be free to accumulate capital—both as a reward for success and to compensate for occasional losses.

The informal sector offers a striking illustration of the strengths and weaknesses of enterprise in Africa. Unregulated and largely unrecorded, its activities comprise the most accessible and competitive part of African economies. These enterprises, many of them very small, are a training ground for entrepreneurial initiative. Faced with restrictive regulations or official neglect, the informal sector has developed its own grassroots institutions to meet the demand for credit and training. But restrictive business environments, weak linkages to formal markets, and poor infrastructure make it hard for entrepreneurs in the informal sector to hire more workers and expand.

An improved business environment and greater support for entrepreneurial capabilities would help enterprises of all sizes to make their contribution to development. Entrepreneurs themselves will need to play an active role in improving the policies, regulations, and institutions that affect them. By evolving a participatory approach that improves the responsiveness of public policies and institutions to the needs of entrepreneurs, governments can build confidence in legal and institutional reforms, raise productivity, and lower the cost of doing business at all levels. Although details will vary from country to country, this approach aims to:

- Improve the business environment by removing undue regulatory constraints, protecting property and contract rights, and improving the public image of entrepreneurs
- Broaden financial and information systems to speed market responses, create employment, and boost productivity for small-scale enterprises
- Stimulate markets through infrastructure linkages, local and regional sourcing of government purchases, and private sector competition to provide public services

• Encourage associations (including trade and professional groups, grassroots organizations, and NGOs) that help entrepreneurs to pool their interests and mobilize resources.

The development of African enterprise

Africa's farmers, traders, artisans, and managers of large-scale enterprises are a seedbed of indigenous entrepreneurship. Because many governments have relaxed controls on competition and trade, these groups are starting to take advantage of new market incentives. There are already some success stories, but the gains in employment and production that are needed over the long term have yet to emerge. To get their economies moving on the road to sustainable growth with equity, African countries will need to take a second look at past experiences, present constraints, and future prospects for enterprise in Africa.

Africa's market tradition

Entrepreneurship has a long history in Sub-Saharan Africa. In parts of the continent long-distance trade on caravan routes dates back to the 11th century. The records of several West African cities—including Kano, Salaga, and Timbuktu—attest to their role as halting places for trans-Saharan caravans of up to 2,000 highly organized traders and supporters. Archeological evidence indicates the presence of "Great Zimbabwe," where mining activities were linked to Arab export markets on Africa's southeastern coast. Tolerant of ethnic and religious diversity, these trading centers developed their own rules and institutions, a liberalized system of exchange, and common languages of trade.

Africa's market traditions are reflected in cities and towns across the continent. Today's traders and artisans continue to organize activities according to long-established customs and rules administered through grassroots institutions. In West and Central Africa women trade clothing, jewelry, and shoes bought wholesale from Europe and sold retail to local markets. "Market queens" are chosen by their peers to regulate the extensive trade in fish, palm oil, and other local commodities. The "Nana Benz" of Togo are famous for their success in textile marketing. In Dakar leatherworkers produce traditional footwear not only for Senegalese markets but also for export to

The Gambia and Mali through informal commercial circuits.

People, capital, and goods have always traveled in Africa, disseminating ideas and technology. Ethnic groups like the Hausa-Fulani have spread through many countries to establish trade links and market their skills. Foreign investment and imported technologies have had a major influence on the development of large-scale industries, both public and private. In many parts of the region resident non-Africans play a significant role in the transfer of capital and technology. Some of these businesses are an important source of training for indigenous entrepreneurs.

Shifting roles of the public and private sectors

During the first three decades of independence policymakers focused mainly on promoting large-scale industrial enterprises. These were deemed the hallmarks of development and were generously supported by public policy. Large firms enjoyed preferential access to credit, foreign exchange concessions, and protection from competition through subsidies, tariffs, quotas, and exclusive licenses. Capacity was often expanded with little regard to cost or profitability.

The state's role as entrepreneur was justified by the argument that the indigenous private sector had neither the capital nor the expertise to drive rapid development and industrialization. Africa was seen as a continent without indigenous entrepreneurial skills, its "progressive" modern sector at odds with a "backward" informal sector that could provide subsistence but nothing more. In viewing activities in the informal sector as marginal to development, however, policymakers have greatly underestimated the depth and potential of African entrepreneurship. Equally, they ignored the extent to which their own policies have driven entrepreneurs into the informal sector.

From time to time nearly every African government has tried to promote small- and medium-scale enterprises (SMEs). But the policy and institutional background has generally been unfavorable. Most of the SMEs that have grown in response to market demand have done so despite official neglect or discouragement. In Ghana and Tanzania, two of the most extreme cases, massive resources were directed to public enterprises, while local entrepreneurs who attempted to circumvent price controls saw their premises destroyed and their property confiscated. Uganda's entire Asian community was expelled in 1972 in an attempt to exert state control over the private sector. These policies crippled economic growth by deterring long-term investment by both foreign and local entrepreneurs. In less extreme cases public enterprises simply crowded local firms out of access to markets and financial resources.

In the 1980s the role of the public and private sectors shifted decisively. As the weaknesses of the postindependence approach to development became clearer, governments began to include local entrepreneurs in their long-term strategies for employment and growth. In most countries the public sector moved away from economic dominance toward greater support for private initiatives, both local and foreign. Controls over foreign investments were relaxed; local capital accumulated through rent-seeking began to move into productive activities. Governments generally became more conscious of the effect of policy on both day-to-day business decisions and long-term private investment.

Prospects and constraints

Outside the informal sector small- and medium-scale enterprises are few and far between. The paucity of businesses that can link imported and local technologies—the "missing middle"—is a major impediment to Africa's development. Despite recent policy reforms entrepreneurial initia-tive is hampered by regulation and limited consumer demand for local products and services. Small-scale entrepreneurs find it hard to raise capital, to pool skills, or to gain access to efficient infrastructure services. Still there are encouraging signs. In some countries new enterprises are emerging despite the difficulties (see Box 6.1).

In other regions, especially in Asia, a middle ground of enterprises between the largest and smallest firms has developed during the past 30 years. The products and services of these enterprises are well suited to the conditions in many developing countries: surplus labor, scarce energy, foreign exchange constraints, lack of technical information and skills, scarce investment capital, and variable weather and soil. SMEs create jobs at a lower cost and use local resources more intensively. These enterprises also contribute to equity by producing goods and services that are widely affordable. They foster entrepreneurship through learning-by-doing. By thus reconciling broad-based consumer demand, available resources, and indigenous and imported technologies, SMEs perform a vital role in development.

PROSPECTS. The 4 percent growth scenario developed in Chapter 2 requires large increases in the labor absorption and productivity of small-scale firms. To bring this about, African governments will need to take steps to support these labor-intensive, high-value-added activities. By

---

Box 6.1 Emerging agricultural entrepreneurs in Côte d'Ivoire

A recently completed study of Côte d'Ivoire notes the emergence of a new group of agricultural entrepreneurs. The group is diverse; it includes women and immigrants as well as entrepreneurs with traditional farming and urban wage-earning backgrounds. By seizing opportunities in both the domestic and export markets, they are establishing enterprises that refute the old dualistic image of separate informal and modern sectors. They use formal banking and marketing facilities as well as up-to-date production techniques, but they also get support from traditional networks, which afford them essential access to labor, land, and savings.

For example, an entrepreneur who trained as a mechanic and agrotechnician was working for an urban-based company when, in 1985, he lost his job and decided to move into full-time farming. He now operates a cocoa and coffee farm of 170 hectares that employs a full range of agricultural machinery to achieve high levels of land productivity. A former plantation worker from Burkina Faso has set up his own family-financed banana planta-tion, with the support of 120 salaried employees and laborers, largely from his home country. Although the farm continues to operate informally, its export capacity has been recognized by the issuance of an official export code number. Among the 28 other emerging agricultural entrepreneurs surveyed are an urban businesswoman who started a poultry farm and a former director of a public works enterprise who developed a 100-hectare pineapple plantation.

By combining advanced agricultural technologies and commercial methods with medium-scale production, these entrepreneurs are able to achieve much higher levels of productivity than small- and large-scale farms. Through learning by doing, they are finding the right balance between investment risk and potential profits. These examples illustrate how both traditional and modern networks stand ready to assist spontaneous entrepreneurial initiatives that emerge in response to market demand.

2020 a substantial share of African value added will have to come from the service sector, where labor intensity is high and proximity to markets affords natural protection not available to the goods-producing sectors. This ought to be feasible. In rural areas, for example, nonfarm enterprises can supply basic financial, construction, health, and educational services. Together with better agricultural productivity these activities can in turn boost demand by raising rural incomes.

Even Kenya, one of Africa's industrially more advanced countries, has recently taken steps to promote its small-scale and rural nonfarm enterprises. In its "Sessional Paper No. 1 of 1986" the government outlined a broad program of support for SMEs.

> For Kenyans to enjoy even modest improvements in their current standard of living, it will be imperative that ... the great majority of jobs be created, not in the cities or in large industry, but on farms and in small-scale industries and services, both rural and urban.

In many other African countries the prospects for large-scale industry are even more limited and the need for productive employment through small-scale enterprises will be much greater.

CONSTRAINTS. Burdensome taxation and regulation deter small-scale entrepreneurs from linking their activities with formal financial and information systems. As a result their ability to pool resources is limited to informal networks. Trade policies have generally favored large-scale, capital-intensive firms while increasing transaction costs for SMEs. Interest rate ceilings and sectoral credit allocations intended to benefit SMEs have, in practice, distorted financial markets and impeded the efficient allocation of financial resources. Banks avoid lending to SMEs because small firms generally lack collateral. Long-term finance remains limited in many countries because interest rates do not favor long-term deposits (see Chapter 8).

Government run extension services and programs of technical assistance to SMEs have largely failed because of unsustainable overhead costs, limited participation, and poorly adapted services. Political instability has also discouraged investment by increasing economic uncertainty. Erratic and arbitrary law enforcement has blurred the "rules of the game" and made many entrepreneurs extremely cautious in their dealings with formal markets and services. Under these condi-

tions graduation from the informal sector may seem too risky even for the most innovative entrepreneurs. In any case the scarcity rents generated by restrictive policies often create higher profits than economically productive investments. Because of these obstacles few small-scale entrepreneurs have the chance to innovate and grow. Many are operating far below their potential.

Entrepreneurs in the informal sector

Small owner-operated enterprises that function outside the official regulatory framework contribute substantially to employment and productivity. Recent estimates by the International Labour Organisation (ILO) indicate that the informal sector accounts for 59 percent of Sub-Saharan Africa's urban labor force and an ILO survey of 17 African countries found that the informal sector contributes, on average, 20 percent of GDP (or $15 billion a year) to the economies studied.

Contrary to their image as "tax evaders," many entrepreneurs in the informal sector pay a significant proportion of their income in some form of tax. The ILO estimated that more than 40 percent of informal sector enterprises in 10 Sub-Saharan countries pay fiscal taxes or registration fees. Taxes on licenses for small repair shops and street vendors provide a large share of municipal revenues in cities such as Bamako and Ouagadougou. These enterprises are also subject to indirect taxes. Because they do not qualify for special tariff reductions on imported equipment and inputs, most must buy from local retailers—absorbing the cost of taxes on sales, fuel, and imports. Since entrepreneurs in the informal sector have only limited access to savings facilities, they are particularly vulnerable to inflation—in effect, a "tax" on holding money.

The informal sector thrives because of its responsiveness to market forces and because of its close links with grassroots institutions. Ease of entry and exit makes these small firms an outlet for the skills of entrepreneurs from all sections of society. For women, the poor, and minority groups, the informal sector is often the only such outlet. Women play a big part in the informal sector largely because their property rights are insecure. In some countries a woman needs her husband's permission to take out a commercial license or to open a bank account. Businesses with low levels of investment and rapid turnover give many disadvantaged groups a way to escape legal and social restrictions of this kind.

Start-up costs in the informal sector are typically low. Small-scale investors obtain much of their initial capital from personal and family savings: amounts from this source range from 92 percent in Kenya to 99 percent in Zaire, according to recent ILO estimates. Most of these enterprises are sole proprietorships with much of their labor provided by proprietors, apprentices, and unpaid family members. Grassroots institutions and family networks provide, on average, four-fifths of the training.

The dynamism of the informal sector

Entrepreneurs in the informal sector engage in a wide range of businesses: agriculture, manufacturing and repairs, trade, and construction. They also provide transportation, water, communications, training, and financial services. Their backgrounds are equally diverse. In rural areas they may be small-scale farmers, agriculturalists engaged in off-season nonfarm activities, or full-time providers of products and services to the countryside. In the cities they may be migrants from rural areas, members of traditionally entrepreneurial ethnic groups, school leavers, workers redeployed from public service or private firms, or public service employees seeking to supplement their official incomes.

EFFICIENT USE OF LOCAL RESOURCES. Manufacturers in the informal sector use domestic labor and raw materials more intensively than the parastatals and transnational corporations that dominate large-scale manufacturing. Lack of working capital and other constraints of small-scale production compel them to produce on a made-to-order basis. As a result they respond almost immediately to shifts in demand. Their technology is simple but flexible. They innovate, particularly in their ability to recycle scrap materials. In Tanzania, for example, artisans make kerosene lamps and charcoal cooking stoves from thin metal plates hammered from old oil drums. In Zaire blacksmiths make agricultural tools with steel salvaged from wrecked trucks.

The demand for small-scale manufacturing and repair services has grown. In Ghana, as foreign exchange dried up in the early 1980s, producers substituted local for imported inputs. Under similar circumstances Uganda's small-scale manufacturers produced spare parts for domestic industries. Nigeria's adjustment program has also stimulated demand for local services specializing in maintenance and repair. Some African governments are adopting policies to build on the strengths of this sector. For example, Kenya's small-scale manufacture and repair shops now qualify for assistance wherever they are located, in contrast to the earlier approach of trying to move them to isolated industrial estates (see Box 6.2).

RESPONSIVENESS TO MARKET SIGNALS. Traders, many of them women, have devised informal distribution networks to keep pace with the growing demand from Africa's expanding urban population. These networks provide an important link for moving food supplies and consumer goods between rural and urban areas and across international borders. In Ghana and Senegal, for example, grassroots agricultural cooperatives have successfully made contact with these networks, thereby reducing their marketing costs and improving their access to inputs. For economies burdened by unfavorable markets, civil unrest, lack of infrastructure, or environmental crises, unrecorded trade across borders is essential both as a source of supply and as an outlet for local goods.

Traders are very skillful in using their informal networks to overcome difficulties. But their initiatives often conflict with government regulations concerning prices, street vending, currency exchange, and trade across borders. Increasingly policymakers have begun to appreciate the traders' vital economic contribution and to change their policies accordingly. For example, the Ghanaian government recently legalized market-based foreign exchange shops that had formerly operated in the black market.

FREEDOM FROM REGULATORY CONSTRAINTS. Through the informal sector entrepreneurs can respond to the demand not met by strictly regulated firms. Most African countries have housing codes and land-use restrictions that increase construction costs beyond levels that most can afford. But although population growth and rural-urban migration have multiplied the population of the largest African cities 10 times during the past 25 years, the number of people living in each house has remained approximately the same, largely because of unregulated construction. According to some estimates, this activity accounts for around 20 percent of gross domestic investment in most African countries. Tanzania and Zambia have

Box 6.2 Small-scale enterprises in Kenya

In the past decade employment in Kenya's urban informal sector has been growing rapidly. The growth of this sector has been the main factor holding down increases in open urban unemployment. Similarly, nonfarm activities appear to be the most rapidly increasing component of rural income and employment. Nonfarm employment will have to be the largest single source of new jobs for the rest of the century; in the next decade small-scale and household activities in cities and market towns must absorb at least 75 percent of the new workers entering the labor market if unemployment is not to rise.

Historically, some small-scale enterprises have suffered harassment and lack of recognition from Kenyan authorities. Under regulations promulgated in 1976, street vendors holding licenses were permitted only one employee; it was the practice of city authorities to arrest additional employees for working without licenses. License fees sometimes quadrupled overnight, causing great hardship to the traders affected. In the transportation sector small-scale *matatu* operators were restricted from competing with bus companies that operated along certain routes. Small-scale manufacturers and repair shops suffered increased production costs because of policies favoring large-scale enterprises and prohibitions against establishing their premises close to consumer markets.

The 1974–78 Development Plan admitted these problems and stated that "there has been some counter-productive harassment of these enterprises, which will be promptly ended." Reform has been slow, however, as indicated by the 1986 Sessional Paper's call for a special task force to investigate legal constraints on small-scale enterprises and local bylaws that continue to restrict their activities. Beginning in the 1970s, Kenya formally opened the transportation sector to competition; the *matatu* were recognized and allowed to organize an association to represent their interests. But a recent executive order banned the *matatu* association after it attempted to raise fares above the ceilings set by the government. Kenya's *matatu* association could play a self-regulating role that promotes improved road conditions and traffic safety, but only if its authority to represent its constituents is consistently recognized.

The government has made sustained progress in encouraging small-scale manufacturing and repair enterprises, known in Kiswahili as *jua kali*, meaning those who work under the hot sun. Simple sheds equipped with power, water, public telephones, and rest rooms have been established through the support of the government, NGOs, and local banks. By providing essential infrastructure while maintaining informal linkages and proximity to local markets, the government is enabling small-scale manufacture and repair services to organize producer or savings cooperatives to improve their access to capital and technology. At least one Nairobi bank has begun lending to *jua kali* cooperatives. Improving the working facilities of the sector has also encouraged linkages to larger enterprises. In 1988 a private Kenyan company, Sparewise Limited, was established to provide the *jua kali* with advanced machinery on special hire-purchase terms.

---

taken steps to encourage low-cost construction by granting property rights and developing infrastructure services in squatter settlements.

Some governments have brought greater competition into public services. As noted in Chapter 2, small-scale entrepreneurs offer inexpensive transportation alternatives that—despite lack of official franchises or subsidies—are competitive with state-owned services. These transport providers reduce costs by adjusting their routes and stops to maximize capacity utilization. Drivers typically wait until their vehicles are full, rather than operate on a fixed timetable. They reach otherwise unserved markets because their vehicles are suited to travel over roads that are inaccessible to conventional public transport.

Institutional development at the grassroots

Enterprises in the informal sector are organized around, and supported by, local values and traditions. This fosters institutional arrangements that are able to adjust quickly to changing conditions, whereas formal organizations, operating further from the grassroots, may be slow to adapt. In finance, training, and policymaking, formal organizations would work better if they could forge better links with the informal activities already underway at the grassroots.

FINANCING. The informal financial system comprises savings clubs, rotating funds, mobile bankers and moneylenders, and financial dealings among family and friends. The services provided are accessible to clients with modest incomes because they rely more on personal relationships than on formal guarantees. Across the continent rotating funds, known in some countries as *tontines* or *susus*, have evolved, which are specially adapted for ease of access. In Ghana, for example, designated collectors make daily tours of the market, accepting deposits from market women in the workplace. In rural areas they do their rounds early in the morning before farmers go to the field and later in the evening after they come back (see Box 6.3).

In several countries informal arrangements have evolved into large-scale financial organizations. In Cameroon, Côte d'Ivoire, Guinea, Mali, and Senegal, savings "clubs" have been established. Like informal arrangements these are based on interpersonal loyalties, but they can also function as effective financial intermediaries with the capacity to make mutual loan guarantees. La Financière, a Senegalese savings club started in 1983, expanded within four years to include almost 400 members with a combined capital of CFA 167 million. Congo and Togo are assisting groups of entrepreneurs to mobilize their savings through similar links with the banking system.

TRAINING. Most entrepreneurs in the informal sector acquire their skills on-the-job through trial and error or by watching and helping others. Many start out as apprentices to experienced entrepreneurs already established in a particular trade. Entry requirements for apprentices are typically low; family ties or friendship are often more decisive than formal education. The average length of apprenticeships may vary from as little as one-and-a-half years (for textile dyers) to five years (for carpenters). Apprentices are a valuable resource for small-scale firms because they are inexpensive to employ; they often receive just room and board plus a small allowance. As they become more skilled, their terms of employment are likely to improve, and they may be permitted to sell some share of what they produce.

Apprenticeship arrangements are successful because they provide training in skills and occupations that are in demand. By combining learning with work, they can reach a broad section of the population, including those already employed. Given the financial and administrative constraints on governments, these low-cost and largely self-financing apprenticeships should be encouraged. Nigeria's recently introduced National Open Apprenticeship Scheme, for example, supports the placement of apprentices in informal workshops by paying a share of costs, monitoring the quality of instruction, and providing supplementary off-the-job theoretical training (see Box 3.9).

SELF-ORGANIZATION AND ADVOCACY. Informal associations regulate business relationships by re-

Box 6.3   The diversity of informal financial institutions

Among the best-known informal financial mechanisms is the system of rotating funds, variously known as *susu* (in Ghana), *sanduk* (in the Sudan), *tontines* (in Cameroon), and *hagbad* (in Somalia), to mention just a few. Participants in rotating funds function as savers, borrowers, and lenders during the cycle of the fund. Typically a rotating fund is organized by a group who know one another either through residential neighborhoods, similar occupations, or extended family relationships. Most rotating savings associations retain a portion of the joint saving for a common insurance fund to cover emergencies and social services. The members meet regularly, determine the amounts to be contributed by each, collect the agreed shares, and decide on the method of allocation. The order of rotation can be determined by seniority, election, drawing lots, negotiation, auction, or the urgency of a member's need—but in every case by common consent.

Fixed-fund associations are similar to savings banks. Participants entrust their savings at regular intervals to a treasurer, who holds them for the agreed period and then returns the lump sum. The funds can be loaned to members or nonmembers with interest payments accruing to the fund. Funds held by these associations are used for a variety of purposes, ranging from food and clothing in times of distress to ceremonial expenditures and consumer durables (such as cars and appliances). They are also used to buy income-generating items (such as trucks, sewing machines, and grain-grinding mills), which are sometimes jointly owned, and to finance trade and capital investment in agriculture and small enterprises.

In addition to their function as mobilizers of resources at the grassroots level, many informal financial institutions also operate as social insurance systems. In Ethiopia's *edirs*, for example, members make periodic contributions that entitle them to benefits in the event of death or sickness, loss of job, or imprisonment. Group ties can be based on community or organizational affiliations. The latter is more common in urban areas where members share some institutional attachment, such as workers in a ministry or firm or graduates of a particular school.

Informal mechanisms are also used to facilitate international trade. In Somalia, for example, a sizable portion of import-export business and foreign exchange remittances are channeled through these mechanisms. Livestock exporters retain a portion of their export earnings in the form of foreign exchange held abroad. Importers buy these foreign exchange retentions at parallel market rates, collect remittances from Somali nationals working in these countries for their families at home, and invest the money in imports.

A major factor behind the success of the informal financial system is its compatibility with the sociocultural environment in which it operates. The amazingly low default rate of informal financial mechanisms is not only because of peer pressure, but also because of the correspondence between loyalty to the group and the functions of the system.

lying on peer pressure to enforce agreements, settle disputes, and promote common goals. In Mali and Togo informal craft associations are improving access to production facilities through joint purchase and leasing of equipment. Rwandan associations originally formed to resist unfavorable government policies now enjoy legal recognition; they routinely negotiate with official authorities on issues such as work permits, credit, taxes, and the right to occupy public land.

As both intermediaries and advocates for their grassroots constituencies, indigenous NGOs are working with informal associations to design, organize, and implement initiatives to support small-scale enterprises. Through consensual decisionmaking, based on local tradition, informal associations can help the smallest enterprises to improve their access to capital and information through links with formal markets. They can also identify specific resource needs and give help where it will do the most good. With increasing official recognition, associations of small-scale entrepreneurs can begin to represent their common interests much as chambers of commerce do for larger enterprises.

The limits of informality

Although the informal sector offers entrepreneurs a competitive environment and grassroots support, it cannot provide all the physical and social infrastructure services that investment and growth require. The informal sector offers limited recourse when contracts are breached, property rights are violated, or merchandise is misrepresented. Small-scale entrepreneurs can ensure that obligations are met and payments made by limiting business contacts to close acquaintances and staying small, but this may raise costs and reduce efficiency. An accessible and predictable legal framework could help entrepreneurs escape the constraints imposed by informality, while also helping to eliminate some of the barriers that prevent graduation to a larger scale of production.

Sometimes even big firms may rely on informal systems to provide water, electricity, communications, and waste disposal. These improvised solutions often offer only second-best alternatives; costs could be considerably reduced if large-scale public utility networks were made more reliable and efficient. Frequent power outages and voltage fluctuations compel Nigerian manufacturers to obtain their own electricity using expensive private generators (see Box 1.2). In Zaire businesses are forced to rely on high-cost radio communications because the telephone system is largely inoperative. Some informal remedies carry unsustainable long-term social costs: illegal house connections impose unfair costs on paying consumers, environmentally unsound methods of waste disposal pose serious health dangers, and uncontrolled exploitation of natural resources threatens the welfare of future generations.

Several governments are trying to build on the demonstrated strengths of the informal sector and to correct its weaknesses. Burkina Faso and Kenya, for example, have incorporated strategies for supporting small-scale enterprises and grassroots institutions in their most recent development plans. Côte d'Ivoire and Senegal have implemented special licensing arrangements to improve the legal status and security of small-scale enterprises. With lower costs of compliance and better support, many entrepreneurs now in the informal sector will have a greater incentive to formalize their activities and to pool their resources through linkages with formal markets and institutions.

Improving the business environment

Entrepreneurs seek a stable business environment *before* they invest or increase their production. Involving representative associations in the policymaking process is the first step toward reducing entrepreneurial uncertainty and confirming the stability of regulatory and institutional reforms. This dialogue requires a change of attitude from all sides. Policymakers need to acknowledge the critical role of the private sector and to avoid arbitrary actions that disrupt its activities. Structural adjustment programs should support broad-based dialogue that encourages associations to participate in the process of regulatory and institutional reform. For their part entrepreneurs must learn to operate on a level playing field on which the ability to compete and produce efficiently, not privilege or evasion, is the key to long-term success.

Tax policies

Taxes should not stifle enterprise. Using them to steer private investment toward officially preferred trade patterns and social objectives can produce undesirable side effects. Tariff and exchange rate policies designed to protect large-scale industry have often discriminated against small firms.

State marketing boards that extracted revenues from rural areas through price controls have sometimes discouraged increased agricultural production. But it does not have to be that way. Incentives can be substantially improved by replacing tariffs on imported industrial inputs and taxes on agricultural exports with consumption taxes and user charges for public services (see Chapter 8).

Special incentives, usually embodied in investment codes, have been used to promote certain investments. Exemptions from import restrictions and preferred access to credit and foreign exchange are often part of such schemes. Most investment codes were initially intended to create large-scale industries through foreign investments. Although explicit biases against local investors have been largely eliminated, the case-by-case approach inherent in many codes still has great drawbacks: it invites corruption, and it limits access for small-scale entrepreneurs who do not have the influence or resources to lobby for discretionary approvals. These incentive schemes need to be reformulated to promote employment through labor-intensive technologies and to increase value added through greater reliance on local resources. Qualifying criteria should be simplified, with the incentives automatically granted to all eligible firms. Benefits should provide real incentives, not merely compensation for other policies that discourage investment.

The regulatory framework

Excessive bureaucratic interference breeds lawlessness. It encourages entrepreneurs to find shortcuts around the rules and causes those that comply to lose their competitive edge. Removing burdensome regulations would help to eliminate the hidden costs that many entrepreneurs must pay to obtain licenses and register their enterprises. Bribes are only one sort of cost; long delays and complicated procedures inflict further costs in lost efficiency and competitiveness.

The purpose of licensing enterprises needs to be reconsidered. Protecting the public from health and environmental hazards may justify government regulation in industries such as pharmaceuticals and chemicals. But using licenses to keep capacity at officially targeted levels is generally counterproductive because it substitutes administrative fiat for entrepreneurial judgement. By creating unnecessary barriers to entry and graduation, restrictive licensing and registration

impede the development of local enterprises and discourage them from achieving the productivity needed to compete in international markets.

Bureaucrats are much addicted to controls. But if the emergence of SMEs is to be encouraged, licensing and other regulations need to be rigorously scrutinized—and retained only if there is compelling justification. The goal should be simple, automatic registration that confers legal status on an enterprise and permits statistical monitoring. For certain types of activities—self-employed persons, for example—registration and licensing should be eliminated unless they serve some valid statistical purpose. Care should be taken, however, to ensure that exemption from registration requirements does not deny these firms their legal status or disqualify them from access to necessary infrastructure services.

Legal and political conditions

A simple and transparent legal framework, properly enforced, is indispensable for the long-term success of an enterprise (see Chapter 2). In most African countries entrepreneurs have had to operate in very unstable legal and political environments. Such conditions, in which the official rules of the game are uncertain, exact a heavy price from firms and the economies in which they operate. Entrepreneurs need consistent and enforceable laws, which subject all parties—from the politically or economically powerful to the microentrepreneur—equally to the rule of law. All enterprises can benefit from a legal framework that defines contract and property rights clearly and provides an equitable forum for settling disputes.

Compliance with legal provisions can be improved by adopting more participatory rule-making procedures. As experiences in the informal sector indicate, effective rules depend more on social pressures than on coercive enforcement. The conventions that have developed to guide financial, political, and commercial practices in the informal sector can help to shape laws that fit each country's own economic and social needs.

Official statements recognizing the value of entrepreneurship, such as Kenya's "Sessional Paper No. 1 of 1986" can help to create a more secure and predictable climate for long-term investment. But a friendlier view of entrepreneurship will be most effective if it changes the official way of doing things. Tariff reforms, for example, will be more reassuring if they follow a realistic, preannounced plan. Small-scale enterprises are particularly vulnerable to inconsistent enforcement. In the most extreme cases businesses that have taken years or generations to build have been disrupted or destroyed by unforeseen new regulations. By proclaiming the economic and social contributions of entrepreneurs—both large and small—officials can reduce uncertainty and promote a more stable and competitive business environment.

Supporting entrepreneurial capabilities

Despite efforts to liberalize Africa's economies, the number of entrepreneurs engaged in long-term productive investments is still small. African countries can help entrepreneurs overcome the barriers that remain by improving the institutions and infrastructure that support enterprise. Both private and public organizations need to speed entrepreneurial responses to market incentives by mobilizing capital and human resources (both locally and internationally) and by stimulating local production of goods and services. Programs that target assistance to specific groups—redeployed workers from the public and private sectors, school leavers, women, and the poor—can also perform a catalytic role.

Mobilizing capital and human resources

FINANCIAL SYSTEMS. Banking systems need to be reformed and strengthened to mobilize savings for investment and to improve access to credit (see Chapter 8). In the past, government policies have attempted to lower financing *costs* for SMEs through interest rate ceilings and directed credit. These policies, however, have largely failed because they did not address the more critical problem of improving *access*. Publicly managed development finance institutions, created to compensate for perceived market failures through subsidized lending programs, have proven either unable or unwilling to recover debts. Access to credit for SMEs will be more sustainable if channeled through commercial banks that are permitted to charge interest rates that reflect the real costs and risks of small-scale lending.

The problem of lack of collateral can be addressed in several ways. Official titling of unregistered land and buildings would increase the supply of collateral for many small-scale entrepreneurs. Training bank loan officers to appraise projects can reduce the demand for collateral by balancing the need for security against more reli-

able estimates of project rates of return. Equipment leasing schemes, such as that recently introduced in Ghana, base payback periods for leased assets on the cost of the equipment and the net cash flow derived from its use. These could be a useful option for many SMEs.

Banks should be given incentives to develop links with SME and microenterprise associations that pool their collateral by providing mutual guarantees for on-lent funds. The Grameen Bank in Bangladesh and the Bedan Kredit Kecamatan program of Indonesia have both demonstrated that such arrangements can be very effective. Rwanda's *banques populaires*, Cameroon's credit unions, and Nigeria's Savanna Bank are successfully using similar approaches to improve access to credit for small-scale borrowers.

INFORMATION SYSTEMS. Entrepreneurs can broaden their markets through cooperative arrangements that disseminate information on local or regional products and services. Extension services based in the public sector have largely failed. The new consensus is that privately managed programs are better at sustaining information flows and technical assistance to local enterprises. The success of these voluntary efforts depends on the ability of locally based trade and professional associations, NGOs, and grassroots organizations—sometimes working with governments and donors—to develop demand-driven mechanisms for delivering these services.

Local consulting firms are well placed to develop the feasibility and implementation studies needed to attract finance. In Ghana and Togo assistance is being provided to improve access to these advisory services. Such programs should reward only consulting firms that turn out bankable projects rather than encourage the mass production of useless studies. These kinds of programs can promote a sustainable information system that provides entrepreneurs with technical expertise specially adapted to local conditions.

Large enterprises should be encouraged to subcontract to smaller ones and to assist their development by helping with credit applications and market studies and by providing equipment, training, and quality control. Private schemes that bring together small firms for joint leasing, purchase, or time sharing of equipment can increase efficiency and economies of scale. Voluntary cooperative arrangements, like those in Kenya and Mali, can help smaller firms to find inputs from local and regional large-scale manufacturers.

Such efforts can also be supported though data banks that help entrepreneurs to locate equipment (including used machinery) or to make licensing arrangements for imported technologies.

The media too can help improve market efficiency. Privately operated newspapers, magazines, journals, and newsletters encourage contacts between potential buyers and sellers. They also help entrepreneurs to share information about investment and technology. More generally, publications give business interests a voice and ensure that governments are accountable for their policies. Governments should permit private groups to disseminate their own publications and should promote an environment of open discussion and press freedom.

Foreign and public sector catalysts

FOREIGN CATALYSTS. Transnational corporations (TNCs) have traditionally been valued for their capital investment. However, their role in the transfer of technical, marketing, and managerial know-how can be much more far-reaching. TNCs can foster enterprise by discovering new business opportunities and by assembling the initial capital and human resources to pursue them. In Madagascar and Mauritius garment industries were established through initial investments by foreign-based firms; TNCs collaborating with domestic counterparts were a catalyst for local entrepreneurs who later followed their successful lead.

Foreign companies and institutions are acting as catalysts in other ways. The African Management Services Company, a nonprofit organization established by 40 TNCs in cooperation with bilateral and multilateral development agencies, supports African enterprises through managerial training provided on a commercial basis. In 1986 the International Finance Corporation, the United Nations Development Programme, and the African Development Bank initiated the African Project Development Facility. Through its regional offices in Abidjan and Nairobi, the facility helps African SMEs to find investors and technical partners but does not itself invest in the projects.

PUBLIC SECTOR CATALYSTS. Governments can assist entrepreneurs directly through specialized agencies. For example, to help new investors overcome bureaucratic obstacles, Mauritius has set up an investment center that centralizes licensing, registrations, approvals, and applications for utilities. Such "one-stop shops" can benefit both for-

eign and domestic investors who may otherwise be reluctant to negotiate the present maze of requirements. These centers should be given full decisionmaking authority, accompanied by a systematic simplification of the approvals and procedures previously assigned to other government offices.

Modified procurement rules, including reasonable preferences, can be used to stimulate local and regional sourcing of publicly purchased goods and services. The size of orders and specific quality requirements should be monitored to ensure that they do not discriminate against small-scale firms unnecessarily. Governments can help private exporters by making export formalities quick and simple, by running ports more efficiently, and by helping to spot foreign markets for nontraditional products. Central banks can help successful exporters to acquire the imported inputs they need by allowing them to retain foreign exchange.

Public enterprises can have a catalytic effect on the development of entrepreneurship and technical skills. In several countries, including Côte d'Ivoire, Kenya, and Zambia, former parastatal managers have formed their own private firms. To fulfill this seedbed role, public enterprises themselves need to become more entrepreneurial. They need to operate with managerial autonomy and on strictly commercial principles. Managers and workers require market incentives for good performance; salary and hiring policies should be designed to reward effective workers and empower managers to fire employees when necessary (see Chapter 2).

Investments in people

Sustainable strategies for fostering enterprise depend on the ability of entrepreneurs to mobilize their own resources. Even if it were possible to "spoon-feed" financing and skills to every entrepreneur, governments alone could not assemble all the capital and human resources required to sustain a vibrant, growing economy. Nevertheless targeted programs to identify and develop the entrepreneurial skills of particular individuals and groups can play an important role. Carefully designed and implemented, these programs can bring economic and social benefits that greatly exceed their cost.

ENTREPRENEURSHIP DEVELOPMENT PROGRAMS. Short-term programs designed to encourage individuals with entrepreneurial potential have proven effective outside of Africa. Candidates typically undergo self-selection procedures or behavioral testing before qualifying for training. The Entrepreneurship Development Institute of India, for example, provides instruction and counseling from the original screening up to the actual operation of an enterprise. In Ghana former public sector employees are receiving advice on investing some of their severance pay in new businesses. Nigeria and Senegal are trying to use such programs to promote self-employment among school leavers and the unemployed. Pilot programs in Kenya and Malawi assist owners of existing enterprises.

Entrepreneurship development programs must ensure that the demand for training is a genuine response to the opportunities of a competitive economy. They should avoid creating new windows for privileged access to subsidized credit and other forms of special treatment. Training for the select few chosen from targeted groups will not by itself solve Africa's long-term employment and productivity challenges, but successful trainees could provide a useful example for others to follow. These programs can also guide governments in identifying and removing the constraints that the business environment unnecessarily imposes on entrepreneurs.

MICROENTERPRISE DEVELOPMENT. Support programs targeted to economically and socially disadvantaged groups are proving to be a cost-effective way to increase incomes and improve productivity. Although experience in this area is still quite recent, a growing body of evidence suggests that the development of Africa's smallest enterprises—typically owned by women, rural residents, and the urban poor—can have a substantial impact on employment and incomes. By increasing the incomes of the poor, these programs can also boost the demand for products and services.

The most effective microenterprise development programs are locally run and aimed at specific objectives. Although the number of prospective recipients is large, the individual assistance required can be quite small. Loans of $300 or less, for example, can make a big difference. Microenterprise associations can screen borrowers and monitor the repayment of loans, and access to credit and information can be quickly improved. Indigenous NGOs can also help to define the needs of targeted groups, to reduce administrative costs, and to improve the distribution of resources. Programs geared toward developing participatory, self-sustaining associations can yield benefits many years after external assistance has ended.

Broad-based infrastructure and services

CONSTRUCTION. House building employs local masons, carpenters, brickmakers, and metalworkers. In rural areas construction provides off-season work for farmers and a smooth transition into rural nonfarm enterprises. Housing construction creates jobs at little capital cost, generates income from rentals, and often provides an entrepreneur's first workshop or warehouse. Contractors who coordinate these activities develop managerial skills. Better access to housing credit and effective protection of property rights could broaden the scope of formal finance and help to increase demand for these services.

After getting their start in housing construction, entrepreneurs can move on to larger projects, such as road construction and maintenance. Governments can ease this transition by contracting civil works projects to local enterprises. Burundi, Ghana, Kenya, and Madagascar, for example, have all begun to shift away from arrangements that rely on public management of civil works. Instead they are giving work to local contractors. This reduces infrastructure costs, and it increases employment through more labor-intensive techniques. Competitive bidding and timely payment can reduce the uncertainties for private contractors. Associations of local construction enterprises should play an active role in planning the technical and scheduling aspects of civil works projects.

RESEARCH AND TECHNOLOGY TRANSFER FACILITIES. Entrepreneurs capable of exploiting the business opportunities presented by local or imported technologies are the vanguard of the "missing middle." Governments and donors should encourage them by funding basic research facilities and by helping to disseminate commercially viable technologies. Schools can support this process by encouraging careers that combine technical expertise with business skills. Programs that bring students into closer contact with local businesses will help build the necessary linkages between academic institutions and the business community.

SERVICES. Privatization of public enterprises engaged in trade, transportation, finance, and social services is under way in many countries. These reforms are opening up fresh opportunities for entrepreneurial initiative. When privatization of public services leads to increased competition, it can become a catalyst for local enterprise. The abolition of Nigeria's cocoa marketing boards, for example, has opened the door to new initiatives led by traders and private farmer associations. In Ghana and Mauritania competition in the transportation sector has created new opportunities for entrepreneurs to run large-scale bus companies.

Education and health services can provide immediate opportunities and long-term support for entrepreneurial initiatives. As public expenditures for human resource development have contracted, Africans from all sections of society—from the wealthy to the poor—have demonstrated their willingness to pay for schools and health care (see Chapter 3). These activities should be encouraged because they promote broad-based access and sustainable systems for achieving social goals. Governments can support them by removing unnecessary barriers to entry. Professional and trade associations, NGOs, and grassroots organizations, in cooperation with official agencies, can certify the quality of social services provided by the private sector.

Answering the need

Enterprises begin with people. The future development strategy should recognize that although governments can facilitate progress, people will make things happen. Africa already has many who will seek out opportunities, take risks, and respond to market incentives. But this is not enough to meet the long-term challenges of productive employment and economic growth. People also need a healthy business environment—one that enables them to plan for the future, that rewards achievement, and that encourages entrepreneurs to invest in themselves and their enterprises. They need financial and information systems that give them access to resources, infrastructure that supports links with the rest of the economy, and institutions that promote the full development of human resources.

By working with governments and local associations to improve the business environment and to support entrepreneurial capabilities, donors can make a valuable contribution to this effort. External resources—financial and technical—will be most effective if they help governments to concentrate on:

• Shifting state spending from public enterprises toward support for infrastructure and services

• Regularizing the legal status of enterprises in the informal sector and building on the grassroots institutions that support them

• Removing barriers to the entry, exit, and expansion of small-scale enterprises, protecting contract and property rights, and ensuring fair settlement of disputes

• Supporting financial and information systems, led by the private sector, that broaden access to capital and technology for all enterprises

• Helping targeted groups to respond to market forces, to create employment, and to improve their productivity.

Entrepreneurs will play the central role in transforming African economies. A consensus, increasingly reflected in policy reforms and other initiatives, is forming around this vision of Africa's future. By creating an environment in which people develop their skills and talents to their full capacity, African countries can make the entrepreneurial catalyst a key strategy for promoting sustainable growth with equity.

7

Regional integration and cooperation: From words to deeds

The preceding chapters have noted many instances in which regional cooperation and trade would assist Africa's long-term development. The most important of these are:

• *Capacity building.* Chapter 3 calls for regional centers of excellence where resources can be concentrated to achieve top-quality training and research in science, technology, agriculture, economic and business management, and a variety of other fields.

• *Food security.* Chapter 4 makes clear that greater trade among African countries would help overcome imbalances in food supplies, thereby reducing Africa's dependence on food imports from overseas. Liberalizing regional trade in food would contribute to food security. Establishing buffer stocks and undertaking joint crop forecasting and livestock disease control are other areas where a regional approach could result in gains for all countries. For better pest control and natural resource management—in particular, river basin development—regional cooperation is also essential.

• *Industry.* Chapter 5 points out that in the framework of a general program of trade liberalization, there are benefits to be gained from a faster rate of liberalization within Africa. This would help existing underutilized and overprotected firms to adjust by increasing markets and competition without exposing them too quickly to international competition. Internal markets in most African countries are not big enough to achieve economies of scale and competition for many intermediate and capital goods industries (such as paper, steel, and pharmaceuticals), and regional cooperation can help these industries to develop efficiently. Neighboring countries can also provide an outlet for excess capacity and experience for tackling larger overseas markets.

• *Energy.* Chapter 5 also argues that the exploration and development of Africa's hydrocarbon reserves can be facilitated if these activities are undertaken simultaneously in several neighboring countries with similar geological structures. Furthermore in the procurement, refining, and distribution of petroleum, costs can be reduced substantially through regional cooperation. And the same is true for the development of natural gas and hydropower, where substantial economies can be realized by interconnecting national power systems.

African leaders have long accorded high priority to regional cooperation and integration. It was a central theme of the 1980 Lagos Plan of Action, the Special UN Session on Africa in 1986, and numerous other high-level statements and reports on African policy and development strategy. This is particularly important for landlocked countries; Africa has more of these than any other continent. The fragmentation of Africa has been arguably viewed as a formidable constraint.

Experience to date

Many institutions for regional integration and cooperation were created soon after independence, although often without much planning or preparation. The Lagos Plan of Action provided a conceptual and planning framework for economic integration. It divided Sub-Saharan Africa into three subregions: west Africa, central Africa, and east and southern Africa. Under the framework envisioned by the plan, each subregion was to pass through three stages: free trade area, customs union, and economic community.

In Africa there are more than 200 organizations for regional cooperation; more than 160 are intergovernmental and the rest nongovernmental, but most receive government support. However, top-heavy structures, politicized appointments, the reluctance to give power to regional executives, and the failure of nearly all member countries to give priority to regional issues have reduced the effectiveness of these regional institutions. Many governments—even the better endowed—have failed to meet the financial obligations of membership in these organizations.

Progress toward market integration has been disappointing, with the share of intraregional trade in total trade still at the level it was 20 or more years ago. This is due partly to the uneven distribution of benefits and costs. When countries face budget and balance of payments problems, they seek to avoid the immediate costs of regional integration. But these costs must be borne if longer-term benefits are to be reaped. The smaller and poorer members are also concerned that most gains from integration will flow to the more developed partners and that compensation procedures will be inadequate.

Regional cooperation efforts have been successful when the objectives were limited and focused and when the benefits accrued quickly to all partners. They are typically cases in which a large part of the financing was borne by external donors.

Lessons from market integration

Among Africa's market integration schemes the West African Economic Community (CEAO) has been most successful. It has achieved a high degree of integration that supports economic specialization and facilitates the flow of labor from the poor Sahelian countries (such as Burkina Faso and Mali) to the richer coastal countries (such as Côte d'Ivoire and Senegal) while supplying goods in the opposite direction. By reducing nontariff barriers and establishing a satisfactory compensation mechanism, trade within the CEAO has expanded significantly and is now around 10 percent of total trade.

All CEAO members, except Mauritania, belong to the West Africa Monetary Union and share the common CFA franc, which is pegged to the French franc. They have a common central bank, which holds their reserves in a French Treasury account. For the privilege of convertibility, the states belonging to the union have accepted limits on budget deficits and domestic credit expansion. But convertibility is not a sufficient catalyst for promoting regional trade; there must also be a supportive regulatory framework and factor mobility.

The Economic Community of West African States (ECOWAS), whose member states include those in the CEAO and the Mano River Union, has made little progress toward economic integration. Because tariff and nontariff barriers have not been reduced, trade among its partners is at the level of the early 1970s—about 3 percent of the group's international trade. The pattern of trade has not changed. Côte d'Ivoire and Nigeria still dominate the export of manufactures. On labor mobility there has been setback rather than progress; in 1981 and 1983 Nigeria expelled more than 1 million Ghanaian guest workers. There is no movement of capital within the region because capital markets remain underdeveloped. Furthermore ECOWAS' rule of product origin has become a source of serious disagreement. To qualify for the organization's tariff preferences, products must be made by firms 51 percent (or more) domestically owned. This rule (which the CEAO does not have) promotes indigenous manufacturers but restricts exports from Côte d'Ivoire and Senegal (since their industrial plants are considered foreign investments) and discourages foreign investment.

In the Central Africa subregion market integration schemes also have been disappointing. The Economic Community of Central African States, the youngest, has had difficulties getting started. The Economic Community of the Great Lakes States has had financial problems, and no serious efforts have been made to implement its trade liberalization program. Although members of the Central African Customs and Economic Union (UDEAC) have a convertible currency—the CFA franc—trade within the group has declined, while trade with nonmembers has increased. For example, the main African trading partner of Congo (a UDEAC member) is Zaire (a nonmember). Almost half of the UDEAC's African trade is with ECOWAS, compared with less than 45 percent within the group.

The slower progress in integration in Central Africa may reflect the absence of regional leadership. In West Africa leadership in the move toward regional integration has been provided by Nigeria, (in ECOWAS) and Côte d'Ivoire and Senegal (in the CEAO).

The collapse of the most promising economic community, the East African Community, demonstrates how the inability to solve political differences can compound the economic problems inherent in any economic integration involving countries at different levels of development. The community began with a shared currency, a regionally coordinated infrastructure, harmonized economic policies, a system of common institutions, and forced labor mobility. It fell apart in the late 1970s over the sharing of benefits, political divisions, and conflict of interest among Kenya, Tanzania, and Uganda.

After a period of disillusionment economic integration has recently been resurrected in the form of the Preferential Trade Area for Eastern and Southern Africa (PTA)—15 heterogeneous sovereign states, stretching from the Horn of Africa to Zimbabwe and the islands in the Indian Ocean. All countries in between are members; Angola, Botswana, Madagascar, Mozambique, and Seychelles have yet to join.

The PTA aims to promote trade within the subregion by reducing tariffs and nontariff barriers, particularly with preferential treatment for certain products. To be eligible for preferential treatment, a commodity must be both of export and import interest to member countries, its producing firm should be 51 percent (or more) locally owned, and not more than 60 percent of its components should originate outside the PTA.

Tariff reduction has been slow and application of the 51 percent ownership criterion difficult. Five states, including Zimbabwe, have been given temporary exemptions. The demands of the economically less-developed countries for equitable distribution of the benefits of liberalization has become a bone of contention even before these benefits have begun to emerge. To facilitate trade payments, a clearinghouse managed by the Central Bank of Zimbabwe has been established, but it is underutilized.

Lessons from regional cooperation

Taking into account the failings of the East African Community, the Southern African Development Coordination Conference (SADCC) has avoided the market integration approach and has, instead, adopted an incremental, project-oriented, regional cooperation approach. SADCC's success as a regional cooperation organization is partly due to its focus on actions rather than on building an elaborate secretariat; governments take responsibility for sectoral programs allocated to them. Its programs aim to reduce economic links with South Africa, and this has led to large transportation and regional industrial projects (with some donor financing) with immediate benefits to member states.

More narrowly, there are regional cooperative institutions strongly supported by national governments and external agencies to address specific problems—for example, the riverblindness program of West Africa supported by a consortium of donors (see Box 7.1). There are also successful regional training and research institutions, such as the Eastern and Southern Africa Management Institute and the African Regional Standards Organization. Similarly the cooperation in the management of hydroelectric interconnections between the Volta River Authority (Ghana) and the power utilities in Benin, Côte d'Ivoire, and Togo, has been remarkably successful.

However, many intergovernmental organizations in Sub-Saharan Africa face a financial crisis. Some regional technical services have been closed—OCLALAV locust control, OICMA migratory cricket control, and the remote sensing organization in Bamako. The largest regional industrial investment, the West Africa Cement Mill (CIMAO), established in part with World Bank financing, was closed in 1984, largely because its clinker was about double the world price.

A strategy for future regional cooperation and integration

How can regionalism work better? The limited achievement of the market integration efforts following independence has opened a debate about its efficacy under present African conditions. Critics have declared market integration a failure. They argue that the model, taken from the experi-

Box 7.1 The control of riverblindness

The Onchocerciasis Control Program (OCP), set up in 1974, illustrates the scope for regional cooperation in tackling a common problem. Onchocerciasis is a parasitic disease that causes debilitation, eye damage, and (eventually) "riverblindness." About 30 million people live in West African areas in which the disease has been (or is) endemic. It is prevalent in the savannah and has contributed to the depopulation of relatively fertile river valleys. It is caused by a thread-like parasitic worm, which lodges in nodules in the human skin and for 10 to 15 years produces millions of embryos. The bite of a female blackfly transmits the disease.

The OCP aims to control the blackfly by destroying its larvae in the river breeding sites with insecticides sprayed from small aircraft and helicopters. The environmental impact of the insecticides is continuously monitored by an ecological group, in cooperation with the beneficiary countries. To complement vector control, the OCP has also collaborated with the pharmaceutical industry to develop a drug, ivermectin. Ivermectin has proved safe and effective in reducing morbidity in large-scale field trials and is being integrated into the OCP's vector operations.

The program required a unique institutional arrangement involving 11 West African governments, the sponsoring agencies, the donors, and an international technical staff. The four sponsoring agencies (the UNDP, the FAO, the World Bank, and the WHO) establish policy and oversee operations. The WHO is responsible for carrying out operations. The World Bank mobilizes donor financing, manages the program's trust fund, and takes the lead in socioeconomic development follow-up. The OCP employs more than 600 staff, 96 percent of whom are Africans. Staff are given precise goals but have considerable flexibility in attaining them. The sustained donor commitment provides relatively long-term employment, helping to create highly motivated staff. At present the program is funded by 20 donor countries and international agencies, with beneficiary countries paying about 1 percent of annual expenditures. The program costs only $1 per person protected per year.

Transmission of the disease has been halted in 95 percent of the original program area—764,000 square kilometers with nearly 20 million inhabitants. The parasite is dying out in the human population. People previously infected are recovering. More than 4 million children born in recent years are growing up without risk of contracting the disease. Increasingly the river valleys freed from onchocerciasis are being resettled. New villages are being established, and agricultural production is increasing. A 1986 report by the US Agency for International Development estimated that the 150,000 square kilometers of cultivable land that has been recovered could potentially feed 10 million people each year.

The program has been successful because:
- Participating countries agreed to pool and share resources to support centralized and technically complex operations
- A plausible, long-term strategy with a clear objective included the target of bringing the program to a successful conclusion
- Donors, impressed by the program's promise of health and economic benefits, committed sufficient resources
- Donor and beneficiary government commitment was reinforced by tangible results—in health and socioeconomic benefits—early during the program
- Program performance and effectiveness have been enhanced through strong management, supported by the involvement of the sponsoring agencies and independent expert committees.

By the late 1990s the reservoir of parasites is expected to have died out in most of the human population throughout the 11-country area. Thereafter, with strengthened health systems, the beneficiary countries should be able to detect any reappearance of riverblindness and to suppress it through the new drug, ivermectin.

---

ence of highly industrialized European countries who have a high level of trade among themselves, is not relevant to Africa, where trade among countries and the level of industrialization are low. The range of tradable commodities is seen as limited, and consequently the transport and communication infrastructure is inadequate. They recommend that the market integration approach be abandoned and that a new approach that emphasizes broadening the regional production base take its place. This would give priority to regional investment in heavy industries (such as chemicals, iron, and steel) and transport and communication infrastructure. The supply of goods is perceived as the main constraint to the increase of trade among African countries.

However, experience suggests that countries are unwilling to buy high-priced goods from their partners when lower-priced goods are available elsewhere. In the past governments have been preoccupied with negotiating preferential agreements and compensation arrangements. Less attention has been given to the real issues: the noncompetitiveness of member states compared with third-country suppliers, the high cost of doing business, the shortage of foreign exchange and credit because of distortions in macroeconomic policy, the limited complementarity of outputs, and the restrictions on food trade.

The production approach does not address this range of issues. It does not identify how and where the capital to be invested in expanding production is to be generated. The sizable volume of informal trade shows that the constraint of poor transport and communications can be overcome. In the absence of market signals, the production approach—implying a state-led development of core industries (such as steel, cement, and chemicals) at whatever cost and without regard to market demand—can force the pace of regional integration. In this approach all investment will come through the public sector. All past experience shows, however, that public sector management combined with protected markets results in costly and unviable projects; this is an unsound basis for integration.

An alternative strategy proposed here has three elements: designing incremental but comprehensive approaches to regional cooperation and integration, strengthening specific functional forms of cooperation, and creating an enabling environment for the free movement of goods, services, labor, and capital.

An incremental but comprehensive approach

A step-by-step approach based on common economic interests offers the best prospects for integration. Even this will fail unless all partners are convinced of the benefits and genuinely committed to a program of implementation. Given the fragmentation and pervasive jealousies and mistrust between countries, the initial steps are likely to be the most difficult.

To overcome this, subgroups of two or more countries should be encouraged to integrate more rapidly than other members whenever they perceive mutual benefits. Such an incremental approach should not involve further proliferation of organizations but would involve bilateral (or multilateral) agreements between governments that perceive benefits from a mutual liberalization of product and factor markets. Donors can help by providing resources to support regional trade across borders by private enterprises.

There is no reason to channel all programs through established organizations; improvised attacks on bottlenecks may be more effective in certain circumstances. But any approach must contain mutually reinforcing, complementary measures. Improved regional infrastructure is of little value in regional integration without policy reforms to increase the demand for goods and services. In turn this will depend on incentives—particularly regarding exchange rates and the liberalization of markets. And policy reform is pointless unless physical and human infrastructure is improved.

Box 7.2 Rationalizing regional institutions

More than 200 regional organizations for cooperation and integration exist in Sub-Saharan Africa. Proliferation and duplication of functions give rise, at the regional level, to conflicts over mandates and to divided loyalty among governments. At the government level, they impose heavy financial and administrative burdens. Even countries such as Côte d'Ivoire and Nigeria are finding it increasingly difficult to meet their financial obligations. Arrears in government contributions to most of those institutions' budgets and special accounts are mounting. As a result, their executives find it difficult to implement the tasks already assigned to them, let alone plan for future activities.

The institutions' budgets are invariably too small for the tasks governments assign to them. Even if governments were to eventually pay, their contributions would not be sufficient to enable the executives to carry out their mandated tasks. Insufficient funding thus prevents institutions from making better use of the resources they receive.

There are other administrative and financial burdens on governments. Most institutions are mandated by charters to hold several high-level conferences annually. In any given year these add up to a sizable agenda. African conferences, together with other regional and international conferences, cost governments money that cannot be justified by the benefits gained from them.

Proliferation also creates an unmanageable problem of coordination. The major African regional and functional organizations have the following structures: a supreme policymaking authority comprised of heads of state, a policy-coordinating body of ministers, and an executive elected by heads of state. In most cases the heads of state meet once every two years and the ministers every year. This is top-heavy and cumbersome.

Recognizing the depth of these problems, the Lagos Plan of Action and subsequent ECA and OAU statements have all expressed concern. The ECA and OAU have made proposals for rationalization that have been endorsed by African governments, but action has been slow. Moribund organizations have not been closed down. Overlapping institutions have not been combined. At the same time regional institutions in critical fields such as agricultural research, river basin planning, higher education and training (including centers of excellence), transportation (airlines and shipping), and pest control need to be strengthened or created.

Phased programs addressing critical barriers to regional integration are essential. Each phase would include advances in harmonizing policy and maintaining and improving infrastructure.

As an urgent first step regional organizations need to be rationalized (see Box 7.2). They should be reformed and consolidated into lean and efficient institutions with a clear mandate and capacity for making decisions. These institutions could then spearhead the creation of a physical, technical, and legal infrastructure that would support regional exchanges in goods, services, labor, and capital. Rationalization would be greatly assisted if donors provided concessional finance to meet transitional costs.

Regional transport, communications, and services

Inefficient highway, airline, railway, shipping, and telecommunications services act as barriers to regional trade and contribute to the high cost of doing business in Africa. Much of the infrastructure has been primarily designed to serve the export and import needs of each country in its trade with non-African countries. After three decades of independence links between Sub-Saharan African countries still remain weak and therefore need to be systematically strengthened.

Large new investments in infrastructure will not stimulate trade within regions when other barriers have not been eased or eliminated. A stark illustration is provided by one of the few concrete achievements of the Mano River Union: a bridge between Liberia and Sierra Leone that is hardly used because of restrictions on both sides of the border.

The preferred sequence is to introduce coordinated incentives and remove administrative barriers to trade and then to improve infrastructure in response to the growth in trade generated by the policy reforms. New investment in infrastructure should be based on a thorough evaluation of current and potential trade and should be the leading element of an action program only where poor infrastructure is the primary barrier to generating new trade or to expanding existing flows. It should be complemented by projects to rehabilitate and upgrade existing infrastructure.

Regional cooperation programs in transport and communications should focus on providing efficient and reliable services. This is particularly important for transit to inland regions and to land-locked countries. Overland transit costs are inflated by cumbersome and antiquated customs procedures, poor operational coordination between modes of transportation—especially at the interface between ports and railways—and weak harmonization of regulations on transit carriers. Furthermore regulations imposed by landlocked countries, particularly regarding reserve cargo rights for national carriers and foreign exchange allocations for transit expenditures, have also contributed to high costs.

Subregional organizations, in particular the PTA, have prepared proposals and plans of action to deal with the nonphysical barriers to transit. Implementation has been slow and plagued with setbacks resulting from unilateral changes. Strong policy commitment is required. Such a commitment has been the main factor behind the progress achieved in developing efficient regional transit along the Beira corridor under the aegis of the Southern Africa Transport and Telecommunications Commission.

The urgent need is for simple and coherent policies designed to encourage more efficient and reliable services. The choice of route and mode, as well as operational coordination along specific corridors, should be left to shippers and carriers. This will require greater reliance on private sector operators, including those in the informal sector. African railways have lost ground to truckers in long-haul overland transit services. To reassert their competitive advantage and to improve their prospects of regaining financial viability, African railways will have to progress quickly toward operational coordination and joint marketing (see Box 2.6).

Civil aviation and maritime shipping stand to gain most from service-oriented regional cooperation. A recent decision to restructure Africa's poorly coordinated national airlines to achieve greater regional integration should be accompanied by decentralization and increased scope for private sector management and operation. A similar approach to national maritime shipping would enable Africa to benefit from the worldwide reorganization of international shipping.

There is considerable scope for national private firms or public corporations to improve regional services. One of the most successful examples of this is the state-owned Ethiopian Airlines. Its African regional network has established an international reputation for technical excellence, managerial efficiency, and entrepreneurial flair (see Box 7.3).

Transportation, electric power, banking, communications, and insurance are some of the areas in which national public and private operations could be extended to the regional level. Better integrated markets and improved transport links would reduce the costs of providing critical inputs and distributing products, which would make them more competitive in African and world markets. Improved telecommunications can fulfill vital needs in Africa by lowering transaction costs, substituting for more expensive transportation, and improving market efficiency by making information more readily available.

The Pan African Telecommunications project is a comprehensive regional approach to integrating the African telecommunications network by linking national networks. Because demand for telecommunications services at the national level is low, strengthening the capability of national telecommunications networks is to be a short-term priority. In the long term, however, this will make it easier to integrate the African network.

Education, training, and research: regional capacity building

Acquiring technical skills is costly. No African country can afford all the higher-level institutions required for training, research, and development. Centers of excellence in various fields are needed in Africa, and they can be most efficiently established and operated on a regional basis (see Box 7.4).

Because technical training and research are specialized, regional cooperation yields significant economies of scale. Quality is also enhanced because regional institutions can achieve a critical mass in staffing and justify the provision of facilities and equipment (such as libraries and laboratories) that smaller institutions cannot afford; this enables them to set higher standards. And, by mixing students and staff from several countries, they broaden perceptions and foster human and

---

Box 7.3 Ethiopian Airlines

Ethiopian Airlines, formed in 1946 as a government-owned enterprise, has established a worldwide reputation for technical excellence, managerial efficiency, entrepreneurial flair, and financial soundness. This reputation has survived the political and economic difficulties that the country faced before and after the revolution in 1973.

The airline has developed a highly profitable network of international and domestic routes. It is the only airline operating a regional "hub" with air links between all corners of Sub-Saharan Africa. Routes within Africa, especially between East and West Africa, now generate 25 percent of its revenues.

The foundations of its success lay in a management agreement with Trans World Airlines during the 1950s. Not only was the technical quality of the fleet of aircraft continuously updated, but the technical capacity to maintain aircraft and to train crews, mechanics, cabin staff, and marketing and financial staff was also built up. These facilities now provide services not only to Ethiopian Airlines but also to other African and Middle Eastern airlines, many of which have seconded Ethiopian air crews and technicians.

Apart from a short period in the late 1970s, political imperatives have not intruded on the selection of senior managers. The directors include cabinet ministers, but they have never interfered with day-to-day management. Route development, pricing policy, and hiring and firing responsibilities have all rested with management. Only on wage and salary levels has there been a political interest in maintaining levels consistent with other local employers.

Beyond technical issues, management's primary success has been in maintaining a purely commercial attitude toward its activities. Financial viability has been the dominant criterion for both old and new routes. The management exacts tight financial discipline and requires timely payment from the Ethiopian government either for transporting officials on scheduled flights or for using its aircraft.

Ethiopian Airlines is competitive on all the routes it operates. When the government considered protecting its domestic routes from foreign competition, the airline management insisted on, and achieved, an open-door policy. It was essential, they argued, for developing the airline's competitive operations in European markets, otherwise the cocoons of protective policies may prove stifling even to the ones being protected. The result has been a net profit almost every year except 1979 and a consequent willingness of international lenders to finance new aircraft. The airline receives no subsidies from the government except a diminishing tax exemption. Its financial independence on both revenue account and capital account has left managers more free to manage and the government less inclined to intrude. The final product is a low-cost and efficient service that both supports national and regional integration and earns foreign exchange from its international operations.

The International Centre of Insect Physiology and Ecology (ICIPE) in Kenya, which carries out research in entomology, is an example of an African center of excellence and of successful regional institution building. It was founded in the belief that basic scientific research is essential if Africans are to control their destiny. The mere transfer of Western technology is not sufficient to solve the crucial problems posed by insects on health and agriculture in the tropics.

Founded in 1970 and originally housed in a Nairobi garage, ICIPE's new headquarters is at Duduville, with a major field station at Lake Victoria. Its current annual operating budget is $10 million. It employs 50 senior scientists, with 63 African graduate and postdoctoral fellows from several disciplines, such as ecology, biochemistry, and toxicology. ICIPE has received extensive support from scientific academies and financial support from many donors, including OPEC and the UNDP. In 1981 it went through a difficult financial period after focusing too little on the practical application of its research. A more realistic approach has since been adopted. Applied rather than theoretical research is now emphasized, and permanent program leaders have replaced visiting directors of research.

The center has now matured into an internationally recognized research and training institute that attracts qualified African scientists. Its success and vitality can be attributed to leadership with a clear sense of purpose and to an enthusiastic and capable staff.

ICIPE's program includes research on crop pests, livestock ticks, tsetse, and other insect vectors of human disease. In its research on crop pests it is trying to learn from Chinese success in the biological control of insects through viruses and microbes that carry toxic bacteria to destroy crop borers, such as a fungus that eats through insect larvae. To move technology from the lab to the field, ICIPE often relies on the cooperation of its neighbors by including their land in field trials. The center's insect-resistant strains of maize mature early and yield before the rain ends. This variety tastes good, but its color does not correspond to local preference—something ICIPE is trying to change.

ICIPE is working on an antitick vaccine and on a way to control the tsetse, which transmits blood parasites that cause trypanosomiasis (sleeping sickness) in both humans and animals. It has adapted a technique developed by Zimbabwean and British scientists that is compatible with a village-based campaign. Young Masai men have made odor-baited traps that have reduced the tsetse population by 50 percent in 62 square miles in the Nguruman highlands. These traps are one example of research on pheromones—the chemical codes for insect communication. ICIPE is trying to identify the pheromone blend used by the female stem borer to attract the male for mating, which could then be used to make it impossible for males and females to find each other.

Another area of research is the study of vectors that transmit parasitic diseases such as leishmaniases, a disease found in semiarid areas. Thousands of people suffer from a form that resembles leprosy or from one that affects internal organs.

institutional links across borders. A promising initiative is the bilingual Inter-African Electrical Engineering College in Côte d'Ivoire, which caters to the training needs of Africa's power utilities.

Institutions serving several countries are of two types: those managed on a regional basis and those run nationally but serving a wider area. The latter presents fewer management and budgetary problems. By creating regional centers of excellence based on national institutions that take students from several countries, the sending country avoids creating and running expensive institutions, while the host country can reduce its unit costs by optimizing the scale of its facilities.

Already 62 national technical institutions in francophone Africa accept foreign students. In addition there are at least 86 regional technical training institutes and no fewer than 60 regional associations concerned with education and research. Nevertheless a sustained effort to coordinate and rationalize the multitude of regional facilities is still needed.

In the early years of independence there were several successful regional universities (for example, the University of East Africa and the University of Botswana, Lesotho, and Swaziland). With rapidly rising enrollments, however, the potential benefits diminished while the additional overhead costs of managing a regional university remained. Consequently they broke up. However, under SADCC a different and more flexible form of cooperation is emerging. To avoid duplication of higher level training in agricultural sciences and to meet the region's human resource development needs, SADCC has agreed to carry out specialized postgraduate training in selected universities. The University of Zimbabwe will specialize in agricultural economics; Sokoine University, Tanzania, in agricultural engineering; University of Malawi, in animal sciences; and the University of Zambia, in crop sciences.

Other areas of cooperation have emerged. The Association of African Universities, the Association of Faculties of Agriculture in Africa, and the

The African Economic Research Consortium is a remarkable example of a successful regional capacity-building program. Twice each year 35 to 50 African economic researchers, often from the universities, governments, and research institutes of more than 15 countries gather to discuss and evaluate their ongoing research.

Launched in 1988, the consortium provides funding and technical support to networks of researchers. The initiative is two-pronged: to promote macroeconomic research and to strengthen local research institutions by developing their staff. It also seeks to make senior policymakers and politicians more aware of applied research and its potential contribution to the decisionmaking process. The consortium is currently supported by several donors and administered by the Rockefeller Foundation. Based in Nairobi, its current annual budget of $1.4 million supports some 20 teams, each with four or five researchers.

In the early 1980s newly trained African economists were challenged to contribute to the far-reaching reviews of domestic policy being undertaken by their governments. At that time, owing to the dearth of experienced local economists and the weakness of African research institutions, most economic policy analysis was conducted by expatriate consultants or staff from multilateral financial institutions; as a result it was poorly internalized and lacked continuity.

The consortium grew out of a venture initiated in 1984 by the Canadian International Development Research Center that provided funding to overcome the hurdles to quality research within the local institutions of Eastern and Southern Africa: lack of equipment, facilities, and library resources; bureaucratic bottlenecks that delayed the transfer of grants made in foreign exchange from central offices to the research teams; and the intellectual isolation of analysts from both academic peers in the region and senior officials.

Leading African researchers and policymakers in the consortium's advisory committee chose the research topics. National teams have so far been concentrating on the issues of balance of payments and domestic financial management, but the advisory committee is now considering adding external debt management, medium-term adjustment, and taxation policy to the research agenda. The common program facilitates comparison and discussion on a regional basis. For example, Tanzanian researchers have directly contributed to recent public debates on structural adjustment in that country. The consortium provides a venue for sharing experiences and assessing their applicability to other nations. The network creates opportunities for international exchanges of ideas and findings, since members of the networks travel and work abroad from time to time; scholars in Europe, North America, and other regions participate through meetings, joint or cooperative research, and as seconded personnel in other African institutions. National meetings to publicize and discuss research findings and their implications for policy also link senior technocrats and politicians so that the latter may better appreciate the economic implications of political decisions. The consortium also supports a scholarly journal, *Eastern Africa Economic Review*, which publishes research emanating from the network.

The consortium's success is largely due to its flexible, pluralistic approach, which tailors programs to the needs of individual groups. By enabling well-trained Africans to remain in contact with colleagues in Africa and overseas, it is helping them to stay at the frontier of their profession. By breaking down the traditional barriers between governments and universities, it is helping policymakers appreciate the potential of local academic resources. It is a model that merits replication in other disciplines.

African Teachers Association might, with modest support, play a key role in promoting communication among African educators and educational institutions. Networking also holds great potential as a highly cost-effective way to enhance professional standards and skills (see Box 7.5).

Another example of regional and subregional cooperation is found in the professional development programs of the Consultative Group on International Agricultural Research (CGIAR) and several of the management development institutes. The CGIAR has strengthened national African agricultural research capacities through institutional support and training of individual researchers. And the Eastern and Southern African Management Institute (ESAMI), the West African Center for Administrative and Management Studies, and the Pan African Institute of Development are developing training programs for a re-

gional clientele and providing assistance to national institutes in, for example, project management and administration. ESAMI is generating its own revenue by providing consulting services (see Box 7.6).

The appeal of regional approaches and organizations is also evident in high-technology areas, such as solar energy, because relevant skills are exceptionally scarce, capital requirements high, and the population to be trained in any one country small. The Solar Energy Research Center, sponsored by the CEAO and based in Bamako, has a matchless physical plant and the potential to be on the cutting edge of applied solar research.

Regional approaches to education, training, and research have a positive long-term effect on economic and political cooperation in the region. It enables institutions to be built that are more indigenous and better suited to local conditions.

Over time this will lessen both the dependence on expatriate teachers and researchers and the need to send students abroad.

Natural resource management

The quality of natural resource management determines whether growth will be sustainable. Much of Africa is caught in a downward spiral of desertification, land degradation, and deforestation that is threatening its economic future. Many of these issues are specific to a particular country, but some, such as pest management, need regional approaches. Regional locust control in west Africa used to be highly effective, but in recent years it has broken down.

The protection of wildlife can also benefit from action at the regional level. The transnational game parks in east Africa, for example, require coordination and joint action to address issues such as poaching. The East African Wildlife Society is a model for building efficient organizations in areas in which wildlife needs protection on a subregional scale.

In watershed management close regional cooperation is also vital. The record of organizations established for this purpose—the Senegal and Gambia river valley organizations, the Niger Basin Authority, the Lake Chad Basin Commission, the Mano River Union, the Great Lakes Electricity Organization, and the Kagera Basin Organization—has been mixed. The main problems are overly ambitious objectives, inadequate finances, and the lack of qualified staff. There has been insufficient attention to river basin planning, and member countries have rarely formulated their national plans with regard to coordinated regional watershed plans.

The river basin organizations should be rehabilitated, but with more limited objectives. They

---

Box 7.6 Eastern and Southern African Management Institute (ESAMI)

In 1974 the member states of the East African Community—Kenya, Tanzania, and Uganda—founded the East Africa Community Management Institute in Arusha, Tanzania, as a management development center for training, consultancy, and research services for public sector organizations. Following the 1977 breakup of the community, membership expanded beyond the three original states to Angola, Botswana, Comoros, Djibouti, Ethiopia, Lesotho, Madagascar, Malawi, Mauritius, Mozambique, Namibia, Seychelles, Somalia, Zambia, and Zimbabwe. In 1980 the institute was renamed the Eastern and Southern African Management Institute (ESAMI).

ESAMI's objective is to improve the performance and effectiveness of management in the region's public and private sectors. Each year it offers about 50 short-term, in-service management development training programs in Arusha and about half as many elsewhere in the region. These are attended by more than 1,500 persons. ESAMI collaborates with national management institutions and enterprises to develop and present their courses and has frequent tailor-made courses for private and public enterprises. With support from the UNDP and other donors, ESAMI has pioneered a women in development program that is unique in Africa.

Training concentrates on core functional management and sectoral areas, such as project planning and management, public finance, transportation policy and management, trade and banking, and data-processing systems. Short-term courses are designed and run in cooperation with client organizations, such as Air Tanzania, Kenya Railways, Kenya and Uganda Commercial Banks, and the Zambia Agricultural Bank.

ESAMI also serves as headquarters of the Association of Management Training Institutions for Eastern and Southern Africa, and trains national trainers, who can in turn offer similar courses in their own institutions—for example, construction management under a project sponsored by the ILO and a workshop on case methods run in cooperation with the Economic Development Institute of the World Bank. Technical assistance activities have included support to the Management Service Board in Zambia and national institutes; staff from national institutions in Lesotho and Uganda have been on short-term assignments at ESAMI.

ESAMI earns about 90 percent of its revenue from course fees and receives 10 percent of its budget in annual contributions from member countries. Some 30 international agencies, with the UNDP as the largest supporter, have contributed to ESAMI's programs through grants, primarily for participant fees, equipment, short-term secondment of staff, and salary support. Other donors are now assisting ESAMI to become self-sufficient and to meet its objective of establishing a quasi-autonomous Center for African Transport Management, an initiative that is already receiving donor and regional support.

ESAMI has a high-quality permanent staff of some 35 African nationals selected on a competitive basis from member countries. Local consultant training staff are hired (as needed) to teach special courses. A director general and a management team oversee management and finances. The director general reports to ESAMI's governing board, which is composed of high-level representatives from member states.

ESAMI offers a viable African alternative that is one-third as expensive as training abroad. And its consultancy fees are far more competitive than those paid to expatriates. With international community support ESAMI expects to be self-sufficient by 1990.

should be given only those responsibilities that member countries cannot discharge independently: planning basinwide and comprehensive river development and monitoring the implementation of river development plans after their adoption by member countries. The regional river basin organizations would integrate national development plans into comprehensive development plans in consultation with national governments. Specific projects would be undertaken by governments either separately or jointly.

An enabling environment for trade, competition, and factor mobility

The most direct way that greater regional economic integration would benefit Africa is through enlarging markets. Some countries produce surplus meat (Ethiopia, Mali, Niger, Somalia, and Sudan), others surplus fish (Côte d'Ivoire, Madagascar, Mauritania, Mauritius, Mozambique, Senegal, and Somalia), and yet others surplus cereals (Burundi, Cameroon, Kenya, and Zimbabwe). Some export cotton (Côte d'Ivoire, Sudan, and Zimbabwe), rubber (Côte d'Ivoire, Liberia, and Nigeria), tea (Kenya, Malawi, Mozambique, and Tanzania), cocoa (Côte d'Ivoire, Ghana, and Nigeria), and sugar (Mauritius, Swaziland, and Zimbabwe). Others have spare hydropower (Ethiopia, Ghana, Zaire, and Zambia) or oil and energy sources (Angola and Nigeria). Some have already developed modern industrial capacity in consumer and intermediate goods (Cameroon, Ethiopia, Côte d'Ivoire, Kenya, Mauritius, Nigeria, Tanzania, and Zimbabwe), while others have not.

The benefits of economic integration through trade could be significant. Official trade among Sub-Saharan African countries amounts to a mere $4 billion—only 6 percent of total African trade estimated to be $65 billion—and has stagnated or declined for most countries since the 1970s, when most of the market integration schemes, such as preferential trade or customs unions, were formed. This has been due mainly to macroeconomic policies—overvalued exchange rates, distorted credit allocation, and heavy domestic market production—that have spurred the growth in Africa's parallel markets and informal border trade. It is estimated that even today up to an additional $5 billion of Africa's imports from the rest of the world could be supplied by other African countries that are already exporting similar products outside the region.

The justification for action also arises from current realities. African economic integration is already extensively practiced through informal trade and other unofficial exchanges. The growth in informal trade across borders partly reestablishes the extensive trade in goods and the migration of people that were a feature of economic and social life before colonization. For many Africans the benefits of greater economic integration are already visible in daily life through this informal exchange that keeps prices down by increasing competition, supplies products across borders that would otherwise be unavailable, provides opportunities for employment in neighboring countries, and encourages entrepreneurial activities. Informal trade also involves profiteering made possible by official barriers and discrepancies in incentives among countries.

TRADE LIBERALIZATION. Raising the returns from integration requires broadening market liberalization from timid tariff cuts on selected products to opening up factor markets, as well as those for goods and services. The challenge is to create market incentives that encourage the private sector to engage in wealth-creating exchanges across borders.

Trade within Africa stimulates economic growth not simply because it permits countries to exchange complementary commodities and services. Trade between countries producing similar goods is most beneficial because it helps increase the efficiency of firms and farms against alternative sources of supply. Japan and Korea are often cited as countries that built industries behind high protective barriers, but they adopted tough policies to ensure that producers became efficient, particularly through domestic competition. This approach needs to be built into Africa's development strategy.

Increased competition would provide an incentive to raise productivity, lower costs, and remove policy distortions. The internal markets for many products are so small, however, that there is no room for competing firms; competition must come from imports. Liberalizing markets within Africa could help greatly to create the conditions for competition among African producers, thereby stimulating efficiency and economic growth.

Overall trade liberalization needs to be a part of the effort to restructure African economies. Unilateral trade liberalization has proceeded slowly, however, and gains have sometimes been reversed. This reflects both the difficulties African producers face in competing on the world market and the opposition of interest groups who have traditionally benefited from trade restrictions. Governments, for example, fear the political costs of lost employment and output, especially in the short run, when weaker firms face retrenchment or closure before new activity has picked up sufficiently to provide an offset. Regional trade liberalization would permit a phased approach by allowing a competitive environment within a region.

A more rapid regional liberalization, in parallel with overall trade liberalization, could accelerate trade expansion and secure benefits that could not be achieved through unilateral liberalization. The greatest benefits are likely to come from combining a phased overall trade liberalization program with a reciprocal phased dismantling of barriers to the free flow of goods, services, capital, and labor within Africa.

By limiting regional preferences, overall trade liberalization will ensure that regional liberalization mainly increases trade rather than diverting it. Further, the more extensive and rapid the overall trade liberalization, the less likely that new resources will be misdirected to produce noncompetitive products for a regional market created by high protection against third parties. Thus the proposed approach should increase regional trade largely by replacing less efficient national production with regional imports. As capacity utilization of the most efficient firms is increased, unit costs would be reduced to lower levels than could be achieved at the national level.

FINANCING REGIONAL TRADE. Increased intra-African trade will also depend on the availability of finance and financial instruments, such as banking networks providing letters of credit, export credits, and other financial services to traders and firms. Even if African suppliers could be competitive on price and quality, inadequate financial arrangements place them at a disadvantage with non-African competitors. At this microeconomic level the banking system should expand and develop, particularly by improving private sector access to hard currencies and credit. This will require the banks to shoulder the commercial risk and donors to assist governments in absorbing noncommercial risks.

The most difficult issues of financing regional trade arise at the macroeconomic level. Imbalances in the flow of trade between member countries are inevitable. Subregional clearinghouses have been established to settle balances between countries. Settlements must ultimately be in convertible currencies because no member can afford to build up balances of other members' currencies. But, given the shortage of convertible currency earnings, members are anxious to use these hard currencies for purchases from non-African sources rather than for settling accounts with neighbors. Governments could help by enabling the private sector to freely hold and dispose of African currency at market clearing prices. To achieve this, the clearinghouses could expand their existing arrangements with central banks to include commercial banks.

MOVEMENT OF LABOR AND CAPITAL. To sustain regional trade liberalization, it will be desirable to free the movement of labor and capital that could compensate for chronic trade deficits. Freeing labor and capital flows within the region would improve growth prospects by creating conditions—through increased competition and wider market access—for mergers, acquisitions, joint ventures, and other forms of horizontal and vertical integration. These would provide additional opportunities for African firms to reduce unit costs and to become more competitive internationally.

Some countries are short of good agricultural land in relation to their population, whereas others are short of labor. The economic prospects for people living in the Sahel region, for example, are limited. Their growing populations can be accommodated only if they are allowed to migrate to the coastal countries where there is greater economic potential (see Box 7.7). Similarly, during the next 30 years, the heavy population pressure around the Great Lakes will need to be relieved by outward migration.

In recent years the migration of skilled workers who cannot find work in their own countries has increased within Sub-Saharan Africa. Ghanaian professionals, for example, are found in Côte d'Ivoire, Gabon, Kenya, and Nigeria. Skilled and semiskilled workers are also moving across borders without formal documentation. Such migrants have made important contributions to innovation and entrepreneurial activity, especially in the informal sector.

A realistic structure of exchange rates is critical to intraregional trade. Trade among members of the CEAO (whose currency is the convertible CFA

Box 7.7 Labor mobility in west Africa

West Africa enjoys a long tradition of labor mobility going back to precolonial times. During this century the relatively more prosperous coastal areas have attracted labor from the poorer interior areas. Although immigration laws imposed after independence have created rigidities, this flow of labor across borders has continued as migrants respond to economic and employment opportunities.

Bilateral agreements, such as the one between Burkina Faso and Côte d'Ivoire that replaced the former system of direct recruitment, have facilitated labor mobility. The CEAO member countries signed an agreement on the free circulation of people, and a 1979 ECOWAS protocol provides for free movement of persons between member states.

Côte d'Ivoire has been particularly welcoming to immigrants. As a matter of government policy, migration and high labor mobility were considered important contributors to economic growth. The population of non-Ivorians practically doubled within a decade, from 720,000 in 1965 to 1.4 million in 1975, as Côte d'Ivoire's employment opportunities in plantation agriculture, industry, commerce, and services attracted workers from neighboring countries. In the mid-1970s migrants helped offset the exodus of rural Ivorians to urban centers, where higher wages in industry and services were more attractive. Migrants came mainly from Burkina Faso, Ghana, Guinea, Mali, and Niger. Initially the Ivorian labor market attracted primarily young, less well-educated males as seasonal workers. But increasingly migrants have stayed longer and have settled with their families.

There are many other examples of such labor mobility. In the 1960s Ghana's prosperity attracted many migrant workers from Burkina Faso, Côte d'Ivoire, Nigeria, and Togo. In 1960 more than 800,000 (12 percent) of its population were immigrants who worked in the cocoa farms and mines and engaged in petty trading. However, this flow reversed during the economic recession in the 1970s; by 1983 Ghana had lost not only the foreigners but also 6 percent of its own population, who had to look for work mainly in Côte d'Ivoire and Nigeria.

Senegal and Sierra Leone have also been important host countries for migrants; in 1975 they had 300,000 and 67,176 immigrants, respectively. The most attractive economy in the late 1970s, however, was Nigeria during its oil boom. Among the Ghanaians migrating to Nigeria were many skilled and semiskilled workers (a 1983 survey shows 25 percent of migrants as skilled and 14 percent as semiskilled laborers). They even found public sector jobs as teachers, doctors, and nurses, filling jobs left vacant by Nigerians, who had taken up higher-paying positions in the private sector. But with the economy's recession from 1981 to 1983, Nigeria expelled more than 1 million foreign workers.

Regional labor mobility benefits both host and source countries. Migrants contribute to the host country's economic growth by helping to exploit its potential more fully. Workers leaving their countries relieve pressure on labor markets and send home remittances. In Burkina Faso these amount to about 8 percent of GDP, which not only augments the scarce foreign exchange earnings but also provides a source of additional savings and capital formation.

But there are costs too. The labor-exporting countries lose output; the more dynamic and able men tend to migrate and leave women behind to manage the family farms. In the host countries government expenditures on social services may rise, and conflicts have occurred when local workers perceived themselves displaced by foreigners, particularly during periods of economic recession.

Experience suggests that taking immigrants has been beneficial to countries in periods of economic growth. Difficulties arise during economic recessions. In the long term, free movement of labor will be central to the development of African economies and the integration of their markets.

---

franc) currently represents 10 percent of their total trade. This compares with less than 1 percent of trade for the other members of ECOWAS, for whom currency convertibility has been suspended because of accumulating debts and delayed settlements.

Monetary convertibility is not sufficient, however. Trade among UDEAC members—the only other union in Africa to have a convertible currency—is 2 percent of total trade, one of the lowest percentages in Africa. Also only these two unions have relatively free internal movement of capital. Currency convertibility and capital mobility are important for sustainable increases in regional trade but are not sufficient.

OTHER BARRIERS TO TRADE. Once a more appropriate regional incentive structure is in place, many regulatory and procedural barriers to intra-African trade should be simplified or eliminated, including quota and licensing arrangements. Simplified procedures that have already been agreed to, such as the PTA Road Transit Customs arrangement, need to be enforced. Border checks and unduly complex transit procedures cause long waiting periods that reduce intraregional trade and contribute to the high cost of doing business in Africa.

Up to 70 administrative steps may be involved in moving goods legally across African borders. In Zaire there are 39 steps for exports and 30 for imports, including signatures, validations, licenses, and authorizations from innumerable administrators, with each official collecting a "fee." An open general license system for imports from regional partners is essential to increased trade and integration.

Lack of information is another barrier to increased trade. Cape Verde, for example, seems unaware that Cameroon could replace Portugal as a source of aluminum discs for making cooking utensils. Private sector manufacturers should help spread information. African producers—both industrial and agricultural—need to take a more activist and aggressive attitude toward marketing and competition. Encouraging such an attitude will require an incentive system that rewards those who move in this direction.

Uniform standards and specifications for products are also necessary. The metric system is not universal in Africa. Beyond this there is a common perception that product specifications are more easily verifiable and quality control and reliability of delivery are better from suppliers outside Africa. Witness the Nigerian bicycle manufacturer whose products became more acceptable to customers in neighboring African countries when sent to the United Kingdom for reexport than when exported directly.

Compensation for unequal benefits

Without explicit sharing of benefits among countries, regional integration is likely to encounter insuperable political obstruction. Experience from successful common markets—for example, the European Economic Community—suggests that creating larger economic units increases specialization and improves overall economic efficiency. African integration too should improve resource allocation; this in turn will raise absolute incomes.

Yet integration may increase the relative incomes of some partners faster than others with new poles of industrialization emerging. For this reason there is a need for compensation mechanisms, such as a direct transfer to the budget of the weaker economies, as happens in the Southern Africa Customs Union. Any compensation mechanism that is not automatic risks failure, since participating governments may withhold payment during a budgetary crisis. It is also important that compensation provide direct benefits to private agents, as well as the state, and that they be geared toward reducing costs arising from market and bureaucratic imperfections.

With scarce foreign exchange and budgets severely constrained for the foreseeable future, the temptation to renege on regional responsibilities may continue to frustrate integration. Donors can help here. This is particularly important for the poorer members of a regional group, especially at the outset.

Promoting a pan-African identity

Beyond actions on policy, infrastructure, and institutions lies a more fundamental need: to mobilize the media and educational and cultural institutions to promote the concept that cooperation within Africa is likely to enhance the progress of all African societies. A systematic program to achieve this could include organizing seminars, workshops, and exchange visits for African journalists; establishing a regional information center to produce and distribute feature articles, pamphlets, videos, and films; and incorporating courses on African history, culture, and economics into school curriculums, especially at the university and postgraduate levels. In addition relaxing travel restrictions and residence requirements would encourage increased contacts within Africa at the personal level.

Only when groups of African teachers, intellectuals, and community leaders are committed to greater cooperation among countries and articulate the steps needed will popular support be built and sustained. Ultimately regional integration cannot be imposed from above; it has to develop from the grassroots. More access to information on other African countries, more exposure to them, and more education about them are vital parts of the process.

Schoolchildren could learn more about their African neighbors. They could also learn that self-reliance does not mean looking inward and depending solely on their own national resources. It means being able to interact competitively with neighboring countries and with other parts of the world. It means making the most of national strengths, but compensating for weaknesses by cooperating with neighbors. It means recognizing that no country, particularly the poorest countries of Sub-Saharan Africa, can go it alone.

In conclusion

Progress toward market integration and increased cooperation in a whole range of areas—economic, technical, environmental, food security, educational, and research—is central to Africa's long-term development strategy. To this end, firm leadership is needed to overcome parochial and entrenched interests and to ensure that benefits are shared equitably. The watchword is pragmatism—to move forward on a step-by-step basis, nurturing new industries supplying regional markets, but avoiding investments that are not clearly justified by a hardheaded analysis of market prospects. An active role for governments and the OAU is critical: initiatives are needed to foster regional and subregional programs. The priorities for action now are:

- To devise compensation arrangements to facilitate rapid progress in rationalizing and strengthening regional and subregional institutions
- To simplify procedures that currently hinder regional trade and investment; in particular, to harmonize fiscal and monetary policies, and to liberalize the flows of goods, labor, and finance.

Donors can facilitate such initiatives by funding regional structural adjustment programs, which would support measures and help meet compensation costs aimed at both promoting market integration and strengthening selected regional institutions.

8

Sustainable funding for development

The future development strategy proposed in this report emphasizes policy reform and institution building. These activities are not resource intensive, but neither can generate a supply response without costly supportive infrastructure—social and physical. The decline in spending on infrastructure during the 1980s has damaged Africa's prospects for growth and must be reversed. Funding for this must be sustainable, and over the long term it will have to come largely from domestic sources. Nonetheless external resource flows will continue to play a crucial role into the next century, falling gradually in importance only after 2010, and then only if the policy reforms and targets proposed in this report are achieved.

Adequate public spending to operate and maintain social and physical infrastructure is as important as new investment, if not more so. In setting targets for savings—both public and private—essential recurrent expenditure must be provided for.

Development expenditure

More and better investment

The evidence of more than two decades suggests that the best performing developing countries have had high rates of investment. As a group the countries with growing per capita incomes have had investment-income ratios of around 20 to 25 percent. East Asian countries, which grew fastest, had investment rates averaging about 25 to 30 percent. China invested roughly 33 percent of GDP to achieve an annual growth rate of more than 9 percent in 1980–86. Yet, despite high average investment rates in Mauritania (30 percent) and Togo (24 percent), the average growth rates achieved were quite low, 1.8 and –0.3 percent, respectively, in 1980–86. Thus it seems that a critical minimum rate of investment is a necessary, but not a sufficient, condition for sustained development.

The rate of return on investment in most Sub-Saharan African countries is low compared with countries in other regions and has been declining (see Chapter 1). The future development strategy aims to raise the efficiency of investment, but this will be slow and difficult. Even if the rate of return on investment can be increased by 50 percent (from about 13 percent in the 1970s to 20 percent by 2000), the rate of investment, both public and private, would have to be about 25 percent of GDP to attain a growth rate of 5 percent a year.

Reorienting investment

The future development strategy emphasizes developing human resources and improving physical infrastructure to provide an enabling environment for producers in the private sector. The composition of investments among sectors should reflect these priorities.

An illustrative level and sectoral composition of projected investment (equal to 25 percent of GDP) is as follows:
• Agriculture (including rural infrastructure). As noted in Chapter 4, public investment should

be related mainly to introducing better technology. The scope for high-cost projects, such as large irrigation schemes, is limited. Instead growth will have to come from improved seed varieties, more and reliable supplies of inputs (such as fertilizer, water, pest control, and agricultural machinery), and better management of livestock. Investments that would most likely yield high returns would be largely in research and extension, small- and medium-scale irrigation, forestry, soil conservation and land development, livestock and fisheries, and low-cost rural infrastructure to serve areas with good agricultural potential. For the agriculture sector as a whole, including rural infrastructure, an investment of 4 percent of GDP would be needed to achieve an annual growth rate of 4 percent..

• Manufacturing. The strategy outlined in Chapter 5 emphasizes that the informal sector (with low capital intensity) would be the dominant source of growth. The main investment components would be selective expansion of key industries, a major expansion of informal manufacturing, development of appropriate technology, technical and managerial capacity building, and the rehabilitation and maintenance of existing equipment. Investment totaling 3 percent of GDP is required to achieve a yearly growth rate of 5 percent in manufacturing.

• Mining and energy. Large investments would be required to open up new areas for exploration and prospecting and to replace aging plant and equipment. In the energy sector there is good potential for investment in hydro power and geothermal plants, natural gas, solid fuels (coal and lignite), petroleum, and the development of energy-efficient technology. An investment of 2.5 percent of GDP in these two sectors is expected to achieve an annual sectoral growth rate of 5 percent.

• Infrastructure (excluding rural). A key component of the enabling environment is sound infrastructure. An investment of 5.5 percent of GDP would be required, with major investment components being to clear the backlog of Africa's maintenance and rehabilitation, to rehabilitate existing facilities to avoid further deterioration, to make infrastructure improvements with high rates of return (such as telecommunications), and to provide new investment to catch up on the shortfall in infrastructure urgently needed to support the productive sectors.

• Human resource development. The investment required for human resource development will be high because of the high proportion of young people in the population and the high priority accorded to investing in people. Achieving the basic goals of human resource development would require total expenditure to rise from 4 to 5 percent of GDP to 8 to 10 percent annually; a substantial part is expected to be of a recurrent nature. New investment would be about 3 percent of GDP, with special emphasis on primary education, improved science and technology, family planning, primary health care, water supply and sewerage, and nutrition.

• Other sectors. An investment of 7 percent of GDP would be required annually to meet the needs of financial, insurance, and business services; housing and construction; hotels; restaurants and tourism; transport and storage; wholesale and retail trade; and other services.

Public spending needs to allow also for operating costs and the replacement of capital. Reviews of public expenditure in Africa have repeatedly confirmed the neglect of operating and maintenance costs. For most countries more analysis is needed to establish the norms for properly maintaining and operating service facilities (such as rural health, water supply, and primary schooling), to maintain existing investments in the road networks, and to estimate the recurrent costs of new investments. Emphasis must continue to be placed on the systematic review of all public investment and spending programs for the appropriateness of size, composition, mix of new and current projects; the funding for operation and maintenance; and the protection of core programs. This is a prerequisite for sound management.

Mobilizing domestic resources

The overall domestic savings rate has declined dramatically in Africa from about 18 percent in 1972 to roughly 13 percent in 1987. For many countries the decline has been even greater. Behind this is a drop in the rate of public savings, which is not only negative but declining (see Table 8.1). Reforms have reduced budget deficits in some countries, but more must be done to raise public savings.

Raising public revenues

In the late 1970s tax revenues in Africa averaged around 20 percent of GDP. Loss of exports and falling export prices in the 1980s have reduced

Table 8.1 Gross domestic savings in Sub-Saharan Africa
(percentage of GDP)

	1972	1981	1987
Gross domestic savings	17.8	15.3	12.6
Public savings[a]	-3.3	-5.9	-7.2
Private savings[b]	21.1	21.2	19.8

a. Current account budget surplus or deficit.
b. Residual.
Source: World Bank data.

these percentages in some countries in which most of the revenues were raised directly or indirectly through taxes on trade. In terms of aggregate revenues raised, both low- and middle-income African countries in general did well until recently. Between 1966 and 1979, when the tax effort peaked, the average annual rate of increase in public revenues was 20 percent faster than the rate of growth of GDP.

RESTRUCTURING TAXATION. Despite the growth in public revenues the pattern of taxes and prices of public services, as well as overall levels of revenue, fall short of what is needed. Taxes on trade retard the development of agriculture and industry and generally work against growth and poverty alleviation. In the 1960s and 1970s they accounted for about 45 percent of total revenue, although their share declined slightly in the 1980s. If the financial transfers from the surpluses of the export marketing boards are counted as an indirect tax, taxes on trade amount to more than 50 percent of revenues. This dependence has arisen because such taxes are easy to administer.

Consumption taxes are preferable because they do not adversely affect production. Unlike import tariffs, they do not draw capital and managerial resources away from agriculture and more employment-intensive local industry and commerce and into capital-intensive industries with poor returns to investments. And they do not reduce the incentives to produce for export. With commodity taxes all domestically consumed goods—whether imported or locally produced—are taxed at one rate. All other goods are tax free, including imports of raw materials and both intermediate and capital goods. Unlike taxes on production, commodity taxes do not "cascade" through the production process, and they enable producers to choose between factors according to their relative cost.

Resource mobilization and development would be better served by a gradual shift from taxes on trade toward taxes on consumption and income. There should be less emphasis on taxing exports and more on carefully targeted domestic sales and excise taxes, revenues from the consumption of public utility services, and an extended use of fees on a selective basis for certain social services. The potential for "rent"—and revenue collection through taxing that rent—has shifted away from producer surplus (taxing exports) to consumer surplus from the use of modern utilities (for example, transport, power, water, and telecommunications). But given the dependence on trade taxes, this shift should be on a selective basis. It also needs careful programming and phasing. Most countries move their tax systems in this direction as per capita GDP grows.

CHARGING FOR SERVICES. Large increases in public revenues are potentially available from full-cost pricing of infrastructure services—roads and drainage, water and sewerage, electricity, and telecommunications. Charges for infrastructure services in most of Africa are lower than economic costs and cannot even finance infrastructure maintenance (see Chapter 2). Moderate increases in financial returns would yield revenue equivalent to about 20 to 30 percent of current public revenues. Such reforms would be relatively easy to administer, monitor, and audit and would entail negligible "deadweight" or efficiency losses. They could also be administered without imposing new burdens on low-income groups. Greater cost sharing is also possible for health and education services (see Chapter 3).

A recent review of Bank-assisted projects in several sectors estimated the difference between actual rates of return and the returns that would be achieved from marginal cost pricing. For electric power, the gap is about 5 to 10 percentage points. For water, financial returns are generally zero or negative, some 10 percentage points below the potential return from marginal cost pricing. Côte d'Ivoire has been an exception. Up to 1985 water charges reflected the long-run marginal cost, about $1.0 per cubic meter, and the sector was financially self-sufficient and generated revenues equivalent to 5 percent of public revenues. This enabled the utility to finance and maintain an extensive water supply program. In most African countries infrastructure services are paid for in part out of general public revenues. For telecommunications, the prices charged are frequently no more than half of marginal costs. Even less is actually collected. For roads, the main forms of user charges are taxes on vehicles and fuel and license fees. These vary greatly between countries and are often greater than actual road expenditures, but well below the requirements for maintenance, rehabilitation, and new investment.

An increase in overall public revenues of 20 to 30 percent is feasible from full-cost pricing of infrastructure services and greater cost sharing for health and education services. Excluding roads, price increases should not be viewed as taxes but rather as charges that reflect their marginal costs of supply. Public services would earn sufficient returns to meet their maintenance and operating expenditures, would show a good return on capital, and would have sufficient resources to finance expansion. Thus, instead of appearing on the debit side of the public accounts, the infrastructure services are capable of earning appreciable income.

The impact of such an increase in charges on the main users of infrastructure services needs to be assessed. An increase of 20 to 30 percent in public revenues is equivalent to about 4 to 6 percent of GDP in a typical Sub-Saharan country and would be about 8 to 12 percent of the income of the modern sector. However, part of the increase could be offset by reductions in trade taxes.

The benefits of infrastructure investment are largely enjoyed by the higher-income groups in the urban areas. There is no social or economic reason not to raise tariffs on power, telecommunications, or other such services. Moreover greater cost recovery for services rendered to the modern sector would not be a great burden for businesses if they were phased in gradually and related to improved service. The likely effect would be to raise incomes by reducing rationing and queuing for services and by minimizing congestion. For example, the efficiency of power service could be improved by reducing demand shedding, which is costly to consumers because it requires them to invest in standby power (see Box 1.2).

This approach has other advantages. The revenues would be relatively easy to collect and administer. They would also tend to rise in line with incomes and would help to stabilize public revenues. They would make labor-intensive, high-yielding programs for rehabilitating and maintaining infrastructure financially feasible. They would also provide a way to generate re-

sources from the informal sector. As economies become larger and stronger, the use of these services would increase, providing a channel for raising revenues—without disincentives and administrative complexities.

The main difficulties of the cost-recovery approach are institutional—improving metering, billing, and accountability, without which extra revenues may not be collected. Hence the need to improve the institutional capacity to collect taxes.

Public finance analysts have paid too little attention to the private sector's willingness to pay for social services. Yet household spending on such items as medicines and education can be considerable and is just as much a "development expenditure" as is public expenditure on the same items. Likewise the propensity of even poor households to invest in productive assets is largely overlooked, although these expenditures are an important element of private savings.

Controlling public expenditure

During the 1960s and 1970s the growth in government revenues led to unsustainably high levels of recurrent expenditure, accompanied by the indiscriminate hiring of staff. The problem was aggravated by donors who financed projects without assessing either how they would affect recurrent budgets or whether they were consistent with a coherent public investment program. Moreover fluctuations in export prices had a ratchet effect on public expenditure: commitments taken on in periods of high revenues could not easily be reduced when tax revenues fell. Worst of all, during the 1980s large and continuing falls in revenues forced many governments to cut back on expenditures, especially on materials. The result is that schools are now short of books, clinics lack medicines, and infrastructure maintenance is neglected. With prudent financial management countries can avoid these problems (see Box 8.1). As revenue measures take effect, much stricter fiscal discipline will be needed to ensure that spending reflects development priorities—particularly human resources—and that a better balance is maintained between expenditures on wages and those on materials.

Expenditure could be reduced through stricter management of public expenditure, particularly by cutting subsidies to the parastatals and public enterprises, tighter control of public sector wages, and lower defense spending. Many public enter-

Box 8.1 Botswana: Managing commodity booms and busts

Commodity booms and busts have had a negative impact on the performance of many exporters of primary products in Africa. Excessive expenditure during the boom period has generally been followed by damaging retrenchment when revenues collapsed. Although Botswana relies greatly on the mining sector, which has few linkages with the rest of the economy, it has been a notable exception. Botswana has been able to manage the boom and bust cycle relatively successfully. During the boom periods the government avoids excessive increases in public expenditure and instead builds up international reserves and balances at the central bank to be used when the boom ends.

When the diamond market weakened in 1981, the severity and duration of the recession were quite uncertain. Quickly the government adopted a variety of adjustment policies, which included lowering the exchange rate, reducing bank lending, raising interest rates, cutting public expenditure, and capping public sector wages. Subsequently, with the continued improvement in the balance of payments, the main challenge facing the government has been how to manage the large resources available from exports to promote sustained economic growth. Faced with current account surpluses of about 13 percent of GDP in 1984–86 (and 37 percent in 1987), the government's policy has been to sterilize about 60 percent of the increase in money supply. A substantial part of the diamond revenues was deflected into a special fund earmarked for use on long-term investments. Unlike other surplus countries, Botswana devalued the exchange rate in real terms by 42 percent in 1980–87 to ensure that its strategy of economic

diversification would not be adversely affected.

The continuity of leadership since independence, with a proven record of successful macroeconomic management, has contributed to Botswana's relative prosperity. Many key policymakers have remained in office and have participated in the long-running debates on economic issues. The top political leaders recognize the importance of the economic dimension of the problems they face and are experienced in weighing economic objectives against other considerations. Botswana's tradition of open discussion of issues facing the community has helped the government reach a consensus on longer run policies. Major policy decisions are made only after extensive consultation within the bureaucracy and in freewheeling debates in Parliament. Policies agreed upon therefore have some staying power.

A sound administrative system has been entrenched, which reinforces the leadership's pragmatic approach to national economic management. Development plans and annual budgets are formulated in an orderly and disciplined manner. Recurrent expenditure is tightly controlled. Criteria for public investment emphasize positive economic rates of return. A strong and widely respected Ministry of Finance and Development Planning ensures that public funds are not misallocated or misspent. Parliamentary oversight of public expenditures has enforced accountability. Long experience with droughts and economic uncertainty helped to secure popular support for the government's prudent financial management measures.

---

prises in Sub-Saharan Africa still run large losses, adding to the pressure on budgets. These enterprises present a depressing picture of inefficiency and poor quality. The noncommercial objectives used to excuse their poor performance are rarely achieved. Reforms introducing better policies, tighter management, more appropriate pricing and user charges, and liquidation or rehabilitation of unviable enterprises are showing results (for example, in The Gambia, Mali, Senegal, Somalia, and Tanzania). Over the longer term these measures, together with some privatization, should result in greater public savings.

The government wage bills in Sub-Saharan Africa are typically high in relation both to GNP and government spending. For some countries, such as Burkina Faso, wages account for almost half of central government expenditures. To contain the wage bill, countries have attempted a variety of measures—hiring freezes, discontinuing the automatic hiring of graduates, early retirement, and even dismissals with compensation—but with

varying success. In most countries wages have fallen in real terms since 1980. This has not resulted in many voluntary departures, but rather in less effort and more "moonlighting." In practice the first and easiest cuts have been in the complementary inputs and materials required for effective delivery of services.

On average African countries spend 37 percent of revenues on salaries. Given tight resources, it is desirable to limit the wage bill. For example, Ghana has decided to limit its civil service wage bill to 5.0 to 5.5 percent of GDP. To this end the civil service (300,000 employees strong) was reduced by 24,000 in 1987–88. As a general rule governments should aim to hold spending on wages to no more than 25 percent of domestic revenue.

Lower military spending could also increase public savings. In Sub-Saharan Africa defense expenditures as a ratio of total expenditure is relatively high. Some countries have inordinately high ratios (see Table 8.2). Most of the countries

Table 8.2 Military spending
(percentage of total government expenditure)

	1980	1981	1985	1986
Sub-Saharan Africa	12.1	11.7	10.0	..
Ethiopia	30.0	34.0	34.6	32.0
Uganda	25.2	31.2	15.6	26.3
Zimbabwe	25.0	20.5	15.2	16.3
Somalia	19.2	22.7	..	..
Burkina Faso	17.0	18.4	19.2	18.3
Kenya	16.4	10.7	8.7	10.6
Senegal	16.8	11.8	10.8	10.6
Sudan	13.2	12.3	12.2	10.2

Source: World Bank data.

with good economic performance (such as Botswana, Ghana, and Mauritius) have low defense expenditures.

There is also potential to increase public savings by tightening procurement for government purchases through competitive bidding, bulk purchases, better handling, and proper audit and accountability. Donors bear a heavy responsibility to help bring about such improvements.

Vigilance can pay off in many ways. The lack of resources facing many African countries means that no opportunity to rationalize public expenditure should be neglected (see Box 8.2).

Mobilizing community savings

The notion that national development in Africa is best pursued through comprehensive planning and state controls has been discredited. Self-reliance and decentralization are now seen as offering more promise. Faced with declining public and private savings, governments are more willing to consider alternatives. In the rural areas health services are increasingly treated as a local affair involving a mixture of modern and traditional health workers. Public utilities, such as water supply, are being taken over by the community. Technologies are being developed with community involvement; so too are approaches to protecting the environment.

Africa has rich traditions of community and group welfare. This is reflected in the widespread practice of sharing among people, with its emphasis on grassroots initiatives and community-based projects. Such cooperation tends to be spontaneous and informal. Community-based development projects provide an avenue for mobilizing

---

Box 8.2 Burkina Faso: Cost-saving procurement of petroleum products

Burkina Faso is a landlocked country located 1,000 kilometers from the nearest port. It therefore felt the consequences of the last oil crisis much faster than other countries. Drawing on this experience, the government took a range of courageous measures to ensure a cost-effective supply of petroleum products. Those measures included diversifying supply sources and ports of entry and improving local infrastructure and stocking facilities significantly.

The process was initiated following a study on the financial implications of fuel supply, transport, and stocking management. The Société Nationale des Hydrocarbures de Burkina (SONABHY), a state-owned company created in 1985, became solely responsible for monitoring all aspects of the petroleum sector. Procurement of petroleum products was based on bilateral negotiations with Algeria, Nigeria, and more recently Brazil. To diversify transport routes and ports of entry, official negotiations were conducted for preferential transit through Lomé, Cotonou, and Tema. To improve storage capacity, private petroleum companies agreed to maintain reserve levels at 60 days, while the government agreed to provide sites for the depositories and to authorize bank loans for improving infrastructure and importing transport vehicles.

These measures have produced several results.
• SONABHY buys petroleum products from the cheapest source by international competitive bidding on the spot market in Rotterdam, by itself or together with a neighboring country. This pooling reduces the purchase price and transport cost.
• The supplies are obtained through the ports of Lomé, Cotonou, and Tema; more outlets for petroleum products have been opened; and railroad tanks are better utilized because each petroleum company uses them.
• The diversification of procurement sources and transport have saved an estimated $6 million a year.

In addition neighboring countries benefit from the initiative— both landlocked (Mali and Niger) and coastal countries (Benin, Côte d'Ivoire, Ghana, and Togo). The southern part of Mali is being supplied from Bobo-Dioulasso, and a part of Niger could potentially be supplied from Ouagadougou, since the distance between Niamey and Ouagadougou is 500 kilometers. Indirect positive effects result from increased economic activity in the transport, banking, and insurance sectors and from improvements in infrastructure. Moreover the scheme so far has been self-financing, without any initial investment cost to the government.

"community savings" in cash or labor for a range of local activities.

Much community development in Africa has been carried out by local self-help—for example, the construction, repair, and maintenance of community facilities. Because those involved are direct beneficiaries, motivation tends to be high. Such projects are an effective means of using free resources to meet the community's most urgent needs. There are many examples.

• In the Jasikan district of Ghana 18 towns and villages raised about $200,000 in 1988 to finance the first phase of a three-year integrated development program devised by the local people. Projects included primary schools, primary health clinics, and drinking water. People provided labor or cash, and the district council provided building materials and technical assistance. Elsewhere farmers are constructing, with assistance from the public works department, a feeder road to facilitate transportation of farm produce to market.

• In Mali the Segou Village Fund has been created from villagers' savings to initiate a system of self-managed development. The village communities have increased output of sorghum, introduced and developed cowpea cultivation, and reintroduced peanuts and maize (abandoned during the drought). Managed by a village credit committee, the fund also provides essential supplies, such as seed and medicines for people and livestock, and improved marketing.

• In Malawi community participation in water supply—one of the most successful programs in Sub-Saharan Africa—is based on strong community involvement and limited, but well-defined, government responsibilities (see Box 3.10).

Many of the themes of this report—human resource development, environmental protection, and self-reliance—are consistent with the concept of community savings and community-based activities. In the future the mobilization of community savings, if encouraged by governments, to finance not only public services and collective goods but also goods-producing and income-generating activities would make a major contribution to development, especially at the local level. Of a total labor force of about 600 million in 2020, a significant number are likely to be seasonally underemployed in the rural areas. Community savings will be useful not only to finance development needs but also to generate productive employment.

Local initiatives cannot flourish without linkages. Small and dispersed, they will have little impact unless they are incorporated into a broader framework. Involving central bureaucracies may stifle local initiative. Thus NGO support structures should be encouraged to serve as a link between the state and thousands of small self-help and community development efforts (see Box 8.3). Such NGOs are closer than government to the rural communities (since their staff often are located in the communities, they develop an empathy that government staff generally lack), highly motivated, cost conscious, and sympathetic to labor-intensive approaches, and flexible—a quality that stems from their small size and decentralized decisionmaking. Both local and foreign-based NGOs should be encouraged.

Boosting private savings

There is potential in Sub-Saharan Africa for mobilizing household savings through a strengthened financial system, both formal and informal. The government has an important role to play in this. Easier access to financial institutions and better financial intermediation would encourage households to defer consumption in favor of investment. Unfortunately many financial systems have deteriorated, and the need for reform is urgent. In contrast the informal sector has shown vitality and could be encouraged to play a greater role in development.

THE FINANCIAL SECTOR IN CRISIS. At independence the financial sector of African countries consisted of banks catering principally to expatriate communities, post office savings banks, cooperative societies, and moneylenders. Since then it has expanded, but the quality of services has evolved differently among countries. In some the banking system has become virtually illiquid. This occurred, for example, in Equatorial Guinea and Guinea in the early 1980s and is occurring now in Angola, Benin, and Mozambique. In contrast, in Kenya and Nigeria financial services have improved and deepened.

Macroeconomic policies have influenced the financial systems. Even when these policies have been inappropriate, commercial banks have been able to operate as long as governments did not use them to finance the public sector deficit. This has been the case in Uganda during the long years of civil unrest, and in Sudan despite acute economic difficulties. In Zaire the commercial banking system has remained liquid even with high inflation and rapid depreciation of the currency.

Box 8.3 Togo: A promising partnership with NGOs

The Togolese government's initiative to strengthen local NGOs is a remarkable partnership aimed at establishing an innovative institutional framework for collaboration with the NGO community, while providing direct financial support for NGO-sponsored development projects. It is part of a local Participatory Development Program for microprojects initiated and implemented at the community level. The program fosters effective community participation in building local capacity and institutions and mobilizes additional concessional resources for small-scale development initiatives.

At the core of this framework is a steering committee in which both government and NGOs are equally represented, with a limited but autonomous mandate to select NGO projects to be financed, provide policy guidance and direction, and serve as a forum for dialogue in carrying out the program. The government created a special division in the Ministry of Planning and Mines to coordinate and administer the program and to serve as a liaison with the NGO community and the NGO association.

During a pilot program the government and the NGO community have grappled with the practical problems of working together and have persevered in their efforts to reach a consensus. Their experience affords valuable insight into the dynamics of forging an effective partnership between government and NGOs.

• Respect for the role and contributions of each partner requires that the collaborative framework sustain an often precarious balance between the independence and autonomy of NGOs and the legitimate concerns and priorities of government.

• Supportive political leadership is critical to reinforce mutual respect and confidence, to foster awareness of the complementarity of the relation, and to direct government agencies to facilitate the NGO's work.

• Partnership and participation are important to the relation between NGOs and their beneficiary communities (as they are to that between NGOs and government). If projects are to be sustainable and yield long-term benefits,

communities must be more explicitly involved in design and implementation and in defining their own contributions.

The experience of the pilot project highlighted two interesting issues. First, selecting NGO representatives for the steering committee proved to be difficult and controversial, which demonstrated that NGOs are independent and autonomous not only from government but also from each other. It became clear that the NGO association can be only a platform for dialogue and a basis for collective participation in a collaborative framework, such as the steering committee, if that role is accepted by the entire NGO community.

Second, the pilot program had defined the role and functions of the steering committee poorly, and its autonomy and decisionmaking authority were initially not fully accepted by the government. This lack of clear lines of authority and decisionmaking led to actions that effectively undermined the authority of the steering committee and were strongly resented by the NGO community. It also revealed the NGO's organizational and operational limitations and emphasized the need to strengthen the capacity for technical reviewing project proposals and for monitoring project implementation.

The pilot program has considerably benefited both parties and as a result the institutional framework for collaboration between the government and NGOs is stronger. The government has reaffirmed its commitment to delegate decisionmaking authority to the steering committee and has reorganized the special division in the Ministry of Planning and Mines. Agreement on NGO eligibility and project selection criteria has been reached, and guidelines for submission and administration of NGO operations have been drawn up. A new Grassroots Development Initiatives Project, financed by IDA, supports NGO development actions at the community level and builds the capacity of local NGOs to design and manage their projects. Thus it will help government and NGOs to consolidate and deepen their promising partnership.

The banking system in the CFA countries has deteriorated in recent years. Although budget deficits and inflation have been generally contained, governments, unable to print money, forced the commercial banks to finance expenditures that would normally have been met by government subsidies. This led to the collapse of the banking system in Benin and has put the system in other CFA countries under strain. The bad debts held by these banks amount to more than $3 billion, representing 30 percent or more of the domestic assets of the banking system. Governments in the CFA franc zone have also interfered with the allocation of credit in several ways. They have induced commercial banks to extend credit to public enterprises that were not creditworthy. They have

financed crop credits on the basis of production costs (inclusive of export taxes) that were greater than export proceeds. Sometimes credits have been extended to individuals because of personal connections. Finally, the accumulation of large government arrears in payments to private sector suppliers and contractors, apart from adversely affecting the banks' portfolios, has been an indirect way to force them to finance the budget deficit. Governments have not been responsible for all bank failures. Private banks have collapsed from mismanagement and disregard of the central bank's regulations and codes of conduct. The rehabilitation and deepening of Africa's financial sectors are necessary if the future development strategy is to succeed.

CREDIT POLICIES. In even the most market-oriented countries credit allocation by commercial banks is affected by political considerations. In many African countries the degree of interference has been too high. Experience suggests that the most efficient way to achieve growth with equity is to use fiscal instruments—taxes and subsidies—and to manage commercial banks on business principles. To reflect the risks and the costs of administering loans, bank margins have to be higher for a customer borrowing a small amount without guarantees than for someone creditworthy borrowing a large amount.

Governments have tried to provide preferential credits to particular sectors and deserving social groups, but these have frequently been misused. Most development finance institutions and specialized banks (such as for housing or agriculture) have gone bankrupt. Moreover in most African countries the market is too small to support many specialized financial institutions in a competitive environment. Established commercial banks are often better placed to provide services to their clientele. With competition banks' costs can be contained—which is rarely the case in state-controlled banks.

The objectives pursued through subsidized or directed credits can be more efficiently achieved through price, trade, and fiscal policies. Thus agricultural income can be increased by raising producer prices and by improving rural infrastructure (notably, feeder roads) and the quality of public services in rural areas generally. Investments by small enterprises can be stimulated through fiscal and trade policies and by technical assistance. Some governments have improved the housing of low-income urban households by providing them with service lots. Concentrating public expenditures on infrastructure has been more beneficial to low-income groups; subsidized housing loans often favor medium- and high-income individuals.

INFORMAL FINANCIAL INSTITUTIONS. Because of high costs the formal commercial banking system may not be willing to provide financial services to remote areas or low-income households. These can generally be provided more efficiently through less formal channels. In some countries of West and Central Africa *tontines* or their equivalent provide an efficient way to mobilize savings and extend small loans to low-income households. The record of loan repayment, not assured by formal guarantees, but induced by social pressures, has generally been excellent (see Box 6.3). These traditional savings and loan associations can be promoted by building links with the formal financial institutions (see Box 8.4).

Banks or informal savings and credit associations should be entrusted with the task of assessing the commercial risks attached to individual credit requests. Monetary authorities will need to ensure that the pace of money creation is consistent with broader economic objectives. This equilibrium should ideally be reached with interest and foreign exchange rates that clear the markets and avoid the need for rationing. This has not been the case in most African countries, but it should be the policy for the future.

INTEREST RATES. When the inflation rate exceeds the nominal interest rate, creditors lose and borrowers gain; no equilibrium therefore can be reached without rationing credit. When the expected rate of depreciation of the domestic currency exceeds the premium of the domestic interest rate over interest rates abroad, holders of financial assets denominated in domestic currency profit by transforming these assets into assets denominated in foreign currencies. This leads to capital flight and further depreciation of the domestic currency—hardly conducive to domestic investment.

Recently some countries have taken measures to bring interest and exchange rates more in line with market equilibrium. Experience has shown that such adjustments cannot succeed without restoring budgetary discipline and that it was often beneficial to relax controls progressively. Despite these difficulties countries should aim to liberalize interest and exchange rates if they are to maximize growth.

REHABILITATION OF THE BANKING SYSTEMS. In the short term the pressing need is to reestablish an operational banking system where it has broken down. Where the public has lost confidence in existing banks, the best solution may be to start from scratch by establishing new ones, as was done in Guinea at the end of 1985. Where the banking system has not yet collapsed, it must be restructured without delay, and the measures must be strong enough to inspire the confidence of the public and the business community.

The package of measures has to be tailored to each country. If political interference in credit allocation is largely responsible for the weakening of the system, steps should be taken to protect

Box 8.4   Rwanda: Banques populaires

The objectives of *Banques populaires* are to mobilize rural savings, to make loans for productive purposes, and to support and stimulate cooperatives. Since they began operations in 1975, they have become Rwanda's fastest growing and most important financial institutions in rural areas. The Banques populaires have been successful because:

•They are based on a "mutualiste" system well suited to its constituency

•They are located mostly in rural areas not served by other financial institutions and thus take advantage of the rural population's relatively high propensity to save

•They offer a suitable mechanism to provide small loans for basic needs, agriculture, and microenterprise activities in rural areas.

The Union Suisse des Banques Raiffeisen has helped the Banques populaires to become established, train technicians, and cover start-up costs. The government has subsidized the agricultural loans since 1983, although this subsidy has declined each year.

The central office staff of the Banques populaires start branches by spending several months in the region educating community members about the purpose of the institution. Those who sign up as members can buy up to 10 shares and are entitled to make deposits, receive loans, and vote at the local Annual General Assembly, at which the Board of Directors and Oversight Board are elected. The branch Board of Directors, in turn, elects representatives to the National Council, which sets general policy.

The Board of Directors approves loans, and, in order to do so, board members receive training in loan analysis, approval, and supervision procedures. Central office supervisors inspect the branches, and a delegate from the central office participates in loan approval meetings. A branch generally has only one Banque populaire staff member, whose prime responsibility is to record transactions, to submit monthly statements to the central office, and to inform the Board of Directors about overdue loan payments.

Branches are mostly located in rural areas, and the principal depositors are small savers with passbook account deposits of about RF13,650 ($170). As of 1988, 102 branches had been established, and the target is to have at least one branch in each of Rwanda's 143 communes. Between 1980 and 1988 deposits in commercial and savings banks increased by 279 percent while deposits in the Banques populaires rose by 726 percent; total assets, equity, and revenues doubled in current terms. Part of the success is explained by the fact that there are few commercial banks in the rural areas; the only other savings system, the *tontines*, often use Banques populaires services to manage their funds.

The central office sets a maximum loan approval amount for each branch, based on its portfolio quality and growth in deposits. The policy is to give smaller loans to more people rather than large loans to a few individuals. Although farmers provide more than one-half of the deposits, until 1988 they received only about 31.4 percent of loans because merchants' and construction activities were favored. The Banques populaires have now begun to change the composition of their loan portfolios. Some of the initiatives are showing encouraging results, but diversification is hampered by lack of project development units and trained staff. Compared with other development financial institutions, the average of 30 to 60 days between loan request and disbursement is favorable. Total administrative expenses and personnel costs also compare favorably with most rural credit programs in developing countries. The operation of branches has been profitable; however, central office costs for supervising the branches have caused the institution as a whole to be unprofitable to date, but net losses have been declining. In 1988 the Banques populaires reached a consolidated financial balance, excluding foreign assistance.

Operating on the "mutualiste" principle well entrenched in Rwandan society, the Banques populaires appear to be well suited to deepen the financial system. They have been very successful in mobilizing savings because the rural population values the convenience and security of passbook accounts. They have also been relatively successful in developing a suitable lending mechanism for small loans for agricultural improvements and microenterprises in rural areas, an inherently difficult activity. Operations have also been helped by the relatively stable environment with low inflation.

---

banks from such interference, if necessary by selling governments' interest in them. Monetary authorities may need to strengthen supervision of banks by requiring regular audits and enforcing prudential ratios. If poor repayment is due to lack of guarantees (or to the difficulties of enforcing them), changes in the legal system may be required. New financial instruments may also be needed; leasing may provide a safer financial device than moneylending.

NEW FINANCIAL INSTRUMENTS. When the banking system is operating securely, financial intermediation should be progressively deepened and diversified to develop flexible money and capital markets. The central bank could then regulate the money supply through an open market policy by purchasing and selling monetary instruments. This would be far better than imposing credit ceilings on individual banks, since they reduce competition and can be discriminatory. An open market policy requires monetary instruments (such as treasury and corporate bonds and bank certificates of deposit) that are liquid and available with maturities corresponding to the needs of the business community. But bonds are liquid only if the market is active, which is not the case in most African countries. The turnover in the secondary bond market in Côte d'Ivoire was 0.7 percent in 1987, compared with an average of 50 percent in industrial countries.

To mobilize savings and to facilitate investment financing, money markets can be supplemented by stock markets. They exist in some African countries, but daily turnover is small. The Abidjan stock market, established in 1976, has been dormant for years because of regulations that favor Ivorians and the depressed economic conditions during most of the 1980s. In addition well-to-do residents invest financial assets abroad rather than at home. If nationals do not trust their own domestic markets, foreigners cannot be expected to do so. The expansion of domestic financial markets requires a climate of confidence in the economy and in the stability of economic and financial policies. The authorities clearly have an essential role to play in creating this climate.

Financial markets could expand sufficiently in countries such as Kenya and Nigeria to enable the monetary authorities to operate an open market policy as a substitute for direct monetary controls, such as credit ceilings. Every government should have a long-term view of the evolution of its financial system and should define the time path realistically. Since most African economies are small, their domestic money and capital markets should be linked to others in Africa and abroad. This would promote trade and joint ventures among African countries as well as exchanges between Africa and the rest of the world. In particular it would stimulate private capital and foreign technology to flow into African countries.

External resources

Export potential

Africa's export performance indicates the continent's unrealized potential. The average annual growth rate of exports from Sub-Saharan Africa fell from 6.6 percent in 1965–80 to –0.8 percent in 1980–87. Africa's share of world markets declined from 2.4 percent in 1970 to 1.3 percent in 1987. The expansion of world trade during the past three decades appears to have largely bypassed Africa. If its economies are to grow, they must improve their share in world markets and diversify their exports.

An argument frequently advanced against vigorously expanding commodity exports is that a generally inelastic world demand implies that aggressive supply behavior by any producer will ultimately hurt the whole sector, initially through lower prices and ultimately perhaps through the forced exit of some producers. From a practical point of view this "fallacy of composition" argument is unconvincing. That producers compete for markets is a fundamental reality, as true for manufactures as it is for primary products. During the 1970s it was aggressive exporting on the part of other developing country producers that eroded Africa's export share, compounded by agricultural subsidies in developed countries.

African production for most commodities (excluding cocoa, coffee, and copper) is a relatively small (less than 20 percent) share of the world market. Even doubling production would have a small effect on world supply. Africa cannot afford to adopt a passive role and lose even larger market shares to more aggressive Asian and Latin American exporters. In negotiating commodity agreements, Africa's loss of market share should be seen as an argument for more favorable treatment.

Since the prospects for significantly higher prices for most primary commodities are poor, export earnings must grow through increasing the supply of existing exports and diversification. Diversification is also the most effective way to protect a country from the impact of large fluctuations in individual commodity prices, as shown by the experience of South and Southeast Asian countries. However, although diversification is an essential long-term goal, in the short and medium term countries must seek to expand traditional exports since it will take time to establish a new product as a major export. In any event it would be best to provide neutral incentives for exports and to avoid targeted policies that may end up misallocating resources. Governments are generally bad at picking winners.

Encouragingly, during the past 15 years or so, some African countries have managed to find new opportunities in world markets for certain primary commodities such as vegetable oils, soybeans, and fishery products. Kenya has had success in exporting fruits, vegetables, and flowers. But except for Mauritius, countries have not diversified significantly into labor-intensive light manufactures, and the few manufactures exported are mostly processed primary products with little value added (see Chapter 5).

Sub-Saharan Africa needs to find new markets. Its traditional market, Europe, has seen declining imports from developing countries (down from 34

Table 8.3 Actual and projected macroeconomic framework for Sub-Saharan Africa
(percentage of GDP unless otherwise specified)

	Actual			Projected		
	1975–80	*1980–85*	*1986–87*	*1990*	*2000*	*2020*
Growth rate of GDP (annual percent)	2.8	–0.3	0.8	2.5	5	5
Investment	21.4	16.2	15.1	17	25	25
Gross domestic savings	19.6	13.9	11.8	12	18	22
Adjustment factor[a]	–3.0	–1.0	–2.9	–3	–2	–2
Net transfers	4.8	3.3	6.2	8	9	5
Imports[b]	29.0	23.7	25.5	30	33	33
Exports	24.2	20.4	19.3	22	24	28
Net transfers	4.8	3.3	6.2	8	9	5
Memorandum items						
Efficiency of investment[c]	13.0	..	5.0	15	20	20
Import elasticity	2.1	..	..	..	1.1	

.. Negligible or negative.
a. Adjustment for interest payments and errors and omissions (discrepancies between national accounts and balance of payments, including treatment of technical assistance).
b. Goods and noninterest service obtained from recorded figures of exports and net transfers; includes items such as technical assistance expenditures abroad not fully reflected in national accounts.
c. Additional value added per unit of investment.
Source: World Bank data.

to 20 percent in 1970–85) compared with the United States, now the biggest market for developing-country exports, and Asian countries. Since the share of Asian markets and the share of nontraditional items in world trade is likely to grow rapidly, special efforts will have to be made to enter this market. Competition in international markets will remain intense, but continued economic growth worldwide could expand demand for African exports. African countries need to expand trade with each other (see Chapter 7). But there are no soft options; Africa will succeed or fail on its ability to compete.

The composition and level of export growth will, of course, vary with the country. In the future development strategy the ratio of exports to GDP is targeted to rise from an annual average of about 19 percent in 1986–87 to about 24 percent by 2000 and to 28 percent by 2020; the growth rate of exports should improve significantly from a negative rate in 1980–87 to about 5 percent a year, thus reversing the decline in Africa's share of primary exports.

Import requirements

Given the modest prospects for expanding exports, Africa will face a foreign exchange shortage well into the next century. The strategy proposed in this report is not capital-intensive, but the emphasis on infrastructure and the higher rates of

investment proposed nonetheless imply substantial imports of capital goods.

African countries have scope for using imports more efficiently as well as for reducing luxury and food imports. As domestic production grows, domestic products can substitute for imports, particularly in high value-added goods. Nonetheless in the early 1990s imports would need to grow faster than GDP to make up for the compression that has occurred during the past decade. Imports in the 1990s will need to grow at least by 1 percent a year over and above the projected GDP growth rate of 4 to 5 percent. This implies an elasticity of 1.2 for the 1990s, which suggests imports of about 33 percent of GDP in 2000. Thereafter imports may be expected to grow in step with GDP. Recent experience of African countries with strong adjustment programs (such as Ghana, Kenya, and Mauritius) suggests an import elasticity of 1.5. It is assumed that success in increasing food production will curb the growth in food imports and, given the projected rise in investment from 15 to 25 percent of GDP, imports of capital goods will rise faster than income.

Overall resource balance

The external resource requirements for a program of growth and social development can be calculated either as the gap between investment and domestic savings or as the gap between import needs and export capacity. *Ex post*, the two are identical.

An initial target for GDP growth of 4 percent a year, rising to 5 percent, has been proposed (see Chapter 2). With the best efforts to reduce population growth, per capita incomes could be raised by between 1 and 2 percent during 1990–2020. The macroeconomic assumptions used to analyze the implications of this target are set out in Table 8.3. Given the weakness of the data base and the impact of exchange rate adjustments on trade to GDP ratios, the parameters given are broad, and the scenario is illustrative. They are not econometric projections based on historical trends and relationships since the objective is to modify the past growth strategy.

The low levels to which savings have plummeted can be raised only slowly given the long time it will take to reorient consumption and behavioral patterns. An overall domestic savings rate of 22 percent of GDP must be attained by 2020 to reduce dependence on external financing. By 2000, however, the savings rate may increase to about 18 percent of GDP, which, after allowance for interest payments, would leave a gap between investment and savings of about 9 percent of GDP.

The effect of measures to promote exports and the likely changes in the world markets for Sub-Saharan Africa's exports can be assessed only country by country. Overall a growth rate of export volume slightly higher than the envisaged GDP growth rate would be a minimum and feasible target to narrow the external resource gap in the region.

Given the decline in African imports during the past decade—and remembering that per capita imports are almost half those of the early 1980s—some recovery in imports is needed in the short term. Over the longer term, however, it is assumed that the ratio of imports to income remains roughly constant.

The net transfer required to close the external gap works out to be roughly the same: about 9 percent of GDP in 2000. Thereafter the need for foreign savings (as a percentage of GDP) is projected to decline to 5 percent of GDP by 2020.

Development assistance in the 1990s

Aid levels

Self-reliance is an important objective of the Lagos Plan of Action and in other statements by Africans. The future development strategy is de-signed to achieve this objective in the long run. By 2020 Africa's reliance on external resources to finance development and on food imports is projected to be much smaller than today (see Table 8.3, above).

A high level of resource transfer may lead to an aid dependency syndrome and a decline in domestic savings, overvalued exchange rates, and high wage rates. With a proper policy framework, however, such transfers can be associated with high growth rates and appropriate wage and exchange rates. In Korea, for example, resource transfers amounted to about 10 percent of GDP throughout the 1960s and 1970s, yet impressive growth rates of GDP and exports as well as high investment rates were achieved while maintaining competitive exchange rates and wages.

The momentum of aid generated in the past few years will have to be maintained during the 1990s for several reasons. First, countries will have to continue the difficult adjustment programs initiated in recent years. Those that have not yet embarked on reform will need to do so. Unless these programs are funded adequately, they cannot be effective or sustained; the successes of The Gambia, Ghana, and Guinea, where funding was adequate, are to be contrasted with Zambia, where inadequate funding made it difficult for the government to stick to its adjustment program.

Second, there will be some major new entrants to the list of IDA-eligible countries. Nigeria has already become eligible and will increasingly depend on official development assistance (ODA) to meet its external resource gap. In the past Nigeria has received a negligible amount of ODA ($0.6 per capita in 1986). If by the year 2000 it were to receive the same level of per capita ODA as other oil-exporting African countries such as Cameroon and Côte d'Ivoire, it will account for about $2.5 billion of ODA a year; this would mean a 17 percent increase in ODA estimated for 1990. In addition Angola can be expected to join IDA.

Third, special efforts are needed in the 1990s to correct the backsliding that has occurred in areas such as food security, human resource development, and infrastructure and to fund initiatives in family planning and the environment. By 2000 food imports are likely to rise to the order of 15 million tons, which will cost about $4 billion at 1988 prices, a large part of which will have to be met through foreign aid. For human resource development, additional expenditures of about $10 billion (1990 prices) a year will be needed by 2000. The backlog of road maintenance itself is estimated to cost $5 billion on top of the $700 million needed annually during the next decade to avoid further deterioration. For family planning and environmental protection, large initial efforts are needed to give momentum to these programs.

As demonstrated above, a net transfer of resources of about 9 percent of GDP on average will be required to achieve sustained growth during the 1990s. The ODA required to meet these targets will depend on such variables as debt relief programs, nonconcessional capital inflows from private and public sources, and reserve requirements—all of which are subject to uncertainties. With sustained policy reforms private capital inflows could improve significantly through increased private remittances, reverse capital flight, and improved inflows of foreign private investment. The evidence of several countries (such as Ghana and Senegal), however, suggests that restoring private sector confidence takes time and that during the next decade only moderate progress can be expected. Moreover, given deteriorating creditworthiness, nonconcessional borrowings should be lower than in the past. It is estimated that the *net* receipts from these sources will be moderate, probably about $6 billion a year.

The external resource requirement of Sub-Saharan Africa during the 1990s could be met if donors achieve two related targets. First, during the 1990s gross ODA continues to increase at about 4 percent a year in real terms. Second, debt relief mechanisms are put in place so that the actual debt service payments for countries with strong reform programs are kept within manageable limits (a menu of options for debt relief is discussed in the following section). For the region as a whole it is estimated that adequate debt relief will be available to keep the debt service payments in the 1990s around the level of the 1980s (that is, about $9 billion a year). If this does not occur, higher levels of external assistance will be necessary. Alternatively, if debt relief exceeds the above estimate, external assistance requirements would be correspondingly reduced.

Multilateral agencies, unable to reschedule their loans, have mobilized special additional finance for low-income African countries. Through the World Bank's Joint Program of Action for Sub-Saharan Africa, the Special Facility for Africa mobilized almost $2 billion in nonproject aid and joint cofinancing of structural adjustment programs from mid-1985 to mid-1988. The World Bank also launched a three-year Special Program of Assistance (SPA) for low-income, debt-dis-

tressed Sub-Saharan African countries at the end of 1987, which provides highly concessional, quick-disbursing finance. To be eligible, a country must have a donor-endorsed economic reform program with the World Bank and the IMF; by mid-1989 22 countries were eligible. The SPA has four main elements: additional disbursements from IDA, concessional adjustment cofinancing from bilateral donors and other multilateral agencies, concessional rescheduling, and concessional financing of interest due on World Bank loans. Eighteen donor governments and agencies pledged an initial $6.4 billion in cofinancing, about half of which can be considered additional to existing aid programs.

In 1986 the IMF established its Structural Adjustment Facility to provide assistance on concessional terms (interest rates of 0.5 percent, with repayments over a 10-year period including 4.5 years' grace) to low-income countries undertaking comprehensive structural adjustment programs. It disbursed about $0.667 billion to the Sub-Saharan Africa countries in 1986–88. To enlarge the pool of concessional resources available to low-income countries, the IMF established the Enhanced Structural Adjustment Facility, which became effective in January 1988. Donor contributions were expected to provide new resources totaling $8.4 billion and to increase the concessionality of IMF resources in Sub-Saharan Africa. By mid-1989 eight African countries had access to the enhanced facilities.

Debt relief: A menu of options

Africa cannot escape its present economic crisis without reducing its debt burden sizably. Several important initiatives have been taken in recent years to provide debt relief, and many new proposals are under consideration. Together they provide a menu of options for keeping the actual debt service payments within manageable limits. These fall into two broad groups: debt reduction and flexible and concessional debt rescheduling, which postpones debt service payments or reduces long-term debt burden, and debt swaps.

DEBT REDUCTION AND DEBT RESCHEDULING. For low-income countries several donors (such as Canada, Finland, Germany, Netherlands, Norway, Sweden, and the United Kingdom) have converted concessional bilateral loans to grants. Sub-Saharan Africa has also benefited from about two-thirds of worldwide cancellations reported two-thirds of worldwide cancellations reported by creditors, far higher than its share of global concessional debt. More recently France has decided to write off concessional debt owed it by 35 of the poorest African countries; the measure is expected to cancel some $2.4 billion of debt. Belgium has also decided to cancel government-to-government debt of 13 African countries. These debts are estimated at about BF7.5 billion (about $200 million). In July 1989 the United States announced that beginning in fiscal 1990 it would forgive development assistance (DA) and Economic Support Fund (ESF) debt owed by Sub-Saharan African countries with reform programs. To be eligible, the debtor country must have in effect an IMF stand-by, a structural adjustment facility or an enhanced facility, or a World Bank structural adjustment program. The total amount forgiven will depend on the number of countries meeting the eligibility requirements, however; 23 Sub-Saharan African countries carry DA or ESF debt amounting to almost $1 billion.

The scope for further relief through this option is limited, however, since scheduled payments on bilateral ODA (concessional) debt is small. In fiscal 1988, IDA used a portion of its repayments to provide supplementary credits to countries no longer receiving World Bank loans to help meet debt service borrowings from their IBRD borrowing. In addition the IBRD has allocated $100 million from its fiscal 1989 net income to fund on a grant basis a new facility to finance the reduction of commercial debt of IDA-only countries with satisfactory medium-term economic programs and comprehensive debt service plans.

At the Venice economic summit in June 1987 the seven major industrial countries (G7) agreed that "for those of the poorest countries that are undertaking adjustment efforts, consideration should be given to the possibility of applying lower interest rates on existing debt, and agreement should be reached, especially in the Paris Club, on longer repayment and grace periods to ease the debt burden." Since then, reschedulings by the Paris Club have reflected that new approach, with Guinea-Bissau, Malawi, Mozambique, Niger, and Somalia receiving 20-year maturities, including 10 years' grace, and seven other Sub-Saharan African countries, 14-year maturities with 6 years' grace. In 1988 the G7 countries further agreed on measures to reduce bilateral debt service obligations of very low-income countries to provide short term balance of payments relief.

Under the terms of the agreement reached at the June 1988 Toronto economic summit, the debts of IDA-eligible countries could be rescheduled, based on individual creditor countries choosing among three options:

• Forgiving one-third of the debt service due on obligations rescheduled through the Paris Club

• Rescheduling all eligible obligations at market interest rates, but over a very long time period (25 years' maturity and a grace period of 14 years)

• Rescheduling all eligible obligations at concessional interest rates with long maturity (14 years, including 8 years' grace).

By mid-1989 the Toronto initiative was applied to seven low-income African countries (Central African Republic, Madagascar, Mali, Niger, and Tanzania in 1988; and Senegal and Uganda in 1989).

In March 1989 the US Secretary of the Treasury called on the IMF and the World Bank to support and encourage efforts aimed at commercial debt reduction for major developing countries by catalyzing new financing. Subsequently the World Bank and the IMF agreed that for the next three years a proportion of their lending may be earmarked for debt reduction. It is expected that the Brady Plan will include several Sub-Saharan African countries.

Beyond these initiatives, proposals have been made to provide long-term relief on debt from official as well as commercial sources. Among these is a proposal from the African Development Bank, jointly with S. G. Warburg of London, which suggests a securitization plan whereby short- and medium-term claims can be exchanged for longer term bonds of the same face value but carrying a lower interest rate for all debt, except concessional loans from bilateral creditors and loans from multilateral agencies. Under this formulation eligible debt would be exchanged for a 20-year bullet (single-payment) bond, with a fixed, below-market rate. The debtor would make annual payments into a redemption fund—to a single entity instead of a multitude of creditors—managed by a board of trustees, which would manage the fund's assets to ensure redemption of the notes at maturity.

SWAPS WITH LOCAL ASSETS. During the past two years proposals have been made to relieve the pressure on foreign exchange resources by swapping local assets—physical or financial—for debts. Nigeria has already converted close to $100 million (as of May 1989) of its promissory notes vary greatly, but there are some common features. Most arrangements enable the debtor to share part of the discount on debt, determine the sectors of the economy in which equity can be purchased, and place restrictions on the dividends and principal that can be repatriated.

The simplest form of swap—debt for equity—has very limited application in Africa because of the lack of perceived investment opportunities and developed markets for financial instruments. The possibility of swapping debt for the assets of a state enterprise is being studied in the Congo and Togo, but so far no arrangements have been concluded.

New and innovative forms of debt conversions are being explored. For example, several debt-for-nature swaps have been proposed. One way would be for debt to be exchanged for local currency or local bonds to be held by a local environmental organization for investment in environmental projects. Alternatively debt might be sold to a multinational corporation to support environmentally sound corporate investments, or, more directly, official debt relief might be tied to support for environmental actions. The first debt-for-nature swap occurred in July 1987 in Bolivia, with an arrangement aimed at protecting Bolivia's tropical rainforest. This approach can be broadened to cover any form of debt-for-development arrangement. For example, in December 1988 the Midland Bank donated to UNICEF its holding of Sudanese debt ($800,000), which the Sudanese government redeemed in local currency to be applied to a water, reforestation, and health program for the Kordofan region. This donation can be treated as a tax deductible expense for the bank.

Another variation would be for a donor to purchase debt (at a discount) and then pass the loans to an NGO, on the understanding that the debtor government will redeem the loans in local currency or bonds. The NGO will subsequently exchange or swap the debt. The value of the assets received in this exchange may be less than the debt's face value but greater than the debt's purchase price. The NGO would then use the proceeds for development purposes. Such local currency swaps are useful only when the country has domestic savings available for that purpose; otherwise they may result in inflationary pressure. In the CFA franc zone the scope for such swaps is particularly limited because of the convertibility of local currency with the French franc.

Impact of debt relief measures

Many of the above initiatives benefit only low-income African countries, and there are no comparable special programs for middle-income African countries with acute debt problems. The middle-income countries in Africa face long-term development problems not significantly different from the low-income countries. And, indeed, when the correction of overvalued currencies—Nigeria's for example—places some of these countries in the low-income category, they should be considered eligible for the same debt relief measures as those granted to low-income African countries, provided they are willing to implement adjustment programs.

There is a range of technical and legal problems to be settled—in addition to the "free riders" and the moral hazard issues. Each debtor country has its specific debt profile and special circumstances, and the solution to its debt problem must be decided on a case-by-case basis. As a general principle debt relief should be given only to countries that are both debt distressed and willing to adopt reforms to improve their capacity for growth and future debt service. To truly benefit debtor countries, special finance for debt relief or concessional debt rescheduling should be genuinely "additional" and not taken out of the aid budgets already allocated to the beneficiary countries. In countries with severe problems of arrears, bridge financing may be needed to make use of debt relief facilities.

While debt relief can never be cost free, Africa's debts, although devastating for Africa, are relatively minor for the creditors in relation to global debts. The kind of debt write-downs arranged with commercial banks for large Latin American debtor countries are not likely to be offered to Africa and, in some important respects, are not relevant to Africa. Significant debt relief from new money cannot be counted on in the near future, and conventional debt restructuring is unlikely to generate the debt relief required to restore growth. For most African countries the predominant problem is the official debt. Although the Toronto arrangements are in the right direction, clearly more far-reaching relief is needed. Given the acuteness of Africa's problems, its poverty and social distress, when put alongside the major benefits enjoyed by consumers in the creditor countries from the fall in commodity prices, it is reasonable to expect that debt relief measures will

Table 8.4 ODA requirements for Sub-Saharan Africa, 1981–2000
(billions of dollars)

	Annual average 1981–85 (current dollars)	1986 (current dollars)	Projected (1990 dollars) 1990	2000
Net transfers	5	8	12	19
(percentage of GDP)	(3)	(5)	(8)	(9)
Debt service payments	9	9	9	9
Other flows[a]	6	6	6	6
Gross ODA	8	11	15	22

a. This includes gross nonconcessional borrowings, net direct foreign private investment, net private transfers, changes in reserves, and errors and omissions.
Source: World Bank data.

keep debt service payments in the 1990s at or below the level actually made in the 1980s (about $9 billion a year).

Need for continued special assistance

The above assumptions lead to gross ODA requirements of $22 billion (1990 prices) a year by 2000 (see Table 8.4). To meet these requirements, ODA would have to grow at 4 percent a year in real terms. This is below the rate of growth that was in fact achieved in the 1980s. Given the present prospects for aid, however, this may not be realized in the 1990s unless the share of low-income countries in ODA can be increased, since reallocating ODA from poor countries in other regions would seriously hamper their development efforts. If adequate funding for Africa is not forthcoming, Africa's decline is likely to continue in the 1990s. If, however, the special programs of assistance for Africa can be continued for another decade, through either higher total ODA or an increased share of ODA going to low-income countries, Africa should be able to reverse its decline and to level off, and eventually reduce aid.

Clearly the needs of Africa for ODA will depend on the number of countries that can introduce and sustain economic programs that both increase the efficiency of resource use and put developmental issues on center stage in these programs. Donors should recognize that their challenge is to ensure that no such reform program collapses because of lack of adequate external funding. Determining what is "adequate" is not easy. There can be too much external assistance in some instances,

thereby undermining the domestic commitment to the program, as well as too little assistance in other cases. These are matters of judgment. They are calls that must be made in a disciplined manner. The judgment call on the optimal level of external assistance for a country should not be influenced by narrow political and bureaucratic pressures in any donor institution.

Impact on consumption

Even with the level of special donor assistance proposed, the improvement in per capita incomes would be modest—less than 1 percent a year during the 1990s. If, at the same time, the savings rate is to be increased by 50 percent, the per capita consumption would remain stagnant during this period. However, income and consumption of the vast majority would increase at a significant rate. As noted in Chapter 2, labor productivity in agriculture and the informal sector (which together account for 95 percent of the labor force) is projected to increase by about 1.5 percent a year. With a deceleration of the population growth rate, the dependency ratio would decline, and per capita income would grow at about 2 percent a year. This would allow per capita consumption of the bottom 95 percent to increase at about 2 percent a year, which would be reflected mostly in increasing food consumption (projected to increase at 1 percent a year) and increasing access to primary health and education facilities.

It is the top 5 percent of income earners belonging to the "modern sector" who would contribute most to the reduction of public dissavings and consequently will see their consumption compressed. Since average value added per worker for the modern sector is not projected to grow, this sector can be expected to experience a stagnant per capita income and a decline in per capita consumption amounting to about 2 percent a year in order to allow for increased savings and investment. This would be largely the result of rationalizing the tax structure, reducing subsidies, and increasing cost sharing in infrastructure services and tertiary health and education facilities. Beyond 2000 the situation would ease. The correction in consumption pattern would have been made, and with rising incomes and declining population growth, aggregate consumption would rise by more than 2 percent, enabling both income groups to benefit.

Downside risks

Given the uncertainties of the world economic environment and the optimistic assumptions about improving the implementation capacity of many African governments, the scenario presented in Table 8.3 (above) is only illustrative, and there are serious downside risks. It assumes that the efficiency of investments will improve about 50 percent over the levels of the 1970s. Also, during the 1990s, domestic savings and net transfers as a percentage of GDP are both projected to rise by 50 percent. If there is no increase in the ratio of net transfers to GDP, the growth rate in per capita income would fall to 0.3 percent. With the domestic savings rate stagnating, per capita incomes would stagnate; and if the efficiency of investment does not improve, per capita incomes would decline. Alternatively if improvement in all these parameters is only half of the projected levels, per capita income would also stagnate. Any greater shortfall in achieving these targets would cause per capita incomes to continue to decline. Moreover, if the top 5 percent is not willing to accept a reduction in per capita consumption, the projected improvements in the consumption levels of the bottom 95 percent will not be achieved, nor will the growth targets. In such an event it would not be possible to effectively tackle the backsliding that has occurred in areas such as food security, human resource development, environmental degradation, and infrastructure—so essential for sustainable growth. Clearly this is not an all-or-nothing situation; but there is a fine margin between modest growth with improved human welfare and a spiraling decline that can easily become politically explosive.

Aid composition

In line with the strategy proposed in this report, ODA should be increasingly focused on supporting public expenditures on social and physical infrastructure. Structural adjustment financing will remain an important component in the 1990s and beyond, but it should be used more selectively. Lending for technical assistance needs restructuring, and NGOs should be used more intensively for channeling ODA, particularly for grassroots development.

One of the central recommendations of this report is to promote a more enabling environment in which agriculture and industry can grow rapidly in response to market opportunities and tech-

nical change. Even in professed socialist African countries these sectors are overwhelmingly dominated by private sector farmers and manufacturing firms—informal, intermediate, and large-scale. There is some, but only limited, scope for direct public sector (including donor) assistance to these productive units. Governments and donors must support private sector farmers and firms indirectly, however. First, this should encourage the development of an incentive system reflected in improved macroeconomic and sector policies. Second, the indirect support should come mainly from the direct funding of the human infrastructure (such as research and extension, education, health, and training) and the physical infrastructure (such as roads, telecommunications, power, and shipping). Improvements in agricultural and industrial production and capacity depend on improvements in policies and infrastructure. The formulation of government expenditure programs to expand human and physical infrastructure is essential both for closing the social gap and for developing the physical and human infrastructure on which growth depends.

Donor strategy before and during the 1970s had focused primarily on financing projects and related technical assistance to help improve human and physical infrastructure. Disappointment with the results of this strategy led in the 1980s to a donor strategy that has emphasized quick-disbursing financial support for policy reform, principally through structural and sectoral adjustment lending led by the World Bank and the IMF. Both strategies have had strengths and weaknesses. How can they be modified during the 1990s to support the changes in development strategies outlined above?

SOCIAL AND INFRASTRUCTURE DEVELOPMENT LOANS. The composition of donor support should increasingly be changed from financing general imports as part of a structural adjustment program to directly financing domestic development expenditure on physical infrastructure and human resource development. Most external financing should not be limited to project lending. This has often led to an overemphasis on investment in bricks and mortar and less on recurrent outlays on instructional materials, medicines, and operation and maintenance. Moreover donor project lending has frequently meant projects that are import-intensive and proceed irrespective of distortions in sectoral policies and programs. External funding of "time slices" of sector and subsector programs allows these programs to be modified during implementation and avoids the potential distortion of project lending. It would also permit the level of donor funding to be varied more easily depending on progress on both macroeconomic and sector policy issues. This approach would have a desirable element of automaticity. Thus if donors agree to finance a specified percentage of development expenditures in the key areas—human resource development and infrastructure—countries that give preference to these sectors would automatically receive a higher share of donor assistance.

STRUCTURAL ADJUSTMENT LENDING. Concern over macro-sector policy will continue into the 1990s and beyond. Structural adjustment is not a one-shot effort but reflects the need for pricing, exchange rate, fiscal, and other macroeconomic and sector policies to be continuously appraised and modified. With population growing at more than 3 percent a year, African countries cannot afford to lose any opportunity to improve the efficiency with which their resources are used through changes in policies. Therefore the question is: how can donors most effectively provide support for structural adjustment programs?

Structural adjustment lending, as it has developed during the 1980s, is still needed. It links World Bank financing and bilateral financing directly to an agreed program of macroeconomic and sector policy reform. Greater efforts should be made to internalize the process and to provide more *ex post* support for measures already adopted rather than *ex ante* conditionality based on promises of action to be taken in the future (see Chapter 9). In the 1980s there was need for *ex ante* conditionality, but in the 1990s Sub-Saharan Africa will most likely be at a different stage. As countries make progress, they need support for measures already in place. To sustain this trend, it will most likely be desirable to strengthen countries' management capacity.

TECHNICAL ASSISTANCE. Donor technical assistance to Africa was reported to be more than $3 billion in 1987. Average technical assistance for 42 African countries amounted to about $7 per capita. Expenditure on volunteers and technical assistance incorporated in capital projects (amounting to $400 million for the World Bank alone) was excluded. It is estimated that more than 80,000 people are working in Africa as technical assistants. They include senior policy advisers to governments, senior managers of operational agencies, and senior technical professionals—technicians, nurses, and teachers. This high level of technical assistance has to be set against the enormous growth in the number of educated, trained, and experienced Africans that has occurred since independence. The human resource capacities of Africans will continue to expand during the next generation. The implications for donor technical assistance policies must be examined—particularly since donor and African government attitudes toward technical assistance changed very little during the past generation. In education most African countries no longer depend on technical assistance for primary or secondary schoolteachers. In many countries, however, education still receives the largest share of such assistance, followed by agriculture and health. There are many expatriate experts in most departments of government and in operational agencies. For instance, despite the education and training of a generation of Africans in economics, ministers of finance and planning still choose expatriates to undertake policy analysis. Many governments lack confidence in local specialists and yield to the offers of expatriates—often at little cost. In the past few years, however, many governments (including Côte d'Ivoire and Kenya) and donors have become aware of the need to change policies toward technical assistance. An encouraging example of what can be done is Tanzania, where capacity building for economic policy analysis is beginning to show results (see Box 2.8).

Technical assistance will still be required. Experts in engineering, agronomy, and finance will continue to be in short supply. But the rush to use expatriates must be resisted by African and donor governments alike. Technical assistance must be increasingly used to build local capacity and institutions, which in the past has taken second place to doing the job. The time has come for donors to switch technical assistance toward building up local capabilities and increasing the supply of qualified people through training programs. Reversing the brain drain from Africa should be part of such a program.

Technical assistance not only reflects the short supply of certain African specialists but the inability of institutions, especially in the public sector, to attract and retain qualified nationals. Reducing reliance on foreign advisers will only be realized when questions of the supply of new talent and the utilization of existing talent are addressed.

With changes in the quality of educational systems and public sector reforms, the technical assistance could be focused more on training and over time be reduced in absolute terms. Donors and African countries should set targets for achieving this.

In the meantime the quality, cost-effectiveness, and management of technical assistance can be improved. A first step is for donors to seek experts from other developing countries. Another is to encourage networks and twinning arrangements, especially with like institutions in developing countries, which would have specialists more likely to be familiar with Third World conditions. Reducing the high cost of advisors and stimulating more local self-reliance may also be achieved by structuring advisory positions on a part-time basis, with periodic visits, instead of full-time residencies. Careful counterpart selection and monitoring of performance also need improvement.

It is widely recognized that technical assistance is poorly managed. Recipient governments rarely have reliable data on the numbers, composition, and disposition of the technical assistants working in their countries. Nor do they have clear policies governing the use and eventual phasing out of technical assistance linked to long-term plans for public sector manpower development. Such plans could guide not only internal training programs but also technical assistance programs. The UNDP has begun studies in several countries with this objective.

NONGOVERNMENTAL ORGANIZATIONS. A strategy of development that stresses the dynamism of farmers, grassroots communities, and other parts of the nonmodern sector needs to be matched by changes in donor financing to reflect that emphasis. The need for change has been recognized. Donors increasingly channel assistance through NGOs—both northern and African. In 1987 official contributions for NGO activities amounted to about $2.2 billion, representing about 5 percent of total ODA. In addition NGOs from the OECD countries collected some $3.3 billion for development through private fund-raising.

This reflects a growing belief that most NGOs are committed to addressing the problems of developing societies and the needs of their poorest members in a manner not matched by government officials. NGOs have learned how to work with grassroots organizations and how to put together projects with minimal financial and external technical assistance, thus helping poor people to help themselves (see Box 5.7). This compares starkly with the widespread concern that official assistance has created dependency. NGOs have demonstrated a flexibility and dynamism within the donor community that is comparable with that of the communities with which they work. In particular they have moved increasingly from emergency assistance to development assistance, particularly in agriculture, water supply, nutrition, education, and health. They have found new support in donor countries, partly because they are seen as helping the poor directly—without the costly bureaucratic intermediation of donors and recipient governments and without the danger of assistance ending up in the pockets of the rich, the military, or the corrupt.

The strengths of NGOs are impressive but can be exaggerated. Local institution building has proved difficult, and it is common for projects to fail when NGO staff have departed. A key issue is how to build on local successes in providing services nationally. The danger is that northern NGOs will be used even more actively as channels for donor assistance, which would threaten to suffocate the flexibility, independence, and low bureaucratic costs that have made them so effective. Some NGOs are responding by establishing field offices to enlarge and decentralize their operations. Others are working either directly or alongside governments to develop the capacity of African NGOs more rapidly (see Box 8.3, above). Training, technical assistance, networking to disseminate technical information among African NGOs, and other activities are being pursued. Many of the difficulties mirror those in the relationship between official donors and governments—the need to be less dirigiste, to have confidence in local agencies, and to move beyond lending for projects to lending in support of broader programs. It is difficult to decide when to extend financial support to a local NGO—too early and it may weaken the self-help motivations; too late and it frustrates attempts to move ahead with schemes for water supply, schools, and so forth. It is not unusual for NGOs in some countries to be critical of government policies, especially when these are seen as hurting the disadvantaged; in such cases an element of tolerance by the government would be desirable. All these are problems of success. Each will take time to resolve. This calls for caution, and money should not be thrown blindly at institutions, projects, and programs.

REGIONAL ECONOMIC INTEGRATION. This report has emphasized the need for regional integration for sustained development in Africa. However, the much-needed rationalization of regional institutions, policy reforms, and social and physical infrastructure building cannot be accomplished without funding, much of which will have to come from donors. Some donor policies will have to be reoriented from country assistance to regional assistance. Already there are innovative proposals to provide funds for harmonized policy reforms in a regional grouping of countries, as in the UDEAC.

All this suggests changes in the allocation of development assistance among sectors in the 1990s. The composition would vary from country to country, donor to donor. It may, however, be useful to indicate the changes implied by the strategy proposed above. In recent years about 20 percent of ODA has gone to each of the following: social infrastructure, physical infrastructure, productive sectors, technical assistance, and program assistance. The proposed strategy calls for increased assistance to social and physical infrastructure and reduced direct public assistance (in relative terms) to agriculture, industry, technical assistance, and program assistance. The suggested composition is 25 percent each for social and physical infrastructure and 50 percent for productive sectors, technical assistance, and program assistance. At these levels ODA would cover about half of all public expenditures on human resource development and on maintenance and improvement of infrastructure. Technical and program assistance would be maintained at current levels for another decade. Investment in productive sectors would rely increasingly on the private sector, both domestic and foreign.

Aid effectiveness

The levels of ODA should be increasingly related to performance. And the development community, including Africa, should be better organized to expose gross misuse of public funds. This implies, among other measures, insistence on transparent procurement procedures, rigorous accounting, and prompt auditing.

The estimates of external resource needs for African countries are large and rising. They would represent about $32 per capita by 2000, compared with $26 per capita in 1986 and with $14 to $18 per capita currently for South Asian countries such as Bangladesh and Nepal. This preference for Africa is justified by the continent's need to improve its physical and human infrastructure and to build its development capability. However, this has to be matched by a conviction that the external resources will be well used.

Will external assistance at the level projected during the 1990s and beyond run the risk of creating or reinforcing dependency? Will generous donor assistance undermine the willingness of governments to make difficult decisions? Difficult economic decisions have often been avoided in industrial and developing countries alike when a windfall has made them seem unnecessary. However, additional ODA for countries that are already receiving high levels of aid is likely to be politically feasible only if it can be shown to promote growth and to alleviate poverty.

Moreover assurance is needed that high and increased levels of ODA do not end up financing military spending, luxury consumption, inefficiency, and capital flight. However, all financial flows are fungible to some extent, some more than others. Linking ODA to specific development expenditure may reduce this fungibility.

If improved economic policy management is to be effectively internalized, then the monitoring of macro performance and the related donor programs should be on parallel tracks. The first track is the dialogue. This should be as disciplined as under structural adjustment lending. But the understandings would be in less high profile ways than under structural adjustment programs. Moreover they should be based more on a government's own internal policy papers than at present—with donors focusing on their analytical quality and on implementation.

The second track would be an agreed program of donor support, which would vary according to performance in implementing the target programs. Donor support should become far more selective. Those pursuing sound programs should receive the external funding required; such external funding should fully reflect the adverse impact of world economic conditions and the debt burden on their import capacity. Countries with weak performance should receive much less assistance, limited where possible to programs important to long-term development (such as research, health, and education).

In summary, donors must increasingly take on a bigger role to support national programs and institutions. This will require less dirigism, a greater willingness to "let go" in day-to-day management, and the recognition that sustainable growth with equity in Africa will be possible only if African governments are willing to establish the necessary enabling environment.

This does not mean that donors should become less concerned about the domestic policy performance of African countries. The outlook for Africa is so bleak in the absence of significant policy action that the concern of donors is justified—more so given their willingness to increase external financial assistance during the 1980s, when ODA in general has stagnated or fallen. The big increase in external support to Africa during the 1990s that is proposed in this report could be anticipated and would be justifiable only if there were confidence that it would lead to sustained growth with equity. But donors need to recognize that this in turn requires a widening and deepening of African strategic thinking and *action* on development issues, as well as a recognition that many of the needed changes will take time to implement, let alone to yield results.

The experience of the 1980s suggests that policy and program reforms need to be not only well formulated but also socially and politically acceptable. That is why the proposed strategy aims to ensure that those who have to implement the difficult economic, social, and political changes during the next decade or more actually believe in the policies and feel that the changes are of their own making. This is the only real basis for donors to be confident that the development programs will be carried out.

9

A strategic agenda for the 1990s

The outlook for Africa is potentially devastating. This threat can only be averted through urgent action. Yet there are no quick fixes, no simple blueprints. Although broad agreement exists on the gravity of the problems, their complexity makes effective collaboration among the many partners in Africa's development—the African governments, the bilateral and multilateral agencies, and the NGOs, both local and foreign—extremely difficult. The time has come to seek out the high ground of agreement and to move from words to deeds.

The search for the high ground

Successful development depends on getting most policies reasonably right and none of them hopelessly wrong, rather than on getting just a few policies perfectly right. In defining joint programs of action, there is no place for fundamentalism. Fortunately disagreements in practice are few. A review of the many official reports on Africa published during the 1980s by the African, UN, and other multilateral agencies reveals many shared positions. Moreover the differences have greatly narrowed during the 1980s. Yet the public perception of disagreement is itself a cause of inaction. Establishing shared viewpoints is essential if collaboration is to work.

Existing areas of agreement cover both the diagnosis and the main objectives. Whatever the political vantage point, there is a broad understanding, in particular, on the absolute priority to be given to human resource and institutional development, on the central role of agriculture in raising incomes and achieving food security, on giving much more attention to protecting the environment, on nurturing small-scale enterprises and grassroots organizations, and on promoting women's role in development. Of course complex problems remain to be solved at the technical level. Professionals will continue to debate—for example, exchange rate policy, the use of protection to promote industrial growth, or even how best to strengthen agricultural research. Such debates are a necessary part of the continuing search for solutions. They in no way diminish the broad consensus on objectives, which is the starting point for working together.

In a few instances the objectives themselves are still being strenuously argued. All in all the common ground is more important than the differences. The emerging consensus can be summarized under three broad headings: restructuring economies, putting people first, and fostering self-reliance.

The need to restructure African economies

In times of economic and financial crisis, the attention of policymakers inevitably shifts from long-term development to short-term stabilization. No government or country can function for long with gross macroeconomic imbalances. Yet it is also now widely accepted that Africa's economic problems are so deep-rooted that conventional stabilization programs are inadequate. Few governments question that Africa's present economic malaise calls for bold reforms. Indeed two-thirds of African countries have embarked on some form of structural adjustment. The success of such programs is a precondition for any long-term strategy. The challenge is to ensure that they go beyond stabilization to achieve a genuine transformation of production structures (as argued for recently by the ECA) and thereby shift Africa's economies from stagnation to robust growth.

The necessary structural adjustment programs are complex and difficult. They demand constant review and modification. Most already aim to put measures in place that will foster private initiative, reduce regulatory controls, and expand the role of market mechanisms. Such reforms are under way across the world. They are designed to promote (rather than control) development. In this context no measure is more controversial in Africa than devaluation. But here too opinion has shifted. Several countries—The Gambia, Ghana, Guinea, and Nigeria, to name but a few—have implemented bold exchange rate policies. The results are mixed, but promising. Growth has generally accelerated. The lesson is that correcting exchange rate overvaluation is a necessary, but not sufficient, condition for renewed growth. If exchange rate adjustments are to be truly beneficial, they must be supported by tough measures—especially wage restraint and fiscal discipline—to control inflation.

There is also universal agreement on the need to combine fiscal and monetary measures with steps to minimize the adverse social impact of adjustment and particularly to reorient public spending in favor of basic education, health, and nutrition. To do this sensibly, governments will need better information on the basic social indicators. Several countries have recently launched programs to address the social dimensions of adjustment. Reducing public sector overstaffing is causing particular distress. To ease the social dislocation resulting from this necessary but painful adjustment, those laid off can be compensated and helped to find work in the private sector; food-for-work programs can also cushion the blow by providing a safety net for those without an alternative source of income.

Many African governments have been reappraising the role of the state. In the past the thinking of African policymakers has been dominated by the dichotomy between capitalist and socialist development models. The Nordic development paradigm (see Box 9.1) offers an alternative development model where the state assumes a leading role in building human resources, administrative, and physical infrastructure capacity, while the goods-producing and noninfrastructure service sectors are left to the flexibility and incentives of private enterprise and market discipline.

People come first

Improving health, expanding education, ensuring food security, creating jobs: these are the priorities shared by all the partners in Africa's development. Everything else—economic growth, fiscal policy, exchange rate management, and so on—is no more than the means to achieve the fundamental objective of improving human welfare. Poverty reduction is widely seen as a central concern of policy matters. UNICEF rightly stresses that when economic policy is in disarray, it is the poor and the children who suffer most. For this reason all the partners in Africa's development support UNICEF's call for structural adjustment with a human face—witness the remarkable support that has been mobilized by the joint program to address the social dimensions of adjustment (see Box 9.2).

Improving human welfare is closely linked to moderating population growth. Few issues are more controversial. Yet during the past decade African governments have rethought their position on family planning. At the conference of African health ministers in Niger in January 1989 almost all endorsed an active population policy; at the World Population Conference in Bucharest 15 years earlier most had been opposed. Several governments have already started to put effective family planning programs in place.

The drive for self-reliance

Fostering self-reliance is widely acclaimed as an objective for Africa; it was enshrined in the Lagos Final Act and is generally respected by Africa's partners. It means building African capacities to take full technical and managerial charge of running Africa's economies—a principal theme of this report. An important measure would be the development of high-level training and professional associations (organized on a regional as well as on a national basis) to attain excellence in

Box 9.1 The Nordic development paradigm

In the mid-1800s the Nordic countries were agrarian economies with low income levels. Starting with Sweden around the 1870s, they have all experienced high growth to become advanced industrial economies. In 1987 the five Nordic countries had an average per capita GDP of $19,670, slightly above that of Japan and the United States, and 48 percent higher than the EC average. Moreover Scandinavia's social indicators are among the best in the world. Like any other countries, the Nordic countries had their own unique circumstances. However, there are two noteworthy factors behind their success: the relative roles of the state and the market and the pattern of trade orientation and regional cooperation.

The roles of the state and the market. At an early stage of development the Nordic states assumed the role of providing infrastructure, high-quality administration, and social services, while the goods-producing sectors were largely left to private enterprise and market discipline. The state actively promoted universal access to social services, encouraged a harmonious partnership between labor and entrepreneurs, and kept a light rein on the private sector.

This was in sharp contrast to the practice in socialist countries, where government took over ownership and direction of the means of production. It was also in contrast to the planned economies in the Third World, where governments tried to capture the "commanding heights" of the economy in the goods-producing sectors. It also differed from the purely market-oriented systems, where free enterprise, without the state provision of social services, led to large income disparities—great wealth alongside acute poverty. It differed too from Japan's and Korea's approach, where the state played lead roles in targeting, establishing, and protecting key industries.

The Nordic countries have consistently sought consensus among organized labor, capital, and government. Sharing economic prosperity was seen as essential for economic development and political stability. Early on the Nordic societies strove for universal literacy, while emphasizing high-quality, although limited, higher education. These policies encouraged informed public participation in social and economic decisionmaking and provided a healthy and well-trained labor force. The public sector's enabling role and respect for market mechanisms allowed the Nordic countries to achieve a high level of economic efficiency. Private entrepreneurship, encouraged but not directed by the state, became the prime mover in the establishment and expansion of the goods-producing sectors and their trading and financial institutions.

Trade orientation and regional cooperation. The Scandinavians have long been open to trade and technical advances from abroad. The patterns of trade orientation emerged as a result of market forces, in contrast to the more top-down mercantilist policies of Japan and Korea, which guided trade. Further the early expansion of Nordic industrial entrepreneurship was linked to the domestic resource base and to demand arising from the agricultural sector and infrastructure investments. However, exports increasingly became the driving force in industrial expansion.

The small Nordic countries have demonstrated the scope for regional cooperation despite relatively homogeneous resource endowment and competitive—rather than complementary—patterns of production. Stable and peaceful political relations fostered economic cooperation, carried out without expensive institutional structures. Trade within the region grew from 12 to 13 percent (of total Nordic trade) before World War I to 30 or more percent thereafter.

The Nordic countries' remarkable transformation from agrarian societies into modern industrial economies offers a distinctive development paradigm. Their success resulted from a social market economy with its combination of free-enterprise economic policies and active social policies.

---

all technical and professional fields. Particular attention needs to be given to expanding top-quality science and technology training so that Africa can keep abreast of the revolutionary advances being made in biotechnology and materials science. At the community level it means empowering people to take fuller charge of their lives.

Self-reliance has sometimes been interpreted as self-sufficiency in food and industrial products. Here a sharp distinction must be made. Framed in these terms, the quest for self-sufficiency ignores the potential gains from trade. That is why any further delinking of Africa from the global economy would enormously hamper its development. However, trade should reflect interdependence, not dependence. It can be convincingly argued that Africa has become too dependent on food imports. Greater trade within Africa in food is one answer; Chapter 7 proposes lifting present barriers to the movement of food from surplus to deficit countries. Yet many African countries now importing food could well meet far more of their own needs if the structure of incentives, and especially exchange rates, were more favorable. The same is true for industry—although it would be naive to pretend that African firms can be transformed overnight into effective competitors on the world market. Industries will need to be nurtured. Liberalization must be phased to allow time to acquire capabilities and to restructure inefficient producers.

The strategy of developing "core" industries, advocated in the early 1980s, poses special problems. Few countries have domestic markets large enough to justify steel, chemical, or fertilizer industries. If investment decisions continue to be made by the public sector without regard for market signals, countries risk incurring heavy losses. Investments of this kind will yield benefits only through regional integration that respects market forces.

Regional integration and cooperation among African states is a strongly held and widely shared objective. It is rightly seen as an integral part of Africa's drive for self-reliance. To yield results, this goal should be pursued in a pragmatic and incremental manner to overcome the many practical obstacles that have slowed progress to date. Donor support could do much to help by easing the transitional costs.

Export-oriented growth has been seen by some policymakers as incompatible with self-reliance. This is incorrect. Although import substitution often offers the most immediate opportunities for industrial investment, a drive for exports can be combined with production for the domestic market and is fully consistent with achieving self-reliance. Viewing Africa as an emerging single market, successful import substitution would serve to build a large industrial base capable of exporting competitively. The key is to achieve

competitiveness. Africa will gain nothing from enterprises that sell products that are more costly than those available in world markets. Moreover Africa has spare capacity in many of the core industries that have already been established; the challenge in the 1990s is to exploit these resources more effectively before investing in new capacity. Meanwhile all can agree that there is enormous scope for Africa's manufacturers to meet the continent's demand for basic consumer goods—building materials, furniture, clothing, kitchenware, and the like—and to do so at internationally competitive prices. This is where industrial capability should first be built.

Promoting local self-reliance is now widely recognized as an essential element of any future development strategy. The aim would be to mobilize local energies to provide basic services. The key is to strengthen local organizations and to find ways to enable women to play a greater role in development. Although there is broad agreement on these objectives, practical measures to pursue them are all too rare. In the 1990s explicit strategies will be needed to develop the capacities of local government and nongovernmental organizations, especially those involving women. The ultimate goal is to empower individuals and communities to take charge of their own development. Clarifying land ownership rights is a vital part of this strategy.

A strategic agenda for the 1990s

This report suggests seven main interconnected themes to shape Africa's strategic agenda for the 1990s—themes that build on the emerging consensus. Despite the great diversity within Africa, enough similarities exist for these themes to be relevant for most countries in drafting their own specific plans (see Box 9.3).

Adjustment for growth

Structural adjustment programs have almost always been mounted in response to an immediate financial crisis. The problems of African economies go much deeper. Evidence in Chapter 1 showed that structural adjustment programs are beginning to produce results, but only slowly. In most instances the process has hardly begun, and too often the efforts have not been maintained. Hesitation and procrastination—repeated cycles of "go-stop-go"—stymie recovery, and greatly extend the period of adjustment and its attendant hardships. The hardest part of all for African governments is to build investor confidence, and even then the supply response inevitably lags.

The challenge is to make African producers competitive in world markets; in other words, to transform Africa from an expensive and difficult place to do business to an efficient one. For this reason the adjustment effort must be both radical and prolonged—a deep transformation of the production structure is required. Structural adjustment is necessary, but it must be sustained—without dogmatism. It must be adjustment with a difference. Different in the sense that greater account is taken of its social impact; different in the drive to encourage competition gradually, by first lowering the barriers to trade within Africa; and different in the use of the exchange rate rather than administrative intervention as the key instrument for bringing costs into line with Africa's principal competitors.

New priorities would call for a new pattern of public expenditure. Switching budgetary allocations usually encounters stiff bureaucratic opposition, but even so development priorities can be most readily changed through the central government budget. The proposed future development strategy elaborated in this report calls for more spending on education, health, science and technology, infrastructure, and environmental protection. Two specific targets are proposed: 8 to 10 percent of GDP to be spent on human resource development and 5 to 6 percent on infrastructure maintenance, rehabilitation, and expansion. These increases will need to be met partly by cuts elsewhere and partly by greater resource mobilization. As the ECA has rightly argued, markedly lower outlays on the military could yield important savings in many African countries. So too would a progressive slimming of the public sector, where overstaffing has become chronic. Public investment in agriculture and industry could be proportionately lower than in the past, with greater reliance placed on private sector outlays. Revenues can be boosted by a more effective and broadly based recovery of costs and by a more determined approach to tax collection.

Developing people

Human resource development should be placed high on the strategic agenda for the 1990s for all countries, thus reflecting a shared determination to reverse the decline witnessed during the past decade. Spending for this purpose should be increased and a major effort made to improve quality. No longer should allocations to basic human services appear as residual items in the budget. Each country should establish monitorable programs to improve basic education, health, family planning, and nutrition, as well as a timetable for achieving universal coverage. Some may be able to achieve that goal by the end of the 1990s; others may need 20 years, but for no country should it take longer than 30 years.

Overcoming hunger and malnutrition is a critical component of the human-centered development strategy. Assuring African food security depends, first and foremost, on increased agricultural productivity. The distribution of food can be improved through increased trade within the region. Food security is also a function of increasing real incomes and enhancing the capacity of the poor to acquire the food they need. In the long run economic growth can be expected to help overcome food insecurity; in the shorter term specific interventions such as food subsidies or employment and income support schemes targeted on vulnerable groups may be necessary.

Donors should see human resource development as a priority for Africa in the next decade. Support for the recurrent costs of wages, salaries,

Box 9.3 The Sahel—A special challenge

The challenges facing Sub-Saharan Africa are most acute in the Sahel. (This region includes Burkina Faso, Chad, The Gambia, Mali, Mauritania, Niger, and Senegal and contains 9 percent of Sub-Saharan Africa's population.) Compared with the rest of Africa, the Sahel has relatively few assets on which to draw. Fully 75 percent of the land is barren desert. Half the countries are completely landlocked, with vast distances separating markets. Since the devastating drought of 1973 rainfall has been below the long-term trend; whether this is a cyclical low or the harbinger of an irreversible trend is uncertain. Rapidly increasing population, exacerbated by internal migration, has accelerated deforestation and soil degradation. The highly dispersed population makes it both difficult and expensive to provide social and infrastructure services. Basic welfare indicators reflect the inadequacy of social services in the Sahel: life expectancy is 10 years less than the average for low-income countries; infant mortality (130 infants per thousand) is twice as high; the primary school enrollment ratio (37 percent) is just half. On average there is one doctor for every 24,000 people.

Barring a worsening of the climate, the Sahel has, however, important development opportunities. There is unexploited agricultural potential, particularly in Mali, Burkina Faso, and Chad. Gold in Burkina Faso and Mali and oil in Chad could become significant sources of revenue. If markets are extended beyond national borders, there is a large potential for small- and medium-scale manufacturing. Sahelian countries are the geographic link between the northern and the western and central regions of Africa. This, combined with the traditional competence of the Sahelian people for commerce and intermediation, are assets for the development of tertiary activities. The challenge is to find a strategy that offsets the liabilities posed by the difficult natural environment and limited resources; the priorities are, nonetheless, very similar to those for other African countries.

First and foremost is the need to invest far more in people. Most important, determined action is needed in three priority areas. Primary education should be improved and expanded to provide children and adults with basic literacy and numeracy skills, thus building the much needed private and public capacities. To further enhance the impact of these qualitative improvements, affordable health services and proper nutrition through food security are critically needed to extend the active life and increase the productivity of the labor force. These actions would in turn support direct efforts to slow population growth, which is essential for translating GDP expansion into per capita income gains, arresting soil degradation, and broadening access to social services while maintaining their quality.

In agriculture traditional production techniques appropriate for the variable rainfall patterns and low-fertility soils included practices to ensure the sustained-yield use of the modest and fragile resource base, notably the natural forest cover. In the face of rapidly rising population, these techniques are no longer effective. Thus the principal task ahead is to stop, and if possible reverse, environmental degradation. In the drier areas of the Sahel the focus will be on water management and soil conservation and on village and pastoral land management, supported by tenure reform. In the better-watered southern areas, agricultural intensification can be pursued as elsewhere, but with integrated village action plans to conserve the increasingly threatened natural resources.

The development of industry and services in the Sahel depends on an integrated market, which should become part of a larger regional market. Official statistics show limited trade so far among the Sahelian countries and with the rest of West Africa (8 percent of exports and 13 percent of imports). Initially, stimulus to industrial development could come from supplying agriculture and transforming agricultural products, from producing low-cost consumer goods and construction materials, and, in the long run, from specializing in selected lines of production, such as cotton-based textiles. Based on current trends, one could well imagine that Senegal becomes a center for services (such as tourism, research, and education), Mali and Niger for trade, and Burkina Faso for banking. For enhanced regional cooperation the barriers of real exchange rate distortions and impediments to capital and labor mobility must be eliminated, and, to facilitate the movement of goods and people, investment in the transport and communications infrastructure is essential.

As for the rest of the continent, important structural reforms are already under way. They aim at reducing the burden of inefficient public sectors, establishing an enabling policy environment for private initiative, and stimulating a supply response. At the same time public expenditure should be shifted not only in favor of programs to protect the environment and develop human resources, but also to provide essential physical infrastructure.

To meet this challenge, the Sahel will require sustained donor assistance as well as far-reaching debt relief. While project aid will be needed for many decades to come, the long-term aim, however, should be to lessen the current dependency on budgetary assistance. With needs so great, nowhere is it more important to ensure that funds be used efficiently; this calls for both streamlining investment programming and improving aid coordination.

---

instruction materials, medicines, and other supplies in the programs should be seen as a higher priority than buildings. This implies a willingness to finance local costs; the preference of donors to fund foreign exchange expenditures might otherwise easily distort priorities.

Building capacity

Africa's lack of technical skills and strong public and private institutions accounts more than anything else for its current predicament. The paradox is that Africa also has people who are educated but unemployed. The suggested remedies are radical.

• First, in education and training, better quality should come above all other considerations. The pursuit of excellence must be ruthless. Africa would be better served if its universities used their present resources to produce fewer but better-trained graduates with a strong bias toward technical and analytical skills. Quality matters right down the line to the primary schools.

• Second, the reform of state enterprises needs to be accelerated. The measures called for are well-known—the most important is to give managers a clear mandate and unfettered authority to meet agreed performance plans.

• Third, every opportunity should be taken to support local, communal, and nongovernmental organizations of all types—village associations, cooperatives, credit unions, professional associations, chambers of commerce and industry, and the like. These initiatives are most likely to succeed if the institutions have local roots. In many countries informal credit organizations (like the *tontines*) have been more successful than the modern commercial banks, and the informal sector is generally more dynamic than the state enterprise sector. The challenge is to build on this solid indigenous base, with a bottom-up approach that places a premium on listening to people and on genuinely empowering the intended beneficiaries of any development program.

• Fourth, public administrations should be drastically overhauled and their role changed as far as possible from that of controlling development to promoting it. Overstaffing should be gradually eliminated, with remaining staff upgraded through systematic retraining. New hiring should be based on competitive examinations and the reward system related to performance. Skilled staff should be adequately paid.

• Fifth, government policy analysis should be strengthened by fuller use of the best-trained nationals, local consultants, and university researchers and by better data collection.

• Sixth, special measures are needed to remove the legal barriers and provide the administrative support to allow women to play a full and equal role in the economy.

Resuming growth and creating jobs

Enhanced capacities and a supportive policy environment provide the underpinnings for greater production. But those measures alone will not suffice. Agricultural growth depends on imaginative research to develop new technologies and on an effective extension service to provide the link between farmer and researcher. Industry and mining development depends on attracting private investors with the resources and expertise to mount viable operations and on the willingness of foreign entrepreneurs to forge genuine partnerships with local businessmen. Private investors are likely to be forthcoming only if a country's investment code (fiscal regime and foreign exchange regulation) recognizes that making profits and paying dividends are necessary rewards for taking risks.

To be competitive, businesses need cost-effective and reliable utilities and other infrastructure services. So the agenda for the 1990s must provide for rehabilitating and maintaining the infrastructure network that has deteriorated during the 1980s and also for building new capacity in critical areas. One of these is telecommunications, in which there is a clear bottleneck and in which the rates of return are demonstrably sufficient for this service to be self-financing. Good telecommunications are the key to Africa's participating in the informatics revolution. The measures needed include improving the management and financing of infrastructure services, some of which can be contracted out to the private sector.

There will be no growth without entrepreneurs. Much can be done to foster African entrepreneurship by recognizing the role and vitality of the informal sector—replacing discriminatory legislation, by unshackling small businessmen from unnecessary and unhelpful regulations and controls, and by facilitating access to credit and markets.

It is not good enough for growth to be sustainable. It must also be equitable. To be equitable, everyone should have some way to earn a livelihood. And growth alone does not ensure that jobs will be created rapidly. Agriculture cannot accommodate all the entrants to the labor force. Much of the increase in the working population will have to be absorbed in nonfarm activities, in small businesses, and in the service sector. The policies that will spur job creation are therefore the same ones that will foster enterprise development. Minimum wage legislation and other restrictive labor regulations that discourage the expansion of employment need to be eased. As a safety net governments may mount food-for-work programs.

Preserving Africa's patrimony

The 1990s will be a critical decade for the environment, as escalating population growth puts increasing stress on Africa's ecological systems. Trees, and the species they sustain, are fast disappearing; fuelwood is becoming increasingly scarce; topsoil is vanishing from fertile slopes and cannot be replaced; and grassland is being overgrazed and turned into desert. Pollution is a fast-growing threat to health in Africa's burgeoning cities.

Measures to address the accelerating destruction of Africa's natural resource base are now increasingly prominent on the agendas of governments and external agencies involved on the continent. Programs to halt, and hopefully reverse, the process of desertification, the devastation of tropical forests, the erosion of arable land, and the pollution of the cities all merit strong support. Achieving faster economic growth for today's population at the cost of an unproductive natural habitat for future generations is not acceptable. No time should be lost in putting in place, country by country, environmental action plans and in mobilizing broadly based popular support for their effective implementation. Extensive community-based programs to plant trees are also urgently required.

Accelerating regional integration and cooperation

The objectives of regional integration and cooperation should be pursued with a new determination to overcome parochial concerns. The Lagos Plan of Action and Final Act establish the basic framework. Decisions are now needed to rationalize regional institutions, to liberalize trade within Africa, to ease transport controls, and to facilitate intra-African payments. Programs to ease infrastructure bottlenecks should be planned in response to identified demand. A more systematic effort is needed to exploit the many opportunities for mutually beneficial cooperation in education, science and technology, health, research, and natural resource management.

Political renewal

Efforts to create an enabling environment and to build local capacities will be wasted if the political context is not favorable. The only way living standards will be raised and basic needs met is through growth in the productive sectors. That requires investment. But a loss of confidence is discouraging investors and producers alike. For too long there has been little stability in policies or public institutions in many African countries. Failure of governance has become so commonplace that expectations are low. Yet there is an evident popularly felt need for renewal—bordering on desperation—that is widely expressed. Too often many of Africa's best-trained minds are in exile or simply underutilized.

It is not just the unpredictability of policies that discourages investment, but also the uncertainty about their interpretation and application by officials. This problem is exacerbated by the frequent lack of a reliable legal framework to enforce contracts. The rule of law needs to be established. In many instances this implies rehabilitation of the judicial system, independence for the judiciary, scrupulous respect for the law and human rights at every level of government, transparent accounting of public monies, and independent public auditors responsible to a representative legislature, not to an executive. Independent institutions are necessary to ensure public accountability.

The widespread perception in many countries is that the appropriation of the machinery of government by the elite to serve their own interests is at the root of this crisis of governance. The willingness of the donor community to tolerate impropriety—by failing to insist on scrupulous conduct by their own suppliers, by not ensuring that funds are properly used, by overlooking inadequate accounting and auditing, and by tolerating generally lax procurement procedures—aggravates the malaise. Everyone avowedly deplores the situation and wishes it were otherwise. But it will not be so until accountability is instituted.

Consensus building within Africa

The need to move from "words to deeds" does not diminish the importance of the "words." Programs of action can be sustained only if they arise out of consensus built on dialogue within each country. Consensus will not be easily achieved. It will require facing up to difficult political, social, and other problems: the vested interests that profit from the present distorted incentives and controls, the political and personal expectations that must be revised, the intellectual and ideological positions that must be questioned.

Within most African countries policymakers have been reluctant to allow open discussion of economic policy issues. This is a mistake; broad and vigorous debate on what has gone right and what has gone wrong since independence is vital if options are to be understood and consensus achieved about future policy directions. This debate needs to be encouraged in the media, in the universities, and in open workshops. It is a precondition for building a genuine and broadly based commitment to a future development strategy.

Since the action programs are country specific, they must reflect national characteristics and be consistent with a country's cultural values if they are to attract popular support. This is obvious in sensitive areas such as education, health, population, and labor management. For example, in Japan the typical Western model of labor management clashes with Japan's culture; Japan's model is based on its own social norms. Africa too will need to search for the models that best fit its culture.

Thus moving from words to action requires a favorable institutional context. It must emerge from, and at the same time support, political consensus. Each country will have to wrestle with this problem in its own way. The most that external agencies can do is to support the search for that consensus.

Building consensus among the donors

Africa faces exceptional difficulties and merits exceptional treatment by the donor community. Just as Europe was seen to be especially needy immediately after World War II and India in the 1960s, so today Africa requires concentrated and coordinated support to overcome its grave difficulties. Donors must work together to focus their efforts in key areas.

• Ways must be found to reduce the debt burden. There is no lack of options; what is missing is collective will on the part of the richer countries to deal decisively with the issue.

• Donors should place their efforts in a longer-term framework; they need to recognize that capacity building is at the heart of the matter and that strengthening institutions and developing capabilities is a long process that demands vision

and persistence over decades, not years. Technical assistance needs to be refocused and better managed to give priority to capacity building.

• External assistance should extend beyond investment to cover development expenditures more broadly defined (including expenditures to improve health and education, to protect the environment, and to maintain and rehabilitate infrastructure). Donors should shift their assistance increasingly from financing projects to financing a "time-slice" of sectoral or subsectoral programs. In the human resource and infrastructure programs support should extend to operation and maintenance expenditures. Donor assistance should not apply just to government-to-government transactions, but also to the activities of nongovernmental and private sector organizations.

• Last, donors should channel resources more selectively to the governments that are already implementing reforms and making good use of the external assistance they receive.

Toward a global coalition for Africa

Many institutional arrangements—notably consultative groups and roundtable meetings—have been developed for coordinating the actions of donors, the UN agencies, and individual African countries. On a range of sectoral and functional issues the UN agencies have special responsibilities. Arrangements such as the Consultative Group for International Agricultural Research (CGIAR) deal with programs that address specific problems. And during the 1980s, as the depth and seriousness of African economic problems were increasingly recognized, institutional arrangements were developed within the framework of the United Nations (such as the UN Programme of Action for African Economic Recovery and Development—UNPAAERD), the Development Committee (such as the World Bank studies of Sub-Saharan Africa and related initiatives), and the OECD's Development Assistance Committee (DAC), and Club du Sahel. These responded flexibly to the immediate need for joint action on issues such as food, drought, and debt. UNPAAERD was an historic North-South compact endorsed by the Special UN General Assembly in 1986, which has demonstrated the potential for united action to assist Africa.

But it is becoming increasingly obvious that the causes of Africa's economic malaise are deep and persistent. Moreover they are so inextricably linked that they demand a coherent set of programs—programs designed by the government concerned and implemented through strengthened institutions. Donor measures are no substitute for sustained political commitment to building institutional capabilities. And without this strengthening, even the best policies and programs will not be carried out effectively.

Can Africa's decline be reversed? The simple answer is yes. It can be and must be. The alternative is too awful to contemplate. But it must happen from within Africa. Like trees, countries cannot be made to grow by being pulled upward from the outside; they must grow from within, from their own roots. But Africa will need sustained and increased external support if it is to meet the challenge without unreasonable hardship. This support should be offered in the context of a compact that does not diminish Africans' right to determine what happens on their continent, but that at the same time responds to the concerns and insights of the external development community.

The need for such a new international compact for Africa, which could build on the work of the UNPAAERD initiative that ends in 1990, is urgent. The UNPAAERD has provided a framework for mobilizing resources to aid Africa's economic re-

form efforts. To take this initiative a step further, a new global coalition is proposed for the 1990s. It should be broader and more permanent and thus widen the scope of consultations to cover both donors and recipients. Its mandate would be to cover the full range of long-term development issues. But "long-term" does not imply that action can be long delayed. On the contrary, movement toward the objectives has to begin *now*.

The proposed global coalition for Africa would be a forum in which African leaders (not just from the public sector, but also from private business, the professions, the universities, and other NGOs) could meet with their key partners—the bilateral and multilateral agencies and major foreign NGOs—to agree on general strategies that would then provide broad guidance for the design of individual country programs. The coalition could seek agreement on actions to tackle the priorities identified in this report: environmental protection, capacity building, population policy, food security, and regional integration and cooperation. It could provide the impetus for channeling external assistance to programs in these areas and for monitoring programs. The creation of this coalition would be a decisive new step forward for Africa and its partners. It would mark a new resolve to work together for a better future.

Bibliographical note

Chapter 1

Data in this chapter were drawn mainly from the IMF, FAO, UNCTAD, and World Bank sources. Sources for the analysis of the high costs of doing business in Sub-Saharan Africa include background papers by Van der Tak and King, and Singh as well as Heller and Tait 1984. The analysis of external debt and price prospects for primary commodities relies on work by the Debt and International Finance Division and International Commodity Markets Division of the International Economics Department of the World Bank. The analysis of recent economic performance also draws on research undertaken by the Trade and Finance Division of the World Bank's Africa Technical Department, particularly from the UNDP project to monitor development programs and aid flows in Africa executed by the World Bank.

Chapter 2

This chapter draws heavily on the World Bank's experience with structural adjustment programs. World Bank country economic reports were a primary reference. The discussion on infrastructure is partly based on the research results of the ongoing multidonor Sub-Saharan African Transport Program. The treatment of public sector management issues stems from the analysis in the *World Development Report 1983* and the program of research undertaken by the World Bank's Public Sector Management Division. The discussion of the role of the state was also influenced by a series of articles in *IDS Bulletin* in 1987 and 1988 and

contributions from Oyje Aboyade, Jonathan Frimpong-Ansah, Goran Hyden, Ali Mazrui, Harris Mule, and Dunstan Wai. The analysis of employment issues draws heavily on ILO publications. Much of the analysis on environmental trends was based on World Resources Institute 1988 and FAO data and publications.

Chapter 3

The discussion on health care, population, and water draws on Birdsall and Sai 1988, Herz and Measham 1987, Whittington and others 1989, Churchill and others 1987, various World Bank policy papers on population and health care, UNICEF 1989, and unpublished material from Althea Hill. The discussion on food security and nutrition is based on the World Bank's "Report of the Task Force on Food Security in Africa," Berg 1987, and unpublished material by Janet Lowenthal and by Judith McGuire and Barry Popkin. The section on education draws heavily on the World Bank's *Education in Sub-Saharan Africa: Policies for Adjustment, Revitalization, and Expansion* and unpublished material from Ralph Harbison, Janet Leno, Peter Moock, and James Socknat.

Chapter 4

A major source of ideas and information for this chapter is the series of studies completed under the World Bank's research project, Managing Agricultural Development in Africa (MADIA). World Bank agricultural sector studies were also used. Additional sources include annual reports of the International Agricultural Research Centers and numerous FAO publications. Of particular importance is FAO's *African Agriculture: The Next 25 Years*. Publications from the International Food Policy Research Institute were also used. Most of the data for the chapter come from the FAO, the World Bank's *World Tables*, and the World Bank's *Price Prospects for Major Primary Commodities, 1988–2000*.

Chapter 5

This chapter draws extensively on World Bank operational and project work. The industry section draws heavily on World Bank experience with industrial development in Africa, some of which has been summarized in Meier and Steel 1989 and the ECA and UNIDO's 1989 review of the Industrial Development Decade for Africa. The formulation of industry issues was influenced by Hawkins 1986, Mytelka 1988, the background paper by Sanjaya Lall , and background work by Howard Pack and Thelma Triche. Sections on competitiveness and exports draw on Frischtak and others 1989 and Rhee 1989. Much of the analysis in the mining section is drawn from World Bank operational experience in Sub-Saharan Africa's mineral-producing countries and from background contributions by Peter Fozzard and John Strongman. Much of the data in the energy section, particularly on oil and gas reserves and exploration and drilling activity, was drawn from a historical database that includes data obtained largely from *Oil and Gas Journal* and the *American Association of Petroleum Geologists Bulletin*. Various other sources were utilized with regard to energy, including World Bank appraisal reports.

Chapter 6

The discussion of entrepreneurship and the business environment is drawn from Elkan 1988, Kilby 1988, Richardson and Ahmed 1987, and de Soto 1989. The ILO's 1988 "African Employment Report" provided information and data on the informal sector. Material on small-scale enterprises and grassroots institutions is based on Maldonado 1989, Sanyal 1988, and the background papers by Ayittey, Gabianu, Giri, and MacGaffey. The section on supporting entrepreneurial capabilities draws on Aiyer 1985, Dessing 1988, Pean 1989, Rhee 1989, Roth 1987, Tiffin and Osotimehin 1988, and Webster 1989.

Chapter 7

This chapter draws extensively on background papers presented at the workshop on "Regional Integration and Cooperation in Sub-Saharan Africa" held at the World Bank in September 1988. (The proceedings of the workshop will be published in a separate volume.) Discussion of the regional trade issues draws heavily on Ali Mansoor and others 1989. The work of Elliot Berg and others 1988 also has been used. The African Development Bank's "African Development Report 1989" was also an important source.

Chapter 8

This chapter is based primarily on the World Bank's country economic reports. The data on growth, investment, savings, public revenues and expenditure, exports, imports, and other macroeconomic variables are mainly derived from World Bank reports, *World Tables*, and World Bank data sources. Analysis on infrastructure pricing and charges for services benefited from the work of Anderson 1987. The section on the financial sector draws on World Bank reports, including the *World Development Report 1989*. The analysis on community savings and informal financial systems benefited from inputs from African development practitioners. The discussions on "development assistance in the 1990s" and "debt relief: a menu of options" benefited from useful contributions from the World Bank's Resource Mobilization Department and the International Economics Department, respectively.

Background papers

The following papers are to be published in a forthcoming series.

Abdallahi, Sidi Ould Cheikh. "Long-Term Perspectives Study for Sub-Saharan Africa: The Situation in Mauritania."

Addo, John S. "Exchange Rate Reforms under Ghana's Economic Recovery Program."

Ake, Claude. "Sustaining Development on the Indigenous."

Ayittey, George B. N. "Indigenous African Systems: An Assessment."

Badri, Balgis Y. "An Analysis of Sudan's Development."

———. "Sudanese Women: Current Status and Future Prospects."

Baldwin, George B. "Non-Governmental Organizations and African Development: An Enquiry."

Bocar Ba, Ibrahim. "Sustained Growth and Development with Equity in Sub-Saharan Africa: Mali."

Chirwa, Gilbert B. "Reflections on the Long-Term Perspective Study for Sub-Saharan Africa with Particular Reference to Malawi."

DeGuefe, Befekadu. "Profile of the Ethiopian Economy."

Diouf, Makhtar. "The Lifestyle of Senegal's Elites and Their Macro-Economic Impact."

Gabianu, A. Sena. "The Susu Credit System: An Ingenious Way of Financing Business Outside the Formal Banking System."

Giri, Jacques. "Formal and Informal Small Enterprises in the Long-Term Future of Sub-Saharan Africa."

Harrison, Paul. "Sustainable Growth in Agriculture."

Hyden, Goran. "The Changing Context of Institutional Development in Sub-Saharan Africa."

———. "Creating an Enabling Environment."

Lall, Sanjaya. "Structural Problems of Industry in Sub-Saharan Africa."

Lemer, Andrew. "Building Firm Foundations: Africa's Infrastructure in Long-Term Perspective."

Lipumba, Nguyuru H. I. "Reflections on the Long-Term Development Strategy in Tanzania."

MacGaffey, Janet (with Gertrud Windsperger). "The Endogenous Economy."

Mitra, M. Radja. "The Social Market Economy Paradigm and Its Relevance to Sub-Saharan Africa—Lessons from the Nordic Development Experience."

Mwanakatwe, John M. "Reflections on Long-Term Perspectives for Sub-Saharan Africa with Particular Reference to Zambia."

Okyere, Asenso. "The Response of Farmers to Ghana's Adjustment Policies."

Park, Eul Young. "Some Lessons from East Asian Development Experience."

Safilios-Rothschild, Constantina. "Women's Groups in Sub-Saharan Africa: An Underutilized Grassroot Institution."

Samater, Ibrahim. "Long-Term Development Prospects for Somalia."

Singh, J. Prasad. "Analysis of Project Costs in Sub-Saharan Africa in Selected Sectors."

Steedman, David W. "The Internalization of the Policy-Making Process."

Tarr, Byron. "Political Developments and Environment in Africa."

Van der Tak, Herman (with Donald King). "High Project Costs in Africa."

Selected bibliography

African Development Bank. 1989a. "Africa and the African Development Bank: Current and Future Challenges—Report of the Committee of Ten." Abidjan. Processed.

———. 1989b. "African Development Report 1989." Abidjan. Processed.

Aiyer, Sri-ram. 1985. "A Strategy for Small-Scale Enterprise Development in Western Africa." Washington, D.C.: World Bank, Western Africa Department. Processed.

Ake, Claude. 1981. *A Political Economy of Africa.* Harlow, Essex: Longman.

Anderson, Dennis. 1987. *The Public Revenue and Economic Policy in African Countries: An Overview of Issues and Policy Options.* World Bank Discussion Paper 19. Washington, D.C.

Anjaria, S. J., S. Eken, and J. F. Laker. 1982. *Payments Arrangements and the Expansion of Trade in Eastern and Southern Africa.* Occasional Paper 11. Washington, D.C.: IMF.

Baxter, M., J. Howell, and R. Slade. 1989. *Aid and Agricultural Extension: Evidence from the World Bank and Other Donors.* World Bank Technical Paper 87. Washington, D.C.

Berg, Alan. 1987. *Malnutrition: What Can Be Done? Lessons from World Bank Experience.* Baltimore, Md.: The Johns Hopkins University Press.

Berg, Elliot. 1985. "Intra-African Trade and Economic Integration." Alexandria, Virginia: Elliot Berg Associates. Processed.

Berg, Elliot, and others. 1988. *Regional Cooperation in Africa.* Alexandria, Va.: Applied Development Economics. Processed.

Birdsall, Nancy, and Frederick T. Sai. 1988. "Family Planning Services in Sub-Saharan Africa." *Finance and Development* 25:28–31.

Birkhaeuser, Dean, Robert E. Evenson, and Gershon Feder. 1988. "The Economic Impact of Agricultural Extension: A Review." Washington, D.C.: World Bank, Agriculture and Rural Development Department. Processed.

Botswana, Government of. 1989. "Botswana Family Health Survey II 1988." Preliminary Report. Gabarone: Ministry of Finance and Development Planning and Ministry of Health. Processed.

Brett, E. A. 1986. "State Power and Economic Inefficiency: Explaining Political Failure in Africa." *IDS Bulletin* 17:22–29.

———. 1987. "States, Markets, and Private Power in the Developing World: Problems and Possibilities." *IDS Bulletin* 18:31–37.

Briscoe, John, and David de Ferranti. 1988. *Water for Rural Communities: Helping People Help Themselves.* Washington, D.C.: World Bank.

Buckley, R., and S. Mayo. 1988. "Housing Policy in Developing Economies: Evaluating the Macroeconomic Impacts." Discussion Paper 19. Washington, D.C.: World Bank, Infrastructure and Urban Development Department. Processed.

Bureau de Recherches Geologiques et Minieres. 1989. "Sub-Saharan African Mineral Potential: Study of Ten Countries." Washington, D.C.: World Bank, Africa Technical Department. Processed.

Churchill, Anthony A., and others. 1987. *Rural Water Supply and Sanitation: Time for a Change.* World Bank Discussion Paper 18. Washington, D.C.

Cleaver, Kevin. 1988. "The Use of Price Policy to Stimulate Agricultural Growth in Sub-Saharan Africa." In Collen Roberts, ed., *Trade, Aid, and Policy Reform: Proceedings of the Eighth Agriculture Sector Symposium.* Washington, D.C.: World Bank.

Cornia, Giovanni, Richard Jolly, and Frances Stewart, eds. 1987. *Adjustment with a Human Face.* Oxford: Clarendon Press.

Cour, J. M. 1988a. "Population Redistribution, Urbanization, and Economic Growth in Côte d'Ivoire." Washington, D.C.: World Bank, Africa Technical Department. Processed.

———. 1988b. "Urban-Rural Linkages: Macroeconomic and Regional Implications." Washington, D.C.: World Bank, Africa Technical Department. Processed.

Dailami, Mansoor, and Michael Walton. 1989. "Private Investment, Government Policy, and Foreign Capital in Zimbabwe." PPR Working Paper 248. Washington, D.C.: World Bank. Processed.

Dessing, Maryke. 1988. "Entrepreneurship and Private Sector Development: Support to Small and Microenterprises." Washington, D.C.: World Bank, Africa Technical Department. Processed.

Economic Development Institute, 1989. *Successful Development in Africa: Case Studies of Projects, Programs, and Policies.* Washington, D.C.: World Bank.

Eicher, Carl K. 1982. "Facing Up to Africa's Food Crisis." *Foreign Affairs* 61, 1 (Fall):151–74.

Elkan, Walter. 1988. "Entrepreneurs and Entrepreneurship in Africa." *Finance and Development* 25 (December):20,41–42.

The Enabling Environment Conference. 1986. "The Nairobi Statement on the Enabling Environment for Effective Private Sector Contribution to Development in Sub-Saharan Africa." Issued at the Enabling Environment Conference, Nairobi, October 24. Processed.

Falloux, Francois, J. R. Mercier, and N. Savine. 1988. "Madagascar Environmental Action Plan." Washington, D.C.: World Bank. Processed.

Falloux, Francois, and Aleki Mukendi, eds. 1987. *Desertification Control and Renewable Resource Management in the Sahelian and Sudanian Zones of West Africa.* World Bank Technical Paper 70. Washington, D.C.

Faruqee, Rashid, and Ravi Gulhati. 1983. *Rapid Population Growth in Sub-Saharan Africa: Issues and Policies.* World Bank Staff Working Paper 559. Washington, D.C.

Frischtak, Claudio, Bita Hadjimichael, and Ulrich Zachau. 1989. "Competition Policies for Industrializing Countries." Washington, D.C.: World Bank, Industry Development Division. Processed.

Gamsonre, P. Emile. 1988. "Entreposage et Diversification des Sources D'Approvisionnement en Hydrocarbures au Burkina Faso." Case study prepared for World Bank, Africa Technical Department. Washington, D. C. Processed.

Goldmark, Susan. 1986. "Financial Sector Review of Rwanda." Washington, D.C.: Development Alternatives, Inc. Processed.

Haggblade, Steven, and Peter B. Hazell. 1988. "Prospects for Equitable Growth in Rural Sub-Saharan Africa." PPR Working Paper 8. Washington, D.C.: World Bank. Processed.

Haggblade, Steven, Peter B. Hazell, and James Brown. 1988. "Farm-Nonfarm Linkages in Rural Sub-Saharan Africa." PPR Working Paper 6. Washington, D.C.: World Bank. Processed.

Hagon, Philippe, and others. 1988. *Les Afriques en l'an 2000: perspectives economiques.* Afrique Contemporaine No. 146 (special).

Hamer, Andrew M. 1986. "Urban Sub-Saharan Africa in Macroeconomic Perspective: Selected Issues and Policy Options." Discussion Paper

96. Washington, D.C.: World Bank, Water Supply and Urban Development Department. Processed.

Harrison, Paul. 1987. *The Greening of Africa: Breaking through in the Battle for Land and Food.* London: Paladin Grafton Books.

Hawkins, A. M. 1986. "Can Africa Industrialize?" In Robert Berg and Jennifer Seymour Whitaker, eds., *Strategies for African Development: A Study for the Committee on African Development Strategies.* Berkeley: University of California Press.

Hazlewood, Arthur. 1979. "The End of the East African Community: What Are the Lessons for Regional Integration Schemes?" *Journal of Common Market Studies* 18, 1 (September):40–58.

Heller, Peter S., and Alan A. Tait. 1984. *Government Employment and Pay: Some International Comparisons.* Occasional Paper 24. Washington, D.C.: International Monetary Fund.

Herz, Barbara, and Anthony R. Measham. 1987. *The Safe Motherhood Initiative: Proposals for Action.* World Bank Discussion Paper 9. Washington, D.C.

Hill, A. 1989. "Population Conditions in Mainland Sub-Saharan Africa." Washington, D.C.: World Bank, Africa Technical Department. Processed.

Hogg, V. 1989. "Sub-Saharan Africa Transport: Perspectives and Policy Options." Washington, D.C.: World Bank, Africa Technical Department. Processed.

Howe, John, and Ian Barwell. "Study of Potential for Intermediate Means of Transport." Report prepared for the Ministry of Transport and Communications, Republic of Ghana, on behalf of the World Bank. Processed.

Hyden, Goran. 1983. *No Shortcuts to Progress: African Development Management in Perspective.* Berkeley: University of California Press.

International Labour Organisation (ILO). 1988. "African Employment Report." Addis Ababa: Jobs and Skills Programme for Africa. Processed.

International Monetary Fund (IMF). Various years. *Government Finance Statistics Yearbook.* Washington, D.C.

Israel, Arturo. 1987. *Institutional Development: Incentives to Performance.* Baltimore, Md.: The Johns Hopkins University Press.

Kenya, Government of. 1986. "Sessional Paper No. 1 of 1986 on Economic Management for Renewed Growth." Nairobi: Government of Kenya. Processed.

Kilby, Peter. 1988. "Breaking the Entrepreneurial Bottle-Neck in Late-Developing Countries: Is There a Useful Role for Government?" *Journal of Development Planning* 18: 221–49.

Klitgaard, Robert. 1988. *Controlling Corruption.* Berkeley: University of California Press.

Lamb, Geoffrey. 1987. *Managing Economic Policy Change: Institutional Dimensions.* World Bank Discussion Paper 14. Washington, D.C.

Lee, Kyu Sik, and Alex Anas. 1989. "Manufacturers' Responses to Infrastructure Deficiencies in Nigeria: Private Alternatives and Policy Options." Report INU 50. Washington, D.C.: World Bank. Processed.

Lele, Uma. 1989a. *Agricultural Growth, Domestic Policies, The External Environment, and Assistance to Africa: Lessons of a Quarter Century.* MADIA Discussion Paper 1. Washington, D.C.: World Bank.

———. 1989b. "Sources of Growth in East African Agriculture." *World Bank Economic Review* 3, 1 (January):119–44.

Lele, Uma, and Robert E. Christiansen. 1989. *Markets, Marketing Boards, and Cooperatives: Issues in Adjustment Policy.* MADIA Discussion Paper 11. Washington, D.C.: World Bank.

Lele, Uma, Robert E. Christiansen, and Kundhavi Kadiresan. 1989. *Fertilizer Policy in Africa: Lessons from Development Programs and Adjustment Lending, 1970–87.* MADIA Discussion Paper 5. Washington, D.C.: World Bank.

Lipton, Michael. 1983. "Is Increased Agricultural Marketing Good for the Rural Poor?" *Development Research Digest* 10 (Winter):55–59.

Ljung, Per Erik, and Catherine Farvacque. 1988. "Addressing the Urban Challenge: A Review of the World Bank FY87 Water Supply and Urban Development Operations." Report INU 13. Washington, D.C.: World Bank. Processed.

Mabbut, Jack. 1984. "A New Global Assessment of the Status and Trends of Desertification." *Environmental Conservation* 11, 2 (Summer):103–13.

Maldonado, Carlos. 1989. "The Underdogs of the Urban Economy Join Forces: Results of an ILO Programme in Mali, Rwanda, and Togo." *International Labour Review* 128, 1:65–84.

Mansoor, Ali, and others. 1989. "Intra-Regional Trade in Sub-Saharan Africa." Washington, D.C.: World Bank, Africa Technical Department. Processed.

Mason, M., and S. Thriscutt. 1989. "Road Deterioration in Sub-Saharan Africa." Washington,

D.C.: World Bank, Africa Technical Department. Processed.

Mazrui, Ali. 1980. *The African Condition: A Political Diagnosis.* New York: Cambridge University Press.

Meier, Gerald. M., and William F. Steel, eds. 1989. *Industrial Adjustment in Sub-Saharan Africa.* EDI Series in Economic Development. New York: Oxford University Press.

Mellor, John W., Christopher L. Delgado, and Malcolm J. Blackie, eds. 1987. *Accelerating Food Production in Sub-Saharan Africa.* Baltimore, Md.: Johns Hopkins University Press.

Mytelka, Lynn. 1988. "The Unfulfilled Promise of African Industrialization." Paper presented at the 31st Annual Meeting of the African Studies Association, Chicago, October 28–31. Processed.

National Research Council. 1988. "Scientific Institution Building in Africa." Summary Report of the Joint Symposium ICIPE Foundation, The African Academy of Sciences, and the US National Academy of Sciences, March 14–18. Nairobi: ICIPE Science Press.

Nellis, John. 1989. "Public Enterprise Reform in Adjustment Lending." PPR Working Paper 233. Washington, D.C.: World Bank. Processed.

Nelson, Ridley. 1988. "Dryland Management: The Desertification Problem." Environmental Department Working Paper 8. Washington, D.C.: World Bank. Processed.

Norgaard, Richard B. 1988. "The Biological Control of Cassava Mealybug in Africa." *American Journal of Agricultural Economics* 70, 2 (May):366–71.

Nunberg, Barbara. 1988. "Public Sector Pay and Employment Reform." PPR Working Paper 113. Washington, D.C.: World Bank. Processed.

Organisation for Economic Cooperation and Development (OECD). 1988a. *Development Cooperation.* Paris.

———. 1988b. *The Sahel Facing the Future: Increasing Dependence or Structural Transformation: Futures Study of the Sahel Countries, 1985–2010.* Paris.

Organization of African Unity (OAU). 1980. *Lagos Plan of Action for the Implementation of the Monrovia Strategy for the Economic Development of Africa.* Addis Ababa.

Paul, Samuel. 1989. "Private Sector Assessment: A Pilot Exercise in Ghana." PPR Working Paper 199. Washington, D.C.: World Bank. Processed.

Péan, Leslie. 1989. "Working Paper on the Urban Informal Sector in the Sahel." Washington, D.C.: World Bank, Sahelian Department. Processed.

Péan, Pierre. 1988. *L'Argent Noir: Corruption et Sous-Developpement.* Paris: Fayard.

Repetto, Robert. 1988. *The Forest for the Trees? Government Policies and the Misuse of Forest Resources.* Washington, D.C.: World Resources Institute.

Rhee, Yung Whee. 1989. "The Role of Catalytic Agents in Entering International Markets." Industry Series Paper 5. Washington, D.C.: World Bank, Industry and Energy Department. Processed.

Richardson, Richard, and Osman Ahmed. 1987. "African Development Symposium: Challenge for Africa's Private Sector." *Challenge* 29 (January/February): 16–25.

Roth, Gabriel. 1987. *The Private Provision of Public Services in Developing Countries.* EDI Series in Economic Development. New York: Oxford University Press.

Russell, Sharon Stanton, and Karen Jacobsen. 1988. "International Migration and Development in Sub-Saharan Africa." Washington, D.C.: World Bank, Africa Technical Department. Processed.

Salam, Abdus, ed. 1987. "The Role of Science and Technology in Development." *Development and South-South Cooperation* 3, 5 (December).

Sanyal, Bishwapriya. 1988. "Urban Informal Sector Revisited: Some Notes on the Relevance of the Concept in the 1980s." *Third World Planning Review* 10 (February): 65–83.

Save-Soderbergh, S. and Per Taxell, eds. 1988. *Recovery in Africa: A Challenge for Development Cooperation in the 1900s.* Swedish Ministry of Foreign Affairs.

Schneider, Bertrand. 1988. *Africa Facing Its Priorities.* Philadelphia: Published for the Club of Rome by Cassell Tycooly.

Schultz, T. Paul. 1989. "Women and Development: Objectives, Frameworks, and Policy Interventions." PPR Working Paper 200. Washington, D.C.: World Bank. Processed.

Soto, Hernando de. 1989. *The Other Path: The Invisible Revolution in the Third World.* New York: Harper and Row.

Southern African Development Coordination Conference (SADCC). 1988. "Annual Progress Report." Gaborone. Processed.

Svedberg, Peter. 1988. *Export Performance of Sub-Saharan Africa 1970–1985.* Seminar Paper 409. Stockholm: Institute for International Economic Studies.

Thriscutt, S. 1989. "Review of Country Experiences with Rural Roads Projects." Draft paper prepared for the SSATP Rural Travel and Transport Project. Washington, D.C.: World Bank, Africa Technical Department. Processed.

Tiffin, Scott, and S. O. A. Osotimehin. 1988. "Technical Entrepreneurship and Technological Innovation in Nigeria." *Journal of Development Planning* 18: 194–220.

United Nations. Administrative Committee on Coordination. Subcommittee on Nutrition. 1989. *Update on the Nutrition Situation: Recent Trends in Nutrition in 33 Countries*. Geneva, Switzerland.

United Nations Development Programme (UNDP) and World Bank. 1984. "Energy Issues and Options in Thirty Developing Countries." Processed.

————. "Issues and Options in the Energy Sector (various African countries)." Processed.

United Nations Economic Commission for Africa (ECA). 1981. "Report of the ECA Mission on the Evaluation of UDEAC and the Feasibility of Enlarging Economic Cooperation in Central Africa." Addis Ababa. Processed.

————. 1983. "ECA and Africa's Development 1983–2008: A Preliminary Perspective Study." Addis Ababa. Processed.

————. 1984. "Proposal for Strengthening Economic Integration in West Africa." Addis Ababa. Processed.

————. 1987a. "The Abuja Statement: The International Conference on Africa: The Challenge of Economic Recovery and Accelerated Development." Abuja, Nigeria. Processed.

————. 1987b. "Proposal for Rationalization of West African Integration Efforts." Addis Ababa. Processed.

————. 1988a. "Africa's Mineral Resources Development and Utilization." Processed.

————. 1988b. "Beyond Recovery: ECA-Revised Perspectives of Africa's Developments, 1988–2008." Addis Ababa. Processed.

————. 1988c. "The Khartoum Declaration: Towards a Human-Focused Approach to Socio-Economic Recovery and Development in Africa." In *Economic Commission for Africa: Annual Report*. New York: United Nations.

————. 1989. "African Alternative Framework to Structural Adjustment Programmes for Socio-Economic Recovery and Transformation (AAF-SAP)." Addis Ababa. Processed.

United Nations Economic Commission for Africa, Organization of African Unity, and United Nations Industrial Development Organization. 1982. *A Programme for the Industrial Development Decade for Africa: A Framework for the Formulation and Implementation of Programmes at the National, Subregional, Regional, and International Levels*. New York: United Nations.

United Nations Economic Commission for Africa and United Nations Industrial Development Organization. 1989. "Report on the Independent Mid-Term Evaluation of the Industrial Development Decade for Africa (IDDA) and the Proclamation of the Second IDDA." Presented at the Ninth Meeting of the Conference of African Ministers of Industry, Harare, Zimbabwe, May 29 – June 1. Processed.

United Nations Economic, Scientific and Cultural Organization (Unesco). Office of Statistics. various years. *Statistical Yearbook*. Paris.

United Nations Food and Agriculture Organisation (FAO). 1986. *African Agriculture: The Next 25 Years*. Rome.

United Nations Inter-Agency Task Force, Africa Recovery Programme/United Nations Economic Commission for Africa. 1989. "South African Destabilization—The Economic Cost of Frontline Resistance to Apartheid." New York. Processed.

United Nations International Children's Emergency Fund (UNICEF). 1989a. *The State of the World's Children*. New York: Oxford University Press.

————. 1989b. *Statistics on Children in UNICEF-Assisted Countries*. New York.

United Nations Statistical Office (UNSO). various years. *Population and Vital Statistics Report*. New York.

————. various years. *Energy Statistics Yearbook*. New York.

United States Bureau of Mines. 1988. *1986 Minerals Yearbook Volume III, Area Reports International*. Washington, D.C.

Van Arkadie, Brian. 1989. "The Role of Institutions in Development." Paper presented at the First Annual World Bank Conference on Development Economics, Washington, D.C., April 27–28. Processed.

Vogel, Ronald J. 1988. *Cost Recovery in the Health Care Sector: Selected Country Studies in West Africa*. World Bank Technical Paper 82. Washington, D.C.

Von Pischke, John, and John Rouse. 1983. "Selected Successful Experiences in Agricultural Credit and Rural Finance in Africa." *Savings and Development* 1:21–44.

Wad, Atulo. 1984. "Science, Technology, and Industrialization in Africa." *Third World Quarterly*
6, 2 (April): 327–50.

Webster, Leila. 1989. "World Bank Lending to
Small and Medium Enterprises: 15 Years of Experience." Washington, D.C.: World Bank, Industry and Energy Department. Processed.

Whitaker, Jennifer Seymour. 1988. *How Can Africa
Survive?* New York: Harper & Row.

Whittington, Dale, Donald T. Lauria, and Xinm-
ing Mu. 1989. "Paying for Urban Services: A
Study of Water Vending and Willingness to Pay
for Water in Onitsha, Nigeria." Report INU 40.
Washington, D.C.: World Bank. Processed.

World Bank. 1983. *The Energy Transition in Developing Countries.* Washington, D.C.

———. 1986. *Population Growth and Policies in Sub-
Saharan Africa.* A World Bank Policy Study.
Washington, D.C.

———. 1987. *Financing Health Services in Developing Countries: An Agenda for Reform.* A World
Bank Policy Study. Washington, D.C.

———. 1988a. "Agricultural Marketing: World
Bank's Experience." World Bank Operations
Evaluation Department, Report 7353. Washing-
ton, D.C. Processed.

———. 1988b. *Education in Sub-Saharan Africa: Policies for Adjustment, Revitalization, and Expansion.*
A World Bank Policy Study. Washington, D.C.

———. 1988c. "The Future of Railway Transport
in Sub-Saharan Africa and the Role of the World
Bank." Washington, D.C.: World Bank, Africa
Technical Department. Processed.

———. 1988d. "Report of the Task Force on Food
Security in Africa." Washington, D.C. Processed.

———. 1988e. *Social Indicators of Development.* Baltimore, Md.: The Johns Hopkins University
Press.

———. 1988f. "Stimulating Agricultural Growth
and Rural Development in Sub-Saharan Africa." PPR Working Paper 15. Washington,
D.C.: World Bank. Processed.

———. 1988g. "Sub-Saharan Africa Railways
Management Workshop." Proceedings of a
Workshop held in Brazzaville, November 21–

25, 1988. Washington, D.C.: World Bank, Africa
Technical Department. Processed.

———. 1988h. *World Debt Tables, 1988–89 Edition.*
Washington, D.C.

———. 1989a. *African Economic and Financial Data.*
Washington, D.C.

———. 1989b. *Africa Region Population Projections,
1988–89 Edition.* Washington, D.C.

———. 1989c. *The Challenge of Hunger in Africa: A
Call to Action.* Washington, D.C.

———. 1989d. *Price Prospects for Major Primary
Commodities, 1988–2000.* 2 Vols. Washington,
D.C.

———. 1989e. "Report of the Africa Region Task
Force on Population FY90–92." Washington,
D.C. Processed.

———. 1989f. *Road Deterioration in Developing
Countries: Causes and Remedies.* World Bank Policy Paper. Washington, D.C.

———. 1989g. *World Tables, 1988–89 Edition.* Baltimore, Md.: The Johns Hopkins University
Press.

———. various years. *World Development Report.*
New York: Oxford University Press.

World Bank and Instituto Italo Africano. 1989.
"Strengthening Local Governments in Sub-
Saharan Africa." Proceedings of Two Work-
shops Held in Poretta Terme, Italy, March 5-17.
Washington, D.C.: World Bank, Africa Techni-
cal Department. Processed.

World Bank and United Nations Development
Programme. 1989. *Africa's Adjustment and
Growth in the 1980s.* Washington, D.C.: World
Bank.

World Resources Institute and International Insti-
tute for Environment and Development. 1988.
World Resources 1988. New York: Basic Books,
Inc.

Zachariah, K. C., and My T. Vu. 1988. *World Pop-
ulation Projections, 1987–88 Edition: Short- and
Long-Term Estimates.* Baltimore, Md.: The Johns
Hopkins University Press.

Zimbabwe, Government of. 1989. "Zimbabwe Demographic and Health Survey 1988." Preliminary Report. Harare: Department of Census and
Statistics. Processed.

Statistical appendix

Contents

Strengthening information systems and basic statistics in Sub-Saharan Africa

In most Sub-Saharan countries before independence, data compilations were mostly limited to periodic censuses of population, records of trade flows, and abstracts of administrative records. Independence brought the desire and commitment to meet economic and social development goals through formal multiyear development plans, and the need for data became pressing. Statistical cells or units were created, staffed initially with expatriates funded from multilateral and bilateral aid programs. Expatriates transplanted concepts and methods current elsewhere without adapting them to prevailing local conditions. The UN System of National Accounts (SNA), with its emphasis on market transactions, was not modified to take into account the predominance of subsistence activities in largely rural Africa. The measurement of agricultural production was attempted in an environment in which cropping patterns were not conducive to scientifically based crop-cutting tests developed in India. And even such demographic concepts as the household, based on non-African situations, were applied without modification.

Not only were the data inappropriate, they reached decisionmakers too late to be useful. Modest human and financial resources were spread thinly over many sectors and fields of statistics.

The emphasis on large-scale collections and on complete enumerations to increase reliability sacrificed the timeliness of information, as did the inadequacy of computing and tabulating capacities. Already stretched, the resources to statistical agencies were further curtailed by austerity measures in the 1970s and the early 1980s. Many people left the statistical services to seek the better pay in other fields. Governments generally gave very low priority to data collection, and in many countries there are virtually no reliable statistics.

The current situation was well summarized in the report by the Economic Commission for Africa (ECA) for the Joint Conference of African Planners, Statisticians, and Demographers. "Data gaps affect every sector and every aspect of the African situation. In the field of demography, even the size and growth rate of population in some of the African countries cannot be unambiguously determined. In the field of social statistics, there are gaps relating to literacy, school enrollment ratios, the institutional status of the child and poverty levels. And in the field of economic statistics, basic economic series like GDP and resource flows are sometimes lacking. Data on national resources and the environment are, if available, in a very rudimentary state." If strategies for sustainable growth with equity are to be developed in Africa, the information systems must be improved, as a matter of urgency.

New development strategy for information systems

This report makes many references to the types of information needed to formulate and implement policies. Its call to address population as a matter of urgency points directly to the need for information on demographic trends, on changing attitudes to fertility, and on variables that influence demographic change. The creation of an enabling environment for higher productivity requires information on incomes, costs, prices, public finances, and investment. And building the capacity for effective economic management involves the ability to undertake policy analysis and to make rational choices based on solid information. The report's emphasis on equity implies the need for information systems to identify the disadvantaged and to monitor the impact of policies on beneficiaries and nonbeneficiaries. To address the issue of sustainability, the concept of capital needs to go beyond the "produced means of production," such as machinery, to include natural resources and human capital—elements that conventional national accounting frameworks do not fully reflect. The need is thus clear: to expand the scope of such frameworks and to collect and analyze data encompassing these elements.

Action is required in four broad data fields:
- Social and demographic data
- Natural resources and environment
- Price and production statistics
- National accounts.

In each priorities need to be articulated more clearly. African governments and the international community need to formulate an action program. The concept of a partnership in development described in the main text applies equally to developing data systems.

Social and demographic data

Most African countries took part in the 1970 and 1980 population censuses, but the African Census Program (funded by UNFPA and other donors) does not appear to have been sustained. The World Fertility Survey in Sub-Saharan Africa generated valuable demographic data. The Demographic and Health Surveys by Westinghouse followed up on the earlier work, but created few indigenous capabilities. The UN's National Household Survey Capability Program and its African variant, the African Household Capability Program, have been launched in a few countries. Household surveys have been conducted on such topics as household expenditures, labor force, and demographic characteristics, but many field surveys have been either suspended or abandoned for want of resources. Other initiatives, not

all successful, have included the Global Early Warning System and UNICEF's surveillance systems covering nutrition and health-related topics.

The emphasis on single-topic enquiries has meant that the data emerging from such surveys has been limited to the particular field of enquiry. Earlier expectations of integrating results from successive surveys have not been met because variations in sample sizes, concepts, and coverage have hampered the production of multidimensional data sets. All in all, the experience to date has been sobering.

The World Bank, recognizing the need for current data to address immediate and pressing policy concerns in the 1980s, launched the Living Standards Measurement Study (LSMS) with three broad objectives: collecting high-quality data through specially designed, multisubject, integrated household surveys; tabulating results rapidly for immediate use; and analyzing the data to address specific policy concerns. The study also was meant to develop national capabilities for the regular collection of data. The LSMS's comprehensive coverage of topics includes savings, housing conditions, educational attainment and enrollment, health status, economic activities at the household level (including income and labor force participation), demographic characteristics, expenditure and consumption patterns, ownership of durable goods, fertility history and anthropometric data to assess nutrition.

The experience of the LSMS in Côte d'Ivoire and Ghana shows that it is indeed feasible to canvass complex questionnaires through successive visits. Further, by using personal computers for data entry, long lags in data processing can be overcome, and basic tabulations of fairly high-quality data can be delivered six to eight months after field operations have been completed. The integration of policy analysis into LSMS operations has also meant that data are rapidly turned into analytical outputs needed and used for policymaking.

The World Bank translated the LSMS experience into an expanded action program to address the social dimensions of adjustment policies. The Social Dimensions of Adjustment (SDA) project (see Box 9.2) incorporates the canvassing of multitopic integrated household surveys—linking the analysis to the design of compensatory programs to mitigate the impact of adjustment on distressed groups, to measures to protect social investment in the face of tighter public finance, and to programs that target groups most in need of support. Central to the SDA project is establishing permanent national survey and analytical capabilities—and creating databases on the basic economic and social conditions of households.

The SDA project, even at this early stage, has attracted widespread and enthusiastic participation from 26 countries in Sub-Saharan Africa. Along with the allocation of modest resources by governments, support from the donor community has been equally enthusiastic. The UN Statistical Office (UNSO) and the ECA have agreed to collaborate with the Bank in countries in which both the National Household Survey Capability Program and the SDA project are active to coordinate the implementation of the two programs. The new partnership between African governments and the donor community represents a fresh effort to address statistical issues in Africa. Of even greater significance, the coordination will ensure that African governments will be full partners in the longer-term development of statistics in Sub-Saharan Africa.

The SDA project holds great promise for statistics in Africa. In addition to transferring new methods and technologies, the project should build institutions through active collaboration in data gathering, analysis, and research, thus drawing together data users and producers at the national level. The SDA project will not only yield immediate and direct household data on various topics, it will also feed its findings into the compilation of timely and more reliable macroeconomic aggregates of household consumption, investment, and savings—shedding light on the interactions between households and the productive sectors of economies. The SDA project will also train African nationals at all levels of the statistical system, and the training of field enumerators and analysts has been assigned high priority.

The SDA project must, however, not crowd out national efforts. The investment in capability building will need to be protected and nurtured beyond the life of the project. External inputs will need to be phased out over time, with governments assuming responsibility for funding the survey operations after the first four or five years and with only modest external technical inputs continuing beyond the initial phase. Unless this happens, the large investment in this effort will be lost.

Natural resources and environment

A greatly enhanced flow of data is needed to manage Africa's natural resources and environment. The World Bank has been active in identifying existing and potential databases on the environment—and has organized a series of workshops with the involvement of the UN Environmental Programme (UNEP). Finding a consensus on an appropriate framework has been difficult, with two distinct approaches in contention. The first is concerned with the physical aspects, and emphasizes the physical measurements of environment and resource variables. The second is concerned with economic data systems that attempt measurement in monetary terms. The physical systems, although somewhat easier to implement, cannot provide measures in common units. The economic systems are based on controversial assumptions and generally are difficult to implement.

The World Bank—working with resource economists, the UNSO, and the UNEP—is seeking consensus on a minimum framework that links a set of satellite accounts to the conventional SNA. Through case studies by the Bank and the United Nations and the testing of alternative accounting frameworks, it should prove possible to evolve a practical set of guidelines.

If income is viewed as the flow of goods and services that can be consumed without depleting capital, basic national accounting concepts require modification. Existing statistical frameworks, such as the SNA, embody narrow concepts of production and capital—and measure capital inadequately. It is heartening to note that national accountants currently revising the SNA are making some needed changes. The new SNA will incorporate recommendations for a set of satellite accounts for compiling adjusted aggregates that take into account the use of nonreplaceable natural resources and expenditures on protecting the environment.

Micro data sets on the environment do not exist for many countries. The reason is that global and national statistical priorities and efforts have been inadequate in developing appropriate conceptual, methodological, and classification schemes. The challenge then is to rapidly develop the micro data systems along with accounting frameworks that incorporate natural resources and address environmental concerns. The application of these systems and guidelines will take time, and national users will need to determine priorities for work in this field.

Price and production statistics

The skillful management of the interconnected system of prices and incentives is critical for achieving sustained and equitable growth. Many countries' consumer price indexes are based on outdated weights that do not reflect current consumption patterns. Price series for compiling these indexes mostly reflect urban prices. Wage statistics, if compiled at all, reflect only the wages in a few narrowly defined sectors of the economy.

Given the importance of prices in government policy, the need for mounting an integrated system to collect prices and to compute indexes is urgent. With assistance from the European Community (EC), many African governments took part in the International Comparison Project (ICP). Twenty-three countries participated in the latest phase (Phase V) of the ICP. Although the information has been used only to compute purchasing power parities for international comparisons, the rich body of data could be exploited more fully. Based on the partnership with the EC, the ICP could be expanded to develop an integrated program for price statistics covering producer, consumer, and import and export prices. With modest increases in funding and expanded effort to train national statistical personnel, progress can be rapid. Additional elements in a program for price statistics should include the preparation of manuals on methods for compiling and analyzing price data.

External trade statistics, although in many countries the oldest and most established set of administrative statistics, have in recent years become less timely and reliable. The Automated System for Customs Data—a computerized system developed by UNCTAD and now being adopted by several Sub-Saharan countries—will rehabilitate work on external trade statistics. In addition to improving data on trade flows and the balance of payments, it will enhance the recording of customs revenues and the ability to compute external trade price and volume indexes.

A program to compile wage statistics in key sectors—the government, state-owned enterprises, large and medium industrial and trading enterprises, and major service trades—is feasible if integrated with the collection of production statistics.

AGRICULTURAL STATISTICS. Agriculture will continue to have an important and large role in Africa. But most analysts and decisionmakers believe that available estimates of agricultural output are unreliable and grossly inadequate. The need for prompt and more reliable production statistics has been reaffirmed at the national, regional, and global levels. Sectoral policy analysis, early warning systems, assessment of food requirements, and the study of nutritional standards all demand basic agricultural production data. And given the size and contribution of agriculture in GDP, production estimates are critical for preparing macroeconomic accounts as well.

Statistics on agricultural production have been compiled in most African countries through agricultural surveys, supplemented by poorly supervised (mostly subjective) crop estimates by extension workers and other local officials. Where measurement techniques have been objective, the principal approach has been to use crop-cuts and physical measurements of plots and areas under cultivation. In many situations, however, the data from crop-cuts can result in systematic overestimation and variance resulting from different of crop conditions in the plots and areas surveyed. Crop-cuts are feasible for cereal crops but inappropriate for tree and root crops. Compounding these problems are the high costs and time requirements of crop-cuts. The need to station enumerators in remote areas for long periods increases costs, which leads to the use of highly clustered sample designs and small sample sizes. The regular collection of production data through a broadly based survey system has not been sustainable and has led to increasing use of subjective methods.

Beyond annual production data, national efforts to develop basic agricultural statistics have included large agricultural censuses. These have been expensive but have not yielded the hoped-for results. Delays in processing censuses have resulted in considerable lags in data availability—often three to five years—which limits the value of the data for users grappling with immediate concerns.

Critics of present methods have argued for simpler, more cost-effective approaches to gathering timely agricultural production data. Some argue that farmers can provide reasonably reliable estimates of outputs, which would enable cheaper and more efficient sample designs. The World Bank, in cooperation with the FAO and with UNICEF support, tested the hypothesis that estimates of production obtained by interviewing farmers soon after a harvest can be at least as accurate as estimates obtained through physical measurement involving crop-cuts. The study found that:

• Square cuts appear to result in serious overestimates—by around 30 percent on average, with a range from 15 to 40 percent.

• Farmers' estimates are remarkably close to actual production figures in all countries, varying from –8 to +7 percent. They also displayed considerably smaller variance than the crop-cut estimates.

The decades-long problems with agricultural production data can be overcome if these research findings are systematically applied and further refined. An initiative is now needed to promote these methods through a program of seminars, training courses, manuals, and practical applications. African governments will require modest financial support for such an effort, in large part from donor resources set aside for monitoring and evaluating agricultural and rural development projects. These resources could be supplemented from nationally funded budget allocations for agricultural censuses and ongoing crop-cutting surveys. The gains from such an effort should materially improve estimates of GDP and of agricultural output.

OTHER PRODUCTION STATISTICS. In many Sub-Saharan countries, production data for other sectors are equally weak, if available at all. Industrial production is inadequately measured. The contribution of services to total output is poorly captured. Public finance data have gaps and long lags. Information on external transactions is imprecise. Addressing these issues requires a long-term program to strengthen accounting systems and to develop the overall capacity of national statistical agencies. It also requires increased user awareness in determining statistical priorities. Conventional statistical enquiries should satisfy specific requirements rather than try to catch everything. Paralleling the household surveys under the SDA project, there is need for a well-designed multisector enterprise or establishment survey covering, in the first instance, a subset of the large- and medium-scale entities in the economy. Such a survey should collect data only on production, employment, wages, and capital formation.

National accounts

The foregoing flows of information would provide African national statistical offices with the basic data sets needed to compile macroeconomic accounts within the framework of the SNA. Without an integrated approach to developing information systems, the goals of setting in place reliable and timely national accounts will remain unfulfilled.

In the context of building up national accounting systems, some key steps can be identified. The SNA framework is complex. Although the SNA revision now under way at the international level acknowledges the urgent need for practical manuals, budgetary constraints faced by the UNSO preclude their early production and publication. The need for a modest increment in resources for the work to proceed is pressing.

Improving the quality and timeliness of national accounts is a long-term program stretching over a decade or more. Most Sub-Saharan Africa countries will find the task beyond their present statistical capabilities. Even when information flows improve, the lags in compilation will compromise the timely availability of national accounts sufficiently disaggregated to meet analytical needs. A collective effort that permits the compilation of preliminary, somewhat aggregative estimates, is called for. This is within the reach of most countries and ought to be done systematically.

Rehabilitating and building statistical systems

The task of building sustainable capabilities to support *a flow of relevant, timely data* to aid decisionmaking is complex and difficult. It depends on strengthening existing institutions by developing a viable statistical infrastructure. It also depends on developing sampling frames, compiling registers of businesses, documenting processes, evolving classifications, and adapting concepts. Equally important is the development of a cadre of professional, middle-level and support staff through training and upgrading skills. Bilateral and multilateral programs of assistance have attempted to deliver a range of inputs and resources toward these goals.

Efforts at institution building have had only a modest impact. This can be attributed to six problems:

- Inadequate counterpart resources by national governments, implying weak commitment to statistical development.
- Improvised or informal programs.
- Loss of trained statisticians to other sectors and fields.
- Low morale of staff in statistical services because of unsatisfactory pay levels, motivation, and image.
- User-driven assistance programs geared to a narrow demand for information for high-profile international statistical activities.
- Absence of a long-term national strategy for information systems.

Efforts at both national and international levels are now needed to build statistical systems in Africa.

National efforts

Most statistical offices in Sub-Saharan Africa are embarking on the task of building and rehabilitating systems. They face a dual challenge of new demands for data and severe resource constraints: tight budgets, a continuing brain drain of trained staff, a weakened statistical infrastructure, and a general incapacity to produce the data on demand. The challenge now is to tackle the different elements of demand by articulating a coherent and focused national program for information flows. Each country also needs to formulate a consensus on a minimum set of priorities. Divergent (and sometimes competing) needs of the different users need to be coordinated to establish a balanced statistical program. In each country a multiyear, incremental program of statistical development would articulate priorities and systematically assess needs, against which the existing capacity for data generation could be evaluated. Beyond this initial set of actions is the crucial need for the leadership to commit—and continue to commit—the needed budgetary resources. A reciprocal commitment from users to commit resources and from producers to generate the needed information will start the long-term task of strengthening statistical institutions.

Progress in developing viable statistical systems will be made only if there is a change in attitudes toward a quantitative approach to decisionmaking. The change has to occur at all levels of government—among decisionmakers,

users, analysts, and statistical staff—and will have to be accompanied by a tangible set of actions.

PRIORITY SETTING. Working with international donors, governments and policymakers must take the lead in determining needs and priorities and in developing an action program. There are several areas in which consensus needs to be reached. First, for long-term institution building, *training* of nationals at all levels of the statistical system should have the highest priority. Many training centers at the national and regional levels already exist but need to be strengthened. Past emphasis on higher-level training has been somewhat misplaced. Future efforts must focus on middle-level personnel—with greater emphasis on practical training and less on statistical theory.

Second, inadequate capabilities for *data processing* have been a significant constraint. Although hardware has, in some instances, been a factor, the more significant issue has been the inability to develop software. The rapid advances in microcomputing technology now provide cost-effective alternatives to mainframe machines. Furthermore commercially developed statistical and survey packages, available at modest cost, satisfy most requirements. And many packages produced by the United Nations and statistical offices in the developed countries are not widely disseminated. Acquisition of these packages, along with the right training, would eliminate the need for customized software requiring time-consuming design and program development by computer specialists.

Third is the issue of *timeliness*, which has a dimension beyond computing capacities. Traditionally, statistical offices have regarded data as proprietary—and have refrained from putting out tabulations without accompanying analysis. But statistical offices often lack the capacity for such analysis. The analytical function should be assigned to data users, who generally have subject-specific specialization; this would enable statistical offices to focus more on statistical issues and to direct their attention to releasing data more rapidly. Nevertheless statistical agencies that have the capability for analytical work should be strengthened.

FUNDING AND INCENTIVES. In addition to translating the broad areas of work into multiyear plans, there must be a commitment of budgetary resources with some assurance of continuity. This commitment, both political and administrative,

211

will send clear signals to those charged with the task of reconstruction.

The existing incentive systems—the salaries and status of statistical personnel—are clearly inadequate. Even with modest improvements in incentives, it should prove possible to rebuild morale and inject new vigor. The brain drain and staff leakages can be checked only if actions are taken to address the issue of incentives. Because the special problems of statistical agencies merit attention, governments should assign high priority to appropriate incentives—both monetary and nonmonetary—for statistical staff. Unless morale is addressed through a better incentive system, statistical institutions will continue to languish.

International efforts

The absence of adequate *coordination* among donors, particularly at the country level, is perhaps the most salient feature of past efforts. Statistical work programs and national priorities have been distorted because of competing interventions by the donors.

- In the choice of statistical fields, a heavy emphasis has been put on demography, with little on agricultural data.
- Technical advisory services provided by donors have tended to station long-term advisors at considerable expense.
- Little has been done to adapt methods and approaches to suit local conditions.
- Considerable amounts have been provided for hardware and equipment without taking into account maintenance and operating costs or the need for associated software.
- Training efforts have been largely focused on postgraduate training abroad.
- Regional centers have fallen into decay as donors largely took a country-by-country approach.
- The courses at both national and regional centers have been biased toward theory rather than practical applications.

Coordination of aid programs is thus essential to get the most from resources, to provide national governments with the means to develop sustainable programs for statistical development, to formulate priorities, and to inject a regional focus and

achieve the benefits of economies of scale. It is suggested that an African consultative group on statistics be established. Such a group, made up of all donors, both bilateral and multilateral, would be concerned with the broader issues of support for statistical development in Africa, including issues that go beyond national statistical concerns. The group could also organize a modest fund through voluntary contributions from participating agencies to channel resources into regional programs—particularly to support regional training centers, the testing and adaptation of methods to meet African requirements, the preparation of guidelines and manuals with an African orientation, and the funding of research and experiments into appropriate statistical techniques.

Following the SDA model, the group could act as the vehicle for the regional and international aspects of the operations pertaining to the development of work in the four areas discussed above: social and demographic statistics, natural resource and environmental statistics, price and production statistics, and national accounts. As part of this effort it could fund an expanded group of consultants in the specialties mentioned above, attached either to the Statistics Division of the ECA or to other subregional agencies. These consultants would deliver technical advisory services to national governments through short-term consultancies and periodic visits, thus obviating the need for long-term consultants in each country.

To elevate the importance of information systems in the framework of national and international programs, the periodic donor country Consultative Group or Round Table meetings should discuss the development of national information systems regularly. The national statistical programs could then be reviewed in a wider context, and pledges of donor support including funding for local costs could be obtained. This would greatly increase the attention of both African governments and donors to statistical issues and would provide the necessary coordination.

Sustainable information systems in Sub-Saharan Africa can be built only gradually over the longer term. Working with international donors, governments and policymakers must take the lead in determining needs and priorities and in developing an action program.

Introduction to the data

The following maps and tables provide information on the main features of social and economic development in Sub-Saharan Africa. Technical notes follow the data.

Content and format

The first section of the data contains four maps which present key information on the 45 countries of Sub-Saharan Africa. The maps show groupings of countries for per capita GNP, population growth, infant mortality, and growth of per capita food production.

The main classifications used in the tables are the 45 countries in all Sub-Saharan Africa, Sub-Saharan Africa excluding Nigeria, 32 low-income economies with per capita incomes of $480 or less in 1987, low-income economies excluding Nigeria, 13 middle-income economies with per capita incomes over $480 in 1987, 6 countries with populations of more than 22 million persons, 9 countries in the Sahel, and 5 oil exporters. Comparator groups presented in the tables are the 52 low-income developing economies, low-income economies excluding China and India, South Asia, and South Asia excluding India. The key preceding Table 1 lists countries included in the various groupings.

The indicators in Table 1 give a summary profile of the economies of Sub-Saharan Africa. Data in the other tables fall into the following broad areas: national accounts, production, external trade, external debt, international transactions, central government finance, monetary statistics, demo-graphic and social indicators, and land use and environmental indicators.

In most of the tables the presentation follows that used in the World Development Indicators in the *World Development Report*. In each group economies are listed in ascending order of GNP per capita, except those for which no such figure can be calculated. These are italicized and in alphabetical order at the end of the group deemed to be appropriate. The alphabetical list in the key shows the reference number for each economy; here, too, italics indicate economies with no estimates of GNP per capita. The colored bands contain summary measures—totals, weighted averages, or median values—calculated for groups of Sub-Saharan Africa economies if data are adequate.

In general the format of the column headings also follows that of the World Development Indicators, with some modifications. Data are given for three years (1965, 1980, and 1987) or periods (1965–73, 1973–80, and 1980–87) rather than for two. In addition all of the tables include Angola and the nine Sub-Saharan Africa countries with populations of less that 1 million. Summary lines for total Sub-Saharan Africa and low-income Africa are shown with and without Nigeria because of Nigeria's large share in weighted averages, especially when population is used as the weight. The tables on official development assistance (Table 18) and on women in development (Table 30) are significantly different from the versions in the World Development Indicators.

Several supplementary tables have been included to show production of major crops (Table

7), major agricultural exports (Table 15), status of children (Table 31), land use (Table 36), and environmental indicators (Table 37). The table on growth of production of major crops (Table 6) contains information for total Sub-Saharan Africa only.

For ease of reference, ratios and rates of growth are shown; absolute values are reported in only a few instances but are often available from other World Bank publications. Growth rates are computed, unless otherwise noted, by using the least-squares method. All growth rates for economic indicators are based on constant price series. Details of the methodology are given in the technical notes following the data. Data in italics are for years or periods other than those specified—up to two years earlier for economic indicators and up to three years on either side for social indicators. All dollar figures are US dollars. The various methods used to convert from national currency figures are described, where appropriate, in the technical notes.

The methodology used to compute the summary measures is described in the technical notes. For these numbers, *w* indicates that the summary measures are weighted averages; *m*, median values; and *t*, totals. The coverage of economies is not uniform for all indicators, and the variation from measures of central tendency can be large; therefore readers should exercise caution in comparing the summary measures for different indicators, groups, and years or periods. The summary measures for most of the indicators are overall estimates: countries for which individual estimates are not shown, because of nonreporting or insufficient history, have been included by assuming they follow the trend of reporting countries during such periods. This gives a more consistent aggregate measure by standardizing country coverage for each period shown. Where missing information accounts for a significant share of the overall estimate, however, the group measure is reported as not available. Footnotes to the tables indicate the procedure used for summary measures and the weights used to calculate weighted averages.

The technical notes and footnotes to tables should be referred to in any use of the data. These notes outline the methods, concepts, definitions, and data sources used in compiling the maps and tables. The bibliography gives details of the data sources, which contain comprehensive definitions and descriptions of concepts used.

Sources and caveats

The data in the maps and tables are drawn from the United Nations and its specialized agencies, the International Monetary Fund (IMF), and the World Bank files. National accounts data are from member countries obtained by Bank missions and, where appropriate, estimates prepared by Bank staff. Data on external debt are compiled directly by the Bank on the basis of reports from developing member countries through the Debtor Reporting System. The data in the environmental indicators table come from the World Resources Institute.

Differences between data given in this appendix and other World Bank publications may reflect updating, revisions to historical series, methodological changes, changes to aggregation procedures, and definitional differences. Most of the tables here are based on the 1989 World Development Indicators, for which data were finalized in April 1989. Data on debt, Tables 18 through 23, were updated in September 1989.

Every effort has been made to standardize the data. Full comparability cannot be ensured, however, and care must be taken in interpreting the indicators. The statistics are drawn from sources thought to be most authoritative, but many of them are subject to considerable margins of error. Variations in national statistical practices also reduce the comparability of data; thus the data should be construed only as indicating trends and characterizing significant differences among economies, rather than taken as being precise quantitative indicators of those differences.

Throughout this report, and especially the section "Strengthening information systems and basic statistics in Sub-Saharan Africa," there are references to gaps and weaknesses in the available statistics and how these gaps have adversely affected policy analysis and the decisionmaking capacity of governments. The indicators presented here confirm many of the gaps and the timeliness and availability of the data.

The data in this appendix should be useful for analyzing past and current trends and for formulating policy. The data should also provide information for increased discussion about solutions to the problems of statistical sources and methods as well as about the critical need for strengthened information systems in Sub-Saharan Africa.

Additional information on Sub-Saharan Africa and other economies may be found in other World

Bank publications, notably *African Economic and Financial Data*, the *Atlas, Social Indicators of Development, World Debt Tables, World Tables,* and the *World Development Report*.

Staff of the World Bank's International Economics Department and the Special Economic Office of the Africa Technical Department have made substantial contributions in the production of this appendix.

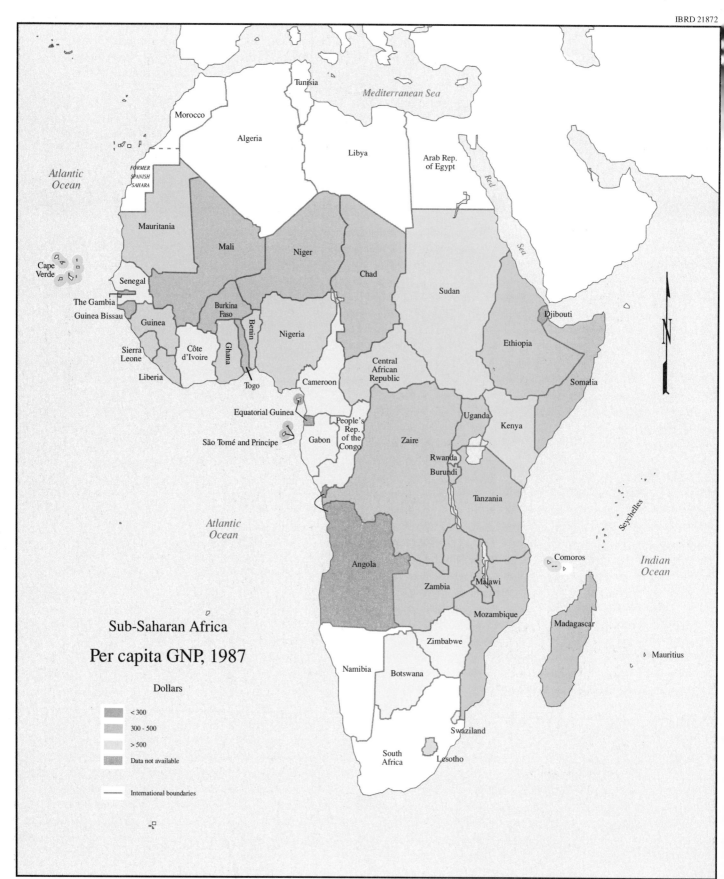

Tunisia

Mediterranean Sea

Morocco

*Atlantic
Ocean*

Algeria

Libya

Arab Rep.
of Egypt

*FORMER
SPANISH
SAHARA*

Mauritania

Mali

Niger

Chad

Sudan

Red

Sea

Cape
Verde

Senegal

The Gambia

Guinea Bissau

Guinea

Sierra
Leone

Liberia

Burkina
Faso

Benin

Côte
d'Ivoire

Ghana

Togo

Nigeria

Djibouti

Ethiopia

Somalia

Cameroon

Central
African
Republic

Equatorial Guinea

People's
Rep.
of the
Congo

Uganda

Kenya

São Tomé and Principe

Gabon

Zaire

Rwanda

Burundi

*Atlantic
Ocean*

Tanzania

Seychelles

Comoros

*Indian
Ocean*

Angola

Zambia

Malawi

Mozambique

Madagascar

ᵇ Mauritius

Sub-Saharan Africa

Per capita GNP, 1987

Zimbabwe

Namibia

Botswana

Dollars

< 300

300 - 500

> 500

Data not available

International boundaries

Swaziland

South
Africa

Lesotho

N

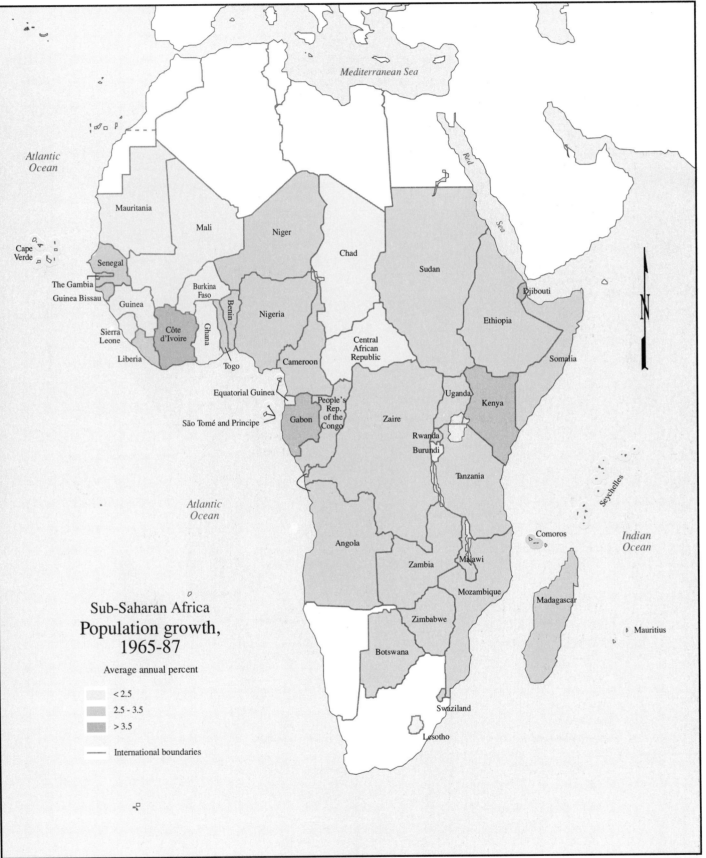

Mediterranean Sea

Atlantic
Ocean

Red Sea

Mauritania

Mali

Niger

Chad

Sudan

Cape
Verde

Senegal

The Gambia

Guinea Bissau

Guinea

Burkina
Faso

Benin

Nigeria

Djibouti

Ethiopia

Sierra
Leone

Côte
d'Ivoire

Ghana

Liberia

Togo

Cameroon

Central
African
Republic

Somalia

Equatorial Guinea

São Tomé and Principe

Gabon

People's
Rep.
of the
Congo

Zaire

Uganda

Kenya

Rwanda
Burundi

Tanzania

Atlantic
Ocean

Seychelles

Comoros

Indian
Ocean

Angola

Zambia

Malawi

Mozambique

Madagascar

Mauritius

Sub-Saharan Africa
Population growth,
1965-87

Average annual percent

- < 2.5
- 2.5 - 3.5
- > 3.5
- International boundaries

Zimbabwe

Botswana

Swaziland

Lesotho

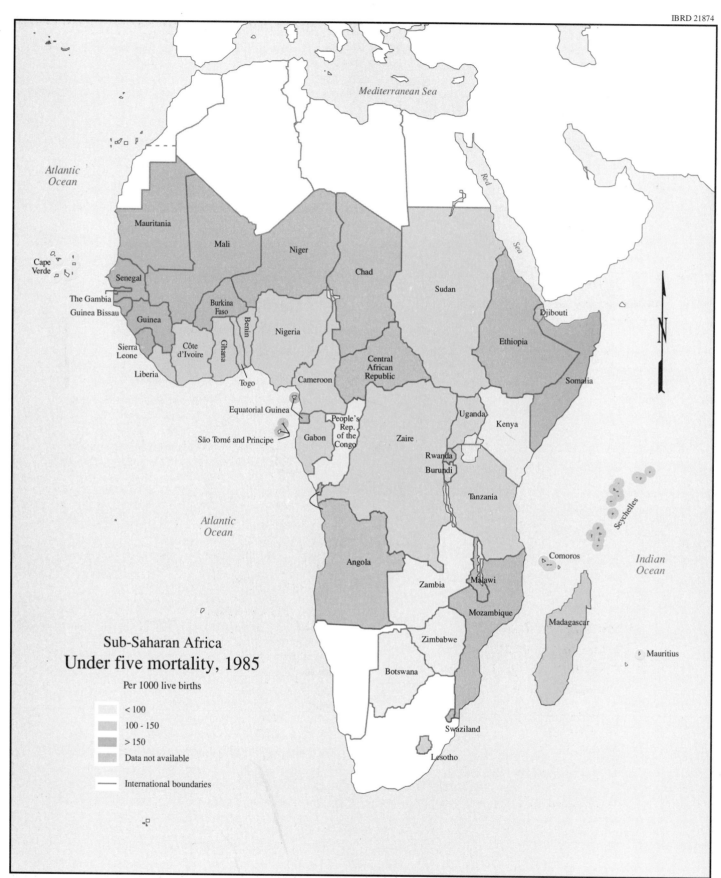

Atlantic
Ocean

Mediterranean Sea

Red

Sea

Mauritania

Mali

Niger

Chad

Sudan

Cape
Verde

Senegal

The Gambia

Guinea Bissau

Guinea

Burkina
Faso

Djibouti

Sierra
Leone

Côte
d'Ivoire

Ghana

Benin

Nigeria

Ethiopia

Liberia

Togo

Cameroon

Central
African
Republic

Somalia

Equatorial Guinea

People's
Rep.
of the
Congo

Uganda

Kenya

São Tomé and Principe

Gabon

Zaire

Rwanda

Burundi

Atlantic
Ocean

Tanzania

Seychelles

Angola

Comoros

Indian
Ocean

Zambia

Malawi

Madagascar

Mozambique

Mauritius

Zimbabwe

Sub-Saharan Africa
Under five mortality, 1985

Botswana

Per 1000 live births

< 100

100 - 150

> 150

Swaziland

Data not available

Lesotho

International boundaries

N

OCTOBER 1989

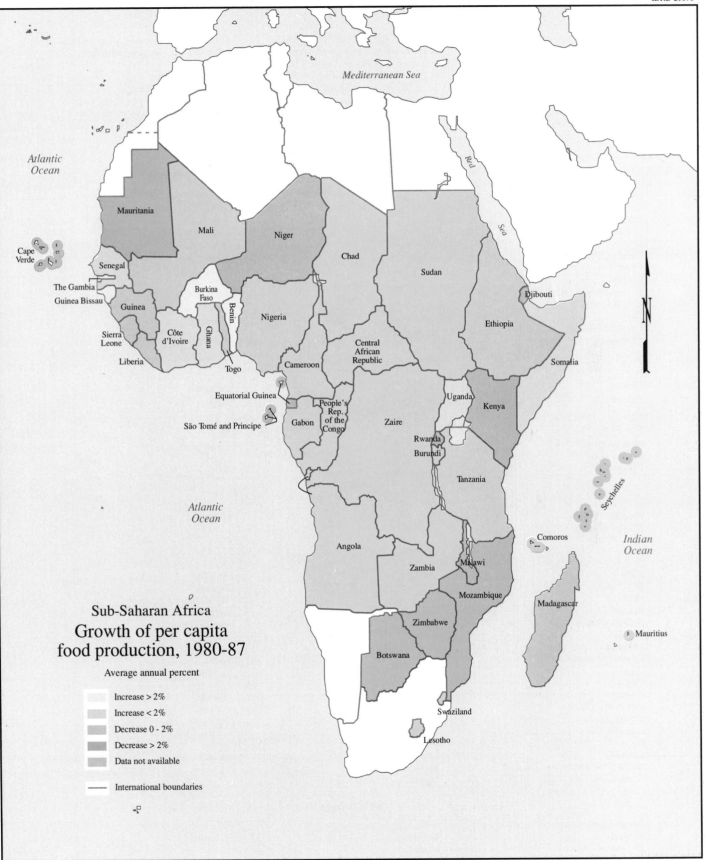

Atlantic
Ocean

Mediterranean Sea

Mauritania

Mali

Niger

Chad

Sudan

Cape
Verde

Senegal

The Gambia

Guinea Bissau

Guinea

Sierra
Leone

Liberia

Côte
d'Ivoire

Burkina
Faso

Benin

Ghana

Togo

Nigeria

Cameroon

Djibouti

Ethiopia

Somalia

Central
African
Republic

Equatorial Guinea

São Tomé and Principe

Gabon

People's
Rep.
of the
Congo

Zaire

Uganda

Kenya

Rwanda

Burundi

Tanzania

Atlantic
Ocean

Angola

Zambia

Malawi

Mozambique

Comoros

Seychelles

*Indian
Ocean*

Madagascar

Mauritius

Zimbabwe

Botswana

Swaziland

Lesotho

Sub-Saharan Africa
Growth of per capita
food production, 1980-87

Average annual percent

Increase > 2%

Increase < 2%

Decrease 0 - 2%

Decrease > 2%

Data not available

International boundaries

*Red
Sea*

OCTOBER 1989

219

Key

In each table, economies are listed in their group in ascending order of GNP per capita except those for which no GNP per capita can be calculated. These are italicized, in alphabetical order, at the end of their groups. The reference numbers below reflect the order in the tables.

Figures in the colored bands are summary measures for groups of economies in Sub-Saharan Africa. The letter *w* after a summary measure indicates that it is a weighted average; *m*, a median value; and *t*, a total.

All growth rates are in real terms.

Figures in italics are for years or periods other than those specified.

.. = not available.

0 and 0.0 = zero or less than half the unit shown (unless otherwise noted).

Sub-Saharan Africa

Angola	44	Gabon	42	Nigeria	27
Benin	21	Gambia, The	11	Rwanda	19
Botswana	40	Ghana	28	São Tomé and Principe	16
Burkina Faso	8	*Guinea*	32	Senegal	34
Burundi	12	Guinea-Bissau	4	Seychelles	43
Cameroon	39	Kenya	23	Sierra Leone	20
Cape Verde	33	Lesotho	26	Somalia	17
Central African Republic	22	Liberia	30	Sudan	24
Chad	2	Madagascar	9	Swaziland	36
Comoros	25	Malawi	5	Tanzania	7
Congo, People's Republic	38	Mali	10	Togo	18
Côte d'Ivoire	37	Mauritania	29	Uganda	15
Djibouti	45	Mauritius	41	Zaire	3
Equatorial Guinea	31	Mozambique	6	Zambia	13
Ethiopia	1	Niger	14	Zimbabwe	35

Six most populous economies

Ethiopia	Nigeria	Tanzania
Kenya	Sudan	Zaire

Sahelian economies

Burkina Faso	Gambia	Mauritania
Cape Verde	Guinea-Bissau	Niger
Chad	Mali	Senegal

Oil exporters

Angola	Congo	Nigeria
Cameroon	Gabon	

All low-income economies

Afghanistan	Haiti	Pakistan
Bangladesh	India	Rwanda
Benin	Indonesia	São Tomé and Principe
Bhutan	Kampuchea	Sierra Leone
Burkina Faso	Kenya	Solomon Islands
Burma	Kiribati	Somalia
Burundi	Lao PDR	Sri Lanka
Central African Rep.	Lesotho	Sudan
Chad	Liberia	Tanzania
China	Madagascar	Togo
Comoros	Malawi	Uganda
Equatorial Guinea	Maldives	Vanuatu
Ethiopia	Mali	Viet Nam
Gambia, The	Mauritania	Yemen, PDR
Ghana	Mozambique	Zaire
Guinea	Nepal	Zambia
Guinea-Bissau	Niger	
Guyana	Nigeria	

South Asia

Bangladesh	India	Pakistan
Bhutan	Maldives	Sri Lanka
Burma	Nepal	

Table 1. Basic indicators

		Population (millions) mid-1987	Area (thousands of square kilometers)	GNP per capita [a] Dollars 1987	GNP per capita [a] Average annual growth rate (percent) 1965-73		1980-87	Average annual inflation rate [a] (percent) 1965-73		1980-87	Life expectancy at birth (years) 1987
						1973-80			1973-80		
Sub-Saharan Africa											
Total		451.2 t	22,245 t	330 w	2.9 w	0.1 w	-2.8 w	7.5 w	6.8 w	15.2 w	51 w
Excluding Nigeria		344.5 t	21,321 t	330 w	1.2 w	-0.7 w	-1.2 w	5.9 w	17.3 w	20.4 w	50 w
Low-income economies		397.3 t	18,377 t	270 w	3.1 w	0.3 w	-3.6 w	8.2 w	17.4 w	17.0 w	50 w
Excluding Nigeria		290.6 t	17,453 t	240 w	0.8 w	-0.6 w	-2.2 w	6.7 w	19.3 w	27.5 w	50 w
1	Ethiopia	44.8	1,222	130	1.1	0.0	-1.6	2.0	5.7	2.6	47
2	Chad	5.3	1,284	150	-1.3	-3.5	2.4	4.6	8.3	5.3	46
3	Zaire	32.6	2,345	150	0.3	-4.7	-2.5	19.0	42.1	53.5	52
4	Guinea-Bissau	0.9	36	160	..	-4.2	0.8	..	5.6	39.2	39
5	Malawi	7.9	118	160	4.3	1.4	0.0	3.7	8.5	12.4	46
6	Mozambique	14.6	802	170	..	..	-8.2	..	..	26.9	48
7	Tanzania	23.9	945	180	2.0	-0.9	-1.7	3.4	15.4	24.9	53
8	Burkina Faso	8.3	274	190	1.2	2.5	2.5	1.9	11.2	4.4	47
9	Madagascar	10.9	587	210	1.1	-1.5	-3.7	4.6	10.2	17.4	54
10	Mali	7.8	1,240	210	..	4.3	0.7	..	10.8	4.2	47
11	Gambia, The	0.8	11	220	1.7	0.2	0.8	3.0	13.5	13.8	43
12	Burundi	5.0	28	250	3.2	1.9	-0.2	3.0	15.4	7.5	49
13	Zambia	7.2	753	250	-0.5	-2.2	-5.6	5.8	8.9	28.7	53
14	Niger	6.8	1,267	260	-3.7	2.6	-4.9	4.1	8.5	4.1	45
15	Uganda	15.7	236	260	0.7	-6.2	-2.4	5.6	45.4	95.2	48
16	São Tomé and Principe	0.1	1	280	..	7.2	-6.0	..	2.1	4.9	65
17	Somalia	5.7	638	290	0.1	4.6	-2.5	4.5	17.6	37.8	47
18	Togo	3.2	57	290	2.0	1.5	-3.9	2.9	8.2	6.6	53
19	Rwanda	6.4	26	300	3.2	2.2	-1.0	7.2	17.1	4.5	49
20	Sierra Leone	3.8	72	300	2.3	-0.8	-2.0	2.1	14.5	50.0	41
21	Benin	4.3	113	310	0.0	-0.3	-0.6	2.9	11.6	8.2	50
22	Central African Republic	2.7	623	330	1.5	-0.5	-0.7	3.0	14.8	7.9	50
23	Kenya	22.1	583	330	4.7	1.3	-0.9	2.4	11.6	10.3	58
24	Sudan	23.1	2,506	330	-1.7	3.5	-4.3	7.2	15.3	31.7	50
25	Comoros	0.4	2	370	..	..	..	..	..	..	56
26	Lesotho	1.6	30	370	4.2	6.6	-0.9	4.1	11.3	12.3	56
27	Nigeria	106.6	924	370	5.3	1.2	-4.8	9.1	16.2	10.1	51
28	Ghana	13.6	239	390	1.0	-2.1	-2.0	8.1	45.4	48.3	54
29	Mauritania	1.9	1,031	440	1.2	-0.6	-1.6	4.1	8.5	9.8	46
30	Liberia	2.3	111	450	2.4	-0.7	-5.2	1.6	9.1	1.5	54
31	*Equatorial Guinea*	0.4	28	..	..	..	..	..	..	..	46
32	*Guinea*	6.5	246	..	1.2	1.3	-0.1	2.9	2.4	55.1	42
Middle-income economies		53.9 t	3,868 t	870 w	1.9 w	-1.2 w	0.3 w	4.7 w	14.2 w	6.8 w	53 w
33	Cape Verde	0.3	4	500	..	7.3	1.2	..	9.7	13.9	65
34	Senegal	7.0	196	520	-0.8	-0.5	0.1	3.0	8.8	9.1	48
35	Zimbabwe	9.0	391	580	2.6	-2.0	-1.3	2.3	10.6	12.4	58
36	Swaziland	0.7	17	700	5.8	0.3	1.2	4.3	13.3	10.2	55
37	Côte d'Ivoire	11.1	322	740	4.5	1.2	-3.0	2.7	16.0	4.4	52
38	Congo, People's Republic	2.0	342	870	4.2	1.1	1.7	4.4	9.2	1.8	59
39	Cameroon	10.9	475	970	-0.4	5.7	4.5	7.5	10.4	8.1	56
40	Botswana	1.1	582	1,050	9.3	7.3	8.0	4.4	11.6	8.4	59
41	Mauritius	1.0	2	1,490	0.8	3.9	4.4	5.5	12.5	8.1	67
42	Gabon	1.1	268	2,700	4.9	-1.2	-3.5	5.8	15.8	2.6	52
43	Seychelles	0.1	0	3,120	2.6	4.5	1.3	7.3	18.3	3.7	70
44	*Angola*	9.2	1,247	..	1.1	-9.8	..	6.9	22.4	..	44
45	*Djibouti*	0.4	22	..	..	..	..	..	..	..	47
Six most populous economies		253.1 t	8,525 t	270 w	3.9 w	0.4 w	-4.0 w	9.0 w	17.5 w	14.7 w	51 w
Sahelian economies		39.0 t	5,344 t	270 w	-1.0 w	1.1 w	-0.4 w	3.4 w	9.4 w	6.6 w	46 w
Oil exporters		129.7 t	3,256 t	460 w	4.4 w	0.5 w	-3.6 w	8.7 w	16.0 w	9.5 w	51 w
All low-income economies											
Total		2,823.2 t	37,015 t	290 w	3.3 w	2.6 w	4.0 w	9.7 w	8.9 w	8.6 w	61 w
Excluding China and India		957.2 t	24,166 t	280 w	3.0 w	1.8 w	-1.1 w	22.1 w	17.1 w	13.3 w	54 w
South Asia		1,080.9 t	5,158 t	290 w	1.5 w	2.0 w	2.6 w	6.1 w	8.0 w	7.8 w	57 w
Excluding India		283.3 t	1,870 t	250 w	0.6 w	2.8 w	2.4 w	5.3 w	12.4 w	8.2 w	55 w

Note: Summary measures include estimates for missing country data. The summary measures for GNP per capita and life expectancy are weighted by population. Those for average annual rates of inflation are weighted by the 1980 share of country GDP valued in current dollars.
a. See the technical notes.

221

Table 2. Growth of production (average annual percent)

		GDP			Agriculture			Industry		
		1965-73	1973-80	1980-87	1965-73	1973-80	1980-87	1965-73	1973-80	1980-87
Sub-Saharan Africa										
Total		5.9 w	2.5 w	0.5 w	2.2 w	-0.3 w	1.3 w	13.8 w	4.3 w	-1.2 w
Excluding Nigeria		4.0 w	1.7 w	2.3 w	1.9 w	0.7 w	1.8 w	..	1.8 w	3.4 w
Low-income economies		6.0 w	2.8 w	-0.4 w	2.2 w	0.0 w	1.0 w	14.3 w	4.4 w	-2.7 w
Excluding Nigeria		3.3 w	1.9 w	1.4 w	..	1.7 w	5.0 w	..	8.0 w	1.6 w
1	Ethiopia	3.9	1.6	0.9	2.1	0.6	-2.1	6.4	1.4	3.8
2	Chad b	0.4	-1.5	5.1	..	0.5	2.6	..	-6.0	10.0
3	Zaire b	3.6	-2.0	1.6	..	0.9	3.2	..	-3.4	3.6
4	Guinea-Bissau b	..	1.2	3.7	..	-3.4	5.7	..	3.6	3.6
5	Malawi	5.9	5.3	2.6	..	4.8	2.5	..	5.6	1.9
6	Mozambique	..	..	-2.6	..	..	-11.1	..	..	-8.4
7	Tanzania	4.8	2.3	1.7	3.1	0.2	3.8	7.0	1.8	-2.4
8	Burkina Faso	..	3.9	5.6	..	1.3	6.1	..	1.5	3.9
9	Madagascar b	3.0	1.0	0.3	..	-0.4	2.2	..	1.6	-2.0
10	Mali b	2.7	6.3	3.4	0.9	7.1	0.3	1.1	1.6	9.8
11	Gambia, The	4.4	2.0	5.0	4.5	0.9	7.1	3.8	-2.1	5.8
12	Burundi	4.6	3.2	2.6	4.7	1.6	1.7	10.4	9.8	4.9
13	Zambia b	2.4	0.3	-0.1	2.0	1.6	3.2	2.7	-0.3	-0.7
14	Niger b	-1.2	5.6	-1.9	-2.9	1.4	2.8	13.2	14.3	-4.3
15	Uganda	3.6	-2.7	0.4	3.6	-2.3	-0.5	3.0	-11.9	1.4
16	São Tomé and Principe	..	6.3	-0.6	..	7.2	-7.3	..	2.3	1.8
17	Somalia	2.1	7.8	2.2	..	10.9	2.8	..	0.2	1.0
18	Togo b	5.5	4.1	-0.5	2.6	1.9	0.8	6.2	6.7	-1.6
19	Rwanda b	6.4	5.7	2.4	..	8.7	1.1	..	..	4.8
20	Sierra Leone	3.5	1.8	0.7	1.5	3.9	1.6	1.9	-4.6	-2.3
21	Benin	1.9	2.3	2.8	..	3.4	2.5	..	0.7	8.3
22	Central African Republic	2.6	2.1	2.0	2.1	1.8	2.4	7.1	3.2	2.2
23	Kenya	7.9	4.8	3.8	6.2	3.7	3.4	12.4	5.7	3.0
24	Sudan	0.2	7.0	-0.1	0.3	3.4	0.8	1.0	6.0	2.1
25	Comoros	..	..	..	..	..	..	..	..	..
26	Lesotho	3.8	7.6	2.3	..	1.1	0.4	..	23.8	0.4
27	Nigeria	8.4	3.4	-1.7	2.8	-1.4	0.6	19.6	5.7	-4.4
28	Ghana b	3.4	-0.3	1.4	4.5	0.0	0.0	4.3	-3.4	0.1
29	Mauritania	2.6	2.6	1.4	-2.1	-0.3	1.5	4.3	1.2	5.1
30	Liberia	5.4	2.0	-1.3	6.5	4.0	1.2	6.2	-1.5	-6.0
31	Equatorial Guinea	..	..	..	..	..	..	..	..	..
32	Guinea b	3.2	4.1	2.1	..	2.5	..	..	9.4	..
Middle-income economies		5.2 w	1.4 w	3.8 w	2.2 w	-1.7 w	2.7 w	11.3 w	3.2 w	5.6 w
33	Cape Verde b	..	4.1	6.6	..	0.4	4.2	..	..	..
34	Senegal b	1.6	2.3	3.3	0.2	0.4	4.2	3.5	6.2	4.3
35	Zimbabwe	8.0	-0.1	2.4	..	-0.3	2.3	..	-1.5	1.4
36	Swaziland	7.6	3.5	3.3	8.0	3.5	3.9	3.1	3.5	1.9
37	Côte d'Ivoire	8.6	4.7	2.2	4.9	3.3	1.6	12.5	11.7	-2.4
38	Congo, People's Republic b	7.0	4.7	5.5	4.1	2.1	1.5	9.3	8.5	10.9
39	Cameroon b	2.4	8.9	7.0	4.6	4.5	2.4	4.7	16.0	11.0
40	Botswana b	14.7	10.5	13.0	12.4	0.6	-7.8	30.3	15.0	19.2
41	Mauritius	2.4	5.7	5.5	..	-6.0	5.2	..	7.5	8.7
42	Gabon b	7.4	3.6	0.6	..	..	..	..	..	..
43	Seychelles	5.0	6.3	2.5	..	..	-2.9	..	..	1.5
44	Angola	3.7	-9.4	..	0.2	-9.7	..	20.2	-7.5	..
45	Djibouti	..	..	..	..	..	..	..	..	..
Six most populous economies		7.0 w	3.0 w	-0.8 w	2.2 w	-0.6 w	1.1 w	16.2 w	4.8 w	-3.2 w
Sahelian economies		1.0 w	3.5 w	2.5 w	-0.8 w	2.1 w	3.0 w	4.7 w	5.2 w	3.3 w
Oil exporters		7.5 w	2.8 w	-0.5 w	2.5 w	-1.9 w	1.0 w	18.9 w	5.3 w	-2.7 w
All low-income economies										
Total		6.0 w	4.6 w	6.1 w	3.0 w	2.1 w	4.0 w	10.6 w	6.9 w	8.6 w
Excluding China and India		5.9 w	4.3 w	1.7 w	2.7 w	1.4 w	1.9 w	13.4 w	5.6 w	0.2 w
South Asia		3.7 w	4.3 w	4.8 w	3.4 w	2.4 w	1.4 w	3.7 w	5.4 w	7.2 w
Excluding India		3.1 w	5.5 w	5.3 w	2.3 w	3.3 w	3.2 w	3.6 w	7.6 w	7.3 w

Note: Summary measures include estimates for missing country data. Summary measures are based on aggregate 1980 dollar values.
a. Because manufacturing is generally the most dynamic part of the industrial sector, its growth rate is shown separately.
b. GDP and its components are at purchaser values.

(Manufacturing)[a]			Services, etc.			
1965-73	1973-80	1980-87	1965-73	1973-80	1980-87	
						Sub-Saharan Africa
10.1 w	8.2 w	0.6 w	4.9 w	3.7 w	1.2 w	Total
..	1.9 w	3.4 w	..	2.5 w	2.4 w	Excluding Nigeria
10.7 w	10.2 w	-1.0 w	4.8 w	4.3 w	0.4	Low-income economies
..	1.5 w	1.4 w	..	2.9 w	1.3	Excluding Nigeria
8.8	2.6	3.8	6.6	3.3	3.5	Ethiopia
..	-5.5	8.5	..	-2.2	6.3	Chad [b]
..	-5.7	0.6	..	-2.8	-1.2	Zaire [b]
..	..	..	..	11.9	1.0	Guinea-Bissau [b]
..	..	..	..	5.5	3.0	Malawi
	..	..	..	..	6.2	Mozambique
8.7	2.6	-3.5	6.9	5.5	0.8	Tanzania
..	..	..	..	9.5	5.8	Burkina Faso
..	..	..	..	1.9	-0.5	Madagascar [b]
..	..	..	8.5	6.4	5.9	Mali [b]
..	..	..	4.6	4.0	3.7	Gambia, The
10.5	4.6	6.6	3.0	4.8	3.5	Burundi
9.8	0.5	0.8	2.3	0.4	-0.6	Zambia [b]
..	..	..	-1.6	7.8	-8.0	Niger [b]
4.0	-12.4	-0.9	3.8	-1.1	3.0	Uganda
..	3.8	-0.8	..	7.8	4.1	São Tomé and Principe
..	2.5	-0.5	..	3.3	0.9	Somalia
..	..	..	7.3	4.2	-0.7	Togo [b]
..	6.3	2.5	..	..	3.9	Rwanda [b]
3.3	3.9	0.6	7.1	4.2	1.3	Sierra Leone
..	-2.6	4.6	..	1.5	1.3	Benin
..	3.8	0.3	1.6	1.9	1.6	Central African Republic
12.4	6.9	4.3	7.6	5.2	4.4	Kenya
..	6.7	1.6	0.5	10.6	-1.3	Sudan
..	..	..	..	..	..	Comoros
..	7.0	12.9	..	7.6	4.0	Lesotho
15.0	17.2	-2.1	6.6	5.4	-0.3	Nigeria
6.5	-2.8	1.3	1.1	0.6	4.2	Ghana [b]
..	..	..	8.1	6.2	-1.3	Mauritania
13.2	4.4	-5.0	3.8	3.3	-0.8	Liberia
..	..	..	..	..	..	*Equatorial Guinea*
..	-1.1	..	..	3.4	..	*Guinea* [b]
..	2.5 w	6.1 w	5.1 w	1.9 w	4.2 w	Middle-income economies
..	..	..	..	..	..	Cape Verde [b]
4.0	1.5	4.3	1.5	1.6	2.4	Senegal [b]
..	0.4	1.8	..	1.1	3.3	Zimbabwe
..	4.7	3.8	12.2	3.6	4.0	Swaziland
10.9	8.3	8.2	11.2	3.6	4.2	Côte d'Ivoire
..	..	9.7	6.7	2.2	-1.9	Congo, People's Republic [b]
7.4	9.0	8.5	0.2	9.0	6.9	Cameroon [b]
6.3	12.7	4.5	9.5	10.9	9.5	Botswana [b]
..	5.0	10.9	..	10.0	4.1	Mauritius
..	..	..	..	..	..	Gabon [b]
..	..	2.3	..	..	2.6	Seychelles
11.5	-15.3	..	2.7	-10.7	..	*Angola*
..	..	..	..	..	..	*Djibouti*
12.0 w	12.9 w	-1.3 w	5.4 w	4.6 w	0.0 w	Six most populous economies
..	..	..	1.8 w	4.1 w	1.9 w	Sahelian economies
13.5 w	15.0 w	-1.0 w	5.5 w	4.5 w	0.5 w	Oil exporters
						All low-income economies
9.1 w	8.1 w	10.3 w	6.2 w	5.1 w	5.1 w	Total
8.3 w	10.7 w	3.9 w	4.7 w	6.0 w	2.9 w	Excluding China and India
4.1 w	5.2 w	8.0 w	3.9 w	5.7 w	6.1 w	South Asia
4.5 w	7.0 w	6.9 w	3.7 w	6.4 w	6.1 w	Excluding India

Table 3. Structure of production

	GDP[a] (millions of dollars)			Distribution of gross domestic product (percent)					
				Agriculture			Industry		
	1965	1980	1987	1965	1980	1987	1965	1980	1987
Sub-Saharan Africa									
Total	27,758 t	202,323 t	134,483 t	43 w	30 w	34 w	18 w	33 w	28 w
Excluding Nigeria	21,908 t	102,176 t	110,093 t	40 w	34 w	35 w	20 w	25 w	24 w
Low-income economies	22,632 t	164,394 t	88,877 t	45 w	31 w	38 w	18 w	33 w	25 w
Excluding Nigeria	16,782 t	64,247 t	64,487 t	42 w	40 w	42 w	19 w	20 w	19 w
1 Ethiopia	1,180	3,683	4,800	58	51	42	14	16	18
2 Chad [c]	290	727	980	42	53	43	15	12	18
3 Zaire [c]	3,140	10,281	5,770	21	29	32	26	29	33
4 Guinea-Bissau [c]	..	105	135	..	52	61	..	20	6
5 Malawi	220	1,122	1,110	50	40	37	13	19	18
6 Mozambique	..	2,111	1,490	..	..	50	..	..	12
7 Tanzania	790	4,565	3,080	46	44	61	14	17	8
8 Burkina Faso	260	1,199	1,650	53	45	38	20	22	25
9 Madagascar [c]	670	3,265	2,070	31	39	43	16	19	16
10 Mali [c]	260	1,629	1,960	65	58	54	9	9	12
11 Gambia, The	37	205	172	35	31	35	9	13	11
12 Burundi	150	851	1,150	..	62	59	..	13	14
13 Zambia [c]	1,060	3,885	2,030	14	14	12	54	41	36
14 Niger [c]	670	2,538	2,160	68	43	34	3	23	24
15 Uganda	1,100	1,688	3,560	52	72	76	13	4	5
16 São Tomé and Principe	..	37	31	..	45	30	..	20	19
17 Somalia	220	630	995	71	68	65	6	8	9
18 Togo [c]	190	1,136	1,230	45	27	29	21	25	18
19 Rwanda [c]	150	1,163	2,100	75	46	37	7	22	23
20 Sierra Leone	320	1,013	900	34	33	45	28	22	19
21 Benin	220	1,041	1,570	59	48	46	8	12	14
22 Central African Republic	140	750	1,010	46	40	41	16	20	13
23 Kenya	920	6,018	6,930	35	32	31	18	22	19
24 Sudan	1,330	6,178	8,210	54	34	37	9	14	15
25 Comoros	..	..	199	..	..	36	..	..	14
26 Lesotho	50	339	270	65	26	21	5	25	28
27 Nigeria	5,850	100,147	24,390	54	26	30	13	42	43
28 Ghana [c]	2,050	4,445	5,080	44	58	51	19	12	16
29 Mauritania	160	666	840	32	31	37	36	26	22
30 Liberia	270	1,001	990	27	36	37	40	28	28
31 *Equatorial Guinea*	65	..	..	..	..	..	..	..	..
32 *Guinea* [c]	520	1,764	2,166	..	42	30	..	23	32
Middle-income economies	5,131 t	37,913 t	50,898 t	33 w	25 w	27 w	21 w	32 w	30 w
33 Cape Verde [c]	..	89	158	..	25	19	..	23	20
34 Senegal [c]	810	2,970	4,720	25	19	22	18	25	27
35 Zimbabwe	960	5,017	5,240	18	14	11	35	39	43
36 Swaziland	67	465	369	35	30	24	33	25	30
37 Côte d'Ivoire	760	8,482	7,650	47	33	36	19	20	25
38 Congo, People's Republic [c]	200	1,706	2,150	19	12	12	19	47	33
39 Cameroon[c]	810	7,499	12,660	33	28	24	20	26	32
40 Botswana [c]	50	913	1,520	34	12	3	19	41	57
41 Mauritius	190	962	1,480	16	12	15	23	26	32
42 Gabon [c]	230	4,281	3,500	26	7	11	34	60	41
43 Seychelles	16	147	256	..	7	6	..	16	17
44 *Angola*	989	5,069	7,740	50	43	46	7	30	23
45 *Djibouti*	..	..	..	..	..	..	..	..	..
Six most populous economies	13,205 t	130,873 t	53,189 t	45 w	28 w	34 w	16 w	37 w	30 w
Sahelian economies	2,576 t	10,128 t	12,772 t	46 w	38 w	34 w	14 w	20 w	20 w
Oil exporters	8,063 t	118,701 t	45,924 t	49 w	26 w	27 w	14 w	41 w	38 w
All low-income economies									
Total	155,452 t	743,934 t	756,127 t	43 w	33 w	31 w	27 w	38 w	37 w
Excluding China and India	42,884 t	302,684 t	239,389 t	45 w	31 w	33 w	17 w	34 w	27 w
South Asia	60,263 t	200,536 t	288,264 t	46 w	38 w	31 w	21 w	25 w	28 w
Excluding India	13,998 t	45,666 t	67,432 t	43 w	39 w	35 w	16 w	20 w	21 w

Note: Summary measures include estimates for missing country data. The weighting process may result in discrepancies between summed subgroup figures and overall totals. Summary measures are based on aggregate current dollar values.
a. See the technical notes.

224

Distribution of gross domestic product (percent)						
(Manufacturing) [b]			Services, etc.			
1965	1980	1987	1965	1980	1987	
						Sub-Saharan Africa
9 w	9 w	10 w	39 w	37 w	39 w	Total
10 w	9 w	12 w	41 w	41 w	43 w	Excluding Nigeria
8 w	9 w	8 w	37 w	35 w	37 w	Low-income economies
9 w	8 w	9 w	39 w	40 w	42 w	Excluding Nigeria
7	11	12	28	34	40	Ethiopia
12	11	15	43	35	39	Chad [c]
16	3	7	53	42	35	Zaire [c]
..	..	..	..	28	33	Guinea-Bissau [c]
..	..	..	37	41	45	Malawi
..	..	..	..	..	38	Mozambique
8	11	5	40	39	31	Tanzania
..	..	15	27	32	38	Burkina Faso
11	..	..	53	42	42	Madagascar [c]
5	4	6	25	32	35	Mali [c]
3	4	6	56	55	55	Gambia, The
..	7	9	..	25	27	Burundi
6	18	23	32	44	52	Zambia [c]
2	4	9	29	35	42	Niger [c]
8	4	5	35	23	19	Uganda
..	9	..	..	35	51	São Tomé and Principe
3	5	5	24	24	26	Somalia
10	7	7	34	48	54	Togo [c]
2	15	16	18	33	40	Rwanda [c]
6	6	4	38	45	36	Sierra Leone
..	6	4	33	40	39	Benin
4	7	8	38	40	46	Central African Republic
11	13	11	47	45	50	Kenya
4	7	8	37	52	48	Sudan
..	..	4	..	..	50	Comoros
1	5	15	30	49	51	Lesotho
6	9	8	33	32	27	Nigeria
10	8	10	38	30	33	Ghana [c]
4	..	..	32	43	41	Mauritania
3	8	5	34	36	35	Liberia
..	..	..	..	..	..	*Equatorial Guinea*
..	2	5	..	35	38	*Guinea* [c]
12 w	11 w	..	46 w	43 w	44 w	Middle-income economies
..	..	4	..	52	60	Cape Verde [c]
14	15	17	56	56	52	Senegal [c]
20	25	31	47	47	46	Zimbabwe
9	..	20	32	45	46	Swaziland
11	11	16	33	47	39	Côte d'Ivoire
..	7	8	62	42	55	Congo, People's Republic [c]
10	8	13	47	46	45	Cameroon [c]
12	4	6	47	47	40	Botswana [c]
14	15	24	61	62	53	Mauritius
..	..	..	40	34	48	Gabon [c]
..	7	9	..	78	77	Seychelles
4	3	3	42	27	31	*Angola*
..	..	..	..	..	..	*Djibouti*
9 w	9 w	8 w	39 w	35 w	35 w	Six most populous economies
9 w	9 w	13 w	40 w	42 w	44 w	Sahelian economies
6 w	9 w	9 w	37 w	33 w	35 w	Oil exporters
						All low-income economies
20 w	22 w	..	30 w	30 w	32 w	Total
9 w	11 w	12 w	38 w	36 w	40 w	Excluding China and India
14 w	17 w	18 w	34 w	37 w	41 w	South Asia
11 w	13 w	13 w	41 w	41 w	44 w	Excluding India

b. Because manufacturing is generally the most dynamic part of the industrial sector, its share of GDP is shown separately.
c. GDP and its components are shown at purchaser values.

Table 4. Structure of demand (percentage of gross domestic product)

	General government consumption			Private consumption, etc.			Gross domestic investment		
	1965	1980	1987	1965	1980	1987	1965	1980	1987
Sub-Saharan Africa									
Total	10 w	13 w	16 w	72 w	66 w	71 w	14 w	20 w	16 w
Excluding Nigeria	12 w	16 w	17 w	69 w	70 w	71 w	15 w	20 w	16 w
Low-income economies	10 w	11 w	14 w	72 w	67 w	75 w	14 w	20 w	16 w
Excluding Nigeria	12 w	15 w	15 w	69 w	76 w	77 w	14 w	19 w	16 w
1 Ethiopia	11	15	19	77	80	77	13	10	14
2 Chad	20	34	8	74	73	104	12	18	18
3 Zaire	9	9	17	61	77	73	14	15	13
4 Guinea-Bissau	..	29	9	..	77	86	..	30	19
5 Malawi	16	19	18	84	70	70	14	25	14
6 Mozambique	..	..	21	..	..	90	..	..	22
7 Tanzania	10	13	8	74	77	98	15	23	17
8 Burkina Faso	9	17	25	87	92	74	12	20	24
9 Madagascar	23	17	14	74	76	79	10	24	14
10 Mali	10	10	10	84	91	90	18	17	16
11 Gambia, The	19	21	20	78	73	74	8	27	19
12 Burundi	7	13	17	89	87	76	6	14	20
13 Zambia	15	26	25	45	55	55	25	23	15
14 Niger	6	10	12	90	67	84	8	37	9
15 Uganda	10	a	7	78	95	88	11	6	12
16 São Tomé and Principe	..	24	40	..	91	66	..	34	44
17 Somalia	8	14	11	84	94	89	11	44	35
18 Togo	8	15	21	76	70	74	22	30	17
19 Rwanda	14	12	12	81	83	83	10	16	17
20 Sierra Leone	8	8	7	83	91	83	12	16	9
21 Benin	11	11	10	87	96	86	11	19	14
22 Central African Republic	22	15	13	67	94	89	21	7	14
23 Kenya	15	20	19	70	61	61	14	30	25
24 Sudan	12	16	15	79	81	79	10	15	11
25 Comoros	..	..	27	..	..	84	..	..	12
26 Lesotho	18	33	16	109	133	158	11	34	25
27 Nigeria	5	9	11	83	62	69	14	20	16
28 Ghana	14	11	9	77	84	87	18	6	11
29 Mauritania	19	25	13	54	68	73	14	36	20
30 Liberia	12	16	17	61	56	65	17	27	10
31 *Equatorial Guinea*	13	..	..	59	..	..	19	..	..
32 *Guinea*	..	21	11	..	58	72	..	16	17
Middle-income economies	13 w	17 w	19 w	70 w	59 w	65 w	15 w	22 w	16 w
33 Cape Verde	..	24	..	..	110	..	..	42	..
34 Senegal	17	22	17	75	78	77	12	16	13
35 Zimbabwe	12	20	20	65	64	59	15	19	18
36 Swaziland	16	25	..	46	68	..	26	41	..
37 Côte d'Ivoire	11	18	17	61	60	65	22	28	13
38 Congo, People's Republic	14	18	21	80	47	58	22	36	24
39 Cameroon	13	9	11	75	76	74	13	19	18
40 Botswana	24	20	..	89	52	..	6	41	..
41 Mauritius	13	14	11	74	75	60	17	21	26
42 Gabon	11	13	23	52	26	43	31	28	31
43 Seychelles	..	29	..	..	44	..	..	38	..
44 *Angola*	11	21	26	77	48	58	10	9	9
45 *Djibouti*	..	..	..	..	..	..	..	..	..
Six most populous economies	8 w	10 w	14 w	76 w	65 w	72 w	13 w	20 w	16 w
Sahelian economies	13 w	18 w	17 w	80 w	78 w	80 w	12 w	24 w	15 w
Oil exporters	7 w	10 w	14 w	81 w	60 w	67 w	14 w	20 w	18 w
All low-income economies									
Total	12 w	13 w	13 w	69 w	63 w	61 w	20 w	25 w	28 w
Excluding China and India	9 w	11 w	12 w	76 w	66 w	73 w	14 w	21 w	19 w
South Asia	9 w	10 w	12 w	76 w	73 w	68 w	18 w	23 w	22 w
Excluding India	..	9 w	11 w	80 w	83 w	80 w	16 w	19 w	16 w

Note: Summary measures include estimates for missing country data. Summary measures are based on aggregate current dollar values.
a. General government consumption figures are not available separately; they are included in private consumption, etc.

Gross domestic savings			Exports of goods and nonfactor services			Resource balance			
1965	1980	1987	1965	1980	1987	1965	1980	1987	
									Sub-Saharan Africa
14 w	22 w	13 w	22 w	26 w	26 w	1 w	1 w	..	Total
15 w	15 w	11 w	26 w	26 w	24 w	-5 w	-6 w	-4 w	Excluding Nigeria
13 w	22 w	10 w	21 w	24 w	22 w	1 w	1 w	-6 w	Low-income economies
14 w	9 w	7 w	24 w	21 w	19 w	0 w	-11 w	-9 w	Excluding Nigeria
12	5	3	12	14	11	-1	-5	-11	Ethiopia
6	-6	-12	19	28	17	-6	-25	-31	Chad
30	14	10	36	24	33	15	-1	-3	Zaire
..	-6	5	..	8	6	..	-36	-14	Guinea-Bissau
0	11	12	19	25	24	-14	-14	-2	Malawi
..	..	-10	..	..	11	..	..	-32	Mozambique
16	10	-6	26	13	13	1	-13	-23	Tanzania
4	-9	1	9	16	17	-8	-29	-23	Burkina Faso
4	6	7	16	16	20	-6	-17	-7	Madagascar
5	-2	0	12	16	17	-13	-19	-17	Mali
3	5	6	43	57	63	-5	-22	-13	Gambia, The
4	0	8	10	9	9	-2	-14	-12	Burundi
40	19	20	49	41	47	15	-4	5	Zambia
3	23	5	9	24	19	-5	-14	-5	Niger
12	..	5	26	2	10	1	-1	-7	Uganda
..	-15	-6	..	46	20	..	-49	-50	São Tomé and Principe
8	-8	1	17	31	11	-3	-52	-34	Somalia
17	15	6	20	32	31	-6	-15	-12	Togo
5	4	5	12	14	8	-5	-12	-12	Rwanda
9	1	10	30	23	9	-3	-15	1	Sierra Leone
3	-6	4	13	28	15	-8	-25	-10	Benin
11	-10	-2	27	26	17	-11	-17	-16	Central African Republic
15	19	20	31	29	21	1	-11	-5	Kenya
9	3	6	15	12	8	-1	-12	-5	Sudan
..	..	-11	..	..	11	..	..	-23	Comoros
-26	-66	-73	16	21	10	-38	-100	-99	Lesotho
12	30	20	13	26	31	-2	9	4	Nigeria
8	5	4	17	8	20	-10	-1	-6	Ghana
27	7	14	42	37	50	13	-29	-7	Mauritania
27	27	18	50	55	43	10	0	9	Liberia
28	..	..	42	..	..	9	..	..	*Equatorial Guinea*
..	22	17	..	28	30	..	6	0	*Guinea*
17 w	24 w	16 w	27 w	36 w	30 w	1 w	2 w	..	Middle-income economies
..	-34	..	..	22	..	..	-77	..	Cape Verde
8	0	6	24	29	28	-4	-16	-7	Senegal
23	16	22	..	30	27	8	-3	3	Zimbabwe
38	7	..	59	77	..	12	-33	..	Swaziland
29	22	19	37	34	34	7	-6	6	Côte d'Ivoire
5	36	21	36	60	43	-17	0	-2	Congo, People's Republic
12	16	15	24	24	16	-1	-3	-4	Cameroon
-13	29	..	32	50	..	-19	-12	..	Botswana
13	10	29	36	51	69	-4	-10	3	Mauritius
37	61	34	43	..	41	6	32	3	Gabon
..	27	..	..	68	..	..	-11	..	Seychelles
12	30	*16*	21	52	*38*	2	22	*6*	*Angola*
..	..	..	..	..	..	..	..	..	*Djibouti*
16 w	25 w	14 w	20 w	25 w	23 w	3 w	5 w	-2 w	Six most populous economies
6 w	4 w	5 w	18 w	25 w	24 w	-5 w	-20 w	-13 w	Sahelian economies
12 w	30 w	20 w	14 w	28 w	31 w	-1 w	10 w	1 w	Oil exporters
									All low-income economies
19 w	25 w	26 w	8 w	14 w	13 w	-1 w	0 w	-2 w	Total
12 w	23 w	15 w	17 w	25 w	20 w	-1 w	2 w	-4 w	Excluding China and India
15 w	18 w	19 w	6 w	8 w	8 w	-3 w	-5 w	-3 w	South Asia
11 w	7 w	9 w	13 w	12 w	11 w	-5 w	-12 w	-7 w	Excluding India

Table 5. Growth of consumption and investment (average annual percent)

	General government consumption			Private consumption, etc.			Gross domestic investment		
	1965-73	1973-80	1980-87	1965-73	1973-80	1980-87	1965-73	1973-80	1980-87
Sub-Saharan Africa									
Total	9.0 w	7.0 w	-0.7 w	3.9 w	2.6 w	1.1 w	9.8 w	4.0 w	-8.2 w
Excluding Nigeria	6.1 w	5.5 w	0.8 w	2.5 w	2.3 w	2.2 w	6.9 w	1.9 w	-3.4 w
Low-income economies	9.7 w	6.5 w	-2.4 w	4.2 w	2.8 w	0.7 w	10.3 w	4.5 w	-9.9 w
Excluding Nigeria	·5.6 w	3.7 w	-1.2 w	2.5 w	2.5 w	1.8 w	6.3 w	1.6 w	-3.5 w
1 Ethiopia	3.7	8.3	5.6	4.0	3.0	1.3	1.5	-1.6	2.0
2 Chad	6.0	-1.6	..	1.6	-4.8	..	..	..	..
3 Zaire	5.8	-4.7	-10.9	4.4	-3.0	0.4	10.2	3.7	1.3
4 Guinea-Bissau	..	-0.5	0.7	..	-4.9	6.3	..	7.0	3.8
5 Malawi	3.0	10.8	4.5	5.5	3.8	2.6	16.0	3.0	-10.5
6 Mozambique	..	..	-10.8	..	..	0.9	..	..	-23.1
7 Tanzania	a	..	-7.1	5.0	..	5.0	9.6	3.8	-5.6
8 Burkina Faso	10.7	4.1	3.4	1.4	6.7	2.5	13.7	-2.1	2.0
9 Madagascar	3.3	4.3	-1.0	2.0	0.2	-0.1	4.2	3.2	-4.5
10 Mali	2.3	4.4	4.3	3.0	6.6	4.1	1.0	6.4	4.2
11 Gambia, The	2.8	12.3	..	4.3	2.7	..	-0.1	36.1	..
12 Burundi	12.3	5	2.9	4.4	3.6	2.1	-1.4	18.5	5.4
13 Zambia	10.4	-0.6	-2.5	-1.9	3.1	1.4	6.2	-16.5	-9.3
14 Niger	2.1	3.8	1.2	-5	5.8	2.3	4.6	5.2	-15
15 Uganda	a	a	..	4	-3.1	..	2.1	-9.8	..
16 São Tomé and Principe	..	6.9	1.5	..	9.5	-1.4	..	29.6	5.8
17 Somalia	16.9	0.0	1.1	-1.0	14.8	1.1	5.6	17.8	2.7
18 Togo	7.9	10.9	1.9	6.5	5.4	-0.3	3.3	12.2	-6.4
19 Rwanda	2.3	3.9	3.2	7.9	6.8	2.0	5.7	9.4	9.2
20 Sierra Leone	a	a	a	2.0	4.3	-2.5	-2.6	1.7	-7.1
21 Benin	5.0	-3.1	3.0	3.1	3.2	1.4	9.1	9.0	-12.7
22 Central African Republic	1.7	-0.9	-3.1	3.4	6.0	1.6	2.3	-10.6	14.6
23 Kenya	13.1	9.7	0.8	5.2	4.8	3.1	15.9	4.4	-2.3
24 Sudan	1.4	3.9	-1.6	-1.1	9.7	-1.4	0.2	5.3	-4.0
25 Comoros	..	..	..	..	..	..	..	..	..
26 Lesotho	5.4	17.8	..	6.0	7.3	..	10.5	20.4	..
27 Nigeria	16.7	9.1	-3.6	5.8	2.9	0.0	15.2	6.6	-14.8
28 Ghana	1.1	8.4	-1.6	2.9	0.0	1.7	-3.5	-3.6	3.2
29 Mauritania	6.1	8.5	-6.2	2.8	0.7	4.7	12.5	12.1	-5.5
30 Liberia	4.5	5.3	1.3	-0.5	3.4	0.8	5.6	10.5	-16.7
31 *Equatorial Guinea*	..	..	..	..	..	..	..	..	..
32 *Guinea*	..	7.5	..	..	2.8	..	..	-2.3	..
Middle-income economies	7.0 w	8.4 w	3.5 w	2.5 w	1.8 w	3.1 w	8.1 w	2.4 w	-3.4 w
33 Cape Verde	..	15.7	..	..	7.0	..	..	13.3	..
34 Senegal	-1.2	8.1	1.5	0.2	3.7	2.2	8.1	-2.1	1.1
35 Zimbabwe	8.3	13.7	7.1	..	..	-2.7	7.6	-11.1	-1.4
36 Swaziland	10.6	5.5	..	5.6	10.6	..	7.4	9.9	..
37 Côte d'Ivoire	14.6	13.4	-5.7	8.6	5.4	3.5	7.8	15.5	-14.2
38 Congo, People's Republic	7.4	3.7	7.1	2.2	1.8	6.7	9.3	-4.9	-3.8
39 Cameroon	4.6	3.7	10.0	1.7	8.1	5.7	8.6	14.4	3.3
40 Botswana	5.5	14.3	13.8	7.4	10.4	4.4	48.1	2.6	-1.5
41 Mauritius	2.3	10.2	2.2	-4.1	10.3	3.2	5.2	-1.2	10.8
42 Gabon	10.2	8.4	4.7	..	..	-2.2	7.3	-0.7	-3.0
43 Seychelles	..	..	..	..	..	..	..	..	..
44 *Angola*	7.2	3.5	..	0.4	-10.2	..	7	-5.6	..
45 *Djibouti*	..	..	..	..	..	..	..	..	..
Six most populous economies	11.7 w	7.5 w	-3.0 w	5.0 w	2.7 w	0.4 w	13.1 w	5.9 w	-11.1 w
Sahelian economies	2.8 w	5.0 w	2.1 w	0.1 w	3.8 w	3.2 w	5.1 w	3.6 w	-3.4 w
Oil exporters	13.4 w	8.1 w	-1.0 w	4.8 w	2.3 w	0.6 w	13.4 w	5.6 w	-11.5 w
All low-income economies									
Total	7.5 w	7.2 w	4.4 w	4.6 w	4.1 w	4.4 w	9.2 w	7.3 w	10.2 w
Excluding China and India	9.1 w	7.7 w	0.7 w	4.4 w	4.1 w	2.4 w	9.3 w	7.1 w	-1.9 w
South Asia	6.5 w	7.0 w	8.6 w	3.4 w	4.0 w	4.9 w	3.2 w	6.3 w	3.7 w
Excluding India	..	5.3 w	7.8 w	..	6.2 w	5.1 w	-0.3 w	9.5 w	3.5 w

Note: Summary measures include estimates for missing country data. Summary measures are based on aggregate 1980 dollar values.
a. Central government consumption figures are not available; they are included in private consumption, etc.

Table 6. Growth of production of major crops (average annual percent)

	Maize			Millet			Rice		
	1965-73	1973-80	1980-87	1965-73	1973-80	1980-87	1965-73	1973-80	1980-87
Sub-Saharan Africa									
Total	3.3	-0.2	3.7	1.2	-1.2	2.5	3.7	2.6	2.7
Excluding Nigeria	3.6	0.5	3.1	-0.6	2.3	1.7	3.2	1.6	2.5
Low-income economies	2.7	0.1	4.8	1.6	-1.2	2.6	4.1	2.5	2.3
Excluding Nigeria	3.0	1.0	4.1	-0.9	4.1	1.6	3.7	1.4	2.0
Middle-income economies	5.2	-1.1	-0.6	-1.7	0.0	4.0	-0.4	3.1	6.2
Six most populous economies	3.0	0.3	6.0	4.3	-4.2	1.5	11.0	8.2	4.1
Sahelian economies	-8.3	5.6	11.4	-2.5	3.5	4.3	-2.9	0.5	6.4
Oil exporters	1.1	-6.6	6.3	4.1	-6.2	3.6	7.7	9.3	4.0

	Sorghum			Wheat			Total cereals		
	1965-73	1973-80	1980-87	1965-73	1973-80	1980-87	1965-73	1973-80	1980-87
Sub-Saharan Africa									
Total	0.2	2.3	1.3	3.9	1.1	1.0	2.0	0.9	2.3
Excluding Nigeria	2.3	4.3	0.1	4.0	1.0	0.4	2.3	2.0	1.7
Low-income economies	0.1	2.5	1.3	3.1	-0.1	0.8	1.9	1.0	2.4
Excluding Nigeria	2.3	4.7	0.1	3.2	-0.2	0.2	2.2	2.4	1.7
Middle-income economies	3.5	-6.8	1.8	20.1	10.8	1.8	2.9	-0.1	1.6
Six most populous economies	-0.2	2.6	0.9	3.4	0.0	0.7	2.3	1.0	2.3
Sahelian economies	-2.8	4.9	4.9	4.5	-1.7	6.7	-2.8	3.5	5.0
Oil exporters	-2.8	-1.0	3.5	-5.5	1.4	15.1	0.9	-3.4	4.0

	Coconuts			Groundnuts			Palm kernels		
	1965-73	1973-80	1980-87	1965-73	1973-80	1980-87	1965-73	1973-80	1980-87
Sub-Saharan Africa									
Total	2.4	0.3	1.3	-1.2	-4.0	0.2	-2.4	0.1	0.2
Excluding Nigeria	2.6	0.3	1.2	1.1	-2.6	-0.6	0.4	-2.2	-0.4
Low-income economies	2.4	-0.8	-0.6	-1.0	-3.1	-0.1	-2.5	0.1	0.3
Excluding Nigeria	2.6	-0.9	-0.8	2.8	-0.9	-1.4	0.9	-2.9	-0.3
Middle-income economies	1.7	11.5	10.5	-2.2	-6.4	1.5	-1.5	0.0	-0.6
Six most populous economies	1.0	0.7	0.9	-2.5	-3.2	-0.4	-4.3	2.0	0.7
Sahelian economies	0.0	2.8	0.1	-4.6	-4.8	0.6	-2.0	3.2	5.5
Oil exporters	-0.7	0.2	2.0	-5.2	-8.9	4.4	-5.3	2.5	0.4

	Pulses			Roots and tubers			Seed cotton		
	1965-73	1973-80	1980-87	1965-73	1973-80	1980-87	1965-73	1973-80	1980-87
Sub-Saharan Africa									
Total	2.1	1.2	3.4	2.7	1.8	3.1	5.2	-3.0	7.3
Excluding Nigeria	2.4	2.6	2.9	2.5	1.8	3.2	5.5	-3.0	7.7
Low-income economies	2.1	1.3	3.4	2.8	1.8	3.1	3.9	-4.6	7.0
Excluding Nigeria	2.4	2.7	2.9	2.6	1.7	3.2	4.1	-4.6	7.6
Middle-income economies	3.0	-0.1	2.8	2.1	1.8	3.1	15.8	3.0	8.1
Six most populous economies	1.7	0.8	4.0	2.5	2.2	2.4	4.1	-4.6	3.4
Sahelian economies	0.7	7.2	-0.8	-0.5	1.7	3.0	7.3	3.3	9.1
Oil exporters	1.1	-4.1	5.0	2.9	1.6	2.7	2.8	-2.0	1.6

Table 7. Production of major crops (thousand metric tons)

	Maize 1965	Maize 1980	Maize 1987	Millet 1965	Millet 1980	Millet 1987	Rice 1965	Rice 1980	Rice 1987
Sub-Saharan Africa									
Total	9,895	12,871	15,588	8,084	9,229	10,125	3,677	6,295	7,593
Excluding Nigeria	8,735	12,227	14,288	5,355	6,142	6,775	3,446	5,205	6,193
Low-income economies	8,013	10,013	13,138	6,850	7,963	8,440	3,245	5,736	6,718
Excluding Nigeria	6,853	9,369	11,838	4,121	4,876	5,090	3,014	4,646	5,318
1 Ethiopia	788	948	1,360	147	205	180	0	0	0
2 Chad	14	25	34	614	450	500	25	47	20
3 Zaire	330	594	777	14	16	37	49	234	313
4 Guinea-Bissau	3	7	25	7	9	20	47	42	155
5 Malawi	890	1,165	1,228	0	0	0	5	60	34
6 Mozambique	390	380	300	10	5	5	93	70	55
7 Tanzania	751	1,726	2,337	117	380	297	73	363	571
8 Burkina Faso	109	105	131	315	351	632	25	40	40
9 Madagascar	123	128	153	0	0	0	1,589	2,109	2,286
10 Mali	88	45	143	720	708	1,130	162	132	190
11 Gambia, The	1	6	18	42	29	104	37	43	35
12 Burundi	108	140	160	21	40	50	2	11	20
13 Zambia	800	937	954	72	50	30	0	2	13
14 Niger	3	10	9	790	1,364	1,020	12	31	60
15 Uganda	270	286	357	511	458	490	5	17	38
16 São Tomé and Principe	0	1	1	0	0	0	0	0	0
17 Somalia	105	111	355	0	0	0	0	17	5
18 Togo	78	138	145	136	43	82	16	15	19
19 Rwanda	44	85	120	2	2	2	0	4	5
20 Sierra Leone	10	12	10	10	14	23	399	513	508
21 Benin	219	271	278	6	7	22	1	10	9
22 Central African Republic	32	41	45	50	46	70	7	13	16
23 Kenya	1,301	1,620	2,170	130	90	50	14	40	40
24 Sudan	12	43	25	253	491	131	1	8	2
25 Comoros	3	5	7	0	0	0	12	14	17
26 Lesotho	110	106	90	0	0	0	0	0	0
27 Nigeria	1,160	644	1,300	2,729	3,087	3,350	231	1,090	1,400
28 Ghana	209	382	553	57	82	121	33	78	88
29 Mauritania	4	5	8	100	37	95	1	11	20
30 Liberia	0	0	0	0	0	0	135	243	280
31 *Equatorial Guinea*	0	0	0	0	0	0	0	0	0
32 *Guinea*	60	47	45	0	0	0	272	480	480
Middle-income economies	1,882	2,858	2,450	1,234	1,266	1,685	432	559	875
33 Cape Verde	13	9	20	0	0	0	0	0	0
34 Senegal	41	57	120	557	553	1,078	122	65	130
35 Zimbabwe	822	1,511	1,094	253	180	102	3	0	0
36 Swaziland	32	97	92	0	0	0	6	5	3
37 Côte d'Ivoire	180	380	415	34	34	44	250	420	595
38 Congo, People's Republic	5	9	8	0	0	0	5	3	3
39 Cameroon	330	414	380	330	441	400	13	46	123
40 Botswana	2	12	2	1	2	1	0	0	0
41 Mauritius	0	1	9	0	0	0	0	0	0
42 Gabon	8	10	10	0	0	0	1	1	1
43 Seychelles	0	0	0	0	0	0	0	0	0
44 *Angola*	450	360	300	60	57	60	32	20	20
45 *Djibouti*	0	0	0	0	0	0	0	0	0
Six most populous economies	4,342	5,575	7,969	3,389	4,268	4,045	368	1,735	2,325
Sahelian economies	273	269	508	3,144	3,500	4,579	430	409	650
Oil exporters	1,953	1,437	1,998	3,119	3,585	3,810	282	1,159	1,546
All low-income economies									
Total	38,726	81,422	98,402	20,745	23,477	23,228	178,999	284,215	323,189
Excluding China and India	14,937	18,722	22,097	14,545	18,032	17,428	88,779	142,835	145,989
South Asia	1,524	1,618	2,252	163	207	345	37,923	49,825	57,339
Excluding India	1,385	1,518	2,147	163	207	345	35,423	48,355	55,639

Sorghum			Wheat			Total cereals			
1965	*1980*	*1987*	*1965*	*1980*	*1987*	*1965*	*1980*	*1987*	
									Sub-Saharan Africa
8,383	11,063	10,667	964	1,460	1,528	32,972	43,680	47,749	Total
4,148	6,760	6,317	944	1,436	1,428	24,559	34,472	37,189	Excluding Nigeria
8,308	10,969	10,580	940	1,258	1,322	29,313	38,670	42,408	Low-income economies
4,073	6,666	6,230	920	1,234	1,222	20,900	29,462	31,848	Excluding Nigeria
740	1,411	1,000	580	614	700	4,010	5,612	5,160	Ethiopia
0	0	0	4	6	3	664	573	602	Chad
24	14	36	3	4	20	428	862	1,182	Zaire
3	18	35	0	0	0	76	80	240	Guinea-Bissau
55	120	154	1	1	1	951	1,346	1,417	Malawi
181	200	150	10	3	3	684	658	513	Mozambique
149	563	663	33	91	72	1,123	3,126	3,945	Tanzania
495	547	848	0	0	0	953	1,048	1,659	Burkina Faso
3	1	2	0	0	0	1,715	2,238	2,441	Madagascar
0	0	0	2	2	2	997	913	1,515	Mali
0	0	0	0	0	0	86	81	159	Gambia, The
122	161	220	8	6	15	261	358	465	Burundi
44	20	26	0	10	13	916	1,019	1,039	Zambia
266	368	360	1	1	8	1,071	1,776	1,460	Niger
272	299	330	0	17	10	1,058	1,077	1,225	Uganda
0	0	0	0	0	0	0	1	1	São Tomé and Principe
110	141	203	0	1	1	215	269	564	Somalia
0	95	135	0	0	0	237	296	387	Togo
130	179	187	0	2	5	178	273	319	Rwanda
10	11	20	0	0	0	430	551	562	Sierra Leone
59	56	87	0	0	0	287	347	399	Benin
0	0	0	0	0	0	89	100	131	Central African Republic
163	200	130	172	216	195	1,794	2,233	2,612	Kenya
1,094	2,068	1,450	56	233	157	1,417	2,843	1,765	Sudan
0	0	0	0	0	0	15	19	23	Comoros
55	59	41	50	28	16	218	195	149	Lesotho
4,235	4,303	4,350	20	24	100	8,413	9,208	10,560	Nigeria
90	132	151	0	0	0	389	674	913	Ghana
0	0	0	0	0	1	105	53	124	Mauritania
0	0	0	0	0	0	135	243	280	Liberia
0	0	0	0	0	0	0	0	0	*Equatorial Guinea*
8	3	4	0	0	0	400	601	599	*Guinea*
75	94	87	24	202	206	3,659	5,010	5,341	Middle-income economies
0	0	0	0	0	0	13	9	20	Cape Verde
0	0	0	0	0	0	723	676	1,331	Senegal
52	42	52	4	191	200	1,135	1,949	1,479	Zimbabwe
3	2	2	0	1	1	40	105	98	Swaziland
11	21	25	0	0	0	482	860	1,084	Côte d'Ivoire
0	0	0	0	0	0	10	12	11	Congo, People's Republic
0	0	0	0	2	1	673	901	904	Cameroon
9	29	8	0	1	1	12	44	12	Botswana
0	0	0	0	0	0	0	1	9	Mauritius
0	0	0	0	0	0	9	11	11	Gabon
0	0	0	0	0	0	0	0	0	Seychelles
0	0	0	20	7	2	562	444	382	*Angola*
0	0	0	0	0	0	0	0	0	*Djibouti*
6,406	8,559	7,629	864	1,181	1,244	17,186	23,884	25,224	Six most populous economies
764	933	1,243	6	9	13	4,687	5,208	7,110	Sahelian economies
4,235	4,303	4,350	40	33	103	9,668	10,576	11,868	Oil exporters
									All low-income economies
23,303	28,000	25,710	45,514	103,201	151,194	321,570	532,466	633,269	Total
16,203	21,225	19,710	20,294	47,991	64,194	159,841	253,706	274,164	Excluding China and India
111	178	253	238	1,363	2,058	40,059	53,295	62,342	South Asia
111	178	253	238	1,363	2,058	37,420	51,725	60,537	Excluding India

Table 7. Production of major crops (thousand metric tons) — continued

		Coconuts			Groundnuts			Palm kernels		
		1965	1980	1987	1965	1980	1987	1965	1980	1987
Sub-Saharan Africa										
Total		1,269	1,545	1,675	5,500	4,083	4,306	844	706	702
	Excluding Nigeria	1,170	1,455	1,575	3,522	3,408	3,566	382	361	342
Low-income economies		1,181	1,348	1,293	4,087	3,231	3,072	749	602	607
	Excluding Nigeria	1,082	1,258	1,193	2,109	2,556	2,332	287	257	247
1	Ethiopia	0	0	0	18	26	50	0	0	0
2	Chad	0	0	0	150	100	90	0	0	0
3	Zaire	0	0	0	180	340	411	82	69	70
4	Guinea-Bissau	25	25	25	42	30	30	9	9	14
5	Malawi	0	0	0	157	177	190	0	0	0
6	Mozambique	275	450	415	120	90	65	0	0	0
7	Tanzania	274	310	340	49	54	60	1	5	6
8	Burkina Faso	0	0	0	73	54	100	0	0	0
9	Madagascar	16	68	81	35	39	33	0	4	6
10	Mali	0	0	0	153	135	60	0	0	0
11	Gambia, The	0	0	0	128	60	120	2	1	2
12	Burundi	0	0	0	4	56	80	1	2	3
13	Zambia	0	0	0	44	16	14	0	0	0
14	Niger	0	0	0	277	126	42	0	0	0
15	Uganda	0	0	0	130	70	120	0	0	0
16	São Tomé and Principe	55	35	35	0	0	0	4	0	1
17	Somalia	1	1	1	4	3	5	0	0	0
18	Togo	20	14	14	21	24	37	22	19	15
19	Rwanda	0	0	0	5	16	18	0	0	0
20	Sierra Leone	2	3	3	23	10	19	52	30	30
21	Benin	40	20	20	33	63	67	50	36	20
22	Central African Republic	0	0	0	61	123	146	1	1	1
23	Kenya	65	90	72	4	8	9	0	0	0
24	Sudan	0	0	0	305	707	360	0	0	0
25	Comoros	55	53	47	0	0	0	0	0	0
26	Lesotho	0	0	0	0	0	0	0	0	0
27	Nigeria	99	90	100	1,978	675	740	462	345	360
28	Ghana	229	160	110	27	142	128	22	30	30
29	Mauritania	0	0	0	1	1	2	0	0	0
30	Liberia	5	7	7	2	3	3	12	7	8
31	*Equatorial Guinea*	6	7	8	0	0	0	2	3	3
32	*Guinea*	15	15	15	65	84	75	27	40	40
Middle-income economies		88	197	382	1,413	852	1,234	95	103	95
33	Cape Verde	10	10	10	1	0	0	0	0	0
34	Senegal	3	4	5	1,121	523	876	5	5	6
35	Zimbabwe	0	0	0	61	78	79	0	0	0
36	Swaziland	0	0	0	3	1	1	0	0	0
37	Côte d'Ivoire	18	153	340	32	81	90	17	41	41
38	Congo, People's Republic	0	0	0	18	14	16	6	0	1
39	Cameroon	6	3	4	141	126	140	48	44	35
40	Botswana	0	0	0	0	1	1	0	0	0
41	Mauritius	18	5	3	1	1	2	0	0	0
42	Gabon	0	0	0	3	7	9	0	0	0
43	Seychelles	34	22	21	0	0	0	0	0	0
44	*Angola*	0	0	0	32	20	20	19	12	12
45	*Djibouti*	0	0	0	0	0	0	0	0	0
Six most populous economies		438	490	512	2,533	1,809	1,629	545	420	436
Sahelian economies		38	39	40	1,945	1,028	1,320	16	15	22
Oil exporters		105	93	104	2,172	842	925	536	402	408
All low-income economies										
Total		7,453	7,939	9,227	11,848	12,882	15,935	763	645	662
	Excluding China and India	7,372	7,850	9,103	9,896	9,279	9,922	753	605	612
South Asia		361	558	956	466	471	904	4	0	1
	Excluding India	330	528	912	442	468	891	4	0	1

232

Pulses			Roots and tubers			Seed cotton			Sugar			
1965	1980	1987	1965	1980	1987	1965	1980	1987	1965	1980	1987	
												Sub-Saharan Africa
3,533	4,546	3,871	59,010	85,656	64,514	1,497	1,747	2,698	1,777	3,208	4,020	Total
2,906	3,878	3,144	37,062	54,881	40,790	1,358	1,657	2,588	1,777	3,172	3,970	Excluding Nigeria
3,347	4,315	3,677	52,623	76,709	57,681	1,379	1,273	1,938	606	1,719	1,944	Low-income economies
2,720	3,647	2,950	30,675	45,934	33,958	1,240	1,183	1,828	606	1,684	1,894	Excluding Nigeria
679	918	723	822	1,468	880	10	89	67	77	166	198	Ethiopia
73	58	60	234	456	278	87	86	110	..	30	20	Chad
118	163	124	9,907	13,793	10,597	19	29	77	..	56	76	Zaire
2	2	1	40	35	38	0	3	5	..	..	..	Guinea-Bissau
146	207	163	208	563	231	20	23	42	..	158	184	Malawi
65	60	65	2,206	3,315	2,427	85	52	52	167	173	25	Mozambique
145	316	171	3,561	6,748	3,740	201	175	147	68	124	117	Tanzania
128	175	144	89	88	96	7	63	142	..	28	25	Burkina Faso
52	48	60	1,559	2,307	1,694	6	23	52	110	118	109	Madagascar
30	47	31	72	122	74	34	151	220	..	19	18	Mali
3	3	3	8	6	8	0	1	3	..	..	..	Gambia, The
317	327	328	1,135	1,071	1,088	6	6	7	..	..	..	Burundi
14	4	16	162	213	173	2	15	57	..	112	132	Zambia
103	283	117	155	205	174	7	3	4	..	..	..	Niger
177	293	254	1,550	4,475	2,746	256	13	36	119	15	20	Uganda
0	0	0	10	15	11	0	0	0	..	..	..	São Tomé and Principe
2	13	5	22	37	26	3	3	3	17	36	36	Somalia
22	26	21	776	922	826	8	20	60	..	..	..	Togo
190	228	185	524	1,786	763	0	0	0	..	2	4	Rwanda
21	32	25	122	130	116	0	0	0	..	..	6	Sierra Leone
20	31	26	1,059	1,273	1,117	8	17	145	..	..	5	Benin
4	6	4	774	1,147	961	24	28	37	..	..	..	Central African Republic
235	200	260	864	1,386	930	14	38	36	29	406	371	Kenya
101	99	84	387	298	327	442	338	525	18	198	533	Sudan
1	2	1	74	103	81	0	0	0	..	..	..	Comoros
8	9	9	4	6	4	0	0	0	..	..	..	Lesotho
627	668	727	21,948	30,775	23,723	139	90	110	..	36	51	Nigeria
10	17	12	3,390	2,874	3,537	0	7	3	..	20	..	Ghana
20	32	19	6	6	6	0	0	0	..	..	..	Mauritania
2	3	2	292	361	297	0	0	0	..	..	3	Liberia
0	0	0	66	87	69	0	0	0	..	..	..	*Equatorial Guinea*
33	45	37	599	642	641	0	0	0	..	20	10	*Guinea*
186	231	194	6,387	8,947	6,833	119	474	760	1,171	1,489	2,076	Middle-income economies
7	1	3	26	17	21	0	0	0	..	..	..	Cape Verde
18	26	20	255	50	195	2	21	60	..	46	72	Senegal
24	21	24	64	71	68	17	158	300	235	364	467	Zimbabwe
3	3	3	10	8	11	6	33	32	121	333	468	Swaziland
6	8	7	2,016	3,486	2,202	10	143	217	..	91	168	Côte d'Ivoire
5	4	6	547	699	550	0	0	0	71	20	36	Congo, People's Republic
48	109	53	1,417	2,099	1,659	58	84	115	..	59	71	Cameroon
10	18	12	5	7	5	6	3	3	..	..	..	Botswana
1	1	1	10	16	9	0	0	0	675	512	745	Mauritius
0	0	0	382	373	376	0	0	0	..	12	19	Gabon
0	0	0	0	0	0	0	0	0	..	..	..	Seychelles
64	40	67	1,655	2,120	1,736	20	33	33	68	51	30	*Angola*
0	0	0	0	0	0	0	0	0	..	..	..	*Djibouti*
1,905	2,364	2,088	37,489	54,468	40,198	825	759	962	193	1,042	1,402	Six most populous economies
384	626	397	885	985	889	137	327	543	..	123	136	Sahelian economies
744	821	853	25,949	36,066	28,044	216	207	258	139	178	207	Oil exporters
												All low-income economies
26,401	21,356	25,028	162,583	243,067	251,383	11,912	15,416	22,815	..	..	..	Total
16,947	14,639	19,338	61,328	94,747	111,719	5,612	7,294	9,679	..	..	..	Excluding China and India
716	856	1,193	3,546	9,017	8,102	95	62	95	..	..	..	South Asia
697	839	1,153	3,491	8,847	7,938	89	62	94	..	..	..	Excluding India

233

Table 8. Agriculture and food

	Value added in agriculture (millions of current dollars)			Cereal imports (thousands of metric tons)		Food aid in cereals (thousands of metric tons)	
	1970	1980	1987	1974	1986	1974/75	1985/86
Sub-Saharan Africa							
Total	15,676 t	60,937 t	45,197 t	4,108 t	8,084 t	910 t	3,107 t
Excluding Nigeria	10,596 t	34,751 t	37,818 t	3,719 t	7,408 t	903 t	3,107 t
Low-income economies	13,523 t	51,576 t	34,189 t	2,977 t	5,704 t	846 t	2,858 t
Excluding Nigeria	8,443 t	25,391 t	26,810 t	2,587 t	5,028 t	839 t	2,858 t
1 Ethiopia	931	1,870	2,031	118	609	54	570
2 Chad [b]	142	388	418	37	71	20	29
3 Zaire [b]	585	2,961	1,857	343	415	1	56
4 Guinea-Bissau [b]	37	47	83	33	32	..	..
5 Malawi	119	393	411	17	11	0	10
6 Mozambique	..	1,129	747	62	406	34	344
7 Tanzania	473	2,030	1,882	431	188	148	55
8 Burkina Faso	126	496	626	99	164	28	22
9 Madagascar [b]	266	1,179	879	114	140	7	115
10 Mali [b]	207	951	1,051	281	86	107	77
11 Gambia, The	16	64	60	13	70	..	..
12 Burundi	159	532	681	7	13	6	2
13 Zambia [b]	191	552	222	93	150	5	116
14 Niger [b]	420	1,080	729	155	83	73	11
15 Uganda	929	1,216	2,710	36	26	..	..
16 São Tomé and Principe	6	17	9	3	7	..	..
17 Somalia	167	415	632	42	343	111	156
18 Togo [b]	85	312	354	6	86	11	6
19 Rwanda [b]	136	533	784	3	11	19	16
20 Sierra Leone	108	334	402	72	152	10	43
21 Benin	121	498	726	7	77	9	8
22 Central African Republic	60	300	415	7	37	1	6
23 Kenya	484	1,951	2,139	15	274	2	107
24 Sudan	757	2,097	3,044	125	707	46	890
25 Comoros	..	..	71	19	19	..	..
26 Lesotho	23	90	57	48	94	14	32
27 Nigeria	5,080	26,186	7,379	389	677	7	0
28 Ghana [b]	1,030	2,575	2,568	177	223	33	64
29 Mauritania	58	202	310	115	206	48	30
30 Liberia	91	359	368	42	117	3	2
31 *Equatorial Guinea*	..	..	..	2	8	..	..
32 *Guinea*	..	748	659	63	203	49	92
Middle-income economies	2,159 t	9,342 t	13,996 t	1,131 t	2,380 t	64 t	249 t
33 Cape Verde [b]	..	28	..	45	54	..	..
34 Senegal [b]	208	568	1,024	341	431	27	80
35 Zimbabwe	214	702	570	56	71	0	38
36 Swaziland	34	116	89	14	44	..	..
37 Côte d'Ivoire	462	2,830	2,728	172	675	4	0
38 Congo, People's Republic [b]	49	199	262	34	97	2	0
39 Cameroon [b]	364	2,089	3,009	81	290	4	6
40 Botswana [b]	28	107	48	21	137	5	44
41 Mauritius	30	119	220	160	197	22	15
42 Gabon [b]	60	310	379	24	56	..	..
43 Seychelles	..	10	13	9	7	..	..
44 *Angola*	685	2,187	..	149	280	0	67
45 *Djibouti*	..	..	..	25	40	..	..
Six most populous economies	8,311 t	37,094 t	18,332 t	1,421 t	2,870 t	258 t	1,678 t
Sahelian economies	1,221 t	3,824 t	4,338 t	1,119 t	1,198 t	303 t	249 t
Oil exporters	6,238 t	30,970 t	12,222 t	678 t	1,399 t	13 t	73 t
All low-income economies							
Total	83,666 t	243,599 t	236,213 t	22,767 t	27,750 t	6,002 t	6,662 t
Excluding China and India	28,413 t	92,719 t	80,006 t	11,472 t	11,807 t	4,420 t	5,871 t
South Asia	32,198 t	76,544 t	88,877 t	9,404 t	2,833 t	4,522 t	2,562 t
Excluding India	8,977 t	17,652 t	23,629 t	4,142 t	2,737 t	2,940 t	2,354 t

Note: Summary measures for value added in agriculture include estimates for missing country data. The weighting process may result in discrepancies between summed subgroup figures and overall totals. Summary measures for the other indicators do not include estimates for missing country data. The summary measures for fertilizer consumption are weighted by total arable land area; the summary measures for food production per capita are weighted by population.

Fertilizer consumption (hundreds of grams of plant nutrient per hectare of arable land)		Irrigated land as a percentage of arable and permanent cropland		Average index of food production per capita (1979-81=100)	
1970 [a]	1986	1974-76	1984-86	1985-87	
					Sub-Saharan Africa
33 w	85 w	..	..	100 w	Total
42 w	83 w	..	..	98 w	Excluding Nigeria
20 w	77 w	..	..	100 w	Low-income economies
27 w	70 w	..	..	98 w	Excluding Nigeria
4	66	1	1	89	Ethiopia
7	13	0	0	104	Chad [b]
8	15	0	0	99	Zaire [b]
..	..	..	..	129	Guinea-Bissau [b]
52	131	1	1	87	Malawi
22	19	1	3	84	Mozambique
31	77	1	2	90	Tanzania
3	61	0	0	118	Burkina Faso
61	23	17	27	97	Madagascar [b]
31	166	6	9	101	Mali [b]
23	..	6	7	126	Gambia, The
5	23	4	5	100	Burundi
73	148	0	0	97	Zambia [b]
1	7	1	1	87	Niger [b]
14	..	0	0	123	Uganda
..	..	..	..	68	São Tomé and Principe
25	16	11	17	102	Somalia
3	78	0	0	89	Togo [b]
3	20	0	0	86	Rwanda [b]
17	22	1	2	98	Sierra Leone
36	63	0	0	114	Benin
12	1	..	..	94	Central African Republic
238	518	2	2	93	Kenya
28	67	14	15	100	Sudan
..	..	0	0	95	Comoros
10	130	..	..	83	Lesotho
2	94	3	3	105	Nigeria
13	27	0	0	106	Ghana [b]
11	50	6	6	90	Mauritania
63	46	1	1	96	Liberia
84	..	..	..	..	*Equatorial Guinea*
19	4	4	4	93	*Guinea*
95 w	123 w	..	..	97 w	Middle-income economies
..	..	5	5	99	Cape Verde [b]
17	40	3	3	105	Senegal [b]
446	571	3	6	91	Zimbabwe
396	..	34	34	104	Swaziland
74	83	1	1	105	Côte d'Ivoire
114	59	0	1	92	Congo, People's Republic [b]
34	75	0	0	94	Cameroon [b]
15	5	0	0	75	Botswana [b]
2,095	2,364	14	16	103	Mauritius
..	22	..	..	97	Gabon [b]
..	..	..	..	..	Seychelles
33	34	..	..	88	*Angola*
..	..	..	..	..	*Djibouti*
17 w	89 w	..	..	100 w	Six most populous economies
11 w	47 w	..	..	107 w	Sahelian economies
11 w	85 w	..	..	103 w	Oil exporters
					All Low-income economies
161 w	706 w		..	115 w	Total
72 w	318 w	..	..	106 w	Excluding China and India
114 w	586 w	..	..	109 w	South Asia
131 w	644 w	..	..	104 w	Excluding India

a. Average for 1969-71.
b. Value added in agriculture data are at purchaser values.

235

Table 9. Structure of manufacturing

| | Value added in manufacturing (millions of current dollars) | | | Distribution of manufacturing value added (percent) | | | | | |
| | | | | Food and agriculture | | | Textiles and clothing | | |
	1970	1980	1986	1970	1980	1986	1970	1980	1986
Sub-Saharan Africa									
Total	3,349 t	18,729 t	16,288 t						
Excluding Nigeria	2,806 t	9,515 t	11,092 t						
Low-income economies	2,417 t	14,575 t	10,461 t						
Excluding Nigeria	1,874 t	5,361 t	5,265 t						
1 Ethiopia	149	401	518	46	49	51	31	29	23
2 Chad [b]	51	81	132	..	45	45	..	40	40
3 Zaire [b]	286	310	96	38	40	40	16	16	16
4 Guinea-Bissau [b]	17	..	..	..	..	..	..	..	..
5 Malawi	..	..	..	51	58	..	17	12	..
6 Mozambique	..	242	..	51	..	..	13	..	..
7 Tanzania	116	500	227	36	23	28	28	33	26
8 Burkina Faso	..	..	174	69	59	62	9	19	18
9 Madagascar [b]	118	..	..	36	27	35	28	44	47
10 Mali [b]	25	70	100	36	29	..	40	51	..
11 Gambia, The	2	8	8	..	35	46	..	2	2
12 Burundi	16	63	102	53	78	..	25	11	..
13 Zambia [b]	181	718	461	49	44	44	9	13	13
14 Niger [b]	30	94	142	..	30	..	..	25	..
15 Uganda	158	72	152	40	..	..	20	..	..
16 São Tomé and Principe	1	3	4	..	..	..	..	..	..
17 Somalia	26	29	48	88	46	46	6	21	21
18 Togo [b]	25	78	49	..	47	..	..	13	..
19 Rwanda [b]	8	178	310	86	93	77	0	2	1
20 Sierra Leone	22	56	47	..	..	65	..	..	1
21 Benin	19	61	48	..	59	58	..	14	16
22 Central African Republic	12	54	59	..	49	..	..	22	..
23 Kenya	174	796	709	31	39	35	9	10	12
24 Sudan	140	424	537	39	22	22	34	25	25
25 Comoros	..	..	6	..	..	..	..	..	..
26 Lesotho	3	18	26	11	12	12	26	20	20
27 Nigeria	543	9,214	5,196	36	21	..	26	11	..
28 Ghana [b]	252	347	639	34	36	..	16	10	..
29 Mauritania	10	..	..	..	..	..	..	..	..
30 Liberia	15	77	47	..	..	..	..	..	..
31 *Equatorial Guinea*	..	..	..	..	..	..	..	..	..
32 *Guinea*	..	38	105	..	..	..	..	..	..
Middle-income economies	957 t	4,178 t	6,061 t						
33 Cape Verde [b]	..	..	4	..	..	..	..	..	..
34 Senegal [b]	141	456	626	51	48	48	19	19	15
35 Zimbabwe	293	1,248	1,444	24	23	28	16	17	16
36 Swaziland	..	102	73	37	41	..	2	3	..
37 Côte d'Ivoire	149	926	1,191	27	35	..	16	15	..
38 Congo, People's Republic [b]	..	128	177	65	..	47	4	..	13
39 Cameroon [b]	119	593	1,321	47	50	50	16	13	13
40 Botswana [b]	5	38	67	..	45	52	..	17	12
41 Mauritius	26	147	284	75	36	35	6	30	39
42 Gabon [b]	..	..	..	37	24	..	7	4	..
43 Seychelles	..	11	19	..	71	79	..	2	2
44 *Angola*	80	131	226	..	..	..	..	..	..
45 *Djibouti*	..	..	..	..	..	..	..	..	..
Six most populous economies	1,407 t	11,645 t	7,283 t						
Sahelian economies	324 t	923 t	1,273 t						
Oil exporters	779 t	10,412 t	7,074 t						
All low-income economies									
Total	42,814 t	163,452 t	163,354 t						
Excluding China and India	6,244 t	32,561 t	31,119 t						
South Asia	9,398 t	33,414 t	46,406 t						
Excluding India	2,439 t	5,981 t	8,094 t						

Note: Summary measures include estimates for missing country data. The weighting process may result in discrepancies between summed subgroup figures and overall totals.

Distribution of manufacturing value added (percent)									
Machinery and transport equipment			Chemicals			Other [a]			
1970	1980	1986	1970	1980	1986	1970	1980	1986	
									Sub-Saharan Africa
									Total
									Excluding Nigeria
									Low-income economies
									Excluding Nigeria
0	0	0	2	3	3	21	19	22	Ethiopia
..	..	..	..	0	0	..	15	15	Chad [b]
7	8	8	10	8	8	29	29	29	Zaire [b]
									Guinea-Bissau [b]
3	4	..	10	5	..	20	20	..	Malawi
5	..	..	3	..	..	28	..	..	Mozambique
5	8	8	4	6	7	26	30	31	Tanzania
2	3	2	1	1	1	19	17	17	Burkina Faso
6	5	3	7	5	..	23	20	*15*	Madagascar [b]
4	8	..	5	3	..	14	8	..	Mali [b]
..	0	0	..	3	2	..	60	49	Gambia, The
0	0	..	*6*	3	..	*16*	8	..	Burundi
5	9	9	10	9	9	27	25	25	Zambia [b]
..	2	..	..	16	..	..	28	..	Niger [b]
2	..	..	4	..	..	34	..	..	Uganda
..	..	..	..	..	..	..	31	..	São Tomé And Principe
0	0	0	1	2	2	6	31	31	Somalia
..	..	..	..	8	..	..	32	..	Togo [b]
3	*0*	0	2	3	12	8	2	*9*	Rwanda [b]
..	..	..	..	..	4	..	..	30	Sierra Leone
..	0	0	..	6	5	..	21	21	Benin
..	..	..	..	11	..	..	18	..	Central African Republic
18	12	14	7	8	9	35	30	29	Kenya
3	1	1	5	21	21	19	31	31	Sudan
..	..	..	..	..	..	..	..	..	Comoros
..	..	..	..	..	..	63	68	68	Lesotho
1	25	..	6	12	..	31	31	..	Nigeria
4	2	..	4	4	..	41	47	..	Ghana [b]
..	..	..	..	..	..	..	..	..	Mauritania
..	..	..	..	..	..	..	..	..	Liberia
..	..	..	..	..	..	..	..	..	*Equatorial Guinea*
..	..	..	..	..	..	..	..	..	*Guinea*
									Middle-income economies
									Cape Verde [b]
2	4	6	6	8	7	· 22	21	24	Senegal [b]
9	9	10	11	9	9	40	42	36	Zimbabwe
..	2	..	..	11	..	60	43	..	Swaziland
10	10	..	5	6	..	42	34	..	Côte d'Ivoire
1	..	3	7	..	9	23	..	29	Congo, People's Republic [b]
5	7	7	4	6	6	28	23	23	Cameroon [b]
..	..	..	..	2	4	..	36	32	Botswana [b]
5	6	3	3	6	4	12	23	19	Mauritius
6	9	..	6	4	..	44	58	..	Gabon [b]
..	0	0	..	2	2	..	25	16	Seychelles
..	..	..	..	..	..	..	..	..	*Angola*
..	..	..	..	..	..	..	..	..	*Djibouti*
									Six most populous economies
									Sahelian economies
									Oil exporters
									All low-income economies
									Total
									Excluding China and India
									South Asia
									Excluding India

a. Includes unallocable data; see the technical notes.
b. Value added in manufacturing data are at purchaser values.

Table 10. Manufacturing earnings and output

| | | Earnings per employee | | | Total earnings as percentage of value added | | | Gross output per employee (1980=100) | |
| | Growth rates | | Index (1980=100) | | | | | | |
	1973-80	1980-86	1973	1986	1973	1980	1986	1973	1986
Sub-Saharan Africa									
Total									
Excluding Nigeria									
Low-income economies									
Excluding Nigeria									
1 Ethiopia	-7.3	-3.1	156	87	24	18	19	75	111
2 Chad	..	..	..	..	..	14	..	..	..
3 Zaire	..	..	..	..	..	..	..	..	..
4 Guinea-Bissau	..	..	..	..	..	..	..	..	..
5 Malawi	..	..	100	..	40	33	..	126	..
6 Mozambique	..	..	..	..	41	..	..	..	..
7 Tanzania	..	-11.5	180	47	37	33	34	136	90
8 Burkina Faso	11.7	2.6	..	118	..	23	20	..	120
9 Madagascar	-0.9	-12.9	113	..	42	38	..	83	..
10 Mali	..	..	160	..	49	28	..	78	..
11 Gambia, The	19.2	4.4	..	..	..	25	..	..	..
12 Burundi	-9.0	..	186	..	25	14	..	91	..
13 Zambia	-5.3	0.2	139	114	30	25	26	126	78
14 Niger	..	..	..	..	..	44	..	..	..
15 Uganda	..	..	..	..	..	..	..	..	..
16 São Tomé and Principe	..	..	..	..	..	..	..	..	..
17 Somalia	-6.1	-8.6	194	61	27	30	30	163	61
18 Togo	4.2	..	..	..	..	..	..	..	..
19 Rwanda	..	..	..	..	44	..	..	..	..
20 Sierra Leone	..	..	..	..	..	..	..	..	..
21 Benin	..	..	..	..	..	25	25	..	..
22 Central African Republic	..	..	57	..	30	47	..	69	..
23 Kenya	-2.5	-3.7	105	81	45	43	46	57	96
24 Sudan	..	..	..	..	..	..	..	..	..
25 Comoros	..	..	..	..	..	..	..	..	..
26 Lesotho	-16.1	..	66	..	48	48	48	55	..
27 Nigeria	-0.4	..	94	..	22	22	..	99	..
28 Ghana	-20.0	..	383	..	20	19	..	190	..
29 Mauritania	..	..	..	..	..	..	..	..	..
30 Liberia	..	1.6	..	99	..	..	..	..	..
31 *Equatorial Guinea*	..	..	..	..	..	..	..	..	..
32 *Guinea*	..	..	..	..	..	..	..	..	..
Middle-income economies									
33 Cape Verde	..	..	..	..	..	..	..	..	..
34 Senegal	-4.9	-0.2	..	93	..	43	44	..	103
35 Zimbabwe	0.6	6.1	90	145	42	42	44	98	120
36 Swaziland	3.3	..	94	..	34	41	..	..	..
37 Côte d'Ivoire	-1.3	..	107	..	28	30	..	63	..
38 Congo, People's Republic	..	..	..	..	44	..	..	..	..
39 Cameroon	5.6	12.6	..	..	..	37	37	..	..
40 Botswana	2.6	-4.2	48	..	..	51	..	..	..
41 Mauritius	2.9	-3.1	97	84	26	52	48	179	74
42 Gabon	..	..	..	..	40	50	..	..	..
43 Seychelles	9.2	5.3	..	..	..	29	..	..	..
44 *Angola*	..	..	..	..	..	..	..	..	..
45 *Djibouti*	..	..	..	..	..	..	..	..	..
Six most populous economies									
Sahelian economies									
Oil exporters									
All low-income economies									
Total									
Excluding China and India									
South Asia									
Excluding India									

Table 11. Commercial energy

	Average annual growth rate (percent)						Energy consumption per capita (kilograms of oil equivalent)			Energy imports as a percentage of merchandise exports		
	Energy production			Energy consumption								
	1965-73	1973-80	1980-86	1965-73	1973-80	1980-86	1965	1980	1986	1965	1980	1987
Sub-Saharan Africa												
Total	28.9 w	1.6 w	0.0 w	7.0 w	4.4 w	2.2 w	72 w	110 w	105 w	7 w	10 w	10 w
Excluding Nigeria	18.8 w	4.5 w	5.9 w	7.0 w	1.9 w	0.6 w	84 w	109 w	96 w	7 w	20 w	13 w
Low-income economies	31.8 w	1.6 w	-2.9 w	7.9 w	4.8 w	2.4 w	50 w	86 w	83 w	7 w	9 w	12 w
Excluding Nigeria	15.0 w	14.4 w	-3.8 w	8.2 w	0.9 w	-0.3 w	56 w	75 w	63 w	7 w	25 w	20 w
1 Ethiopia	11.1	5.5	5.3	11.4	2.5	2.1	10	20	21	8	42	55
2 Chad	..	..	..	..	..	..	..	..	..	22		..
3 Zaire	4.8	14.7	2.7	6.0	1.4	0.8	74	83	73	6	4	2
4 Guinea-Bissau	..	..	..	2.0	0.0	1.5	40	38	37	..	..	..
5 Malawi	31.1	9.9	5.0	8.3	7.5	-0.7	25	55	41	7	24	10
6 Mozambique	4.6	46.8	-50.1	9.3	-1.8	1.8	81	95	86	13	..	..
7 Tanzania	6.8	9.3	2.5	10.5	-3.8	2.0	37	39	35	10	48	56
8 Burkina Faso	..	..	..	8.0	14.8	0.2	7	21	18	11	37	7
9 Madagascar	8.6	-3.9	11.0	13.6	-4.8	1.2	34	45	40	8	25	36
10 Mali	80.5	11.2	9.4	4.6	8.4	2.3	14	25	23	16	36	32
11 Gambia, The	..	..	..	10.6	16.4	0.9	23	83	68	3	29	12
12 Burundi	..	23.3	15.7	5.6	9.5	10.4	5	14	21	11	41	8
13 Zambia	41.1	8.7	1.0	-0.1	2.5	-0.4	464	462	380	6	14	11
14 Niger	..	..	17.6	14.7	11.8	3.3	8	38	42	9	27	9
15 Uganda	3.7	-4.5	2.7	8.4	-7.4	4.4	36	25	26	1	19	17
16 São Tomé and Principe	12.0	15.6	-2.5	4.8	13.5	-0.3	48	140	113	..	..	..
17 Somalia	..	..	..	9.3	23.1	1.8	14	83	82	8	3	9
18 Togo	-6.1	8.6	11.4	12.9	9.4	-3.2	27	76	52	4	26	8
19 Rwanda	15.7	0.4	8.2	11.4	18.5	4.9	8	37	42	10	17	53
20 Sierra Leone	..	..	..	4.6	6.4	-1.8	109	95	77	11	29	10
21 Benin	..	..	11.4	19.7	1.1	5.4	21	45	46	10	5	97
22 Central African Republic	10.6	5.3	1.0	9.8	2.0	4.6	22	26	30	9	3	1
23 Kenya	9.9	16.5	10.4	7.1	1.7	-0.8	110	131	100	13	63	39
24 Sudan	14.7	13.9	0.6	12.1	-6.9	0.3	67	68	59	5	32	38
25 Comoros	..	..	..	8.1	1.6	1.1	21	46	40	..	..	..
26 Lesotho	..	..	..	..	..	..	..	..	..	10	52	1
27 Nigeria	33.4	0.8	-2.8	7.1	16.2	6.5	34	115	134	7	1	3
28 Ghana	43.4	4.3	-10.7	15.0	1.5	-4.9	76	187	132	6	24	14
29 Mauritania	..	..	..	16.0	4.7	-0.2	48	138	114	2	16	8
30 Liberia	37.0	1.6	-3.2	16.1	2.5	-12.4	182	427	167	6	25	11
31 *Equatorial Guinea*	7.8	-0.2	0.0	13.8	2.3	5.6	28	56	72	..	..	..
32 *Guinea*	17.1	9.6	1.8	2.3	3.3	0.6	56	65	59	..	..	..
Middle-income economies	19.8 w	1.9 w	8.7 w	5.3 w	3.4 w	1.9 w	..	286 w	265 w	6 w	14 w	7 w
33 Cape Verde	..	..	..	-5.3	-18.6	0.1	..	355	304	..	..	..
34 Senegal	..	..	..	6.0	6.8	-2.3	79	150	116	8	55	24
35 Zimbabwe	1.1	-2.3	-0.9	10.7	0.8	0.4	441	626	516	7	17	6
36 Swaziland	13.2	4.0	0.5	7.5	5.9	0.9	198	339	292	..	..	..
37 Côte d'Ivoire	0.5	33.0	17.0	10.9	5.9	2.7	101	189	174	5	16	11
38 Congo, People's Republic	39.5	5.7	10.1	10.9	5.7	5.0	90	208	225	10	7	5
39 Cameroon	1.2	43.4	20.2	6.5	8.0	6.8	67	114	143	6	12	1
40 Botswana	8.4	9.6	2.7	7.8	10.9	2.2	191	426	432	16	18	6
41 Mauritius	3.1	3.1	6.6	11.9	2.5	3.0	160	351	378	6	20	7
42 Gabon	23.9	1.4	0.2	23.0	8.3	3.0	153	1,174	1,125	3	0	1
43 Seychelles	..	..	..	47.8	17.5	9.3	43	1,118	1,451	19	114	90
44 *Angola*	47.1	-2.3	12.1	10.6	2.8	2.7	114	208	203	..	..	..
45 *Djibouti*	..	..	..	-16.3	4.0	-0.4	..	1,723	1,383	..	..	..
Six most populous economies	32.4 w	1.0 w	-2.6 w	8.1 w	6.5 w	4.2 w	44 w	83 w	87 w	8 w	6 w	11 w
Sahelian economies	80.5 w	16.0 w	13.2 w	2.5 w	3.5 w	-0.3 w	51 w	63 w	54 w	9 w	36 w	17 w
Oil exporters	32.5 w	1.0 w	0.3 w	8.4 w	12.4 w	5.8 w	45 w	131 w	149 w	6 w	2 w	2 w
All low-income economies												
Total	12.9 w	6.3 w	4.8 w	9.3 w	7.1 w	5.5 w	128 w	250 w	301 w	6 w	17 w	10 w
Excluding China and India	20.3 w	3.4 w	-0.3 w	5.0 w	5.7 w	4.0 w	81 w	107 w	116 w	8 w	14 w	16 w
South Asia	4.0 w	7.9 w	8.9 w	5.0 w	7.0 w	6.5 w	99 w	143 w	183 w	7 w	65 w	20 w
Excluding India	7.2 w	8.6 w	8.4 w	4.2 w	6.3 w	6.9 w	95 w	89 w	112 w	6 w	51 w	25 w

Note: Summary measures include estimates for missing country data. The summary measures for energy production, energy consumption, and energy imports as a percentage of merchandise exports are based on aggregate values in current dollars. The summary measures for energy consumption per capita are weighted by population.

Table 12. Growth of merchandise trade

	Merchandise trade (millions of dollars)					
	Exports			Imports		
	1965	*1980*	*1987*	*1965*	*1980*	*1987*
Sub-Saharan Africa						
Total	4,891 t	51,729 t	30,258 t	5,182 t	46,147 t	33,596 t
Excluding Nigeria	4,154 t	25,761 t	22,893 t	4,411 t	29,505 t	25,780 t
Low-income economies	3,552 t	39,062 t	16,802 t	3,887 t	34,340 t	21,998 t
Excluding Nigeria	2,814 t	13,094 t	9,437 t	3,117 t	17,698 t	14,182 t
1 Ethiopia	113	425	396	150	721	1,150
2 Chad	27	72	..	31	74	..
3 Zaire	336	2,507	1,594	321	1,117	1,149
4 Guinea-Bissau	..	11	..	..	53	72
5 Malawi	38	285	264	57	440	281
6 Mozambique	108	281	*89*	173	800	*486*
7 Tanzania	175	537	347	197	1,227	1,150
8 Burkina Faso	18	161	198	46	446	540
9 Madagascar	92	402	310	138	676	386
10 Mali	16	205	216	43	439	447
11 Gambia, The	13	31	45	16	132	109
12 Burundi	16	65	84	32	167	206
13 Zambia	525	1,360	869	295	1,111	745
14 Niger	25	580	361	38	608	417
15 Uganda	176	345	320	161	293	477
16 São Tomé and Principe	..	18	*9*	5	19	..
17 Somalia	34	133	94	56	461	452
18 Togo	35	476	297	47	638	417
19 Rwanda	89	134	121	108	277	352
20 Sierra Leone	18	207	129	34	425	132
21 Benin	12	223	168	18	331	418
22 Central African Republic	33	147	130	41	221	186
23 Kenya	228	1,389	961	282	2,590	1,755
24 Sudan	196	594	482	208	1,499	694
25 Comoros	..	11	*18*	..	55	*71*
26 Lesotho	7	58	47	25	490	456
27 Nigeria	737	25,968	7,365	770	16,642	7,816
28 Ghana	292	1,257	1,056	447	1,129	836
29 Mauritania	58	196	428	44	363	474
30 Liberia	135	597	382	105	534	208
31 *Equatorial Guinea*	..	15	*20*	..	63	*115*
32 *Guinea*	..	374	..	..	299	..
Middle-income economies	1,339 t	12,667 t	13,456 t	1,294 t	11,807 t	11,598 t
33 Cape Verde	..	9	*3*	..	68	..
34 Senegal	129	477	645	164	1,038	1,174
35 Zimbabwe	399	1,423	1,358	335	1,448	1,055
36 Swaziland	..	368	311	..	538	365
37 Côte d'Ivoire	277	3,142	2,982	236	3,015	2,168
38 Congo, People's Republic	38	980	884	65	500	570
39 Cameroon	119	1,447	1,714	135	1,538	2,168
40 Botswana	14	503	1,521	23	691	849
41 Mauritius	62	431	918	77	619	1,010
42 Gabon	100	2,173	1,286	62	686	836
43 Seychelles	2	21	22	2	99	114
44 *Angola*	200	1,682	*1,787*	195	1,353	*1,080*
45 *Djibouti*	..	12	*25*	..	213	*210*
Six most populous economies	1,785 t	31,419 t	11,144 t	1,929 t	23,796 t	13,714 t
Sahelian economies	286 t	1,741 t	1,897 t	382 t	3,220 t	3,233 t
Oil exporters	1,194 t	32,249 t	13,036 t	1,226 t	20,719 t	12,470 t
All low-income economies						
Total	9,948 t	95,457 t	95,802 t	12,032 t	97,820 t	116,254 t
Excluding China and India	6,027 t	68,860 t	43,712 t	7,200 t	64,180 t	53,877 t
South Asia	2,910 t	13,368 t	19,616 t	4,521 t	25,039 t	30,871 t
Excluding India	1,219 t	5,036 t	7,068 t	1,708 t	10,949 t	11,886 t

Note: Summary measures do not include estimates for missing country data. The summary measures are calculated from aggregated 1980 constant dollar values. These values do not include trade in services.

Average annual growth rate [a] (percent)						Terms of trade (1980=100)		
Exports			Imports					
1965-73	1973-80	1980-87	1965-73	1973-80	1980-87	1985	1987	
15.1 w	0.2 w	-1.3 w	3.7 w	7.6 w	-5.8 w	91 m	84 m	**Sub-Saharan Africa** Total
5.7 w	2.0 w	1.7 w	3.4 w	2.9 w	-1.5 w	92 m	84 m	Excluding Nigeria
16.9 w	-0.6 w	-3.6 w	3.4 w	8.1 w	-7.8 w	91 m	84 m	Low-income economies
4.8 w	0.6 w	-1.1 w	2.9 w	1.4 w	-2.5 w	91 m	84 m	Excluding Nigeria
3.4	-5.2	-0.7	-0.5	4.1	7.6	99	83	Ethiopia
..	..	..	..	..	..	..	..	Chad
10.6	5.9	-3.4	7.8	-9.1	-0.4	82	74	Zaire
..	..	..	..	..	..	..	..	Guinea-Bissau
6.3	5.0	3.4	7.6	3.0	-6.1	73	67	Malawi
..	..	..	..	..	..	..	..	Mozambique
4.2	-5.6	-7.4	4.6	-0.2	-0.5	90	89	Tanzania
2.0	10.9	5.6	8.7	5.6	2.0	80	74	Burkina Faso
6.2	-3.1	-3.1	1.5	4.5	-2.7	104	105	Madagascar
12.5	15.8	6.6	8.0	6.3	3.4	82	86	Mali
-4.0	1.8	12.5	0.8	12.7	-2.4	97	83	Gambia, The
6.9	0.9	8.3	-2.3	14.1	2.4	100	75	Burundi
5.5	-0.3	-3.3	0.8	-7.5	-6.2	72	79	Zambia
4.7	31.0	-4.8	3.8	20.0	-6.2	109	86	Niger
3.0	-9.5	2.7	-4.1	-2.9	3.0	96	67	Uganda
..	..	..	..	..	..	..	..	São Tomé and Principe
0.1	2.2	-7.7	2.3	9.7	-1.3	91	84	Somalia
6.2	14.5	-3.0	5.3	18.1	-4.6	90	86	Togo
11.4	5.9	2.5	5.2	13.2	5.4	102	87	Rwanda
0.5	-3.7	-2.1	-2.5	1.6	-15.1	100	93	Sierra Leone
16.3	1.4	-0.1	10.1	2.6	0.4	90	87	Benin
-0.6	3.5	1.0	-4.8	5.5	-1.8	88	84	Central African Republic
4.4	-0.1	-0.6	4.0	3.5	-3.0	92	80	Kenya
3.9	-0.5	4.2	6.3	0.3	-8.7	90	84	Sudan
..	..	..	..	..	..	..	..	Comoros
0.4	15.2	-8.4	9.1	12.7	-7.6	100	77	Lesotho
27.0	-1.0	-5.1	5.9	21.2	-14.0	90	54	Nigeria
1.0	-4.1	-1.6	-2.5	-2.8	-2.9	91	85	Ghana
12.5	-7.5	11.2	7.2	1.8	1.7	112	98	Mauritania
8.8	0.7	-2.7	1.4	1.8	-10.2	91	93	Liberia
..	..	..	..	..	..	..	..	*Equatorial Guinea*
..	..	..	..	..	..	..	..	*Guinea*
7.2 w	3.8 w	4.5 w	4.7 w	6.0 w	-0.1 w	94 m	84 m	Middle-income economies
..	..	..	..	..	..	..	..	Cape Verde
2.1	1.4	6.7	4.6	3.7	2.7	100	96	Senegal
3.3	0.5	0.9	1.3	-3.3	-6.8	84	84	Zimbabwe
..	..	..	..	..	..	..	..	Swaziland
7.4	3.3	3.4	6.4	9.6	-3.1	96	85	Côte d'Ivoire
5.3	7.9	3.9	-3.0	7.2	-0.7	94	65	Congo, People's Republic
6.8	6.2	9.7	6.9	10.0	3.4	92	66	Cameroon
20.4	18.7	16.2	20.6	8.3	0.5	98	106	Botswana
3.1	3.4	11.1	3.7	5.6	6.7	90	108	Mauritius
13.4	2.4	-2.1	4.0	6.5	3.0	90	64	Gabon
11.6	9.4	13.4	20.9	9.0	3.9	103	64	Seychelles
..	..	..	..	..	..	..	..	*Angola*
..	..	..	..	..	..	..	..	*Djibouti*
21.2 w	-0.8 w	-4.4 w	5.2 w	10.8 w	-9.9 w	90 m	82 m	Six most populous economies
4.8 w	6.6 w	4.5 w	5.6 w	6.5 w	0.8 w	99 m	86 m	Sahelian economies
24.5 w	0.4 w	-3.2 w	5.3 w	18.5 w	-10.7 w	91 m	64 m	Oil exporters
								All low-income economies
9.6 w	2.3 w	3.5 w	1.1 w	8.0 w	2.3 w	92 m	84 m	Total
12.3 w	0.8 w	-0.1 w	1.5 w	8.2 w	-3.9 w	91 m	84 m	Excluding China and India
-0.7 w	5.8 w	4.8 w	-2.8 w	6.0 w	3.7 w	95 m	97 m	South Asia
-4.2 w	6.0 w	6.5 w	-5.3 w	7.5 w	2.4 w	91 m	96 m	Excluding India

a. See the technical notes.

Table 13. Structure of merchandise imports (percentage share)

	Food 1965	Food 1980	Food 1987	Fuels 1965	Fuels 1980	Fuels 1987	Other primary commodities 1965	Other primary commodities 1980	Other primary commodities 1987
Sub-Saharan Africa									
Total	14 w	16 w	12 w	6 w	12 w	10 w	4 w	3 w	4 w
Excluding Nigeria	15 w	15 w	13 w	6 w	18 w	12 w	4 w	4 w	4 w
Low-income economies	13 w	16 w	10 w	6 w	10 w	10 w	4 w	3 w	3 w
Excluding Nigeria	14 w	14 w	11 w	6 w	19 w	14 w	4 w	4 w	4 w
1 Ethiopia	6	7	4	6	25	18	6	4	3
2 Chad	13	..	..	19	..	..	3	..	..
3 Zaire	18	19	13	7	8	3	5	5	5
4 Guinea-Bissau	..	..	..	..	..	..	..	..	..
5 Malawi	15	7	5	5	15	9	3	3	3
6 Mozambique	17	..	..	8	..	..	7	..	..
7 Tanzania	10	13	6	9	21	17	2	3	2
8 Burkina Faso	23	19	16	4	13	3	14	4	5
9 Madagascar	19	8	9	5	15	29	2	4	2
10 Mali	20	16	12	6	17	16	5	2	2
11 Gambia, The	19	11	43	3	7	4	7	3	14
12 Burundi	16	14	12	6	16	5	9	4	5
13 Zambia	9	8	7	10	18	12	3	2	1
14 Niger	12	13	18	6	26	6	6	4	11
15 Uganda	7	5	5	1	23	9	3	2	2
16 São Tomé and Principe	..	..	..	..	..	..	..	..	..
17 Somalia	31	31	13	5	1	3	8	6	6
18 Togo	15	19	20	3	20	6	5	3	6
19 Rwanda	12	9	12	7	8	15	5	8	7
20 Sierra Leone	17	19	17	9	14	9	3	5	4
21 Benin	18	19	11	6	4	34	7	8	2
22 Central African Republic	13	20	13	7	2	1	2	4	4
23 Kenya	10	8	9	11	34	21	3	3	4
24 Sudan	23	26	17	5	13	22	4	2	3
25 Comoros	..	..	..	..	..	..	..	..	..
26 Lesotho	49	17	-7	3	6	-1	7	14	-8
27 Nigeria	9	17	8	6	2	3	3	3	3
28 Ghana	12	9	6	4	27	17	3	4	3
29 Mauritania	9	29	26	4	9	10	1	3	2
30 Liberia	16	18	19	8	28	21	3	3	3
31 *Equatorial Guinea*	..	..	..	..	..	..	..	..	..
32 *Guinea*	..	..	..	..	..	..	..	..	..
Middle-income economies	19 w	16 w	18 w	6 w	15 w	9 w	3 w	4 w	5 w
33 Cape Verde	..	..	..	..	..	..	..	..	..
34 Senegal	36	24	32	6	25	16	4	2	2
35 Zimbabwe	13	15	10	8	17	8	3	3	3
36 Swaziland	..	..	..	..	..	..	..	..	..
37 Côte d'Ivoire	18	17	19	6	17	15	3	3	4
38 Congo, People's Republic	15	18	16	6	14	7	1	3	3
39 Cameroon	11	8	13	5	12	1	4	2	3
40 Botswana	9	8	9	10	13	7	18	17	16
41 Mauritius	34	26	19	5	14	7	3	5	5
42 Gabon	16	19	18	5	1	1	2	2	3
43 Seychelles	36	20	14	13	24	18	3	3	1
44 *Angola*	..	..	..	..	..	..	..	..	..
45 *Djibouti*	..	..	..	..	..	..	..	..	..
Six most populous economies	12 w	16 w	9 w	7 w	8 w	10 w	4 w	3 w	3 w
Sahelian economies	25 w	20 w	23 w	5 w	20 w	10 w	5 w	3 w	4 w
Oil exporters	10 w	16 w	10 w	6 w	3 w	3 w	3 w	3 w	3 w
All low-income economies									
Total	22 w	14 w	7 w	5 w	17 w	9 w	10 w	8 w	7 w
Excluding China and India	17 w	15 w	9 w	7 w	16 w	14 w	4 w	4 w	4 w
South Asia	29 w	12 w	10 w	4 w	35 w	13 w	11 w	7 w	7 w
Excluding India	28 w	16 w	15 w	4 w	23 w	15 w	6 w	6 w	6 w

Note: Summary measures include estimates for missing country data. Summary measures are weighted by total merchandise imports of individual countries in current dollars.

Machinery and transport equipment			Other manufactures			
1965	1980	1987	1965	1980	1987	
						Sub-Saharan Africa
30 w	31 w	32 w	45 w	39 w	41 w	Total
29 w	29 w	32 w	44 w	35 w	39 w	Excluding Nigeria
30 w	31 w	34 w	44 w	39 w	41 w	Low-income economies
30 w	30 w	34 w	44 w	33 w	37 w	Excluding Nigeria
37	28	37	44	36	39	Ethiopia
23	..	..	42	..	..	Chad
33	32	37	37	36	42	Zaire
..	..	..	..	..	..	Guinea-Bissau
21	34	33	57	41	49	Malawi
24	..	..	45	..	..	Mozambique
34	35	44	45	28	31	Tanzania
19	29	34	40	34	42	Burkina Faso
25	34	30	48	39	30	Madagascar
23	39	44	47	26	27	Mali
19	19	10	52	60	30	Gambia, The
15	20	23	55	47	55	Burundi
33	35	39	45	37	41	Zambia
21	27	31	55	29	20	Niger
38	39	46	51	32	38	Uganda
..	..	..	..	..	..	São Tomé and Principe
24	35	47	33	27	32	Somalia
31	20	28	45	38	40	Togo
28	30	30	50	45	35	Rwanda
30	18	20	41	44	49	Sierra Leone
17	21	16	53	49	37	Benin
29	34	39	49	41	43	Central African Republic
34	28	34	42	28	33	Kenya
21	29	26	47	31	32	Sudan
..	..	..	..	..	..	Comoros
6	14	26	35	49	90	Lesotho
34	33	36	48	45	50	Nigeria
33	30	36	48	31	37	Ghana
56	36	35	30	25	27	Mauritania
34	28	29	39	23	29	Liberia
..	..	..	..	..	..	*Equatorial Guinea*
..	..	..	..	..	..	*Guinea*
27 w	28 w	30 w	45 w	37 w	43 w	Middle-income economies
..	..	..	..	..	..	Cape Verde
15	23	16	38	25	33	Senegal
31	30	36	46	35	43	Zimbabwe
..	..	..	..	..	..	Swaziland
28	28	28	46	35	35	Côte d'Ivoire
34	23	27	44	42	46	Congo, People's Republic
28	34	36	51	44	46	Cameroon
18	17	20	46	45	48	Botswana
16	16	20	43	39	48	Mauritius
38	37	38	40	41	39	Gabon
16	29	25	33	24	41	Seychelles
..	..	..	..	..	..	*Angola*
..	..	..	..	..	..	*Djibouti*
33 w	32 w	36 w	45 w	41 w	42 w	Six most populous economies
19 w	28 w	27 w	39 w	29 w	31 w	Sahelian economies
33 w	33 w	34 w	47 w	45 w	46 w	Oil exporters
						All low-income economies
28 w	27 w	34 w	34 w	34 w	43 w	Total
29 w	30 w	33 w	40 w	35 w	37 w	Excluding China and India
32 w	19 w	26 w	26 w	28 w	43 w	South Asia
26 w	26 w	30 w	33 w	30 w	35 w	Excluding India

Table 14. Structure of merchandise exports (percentage share)

	Fuels, minerals, and metals			Other primary commodities			Machinery and transport equipment		
	1965	1980	1987	1965	1980	1987	1965	1980	1987
Sub-Saharan Africa									
Total	34 w	71 w	47 w	58 w	25 w	39 w	1 w	1 w	2 w
Excluding Nigeria	36 w	43 w	33 w	60 w	49 w	52 w	1 w	1 w	2 w
Low-income economies	37 w	80 w	61 w	55 w	18 w	33 w	0 w	0 w	1 w
Excluding Nigeria	39 w	44 w	38 w	54 w	50 w	54 w	0 w	1 w	1 w
1 Ethiopia	1	7	3	98	92	96	1	0	0
2 Chad	4	..	..	93	..	..	0	..	..
3 Zaire	72	59	63	20	35	31	0	1	1
4 Guinea-Bissau	..	..	..	..	..	..	..	..	..
5 Malawi	0	0	0	99	89	84	0	4	5
6 Mozambique	14	..	..	83	..	..	0	..	..
7 Tanzania	4	10	7	83	74	75	0	1	3
8 Burkina Faso	1	0	0	94	89	98	1	2	1
9 Madagascar	4	9	11	90	85	78	1	2	2
10 Mali	1	0	0	96	83	71	1	0	1
11 Gambia, The	0	1	1	100	96	92	0	0	0
12 Burundi	1	1	1	94	92	85	0	0	0
13 Zambia	97	98	93	3	1	4	0	0	1
14 Niger	0	86	86	95	12	13	1	1	0
15 Uganda	14	3	4	86	97	96	0	0	0
16 São Tomé and Principe	..	..	..	..	..	..	..	..	..
17 Somalia	6	5	1	80	94	98	4	0	0
18 Togo	49	76	66	48	16	26	1	1	1
19 Rwanda	40	36	9	60	63	90	0	0	0
20 Sierra Leone	25	13	22	14	31	19	0	0	1
21 Benin	1	51	42	94	45	38	2	1	6
22 Central African Republic	1	0	0	45	74	66	0	0	0
23 Kenya	13	34	21	81	50	62	0	3	2
24 Sudan	1	1	14	98	96	79	1	2	3
25 Comoros	..	..	..	..	..	..	..	..	..
26 Lesotho	0	0	0	91	76	64	0	0	0
27 Nigeria	32	96	91	65	3	8	0	0	0
28 Ghana	13	31	37	85	67	60	1	0	0
29 Mauritania	94	76	31	5	23	66	1	0	0
30 Liberia	72	59	57	25	38	41	1	1	0
31 *Equatorial Guinea*	..	..	..	..	..	..	..	..	..
32 *Guinea*	..	..	..	..	..	..	..	..	..
Middle-income economies	25 w	41 w	29 w	70 w	48 w	51 w	1 w	2 w	3 w
33 Cape Verde	..	..	..	..	..	..	..	..	..
34 Senegal	9	39	25	88	46	60	1	3	4
35 Zimbabwe	45	22	17	40	49	43	1	2	3
36 Swaziland	..	..	..	..	..	..	..	..	..
37 Côte d'Ivoire	2	6	4	93	84	86	1	2	2
38 Congo, People's Republic	5	88	67	32	6	17	2	0	1
39 Cameroon	17	37	51	77	60	40	3	1	5
40 Botswana	18	21	20	78	9	17	2	2	3
41 Mauritius	0	0	0	100	71	59	0	4	2
42 Gabon	50	91	63	39	7	26	1	0	2
43 Seychelles	12	74	80	85	23	16	0	1	5
44 *Angola*	..	..	..	..	..	..	..	..	..
45 *Djibouti*	..	..	..	..	..	..	..	..	..
Six most populous economies	29 w	86 w	72 w	66 w	12 w	24 w	0 w	0 w	1 w
Sahelian economies	24 w	50 w	31 w	68 w	41 w	57 w	1 w	1 w	2 w
Oil exporters	28 w	93 w	73 w	57 w	7 w	14 w	0 w	0 w	1 w
All low-income economies									
Total	22 w	58 w	29 w	53 w	23 w	22 w	1 w	2 w	4 w
Excluding China and India	30 w	73 w	48 w	58 w	22 w	27 w	1 w	1 w	3 w
South Asia	6 w	7 w	8 w	57 w	38 w	28 w	1 w	5 w	8 w
Excluding India	2 w	8 w	5 w	74 w	51 w	37 w	0 w	2 w	5 w

Note: Summary measures include estimates for missing country data. The summary measures are weighted by total merchandise exports of individual countries in current dollars.

Other manufactures			(Textiles and clothing)[a]			
1965	1980	1987	1965	1980	1987	
						Sub-Saharan Africa
6 w	4 w	10 w	0 w	1 w	..	Total
7 w	9 w	14 w	0 w	1 w	..	Excluding Nigeria
5 w	2 w	5 w	0 w	0 w	..	Low-income economies
6 w	6 w	7 w	0 w	1 w	..	Excluding Nigeria
0	0	1	0	0	0	Ethiopia
4	..	..	0	..	..	Chad
8	6	5	0	0	..	Zaire
..	..	..	..	..	..	Guinea-Bissau
1	7	11	0	5	..	Malawi
2	..	..	1	..	..	Mozambique
13	14	15	0	8	..	Tanzania
4	8	1	2	1	..	Burkina Faso
4	4	9	1	2	3	Madagascar
2	16	28	1	1	..	Mali
0	4	7	..	1	..	Gambia, The
6	7	15	0	0	..	Burundi
0	1	2	0	0	..	Zambia
4	2	1	1	1	..	Niger
1	0	0	0	0	..	Uganda
..	..	..	..	..	..	São Tomé and Principe
10	1	1	0	0	..	Somalia
3	6	7	0	1	..	Togo
1	1	1	0	0	..	Rwanda
60	56	58	0	0	..	Sierra Leone
3	3	15	0	0	..	Benin
54	26	33	0	..	..	Central African Republic
6	12	15	0	1	..	Kenya
0	1	4	0	1	..	Sudan
..	..	..	..	..	..	Comoros
9	24	36	..	..	..	Lesotho
2	0	1	0	0	..	Nigeria
2	2	2	0	0	..	Ghana
0	2	2	0	0	..	Mauritania
3	2	1	0	0	..	Liberia
..	..	..	..	..	..	*Equatorial Guinea*
..	..	..	..	..	..	*Guinea*
10 w	12 w	19 w	..	..	..	Middle-income economies
..	..	..	..	..	..	Cape Verde
2	12	11	1	1	..	Senegal
15	26	37	6	0	..	Zimbabwe
..	..	..	..	..	..	Swaziland
4	7	7	1	1	1	Côte d'Ivoire
61	6	15	0	0	0	Congo, People's Republic
2	3	4	0	1	1	Cameroon
2	68	61	..	..	..	Botswana
0	25	38	0	19	..	Mauritius
10	1	8	0	..	..	Gabon
3	3	0	..	0	0	Seychelles
..	..	..	..	..	..	*Angola*
..	..	..	..	..	..	*Djibouti*
5 w	2 w	4 w	0 w	0 w	..	Six most populous economies
2 w	7 w	8 w	..	1 w	..	Sahelian economies
5 w	1 w	3 w	0 w	0 w	..	Oil exporters
						All low-income economies
23 w	17	45	11 w	5 w	7 w	Total
8 w	5	21	4 w	3 w	9 w	Excluding China and India
36 w	49	56	27 w	24 w	23 w	South Asia
20 w	39	52	15 w	31 w	37 w	Excluding India

a. Textiles and clothing is a subgroup of other manufactures.

Table 15. Major agricultural exports

	Volume (thousands of metric tons)			Volume growth (percent)			Percentage of total merchandise exports value		
	1965	1980	1987	1965-73	1973-80	1980-87	1965	1980	1987
Ethiopia									
Coffee	82	76	73	0.2	2.9	1.2	66.5	64.1	50.5
Sesame seed	22	8	7	17.3	-37.8	-8.7	3.6	1.6	1.2
Sugar	(.)	11	11	173.3	-30.5	11.5	0.0	0.5	0.5
Chad									
Cotton	38	35	30	0.1	0.9	2.2	78.1	54.2	..
Oilseed cake and meal	1	2	0	-8.5	19.4	4.6	0.2	0.4	..
Zaire									
Cocoa	5	4	5	3.4	-3.8	3.5	0.5	0.3	0.5
Coffee	23	74	99	13.8	-0.1	6.7	4.3	6.6	10.9
Palm kernel oil	33	19	10	1.8	-10.7	-5.8	2.7	0.4	0.2
Guinea–Bissau									
Cotton	0	0	(.)	0.0	0.0	0.0	..	..	..
Groundnuts (shelled)	15	7	5	-3.0	-2.0	-7.5	..	25.7	..
Palm kernels	9	6	5	-10.2	7.7	-6.5	..	17.6	..
Malawi									
Tea	13	31	33	5.7	4.5	2.3	27.8	12.9	10.5
Tobacco	17	61	61	5.5	13.7	3.9	37.6	44.2	64.2
Sugar	(.)	92	66	89.4	24.0	-4.0	..	16.3	8.4
Mozambique									
Cotton	31	6	20	4.0	-21.5	5.8	17.8	2.9	..
Groundnut oil	9	0	3	-3.5	0.0	0.0	3.1	..	..
Sugar	95	64	25	8.5	-12.7	-15.8	9.4	8.8	..
Tanzania									
Coffee	28	43	47	4.5	-2.6	-1.0	13.7	26.8	39.1
Cotton	56	31	41	-1.3	-6.5	-1.6	19.5	9.1	12.4
Tobacco	3	8	7	11.2	-1.5	-5.3	1.8	2.4	4.6
Burkina Faso									
Cotton	2	28	49	21.7	14.9	10.6	5.8	24.6	21.3
Groundnuts (shelled)	4	1	4	8.3	-46.0	-47.4	3.6	0.3	0.5
Sesame seed	3	4	4	8.5	0.9	5.3	2.0	1.3	0.5
Madagascar									
Coffee	50	69	46	11.0	6.0	7.4	31.4	53.3	31.2
Cotton	(.)	1	6	0.0	0.0	12.7	0.2	0.4	1.8
Sugar	36	26	52	-6.4	-3.4	0.0	5.1	2.9	6.0
Mali									
Cotton	9	53	41	16.5	16.5	2.2	16.6	38.5	21.3
Groundnut oil	0	5	1	141.6	22.7	-25.7	..	1.7	0.3
Oilseed cake and meal	3	15	12	26.0	2.5	-3.8	3.6	1.0	0.8
Gambia									
Groundnut oil	16	10	10	-1.7	-9.4	-3.3	14.6	23.2	20.6
Groundnuts (shelled)	34	44	23	-0.3	-0.6	-6.8	51.8	57.7	40.0
Oilseed cake and meal	16	13	13	-4.1	-7.5	0.5	14.6	8.2	2.3
Burundi									
Coffee	13	19	27	7.0	-1.0	5.7	62.7	89.5	41.8
Cotton	3	1	3	-0.4	-5.2	-7.5	14.1	2.0	7.0
Tea	0	1	4	58.6	11.2	16.6	..	2.3	3.6
Zambia									
Coffee	0	0	1	0.0	0.0	0.0	..	..	0.3
Tobacco	10	3	6	-6.2	-15.3	13.4	1.3	0.3	1.4
Sugar	2	0	24	0.0	0.0	145.3	0.1	..	0.8
Niger									
Cotton	2	(.)	2	-7.8	13.9	0.0	4.2	0.1	0.6
Oilseed cake and meal	7	1	1	14.1	-27.5	-1.1	1.5	0.0	0.0
Uganda									
Coffee	158	110	150	4.3	-9.6	2.6	48.4	98.2	136.8
Cotton	69	2	4	-0.4	-36.3	16.7	26.7	1.2	2.0
Tea	7	1	3	13.9	-37.3	28.2	3.9	0.1	1.3

Note: (.) indicates amount less than 500 metric tons.

	Volume (thousands of metric tons)			Volume growth (percent)			Percentage of total merchandise exports value		
	1965	1980	1987	1965-73	1973-80	1980-87	1965	1980	1987
São Tomé and Principe									
Cocoa	9	7	3	2.3	-4.2	-14.4	..	97.2	..
Coffee	(.)	(.)	(.)	-12.9	-11.1	-4.1	..	0.3	..
Palm kernels	4	(.)	0	-8.3	-18.2	0.0	..	0.8	..
Somalia									
Bananas	99	50	55	3.5	-12.4	3.3	44.5	8.2	13.6
Togo									
Cocoa	17	15	12	5.4	-2.5	-4.1	19.5	8.1	8.8
Coffee	11	9	9	2.3	-3.2	-2.1	15.8	5.0	8.1
Cotton	2	5	30	-6.6	15.5	27.4	3.3	1.7	12.5
Rwanda									
Coffee	10	22	46	7.1	1.5	9.4	61.3	32.8	69.2
Tea	(.)	7	9	34.8	12.5	7.1	1.9	9.6	9.2
Sierra Leone									
Cocoa	3	9	9	9.9	3.5	0.8	1.4	11.0	18.8
Coffee	4	10	6	16.8	6.6	-6.3	2.1	13.5	9.2
Tobacco	0	0	(.)	0.0	0.0	46.3	..	..	1.9
Benin									
Cocoa	0	5	6	0.0	-6.9	0.0	..	6.4	9.0
Cotton	1	8	42	39.5	-15.1	34.2	3.5	5.2	40.5
Palm oil	13	13	12	-4.0	6.3	7.7	16.7	2.9	2.7
Central African Republic									
Coffee	8	11	12	-3.9	4.7	-0.1	12.3	21.5	11.2
Cotton	9	14	10	5.3	-2.2	1.8	15.2	12.3	6.5
Tobacco	(.)	1	1	8.1	3.6	-12.5	0.6	0.7	1.0
Kenya									
Coffee	39	80	100	6.3	2.6	4.4	17.4	20.9	24.1
Maize	(.)	(.)	280	22.3	-56.3	244.4	0.0	0.0	2.6
Tea	23	84	150	11.4	10.1	9.5	10.0	12.3	22.0
Sudan									
Cotton	106	132	174	9.7	-1.3	10.8	45.7	39.7	38.4
Oilseed cake and meal	166	212	106	0.3	8.3	-17.0	5.5	5.1	3.2
Sesame seed	71	57	60	3.9	-13.9	-4.6	7.0	8.4	9.3
Comoros									
Lesotho									
Wheat	3	0	0	1.5	..	..	0.9	..	..
Nigeria									
Cocoa	306	154	97	0.3	-7.5	-6.3	16.2	1.2	2.2
Palm kernels	422	96	84	-8.7	-10.5	-0.6	10.1	0.1	0.1
Rubber	69	15	48	-4.6	-15.6	13.2	4.2	0.1	0.5
Ghana									
Bananas	1	(.)	(.)	-47.0	..	..	0.0	0.0	0.0
Cocoa	554	223	224	-1.6	-9.4	-1.0	70.4	58.9	46.4
Coffee	2	(.)	1	2.8	-32.2	7.8	0.3	0.0	0.1
Mauritania									
Liberia									
Cocoa	1	4	3	14.2	4.5	-4.2	0.2	1.8	1.6
Coffee	1	4	3	3.8	14.9	-8.0	1.3	5.5	2.5
Rubber	53	77	84	6.9	-2.2	2.7	20.7	17.1	22.1
Equatorial Guinea									
Cocoa	28	7	6	-13.6	-4.0	-2.8	..	74.7	..
Coffee	7	(.)	1	-2.3	-41.7	21.0	..	4.7	..
Guinea									
Cocoa	2	4	4	0.0	11.5	0.0	..	1.9	..
Coffee	11	3	5	-5.7	-8.5	-3.1	..	2.5	..
Oilseed cake and meal	0	0	10	0.0	0.0	114.9	..	..	..
Cape Verde									
Bananas	3	1	1	-6.2	5.4	1.9	..	5.5	..

Table 15. Major agricultural exports — continued

	Volume (thousands of metric tons)			Volume growth (percent)			Percentage of total merchandise exports value		
	1965	1980	1987	1965-73	1973-80	1980-87	1965	1980	1987
Senegal									
Cotton	0	6	5	73.5	6.2	5.7	..	2.1	0.9
Groundnut oil	143	74	105	-4.9	-2.8	5.4	41.6	12.8	7.1
Oilseed cake and meal	197	104	158	-0.6	-4.6	4.5	8.1	4.6	2.8
Zimbabwe									
Cotton	1	54	66	55.9	5.2	5.5	0.1	6.3	5.9
Tobacco	123	93	100	1.9	1.6	-0.4	33.5	12.8	21.3
Sugar	254	169	283	2.5	3.2	6.6	5.0	5.2	4.1
Swaziland									
Cotton	1	4	5	10.4	11.0	-3.9	..	1.9	1.5
Tobacco	0	(.)	(.)	14.8	-0.5	-18.5	..	0.1	0.0
Sugar	100	300	436	6.8	7.6	5.8	..	44.9	35.1
Côte d' Ivoire									
Cocoa	140	338	543	4.6	6.1	6.2	17.6	29.9	36.6
Coffee	186	210	163	1.7	-1.1	-2.9	36.6	22.0	13.7
Cotton	2	39	68	26.3	14.1	10.7	0.2	2.2	2.5
Congo									
Cocoa	1	2	1	7.6	2.0	-7.2	0.7	0.6	0.3
Coffee	(.)	2	1	2.9	21.0	-11.3	0.8	0.6	0.2
Sugar	7	(.)	24	7.3	-58.9	85.6	1.2	0.0	1.0
Cameroon									
Cocoa	94	106	133	1.7	-1.7	3.1	31.1	20.1	13.9
Coffee	48	92	50	3.3	-0.2	-6.4	26.7	21.0	7.5
Cotton	16	26	21	-1.9	11.5	-4.4	7.6	2.9	1.6
Botswana									
Cotton	2	1	0	0.0	0.0	0.0	2.2	0.1	..
Groundnuts (shelled)	(.)	(.)	(.)	0.0	0.0	0.0	0.0	0.0	0.0
Mauritius									
Maize	(.)	(.)	5	0.0	0.0	0.0	0.0	0.0	0.1
Tea	1	4	7	18.0	2.8	10.6	2.0	1.3	0.8
Sugar	569	618	657	1.9	-0.6	2.1	96.0	65.4	36.6
Gabon									
Cocoa	3	4	2	1.5	2.9	-12.4	1.0	0.5	0.3
Coffee	1	1	1	-15.2	15.9	2.5	0.4	0.1	0.1
Palm oil	1	0	2	-15.3	0.0	0.0	0.3	..	0.0
Seychelles									
Angola									
Coffee	159	47	11	2.4	-21.9	-19.0	46.7	9.7	..
Cotton	5	0	1	25.0	-11.9	0.0	1.5	..	..
Tobacco	2	2	0	3.0	-15.5	5.9	0.7	0.2	..
Djibouti									

Note: (.) indicates amount less than 500 metric tons.

Table 16. Origin and destination of merchandise exports

	Merchandise exports (millions of dollars)			Destination of merchandise exports (percentage of total)								
				High-income economies			Middle- and low-income economies			Nonreporting nonmember economies		
	1965	1980	1987	1965	1980	1987	1965	1980	1987	1965	1980	1987
Sub-Saharan Africa												
Total	4,910 t	51,729 t	30,463 t	81 w	83 w	..	18 w	16 w	..	..	..	..
Excluding Nigeria	4,173 t	25,761 t	22,988 t	79 w	71 w	..	21 w	27 w	..	..	..	..
Low-income economies	3,595 t	39,062 t	17,332 t	80 w	85 w	..	19 w	14 w	..	..	..	..
Excluding Nigeria	2,858 t	13,094 t	9,857 t	..	66 w	..	..	31 w	..	..	..	..
1 Ethiopia	113	425	402	84	64	74	13	25	17	3	11	8
2 Chad	27	72	..	65	57	..	35	43	..	..	..	..
3 Zaire	336	2,507	1,594	93	45	..	7	55	..	0	..	..
4 Guinea-Bissau	..	11	..	..	51	..	..	49	..	..	..	..
5 Malawi	38	285	264	71	75	..	29	25	..	0	..	..
6 Mozambique	108	281	..	25	62	..	71	38	..	4	..	..
7 Tanzania	175	537	348	76	60	..	24	37	..	0	3	..
8 Burkina Faso	18	161	202	17	45	..	83	55	..	..	..	..
9 Madagascar	92	402	310	85	78	84	15	21	13	0	1	3
10 Mali	16	205	216	7	68	..	89	32	..	4	..	..
11 Gambia, The	13	31	35	90	92	..	10	8	..	5	..	..
12 Burundi	16	65	139	24	74	..	76	26	..	..	..	..
13 Zambia	525	1,360	869	..	..	..	..	..	..	..	..	..
14 Niger	25	580	361	61	80	..	39	20	..	0	..	..
15 Uganda	176	345	221	74	89	..	26	11	..	0	..	..
16 São Tomé and Principe	..	18	..	..	90	..	..	10	..	..	..	..
17 Somalia	34	133	118	43	92	..	57	8	..	0	0	..
18 Togo	35	476	272	92	60	..	6	40	..	2	0	..
19 Rwanda	12	134	133	96	86	..	4	14	..	..	..	..
20 Sierra Leone	88	207	120	92	95	..	8	5	..	0	..	..
21 Benin	18	223	121	88	74	..	12	26	..	0	..	..
22 Central African Republic	33	147	154	94	93	..	6	7	..	0	..	..
23 Kenya	228	1,389	985	71	51	..	28	49	..	1	0	..
24 Sudan	196	594	482	61	66	..	31	31	..	9	2	..
25 Comoros	..	11	..	87	91	..	13	9	..	..	..	..
26 Lesotho	7	58	28	..	93	..	7	7	..	1	..	..
27 Nigeria	737	25,968	7,475	91	93	..	7	7	..	14	18	..
28 Ghana	292	1,257	1,056	75	76	..	11	7	..	0	..	..
29 Mauritania	58	196	428	96	86	..	4	14	..	..	0	0
30 Liberia	135	597	385	98	93	92	2	7	8	..	0	0
31 *Equatorial Guinea*	..	15	..	..	74	..	..	26	..	..	..	..
32 *Guinea*	..	374	..	..	91	..	..	9	..	..	..	..
Middle-income economies	1,314 t	12,667 t	13,086 t	84 w	77 w	..	..	23 w	..	..	1 w	..
33 Cape Verde	..	9	..	4	19	2	95	79	98	0	2	0
34 Senegal	128	477	723	92	50	..	7	49	..	0	0	..
35 Zimbabwe	399	1,423	1,358	51	79	..	47	21	..	1	..	..
36 Swaziland	..	368	311	..	..	..	..	..	..	..	..	..
37 Côte d'Ivoire	277	3,142	2,961	85	79	71	14	21	24	1	0	5
38 Congo, People's Republic	38	980	884	90	80	94	9	20	4	1	0	1
39 Cameroon	119	1,447	1,714	93	94	77	7	5	22	0	0	2
40 Botswana	14	503	1,010	..	..	..	..	..	..	..	..	..
41 Mauritius	62	431	918	95	96	..	5	4	..	..	0	..
42 Gabon	100	2,173	1,285	91	65	..	8	35	..	0	0	..
43 Seychelles	2	21	24	43	19	15	57	81	85	..	..	0
44 *Angola*	200	1,682	..	55	75	..	45	21	..	0	3	..
45 *Djibouti*	..	12	..	..	28	..	..	72	..	..	..	..
Six most populous economies	1,785 t	31,419 t	11,285 t	82 w	86 w	..	19 w	14 w	..	..	..	..
Sahelian economies	289 t	1,741 t	2,123 t	..	68 w	..	..	32 w	..	..	..	..
Oil exporters	1,166 t	32,249 t	13,272 t	87 w	90 w	..	9 w	10 w	..	..	..	..
All low-income economies												
Total	10,202 t	95,465 t	97,357 t	68 w	81	..	..	16 w	..	..	..	..
Excluding China and India	6,263 t	68,868 t	45,029 t	71 w	84	..	27 w	15 w	..	..	..	..
South Asia	3,171 t	13,368 t	19,621 t	57 w	56	..	32 w	31 w	..	11 w	13 w	..
Excluding India	1,549 t	5,036 t	7,073 t	53 w	53	71	41 w	44 w	26 w	..	4 w	4 w

Note: Summary measures include estimates for missing country data. The weighting process may result in discrepancies between summed subgroup figures and overall totals. Summary measure percentages are weighted by merchandise exports of individual countries in current dollars.

Table 17. Origin and destination of manufactured exports

| | Manufactured exports (millions of dollars) | | | Destination of manufactured exports (percentage of total) | | | | | | | | |
| | | | | High-income economies | | | Middle- and low-income economies | | | Nonreporting nonmember economies | | |
	1965	1980	1987	1965	1980	1987	1965	1980	1987	1965	1980	1987
Sub-Saharan Africa												
Total	332 t	2,556 t	3,629 t	..	48 w	..	..	52 w	..	..	..	..
Excluding Nigeria	315 t	2,426 t	3,509 t	..	46 w	..	..	54 w	..	..	..	..
Low-income economies	194 t	1,027 t	923 t	..	33 w	..	..	67 w	..	..	..	..
Excluding Nigeria	177 t	897 t	803 t	..	29 w	..	..	71 w	..	..	..	..
1 Ethiopia	1	1	4	87	52	67	13	40	13	0	8	21
2 Chad	1	..	..	6	21	..	94	79	..	..	..	..
3 Zaire	28	158	94	93	15	..	7	85	..	0	..	..
4 Guinea-Bissau	..	..	..	..	47	..	..	53	..	..	..	..
5 Malawi	0	31	42	3	19	..	97	81	..	1	..	..
6 Mozambique	3	..	..	27	31	..	68	69	..	5	..	..
7 Tanzania	23	83	63	93	59	..	7	41	..	0	0	..
8 Burkina Faso	1	17	4	2	27	..	98	73	..	..	..	..
9 Madagascar	5	24	34	81	93	79	19	7	21	..	0	0
10 Mali	0	34	61	14	9	..	78	91	..	8	..	..
11 Gambia, The	0	1	3	98	51	..	2	49	..	..	..	..
12 Burundi	1	4	20	0	5	..	100	95	..	..	..	..
13 Zambia	1	13	23	..	..	..	..	..	..	..	..	..
14 Niger	1	12	6	43	31	..	57	69	..	..	..	..
15 Uganda	1	1	1	7	53	..	93	47	..	0	..	..
16 São Tomé and Principe	..	..	..	..	80	..	..	20	..	..	..	..
17 Somalia	5	1	1	23	72	..	77	26	..	0	3	..
18 Togo	1	35	22	37	12	..	62	88	..	0	..	..
19 Rwanda	0	1	2	95	70	..	5	30	..	..	..	..
20 Sierra Leone	53	116	70	99	89	..	1	11	..	0	..	..
21 Benin	1	10	25	15	12	..	85	88	..	0	..	..
22 Central African Republic	18	39	52	99	99	..	1	1	..	..	..	..
23 Kenya	14	210	164	26	13	..	74	87	..	0	0	..
24 Sudan	2	15	35	80	52	..	20	48	..	0	0	..
25 Comoros	..	..	..	100	99	..	0	1	..	..	..	..
26 Lesotho	1	14	11	..	..	..	..	..	..	..	..	..
27 Nigeria	17	130	120	85	101	..	14	-1	..	0	..	..
28 Ghana	7	25	28	61	82	..	29	18	..	10	0	..
29 Mauritania	1	4	10	61	69	..	39	31	..	..	..	..
30 Liberia	4	20	5	78	51	61	22	49	39	..	..	0
31 *Equatorial Guinea*	..	..	..	..	84	..	..	16	..	..	..	..
32 *Guinea*	..	..	..	..	39	..	..	61	..	..	..	..
Middle-income economies	149 t	1,703 t	3,056 t	..	77 w	..	..	23 w	..	..	..	..
33 Cape Verde	..	..	..	4	..	1	95	65	99	0	35	..
34 Senegal	4	72	108	48	31	..	52	69	..	0	0	..
35 Zimbabwe	61	404	550	12	81	..	86	19	..	2	..	..
36 Swaziland	..	..	..	..	..	..	..	..	..	..	..	..
37 Côte d'Ivoire	15	295	283	50	51	32	50	49	68	0	0	0
38 Congo, People's Republic	24	64	137	93	88	52	6	12	17	1	0	31
39 Cameroon	6	50	152	46	77	28	54	23	72	0	0	0
40 Botswana	1	353	641	..	..	..	..	..	..	..	..	..
41 Mauritius	0	125	486	16	89	..	84	11	..	..	0	..
42 Gabon	10	26	135	73	..	..	27	..	..	0	..	..
43 Seychelles	0	1	1	43	71	69	57	29	31	..	..	0
44 *Angola*	..	..	..	3	98	..	97	2	..	0	0	..
45 *Djibouti*	..	..	..	..	53	..	..	47	..	..	..	..
Six most populous economies	86 t	597 t	480 t	..	25 w	..	..	75 w	..	..	..	..
Sahelian economies	8 t	148 t	203 t	..	26 w	..	..	74 w	..	..	..	..
Oil exporters	61 t	287 t	579 t	..	95 w	..	..	5 w	..	..	..	..
All low-income economies												
Total	2,478 t	18,257 t	47,468 t	59 w	59 w	..	..	32 w	..	..	..	..
Excluding China and India	572 t	3,978 t	10,371 t	61 w	57 w	..	..	41 w	..	..	..	..
South Asia	1,156 t	7,256 t	12,714 t	55 w	62 w	..	35 w	25 w	..	10 w	14	..
Excluding India	308 t	2,079 t	4,053 t	44 w	65 w	80 w	..	31 w	17 w	8 w	5	4

Note: Summary measures include estimates for missing country data. The weighting process may result in discrepancies between summed subgroup figures and overall totals. Summary measure percentages are weighted by manufactured exports of individual countries in current dollars.

Table 18. Official development assistance

| | Millions of dollars | | | | | Bilateral (percentage of total) | | Per capita (dollars) | | Grants as percentage of net ODA | | | |
| | | | | | | | | | | Total grants | | Technical assistance | |
	1975	1980	1985	1986	1987	1980	1987	1980	1987	1980	1987	1980	1987
Sub-Saharan Africa													
Total	3,237	7,126	8,222	10,016	11,066	68	66	20	25	71	66	30	26
Excluding Nigeria	3,155	7,091	8,190	9,957	10,996	68	66	25	32	71	66	30	26
Low-income economies	2,618	5,729	6,952	8,179	8,965	66	63	18	23	71	67	27	25
Excluding Nigeria	2,536	5,694	6,920	8,120	8,895	66	63	24	31	70	66	27	25
1 Ethiopia	134	212	715	636	635	43	49	6	14	80	78	21	23
2 Chad	70	35	182	165	198	57	60	8	37	94	80	34	26
3 Zaire	205	428	325	448	620	75	54	16	19	62	43	39	25
4 Guinea-Bissau	19	59	58	71	104	61	48	73	116	83	65	20	26
5 Malawi	63	143	113	198	280	52	61	24	35	59	69	25	20
6 Mozambique	..	..	..	..	..	..	..	..	..	..	..	..	..
7 Tanzania	295	679	487	681	882	81	81	36	37	97	75	26	21
8 Burkina Faso	89	212	197	284	283	71	71	31	34	76	74	34	35
9 Madagascar	85	230	187	316	327	60	54	26	30	35	39	22	18
10 Mali	144	267	380	372	364	61	63	41	47	67	71	29	24
11 Gambia, The	8	54	50	101	103	43	49	85	129	72	66	22	20
12 Burundi	48	117	142	187	192	54	51	28	38	72	44	39	27
13 Zambia	87	318	328	464	429	81	80	56	60	50	73	27	24
14 Niger	140	170	304	307	348	62	62	31	51	67	66	37	27
15 Uganda	48	114	182	198	276	39	32	9	18	73	55	18	20
16 São Tomé and Principe	1	4	12	12	18	25	22	42	180	100	67	25	17
17 Somalia	152	433	353	511	580	62	69	93	102	85	76	22	25
18 Togo	42	91	114	174	123	57	72	35	38	48	70	32	36
19 Rwanda	91	155	181	211	242	63	58	30	38	79	62	36	31
20 Sierra Leone	18	91	66	87	68	67	69	28	18	51	82	23	41
21 Benin	54	90	95	138	136	41	57	26	32	74	79	29	99
22 Central African Republic	57	111	104	139	173	69	68	49	64	81	53	31	28
23 Kenya	129	397	438	455	565	70	78	24	26	63	71	32	27
24 Sudan	265	583	1,128	945	901	67	72	31	39	84	79	18	16
25 Comoros	22	43	47	46	53	70	60	129	133	58	76	16	34
26 Lesotho	30	94	94	88	108	64	54	69	68	89	80	34	36
27 Nigeria	82	35	32	59	69	49	74	0	1	143	99	134	77
28 Ghana	126	191	203	371	373	69	34	18	27	34	39	22	12
29 Mauritania	68	176	207	221	178	80	57	114	94	51	64	17	26
30 Liberia	21	98	90	97	78	70	65	53	34	48	65	25	40
31 *Equatorial Guinea*	2	9	17	22	42	11	50	26	105	33	52	22	14
32 *Guinea*	25	89	119	175	214	36	61	16	33	49	47	21	17
Middle-income economies	619	1,397	1,270	1,837	2,101	74	77	33	39	73	62	41	31
33 Cape Verde	9	64	70	109	86	64	71	216	287	81	94	19	31
34 Senegal	140	263	294	567	642	70	60	46	92	76	53	46	20
35 Zimbabwe	4	164	237	225	295	71	90	23	33	120	72	43	30
36 Swaziland	16	50	25	35	45	64	64	89	64	68	87	44	47
37 Côte d'Ivoire	101	210	124	186	254	72	87	25	22	60	47	47	31
38 Congo, People's Republic	56	92	71	110	152	76	86	57	76	62	36	40	32
39 Cameroon	111	265	159	224	211	73	85	31	19	43	67	32	43
40 Botswana	51	106	96	102	154	78	80	118	140	93	96	44	32
41 Mauritius	29	33	28	56	65	76	82	34	65	73	63	33	35
42 Gabon	60	55	61	79	81	89	91	69	74	75	61	67	49
43 Seychelles	7	21	22	28	24	86	79	333	240	62	67	38	38
44 *Angola*	..	..	..	..	..	..	..	..	..	..	..	..	..
45 *Djibouti*	34	73	81	115	92	88	76	243	230	78	76	38	40
Six most populous economies	1,110	2,333	3,125	3,224	3,673	71	68	12	15	81	71	28	23
Sahelian economies	687	1,301	1,741	2,196	2,307	67	62	40	59	71	66	32	25
Oil exporters	310	448	323	473	514	74	85	4	4	58	61	46	45
All low-income economies													
Total													
Excluding China and India													
South Asia	3,531	5,539	4,630	5,849	5,576	54	55	6	5	54	51	10	16
Excluding India	1,953	3,346	3,038	3,725	3,723	70	57	14	13	66	55	13	17

Note: Summary measures are computed from aggregate values; they do not include estimates for missing country data.

Table 19. Total external debt (millions of dollars)

| | | Long-term debt | | | | | | | | |
| | | Public and publicly guaranteed | | | Private nonguaranteed | | | Use of IMF credit | | |
		1970	1980	1987	1970	1980	1987	1970	1980	1987
Sub-Saharan Africa										
Total										
	Excluding Nigeria										
Low-income economies										
	Excluding Nigeria										
1	Ethiopia	169	701	2,434	0	0	0	0	46	63
2	Chad	33	201	270	0	0	0	3	7	10
3	Zaire	311	4,294	7,334	0	0	0	0	233	833
4	Guinea-Bissau	..	125	391	0	0	0	0	1	2
5	Malawi	122	644	1,155	0	0	0	0	61	110
6	Mozambique	..	..	..	..	..	..	..	..	..
7	Tanzania	250	2,044	4,068	15	93	11	0	119	65
8	Burkina Faso	21	299	794	0	0	0	0	0	0
9	Madagascar	89	956	3,113	0	0	0	0	55	144
10	Mali	238	685	1,847	0	0	0	9	11	75
11	Gambia, The	5	106	273	0	0	0	0	8	23
12	Burundi	7	141	718	0	0	0	8	12	0
13	Zambia	623	2,187	4,354	30	87	0	0	393	957
14	Niger	32	399	1,259	..	305	254	0	0	91
15	Uganda	138	603	1,116	0	0	0	0	61	229
16	São Tomé and Principe	..	23	84	0	0	0	0	0	0
17	Somalia	77	601	1,719	0	0	0	0	4	154
18	Togo	40	913	1,042	0	0	0	0	14	78
19	Rwanda	2	164	544	0	0	0	3	0	0
20	Sierra Leone	59	351	513	0	0	0	0	28	83
21	Benin	41	348	929	0	0	0	0	0	0
22	Central African Republic	24	160	520	0	0	0	0	7	37
23	Kenya	319	2,238	4,482	88	437	496	0	194	381
24	Sudan	307	3,805	8,024	..	325	405	31	342	859
25	Comoros	1	43	188	0	0	0	0	0	0
26	Lesotho	8	63	237	0	0	0	0	0	0
27	Nigeria	452	4,204	27,769	115	1,097	352	0	0	0
28	Ghana	487	1,128	2,207	10	10	30	46	43	778
29	Mauritania	27	734	1,868	0	0	0	0	34	47
30	Liberia	158	573	1,152	0	0	0	4	53	291
31	*Equatorial Guinea*	5	58	175	0	0	0	0	10	8
32	*Guinea*	312	1,032	2,010	0	0	0	3	5	30
Middle-income economies										
33	Cape Verde	..	20	121	0	0	0	0	0	0
34	Senegal	100	958	3,068	31	9	42	0	98	267
35	Zimbabwe	229	695	2,044	..	..	51	0	0	156
36	Swaziland	37	166	273	0	0	0	0	0	3
37	Côte d'Ivoire	255	4,328	8,450	11	414	3,264	0	0	576
38	Congo, People's Republic	124	1,427	3,679	0	0	0	0	6	13
39	Cameroon	131	2,049	2,785	9	178	520	0	15	0
40	Botswana	17	152	514	0	0	0	0	0	0
41	Mauritius	32	296	545	0	24	46	0	90	150
42	Gabon	91	1,308	1,605	0	0	0	0	15	60
43	Seychelles	..	25	124	0	0	0	0	0	0
44	*Angola*	..	..	..	..	..	..	..	..	..
45	*Djibouti*	..	26	152	0	0	0	0	0	0
Six most populous economies										
Sahelian economies										
Oil exporters										
All low-income economies										
Total										
	Excluding China and India										
South Asia										
	Excluding India										

Note: Total external debt for 1970 is presented as .. because there are no data for short-term debt for 1970.

Short-term debt			Total external debt			
1970	1980	1987	1970	1980	1987	
						Sub-Saharan Africa
						Total
						Excluding Nigeria
						Low-income economies
						Excluding Nigeria
..	56	94	..	803	2,590	Ethiopia
..	11	38	..	218	318	Chad
..	296	462	..	4,824	8,630	Zaire
..	5	31	..	131	424	Guinea-Bissau
..	116	98	..	821	1,363	Malawi
..	..	..	..	..	..	Mozambique
..	307	192	..	2,564	4,335	Tanzania
..	35	67	..	334	861	Burkina Faso
..	244	119	..	1,255	3,377	Madagascar
..	24	94	..	720	2,016	Mali
..	23	24	..	137	319	Gambia, The
..	12	37	..	165	755	Burundi
..	586	1,089	..	3,253	6,400	Zambia
..	159	75	..	863	1,679	Niger
..	66	60	..	730	1,405	Uganda
..	0	4	..	23	87	São Tomé and Principe
..	51	92	..	656	1,965	Somalia
..	113	102	..	1,041	1,223	Togo
..	26	39	..	190	583	Rwanda
..	54	63	..	433	659	Sierra Leone
..	68	204	..	416	1,133	Benin
..	24	28	..	191	585	Central African Republic
..	638	591	..	3,507	5,950	Kenya
..	585	2,100	..	5,057	11,388	Sudan
..	1	15	..	44	203	Comoros
..	8	4	..	71	241	Lesotho
..	3,553	1,657	..	8,854	29,778	Nigeria
..	131	108	..	1,312	3,124	Ghana
..	65	119	..	833	2,035	Mauritania
..	81	175	..	708	1,618	Liberia
..	7	11	..	75	193	*Equatorial Guinea*
..	80	138	..	1,117	2,177	*Guinea*
						Middle-income economies
..	0	11	..	20	131	Cape Verde
..	219	319	..	1,284	3,695	Senegal
..	90	260	..	..	2,512	Zimbabwe
..	15	17	..	181	293	Swaziland
..	1,059	1,265	..	5,801	13,555	Côte d'Ivoire
..	244	944	..	1,677	4,636	Congo, People's Republic
..	270	722	..	2,512	4,028	Cameroon
..	4	3	..	156	518	Botswana
..	47	34	..	457	775	Mauritius
..	228	406	..	1,550	2,071	Gabon
..	59	35	..	84	159	Seychelles
..	..	..	..	..	..	*Angola*
..	6	29	..	32	181	*Djibouti*
						Six most populous economies
						Sahelian economies
						Oil exporters
						All low-income economies
						Total
						Excluding China and India
						South Asia
						Excluding India

Table 20. Flow of public and private external capital (millions of dollars)

| | | Disbursements | | | | | | Repayment of principal | | |
| | | Public and publicly guaranteed | | | Private nonguaranteed | | | Public and publicly guaranteed | | |
		1970	1980	1987	1970	1980	1987	1970	1980	1987
Sub-Saharan Africa											
Total											
Excluding Nigeria											
Low-income economies											
Excluding Nigeria											
1	Ethiopia	28	110	403	0	0	0	15	17	130
2	Chad	6	5	51	0	0	0	3	3	3
3	Zaire	32	492	493	0	0	0	28	167	127
4	Guinea-Bissau	..	69	52	0	0	0	..	3	5
5	Malawi	40	158	132	0	0	0	3	33	45
6	Mozambique	..	..	..	..	..	..	..	..	..
7	Tanzania	51	385	107	..	..	..	10	39	46
8	Burkina Faso	2	73	112	0	0	0	2	11	17
9	Madagascar	11	392	229	0	0	0	5	31	64
10	Mali	23	103	117	0	0	0	0	6	19
11	Gambia, The	1	54	37	0	0	0	0	0	10
12	Burundi	1	45	140	0	0	0	0	4	27
13	Zambia	351	631	130	..	..	..	35	182	73
14	Niger	12	177	156	..	113	50	2	23	47
15	Uganda	27	134	187	0	0	0	4	20	46
16	São Tomé and Principe	..	10	9	0	0	0	..	1	2
17	Somalia	4	127	74	0	0	0	0	7	7
18	Togo	5	105	50	0	0	0	2	27	35
19	Rwanda	0	34	91	0	0	0	0	3	13
20	Sierra Leone	8	95	2	0	0	0	11	32	4
21	Benin	2	72	68	0	0	0	1	6	19
22	Central African Republic	2	41	76	0	0	0	2	1	13
23	Kenya	35	538	449	41	87	90	17	120	291
24	Sudan	53	730	205	..	..	..	22	52	40
25	Comoros	0	13	13	0	0	0	0	0	0
26	Lesotho	0	15	41	0	0	0	0	3	9
27	Nigeria	56	1,141	1,138	25	565	75	38	64	304
28	Ghana	42	198	365	..	..	0	14	71	117
29	Mauritania	4	134	140	0	0	0	3	17	58
30	Liberia	7	85	32	0	0	0	11	16	5
31	*Equatorial Guinea*	0	25	24	0	0	0	0	2	6
32	*Guinea*	90	120	139	0	0	0	11	72	94
Middle-income economies											
33	Cape Verde	..	3	7	0	0	0	..	0	4
34	Senegal	19	318	360	1	0	6	5	122	161
35	Zimbabwe	..	130	277	..	..	..	5	34	274
36	Swaziland	4	29	30	0	0	0	2	5	19
37	Côte d'Ivoire	78	1,429	602	4	262	900	28	520	289
38	Congo, People's Republic	20	577	532	0	0	. 0	6	49	150
39	Cameroon	28	573	302	11	50	217	5	82	203
40	Botswana	6	24	102	0	0	0	0	6	38
41	Mauritius	2	86	70	0	4	21	1	14	45
42	Gabon	26	170	265	0	0	0	9	286	13
43	Seychelles	..	12	4	0	0	0	..	0	5
44	*Angola*	..	..	..	..	..	..	..	..	..
45	*Djibouti*	..	10	28	0	0	0	..	2	9
Six most populous economies											
Sahelian economies											
Oil exporters											
All low-income economies											
Total											
Excluding China and India											
South Asia											
Excluding India											

Note: Data are for long-term loans.

a. Disbursements less repayments of principal may not equal net flow because of rounding.

Repayment of principal			Net flow [a]						
Private nonguaranteed			Public and publicly guaranteed			Private nonguaranteed			
1970	1980	1987	1970	1980	1987	1970	1980	1987	
									Sub-Saharan Africa Total Excluding Nigeria
									Low-income economies Excluding Nigeria
0	0	0	13	92	273	0	0	0	Ethiopia
0	0	0	3	3	48	0	0	0	Chad
0	0	0	3	325	365	0	0	0	Zaire
0	0	0	..	66	47	0	0	0	Guinea-Bissau
0	0	0	37	125	87	0	0	0	Malawi
..	..	..	..	..	..	..	..	..	Mozambique
..	..	..	40	346	61	..	..	..	Tanzania
0	0	0	0	62	95	0	0	0	Burkina Faso
0	0	0	5	361	165	0	0	0	Madagascar
0	0	0	23	97	99	0	0	0	Mali
0	0	0	1	53	27	0	0	0	Gambia, The
0	0	0	1	41	113	0	0	0	Burundi
..	..	..	316	449	58	..	..	..	Zambia
..	35	30	11	154	109	..	79	20	Niger
0	0	0	23	114	141	0	0	0	Uganda
0	0	0	..	9	7	0	0	0	São Tomé and Principe
0	0	0	4	120	66	0	0	0	Somalia
0	0	0	3	78	15	0	0	0	Togo
0	0	0	0	31	78	0	0	0	Rwanda
0	0	0	-3	63	-2	0	0	0	Sierra Leone
0	0	0	1	66	49	0	0	0	Benin
0	0	0	-1	40	63	0	0	0	Central African Republic
12	88	53	17	419	158	30	-1	37	Kenya
..	..	..	30	678	164	..	..	..	Sudan
0	0	0	0	13	13	0	0	0	Comoros
0	0	0	0	12	31	0	0	0	Lesotho
30	177	123	18	1,078	834	-5	388	-48	Nigeria
0	0	8	28	127	248	..	..	-8	Ghana
0	0	0	1	117	82	0	0	0	Mauritania
0	0	0	-4	69	27	0	0	0	Liberia
0	0	0	0	23	18	0	0	0	*Equatorial Guinea*
0	0	0	80	48	46	0	0	0	*Guinea*
									Middle-income economies
0	0	0	..	3	4	0	0	0	Cape Verde
3	4	8	14	196	199	-2	-4	-2	Senegal
..	..	..	..	96	3	..	..	..	Zimbabwe
0	0	0	2	24	11	0	0	0	Swaziland
2	38	591	49	909	314	2	224	309	Côte d'Ivoire
0	0	0	15	528	382	0	0	0	Congo, People's Republic
2	32	210	24	492	99	9	18	7	Cameroon
0	0	0	6	18	64	0	0	0	Botswana
0	4	3	1	72	25	0	0	19	Mauritius
0	0	0	17	-115	252	0	0	0	Gabon
0	0	0	..	12	8	0	0	0	Seychelles
..	..	..	..	..	..	..	..	..	*Angola*
..	0	0	..	8	19	..	0	0	*Djibouti*
									Six most populous economies Sahelian economies Oil exporters

									All low-income economies
									Total
									  Excluding China and India
									South Asia
									  Excluding India

Table 21. Total external public and private debt and debt service ratios

		Total long-term debt disbursed and outstanding						Total interest payments on long-term debt (millions of dollars)		
		Millions of dollars			As a percentage of GNP					
		1970	1980	1987	1970	1980	1987	1970	1980	1987
Sub-Saharan Africa										
Total										
	Excluding Nigeria									
Low-income economies										
	Excluding Nigeria									
1	Ethiopia	169	701	2,434	10	17	46	6	17	51
2	Chad	33	201	270	10	28	28	0	0	3
3	Zaire	311	4,294	7,334	9	43	140	9	197	119
4	Guinea-Bissau	..	125	391	..	119	321	..	1	4
5	Malawi	122	644	1,155	43	56	98	4	35	26
6	Mozambique	..	..	..	..	..	..	..	..	..
7	Tanzania	265	2,137	4,079	21	42	144	..	..	..
8	Burkina Faso	21	299	794	7	21	44	0	6	14
9	Madagascar	89	956	3,113	10	30	163	2	27	83
10	Mali	238	685	1,847	71	42	96	0	3	13
11	Gambia, The	5	106	273	10	44	151	0	0	5
12	Burundi	7	141	718	3	16	60	0	2	15
13	Zambia	653	2,274	4,354	38	63	228	..	..	..
14	Niger	..	704	1,513	..	28	73	..	65	73
15	Uganda	138	603	1,116	7	35	30	5	2	24
16	São Tomé and Principe	..	23	84	..	51	337	..	0	2
17	Somalia	77	601	1,719	24	111	237	0	2	4
18	Togo	40	913	1,042	16	82	91	1	19	29
19	Rwanda	2	164	544	1	14	26	0	2	7
20	Sierra Leone	59	351	513	14	33	55	2	8	1
21	Benin	41	348	929	15	30	57	0	3	15
22	Central African Republic	24	160	520	14	20	49	1	0	9
23	Kenya	406	2,675	4,978	26	39	64	17	173	244
24	Sudan	..	4,130	8,429	..	61	102	..	..	..
25	Comoros	1	43	188	5	36	95	0	0	1
26	Lesotho	8	63	237	8	10	37	0	2	5
27	Nigeria	567	5,301	28,121	4	5	111	28	551	569
28	Ghana	497	1,138	2,237	23	26	45	..	..	58
29	Mauritania	27	734	1,868	14	109	215	0	13	28
30	Liberia	158	573	1,152	39	53	108	6	23	6
31	*Equatorial Guinea*	5	58	175	8	..	..	0	0	3
32	*Guinea*	312	1,032	2,010	47	63	78	4	23	37
Middle-income economies										
33	Cape Verde	..	20	121	..	15	69	..	0	3
34	Senegal	131	967	3,109	16	34	69	2	57	116
35	Zimbabwe	..	..	2,095	..	..	37	..	..	..
36	Swaziland	37	166	273	33	31	46	2	7	12
37	Côte d'Ivoire	266	4,742	11,714	20	48	124	12	385	597
38	Congo, People's Republic	124	1,427	3,679	47	90	195	3	42	45
39	Cameroon	140	2,227	3,306	13	33	27	5	119	176
40	Botswana	17	152	514	21	18	38	0	7	32
41	Mauritius	32	320	591	14	29	34	2	22	31
42	Gabon	91	1,308	1,605	29	34	53	3	123	57
43	Seychelles	..	25	124	..	18	35	..	0	3
44	*Angola*	..	..	..	..	..	..	..	..	..
45	*Djibouti*	..	26	152	..	8	..	..	1	3
Six most populous economies										
Sahelian economies										
Oil exporters										
All low-income economies										
Total										
	Excluding China and India									
South Asia										
	Excluding India									

Note: Public and private debt includes public, publicly guaranteed, and private nonguaranteed debt; data are shown only when they are available for all categories.

Total long-term debt service as a percentage of						
GNP			Exports of goods and services			
1970	1980	1987	1970	1980	1987	
						Sub-Saharan Africa Total Excluding Nigeria
						Low-income economies Excluding Nigeria
1.2	0.8	3.4	11.4	5.8	28.4	Ethiopia
0.9	0.4	0.7	4.2	3.6	3.9	Chad
1.1	3.6	4.7	4.4	15.2	12.8	Zaire
..	3.8	7.2	..	..	37.0	Guinea-Bissau
2.3	5.9	6.0	7.8	21.5	23.3	Malawi
..	..	..	..	..	..	Mozambique
..	..	..	..	..	..	Tanzania
0.7	1.2	1.7	6.8	7.5	..	Burkina Faso
0.8	1.8	7.7	3.7	11.1	35.3	Madagascar
0.2	0.6	1.7	1.4	3.6	9.9	Mali
0.2	0.3	8.2	0.5	1.2	12.9	Gambia, The
0.3	0.7	3.6	2.3	6.7	38.5	Burundi
..	..	..	..	..	..	Zambia
..	4.9	7.2	..	19.0	46.9	Niger
0.5	1.3	1.9	2.9	6.7	19.5	Uganda
..	2.2	15.3	..	4.4	41.5	São Tomé and Principe
0.3	1.4	0.9	2.1	4.4	8.3	Somalia
1.0	4.2	5.5	3.1	8.1	14.2	Togo
0.1	0.4	1.0	1.2	2.4	11.3	Rwanda
3.1	3.8	0.5	10.8	14.3	..	Sierra Leone
0.6	0.8	2.0	2.4	2.9	15.9	Benin
1.7	0.2	2.1	5.1	0.8	12.1	Central African Republic
3.0	5.5	7.6	9.1	18.5	33.8	Kenya
..	..	..	..	..	..	Sudan
0.4	0.2	0.6	..	2.1	5.2	Comoros
0.5	0.7	2.3	4.5	1.3	4.4	Lesotho
0.7	0.8	3.9	7.1	2.8	11.7	Nigeria
1.2	2.3	3.7	5.5	8.3	20.3	Ghana
1.8	4.5	9.9	3.4	11.1	18.2	Mauritania
4.3	3.5	1.0	8.1	6.3	2.5	Liberia
0.0	..	..	0.0	13.6	23.1	*Equatorial Guinea*
2.2	5.8	5.4	..	17.2	..	*Guinea*
						Middle-income economies
..	0.2	4.0	..	..	..	Cape Verde
1.1	6.4	6.4	4.0	22.1	22.3	Senegal
..	..	..	..	..	..	Zimbabwe
3.1	2.3	5.2	..	2.7	6.1	Swaziland
3.1	9.5	15.6	7.5	25.9	40.8	Côte d'Ivoire
3.4	5.7	10.3	11.5	8.8	18.6	Congo, People's Republic
1.0	3.4	4.8	4.0	12.8	27.9	Cameroon
0.7	1.5	5.2	1.0	1.7	3.7	Botswana
1.4	3.6	4.6	3.2	7.0	6.5	Mauritius
3.8	10.8	2.3	5.7	16.8	5.1	Gabon
..	0.2	4.2	..	0.3	..	Seychelles
..	..	..	..	..	..	*Angola*
..	1.0	..	..	..	..	*Djibouti*
						Six most populous economies **Sahelian economies** **Oil exporters**

						All low-income economies
						Total
						  Excluding China and India
						South Asia
						  Excluding India

Table 22. External public debt and debt service ratios

	External public debt outstanding and disbursed						Interest payments on external public debt (millions of dollars)		
	Millions of dollars			Percentage of GNP					
	1970	1980	1987	1970	1980	1987	1970	1980	1987
Sub-Saharan Africa									
Total	5,373 t	41,273 t	105,949 t	13 w	21 w	81 w	168 t	1,919 t	2,428 t
Excluding Nigeria	4,921 t	37,069 t	78,180 t	18 w	38 w	74 w	148 t	1,479 t	1,906 t
Low-income economies	4,357 t	29,823 t	82,589 t	12 w	18 w	92 w	135 t	1,194 t	1,465 t
Excluding Nigeria	3,905 t	25,619 t	54,820 t	18 w	40 w	86 w	115 t	754 t	943 t
1 Ethiopia	169	701	2,434	10	17	46	6	17	50
2 Chad	33	201	270	10	28	28	0	0	3
3 Zaire	311	4,294	7,334	9	43	140	9	197	119
4 Guinea-Bissau	..	125	391	..	119	321	..	1	4
5 Malawi	122	644	1,155	43	56	98	4	35	26
6 Mozambique	..	..	..	..	..	..	..	..	..
7 Tanzania	250	2,044	4,068	20	40	144	7	35	37
8 Burkina Faso	21	299	794	7	21	44	0	6	14
9 Madagascar	89	956	3,113	10	30	163	2	27	83
10 Mali	238	685	1,847	71	42	96	0	3	13
11 Gambia, The	5	106	273	10	44	151	0	0	5
12 Burundi	7	141	718	3	16	60	0	2	15
13 Zambia	623	2,187	4,354	36	61	228	29	107	56
14 Niger	32	399	1,259	5	16	60	1	16	60
15 Uganda	138	603	1,116	7	35	30	5	2	24
16 São Tomé and Principe	..	23	84	..	51	337	..	0	2
17 Somalia	77	601	1,719	24	111	237	0	2	4
18 Togo	40	913	1,042	16	82	91	1	19	29
19 Rwanda	2	164	544	1	14	26	0	2	7
20 Sierra Leone	59	351	513	14	33	55	2	8	1
21 Benin	41	348	929	15	30	57	0	3	15
22 Central African Republic	24	160	520	14	20	49	1	0	9
23 Kenya	319	2,238	4,482	21	33	58	13	134	211
24 Sudan	307	3,805	8,024	15	56	97	13	47	21
25 Comoros	1	43	188	5	36	95	0	0	1
26 Lesotho	8	63	237	8	10	37	0	2	5
27 Nigeria	452	4,204	27,769	3	4	110	20	440	522
28 Ghana	487	1,128	2,207	23	26	45	12	30	56
29 Mauritania	27	734	1,868	14	109	215	0	13	28
30 Liberia	158	573	1,152	39	53	108	6	23	6
31 *Equatorial Guinea*	5	58	175	8	..	..	0	0	3
32 *Guinea*	312	1,032	2,010	47	63	78	4	23	36
Middle-income economies	1,016 t	11,450 t	23,360 t	18 w	34 w	57 w	33 t	725 t	963 t
33 Cape Verde	..	20	121	..	15	69	..	0	3
34 Senegal	100	958	3,068	12	33	68	2	57	113
35 Zimbabwe	229	695	2,044	16	13	36	5	10	109
36 Swaziland	37	166	273	33	31	46	2	7	12
37 Côte d'Ivoire	255	4,328	8,450	19	44	90	12	354	422
38 Congo, People's Republic	124	1,427	3,679	47	90	195	3	42	45
39 Cameroon	131	2,049	2,785	12	30	23	4	104	133
40 Botswana	17	152	514	21	18	38	0	7	32
41 Mauritius	32	296	545	14	26	31	2	20	30
42 Gabon	91	1,308	1,605	29	34	53	3	123	57
43 Seychelles	..	25	124	..	18	35	..	0	4
44 *Angola*	..	..	..	..	..	..	..	..	..
45 *Djibouti*	..	26	152	..	8	..	..	1	3
Six most populous economies	1,808 t	17,286 t	54,111 t	8 w	13 w	99 w	68 t	870 t	960 t
Sahelian economies	456 t	3,527 t	9,891 t	17 w	34 w	78 w	3 t	93 t	243 t
Oil exporters	798 t	8,988 t	35,838 t	5 w	8 w	83 w	30 t	709 t	757 t
All low-income economies									
Total	18,259 t	84,081 t	218,245 t	15 w	11 w	28 w	..	..	..
Excluding China and India	10,442 t	61,916 t	157,261 t	16 w	21 w	69 w	..	..	..
South Asia	11,327 t	33,027 t	68,732 t	15 w	15 w	22 w	279 t	766 t	1,966 t
Excluding India	3,490 t	15,366 t	31,407 t	16 w	32 w	44 w	92 t	376 t	719 t

Note: Data are for long-term loans. Summary measures do not include estimates for missing country data. Summary measure percentages are computed from group aggregates of external public debt outstanding and disbursed, debt service, GNP, and exports of goods and services in current dollars.

	Debt service as a percentage of						
	GNP			*Exports of goods and services*			
	1970	1980	1987	1970	1980	1987	
							Sub-Saharan Africa
	1.2 w	2.1 w	4.1 w	5.3 w	7.2 w	14.7 w	Total
	1.5 w	3.6 w	4.2 w	5.5 w	12.3 w	16.1 w	Excluding Nigeria
	1.1 w	1.4 w	3.5 w	5.5 w	5.1 w	14.8 w	Low-income economies
	1.5 w	2.7 w	3.6 w	5.8 w	11.1 w	17.9 w	Excluding Nigeria
	1.2	0.8	3.4	11.4	5.8	28.4	Ethiopia
	0.9	0.4	0.7	4.2	3.6	3.9	Chad
	1.1	3.6	4.7	4.4	15.2	12.8	Zaire
	..	3.8	7.2	..	..	37.0	Guinea-Bissau
	2.3	5.9	6.0	7.8	21.5	23.3	Malawi
	..	..	..	..	..	..	Mozambique
	1.3	1.5	2.9	5.3	10.9	18.5	Tanzania
	0.7	1.2	1.7	6.8	7.5	..	Burkina Faso
	0.8	1.8	7.7	3.7	11.1	35.3	Madagascar
	0.2	0.6	1.7	1.4	3.6	9.9	Mali
	0.2	0.3	8.2	0.5	1.2	12.9	Gambia, The
	0.3	0.7	3.6	2.3	6.7	38.5	Burundi
	3.7	8.0	6.7	6.4	17.8	13.5	Zambia
	0.4	1.6	5.1	4.0	6.0	33.5	Niger
	0.5	1.3	1.9	2.9	6.7	19.5	Uganda
	..	2.2	15.3	..	4.4	41.5	São Tomé and Principe
	0.3	1.4	0.9	2.1	4.4	8.3	Somalia
	1.0	4.2	5.5	3.1	8.1	14.2	Togo
	0.1	0.4	1.0	1.2	2.4	11.3	Rwanda
	3.1	3.8	0.5	10.8	14.3	..	Sierra Leone
	0.6	0.8	2.0	2.4	2.9	15.9	Benin
	1.7	0.2	2.1	5.1	0.8	12.1	Central African Republic
	1.9	3.7	6.5	6.0	12.3	28.8	Kenya
	1.7	1.5	0.6	10.7	12.0	6.8	Sudan
	0.4	0.2	0.6	..	2.1	5.2	Comoros
	0.5	0.7	2.3	4.5	1.3	4.4	Lesotho
	0.4	0.5	3.3	4.3	1.8	10.0	Nigeria
	1.2	2.3	3.5	5.5	8.3	19.2	Ghana
	1.8	4.5	9.9	3.4	11.1	18.2	Mauritania
	4.3	3.5	1.0	8.1	6.3	2.5	Liberia
	0.0	..	..	0.0	13.6	23.1	*Equatorial Guinea*
	2.2	5.8	5.4	..	17.2	..	*Guinea*
	1.6 w	5.5 w	5.3 w	4.6 w	13.8 w	14.6 w	**Middle-income economies**
	..	0.2	4.0	..	..	..	Cape Verde
	0.8	6.2	6.1	2.9	21.6	21.4	Senegal
	0.6	0.8	6.8	2.3	2.5	23.2	Zimbabwe
	3.1	2.3	5.2	..	2.7	6.1	Swaziland
	2.9	8.8	7.5	7.1	24.0	19.6	Côte d'Ivoire
	3.4	5.7	10.3	11.5	8.8	18.6	Congo, People's Republic
	0.8	2.7	2.8	3.2	10.2	15.9	Cameroon
	0.7	1.5	5.2	1.0	1.7	3.7	Botswana
	1.4	3.0	4.3	3.2	5.8	6.1	Mauritius
	3.8	10.8	2.3	5.7	16.8	5.1	Gabon
	..	0.2	4.2	..	0.3	..	Seychelles
	..	..	..	..	..	..	*Angola*
	..	1.0	..	..	..	..	*Djibouti*
	0.9 w	1.0 w	3.5 w	5.6 w	3.9 w	13.9 w	Six most populous economies
	0.7 w	2.7 w	4.5 w	3.3 w	11.7 w	19.6 w	Sahelian economies
	0.6 w	1.1 w	3.4 w	4.6 w	3.6 w	11.2 w	Oil exporters
							All low-income economies
	1.0 w	0.9 w	2.2 w	9.8 w	6.6 w	15.7 w	Total
	1.1 w	1.7 w	4.7 w	7.1 w	6.8 w	21.9 w	Excluding China and India
	1.0 w	0.9 w	1.7 w	17.9 w	10.5 w	20.8 w	South Asia
	1.1 w	1.8 w	2.9 w	13.0 w	14.1 w	24.8 w	Excluding India

Table 23. Terms of external public borrowing

		Commitments (millions of dollars)			Average interest rate (percent)			Average maturity (years)		
		1970	1980	1987	1970	1980	1987	1970	1980	1987
Sub-Saharan Africa										
Total		1,903 t	13,496 t	7,284 t	3.7 w	7.1 w	3.4 w	26 w	17 w	29 w
Excluding Nigeria		1,838 t	11,633 t	6,961 t	3.6 w	6.6 w	3.4 w	26 w	18 w	29 w
Low-income economies		1,665 t	8,644 t	4,964 t	3.6 w	6.1 w	2.1 w	26 w	19 w	34 w
Excluding Nigeria		1,600 t	6,781 t	4,641 t	3.5 w	4.9 w	2.0 w	26 w	22 w	34 w
1	Ethiopia	21	181	561	4.4	3.5	4.4	32	18	24
2	Chad	10	0	116	5.7	0.0	1.3	8	0	34
3	Zaire	258	445	431	6.5	4.7	1.1	13	22	38
4	Guinea-Bissau	..	38	51	..	2.4	1.2	..	19	39
5	Malawi	14	137	117	3.8	5.8	0.9	29	23	47
6	Mozambique	..	..	..	..	..	..	..	..	..
7	Tanzania	284	502	201	1.2	4.7	1.2	39	21	32
8	Burkina Faso	9	127	74	2.3	4.0	2.9	36	23	24
9	Madagascar	23	458	293	2.3	5.3	1.5	39	18	42
10	Mali	34	148	63	1.1	2.1	2.4	25	23	33
11	Gambia, The	2	75	33	0.7	3.6	0.7	50	16	40
12	Burundi	1	109	30	2.9	1.3	2.2	5	40	35
13	Zambia	557	674	267	4.2	6.5	3.0	27	17	28
14	Niger	19	362	131	1.2	7.0	1.1	40	18	40
15	Uganda	12	224	248	3.8	3.7	2.5	28	26	29
16	São Tomé and Principe	..	8	27	..	4.0	0.7	..	11	50
17	Somalia	22	202	154	0.0	3.1	1.1	20	24	41
18	Togo	3	103	48	4.6	3.9	1.5	17	24	40
19	Rwanda	9	55	107	0.8	1.4	1.6	50	36	39
20	Sierra Leone	25	78	0	2.9	4.7	0.0	27	24	0
21	Benin	7	457	76	1.8	8.1	1.0	32	12	45
22	Central African Republic	7	54	21	2.0	0.5	1.2	36	11	38
23	Kenya	50	556	286	2.6	3.5	1.4	37	31	37
24	Sudan	95	933	251	1.8	5.7	1.7	17	20	31
25	Comoros	0	23	20	0.0	1.3	1.4	0	43	39
26	Lesotho	0	60	42	5.0	5.8	3.1	25	24	29
27	Nigeria	65	1,863	323	6.0	10.6	8.2	14	11	13
28	Ghana	51	199	630	2.0	1.6	1.9	37	39	29
29	Mauritania	7	216	124	6.0	3.5	1.0	11	21	45
30	Liberia	12	45	10	6.6	6.0	2.8	19	18	40
31	*Equatorial Guinea*	0	33	38	0.0	5.5	2.0	0	13	36
32	*Guinea*	68	279	191	2.9	4.8	2.6	13	19	37
Middle-income economies		238 t	4,852 t	2,320 t	3.8 w	8.9 w	6.1 w	23 w	12 w	20 w
33	Cape Verde	..	44	21	..	3.1	0.9	..	18	32
34	Senegal	7	400	443	3.8	6.3	3.3	23	21	32
35	Zimbabwe	..	169	410	..	7.1	7.6	..	15	12
36	Swaziland	3	20	28	0.0	6.3	3.1	26	21	26
37	Côte d'Ivoire	70	1,683	490	5.8	11.2	6.6	19	10	18
38	Congo, People's Republic	31	1,932	258	2.8	7.9	7.8	17	10	15
39	Cameroon	42	176	412	4.7	6.5	6.5	29	23	18
40	Botswana	38	69	34	0.6	6.0	5.2	39	18	38
41	Mauritius	14	121	97	0.0	10.4	8.2	24	14	18
42	Gabon	33	197	90	5.1	11.2	6.7	11	11	13
43	Seychelles	..	11	4	..	6.6	7.3	..	16	10
44	*Angola*	..	..	..	..	..	..	..	..	..
45	*Djibouti*	..	30	33	..	2.0	1.5	..	18	34
Six most populous economies		773 t	4,480 t	2,053 t	3.6 w	7.2 w	3.2 w	25 w	18 w	28 w
Sahelian economies		88 t	1,410 t	1,056 t	2.3 w	5.1 w	2.3 w	27 w	20 w	35 w
Oil exporters		171 t	4,168 t	1,083 t	4.9 w	9.2 w	7.3 w	18 w	11 w	15 w
All low-income economies										
Total		4,314 t	26,809 t	31,171 t	3.0 w	6.3 w	5.1 w	30 w	22 w	23 w
Excluding China and India		3,360 t	17,376 t	14,030 t	3.2 w	5.8 w	3.7 w	29 w	22 w	29 w
South Asia		2,052 t	9,490 t	11,454 t	2.7 w	4.1 w	4.7 w	32 w	30 w	27 w
Excluding India		1,098 t	3,884 t	3,523 t	2.9 w	3.1 w	2.5 w	30 w	30 w	34 w

Note: Data are for long-term loans. Summary measures do not include estimates for missing country data. Summary measure percentages and years are weighted by the amounts of the loans.

Average grace period (years)			Public loans with variable interest rates (percentage of public debt)			
1970	1980	1987	1970	1980	1987	
						Sub-Saharan Africa
8 w	5 w	7 w	0.9 w	17.8 w	21.7 w	Total
8 w	5 w	7 w	0.7 w	12.0 w	12.5 w	Excluding Nigeria
8 w	5 w	8 w	0.5 w	15.3 w	19.1 w	Low-income economies
8 w	6 w	8 w	0.3 w	6.5 w	4.8 w	Excluding Nigeria
7	4	6	0.0	1.4	5.8	Ethiopia
1	0	8	0.0	0.2	0.1	Chad
4	6	9	0.0	11.8	5.3	Zaire
..	4	9	..	1.7	0.0	Guinea-Bissau
6	6	10	0.0	22.6	2.7	Malawi
						Mozambique,
11	6	10	1.6	0.3	2.5	Tanzania
8	7	8	0.0	4.1	0.4	Burkina Faso
9	5	9	0.0	8.5	7.8	Madagascar
10	6	7	0.0	0.0	0.3	Mali
10	5	9	0.0	7.2	7.3	Gambia, The
2	9	9	0.0	0.0	0.0	Burundi
9	4	9	0.0	9.1	14.7	Zambia
8	5	9	0.0	20.7	11.0	Niger
7	6	7	0.0	0.9	0.0	Uganda
..	4	10	..	0.0	0.0	São Tomé and Principe
16	6	10	0.0	0.0	1.2	Somalia
4	7	10	0.0	11.6	4.2	Togo
11	8	9	0.0	0.0	0.0	Rwanda
6	6	0	10.6	0.1	0.7	Sierra Leone
7	4	10	0.0	0.4	3.7	Benin
8	4	10	0.0	1.8	0.0	Central African Republic
8	8	10	0.1	11.3	4.0	Kenya
9	5	8	0.0	3.0	0.8	Sudan
0	9	10	0.0	0.0	0.0	Comoros
2	6	7	0.0	3.2	1.2	Lesotho
4	4	3	2.8	69.1	42.6	Nigeria
10	9	8	0.0	0.0	5.7	Ghana
3	8	10	0.0	2.4	6.7	Mauritania
5	5	10	0.0	17.5	10.7	Liberia
0	4	10	0.0	0.0	3.8	*Equatorial Guinea*
5	6	9	0.0	0.3	10.8	*Guinea*
6 w	4 w	6 w	2.5 w	24.6 w	30.7 w	Middle-income economies
..	5	9	..	0.0	0.0	Cape Verde
7	6	8	0.0	13.0	4.1	Senegal
..	5	4	0.0	1.1	26.6	Zimbabwe
8	6	7	0.0	14.4	5.4	Swaziland
5	5	6	9.1	37.1	51.4	Côte d'Ivoire
6	3	4	0.0	7.4	40.4	Congo, People's Republic
8	6	5	0.0	15.7	5.9	Cameroon
10	4	8	0.0	0.0	12.8	Botswana
2	4	3	6.0	42.4	14.1	Mauritius
2	3	4	0.0	38.2	20.6	Gabon
..	5	4	..	0.0	5.6	Seychelles
..	..	..	..	..	..	*Angola*
..	7	8	..	0.0	0.0	*Djibouti*
7 w	5 w	7 w	0.9 w	22.0 w	22.7 w	Six most populous economies
7 w	6 w	8 w	0.0 w	7.0 w	4.2 w	Sahelian economies
5 w	4 w	4 w	1.6 w	42.4 w	38.5 w	Oil exporters
						All low-income economies
9 w	6 w	7 w	0.1 w	12.5 w	17.8 w	Total
9 w	6 w	8 w	0.2 w	11.9 w	17.4 w	Excluding China and India
10 w	7 w	7 w	0.0 w	2.2 w	8.6 w	South Asia
11 w	8 w	9 w	0.0 w	1.7 w	3.3 w	Excluding India

Table 24. Balance of payments and reserves

| | Current account balance (million of dollars) | | | | | | Net workers' remittances (millions of dollars) | | |
| | After official transfers | | | Before official transfers | | | | | |
	1970	1980	1987	1970	1980	1987	1970	1980	1987
Sub-Saharan Africa									
Total									
Excluding Nigeria									
Low-income economies									
Excluding Nigeria									
1 Ethiopia	-32	-126	-264 [a]	-43	-186	-475	0	0	..
2 Chad	2	12	-83	-33	-16	-324	-6	-4	-26
3 Zaire	-64	-292	-705	-141	-559	-851	-98	0	0
4 Guinea-Bissau	..	..	-26	..	..	-66	..	..	-2
5 Malawi	-35	-264	-24	-46	-315	-53	-4	0	0
6 Mozambique	..	-367	-372 [a]	..	-423	-676	..	53	33 [a]
7 Tanzania	-36	-502	-128 [a]	-37	-606	-605	0	0	0
8 Burkina Faso	9	-49	-124	-21	-259	-124	16	100	110
9 Madagascar	10	-568	-135 [a]	-42	-635	-241	-26	-31	..
10 Mali	-2	-124	-111	-22	-234	-313	-1	40	26
11 Gambia, The	0	-74	6	0	-112	-40	0	0	0
12 Burundi	2 [a]	-84	-132 [a]	-8 [a]	-129	-185	-7 [a]	-14	..
13 Zambia	108	-537	21	107	-545	-12	-48	-61	1
14 Niger	0	-276	-67	-32	-429	-201	-3	-48	-43
15 Uganda	20	-83	-107	19	-121	-200	-5	-4	0
16 São Tomé and Principe	..	1	-17	..	1	-28	..	1	0
17 Somalia	-6	-136	248 [a]	-18	-279	-59	0	57	0
18 Togo	3	-95	-73	-14	-181	-147	-3	1	1
19 Rwanda	7	-48	-131	-12	-155	-250	-4	-14	-15
20 Sierra Leone	-16	-165	-5	-20	-209	-9	0	-2	0
21 Benin	-3	-197	-208 [a]	-23	-261	-223	0	44	37 [a]
22 Central African Republic	-12	-43	-96 [a]	-24	-141	-214	-4	-19	-24 [a]
23 Kenya	-49	-886	-497	-86	-1,006	-639	0	0	0
24 Sudan	-42	-564	-422 [a]	-43	-648	-702	0	209	0
25 Comoros	..	-9	-23	..	-20	-61	..	0	1
26 Lesotho	18 [a]	-11	-12	-1 [a]	-117	-16	29 [a]	0	0
27 Nigeria	-368	5,131	-380	-412	5,299	-380	0	0	0
28 Ghana	-68	29	-275	-76	-54	-275	-9	-4	-2
29 Mauritania	-5	-134	-73 [a]	-13	-251	-164	-6	-27	2 [a]
30 Liberia	-16 [a]	46	-118	-27 [a]	10	-163	-18 [a]	-32	-51
31 *Equatorial Guinea*	-6	..	-8	-6	..	-36	-2	..	..
32 *Guinea*	..	-9	-53 [a]	..	-26	-114	..	-8	..
Middle-income economies									
33 Cape Verde	..	-25	..	..	-25	..	..	..	..
34 Senegal	-16	-386	-316 [a]	-66	-526	-608	-16	-15	10 [a]
35 Zimbabwe	-14 [a]	-244	50	-13 [a]	-302	-22	..	8	0
36 Swaziland	..	-135	40	..	-211	-2	..	-1	-5
37 Côte d'Ivoire	-38	-1,826	-624 [a]	-73	-1,836	-641	-56	-716	0
38 Congo, People's Republic	-45 [a]	-166	-245	-53 [a]	-230	-298	-3 [a]	-38	-39
39 Cameroon	-30	-395	-1,112 [a]	-47	-499	-1,112	-11	-70	3 [a]
40 Botswana	-30 [a]	-75	597	-35 [a]	-207	458	-9	-17	-29
41 Mauritius	8	-119	72	5	-130	47	0	0	0
42 Gabon	-3	384	-210	-15	350	-231	-8	-143	-143
43 Seychelles	0	-16	-31	0	-30	-48	..	0	0
44 *Angola*	..	..	..	..	..	..	..	..	..
45 *Djibouti*	..	..	..	..	..	..	..	..	..
Six most populous economies									
Sahelian economies									
Oil exporters									
All low-income economies									
Total									
Excluding China and India									
South Asia									
Excluding India									

Note: Summary measures do not include estimates for missing country data.
a. World Bank estimates.

Net direct private investment (millions of dollars)			Gross international reserves				
			Millions of dollars			Months of import coverage	
1970	1980	1987	1970	1980	1987	1987	
			2,028 t	15,056 t	8,030 t	2.1 w	**Sub-Saharan Africa** Total
			1,804 t	4,416 t	6,532 t	2.0 w	Excluding Nigeria
			1,677 t	13,481 t	4,821 t	2.0 w	Low-income economies
			1,454 t	2,841 t	3,323 t	1.8 w	Excluding Nigeria
4	..	..	72	262	245	2.3	Ethiopia
1	0	4	2	12	57	1.4	Chad
42	6	10	189	380	417	1.8	Zaire
..	..	..	..	..	..	..	Guinea-Bissau
9	9	..	29	76	58	1.8	Malawi
..	0	0	..	..	..	..	Mozambique
..	..	..	65	20	32	0.3	Tanzania
0	0	..	36	75	328	4.4	Burkina Faso
10	-7	0	37	9	185	3.1	Madagascar
-1	2	4	1	26	25	0.5	Mali
0	12	3	8	6	14	1.6	Gambia, The
0 [a]	1	2 [a]	15	105	69	2.8	Burundi
-297	62	0	515	206	111	1.4	Zambia
0	44	..	19	132	254	6.4	Niger
4	2	1	57	3	55	1.0	Uganda
..	..	..	..	..	..	..	São Tomé and Principe
5	..	0	21	26	17	0.4	Somalia
0	42	12	35	85	361	7.3	Togo
0	16	23	8	187	164	4.6	Rwanda
8	-19	-6	39	31	6	1.0	Sierra Leone
7	4	..	16	15	9	0.2	Benin
1	5	20 [a]	1	62	102	3.2	Central African Republic
14	78	0	220	539	294	1.4	Kenya
-1	0	..	22	49	12	0.1	Sudan
..	..	8	..	6	31	4.3	Comoros
..	4	2	..	50	68	1.9	Lesotho
205	-740	386	223	10,640	1,498	2.3	Nigeria
68	16	5	43	330	332	3.0	Ghana
1	27	5 [a]	3	146	77	1.5	Mauritania
28 [a]	..	39	..	5	1	0.0	Liberia
..	..	..	..	..	1	0.1	*Equatorial Guinea*
..	34	5 [a]	..	..	..	..	*Guinea*
			351 t	1,574 t	3,209 t	2.2 w	Middle-income economies
..	..	..	..	36	57	..	Cape Verde
5	13	-50 [a]	22	25	23	0.1	Senegal
..	2	-24	59	419	370	2.7	Zimbabwe
..	17	10	..	159	127	3.0	Swaziland
31	95	0	119	46	30	0.1	Côte d'Ivoire
30 [a]	40	-40	9	93	9	0.1	Congo, People's Republic
16	105	31 [a]	81	206	78	0.3	Cameroon
6 [a]	109	125	..	344	2,057	17.6	Botswana
2	1	44	46	113	362	3.5	Mauritius
-1	24	121	15	115	18	0.1	Gabon
..	6	8	..	18	14	0.5	Seychelles
..	..	..	..	..	..	..	*Angola*
..	..	..	..	..	64	..	*Djibouti*
			791 t	11,890 t	2,498 t	1.7 w	Six most populous economies
			92 t	458 t	835 t	1.2 w	Sahelian economies
			328 t	11,054 t	1,603 t	1.4 w	Oil exporters
							All low-income economies
			3,673 t	46,515 t	50,173 t	4.5 w	Total
			2,650 t	24,415 t	16,208 t	2.7 w	Excluding China and India
			1,453 t	14,873 t	14,547 t	4.6 w	South Asia
			430 t	2,863 t	3,035 t	2.5 w	Excluding India

Table 25. Central government expenditure

	Percentage of total expenditure											
	Defense			Education			Health			Housing, amenities; social security and welfare [a]		
	1972	1980	1987	1972	1980	1987	1972	1980	1987	1972	1980	1987
Sub-Saharan Africa												
Total												
Excluding Nigeria												
Low-income economies												
Excluding Nigeria												
1 Ethiopia	14.3	..	..	14.4	9.3	..	5.7	3.4	..	4.4	5.0	..
2 Chad	24.6	..	..	14.8	..	..	4.4	..	..	1.7	..	..
3 Zaire	11.1	8.5	..	15.2	18.9	..	2.3	2.5	..	2.0	0.8	..
4 Guinea-Bissau [b]	..	..	4.4	..	..	5.2	..	..	5.4	..	..	17.1
5 Malawi [b]	3.1	12.8	6.6	15.8	9.0	10.8	5.5	5.5	7.1	5.8	1.6	2.3
6 Mozambique	..	..	..	..	..	..	..	..	..	..	..	..
7 Tanzania	11.9	9.2	15.8	17.3	13.3	8.3	7.2	6.0	5.7	2.1	2.5	1.7
8 Burkina Faso	11.5	17.0	17.3	20.6	15.5	19.0	8.2	5.8	5.8	6.6	7.6	3.4
9 Madagascar	3.6	..	..	9.1	..	..	4.2	..	..	9.9	..	..
10 Mali	..	11.0	..	..	15.7	..	..	3.1	..	..	3.0	..
11 Gambia, The	0.0	0.0	..	13.1	12.3	..	9.9	7.4	..	7.1	3.3	..
12 Burundi	10.3	..	..	23.4	..	..	6.0	..	..	2.7	..	..
13 Zambia [b]	0.0	0.0	0.0	19.0	11.4	8.3	7.4	6.1	4.7	1.3	3.4	2.3
14 Niger	..	3.8	..	..	18.0	..	..	4.1	..	..	3.8	..
15 Uganda	23.1	25.2	26.3	15.3	14.9	15.0	5.3	5.1	2.4	7.3	4.2	2.9
16 São Tomé and Principe	..	..	..	..	..	..	..	..	..	..	..	..
17 Somalia [b]	23.3	25.0	..	5.5	8.1	..	7.2	3.2	..	1.9	1.7	..
18 Togo	..	7.0	7.6	..	12.6	13.1	..	5.6	3.8	..	5.2	9.9
19 Rwanda	25.6	13.1	..	22.2	18.8	..	5.7	4.5	..	2.6	4.1	..
20 Sierra Leone [b]	3.6	2.7	..	15.5	10.2	..	5.3	3.5	..	2.7	3.9	..
21 Benin [b]	..	8.7	..	..	20.5	..	..	5.6	..	..	11.2	..
22 Central African Republic	..	..	..	..	..	..	..	..	..	..	..	..
23 Kenya [b]	6.0	16.4	9.1	21.9	19.6	23.1	7.9	7.8	6.6	3.9	5.1	1.7
24 Sudan [b]	24.1	13.2	..	9.3	9.8	..	5.4	1.4	..	1.4	0.9	..
25 Comoros	..	..	..	..	..	..	..	..	..	..	..	..
26 Lesotho	0.0	..	9.6	22.4	..	15.5	7.4	..	6.9	6.0	..	1.5
27 Nigeria [b]	40.2	23.5	2.8	4.5	4.5	2.8	3.6	2.5	0.8	0.8	6.6	1.5
28 Ghana [b]	7.9	3.7	6.5	20.1	22.0	23.9	6.3	7.0	8.3	4.1	6.8	7.3
29 Mauritania	..	29.4	..	..	10.4	..	..	2.8	..	..	3.9	..
30 Liberia	5.3	5.8	8.9	15.2	11.9	16.2	9.8	5.2	7.1	3.5	4.3	1.9
31 *Equatorial Guinea*	..	..	..	..	..	..	..	..	..	..	..	..
32 *Guinea*	..	..	..	..	..	..	..	..	..	..	..	..
Middle-income economies												
33 Cape Verde	..	..	..	..	..	..	..	..	..	..	..	..
34 Senegal	..	16.8	..	..	23.0	..	..	4.7	..	..	9.5	..
35 Zimbabwe	..	25.0	14.2	..	15.5	20.3	..	5.4	6.1	..	7.8	4.6
36 Swaziland [b]	0.0	8.5	5.3	20.5	24.6	24.8	8.4	7.2	9.4	3.8	7.4	2.3
37 Côte d'Ivoire	..	3.9	..	..	16.3	..	..	3.9	..	..	4.3	..
38 Congo, People's Republic	..	..	..	..	..	..	..	..	..	..	..	..
39 Cameroon	..	9.1	8.1	..	12.4	12.7	..	5.1	3.5	..	8.0	11.9
40 Botswana [b]	0.0	9.8	7.9	10.0	22.2	18.4	6.0	5.4	5.9	21.7	7.9	10.1
41 Mauritius	0.8	0.8	0.8	13.5	17.6	12.4	10.3	7.5	7.6	18.0	21.4	17.4
42 Gabon	..	..	..	..	..	..	..	..	..	..	..	..
43 Seychelles [b]	0.0	..	..	9.2	..	..	5.5	..	..	7.0	..	..
44 *Angola*	..	..	..	..	..	..	..	..	..	..	..	..
45 *Djibouti*	..	28.0	..	..	6.7	..	..	5.8	..	..	13.2	..
Six most populous economies												
Sahelian economies												
Oil exporters												
All low-income economies												
Total												
Excluding China and India												
South Asia												
Excluding India												

a. See the technical notes.

Percentage of total expenditure						Percentage of GNP						
Economic services			Other[a]			Total expenditure			Overall surplus/deficit			
1972	1980	1987	1972	1980	1987	1972	1980	1987	1972	1980	1987	
												Sub-Saharan Africa
												Total
												Excluding Nigeria
												Low-income economies
												Excluding Nigeria
22.9	22.0	..	38.3	60.3	..	13.7	25.3	..	-1.4	-4.5	..	Ethiopia
21.8	..	..	32.7	..	..	14.9	..	9.0	-2.7	..	-1.3	Chad
13.3	13.2	..	56.1	56.1	..	19.8	17.8	..	-3.8	-1.2	..	Zaire
..	..	40.0	..	..	27.9	..	..	71.5	..	..	-26.2	Guinea-Bissau[b]
33.1	43.7	33.7	36.7	27.3	39.6	22.1	37.2	35.1	-6.2	-17.2	-10.3	Malawi[b]
												Mozambique
39.0	42.9	27.5	22.6	26.1	41.2	19.7	28.8	20.9	-5.0	-8.4	-4.9	Tanzania
15.5	19.3	7.7	37.6	34.8	46.8	11.1	14.5	16.3	0.3	0.3	1.6	Burkina Faso
40.5	..	..	32.7	..	..	20.8	..	..	-2.5	..	..	Madagascar
..	11.3	..	..	55.9	..	..	21.2	35.5	..	-4.6	-10.0	Mali
19.3	44.9	..	50.6	32.2	..	17.4	31.2	..	0.2	-4.3	..	Gambia, The
33.9	..	..	23.8	..	..	19.9	21.6	..	0.0	-3.9	..	Burundi
26.7	32.6	21.0	45.7	46.6	63.7	34.0	40.0	40.3	-13.8	-20.0	-15.8	Zambia[b]
..	32.4	..	..	38.0	..	..	18.7	..	..	-4.8	..	Niger
12.4	11.1	14.8	36.6	39.5	38.6	0.2	0.1	0.1	-0.1	0.0	0.0	Uganda
												São Tomé and Principe
21.6	11.5	..	40.5	50.5	..	13.5	25.1	..	0.6	-8.6	..	Somalia[b]
..	43.5	31.8	..	26.1	33.8	..	31.5	41.5	..	-2.0	-5.0	Togo
22.9	41.4	..	21.9	18.0	..	12.5	14.3	..	-2.7	-1.7	..	Rwanda
24.6	21.7	..	48.3	58.0	..	23.9	30.0	13.7	-4.4	-13.3	-8.9	Sierra Leone[b]
..	20.8	..	..	33.1	..	..	20.4	..	..	-0.5	..	Benin[b]
												Central African Republic
30.1	22.7	22.8	30.2	28.2	36.8	21.0	26.7	25.0	-3.9	-4.7	-4.6	Kenya[b]
15.8	19.8	..	44.1	54.9	..	19.2	19.8	..	-0.8	-3.3	..	Sudan[b]
..	..	..				..	..	..				Comoros
21.6	..	25.5	42.7	..	41.1	14.5	..	24.3	3.5	..	-2.6	Lesotho
19.6	32.3	35.9	31.4	30.6	56.2	8.3	13.1	27.7	-0.7	-1.6	-10.3	Nigeria[b]
15.1	20.7	15.7	46.6	39.8	38.3	19.5	10.9	14.1	-5.8	-4.2	0.6	Ghana[b]
..	13.5	..	..	39.9	..	..	40.1	..	..	-5.3	..	Mauritania
25.8	37.6	27.6	40.5	35.2	38.2	16.7	25.7	24.8	1.1	-8.1	-7.9	Liberia
..	..	..	..	..	..	..	..	..	..	..	..	Equatorial Guinea
..	..	..	..	..	..	..	..	..	..	..	..	Guinea
												Middle-income economies
												Cape Verde
..	14.4	..	..	31.6	..	18.8	24.3	..	-2.8	0.9	..	Senegal
..	28.1	41.4	..	18.2	13.3	..	35.3	40.3	..	-11.1	-10.8	Zimbabwe
23.0	30.0	25.1	44.3	22.4	33.0	21.4	28.2	24.9	-4.2	6.6	1.8	Swaziland[b]
..	13.4	..	..	58.1	..	..	32.4	..	..	-11.1	..	Côte d'Ivoire
..	..	..	..	..	..	..	53.1	..	..	-5.6	..	Congo, People's Republic
..	24.0	35.7	..	41.4	28.0	..	15.5	23.4	..	0.5	-3.5	Cameroon
28.0	26.9	28.4	34.5	27.9	29.2	33.7	40.0	47.5	-23.8	-0.2	28.2	Botswana[b]
13.9	11.7	21.6	43.4	41.0	40.3	16.3	27.4	23.0	-1.2	-10.4	0.2	Mauritius
..	..	..	..	..	..	40.1	41.1	45.9	-12.9	6.9	0.1	Gabon
27.8	..	..	50.5	..	..	45.5	39.2	..	3.4	-5.2	..	Seychelles[b]
..	..	..	..	..	..	..	..	..	..	..	..	Angola
..	14.6	..	..	31.6	..	..	48.5	..	..	7.3	..	Djibouti
												Six most populous economies
												Sahelian economies
												Oil exporters
												All low-income economies
												Total
												Excluding China and India
												South Asia
												Excluding India

b. Refers to budgetary data.

Table 26. Central government current revenue

	Taxes on income profit, and capital gain			Social security contributions			Domestic taxes on goods and services		
	1972	1980	1987	1972	1980	1987	1972	1980	1987

Percentage of total current revenue

Sub-Saharan Africa
Total
 Excluding Nigeria

Low-income economies
 Excluding Nigeria

	1972	1980	1987	1972	1980	1987	1972	1980	1987
1 Ethiopia	23.0	20.9	..	0.0	0.0	..	29.8	24.3	..
2 Chad	16.7	..	20.8	0.0	..	0.0	12.3	..	8.6
3 Zaire	22.2	30.4	29.9	2.2	2.0	0.9	12.7	12.4	15.1
4 Guinea-Bissau b	..	..	7.2	..	..	1.2	..	..	30.3
5 Malawi b	31.4	33.9	35.5	0.0	0.0	0.0	24.2	30.9	28.9
6 Mozambique	..	..	..	..	..	..	..	..	..
7 Tanzania	29.9	32.5	25.8	0.0	0.0	0.0	29.1	40.8	57.4
8 Burkina Faso	16.8	17.8	20.6	0.0	7.8	7.6	18.0	15.9	22.7
9 Madagascar	13.1	16.6	..	7.2	11.3	..	29.9	39.3	..
10 Mali	..	17.9	8.2	..	6.1	4.6	..	36.8	22.2
11 Gambia, The	7.5	15.5	16.1	0.0	0.0	0.0	1.9	3.2	9.9
12 Burundi	18.1	19.3	..	1.2	1.0	..	18.3	25.3	..
13 Zambia b	49.7	38.1	23.5	0.0	0.0	0.0	20.2	43.1	40.2
14 Niger	..	23.8	..	..	4.0	..	..	18.0	..
15 Uganda	22.1	11.5	5.5	0.0	0.0	0.0	32.8	41.0	19.1
16 São Tomé and Principe	..	..	..	..	..	..	..	..	..
17 Somalia b	10.7	5.5	..	0.0	0.0	..	24.7	16.9	..
18 Togo	..	34.4	30.5	..	5.8	6.3	..	15.3	7.7
19 Rwanda	17.9	17.8	..	4.4	4.1	..	14.1	19.3	..
20 Sierra Leone b	32.7	22.4	28.0	0.0	0.0	0.0	14.6	16.3	25.0
21 Benin b	..	13.0	..	..	7.8	..	..	11.4	..
22 Central African Republic	..	..	..	..	..	..	..	..	..
23 Kenya b	35.6	29.1	30.4	0.0	0.0	0.0	19.9	38.8	38.0
24 Sudan b	11.8	14.4	..	0.0	0.0	..	30.4	26.0	..
25 Comoros	..	..	..	..	..	..	..	..	..
26 Lesotho	10.2	..	11.1	0.0	..	0.0	2.3	..	10.3
27 Nigeria b	43.0	59.8	39.9	0.0	0.0	0.0	26.3	4.8	5.1
28 Ghana b	18.4	20.5	21.5	0.0	0.0	0.0	29.4	28.2	25.3
29 Mauritania	..	27.2	..	..	7.5	..	..	20.6	..
30 Liberia	40.4	32.9	34.1	0.0	0.0	0.0	20.3	23.0	32.0
31 *Equatorial Guinea*	..	..	..	..	..	..	..	..	..
32 *Guinea*	..	..	..	..	..	..	..	..	..

Middle-income economies

	1972	1980	1987	1972	1980	1987	1972	1980	1987
33 Cape Verde	..	..	..	..	..	..	..	..	..
34 Senegal	17.5	18.4	..	0.0	3.7	..	24.5	26.0	..
35 Zimbabwe	..	46.2	42.8	..	0.0	0.0	..	27.9	30.6
36 Swaziland b	35.7	24.0	38.2	0.0	0.0	0.0	4.8	1.7	11.4
37 Côte d'Ivoire	..	13.0	..	..	5.8	..	..	24.8	..
38 Congo, People's Republic	19.4	48.8	..	0.0	4.4	..	40.3	7.6	..
39 Cameroon	..	21.7	31.3	..	8.0	5.4	..	18.0	14.9
40 Botswana b	19.9	33.3	38.1	0.0	0.0	0.0	2.4	0.7	1.2
41 Mauritius	22.7	15.3	10.0	0.0	0.0	4.3	23.3	17.2	18.3
42 Gabon	18.2	39.9	44.2	6.0	0.0	0.0	9.5	4.8	6.5
43 Seychelles b	13.7	..	..	0.0	..	..	4.5	..	..
44 *Angola*	..	..	..	..	..	..	..	..	..
45 *Djibouti*	..	16.9	..	..	9.3	..	..	58.6	..

Six most populous economies
Sahelian economies
Oil exporters

All low-income economies
Total
 Excluding China and India
South Asia
 Excluding India

a. See the technical notes.

Percentage of total current revenue												
Taxes on international trade and transactions			Other taxes [a]			Nontax revenue			Total current revenue (percentage of GNP)			
1972	1980	1987	1972	1980	1987	1972	1980	1987	1972	1980	1987	
												Sub-Saharan Africa
												Total
												Excluding Nigeria
												Low-income economies
												Excluding Nigeria
30.4	35.7	..	5.6	3.7	..	11.1	15.4	..	10.5	18.6	..	Ethiopia
45.2	..	46.2	20.5	..	12.7	5.3	..	11.6	10.8	..	5.7	Chad
57.9	38.4	33.4	1.4	4.9	5.6	3.7	11.9	15.2	14.3	13.5	16.3	Zaire
..	..	39.8	..	..	-14.1	..	..	35.6	..	..	17.8	Guinea-Bissau [b]
20.0	22.0	16.8	0.5	0.3	0.6	23.8	12.9	18.2	16.0	20.5	22.6	Malawi [b]
..	..	..	..	..	..	..	..	..	..	..	..	Mozambique
21.7	17.3	8.6	0.5	1.6	3.1	18.8	7.8	5.1	15.8	17.6	16.3	Tanzania
51.8	43.7	39.4	3.2	4.3	6.8	10.2	10.5	10.5	11.4	14.0	15.3	Burkina Faso
33.6	27.6	..	5.5	2.7	..	10.8	2.4	..	18.3	16.6	..	Madagascar
..	17.9	28.1	..	19.5	26.9	..	8.0	10.1	..	10.8	15.1	Mali
70.7	65.3	66.4	0.4	1.5	1.1	19.4	14.5	6.5	16.3	22.7	17.7	Gambia, The
40.3	40.4	..	15.6	8.4	..	6.5	5.6	..	11.5	14.0	..	Burundi
14.3	8.3	32.9	0.1	3.1	0.5	15.6	7.3	3.0	23.2	27.0	24.4	Zambia [b]
..	36.4	..	..	2.6	..	..	15.3	..	..	14.7	..	Niger
36.3	44.3	75.3	0.3	0.2	0.0	8.5	3.1	0.0	0.1	0.0	0.0	Uganda
..	..	..	..	..	..	..	..	..	..	..	..	São Tomé and Principe
45.3	52.5	..	5.2	11.0	..	14.0	14.1	..	13.7	16.4	..	Somalia [b]
..	32.0	32.3	..	1.4	1.1	..	11.1	22.2	..	31.1	31.8	Togo
41.7	42.4	..	13.8	2.4	..	8.1	14.0	..	9.8	12.8	..	Rwanda
42.4	49.6	40.4	0.3	1.5	1.0	9.9	10.1	5.6	19.5	17.1	6.5	Sierra Leone [b]
..	56.0	..	..	3.1	..	..	8.8	..	..	15.8	..	Benin [b]
..	..	..	..	..	..	..	..	..	..	..	..	Central African Republic
24.3	18.5	19.2	1.4	1.0	1.5	18.8	12.6	10.9	18.0	23.2	20.8	Kenya [b]
40.5	42.6	..	1.5	0.7	..	15.7	16.3	..	18.0	14.0	..	Sudan [b]
..	..	..	..	..	..	..	..	..	..	..	..	Comoros
73.7	..	67.8	5.9	..	0.2	7.8	..	10.5	15.4	..	22.0	Lesotho
17.5	22.4	6.6	0.2	0.0	-14.5	13.0	13.1	62.9	9.4	15.2	18.5	Nigeria [b]
40.6	44.2	42.5	0.2	0.2	0.1	11.5	6.9	10.6	15.1	6.9	14.5	Ghana [b]
..	30.1	..	..	1.2	..	..	13.5	..	..	20.8	..	Mauritania
31.6	33.6	26.9	3.1	2.9	2.5	4.6	7.6	4.4	17.0	18.5	17.0	Liberia
..	..	..	..	..	..	..	..	..	..	..	..	Equatorial Guinea
..	..	..	..	..	..	..	..	..	..	..	..	Guinea
												Middle-income economies
												Cape Verde
30.9	34.2	..	23.9	11.4	..	3.2	6.3	..	16.9	25.3	..	Senegal
..	4.4	15.6	..	1.2	1.1	..	20.2	10.0	..	24.4	28.9	Zimbabwe
49.7	67.4	42.2	1.2	0.5	1.0	8.6	6.3	7.3	19.5	35.7	27.3	Swaziland [b]
..	42.8	..	..	6.1	..	..	7.5	..	..	23.4	..	Côte d'Ivoire
26.5	13.0	..	6.3	2.7	..	7.5	23.5	..	18.4	38.0	..	Congo, People's Republic
..	38.4	18.7	..	5.9	4.0	..	7.9	25.8	..	16.2	18.8	Cameroon
47.2	39.1	13.4	0.4	0.1	0.1	30.0	26.7	47.2	30.7	40.0	75.2	Botswana [b]
40.2	51.6	50.5	5.5	4.3	4.2	8.2	11.6	12.8	15.6	21.0	23.3	Mauritius
44.9	19.7	16.2	4.2	2.0	1.9	17.2	33.7	31.2	28.3	40.0	47.1	Gabon
53.2	..	..	9.8	..	..	18.8	..	..	21.9	..	..	Seychelles [b]
..	..	..	..	..	..	..	..	..	..	..	..	Angola
..	4.6	..	..	5.3	..	..	14.6	..	..	29.1	..	Djibouti
												Six most populous economies
												Sahelian economies
												Oil exporters
												All low-income economies
												Total
												Excluding China and India
												South Asia
												Excluding India

b. Refers to budgetary data.

Table 27. Money and interest rates

| | Monetary holdings, broadly defined | | | | | | Average annual inflation (GDP deflator) | Nominal interest rates of banks (average annual percentage) | | | |
| | Average annual nominal growth rate (percent) | | | Average outstanding (percentage of GDP) | | | | Deposit rate | | Lending rate | |
	1965-73	1973-80	1980-87	1965	1980	1987	1980-87	1980	1987	1980	1987
Sub-Saharan Africa											
Total											
Excluding Nigeria											
Low-income economies											
Excluding Nigeria											
1 Ethiopia	10.0	12.8	12.2	12.5	25.3	41.4	2.6	..	1.0	..	6.0
2 Chad	7.0	16.1	17.4	9.3	20.0	25.3	5.3	5.5	5.3	11.0	10.5
3 Zaire	23.6	36.1	53.9	11.1	8.9	8.8	53.5	..	..	..	..
4 Guinea-Bissau	..	..	..	..	..	16.3	39.2	..	..	..	..
5 Malawi	15.5	10.8	17.7	17.6	20.3	25.0	12.4	7.9	14.3	16.7	19.5
6 Mozambique	..	..	..	..	..	..	26.9				
7 Tanzania	14.8	24.5	19.8	..	37.2	25.9	24.9	4.0	15.8	11.5	27.5
8 Burkina Faso	9.9	20.6	12.6	9.3	18.5	23.1	4.4	6.2	5.3	9.4	8.0
9 Madagascar	10.0	16.8	15.4	19.6	27.6	25.7	17.4	5.6	11.5	9.5	14.5
10 Mali	7.3	18.6	13.7	..	17.9	22.5	4.2	6.2	5.3	9.4	8.0
11 Gambia, The	12.7	14.1	21.1	16.9	20.3	24.3	13.8	5.0	15.8	15.0	27.9
12 Burundi	10.1	24.4	10.3	10.1	13.3	15.6	7.5	2.5	5.3	12.0	12.0
13 Zambia	15.6	11.4	28.9	..	32.6	30.6	28.7	7.0	13.2	9.5	21.2
14 Niger	10.7	26.9	6.1	3.8	13.3	18.1	4.1	6.2	5.3	9.4	8.0
15 Uganda	14.6	29.3	77.8	..	0.1	..	95.2	6.8	30.0	10.8	34.7
16 São Tomé and Principe	..	..	..	..	..	113.9	4.9	3.0	..	..	..
17 Somalia	13.8	28.1	37.2	12.7	17.9	16.1	37.8	4.5	15.3	7.5	22.0
18 Togo	15.5	22.7	11.2	10.9	29.0	44.5	6.6	6.2	5.3	9.4	8.0
19 Rwanda	14.4	21.3	10.4	15.8	13.6	16.7	4.5	6.3	6.3	13.5	13.0
20 Sierra Leone	11.0	20.9	47.8	11.7	20.6	10.3	50.0	9.2	12.7	11.0	28.5
21 Benin	13.2	19.1	6.8	10.6	21.1	20.4	8.2	6.2	5.3	9.4	8.0
22 Central African Republic	8.0	17.8	6.9	13.5	18.9	18.3	7.9	5.5	7.2	10.5	11.4
23 Kenya	16.2	21.3	15.3	..	37.7	39.9	10.3	5.8	10.3	10.6	14.0
24 Sudan	12.9	29.7	34.8	14.1	28.2	35.5	31.7	6.0	..	..	..
25 Comoros	..	..	..	..	..	16.3	..	..	6.5	..	13.0
26 Lesotho	..	..	18.9	..	..	49.3	12.3	..	7.0	11.0	11.1
27 Nigeria	17.1	33.5	10.2	9.9	21.5	26.3	10.1	5.3	13.1	8.4	14.0
28 Ghana	12.6	41.9	44.2	20.3	16.2	11.7	48.3	11.5	17.6	19.0	25.5
29 Mauritania	17.6	18.0	12.5	5.7	20.5	23.5	9.8	..	6.0	..	12.0
30 Liberia	..	11.6	11.8	..	12.1	19.1	1.5	10.3	5.9	18.4	13.6
31 Equatorial Guinea	..	..	..	..	..	..	..	..	6.0	..	13.0
32 Guinea	..	..	..	..	..	5.5	55.1	..	..	..	..
Middle-income economies											
33 Cape Verde	..	..	..	..	63.3	..	13.9	..	..	..	..
34 Senegal	7.8	18.4	8.7	15.3	27.0	23.5	9.1	6.2	5.3	9.4	8.0
35 Zimbabwe	..	..	18.1	..	54.6	61.6	12.4	3.5	9.6	17.5	13.0
36 Swaziland	..	16.2	15.0	..	34.0	..	10.2	..	..	..	..
37 Côte d'Ivoire	15.6	22.8	8.1	21.8	25.8	31.0	4.4	6.2	5.3	9.4	8.0
38 Congo, People's Republic	11.0	15.3	10.3	16.5	14.7	20.8	1.8	6.5	7.8	11.0	11.1
39 Cameroon	14.0	23.9	13.8	11.7	18.3	18.7	8.1	7.5	7.2	13.0	13.0
40 Botswana	..	..	23.5	..	30.7	29.5	8.4	5.0	7.5	8.5	10.0
41 Mauritius	15.6	19.3	18.3	27.3	41.1	50.0	8.1	..	9.4	..	14.1
42 Gabon	13.3	25.1	8.4	16.2	15.2	24.4	2.6	7.5	7.9	12.5	11.1
43 Seychelles	..	23.9	5.7	..	29.0	29.5	3.7	..	10.0	..	13.0
44 Angola	..	..	..	..	..	..	..	..	..	..	..
45 Djibouti	..	20.5	..	..	..	..	..	..	..	..	..
Six most populous economies											
Sahelian economies											
Oil exporters											
All low-income economies											
Total											
Excluding China and India											
South Asia											
Excluding India											

Table 28. Population growth and projections

	Average annual population growth (percent)				Population (millions of persons)			Hypothetical size of stationary population (millions of persons)	Assumed year of reaching net reproduction rate of 1	Population momentum 1990
	1965-73	1973-80	1980-87	1987-2000	1987	2000[a]	2025[a]			
Sub-Saharan Africa										
Total	2.6 w	2.8 w	3.1 w	3.1 w	451 t	673 t	1,286 t			
Excluding Nigeria	2.6 w	2.9 w	3.1 w	3.1 w	345 t	516 t	1,000 t			
Low-income economies	2.6 w	2.7 w	3.1 w	3.1 w	397 t	592 t	1,131 t			
Excluding Nigeria	2.6 w	2.8 w	3.0 w	3.1 w	291 t	435 t	845 t			
1 Ethiopia	2.6	2.8	2.4	3.1	44	66	122	220	2040	1.9
2 Chad	1.9	2.1	2.3	2.6	5	7	13	26	2045	1.8
3 Zaire	2.3	3.3	3.1	3.1	33	49	97	200	2045	1.9
4 Guinea-Bissau	1.1	5.2	1.7	2.1	1	1	2	4	2045	1.8
5 Malawi	2.8	3.0	3.8	3.5	8	12	29	96	2060	1.9
6 Mozambique	2.3	2.6	2.7	3.2	15	22	42	87	2045	1.9
7 Tanzania	3.2	3.3	3.5	3.4	24	37	75	155	2045	2.0
8 Burkina Faso	1.9	2.3	2.6	2.9	8	12	23	48	2045	1.8
9 Madagascar	2.3	2.7	3.3	3.0	11	16	28	49	2035	1.9
10 Mali	2.1	2.2	2.4	3.0	8	11	24	59	2050	1.8
11 Gambia, The	2.8	3.4	3.3	3.0	1	1	2	5	2050	1.8
12 Burundi	1.7	2.0	2.8	3.2	5	7	14	29	2045	1.9
13 Zambia	3.0	3.1	3.6	3.5	7	11	23	50	2045	2.0
14 Niger	2.3	2.9	3.0	3.2	7	10	22	69	2060	1.9
15 Uganda	3.4	2.6	3.1	3.3	16	24	46	97	2045	2.0
16 São Tomé and Principe	2.3	1.8	3.0	2.5	(.)	(.)	(.)	(.)	2025	1.8
17 Somalia	2.6	2.6	2.9	3.0	6	8	16	37	2050	1.9
18 Togo	3.8	2.5	3.4	3.1	3	5	9	15	2035	2.0
19 Rwanda	3.1	3.4	3.3	3.8	6	10	23	63	2055	1.9
20 Sierra Leone	1.9	2.1	2.4	2.6	4	5	10	24	2050	1.8
21 Benin	2.7	2.7	3.2	2.9	4	6	11	19	2035	2.0
22 Central African Republic	1.5	2.2	2.5	2.6	3	4	6	11	2035	1.8
23 Kenya	3.4	3.8	4.1	3.9	22	37	83	196	2050	2.1
24 Sudan	2.5	3.1	3.1	2.7	23	33	56	98	2035	1.8
25 Comoros	2.3	2.2	3.6	3.4	(.)	1	1	3	2040	2.0
26 Lesotho	2.1	2.5	2.7	2.6	2	2	4	6	2030	1.8
27 Nigeria	2.5	2.5	3.4	3.0	107	157	286	500	2035	1.9
28 Ghana	2.3	1.8	3.4	3.0	14	20	35	60	2035	1.9
29 Mauritania	2.2	2.5	2.7	2.7	2	3	5	12	2050	1.8
30 Liberia	2.9	3.1	3.3	3.0	2	3	6	11	2035	1.9
31 *Equatorial Guinea*	1.7	1.7	1.9	2.3	(.)	1	1	1	2035	1.7
32 *Guinea*	1.8	2.0	2.4	2.4	6	9	16	34	2045	1.8
Middle-income economies	2.8 w	3.3 w	3.3 w	3.2 w	54 t	81 t	155 t			
33 Cape Verde	2.0	1.2	2.2	2.7	(.)	(.)	1	1	2025	1.9
34 Senegal	2.3	2.8	2.9	3.1	7	10	20	42	2045	1.9
35 Zimbabwe	3.5	2.9	3.7	3.0	9	13	22	32	2025	2.0
36 Swaziland	2.6	3.1	3.4	3.2	1	1	2	3	2035	2.0
37 Côte d'Ivoire	4.1	4.3	4.2	3.6	11	18	36	83	2050	1.9
38 Congo, People's Republic	2.5	3.0	3.3	3.6	2	3	7	17	2050	1.9
39 Cameroon	2.4	3.1	3.2	3.2	11	16	33	67	2045	1.9
40 Botswana	3.1	3.7	3.4	2.3	1	2	2	3	2010	2.0
41 Mauritius	1.6	1.8	1.0	1.1	1	1	1	2	1985	1.6
42 Gabon	1.9	4.7	4.3	2.6	1	1	3	6	2045	1.7
43 Seychelles	2.3	1.5	0.9	1.1	(.)	(.)	(.)	(.)	2005	1.6
44 *Angola*	2.0	3.5	2.5	3.0	9	13	27	61	2050	1.9
45 *Djibouti*	8.1	5.1	3.0	3.0	(.)	1	1	2	2040	1.9
Six most populous economies	2.6 w	2.9 w	3.2 w	3.1 w	253 t	378 t	717 t			
Sahelian economies	2.1 w	2.5 w	2.6 w	3.0 w	39 t	57 t	113 t			
Oil exporters	2.5 w	2.6 w	3.3 w	3.0 w	130 t	192 t	355 t			
All low-income economies										
Total	2.6 w	2.1 w	2.0 w	1.9 w	2,823 t	3,625 t	5,161 t			
Excluding China and India	2.6 w	2.6 w	2.8 w	2.7 w	957 t	1,346 t	2,268 t			
South Asia	2.4 w	2.4 w	2.3 w	2.1 w	1,081 t	1,408 t	2,004 t			
Excluding India	2.7 w	2.7 w	2.7 w	2.6 w	283 t	397 t	639 t			

Note: Summary measures are weighted by each country's share in the aggregate population. (.) indicates population less than 0.5 million.
a. For the assumptions used in the projections, see the technical notes.

Table 29. Demography and fertility

	Crude birth rate per thousand population			Crude death rate per thousand population			Percentage of women of childbearing age (15-49)			Total fertility rate			Percentage of women of childbearing age using contraception [a]
	1965	1980	1987	1965	1980	1987	1965	1980	1987	1965	1987	2000	1985
Sub-Saharan Africa													
Total	48 w	48 w	47 w	23 w	18 w	16 w	45 w	44 w	44 w	6.6 w	6.6 w	5.8 w	..
Excluding Nigeria	48 w	47 w	48 w	22 w	18 w	16 w	45 w	45 w	44 w	6.5 w	6.6 w	6.0 w	..
Low-income economies	49 w	48 w	48 w	23 w	18 w	16 w	45 w	44 w	44 w	6.6 w	6.6 w	5.8 w	..
Excluding Nigeria	48 w	47 w	48 w	23 w	19 w	16 w	46 w	45 w	44 w	6.5 w	6.6 w	6.0 w	..
1 Ethiopia	43	43	48	20	20	18	46	46	46	5.8	6.5	5.7	2
2 Chad	45	44	44	28	22	20	47	46	46	6.0	5.9	6.0	..
3 Zaire	47	45	45	21	16	14	46	45	45	6.0	6.1	5.8	1
4 Guinea-Bissau	46	46	46	29	27	25	48	48	47	5.9	6.0	6.0	..
5 Malawi	56	54	53	26	22	20	46	45	44	7.8	7.6	7.6	..
6 Mozambique	49	46	45	27	20	17	47	46	46	6.8	6.3	6.1	..
7 Tanzania	49	50	50	22	17	14	45	43	43	6.6	7.0	6.0	..
8 Burkina Faso	48	47	47	26	20	18	47	47	46	6.4	6.5	6.2	..
9 Madagascar	47	46	46	22	16	14	47	45	44	6.6	6.4	5.1	..
10 Mali	50	49	51	27	22	20	46	45	45	6.5	7.0	6.9	6
11 Gambia, The	50	49	49	30	24	21	48	46	47	6.5	6.5	6.5	..
12 Burundi	47	47	49	24	20	18	48	47	46	6.4	6.8	6.0	9
13 Zambia	49	49	50	20	16	13	45	44	44	6.6	6.8	6.0	..
14 Niger	48	51	51	29	23	20	43	43	44	6.8	7.0	7.2	..
15 Uganda	49	50	50	19	19	17	44	44	43	6.9	6.9	6.1	1
16 São Tomé and Principe	..	39	37	..	10	9	..	..	44	..	5.3	4.0	2
17 Somalia	50	50	49	26	21	19	45	45	44	6.7	6.8	6.5	2
18 Togo	50	50	49	23	17	14	46	45	44	6.5	6.5	5.2	..
19 Rwanda	52	52	52	17	20	18	45	43	43	7.5	8.0	7.2	1
20 Sierra Leone	48	48	48	32	26	23	47	46	46	6.4	6.5	6.5	4
21 Benin	49	49	48	25	19	16	44	..	44	6.8	6.5	5.2	6
22 Central African Republic	34	41	43	24	17	16	47	46	46	4.5	5.8	5.2	..
23 Kenya	52	54	52	20	14	11	40	40	40	8.0	7.7	6.5	17
24 Sudan	47	46	44	24	18	16	46	45	45	6.7	6.4	5.4	..
25 Comoros	49	49	50	20	16	13	45	45	43	7.0	7.0	5.7	..
26 Lesotho	42	41	41	18	15	13	47	47	45	5.8	5.8	4.5	..
27 Nigeria	51	50	47	23	18	15	45	43	43	6.9	6.5	5.4	5
28 Ghana	47	45	46	17	15	13	45	..	44	6.8	6.4	5.1	..
29 Mauritania	47	47	48	27	21	19	47	46	45	6.5	6.5	6.5	1
30 Liberia	46	45	45	20	15	13	46	44	44	6.4	6.5	5.2	7
31 *Equatorial Guinea*	40	40	42	27	22	20	46	..	48	5.0	5.5	5.2	..
32 *Guinea*	46	46	47	30	23	23	47	..	46	5.9	6.2	6.2	..
Middle-income economies	47 w	47 w	46 w	21 w	17 w	15 w	45 w	45 w	44 w	6.5 w	6.4 w	5.8 w	..
33 Cape Verde	41	39	39	11	8	9	41	44	46	7.2	5.2	3.9	..
34 Senegal	47	46	46	23	20	18	46	45	44	6.4	6.5	6.2	12
35 Zimbabwe	55	49	44	17	13	11	42	44	45	8.0	5.9	4.3	40
36 Swaziland	48	47	47	21	15	13	45	44	43	6.5	6.5	5.2	9
37 Côte d'Ivoire	52	51	51	22	16	15	44	..	44	7.4	7.4	6.4	..
38 Congo, People's Republic	42	43	47	18	13	11	47	45	43	5.7	6.5	6.3	..
39 Cameroon	40	47	45	20	15	13	46	45	42	5.2	6.5	5.8	..
40 Botswana	53	48	35	19	14	10	45	44	45	6.9	5.0	3.1	29
41 Mauritius	36	24	20	8	7	7	45	53	54	4.8	2.2	2.1	78
42 Gabon	31	33	42	22	18	16	49	49	47	4.1	5.5	6.0	..
43 Seychelles	..	29	27	..	7	7	..	..	47	..	3.2	2.3	..
44 *Angola*	49	47	47	29	23	20	47	45	45	6.4	6.4	6.6	..
45 *Djibouti*	49	48	47	24	20	18	46	46	44	6.6	6.6	5.8	..
Six most populous economies	49 w	48 w	47 w	22 w	18 w	15 w	45 w	44 w	44 w	6.6 w	6.6 w	5.7 w	..
Sahelian economies	48 w	47 w	48 w	26 w	21 w	19 w	46 w	45 w	45 w	6.4 w	6.6 w	6.5 w	..
Oil exporters	50 w	49 w	46 w	23 w	18 w	15 w	45 w	43 w	44 w	6.7 w	6.5 w	5.5 w	..
All low-income economies													
Total	42 w	31 w	31 w	16 w	11 w	10 w	46 w	49 w	50 w	6.3 w	4.0 w	3.3 w	..
Excluding China and India	46 w	43 w	41 w	21 w	16 w	13 w	46 w	47 w	46 w	6.4 w	5.6 w	4.7 w	..
South Asia	45 w	37 w	34 w	20 w	14 w	12 w	47 w	..	28 w	6.3 w	4.6 w	3.5 w	..
Excluding India	45 w	43 w	41 w	20 w	15 w	13 w	44 w	..	46 w	6.5 w	5.6 w	4.5 w	..

Note:: Summary measures are weighted by each country's share in the aggregate population. Summary measures do not include estimates for missing country data.

a. Figures include women whose husbands practice contraception; see the technical notes.

Table 30. Women in development

		Female percentage of population, 1985			Life expectancy at birth, 1987 (years)		Average age at first marriage a		Projected economically active population, 1985 (percentage of labor force)		Women in government, 1984 (percent women in national legislature)	Maternal mortality, 1980 (per 100,000 live births)
		Total	Under age 15	Over age 64	Female	Male	Female	Male	Female	Male		
Low-income Sub-Saharan Africa												
1	Ethiopia	50	49	53	48	45	17.7	25.5	38	62	..	2,000 b
2	Chad	51	50	55	46	44	..	..	22	78	..	700
3	Zaire	51	50	55	54	50	21.9	25.4	37	63	..	800 b
4	Guinea-Bissau	52	48	52	40	38	..	..	42	58	..	400
5	Malawi	51	51	49	47	44	17.8	22.9	43	57	13	250
6	Mozambique	51	50	55	49	46	17.6	22.7	49	51	..	479 b
7	Tanzania	51	50	56	55	51	..	..	49	51	..	370 b
8	Burkina Faso	54	56	42	49	45	17.4	27.0	47	53	..	600
9	Madagascar	50	49	48	55	52	20.3	23.5	40	60	..	300
10	Mali	52	49	51	48	45	18.1	28.2	17	83	1	..
11	Gambia, The	50	50	50	44	42	..	..	41	59	..	..
12	Burundi	51	49	54	50	47	20.8	24.4	48	52	9	..
13	Zambia	51	50	53	54	51	19.4	25.1	28	72	3	110
14	Niger	51	50	54	46	43	..	..	47	53	..	420 b
15	Uganda	50	48	53	49	46	..	..	42	58	1	300
16	São Tomé and Principe	50	49	52	67	63	..	..	..	..	..	..
17	Somalia	50	49	50	48	45	20.1	26.5	40	60	..	1,100
18	Togo	52	51	45	54	51	..	..	37	63	8	476 b
19	Rwanda	51	50	52	50	47	21.2	..	49	51	13	210
20	Sierra Leone	50	49	55	42	40	..	..	34	66	..	450
21	Benin	52	50	46	52	48	18.3	24.9	48	52	0	1,680 b
22	Central African Republic	52	50	51	51	48	..	..	47	53	..	600
23	Kenya	50	49	49	59	56	20.4	25.8	41	59	2	510 b
24	Sudan	49	49	53	51	48	..	..	21	79	..	607 b
25	Comoros	50	49	61	57	54	19.5	25.8	42	59	..	..
26	Lesotho	51	50	53	57	53	20.5	26.3	45	55	..	..
27	Nigeria	50	49	55	52	49	18.7	..	36	64	..	1,500
28	Ghana	50	49	50	55	52	..	..	41	59	..	1,070 b
29	Mauritania	51	51	54	47	44	19.4	26.9	21	79	..	119
30	Liberia	50	49	53	56	53	..	..	31	69	..	173
31	*Equatorial Guinea*	51	50	55	46	44	..	..	41	59	3	..
32	*Guinea*	52	50	53	43	40	..	..	41	59	..	..
Middle-income Sub-Saharan Africa												
33	Cape Verde	54	50	57	67	63	..	..	29	71	..	..
34	Senegal	50	49	54	49	46	18.3	28.3	40	60	11	530 c
35	Zimbabwe	50	49	44	60	56	20.4	25.4	36	64	8	150 b
36	Swaziland	49	45	63	57	53	..	..	40	60	..	..
37	Côte d'Ivoire	48	49	53	54	50	18.9	27.1	35	65	5	..
38	Congo, People's Republic	51	49	56	60	56	..	..	39	61	..	..
39	Cameroon	51	49	55	58	54	18.8	26.2	34	66	14	303
40	Botswana	53	49	54	62	56	26.4	30.8	36	64	5	300
41	Mauritius	50	48	62	70	63	21.7	24.7	25	75	6	99
42	Gabon	55	58	50	54	50	..	..	38	62	..	124 b
43	Seychelles	50	50	57	73	67	..	..	..	..	..	..
44	*Angola*	51	49	55	..	..	..	..	40	60	..	..
45	*Djibouti*	49	48	54	48	45	..	..	..	..	..	..

a. See the technical notes.
b. Data refer to maternal mortality in hospitals and other medical institutions only.
c. Community data from rural areas only.

Table 31. Status of children

		Children under age five as a percentage of the total population			Infant mortality (per 1,000 live births)			Percentage of age group affected by		Children under age five suffering from malnutrition 1980-86 average (percentage of age group)
		1965	1980	1987	1965	1980	1987	Wasting (12-23 months)	Stunting (24-59 months)	
Low-income Sub-Saharan Africa										
1	Ethiopia	19	19	19	165	155	155	19	43	..
2	Chad	17	16	16	183	147	134	..	..	..
3	Zaire	18	19	19	141	111	100	11	40	20
4	Guinea-Bissau	..	18	18	196	164	148	..	..	..
5	Malawi	20	20	22	200	169	153	8	61	..
6	Mozambique	17	18	20	179	156	143	..	..	..
7	Tanzania	18	19	19	138	119	108	17	..	48
8	Burkina Faso	18	18	18	193	152	140	17	..	40
9	Madagascar	18	19	19	201	38	122	..	..	..
10	Mali	19	19	19	207	184	171	18	23	..
11	Gambia, The	18	18	18	199	159	145	..	..	..
12	Burundi	18	18	19	142	126	114	36	52	35
13	Zambia	19	20	20	121	90	82	12	41	..
14	Niger	20	19	20	180	150	137	26	32	26
15	Uganda	18	20	20	121	113	105	3	27	19
16	São Tomé and Principe	..	16	18	..	71	53	..	..	..
17	Somalia	21	19	18	165	145	134	..	27	8
18	Togo	19	19	20	153	106	96	9	36	25
19	Rwanda	19	20	21	141	172	124	23	45	37
20	Sierra Leone	18	18	18	209	124	154	26	46	27
21	Benin	19	19	20	166	135	117	14	..	..
22	Central African Republic	16	17	17	167	143	134	..	..	30
23	Kenya	20	23	23	112	83	74	10	41	32
24	Sudan	18	19	18	160	123	110	48	63	41
25	Comoros	19	19	19	119	92	82	..	..	..
26	Lesotho	16	17	18	142	116	102	7	23	..
27	Nigeria	20	20	20	177	118	107	21	..	..
28	Ghana	19	20	21	119	100	92	28	31	30
29	Mauritania	19	18	17	178	142	129	..	..	40
30	Liberia	20	17	21	138	100	89	7	38	35
31	*Equatorial Guinea*	16	15	15	177	142	129	..	..	..
32	*Guinea*	18	18	18	196	164	149	..	..	..
Middle-income Sub-Saharan Africa										
33	Cape Verde	18	17	16	..	94	71	..	..	..
34	Senegal	18	19	18	171	147	131	8	27	30
35	Zimbabwe	19	22	23	103	82	74	..	..	..
36	Swaziland	19	21	21	148	133	120	..	..	..
37	Côte d'Ivoire	19	19	19	149	109	98	21	..	..
38	Congo	17	18	19	118	83	75	5	27	22
39	Cameroon	16	20	19	143	106	96	2	43	..
40	Botswana	20	19	19	112	78	69	19	56	32
41	Mauritius	17	13	12	65	32	24	20	..	24
42	Gabon	13	14	15	153	116	105	..	27	..
43	Seychelles	..	13	13	..	..	17	..	..	..
44	*Angola*	18	19	18	..	153	..	..	..	..
45	*Djibouti*	..	19	20	172	136	124	..	..	..

One-year-old children fully immunized (percentage)

Tuberculosis		DPT		Poliomyelitis		Measles		
1981	1986-87	1981	1986-87	1981	1986-87	1981	1986-87	
								Low-income Sub-Saharan Africa
10	28	6	16	7	15	7	13	Ethiopia
..	40	..	12	..	12	..	33	Chad
34	54	18	36	18	36	23	39	Zaire
..	82	..	47	..	48	..	60	Guinea-Bissau
86	92	66	55	68	50	65	53	Malawi
46	59	56	51	32	38	32	46	Mozambique
78	95	58	81	49	80	76	78	Tanzania
16	67	2	34	2	34	23	68	Burkina Faso
25	42	40	30	..	24	..	10	Madagascar
19	29	..	8	..	8	..	11	Mali
..	..	..	..	..	..	..	..	Gambia, The
65	89	38	73	6	76	30	58	Burundi
72	92	44	66	77	61	21	58	Zambia
28	28	6	5	6	4	19	27	Niger
18	74	9	39	8	40	22	48	Uganda
..	..	..	..	..	..	..	..	São Tomé and Principe
3	33	2	25	2	25	3	29	Somalia
44	66	9	41	9	40	47	48	Togo
51	85	17	78	15	80	42	63	Rwanda
35	73	15	30	13	30	28	50	Sierra Leone
..	67	..	52	..	52	..	38	Benin
26	53	12	24	12	24	16	30	Central African Republic
..	86	..	75	..	75	..	60	Kenya
3	46	1	29	1	29	1	22	Sudan
..	..	..	..	..	..	..	..	Comoros
81	84	56	77	54	77	49	79	Lesotho
23	41	24	20	24	21	55	31	Nigeria
67	71	22	37	25	34	23	51	Ghana
57	91	18	32	18	61	45	69	Mauritania
87	68	39	28	26	28	99	55	Liberia
..	..	..	..	..	..	..	..	*Equatorial Guinea*
4	46	..	15	..	8	15	43	*Guinea*
								Middle-income Sub-Saharan Africa
..	..	..	..	..	..	..	..	Cape Verde
..	92	..	53	..	53	..	70	Senegal
64	86	39	77	38	77	56	73	Zimbabwe
..	..	..	..	..	..	..	..	Swaziland
70	53	42	71	34	71	28	85	Côte d'Ivoire
92	86	42	71	42	71	49	69	Congo
8	77	5	45	5	43	16	44	Cameroon
80	99	64	86	71	88	68	91	Botswana
87	87	82	85	82	85	..	68	Mauritius
..	79	..	48	..	48	..	55	Gabon
..	..	..	..	..	..	..	..	Seychelles
..	29	..	10	..	16	..	55	*Angola*
..	..	..	..	..	..	..	..	*Djibouti*

Table 32. Education (percentage of age group enrolled)

	Primary								
	Total			Male			Female		
	1965	1980	1986	1965	1980	1986	1965	1980	1986
Sub-Saharan Africa									
Total	41 w	79 w	73 w	52 w	87 w	80 w	30 w	67 w	63 w
Excluding Nigeria	44 w	73 w	67 w	56 w	80 w	73 w	32 w	61 w	58 w
Low-income economies	37 w	76 w	68 w	47 w	87 w	77 w	27 w	66 w	60 w
Excluding Nigeria	39 w	69 w	60 w	50 w	78 w	68 w	28 w	59 w	53 w
1 Ethiopia	11	35	36	16	46	44	6	29	28
2 Chad	34	..	43	56	..	61	13	..	24
3 Zaire	70	98	..	95	114	..	45	82	..
4 Guinea-Bissau	26	67	60	38	95	81	13	41	40
5 Malawi	44	61	64	55	74	72	32	49	55
6 Mozambique	37	99	82	48	114	92	26	84	73
7 Tanzania	32	93	69	40	100	70	25	86	69
8 Burkina Faso	12	21	35	16	26	45	8	15	26
9 Madagascar	65	148	121	70	154	125	59	144	118
10 Mali	24	25	22	32	32	27	16	18	16
11 Gambia, The	21	52	75	29	68	92	12	36	58
12 Burundi	26	29	59	36	35	68	15	22	50
13 Zambia	53	98	104	59	103	112	46	92	101
14 Niger	11	27	29	15	35	37	7	19	20
15 Uganda	67	50	..	83	56	..	50	43	..
16 São Tomé and Principe	..	..	..	..	..	..	..	..	..
17 Somalia	10	34	20	16	43	26	4	24	13
18 Togo	55	122	102	78	150	125	32	93	78
19 Rwanda	53	63	67	64	66	68	43	60	66
20 Sierra Leone	29	54	..	37	64	..	21	45	..
21 Benin	34	64	65	48	88	87	21	40	43
22 Central African Republic	56	71	66	84	93	81	28	51	50
23 Kenya	54	110	94	69	115	97	40	104	91
24 Sudan	29	50	50	37	59	59	21	41	41
25 Comoros	24	93	80	36	109	90	12	78	70
26 Lesotho	94	102	115	74	85	102	114	120	127
27 Nigeria	32	97	..	39	110	..	24	84	..
28 Ghana	69	73	63	82	80	75	57	65	59
29 Mauritania	13	34	46	19	44	57	6	24	35
30 Liberia	41	76	..	59	95	..	23	57	..
31 *Equatorial Guinea*	65	84	..	79	..	..	52	..	..
32 *Guinea*	31	31	29	44	42	40	19	21	17
Middle-income economies	73 w	99 w	95 w	89 w	94 w	104 w	58 w	78 w	88 w
33 Cape Verde	..	112	108	..	117	112	..	..	105
34 Senegal	40	46	55	52	55	66	29	36	45
35 Zimbabwe	110	88	129	128	..	132	92	..	126
36 Swaziland	74	106	110	76	106	110	71	106	109
37 Côte d'Ivoire	60	80	78	80	97	92	41	..	65
38 Congo, People's Republic	114	..	..	134	..	..	94	..	..
39 Cameroon	94	104	107	114	113	116	75	95	97
40 Botswana	65	91	105	59	82	101	71	100	109
41 Mauritius	101	108	106	105	109	105	97	108	106
42 Gabon	134	115	126	146	117	127	122	113	125
43 Seychelles	..	..	..	..	..	..	..	..	..
44 *Angola*	39	158	93	53	..	..	26	..	..
45 *Djibouti*	..	..	..	..	..	..	..	..	..
Six most populous economies	34 w	82 w	69 w	44 w	93 w	77 w	24 w	71 w	61 w
Sahelian economies	23 w	32 w	39 w	32 w	40 w	49 w	14 w	23 w	28 w
Oil exporters	40 w	102 w	95 w	48 w	110 w	108 w	30 w	85 w	88 w
World low-income economies									
Total	73 w	93 w	102 w	74 w	105 w	112 w	47 w	79 w	91 w
Excluding China and India	49 w	79 w	78 w	60 w	89 w	86 w	37 w	68 w	69 w
South Asia	68 w	78 w	84 w	83 w	92 w	98 w	52 w	62 w	69 w
Excluding India	50 w	62 w	57 w	66 w	71 w	68 w	34 w	43 w	46 w

Note: Summary measures are weighted by each country's share in the aggregate population. Summary measures do not include estimates for missing country data.

	Secondary									Tertiary total			
	Total			Male			Female						
1965	1980	1986	1965	1980	1986	1965	1980	1986	1965	1980	1986	
													Sub-Saharan Africa
4 w	16 w	20 w	6 w	21 w	27 w	2 w	10 w	13 w	0 w	1 w	2 w	Total
4 w	15 w	16 w	6 w	19 w	20 w	2 w	10 w	12 w	0 w	1 w	1 w	Excluding Nigeria
4 w	16 w	19 w	6 w	20 w	25 w	2 w	10 w	12 w	0 w	1 w	2 w	Low-income economies
4 w	14 w	14 w	6 w	19 w	17 w	2 w	9 w	10 w	0 w	1 w	1 w	Excluding Nigeria
2	9	12	3	11	14	1	6	9	0	0	1	Ethiopia
1	..	6	3	..	10	0	..	2	..	..	0	Chad
5	35	..	8	51	..	2	19	..	0	1	2	Zaire
2	6	11	2	10	18	2	2	4	..	..	..	Guinea-Bissau
2	4	4	3	5	6	1	2	3	0	1	1	Malawi
3	5	7	3	8	9	2	3	5	0	0	0	Mozambique
2	3	3	3	4	4	1	2	3	0	..	0	Tanzania
1	3	6	2	4	8	1	2	4	0	0	1	Burkina Faso
8	..	36	10	..	43	5	..	30	1	3	5	Madagascar
4	8	7	5	12	9	2	5	4	0	0	1	Mali
6	13	20	8	19	29	4	8	12	..	..	..	Gambia, The
1	3	4	2	5	6	1	2	3	0	1	1	Burundi
7	17	19	11	22	24	3	12	14	..	2	2	Zambia
1	5	6	1	7	9	0	3	3	..	0	1	Niger
4	5	..	6	7	..	2	3	..	0	1	1	Uganda
..	..	..	..	..	..	..	..	..	..	..	..	São Tomé and Principe
2	13	12	4	19	15	1	7	8	0	..	4	Somalia
5	34	21	8	..	32	2	..	10	0	2	2	Togo
2	2	3	3	2	4	1	1	2	0	0	0	Rwanda
5	14	..	8	20	..	3	8	..	0	1	..	Sierra Leone
3	16	16	5	24	23	2	9	9	0	2	..	Benin
2	14	13	4	21	19	1	7	7	..	1	1	Central African Republic
4	19	20	6	22	25	2	15	15	0	1	1	Kenya
4	16	20	6	20	23	2	12	17	1	2	2	Sudan
3	24	30	5	31	36	1	16	24	..	..	..	Comoros
4	17	22	4	14	18	4	20	26	0	2	2	Lesotho
5	19	..	7	24	..	3	13	..	0	2	3	Nigeria
13	37	35	19	46	45	7	28	27	1	..	2	Ghana
1	10	15	2	16	21	0	4	8	..	..	0	Mauritania
5	23	..	8	33	..	3	13	..	1	..	..	Liberia
7	..	..	11	..	..	4	..	..	..	..	..	*Equatorial Guinea*
5	14	9	9	21	14	2	8	5	0	4	1	*Guinea*
7 w	17 w	24 w	9 w	24 w	33 w	4 w	13 w	21 w	0 w	2 w	2 w	Middle-income economies
..	8	14	..	9	15	..	7	12	..	..	..	Cape Verde
7	11	13	10	15	18	3	7	9	1	3	2	Senegal
6	8	46	8	..	55	5	..	37	0	1	4	Zimbabwe
8	39	43	9	40	44	7	38	43	..	4	4	Swaziland
6	19	20	10	26	27	2	12	12	0	3	3	Côte d'Ivoire
10	..	..	15	..	..	5	..	..	1	6	..	Congo, People's Republic
5	19	23	8	24	29	2	13	18	0	2	2	Cameroon
3	19	31	5	18	29	3	21	33	..	1	2	Botswana
26	48	51	34	49	53	18	47	49	3	1	1	Mauritius
11	21	27	16	25	31	5	17	22	..	..	4	Gabon
..	..	..	..	..	..	..	..	..	..	..	..	Seychelles
5	19	13	6	..	..	4	..	..	0	0	1	*Angola*
..	..	..	..	..	..	..	..	..	..	..	..	*Djibouti*
4 w	17 w	21 w	6 w	23 w	28 w	2 w	12 w	13 w	0 w	2 w	2 w	Six most populous economies
3 w	7 w	8 w	4 w	10 w	12 w	1 w	4 w	5 w	0 w	1 w	1 w	Sahelian economies
5 w	19 w	26 w	7 w	24 w	39 w	3 w	13 w	18 w	0 w	2 w	3 w	Oil exporters
												World low-income economies
20 w	34 w	35 w	27 w	42 w	42 w	9 w	26 w	26 w	2 w	1 w	3 w	Total
9 w	21 w	26 w	13 w	26 w	32 w	5 w	15 w	20 w	1 w	2 w	4 w	Excluding China and India
24 w	29 w	32 w	36 w	38 w	41 w	12 w	20 w	22 w	4 w	3 w	5 w	South Asia
14 w	20 w	22 w	21 w	26 w	28 w	7 w	12 w	15 w	1 w	3 w	5 w	Excluding India

Table 33. Health and nutrition

		Population per				Daily calorie supply per capita			Babies with low birth weights (percent)
		Physician		Nursing person					
		1965	1984	1965	1984	1965	1980	1986	1985
Sub-Saharan Africa									
Total		33,390 w	23,610 w	5,420 w	2,100 w	2,092 w	2,152 w	2,097 w	..
	Excluding Nigeria	34,630 w	29,820 w	5,160 w	2,560 w	2,062 w	2,120 w	2,081 w	..
Low-income economies		35,280 w	24,760 w	5,710 w	2,200 w	2,084 w	2,132 w	2,078 w	..
	Excluding Nigeria	37,430 w	32,340 w	5,520 w	2,760 w	2,045 w	2,087 w	2,052 w	..
1 Ethiopia		70,190	77,360	5,970	5,290	1,824	1,807	1,749	..
2 Chad		72,480	38,360	13,610	3,390	2,399	1,799	1,717	11
3 Zaire		35,130	..	..	..	2,187	2,123	2,163	..
4 Guinea-Bissau		..	7,260	..	1,130	1,910	1,906	2,186	20
5 Malawi		47,320	11,560	40,980	3,130	2,244	2,406	2,310	10
6 Mozambique		18,000	37,950	5,370	5,760	1,979	1,810	1,595	15
7 Tanzania		21,700	..	2,100	..	1,832	2,310	2,192	14
8 Burkina Faso		73,960	57,180	4,150	1,680	2,009	2,029	2,139	18
9 Madagascar		10,620	10,000	3,650	..	2,462	2,491	2,440	10
10 Mali		51,510	25,390	3,360	1,350	1,859	1,720	2,074	17
11 Gambia, The		..	11,690	1,730	..	2,194	2,154	2,517	..
12 Burundi		55,910	21,120	7,320	3,040	2,391	2,304	2,343	14
13 Zambia		11,380	7,100	5,820	740	..	..	..	14
14 Niger		65,540	38,770	6,210	450	1,994	2,363	2,432	20
15 Uganda		11,110	21,900	3,130	2,060	2,360	2,151	2,344	10
16 São Tomé and Principe		..	1,990	650	290	2,186	2,297	2,338	..
17 Somalia		36,840	16,090	3,950	1,530	2,167	2,099	2,138	..
18 Togo		23,240	8,720	4,990	1,240	2,378	2,178	2,207	20
19 Rwanda		72,480	34,680	7,450	3,650	1,665	2,007	1,830	17
20 Sierra Leone		16,840	13,630	4,470	1,090	1,837	2,034	1,855	14
21 Benin		32,390	15,940	2,540	1,750	2,009	2,041	2,184	10
22 Central African Republic		34,020	23,070	3,000	2,170	2,135	2,136	1,949	15
23 Kenya		13,280	10,100	1,930	950	2,289	2,225	2,060	13
24 Sudan		23,500	10,110	3,360	1,250	1,938	2,417	2,208	15
25 Comoros		..	12,260	3,780	2,260	2,296	2,074	2,109	..
26 Lesotho		20,060	18,610	4,700	..	2,065	2,400	2,303	10
27 Nigeria		29,530	7,980	6,160	1,020	2,185	2,254	2,146	25
28 Ghana		13,740	14,890	3,730	640	1,950	1,795	1,759	17
29 Mauritania		36,470	12,110	..	1,200	2,064	2,065	2,322	10
30 Liberia		12,360	9,240	2,290	1,360	2,154	2,375	2,381	..
31 *Equatorial Guinea*		..	..	..	..	..	..	..	..
32 *Guinea*		54,430	57,390	4,750	6,380	1,923	1,806	1,777	18
Middle-income economies		17,870 w	11,430 w	3,330 w	1,160 w	2,157 w	2,294 w	2,234 w	
33 Cape Verde		..	5,220	..	730	1,767	2,567	2,717	..
34 Senegal		21,130	13,450	2,640	2,090	2,479	2,401	2,350	10
35 Zimbabwe		8,010	6,700	990	1,000	2,105	2,137	2,132	15
36 Swaziland		..	18,850	1,250	1,050	2,100	2,483	2,578	..
37 Côte d'Ivoire		20,640	..	2,000	..	2,360	2,546	2,562	14
38 Congo, People's Republic		14,210	8,140	950	570	2,259	2,472	2,619	12
39 Cameroon		26,720	..	5,830	..	2,079	2,130	2,028	13
40 Botswana		27,460	6,910	17,720	700	2,019	2,152	2,201	8
41 Mauritius		3,930	1,900	2,030	580	2,272	2,715	2,748	9
42 Gabon		..	2,790	760	270	1,881	2,274	2,521	16
43 Seychelles		..	2,200	570	..	1,735	2,306	2,219	..
44 *Angola*		13,150	17,780	3,820	1,010	1,897	2,177	1,880	17
45 *Djibouti*		..	4,150	790	500	..	..	..	..
Six most populous economies		35,510 w	42,540 w	5,070 w	2,030 w	2,072 w	2,172 w	2,080 w	..
Sahelian economies		56,110 w	32,590 w	5,490 w	1,660 w	2,113 w	2,063 w	2,180 w	..
Oil exporters		27,860 w	8,720 w	5,850 w	1,000 w	2,154 w	2,241 w	2,128 w	..
All low-income economies									
Total		9,790 w	5,410 w	6,010 w	2,150 w	1,993 w	2,197 w	2,384 w	..
	Excluding China and India	28,190 w	13,550 w	10,170 w	3,130 w	1,976 w	2,166 w	2,227 w	..
South Asia		6,220 w	3,570 w	8,380 w	2,710 w	2,060 w	2,048 w	2,228 w	..
	Excluding India	12,520 w	6,570 w	17,690 w	5,630 w	1,901 w	2,073 w	2,199 w	..

Note: Summary measures are weighted by each country's share in the aggregate population. Summary measures do not include estimates for missing country data.

Table 34. Labor force

	Percentage of population of working age (15-64 years)			Percentage of labor force in						Average annual growth of labor force (percent)		
				Agriculture		Industry		Services				
	1965	1980	1985	1965	1980	1965	1980	1965	1980	1965-73	1973-80	1980-85
Sub-Saharan Africa												
Total	52 w	51 w	50 w	77 w	71 w	6 w	8 w	11 w	15 w	2.3 w	2.6 w	2.3 w
Excluding Nigeria	52 w	51 w	50 w	78 w	72 w	5 w	7 w	9 w	13 w	2.2 w	2.5 w	2.2 w
Low-income economies	52 w	51 w	50 w	77 w	71 w	6 w	8 w	10 w	14 w	2.3 w	2.7 w	2.4 w
Excluding Nigeria	52 w	51 w	50 w	78 w	72 w	5 w	7 w	8 w	12 w	2.2 w	2.5 w	2.2 w
1 Ethiopia	52	51	51	86	80	5	8	9	12	2.2	2.0	1.8
2 Chad	55	56	56	92	83	3	5	5	12	1.6	1.8	1.9
3 Zaire	52	51	51	82	72	9	13	9	16	1.6	1.9	2.3
4 Guinea-Bissau	..	53	52	86	82	2	4	12	14	0.9	4.2	1.2
5 Malawi	51	51	47	92	83	3	7	5	9	2.1	2.4	2.6
6 Mozambique	55	52	51	87	85	6	7	7	8	2.3	4.2	..
7 Tanzania	53	50	50	..	..	..	..	..	..	2.7	2.9	2.8
8 Burkina Faso	53	52	52	89	87	3	4	7	9	1.5	1.8	2.0
9 Madagascar	54	50	51	85	81	4	6	11	13	2.0	2.2	2.0
10 Mali	53	50	50	90	86	1	2	8	13	1.6	1.8	2.5
11 Gambia, The	53	55	55	88	84	5	7	7	9	2.0	1.9	1.3
12 Burundi	53	52	52	94	93	2	2	4	5	1.1	1.3	2.1
13 Zambia	51	49	49	79	73	8	10	13	17	2.6	2.8	3.3
14 Niger	51	52	51	95	91	1	2	4	7	1.8	2.0	2.3
15 Uganda	53	49	49	91	86	3	4	6	10	3.3	2.8	2.8
16 São Tomé and Principe	..	55	54	..	..	..	..	..	..	..	..	..
17 Somalia	49	52	53	81	76	6	8	13	16	2.6	3.6	1.9
18 Togo	52	50	50	78	73	9	10	13	17	3.3	2.1	2.3
19 Rwanda	51	51	49	94	93	2	3	3	4	2.7	3.2	2.8
20 Sierra Leone	54	55	54	78	70	11	14	11	16	0.8	1.0	1.2
21 Benin	52	50	49	83	70	5	7	12	23	1.7	2.1	2.1
22 Central African Republic	57	54	55	88	72	3	6	9	21	1.1	1.3	1.4
23 Kenya	48	46	45	86	81	5	7	9	12	3.5	3.7	3.5
24 Sudan	53	52	52	82	71	5	8	14	21	2.2	2.7	2.9
25 Comoros	51	51	51	88	83	4	6	8	11	2.6	3.1	2.4
26 Lesotho	56	54	53	92	86	3	4	6	10	1.6	2.0	2.0
27 Nigeria	51	50	49	72	68	10	12	18	20	2.9	3.2	2.7
28 Ghana	52	49	48	61	56	15	18	24	26	1.4	2.5	2.7
29 Mauritania	52	53	53	89	69	3	9	8	22	1.9	1.8	2.7
30 Liberia	51	55	52	79	74	10	9	11	16	2.5	2.7	2.2
31 *Equatorial Guinea*	55	58	58	79	66	7	11	14	23	1.0	1.2	1.4
32 *Guinea*	55	52	53	87	81	6	9	7	10	1.7	1.8	1.6
Middle-income economies	54 w	51 w	51 w	80 w	71 w	7 w	9 w	13 w	20 w	2.3 w	2.5 w	2.2 w
33 Cape Verde	50	47	51	67	52	14	23	19	26	2.5	1.0	3.4
34 Senegal	53	52	52	83	81	6	6	11	13	3.0	3.3	1.9
35 Zimbabwe	51	46	45	79	73	8	11	13	17	3.1	2.9	2.8
36 Swaziland	53	50	49	85	74	5	9	10	17	1.9	2.2	2.2
37 Côte d'Ivoire	54	53	53	81	65	5	8	15	27	3.0	2.5	2.7
38 Congo, People's Republic	55	51	51	66	62	11	12	23	26	1.9	2.1	1.9
39 Cameroon	55	52	50	86	70	4	8	9	22	1.7	1.6	1.9
40 Botswana	50	47	48	89	70	4	13	8	17	1.9	2.9	3.5
41 Mauritius	52	61	62	37	28	25	24	38	48	2.3	3.1	3.1
42 Gabon	61	58	58	83	75	8	11	10	14	0.7	0.9	0.6
43 Seychelles	..	55	57	..	..	..	..	13	17	1.7	2.8	1.8
44 *Angola*	54	52	52	79	74	8	10	..	..	..	..	..
45 *Djibouti*	..	52	51	..	..	..	..	..	..	..	..	..
Six most populous economies	52 w	50 w	50 w	70 w	65 w	7 w	9 w	11 w	15 w	2.5 w	2.8 w	2.6 w
Sahelian economies	52 w	52 w	52 w	90 w	85 w	3 w	4 w	7 w	11 w	1.9 w	2.2 w	2.1 w
Oil exporters	52 w	50 w	50 w	74 w	69 w	9 w	11 w	16 w	20 w	2.6 w	3.0 w	2.5 w
All low-income economies												
Total	53	56	58	77	71	9	13	13	15	2.1	2.2	2.3
Excluding China and India	49	53	53	74	66	8	10	15	20	2.1	2.1	2.4
South Asia	53	55	56	73	68	12	13	16	19	1.7	1.6	2.1
Excluding India	52	54	54	71	64	11	12	17	24	2.0	1.4	2.4

Note: The population of working age summary measures are weighted by each country's share in the aggregate population. Summary measures for the sectoral distribution of the labor force are weighted by each country's share in the aggregate labor force. Summary measures for labor force growth rates are weighted by each country's share in the aggregate labor force in 1980. Summary measures do not include estimates for missing country data.

Table 35. Urbanization

| | Urban population | | | | | | Percentage of urban population | | | | Number of cities of over 500,000 persons | |
| | As a percentage of total population | | | Average annual growth rate (percent) | | | In largest city | | In cities over 500,000 persons | | | |
	1965	1980	1987	1965-73	1973-80	1980-87	1960	1980	1960	1980	1960	1980
Sub-Saharan Africa												
Total	14 w	22 w	27 w	5.5 w	5.7 w	6.9 w	28 w	36 w	6.2 w	41 w	3 t	28 t
Excluding Nigeria	13 w	21 w	26 w	5.7 w	6.0 w	5.9 w	34 w	43 w	1 w	36 w	1 t	19 t
Low-income economies	13 w	21 w	26 w	5.4 w	5.5 w	7.1 w	27 w	35 w	7 w	41 w	3 t	23 t
Excluding Nigeria	12 w	19 w	23 w	5.7 w	5.9 w	5.9 w	33 w	42 w	2 w	35 w	1 t	14 t
1 Ethiopia	8	11	12	5.2	4.8	4.6	30	37	0	37	0	1
2 Chad	9	21	30	7.0	8.5	7.8	..	39	0	0	0	0
3 Zaire	26	34	38	4.7	4.5	4.6	14	28	14	38	1	2
4 Guinea-Bissau	16	24	29	3.8	8.1	4.4	..	..	..	..	..	..
5 Malawi	5	10	13	6.6	7.9	8.6	..	19	0	0	0	0
6 Mozambique	5	13	23	8.5	11.5	10.7	75	83	0	83	0	1
7 Tanzania	5	17	29	9.1	13.4	11.3	34	50	0	50	0	1
8 BurkinaFaso	5	7	8	3.9	4.4	5.3	..	41	0	0	0	0
9 Madagascar	12	19	23	5.2	5.7	6.4	44	36	0	36	0	1
10 Mali	13	17	19	4.6	3.8	3.4	32	24	0	0	0	0
11 Gambia, The	..	26	36	..	10.7	8.5	..	..	..	..	..	..
12 Burundi	2	5	7	4.7	11.8	9.2	..	..	0	0	0	0
13 Zambia	23	43	53	7.6	6.6	6.6	..	35	0	35	0	1
14 Niger	7	13	18	6.3	7.5	7.5	..	31	0	0	0	0
15 Uganda	7	9	10	8.4	3.8	5.0	38	52	0	52	0	1
16 São Tomé and Principe	18	30	40	6.0	5.1	7.3	..	..	..	..	..	..
17 Somalia	20	30	36	5.5	5.3	5.5	..	34	0	0	0	0
18 Togo	11	19	24	7.0	6.1	6.9	..	60	0	0	0	0
19 Rwanda	3	5	7	6.6	8.1	8.1	..	..	0	0	0	0
20 SierraLeone	15	22	26	4.5	3.8	5.0	37	47	0	0	0	0
21 Benin	11	28	39	8.0	8.5	7.9	..	63	0	63	0	1
22 Central African Republic	27	38	45	4.2	4.5	4.7	40	36	0	0	0	0
23 Kenya	9	16	22	7.2	8.5	8.6	40	57	0	57	0	1
24 Sudan	13	20	21.	6.7	4.4	4.2	30	31	0	31	0	1
25 Comoros	6	20	26	6.4	16.1	7.5	..	..	..	..	..	..
26 Lesotho	6	14	19	8.7	7.3	7.2	..	..	0	0	0	0
27 Nigeria	17	27	33	4.7	4.8	6.3	13	17	22	58	2	9
28 Ghana	26	31	32	3.9	2.4	4.1	25	35	0	48	0	2
29 Mauritania	10	27	38	9.0	9.2	7.9	..	39	0	0	0	0
30 Liberia	22	35	42	6.2	6.1	5.9	..	..	0	0	0	0
31 *Equatorial Guinea*	32	54	62	5.6	4.8	4.0	..	..	..	..	..	..
32 *Guinea*	12	19	24	5.1	5.3	5.7	37	80	0	80	0	1
Middle-income economies	20 w	31 w	37 w	5.7 w	6.3 w	6.1 w	39 w	45 w	0 w	43 w	0 t	5 t
33 Cape Verde	18	23	27	3.5	3.0	4.2	..	..	..	..	..	..
34 Senegal	33	35	37	2.8	3.2	3.8	53	65	0	65	0	1
35 Zimbabwe	14	22	26	6.7	5.5	6.3	40	50	0	50	0	1
36 Swaziland	7	14	30	5.1	13.3	13.9	..	..	..	..	..	..
37 Côte d'Ivoire	23	37	44	7.6	7.3	6.9	27	34	0	34	0	1
38 Congo, People's Republic	35	53	41	5.1	6.0	4.6	77	56	0	0	0	0
39 Cameroon	16	35	46	6.8	8.6	7.4	26	21	0	21	0	1
40 Botswana	4	19	21	18.4	10.3	8.1	..	..	..	..	..	..
41 Mauritius	37	43	42	3.6	1.7	0.8	..	..	..	..	..	..
42 Gabon	21	36	43	4.5	6.8	6.7	..	..	..	..	..	..
43 Seychelles	..	..	56	..	..	..	..	..	..	..	..	..
44 *Angola*	13	21	26	5.6	7.0	5.8	44	64	0	64	0	1
45 *Djibouti*	..	..	79	..	..	..	..	..	..	..	..	..
Six most populous economies	14 w	22 w	28 w	5.2 w	5.4 w	7.5 w	22 w	30 w	11 w	48 w	3 t	15 t
Sahelian economies	13 w	19 w	23 w	4.4 w	5.3 w	5.4 w	41 w	40 w	0 w	12 w	0 t	1 t
Oil exporters	17 w	28 w	34 w	5.0 w	5.4 w	9.1 w	17 w	21 w	18 w	54 w	2 t	11 t
All low-income economies												
Total	17 w	21 w	30 w	3.3 w	3.9 w	8.8 w	11 w	13 w	30 w	43 w	59 t	165 t
Excluding China andIndia	14 w	20 w	24 w	4.8 w	4.8 w	5.6 w	24 w	29 w	17 w	43 w	10 t	51 t
South Asia	18 w	22 w	25 w	3.8 w	4.0 w	4.1 w	11 w	11 w	25 w	40 w	15 t	49 t
Excluding India	15 w	19 w	21 w	4.5 w	4.1 w	4.3 w	22 w	25 w	22 w	41 w	4 t	13 t

Note: Summary measures for urban population as a percentage of total population are weighted by each country's share in the aggregate population. Summary measures for the other indicators are weighted by each country's share in the urban population. Summary measures do not include estimates for missing country data.

278

Table 36. Land use

	Total land area (thousand hectares)	Cropland			Pasture			Forest			Other		
		1965	*1980*	*1987*	*1965*	*1980*	*1987*	*1965*	*1980*	*1987*	*1965*	*1980*	*1987*
Low-income Sub-Saharan Africa													
1 Ethiopia	110,100	11	13	13	42	41	41	27	26	25	20	21	22
2 Chad	125,920	2	3	3	36	36	36	12	11	10	50	51	51
3 Zaire	226,760	3	3	3	4	4	4	80	78	77	13	15	16
4 Guinea-Bissau	2,812	9	10	12	38	38	38	39	38	38	13	13	12
5 Malawi	9,408	21	25	25	20	20	20	54	54	46	5	2	9
6 Mozambique	78,409	3	4	4	56	56	56	22	20	19	18	20	21
7 Tanzania	88,604	4	6	6	40	40	40	51	49	48	5	6	7
8 Burkina Faso	27,380	8	10	11	37	37	37	30	26	25	26	27	27
9 Madagascar	58,154	4	5	5	58	58	58	31	27	25	7	9	11
10 Mali	122,019	1	2	2	25	25	25	8	7	7	66	67	67
11 Gambia, The	1,000	13	16	17	9	9	9	30	22	17	48	54	57
12 Burundi	2,565	39	51	52	24	35	36	2	2	3	35	11	10
13 Zambia	74,072	7	7	7	47	47	47	42	40	39	4	6	6
14 Niger	126,670	2	3	3	8	8	7	3	2	2	87	87	88
15 Uganda	19,955	24	28	34	25	25	25	32	30	29	19	16	13
16 São Tomé and Principe	96	35	38	39	1	1	1	..	..	..	64	61	60
17 Somalia	62,734	1	1	1	46	46	46	16	15	14	37	38	38
18 Togo	5,439	20	26	26	4	4	4	45	31	25	31	39	45
19 Rwanda	2,495	26	41	45	34	19	16	23	21	20	17	20	19
20 Sierra Leone	7,162	20	25	25	31	31	31	30	30	29	19	15	15
21 Benin	11,062	13	16	17	4	4	4	44	36	33	39	44	47
22 Central African Republic	62,298	3	3	3	5	5	5	58	58	58	34	34	34
23 Kenya	56,697	3	4	4	7	7	7	8	7	6	82	83	83
24 Sudan	237,600	5	5	5	24	24	24	24	21	20	47	51	51
25 Comoros	223	38	41	44	7	7	7	16	16	16	39	37	34
26 Lesotho	3,035	12	10	11	73	66	66	..	..	..	15	24	24
27 Nigeria	91,077	32	33	34	21	23	23	23	18	16	24	26	27
28 Ghana	23,002	11	12	12	16	15	15	43	38	36	31	35	37
29 Mauritania	102,522	0	0	0	38	38	38	15	15	15	47	47	47
30 Liberia	9,632	4	4	4	2	2	2	22	22	22	72	72	72
31 *Equatorial Guinea*	2,805	8	8	8	4	4	4	46	46	46	42	42	42
32 *Guinea*	24,586	6	6	6	12	12	12	49	43	41	33	38	41
Middle-income Sub-Saharan Africa													
33 Cape Verde	403	10	10	10	6	6	6	0	0	0	84	84	84
34 Senegal	19,253	23	27	27	30	30	30	35	31	31	12	12	12
35 Zimbabwe	38,667	5	7	7	13	13	13	52	52	52	30	29	29
36 Swaziland	1,720	8	11	10	78	64	68	8	6	6	6	19	16
37 Côte d'Ivoire	31,800	8	10	11	9	9	9	60	31	20	22	50	59
38 Congo, People's Republic	34,150	2	2	2	29	29	29	64	63	62	5	6	7
39 Cameroon	46,540	12	15	15	19	18	18	59	55	53	10	12	14
40 Botswana	56,673	2	2	2	74	78	78	2	2	2	23	18	18
41 Mauritius	185	51	58	58	4	4	4	34	31	31	12	7	7
42 Gabon	25,767	1	2	2	20	18	18	78	78	78	2	2	2
43 Seychelles	27	19	19	22	..	..	..	19	19	19	63	63	59
44 *Angola*	124,670	3	3	3	23	23	23	44	43	43	30	31	31
45 *Djibouti*	2,318	..	..	..	9	9	9	0	0	0	91	91	91

Table 37. Environmental indicators

	Forest and woodland, 1980s (thousand hectares)	Deforestation, 1980s		Reforestation 1980s (thousand hectares per year)	Average annual production of roundwood (thousand cubic meters) Fuelwood and charcoal	
		Percent per year	Thousand hectares per Year		1984-86	Percentage change since 1974-76
Low-income Sub-Saharan Africa						
1 Ethiopia	27,150	0.3	88	6	36,132	27
2 Chad	13,500	0.6	80	0	3,063	25
3 Zaire	177,590	0.2	347	0	27,989	34
4 Guinea-Bissau	2,105	2.7	57	0	422	7
5 Malawi	4,271	3.5	150	6	6,211	34
6 Mozambique	15,435	0.8	120	1	14,203	54
7 Tanzania	42,040	0.3	130	7	21,604	41
8 Burkina Faso	4,735	1.7	80	2	6,452	25
9 Madagascar	13,200	1.2	156	12	6,083	32
10 Mali	7,250	0.5	36	0	4,599	29
11 Gambia, The	215	2.4	5	0	829	9
12 Burundi	41	2.7	1	1	3,593	26
13 Zambia	29,510	0.3	80	3	9,418	29
14 Niger	2,550	2.6	67	2	3,680	31
15 Uganda	6,015	0.8	50	0	10,868	38
16 São Tomé and Principe	..	..	..	..	..	..
17 Somalia	9,050	0.1	13	1	4,358	43
18 Togo	1,684	0.7	12	0	603	31
19 Rwanda	230	2.3	5	2	5,535	12
20 Sierra Leone	2,055	0.3	6	0	7,635	18
21 Benin	3,867	1.7	67	0	4,181	33
22 Central African Republic	35,890	0.2	55	..	2,925	32
23 Kenya	2,360	1.7	39	0	30,874	50
24 Sudan	47,650	0.2	104	11	17,690	35
25 Comoros	..	..	0	0	..	..
26 Lesotho	..	..	..	0	525	28
27 Nigeria	14,750	2.7	400	14	87,656	41
28 Ghana	8,693	0.8	72	3	8,219	38
29 Mauritania	554	2.4	13	0	7	40
30 Liberia	2,040	2.3	46	1	3,913	43
31 *Equatorial Guinea*	..	0.2	3	..	447	16
32 *Guinea*	10,650	0.8	86	0	3,647	25
Middle-income Sub-Saharan Africa						
33 Cape Verde	..	..	..	0	..	..
34 Senegal	11,045	0.5	50	2	3,505	33
35 Zimbabwe	19,820	0.4	80	5	5,867	41
36 Swaziland	74	..	0	5	560	20
37 Côte d'Ivoire	9,834	5.2	510	3	7,970	45
38 Congo, People's Republic	..	0.1	22	2	1,585	29
39 Cameroon	25,620	0.4	110	1	9,134	30
40 Botswana	32,560	0.1	20	..	1,107	46
41 Mauritius	..	..	0	1	14	-36
42 Gabon	20,575	0.1	15	..	2,525	15
43 Seychelles	..	..	..	..	..	..
44 *Angola*	53,600	0.2	84	0	3,903	34
45 *Djibouti*	106	..	..	..	..	..

Note: NM indicates not meaningful.
a. Refers only to areas larger than 4,000 square kilometers.

Average annual production of roundwood (thousand cubic meters)			Coastline areas and resources			
Industrial roundwood		Wilderness area [a] as a percentage of total land area 1985	Length of marine coastline 1987 (kilometers)	Average annual marine catch		
1984-86	Percentage change since 1974-76			1983-85 (thousand metric tons)	Percentage change since 1974-76	
						Low-income Sub-Saharan Africa
1,813	38	22	1,094	1	-76	Ethiopia
505	25	52	..	..	..	Chad
2,501	29	6	37	1	-91	Zaire
137	26	0	350	3	30	Guinea-Bissau
302	8	10	..	..	..	Malawi
966	4	9	2,470	34	39	Mozambique
1,454	51	10	1,424	38	-10	Tanzania
306	24	3	..	..	..	Burkina Faso
807	139	2	4,828	13	-22	Madagascar
309	26	49	..	..	..	Mali
21	110	0	80	9	-13	Gambia, The
45	41	0	..	..	..	Burundi
515	34	24	..	..	..	Zambia
242	32	53	..	..	..	Niger
1,633	31	4	..	..	..	Uganda
..	..	..	..	..	..	São Tomé and Principe
67	29	24	3,025	16	92	Somalia
163	27	0	56	14	47	Togo
237	295	0	..	..	..	Rwanda
140	2	0	402	36	-42	Sierra Leone
223	29	15	121	4	-38	Benin
466	-7	39	..	..	..	Central African Republic
1,555	59	25	536	6	60	Kenya
1,841	32	40	853	2	165	Sudan
..	..	NM	340	5	38	Comoros
..	..	80	..	..	..	Lesotho
7,765	106	2	853	214	-10	Nigeria
1,111	-40	0	539	212	8	Ghana
5	25	74	754	44	97	Mauritania
557	-6	17	579	10	61	Liberia
140	218	0	296	3	-24	*Equatorial Guinea*
604	17	0	320	26	143	*Guinea*
						Middle-income Sub-Saharan Africa
..	..	0	965	11	248	Cape Verde
546	37	11	531	235	-30	Senegal
1,347	55	0	..	..	..	Zimbabwe
1,663	-10	0	..	..	..	Swaziland
4,030	-19	16	515	67	-2	Côte d'Ivoire
849	49	42	169	20	22	Congo, People's Republic
2,702	71	3	402	32	-14	Cameroon
73	49	63	..	..	..	Botswana
5	-72	NM	177	11	55	Mauritius
1,484	-6	35	885	49	838	Gabon
..	..	..	491	4	11	Seychelles
997	-8	26	1,600	78	-62	*Angola*
..	..	0	314	0	32	Djibouti

Technical notes

The Statistical appendix provides economic and social indicators for selected periods or years in a form suitable for comparing economies and groups of economies. Economies are classified by GNP per capita levels. There are several groupings of Sub-Saharan Africa countries and two main comparator country groups. The tables include data on 45 economies in Sub-Saharan Africa. The introduction to the data and key provide details of country composition of the groups and other related information.

In addition to 37 tables there are 4 maps, which illustrate key statistics and measures. The indicators give a broad perspective on development in countries of Sub-Saharan Africa during the past two decades.

Considerable effort has been made to standardize the data; nevertheless statistical methods, coverage, practices, and definitions differ widely. In addition the statistical systems in many Sub-Saharan Africa economies are still weak, and this affects the availability and reliability of the data. Moreover intercountry and intertemporal comparisons always involve complex technical problems, which cannot be fully and unequivocally resolved. The data are drawn from sources thought to be most authoritative, but many of them are subject to considerable margins of error. Readers are urged to take these limitations into account in interpreting the indicators, particularly when making comparisons across economies.

To facilitate international comparisons, national accounts constant price data series based on years other than 1980 have been partially rebased to the 1980 base. This is accomplished by *rescaling*, which moves the year in which current and constant price versions of the same time series have the same value, without altering the trend of either. Components of GDP are individually rescaled and are summed to provide GDP and its subaggregates. In this process a rescaling deviation may occur between constant price GDP by industrial origin and GDP by expenditure. Such rescaling deviations are absorbed under the heading *private consumption, etc.*, on the assumption that GDP by industrial origin is a more reliable estimate than GDP by expenditure.

This approach takes into account the effects of changes in intersectoral relative prices between the original and the new base period. Because private consumption is calculated as a residual, the national accounting identities are maintained. It does, however, involve incorporating in private consumption whatever statistical discrepancies arise for *expenditure* in the rebasing process. The value added in the services sector also includes a statistical discrepancy as reported by the original source.

The summary measures are calculated by simple addition when a variable is expressed in reasonably comparable units of account. Indicators that do not seem naturally additive are usually combined by a price weighting scheme. However, the use of a single base year raises problems over a period encompassing profound structural changes and significant changes in relative prices, such as have occurred from 1965 to 1987.

The Statistical appendix does not present time series; growth rates and ratios are shown. For summary measures that cover many years, it is important that the calculation is based on the same country composition over time and across topics. This is done by permitting group measures to be compiled only if the country data available for a given year account for at least two-thirds of the full group, as defined by the 1980 benchmarks. So long as that criterion is met, uncurrent reporters (and those not providing ample history) are, for years with missing data, assumed to behave like the sample of the group that does provide estimates. Readers should keep in mind that the purpose is to maintain an appropriate relationship across indicators, despite myriad problems with country data and that nothing meaningful can be deduced about behavior at the country level by working back from group indicators. In addition the weighting process may result in discrepancies between summed subgroup figures and overall totals.

All growth rates shown are calculated from constant price series and, unless otherwise noted, have been computed using the least-squares method. The least-squares growth rate, r, is estimated by fitting a least-squares linear regression trend line to the logarithmic annual values of the variable in the relevant period. More specifically, the regression equation takes the form: $\log X_t = a + bt + e_t$, where this is equivalent to the logarithmic transformation of the compound growth rate equation, $X_t = X_0(1 + r)^t$. In these equations, X is the variable, t is time, and $a = \log X_0$ and $b = \log(1 + r)$ are the parameters to be estimated; e is the error term. If b^* is the least-squares estimate of b, then the annual average growth rate, r, is obtained as [antilog (b^*)]-1, and multiplied by 100 to express it in percentage terms.

The maps

The data source for the first three maps is the World Bank. For the first map, per capita GNP, 1987, GNP per capita figures in current dollars are calculated according to the World Bank Atlas method. See Table 1 and the technical notes for further explanation. For the second map, population growth, 1965–87, the least-squares growth rate is applied to total population figures. For the third map, under five mortality per 1,000 live births, 1985, data for Cape Verde, Comoros, Equatorial Guinea, Gabon, The Gambia, Guinea-Bissau, and Swaziland are for 1982. For the fourth map, growth of per capita food production, 1980-87, the least-squares growth rate is applied to the FAO index of food production which is based in international dollars.

Table 1. Basic indicators

Population estimates for mid-1987 are based on data from the Population Division of the United Nations or from World Bank sources. These are normally estimates, usually based on data from the most recent population censuses or surveys, which, in some cases, are neither recent nor very accurate. Refugees not permanently settled in the country of asylum are generally considered to be part of the population of their country of origin.

The data on *area* are from the Food and Agriculture Organization (FAO).

Gross national product (GNP) measures the total domestic and foreign value added claimed by residents and is calculated without making deductions for depreciation. It comprises GDP (defined in the note for Table 2) plus net factor income from abroad, which is the income residents receive from abroad for factor services (labor and capital) less similar payments made to nonresidents who contributed to the domestic economy.

GNP per capita figures in dollars are calculated according to the World Bank Atlas method. The *Atlas* conversion factor for any year is the average of the exchange rate for that year and the exchange rates for the two preceding years, after adjusting them for differences in relative inflation between the country and the United States. This three-year average smooths fluctuations in prices and exchange rates for each country. The resulting GNP in dollars is divided by the midyear population for the latest year to derive GNP per capita. The following formulas describe the procedures for computing the conversion factor for year t:

$$(e^*_{t-2,t}) = \frac{1}{3} \left[e_{t-2} \left(\frac{P_t}{P_{t-2}} \Big/ \frac{P_t^\$}{P_{t-2}^\$} \right) + \right.$$

$$\left. e_{t-1} \left(\frac{P_t}{P_{t-1}} \Big/ \frac{P_t^\$}{P_{t-1}^\$} \right) + e_t \right]$$

and for calculating GNP per capita in U.S. dollars for year t:

$$(Y_t^\$) = ([Y_t/N_t] / e^*_{t-2,t})$$

where

Y_t	=	current GNP (local currency) for year t
P_t	=	GNP deflator for year t
e_t	=	annual average exchange rate (local currency/dollar) for year t
N_t	=	midyear population for year t
$P_t^\$$	=	US GNP deflator for year t.

Through its regular review of member countries' national accounts, the Bank systematically evaluates the GNP estimates, focusing on the coverage and concepts employed and, where appropriate, making adjustments to improve comparability. As part of the review Bank staff estimates of GNP (and sometimes of population) may be developed for the most recent period. The Bank also systematically assesses the appropriateness of official exchange rates as conversion factors. An alternative conversion factor is used when the official exchange rate is judged to diverge by an exceptionally large margin from the rate effectively applied to foreign transactions. This applies to only a small number of countries.

The *average annual inflation rate* is measured by the growth rate of the implicit GDP deflator for each of the periods shown. The GDP deflator is first calculated by dividing, for each year of the period, the value of GDP at current values by the value of GDP at constant values, both in national currency. The least-squares method is then used to calculate the growth rate of the GDP deflator for the period.

Life expectancy at birth indicates the number of years a newborn infant would live if patterns of mortality prevailing for all people at the time of the birth were to stay the same throughout the lifetime of the infant. Data are from the UN Population Division, supplemented by World Bank estimates.

The *summary measures* for GNP per capita and life expectancy in this table are weighted by population. Those for average annual inflation rate are weighted by the 1980 share of country GDP valued in current dollars.

Tables 2 and 3. Growth of production; Structure of production

Most of the definitions used are those of the UN *System of National Accounts* (SNA). Estimates are obtained from national sources, sometimes reaching the World Bank through other international agencies but more often collected by World Bank staff during missions.

World Bank staff review the quality of national accounts data and in some instances, through mission work or technical assistance, help adjust national series. Because of the limited capabilities of statistical offices in some countries, strict international comparability cannot be achieved, especially in economic activities that are difficult to measure, such as the informal sector and subsistence agriculture.

GDP measures the total value of output of goods and services produced by an economy, by residents and nonresidents, regardless of the allocation to domestic and foreign claims. It is calculated without making deductions for depreciation. While the SNA envisages estimates of GDP by industrial origin to be at producer prices, many countries still report such details at factor cost, which differs from producer prices because of the treatment of certain commodity taxes at the sector level. Overall, GDP at producer prices is equal to GDP at purchaser values, less import duties. For individual sectors, say agriculture, values at producer prices differ from purchaser values because of indirect taxes less subsidies and, at least in theory, because purchaser prices include retail and wholesale margins and transport costs. International comparability of the estimates is affected by the use of differing country practices in valuation systems for reporting value added by production sectors. As a partial solution GDP estimates are shown at purchaser values if the components are on this basis, and such instances are footnoted. However, for a few countries in Tables 2 and 3, GDP at purchaser values has been replaced by GDP at factor cost.

The figures for GDP are dollar values converted from domestic currencies using single-year official exchange rates. For a few countries where the official exchange rate does not reflect the rate effectively applied to actual foreign exchange transactions, an alternative conversion factor is used. This table does not use the three-year averaging technique applied for GNP per capita in Table 1.

Agriculture covers forestry, hunting, and fishing, as well as agriculture. In developing countries with high levels of subsistence farming, much of agricultural production is not marketed. This increases the difficulty of measuring the contribution of agriculture to GDP and reduces the reliability and comparability of such numbers. *Industry* comprises value added in mining; *manufacturing* (also reported as a sub-group); construction; and electricity, water, and gas. Value added in all other branches of economic activity, including imputed bank service charges, import duties, and any statistical discrepancies noted by national compilers, are included in the *services, etc.* category.

Partially rebased 1980 series in domestic currencies, as explained in the introduction to the technical notes, are used to compute growth rates in Table 2. The sectoral shares of GDP in Table 3 are based on current price series.

In calculating the *summary measures* for each indicator in Table 2, partially rebased constant 1980 dollar values for each economy are calculated for each of the years of the periods covered, the values are aggregated across countries for each year, and the least-squares procedure is used to compute the growth rates. The average sectoral percentage shares in Table 3 are computed from group aggregates of sectoral GDP in current dollars.

Tables 4 and 5. Structure of demand; Growth of consumption and investment

General government consumption includes all current expenditures for purchases of goods and services by all levels of government. Capital expenditure on national defense and security is regarded as consumption expenditure.

Private consumption, etc. is the market value of all goods and services purchased or received as income in kind and the value of own account production consumed by households and nonprofit institutions. It excludes purchases of dwellings but includes imputed rent for owner-occupied dwellings. In practice it includes any statistical discrepancy in the use of resources. At constant prices this means it also includes the rescaling deviation from partial rebasing.

Gross domestic investment consists of outlays on additions to the fixed assets of the economy, plus net changes in the level of inventories.

Gross domestic savings are calculated by deducting total consumption from gross domestic product.

Exports of goods and nonfactor services represent the value of all goods and nonfactor services provided to the rest of the world; they include merchandise, freight, insurance, travel, and other nonfactor services. The value of factor services, such as investment income, interest, and labor income, is excluded from the measure of GDP.

The *resource balance* is the difference between exports of goods and nonfactor services and imports of goods and nonfactor services.

The national accounts series in current domestic currency units are used to calculate the shares of GDP in Table 4. The growth rates in Table 5 are calculated from the partially rebased 1980 series in constant domestic currency units (see the introduction to the technical notes).

The *summary measures* are calculated by the method explained in the note for Tables 2 and 3.

Table 6. Growth of production of major crops

Growth rates are calculated for the volume of production of major crops for total Sub-Saharan Africa. Data on agricultural production, except for sugar production, are from the FAO, based on country reports of output. These estimates should be used with caution, because for several countries the data are weak. Production data for sugar are from the International Sugar Organization. See the commodity notes for Table 7. Data for individual countries are added to obtain the aggregates for Sub-Saharan Africa. Growth rates are calculated using the least-squares method.

Table 7. Production of major crops

Data on agricultural production are from the FAO except for production data for sugar, which is from the International Sugar Organization. Data are in thousands of metric tons for the years indicated. The data for any particular crop refer to the calendar year in which the entire harvest or the bulk of it took place. Data are probably underestimated because it is difficult to estimate production levels of staple food crops, especially roots and tubers, when much of the output is consumed directly by farmers, rather than marketed.

Production data on cereals relate to crops harvested for dry grain only. Cereal crops harvested for hay or harvested green for food, feed, or silage or used for grazing are, therefore, excluded. Many countries, especially in Africa, make no distinction between *millet* and *sorghum* in their reports; in such cases combined figures are given in the table on millet. *Rice* refers to paddy paddy rice. *Total cereals* includes maize, millet, rice, sorghum, wheat, barley, oats, corn, and rye, expressed as bulk adding of tonnage. *Coconuts* refers to total production of coconuts, whether ripe or unripe, whether consumed fresh or processed into copra or desiccated coconut. Production is expressed in terms of weight of the whole nut, excluding only the fibrous outer husk. *Groundnuts* are in the shell. *Pulses* refers to total pulses and shows production of crops harvested for dry grain only, whether used for food or feed. *Roots and tubers* does not include root crops grown principally for feed. *Sugar* is sugar cane and sugar beets.

Table 8. Agriculture and food

The basic data for *value added in agriculture* are from the World Bank's national accounts series at current prices in national currencies, which are then converted into dollar values by using single-year official exchange rates. The figures for the remainder of this table are from the FAO.

Cereal imports are measured in grain equivalents and defined as comprising all cereals in the *Standard International Trade Classification* (SITC), revision 2, groups 041–046. *Food aid in cereals* covers wheat and flour, bulgur, rice, coarse grains, and the cereal component of blended foods. The figures are not directly comparable since cereal imports are based on calendar-year data, whereas food aid in cereals is based on data for crop years reported by donor countries and international organizations, including the International Wheat Council and the World Food Programme. Furthermore food aid information by donors may not correspond to actual receipts by beneficiaries during a given period because of delays in transportation and recording or because it is sometimes not reported to the FAO or other relevant international organizations. The earliest available food aid data are for 1974. The time reference for food aid is the crop year, July to June.

Fertilizer consumption measures the plant nutrients used in relation to arable land. Fertilizer products cover nitrogenous phosphate, which includes ground rock phosphate and potash fertilizers. Arable land is defined as land under temporary crops (double-cropped areas are counted once), temporary meadows for mowing or pastures, and land under market or kitchen gardens and land temporarily fallow or lying idle, as well as land under permanent crops. The time reference for fertilizer consumption is the crop year, July to June.

The *index of food production per capita* shows the average annual quantity of food produced per capita in 1985–87 in relation to that produced in 1979–81. The estimates are derived by dividing the

quantity of food production by the total population. For this index *food* is defined as comprising nuts, pulses, fruits, cereals, vegetables, sugar cane, sugar beet, starchy roots, edible oils, livestock, and livestock products. Quantities of food production are measured net of animal feed, seeds for use in agriculture, and food lost in processing and distribution.

The *summary measures* for fertilizer consumption are weighted by total arable land area; the *summary measures* for food production per capita are weighted by population.

Table 9. Structure of manufacturing

The basic data for *value added in manufacturing* are from the World Bank's national accounts series at *current* prices in national currencies, which are then converted into dollar values by using single-year official exchange rates. For a few countries where the official exchange rate does not reflect the rate effectively applied to actual foreign exchange transactions, an alternative conversion factor is used.

The data for *distribution of value added* among manufacturing industries are provided by the United Nations Industrial Development Organization (UNIDO), and the calculations are based on national currencies in current prices.

The classification of manufacturing industries is in accord with the UN *International Standard Industrial Classification of All Economic Activities* (ISIC). *Food and agriculture* comprise ISIC division 31; *textiles and clothing*, division 32; *machinery and transport equipment*, major groups 382–84; and *chemicals*, major groups 351 and 352. *Other* comprises wood and related products (division 33), paper and related products (division 34), petroleum and related products (major groups 353–56), basic metals and mineral products (divisions 36 and 37), fabricated metal products and professional goods (major groups 381 and 385), and other industries (major group 390). When data for textiles, machinery, or chemicals are shown as not available, they are also included in *other*.

Summary measures given for value added in manufacturing are totals calculated by the aggregation method noted in the beginning of the technical notes.

Table 10. Manufacturing earnings and output

Four indicators are shown—two relate to real earnings per employee, one to labor's share in total value added generated, and one to labor productivity in the manufacturing sector. The indicators are based on data from UNIDO, although the deflators are from other sources, as explained below.

Earnings per employee are in constant prices and are derived by deflating nominal earnings per employee, by the country's consumer price index as reported in the IMF's *International Financial Statistics* (IFS). *Total earnings as percentage of value added* are derived by dividing total earnings of employees by value added in current prices, to show labor's share in income generated in the manufacturing sector. *Gross output per employee* is in constant prices and is presented as an index of overall labor productivity in manufacturing with 1980 as the base year. To derive this indicator, UNIDO data on *gross output per employee* in current prices are adjusted using the implicit deflators for value added in manufacturing or in industry taken from the World Bank's national accounts data files. To improve cross-country comparability, UNIDO has, where possible, standardized the coverage of establishments to those with five or more employees.

The concepts and definitions are in accordance with the *International Recommendations for Industrial Statistics* published by the United Nations. *Earnings* (wages and salaries) cover all remuneration to employees paid by the employer during the year. The payments include all regular and overtime cash payments and bonuses and cost of living allowances; wages and salaries paid during vacation and sick leave; taxes and social insurance contributions and the like, payable by the employees and deducted by the employer; and payments in kind.

The value of *gross output* is estimated on the basis of either production or shipments. On the production basis it consists of the value of all products of the establishment, the value of industrial services rendered to others, the value of goods shipped in the same condition as received, the value of electricity sold, and the net change in the value of work-in-progress between the beginning and the end of the reference period. In the case of estimates compiled on a shipment basis, the net change between the beginning and the end of the reference period in the value of stocks of finished goods is also included. *Value added* is defined as the current value of gross output less the current cost of materials, fuels, and other supplies consumed; contract and commission work done by others; repair and maintenance work

done by others; and goods shipped in the same condition as received.

The term *employees* in this table combines two categories defined by the United Nations, *regular employees* and *persons engaged*. Together these groups comprise regular employees, working proprietors, active business partners, and unpaid family workers; they exclude homeworkers. The data refer to the average number of employees working during the year.

Table 11. Commercial energy

The data on energy are primarily from UN sources. They refer to commercial forms of primary energy—petroleum and natural gas liquids, natural gas, solid fuels (coal, lignite, and so on), and primary electricity (nuclear, geothermal, and hydroelectric power)—all converted into oil equivalents. Figures on liquid fuel consumption include petroleum derivatives that have been consumed in nonenergy uses. For converting primary electricity into oil equivalents, a notional thermal efficiency of 34 percent has been assumed. The use of firewood, dried animal excrement, and other traditional fuels, although substantial in some developing countries, is not taken into account because reliable and comprehensive data are not available.

Energy imports refer to the dollar value of energy imports—section 3 in the SITC, revision 1—and are expressed as a percentage of earnings from merchandise exports.

Because data on energy imports do not permit a distinction between petroleum imports for fuel and for use in the petrochemicals industry, these percentages may overestimate the dependence on imported energy.

The *summary measures* of *energy production* and *consumption* are computed by aggregating the respective volumes for each of the years covered by the periods and then applying the least-squares growth rate procedure. For *energy consumption per capita*, population weights are used to compute *summary measures* for the specified years.

The *summary measures* of *energy imports as a percentage of merchandise exports* are computed from group aggregates for energy imports and merchandise exports in current dollars.

Table 12. Growth of merchandise trade

The statistics on merchandise trade, Tables 12 through 14, are primarily from the UN trade data system, which accords with the UN, *Yearbook of International Trade Statistics*—that is, the data are based on countries' customs returns. However, more recent statistics are often from secondary sources, notably the IMF. World Bank estimates are also reported. Secondary sources and World Bank estimates are based on preliminary estimates of aggregate imports and exports. In some cases these permit coverage adjstments for significant components of a country's foreign trade not subject to regular customs reports. Values in these tables are in current dollars.

Merchandise exports and imports, with some exceptions, cover international movements of goods across customs borders. Exports are valued f.o.b. (free on board) and imports, c.i.f. (cost, insurance, and freight), unless otherwise specified in the foregoing sources. These values are in current dollars; that they do not include trade in services.

The *growth rates of merchandise exports and imports* are in constant terms and are calculated from quantum indexes of exports and imports. Quantum indexes are obtained from the export or import value indexes as deflated by the corresponding price index. To calculate these quantum indexes, the World Bank uses its own price indexes, which are based on international prices for primary commodities and unit value indexes for manufactures. These price indexes are country-specific and disaggregarted by broad commodity groups. This ensures consistency between data for a group of countries and those for individual countries. These growth rates can differ from those published by national statistical offices because national price indexes may use different base years and weighting procedures from those used by the World Bank.

The *terms of trade*, or the net barter terms of trade, measure the relative movement of export prices against that of import prices. Calculated as the ratio of a country's index of average export prices to its average import price index, this indicator shows changes over a base year in the level of export prices as a percentage of import prices. The terms of trade index numbers are shown for 1985 and 1987, where 1980 = 100. The price indexes are from the source cited above for the growth rates of exports and imports.

The *summary measures* for the growth rates are calculated by aggregating the 1980 constant dollar price series for each year and then applying the least-squares growth rate procedure for the periods shown. Again, these values do not include trade in services.

Tables 13 and 14. Structure of merchandise imports; Structure of merchandise exports

The shares in these tables are derived from trade values in current dollars reported in the UN trade data system, supplemented by other secondary sources and World Bank estimates as explained in the note to Table 12.

Merchandise exports and imports are defined in the note to Table 12. The categorization of exports and imports follows the SITC. Estimates from secondary sources also broadly follow this definition.

In Table 13 *food* commodities are those in SITC sections 0, 1, and 4 and division 22 (food and live animals, beverages, oils and fats, and oilseeds and nuts), less division 12 (tobacco). *Fuels* are the commodities in SITC section 3 (mineral fuels, lubricants, and related materials). *Other primary commodities* comprise SITC section 2 (crude materials, excluding fuels), less division 22 (oilseeds and nuts) plus divisions 12 (tobacco) and 68 (nonferrous metals). *Machinery and transport equipment* are the commodities in SITC section 7. *Other manufactures*, calculated residually from the total value of manufactured imports, represent SITC sections 5 through 9, less section 7 and division 68.

In Table 14, *fuels, minerals, and metals* are the commodities in SITC section 3 (mineral fuels and lubricants and related material) divisions 27 and 28 (minerals and crude fertilizers, and metalliferous ores) and division 68 (nonferrous metals). *Other primary commodities* comprise SITC sections 0, 1, 2, and 4 (food and live animals, beverages and tobacco, inedible crude materials, oils, fats, and waxes) less divisions 27 and 28. *Machinery and transport equipment* are the commodities in SITC section 7. *Other manufactures* represent SITC sections 5 through 9 less section 7 and division 68. *Textiles and clothing*, representing SITC divisions 65 and 84 (textiles, yarns, fabrics, and clothing), are shown as a subgroup of *other manufactures*.

The *summary measures* in Table 13 are weighted by total merchandise imports of individual countries in current dollars; those in Table 14, by total merchandise exports of individual countries in current dollars.

Table 15. Major agricultural exports

For each country the three major agricultural exports are determined by share in merchandise exports in current dollars. For several countries fewer than three agricultural export crops are listed because their exports of major crops are insignificant.

Volume of exports is expressed in thousands of metric tons. Data are for calendar years. *Export volume growth* is expressed in average annual rates and is calculated using the least-squares procedure. *Share of total merchandise exports* percentages are calculated on the basis of current dollar values.

Volume and value data for agricultural exports are from the FAO. Export data are probably underestimated because parallel market activity, including trade, may not be fully accounted for. See the notes to Table 12 for information on value of merchandise exports.

Table 16. Origin and destination of merchandise exports

Merchandise exports are defined in the note for Table 12. Trade shares in this table are based on statistics from the United Nations and the IMF on the value of trade in current dollars. *High-income economies* also include Gibraltar, Iceland, and Luxembourg. See the *World Development Report 1989* for lists of countries included in *high-income economies, middle- and low-income economies,* and *nonreporting nonmembr economies.*

The *summary measures* are weighted by the value ot total merchandise exports of individual countries in current dollars.

Table 17. Origin and destination of manufactured exports

The value of *manufactured exports,* reported by country of origin, conforms to Table 14, where separate shares in total merchandise exports are given for machinery and transport equipment and for other manufactures. The *destination of manufactured exports* is based on the UN's Commodity Trade files. Although the two are conceptually the same, differences may arise because aggregate estimates by country of origin (included in Table 14) tend to be more current and comprehensive. When data on values of manufactured exports are not available from the United Nations, supplementary sources, including IMF and World Bank data files, are used.

Manufactured goods are the commodities in SITC, revision 1, sections 5 through 9 (chemicals and related products, basic manufactures, manufactured articles, machinery and transport equipment, and other manufactured articles and goods

not elsewhere classified) excluding division 68 (nonferrous metals).

In the *destination* columns, *high-income economies* also include Gibraltar, Iceland, and Luxembourg. See the *World Development Report 1989* for lists of countries included in *high-income economies, middle- and low-income economies,* and *nonreporting nonmembr economies.* The *summary measures* are weighted by manufactured exports of individual countries in current dollars.

Table 18. Official development assistance

Official development assistance (ODA) consists of net disbursements of loans and grants made on concessional financial terms by all donors to promote economic development and welfare. They include the value of technical cooperation and assistance. Net disbursements equal gross disbursements less payments to the originators of aid for amortization of past receipts. Although this definition aims at excluding purely military assistance, the borderline is sometimes blurred; the definition used by the country of origin usually prevails. All data shown are supplied by the Organisation for Economic Co-operation and Development (OECD), and all dollar values are converted at official exchange rates.

Amounts shown are net disbursements to developing countries and multilateral institutions.

Bilateral net disbursements of ODA are shown as a percentage of the total, net disbursements of ODA are shown *per capita,* and *total grants* and *technical assistance* are shown as a percentage of net ODA. Percentages are calculated based on current dollar values.

The *summary measures* of per capita ODA are computed from group aggregates. *Summary measures* for bilateral ODA as a percentage of net ODA, and grants and technical assistance as a percentage of net ODA are computed from group totals in current dollar values.

Table 19. Total external debt

The data on debt in Tables 19 through 23 are from national sources and as reported through the World Bank Debtor Reporting System, supplemented by World Bank estimates. That system is concerned solely with developing economies and does not collect data on external debt for other groups of borrowers, nor from economies that are not members of the World Bank. The dollar figures on debt shown in Tables 19 through 23 are in dollars converted at official exchange rates.

Public loans are external obligations of public debtors, including the national government, its agencies, and autonomous public bodies. *Publicly guaranteed loans* are external obligations of private debtors that are guaranteed for repayment by a public entity. These two categories are aggregated in the tables. *Private nonguaranteed loans* are external obligations of private debtors that are not guaranteed for repayment by a public entity.

Use of IMF credit denotes repurchase obligations to the IMF for all uses of IMF resources, excluding those resulting from drawings in the reserve tranche and on the IMF Trust Fund and the Structural Adjustment Facility. It is shown for the end of the year specified. It comprises purchases outstanding under the credit tranches, including enlarged access resources, and all of the special facilities (the buffer stock, compensatory financing, and Extended Fund Facility). Trust Fund and Structural Adjustment Facility loans are included individually in the Debtor Reporting System and are thus shown within the total of public long-term debt. Use of IMF credit outstanding at year end (a stock) is converted to dollars at the dollar-SDR exchange rate in effect at year end.

Short-term external debt is debt with an original maturity of one year or less. Available data permit no distinctions between public and private nonguaranteed short-term debt.

Total external debt is defined for the purpose of this report as the sum of public, publicly guaranteed, and private nonguranteed long-term debt, use of IMF credit, and short-term debt.

Table 20. Flow of public and private external capital

Data on *disbursements* and *repayment of principal* (amortization) are for public, publicly guaranteed, and private nonguaranteed long-term loans. The *net flow* estimates are disbursements less the repayments of principal.

Table 21. Total external public and private debt and debt service ratios

Total long-term debt data in this table cover public and publicly guaranteed debt and private nonguaranteed debt. *Interest payments* are actual payments on outstanding and disbursed long-term debt; they include commitment charges on undisbursed debt if information on those charges

is available. *Total long-term debt service as a percentage of GNP* and *as a percentage of exports of goods and services* are calculated based on current dollar values. (See the notes to Table 22.)

Table 22. External public debt and debt service ratios

External public debt outstanding and disbursed represents public and publicly guaranteed loans drawn at year-end, net of repayments of principal and write-offs. For estimating external public debt as a percentage of GNP, the debt figures are converted into dollars from currencies of repayment at end-of-year official exchange rates. GNP is converted from national currencies to dollars by using single-year official exchange rates. For a few countries where the official exchange rate does not reflect the rate effectively applied to actual foreign transactions, an alternative conversion factor is used.

Interest payments are actual payments made on the outstanding and disbursed public and publicly guaranteed debt in foreign currencies, goods, or services; they include commitment charges on undisbursed debt if information on those charges is available.

Debt service is the sum of actual repayments of principal (amortization) and actual payments of interest made in foreign currencies, goods, or services on external public and publicly guaranteed debt. Debt service as a percentage of GNP and debt service as a percentage of exports of goods and services are the same as those for estimating external public debt as a percentage of GNP, which is described above.

The *summary measures* are computed from group aggregates of external public debt, debt service, and GNP in current dollars.

Table 23. Terms of external public borrowing

Commitments refer to the public and publicly guaranteed loans for which contracts were signed in the year specified. They are reported in currencies of repayment and converted into dollars at average annual official exchange rates.

Figures for *interest rates*, *maturities*, and *grace periods* are averages weighted by the amounts of the loans. Interest is the major charge levied on a loan and is usually computed on the amount of principal drawn and outstanding. The maturity of a loan is the interval between the agreement date, when a loan agreement is signed or bonds are issued, and the date of final repayment of principal. The grace period is the interval between the agreement date and the date of the first repayment of principal.

Public loans with variable interest rates, as a percentage of public debt, refer to interest rates that float with movements in a key market rate; for example, the London interbank offered rate (LIBOR) or the US prime rate. This column shows the borrower's exposure to changes in international interest rates.

The *summary measures* in this table are weighted by the amounts of the loans.

Table 24. Balance of payments and reserves

The statistics for this table are mostly as reported by the IMF but do include estimates by World Bank staff for the recent past and, in rare instances, the Bank's own coverage or classification adjustments to enhance international comparability. Values in this table are in current dollars.

The *current account balance after official transfers* is the difference between exports of goods and services (factor and nonfactor) as well as inflows of unrequited transfers (private and official), and imports of goods and services as well as unrequited transfers to the rest of the world.

The *current account balance before official transfers* is the current account balance that treats net official unrequited transfers as akin to official capital movements. The difference between the two balance of payment measures is essentially foreign aid in the form of grants, technical assistance, and food aid, which, for most developing countries, tends to make current account deficits smaller than the financing requirement.

Net workers' remittances cover payments and receipts of income by migrants who are employed or expect to be employed for more than a year in a foreign economy, where they are considered residents. These remittances are classified as private unrequited transfers and are included in the balance of payments current account balance, while those derived from shorter-term stays are included in services, as labor income. The distinction accords with internationally agreed guidelines, but many developing countries classify workers' remittances as a factor income receipt (and hence a component of GNP). The World Bank adheres to international guidelines in defining GNP and, therefore, may differ from national practices.

Net direct private investment is the net amount invested or reinvested by nonresidents in enterprises in which they or other nonresidents exercise significant managerial control, including equity capital, reinvested earnings, and other capital. The net figures are obtained by subtracting the value of direct investment abroad by residents of the reporting country.

Gross international reserves comprise holdings of monetary gold, special drawing rights (SDRs), the reserve position of members in the IMF, and holdings of foreign exchange under the control of monetary authorities. The data on holdings of international reserves are from IMF data files. The gold component of these reserves is valued throughout at year-end (December 31) London prices: that is, $37.37 an ounce in 1970, $589.50 an ounce in 1980, and $484.10 an ounce in 1987. The reserve levels for 1970, 1980, and 1987 refer to the end of the year indicated and are in current dollars at prevailing exchange rates. Because of differences in the definition of international reserves, in the valuation of gold, and in reserve management practices, the levels of reserve holdings published in national sources do not have strict comparability. Reserve holdings at the end of 1987 are also expressed in terms of the number of months of imports of goods and services they could pay for, with total imports level for 1987.

The *summary measures* are computed from group aggregates for gross international reserves and total imports of goods and services, in current dollars.

Table 25. Central government expenditure

The data on central government finance in Tables 25 and 26 are from the IMF, *Government Finance Statistics Yearbook, 1988* and IMF data files. The accounts of each country are reported using the system of common definitions and classifications found in the IMF, *Manual on Government Finance Statistics* (1986).

The shares of total expenditure and revenue by category are calculated from series in national currencies. Because of differences in coverage of available data, the individual components of central government expenditure and current revenue shown in these tables may not be strictly comparable across all economies.

Moreover inadequate statistical coverage of state, provincial, and local governments dictates the use of central government data; this may seriously understate or distort the statistical portrayal of the allocation of resources for various purposes, especially in countries where lower levels of government have considerable autonomy and are responsible for many economic and social services. In addition, *central government* can mean either of two accounting concepts: *consolidated* or *budgetary*. For most countries central government finance data have been consolidated into one overall account, but for others only the budgetary central government accounts are available. Since all central government units are not included in the budgetary accounts, the overall picture of central government activities is incomplete. Countries reporting budgetary data are footnoted.

For these and other reasons the data presented, especially those for education and health, are not comparable across countries. In many economies private health and education services provided by central governments are substantial; in some others these services may be financed by lower levels of government. In a small number of countries education and health services are privately financed. Caution should therefore be exercised in using the data for cross-country comparisons.

Central government expenditure comprises the expenditure by all government offices, departments, establishments, and other bodies that are agencies or instruments of the central authority of a country. It includes both current and capital (development) expenditure.

Defense comprises all expenditure, whether by defense or other departments, on the maintenance of military forces, including the purchase of military supplies and equipment, construction, recruiting, and training. Also in this category are closely related items such as military aid programs.

Education comprises expenditure on the provision, management, inspection, and support of preprimary, primary, and secondary schools; of universities and colleges; and of vocational, technical, and other training institutions. Also included is expenditure on the general administration and regulation of the education system; on research into its objectives, organization, administration, and methods; and on such subsidiary services as transport, school meals, and school medical and dental services.

Health covers public expenditure on hospitals, health, maternity and dental centers, and clinics with a major medical component; on national health and medical insurance schemes; and on family planning and preventive care.

Housing and community amenities and social security and welfare cover expenditures on housing, on the provision and support of housing and slum clearance activities, on community development, and on sanitary services. They also cover compensation for loss of income to the sick and temporarily disabled; payments to the elderly, the permanently disabled, and the unemployed; family, maternity, and child allowances; and the cost of welfare services, such as care of the aged, the disabled, and children. Many expenditures relevant to environmental defense, such as pollution abatement, water supply, sanitary affairs, and refuse collection, are included indistinguishably in this category.

Economic services comprise expenditure associated with the regulation, support, and more efficient operation of business, economic development, redress of regional imbalances, and creation of employment opportunities. Research, trade promotion, geological surveys, and inspection and regulation of particular industry groups are among the activities included.

Other covers items not included elsewhere; for a few economies it also includes amounts that could not be allocated to other components (or adjustments from accrual to cash accounts).

Total expenditure (as a percentage of GNP) is more narrowly defined than the measure of general government consumption (percentage of GDP) given in Table 4, because it excludes consumption expenditure by state and local governments. At the same time central government expenditure is more broadly defined because it includes government's gross domestic investment and transfer payments.

Overall surplus/deficit is defined as current and capital revenue and grants received, less total expenditure and lending minus repayments.

Table 26. Central government current revenue

Information on data sources and comparability is given in the note to Table 25. Current revenue by source is expressed as a percentage of total current revenue, which is the sum of tax and nontax revenue.

The first five indicators of tax revenue comprise compulsory, unrequited, and nonrepayable receipts for public purposes. They include interest collected on tax arrears and penalties collected on nonpayment or late payment of taxes and are shown net of refunds and other corrective transactions. *Taxes on income, profit, and capital gain* are taxes levied on the actual or presumptive net income of individuals, on the profits of enterprises, and on capital gains, whether realized on land sales, securities, or other assets. *Social security contributions* include employers' and employees' social security contributions, as well as those of self-employed and unemployed persons. *Domestic taxes on goods and services* include general sales, turnover or value added taxes, selective excises on goods, selective taxes on services, taxes on the use of goods or property, and profits of fiscal monopolies. *Taxes on international trade and transactions* include import duties, export duties, profits of export or import monopolies, exchange profits, and exchange taxes. *Other taxes* include employers' payroll or labor taxes, taxes on property, and taxes not allocable to other categories. They may include negative values that are adjustments, for instance, for taxes collected on behalf of state and local governments and not allocable to individual tax categories.

Nontax revenue comprises receipts that are not a compulsory nonrepayable payment for public purposes, such as administrative fees or entrepreneurial income from government ownership of property. Proceeds of grants and borrowing, funds arising from the repayment of previous lending by governments, incurrence of liabilities, and proceeds from the sale of capital assets are not included.

Total current revenue (as a percentage of GNP) is based on total current revenue and GNP in current dollar values.

Table 27. Money and interest rates

The data on monetary holdings are drawn from the IMF's *International Financial Statistics* (IFS). *Monetary holdings, broadly defined,* comprise the monetary and quasi-monetary liabilities of a country's financial institutions to residents other than the central government. For most countries monetary holdings are the sum of money (IFS line 34) and quasi-money (IFS line 35). Money comprises the economy's means of payment: currency outside banks and demand deposits. Quasi-money comprises time and savings deposits and similar bank accounts that the issuer will readily exchange for money. Where nonmonetary financial institutions are important issuers of quasi-monetary liabilities, these are also included in the measure of monetary holdings.

The growth rates for monetary holdings are calculated from year-end figures, while the aver-

age of the year-end figures for the specified year and the previous year is used for the ratio of monetary holdings to GDP.

Since interest rates (and growth rates for monetary holdings) are expressed in nominal terms, much of the variation between countries stems from differences in inflation. For easy reference the Table 1 indicator *average inflation* is repeated in this table.

The *nominal interest rates of banks*, also from IFS, represent the rates paid by commercial or similar banks to holders of their quasi-monetary liabilities (deposit rates) and charged by the banks on loans to prime customers (lending rates). They are, however, of limited international comparability partly because coverage and definitions vary and partly because countries differ in the scope available to banks for adjusting interest rates to reflect market conditions.

Table 28. Population growth and projections

Population growth rates are period averages calculated from midyear estimates of population.

Population estimates for mid-1987 are based on official estimates made by country statistical offices, the UN Population Division, and the World Bank. They take into account the results of population censuses, which, in some cases, are neither recent nor accurate. Refugees not permanently settled in the country of asylum are generally considered to be part of the population of their country of origin.

The *projections of population* for 2000, 2025, and the year in which the population will eventually become stationary (see definition below) are made for each economy separately. Information on total population by age and sex, fertility, mortality, and international migration is projected on the basis of generalized assumptions until the population becomes stationary. The base-year estimates are from updated printouts of the UN *World Population Prospects: 1988*; recent issues of the UN, *Population and Vital Statistics Report*; World Bank estimates; and national censuses and surveys.

The *net reproduction rate* (NRR), which measures the number of daughters a newborn girl will bear during her lifetime, assuming fixed age-specific fertility and mortality rates, reflects the extent to which a cohort of newborn girls will reproduce themselves. A NRR of 1 indicates that fertility is at replacement level: at this rate women will bear, on average, only enough daughters to replace themselves in the population.

A *stationary population* is one in which age- and sex-specific mortality rates have not changed over a long period, while age-specific fertility rates have simultaneously remained at replacement level (NRR=1). In such a population the birth rate is constant and equal to the death rate, the age structure is constant, and the growth rate is zero.

Population momentum is the tendency for population growth to continue beyond the time that replacement-level fertility has been achieved; that is, even after the NRR has reached 1. The momentum of a population in any given year is measured as a ratio of the ultimate stationary population to the population of that year, given the assumption that fertility drops to replacement level by that year and remains there.

A population tends to grow even after fertility has declined to replacement level because past high growth rates will have produced an age distribution with a relatively high proportion of women in, or still to enter, the reproductive ages. Consequently, the birth rate will remain higher than the death rate, and the growth rate will remain positive for several decades.

Population projections are made component by component. Mortality, fertility, and migration are projected separately, and the results are applied iteratively to the 1985 base year age structure. For the projection period 1985 to 2005, the changes in mortality are country specific: increments in life expectancy and decrements in infant mortality are based on previous trends for each country. When female secondary school enrollment is high, mortality is assumed to decline more quickly. Infant mortality is projected separately from adult mortality.

Projected fertility rates are also based on previous trends. For countries in which fertility has started to decline (fertility transition), this trend is assumed to continue. It has been observed that no country with a life expectancy of less than 50 years experienced a fertility decline; for these countries the average decline of the group of countries in fertility transition is applied. Countries with below-replacement fertility are assumed to have constant total fertility rates until 1995–2000 and then to regain replacement levels by 2030.

International migration rates are based on past and present trends in migration flows and migration policy. Among the sources consulted are estimates and projections made by national statistical offices, international agencies, and research institutions. Because of the uncertainty of future migration trends, it is assumed in the projections that net migration rates will reach zero by 2025.

The estimates of the size of the stationary population and the assumed year of reaching replacement-level fertility are speculative. *They should not be regarded as predictions.* They are included to show the implications of recent fertility and mortality trends on the basis of generalized assumptions. A fuller description of the methods and assumptions used to calculate the estimates will be available from the World Bank's forthcoming *World Population Projections, 1989–90 Edition.*

Table 29. Demography and fertility

The *crude birth and death rates* indicate, respectively, the number of live births and deaths occuring per thousand population in a year. They come from the sources mentioned in the note to Table 28.

The *percentage of women of childbearing age* provides a more complete picture of fertility patterns. *Childbearing age* is generally defined as 15 to 49.

The *total fertility rate* represents the number of children that would be born to a woman if she were to live to the end of her childbearing years and bear children at each age in accordance with prevailing age-specific fertility rates. The rates given are from the sources mentioned in Table 28.

The *percentage of married women of childbearing age using contraception* refers to women who are practicing, or whose husbands are practicing, any form of contraception. Contraceptive usage is generally measured for women age 15–49. A few countries use measures relating to other age groups such as 15 to 44, 18 to 44, and 19 to 49.

Data are mainly derived from the World Fertility Surveys, the Contraceptive Prevalence Surveys, the Demographic and Health Surveys, World Bank country data, and the UN *Recent Levels and Trends of Contraceptive Use as Assessed in 1983.* For several African countries for which no survey data are available, program statistics are used. Program statistics may understate contraceptive prevalence because they do not measure use of methods such as rhythm, withdrawal, or abstinence, or contraceptives not obtained through the official family planning program. The data refer to rates prevailing in a variety of years, generally not more than three years before the year specified in the tables.

All *summary measures* are country data weighted by each country's share in the aggregate population.

Table 30. Women in development

For information on the source for *female percentage of total population,* see the notes to Table 28.

Information on source and definition for *life expectancy at birth* is given in the notes to Table 1.

Average age at first marriage is from the United Nations Women's Indicators and Statistics Data Base, 1988. Data are for years between 1975 and 1983.

Projected economically active population data are given as female and male percentages of the labor force. Data are for all ages and are projections for 1985 from the United Nations Women's Indicators and Statistics Data Base, 1988.

Women in government data refer to the percent of women in the total membership of the national legislature. Data are from Sivard 1985.

Maternal mortality refers to the number of female deaths that occur during childbirth per 100,000 live births. Because "childbirth" is defined more widely in some countries, to include complications of pregnancy or of abortion, and since many pregnant women die because of lack of suitable health care, maternal mortality is difficult to measure consistently and reliably across countries. The data are drawn from diverse national sources and collected by the WHO. Many national administrative systems are weak and do not record vital events systematically. The data are derived mostly from official community reports and hospital records, and some reflect only deaths in hospitals and other medical institutions. Sometimes smaller private and rural hospitals are excluded, and sometimes even relatively primitive local facilitites are included. The coverage is therefore not always comprehensive, and the figures should be treated with extreme caution.

Clearly, many maternal deaths go unrecorded, particularly for remote rural populations; this accounts for some of the very low numbers shown in the table. The WHO warns that there are "inevitably gaps" in the series, and it has invited countries to provide more comprehensive figures. They are reproduced here from WHO, *Maternal Mortality Rates* (1986), supplemented by UNICEF, *The State of the World's Children 1989,* as part of the international effort to highlight data in this field. The data refer to years between 1977 and 1984.

Table 31. Status of children

For information on the source for *children as a percentage of the total population* see the notes to Table 28.

The *infant mortality rate* is the number of infants who die before reaching 1 year of age per thousand live births in a given year. The data are from UN, *Mortality of Children under Age 5: Projections, 1950–2025,* as well as from the World Bank's data files.

Data for the remaining indicators in the table are from UNICEF 1989. Much of the data cover somewhat different age groups.

Percentage of age group affected by wasting indicates the extent of accute malnutrition; data are given for children age 12 to 23 months. *Percentage of age group affected by stunting* indicates extent of chronic malnutrition; data are given for children age 24 to 59 months. Data refer to the percentage of children with greater than minus two standard deviations from the 50th percentile of the weight-for-height reference population (wasting) or the height-for-age reference population (stunting). Wasting/stunting therefore means less than 77 percent of the median weight-for-height (wasting) or height-for-age (stunting) of the reference population of the United States National Center for Health Statistics.

Percentage of children under age five suffering from malnutrition is the total for mild and moderate malnutrition (between 60 and 80 percent of the desirable weight-for-age) and severe malnutrition (less than 60 percent desirable weight-for-age).

Data for *percentage of one-year-old children fully immunized* is given for immunization against *tuberculosis, DPT, poliomyelitis,* and *measles.*

Table 32. Education

The data in this table refer to a variety of years, generally not more than two years distant from those specified, and are mostly from Unesco. However, disaggregated figures for males and females sometimes refer to a year earlier than that for overall totals.

The data on *primary school enrollments* are estimates of children of all ages enrolled in primary school. Figures are expressed as the ratio of pupils to the population of school-age children. While many countries consider primary school age to be 6 to 11 years, others do not. The differences in country practices in the ages and duration of schooling are reflected in the ratios given. For some countries with universal primary education, the gross enrollment raios may exceed 100 percent because some pupils are younger or older than the country's standard primary school age. The data on *secondary school enrollments* are calculated in the same manner, but again the definition of secondary school age differs among countries. It is most commonly considered 12 to 17 years. Late entry of more mature students, as well as repetition and the phenomenon of *bunching* in the final grades, can influence these ratios.

The *tertiary enrollment* ratio is calculated by dividing the number of pupils enrolled in all postsecondary schools and universities by the population in the 20–24 age group. Pupils attending vocational schools, adult education programs, two-year community colleges, and distance education centers (primarily correspondence courses) are included. The distribution of pupils across these different types of institutions varies among countries. The *youth* population, that is 20 to 24 years, is used as the denominator since it represents an average tertiary level cohort. Although in higher-income countries youths age 18 to 19 may be enrolled in a tertiary institution (and are included in the numerator), in both low- and middle-income economies, many people older than 25 years are also enrolled in such institutions.

The *summary measures* in this table are country enrollment rates weighted by each country's share in the aggregate population.

Table 33. Health and nutrition

The estimates of *population per physician and nursing person* are derived from World Health Organization (WHO) data. The data refer to a variety of years, generally no more than two years before the year specified. The figure for *physicians*, in addition to the total number of registered practitioners in the country, includes medical assistants whose medical training is less than that of qualified physicians, but who nevertheless dispense similar medical services, including simple operations. The numbers include "barefoot doctors." *Nursing persons* include graduate, practical, assistant, and auxilliary nurses, as well as paraprofessional personnel such as health workers, first aid workers, and traditional birth attendants. The inclusion of auxilliary and paraprofessional personnel provides more realistic estimates of available nursing care. Because definitions of doctors and nursing personnel vary—and because the data

shown are for a variety of years—these two indicators are not strictly comparable across countries.

The *daily calorie supply per capita* is calculated by dividing the calorie equivalent of the food supplies in an economy by the population. Food supplies comprise domestic production, imports less exports, and changes in stocks; they exclude animal feed, seeds for use in agricultrure, and food lost in processing and distribution. These estimates are from the FAO.

The percentage of *babies with low birth weights* relates to children born weighing less than 2,500 grams. Low birth weight is frequently associated with maternal malnutrition and tends to raise the risk of infant mortality and to lead to poor growth in infancy and childhood, thus increasing the incidence of other forms of retarded development. The figures are derived from WHO and UNICEF sources and are based on national data. The data are not strictly comparable across countries, as they are compiled from a combination of surveys and administrative records and other such sources.

The *summary measures* in this table are country figures weighted by each country's share in the aggregate population.

Table 34. Labor force

The *population of working age* refers to the population aged 15 to 64. The estimates are from the International Labour Organisation (ILO), based on UN population estimates.

The *labor force* comprises economically active persons aged 10 years and over, including the armed forces and the unemployed, but excluding *economically inactive* groups. The concept of *economically active* is restrictive and does not, for example, include activities of homemakers and other care-givers. *Agriculture, industry,* and *services* are defined as in Table 2. The estimates of the sectoral distribution of the labor force are from the ILO, *Labour Force Estimates and Projections, 1950–2000* (1986) and, in a few instances, from the World Bank. Labor force numbers in several developing countries appear to reflect a significant underestimate of female participation rates and are therefore themselves underestimates.

The *labor force growth rates* are from ILO data and are based on age-specific activity rates reported in the source cited above.

The application of ILO activity rates to the Bank's latest population estimates may be inappropriate for some economies in which there have been significant changes in unemployment and underemployment, as well as in international and internal migration.

Summary measures for population of working age are weighted by each country's share in aggregate population. *Summary measures* for the sectoral distribution of the labor force are weighted by each country's share in the aggregate labor force. *Summary measures* for labor force growth rates are weighted by each country's share in the aggregate labor force in 1980.

Table 35. Urbanization

The data on *urban population as a percentage of total population* are from the forthcoming UN publication, *The Prospects of World Urbanization*, supplemented by data from the World Bank.

The growth rates of urban population are calculated from the World Bank's population estimates; the estimates of urban population shares are calculated from the sources cited above. Data on urban agglomeration in large cities are from the UN, *Patterns of Urban and Rural Population Growth, 1980*.

Because the estimates in this table are based on different national definitions of what is *urban*, cross-country comparisons should be interpreted with caution. Data on urban agglomeration in large cities are from population censuses, which are conducted at 10-year intervals in most countries.

The *summary measures* for urban population, as a percentage of total population are weighted by each country's share in the aggregate population; the other *summary measures* in this table are weighted by each country's share in aggregate urban population.

Table 36. Land use

Data for *land area* and *land use as a percentage of total land area* are from the FAO.

Total land area refers to the total area of the country, including area under inland water bodies.

Cropland refers to arable land and land under permanent crops. Arable land includes land under temporary crops (double-cropped areas are counted only once), temporary meadows for mowing or pasture, land under market and kitchen gardens (including cultivation under glass), and land temporarily fallow or lying idle.

Land under permanent crops includes land cultivated with crops that occupy the land for long periods and need not be replanted after each harvest, such as cocoa, coffee, and rubber; it includes land under shrubs, fruit trees, nut trees and vines, but excludes land under trees grown for wood or timber.

Pasture refers to permanent meadows and pastures, land used permanently (five years or more) for herbaceous forage crops, either cultivated or growing wild (wild prairie or grazing land).

Forest refers to forests and woodland. It includes land under natural or planted stands of trees, whether productive or not, and includes land from which forests have been cleared but that will be reforested in the foreseeable future.

Other refers to unused but potentially productive land, built-on areas, wasteland, parks, ornamental gardens, roads, lanes, barren land, and any other land not specifically listed under the other three categories.

Table 37. Environmental indicators

Data are from the World Resources Institute, 1988–89.

Most data on forest and woodland, deforestation, and reforestation refer to the period around 1980, but no attempt has been made to adjust the data to a baseline year. *Forest and woodland* refers to natural stands of woody vegetation in which trees predominate. This includes all stands except plantations and includes stands that have been degraded to some degree by catastrophic fire, logging, or agriculture. *Deforestation* refers to the clearing of forest lands for use in shifting cultivation, permanent agriculture, or settlements. As defined here, deforestation does not include other alterations, such as selective logging, which can substantially affect forests, forest soil, wildlife and its habitat, and the global carbon cycle. *Reforestation* refers to the establishment of plantations for industrial and nonindustrial uses. Reforestation does not include regeneration of old tree crops (through either natural regeneration or forest management), although some countries may report regeneration as reforestation. Many trees are also planted for nonindustiral uses, such as village wood lots. Reforestation data often exclude this component.

Production of roundwood refers to all wood in the rough, whether destined for industrial uses or for use as fuelwood. *Fuelwood and charcoal* production includes all rough wood used for cooking, heating, and power production. Wood intended for charcoal production, pit kilns, and portable ovens is included. *Industrial roundwood* production refers to all roundwood products other than fuelwood and charcoal: sawlogs, veneer logs, sleepers, pitprops, pulpwood, and other industrial products.

Wilderness area refers to land showing no evidence of development, such as settlements, roads, buildings, airports, railroads, pipelines, powerlines, and reservoirs. The minimum unit of wilderness surveyed was 4,000 square kilometers.

Wilderness areas include areas classified as forest and woodlands or other lands by FAO.

The *average annual marine catch* data are for calendar years. Figures are national totals averaged over a three-year period; they include fish caught by a country's fleet anywhere in the world. Catch refer to marine fish killed, caught, trapped, collected, bred, or cultivated for commercial, industrial, and subsistence use. Crustaceans, molluscs, and miscellaneous aquatic animals are included. Quantities taken in recreational activities are excluded.

Bibliography

FAO, IMF, OECD, UN, UNIDO, and World Bank data; the World Bank Debtor Reporting System; and national sources.

Food and Agriculture Organization. (FAO). 1981. *Fertilizer Yearbook 1982.* Rome.

———. 1983. *Food Aid in Figures* (December). Rome.

———. 1987. *Trade Yearbook 1986.* Vol. 40. Rome.

———. 1989. *Production Yearbook 1988.* Vol. 42. Rome.

Institute for Resource Development/Westinghouse. 1987. *Child Survival: Risks and the Road to Health.* Columbia, Md.

International Union for Conservation of Nature and Natural Resources. 1986. *Review of the Protected Areas System in the Afro-tropical Realm.* Prepared in collaboration with the UN Environment Programme. John and Kathy MacKinnon, consultants. Cambridge, UK.

International Monetary Fund. 1988. *Government Finance Statistics Yearbook.* Vol. 12. Washington, D.C.

———. Various years. *International Finance Statistics.* Washington, D.C.

International Sugar Organization. Various years. *Sugar Yearbook.* London.

Organisation for Economic Co-operation and Development (OECD). 1987. *Geographical Distribution of Financial Flows to Developing Countries.* Paris.

———. Various years. *Development Co-operation.* Paris.

Sivard, Ruth. 1985. *Women—A World Survey.* Washington, D.C.: World Priorities.

United Nations. Department of International Economic and Social Affairs. 1980. *Patterns of Urban and Rural Population Growth.* New York.

———. 1984. *Recent Levels and Trends of Contraceptive Use as Assessed in 1983.* New York.

———. 1988. *Mortality of Children under Age 5: Projections 1950–2025.* New York.

———. Updated printouts. *World Population Prospects: 1988.* New York.

———. Various years. *Demographic Yearbook.* New York.

———. Various years. *Monthly Bulletin of Statistics.* New York.

———. Various years. *Population and Vital Statistics Report.* New York.

———. Various years. *Statistical Yearbook,* New York.

———. Various years. *World Energy Supplies.* Statistical Papers, series J. New York.

———. Various years. *Yearbook of International Trade Statistics.* New York.

———. Forthcoming. *The Prospects of World Urbanization.* New York.

United Nations Conference on Trade and Development (UNCTAD). Various years. *Handbook of International Trade and Development Statistics.* Geneva.

United Nations Development Programme (UNDP) and the World Bank. 1989. *African Economic and Financial Data.* Washington, D.C.

United Nations Educational, Scientific, and Cultural Organization (Unesco). Various years. *Statistical Yearbook.* Paris.

United Nations International Childrens' Emergency Fund (UNICEF). 1989. *The State of the*

World's Children 1989. Oxford: Oxford University Press.

World Health Organization (WHO). 1986. *Maternal Mortality Rates: A Tabulation of Available Information,* 2nd edition. Geneva.

———. Various years. *World Health Statistics Annual.* Geneva.

———. Various years. *World Health Statistics Report.* Geneva.

World Resources Institute and the International Institute for Environment and Development, in collaboration with the United Nations Environment Programme. 1988. *World Resources 1988–89.* New York: Basic Books.